Death, Mourning, and Burial

Death, Mourning, and Burial

A Cross-Cultural Reader

Edited by

Antonius C. G. M. Robben

Blackwell
Publishing

Editorial material and organization © 2004 by Blackwell Publishing Ltd

BLACKWELL PUBLISHING
350 Main Street, Malden, MA 02148-5020, USA
9600 Garsington Road, Oxford OX4 2DQ, UK
550 Swanston Street, Carlton, Victoria 3053, Australia

First published 2004 by Blackwell Publishing Ltd

7   2010

Library of Congress Cataloging-in-Publication Data

Death, mourning, and burial : a cross-cultural reader / edited by Antonius C.G.M.
Robben.
     p. cm.
   Includes bibliographical references and index.
   ISBN 978-1-4051-1470-7 (hardback : alk. paper) – ISBN 978-1-4051-1471-4 (pbk. : alk. paper)
   1. Funeral rites and ceremonies–Cross-cultural studies.   2. Mourning customs–Cross-cultural studies.
   3. Death–Social aspects–Cross-cultural studies.   I. Robben, Antonius C. G. M.
   GN486.D43 2004
   393–dc22

                                                                        2004012938

A catalogue record for this title is available from the British Library.

Set in 10/12½ pt Perpetua
by Kolam Information Services Pvt. Ltd, Pondicherry, India
Printed and bound in Singapore
by Fabulous Printers Pte Ltd

The publisher's policy is to use permanent paper from mills that operate a sustainable forestry policy,
and which has been manufactured from pulp processed using acid-free and elementary chlorine-free
practices. Furthermore, the publisher ensures that the text paper and cover board used have met
acceptable environmental accreditation standards.

For further information on
Blackwell Publishing, visit our website:
www.blackwellpublishing.com

Contents

Contents

Acknowledgments

I owe a considerable debt to Parker Shipton who, generous as always, invited me to edit a volume for Blackwell and introduced me to Jane Huber, that whirlwind of an editor, who sharpened my ideas about this project, provided sound advice, and always answered my e-mails with wit and wisdom. This book would not have been possible without her unfailing support. I also want to express my gratitude to the three anonymous reviewers for their helpful comments. I am certain that they recognize their hand in the texts selected here. I want to thank Ellen Badone, Jan van den Bout, Beth Conklin, Johannes Fabian, Sergei Kan, Sonja Leferink, Yvon van der Pijl, Sergio Visacovsky, and Jan de Wolf for their bibliographic suggestions and comments on the introduction. Their collegiality made the task much lighter and more enjoyable. Nathan Brown at Blackwell's offices in Malden, Massachusetts, and Angela Cohen in Oxford, England, guided me expertly through the publishing process. Lastly, I thank my wife Ellen for her patience in listening to innumerable accounts of burial practices, and for her overall support and encouragement.

3 Extract from *Living and Dying*, by Robert Jay Lifton and Eric Olson, published in The United States of America by Praeger Publishing Inc. Copyright © 1974 by Robert Jay Lifton and Eric Olson.

4 Extract from *The Hour of Our Death*, by Philippe Ariès. Copyright © 1981 by Alfred A. Knopf, Inc., originally published in France as *L'Homme Devant la Mort*. Copyright © 1977 by Les Editions du Seuil. Reprinted by permission of Georges Borchardt, Inc. for Les Editions du Seuil, and Alfred A. Knopf, a Division of Random House, Inc.

5 "How Others Die: Reflections on the Anthropology of Death," by Johannes Fabian, from *Death in American Experience* edited by Arien Mack. First published in *Social Research Journal*, 39:3 (1972) pp. 543–70. Reprinted with permission of *Social Research*.

6 "Death Omens in a Breton Memorate", by Ellen Badone, *Folklore*, Volume 98d, 1987. Copyright © Ellen Badone. Reprinted with the kind permission of the author.

7 "The Meaning of Death in Northern Cheyenne Culture," by Anne S. Straus, Plains Anthropologist, *Journal of the Plains Conference*, Volume 23, February 1978, No. 79. Reprinted with the kind permission of the author.

8 Extracts from *This World, Other Worlds: Sickness, Suicide, Death and the Afterlife Among the Vaqueiros de Alzada of Spain*, by M. Cátedra (1992), W. A. Christian, Jr., translator. Reprinted with permission of the University of Chicago Press.

9 "Displacing Suffering: The Reconstruction of Death in North America and Japan," by Margaret Lock, from *Social Suffering* edited by Arthur Kleinman, Veena Das, and Margaret Lock, published by The University of California Press, 1997. Copyright © 1997 by The Regents of the University of California. Reprinted with permission of the author and The University of California Press.

10 Extract from *Witchcraft, Oracles and Magic Among the Azande*, by E. E. Evans-Pritchard, published by Oxford University Press, 1937. Reprinted with permission of Oxford University Press.

11 Extract from *Divinity and Experience: The Religion of the Dinka*, by Godfrey Lienhardt, published by Oxford University Press, 1961. Reprinted with permission of Oxford University Press.

12 "State Terror in the Netherworld: Disappearance and Reburial in Argentina," by Antonius C. G. M. Robben, from *Death Squad: The Anthropology of State Terror* edited by Jeffrey A. Sluka, published by University of Pennsylvania Press, 2000. Copyright © 2000 University of Pennsylvania Press. Reprinted with permission of the publishers.

13 Extract from *The Andaman Islanders*, by A. R. Radcliffe-Brown, published by Cambridge University Press. Reprinted with permission of the publishers.

14 Extract from *The Death Rituals of Rural Greece*, by Loring M. Danforth. Copyright © 1982 Princeton University Press. Reprinted by permission of Princeton University Press.

15 Extracts from *Culture and Truth: The Remaking of Social Analysis*, by Renato Rosaldo. Copyright © 1989, 1993 Renato Rosaldo. Reprinted with permission of Taylor & Francis UK, and Beacon Press, Boston, USA.

16 Extract from *Death Without Weeping: The Violence of Everyday Life in Brazil*, by Nancy Scheper-Hughes, published by the University of California Press. Copyright © 1992 by The Regents of the University of California Press. Reprinted with permission of the author and the publishers.

17 Extracts from *Death and the Right Hand*, by Robert Hertz, (1881–1915), translated by Rodney and Claudia Needham, published by Cohen & West in 1960. © English translation by Rodney and Claudia Needham 1960. Reprinted by permission of Taylor & Francis UK.

18 Extract from *The Rites of Passage*, by Arnold van Gennep, translated by Monika B. Vizedom and Gabrielle L. Caffee, published by University of Chicago Press 1960. Copyright © 1960 by Monika B. Vizedom and Gabrielle L. Caffee. Reprinted by permission of the University of Chicago Press.

19 Extract from *The Price of Death: The Funeral Industry in Contemporary Japan*, by Hikaru Suzuki. Copyright © 2002 by the Board of Trustees of the Leland Stanford Jr., University. Reprinted with permission of the author and the publishers.

20 "Thus Are Our Bodies, Thus Was Our Custom," by Beth A. Conklin, from *American Ethnologist*, Volume 22, No. 1, Issue February 1995, pp. 75–101. Copyright © 1995 by the American Anthropological Society. Reprinted by permission of the author and American Anthropological Society.

21 "Sacrificial Death and the Necrophagous Ascetic," by Jonathan Parry, from *Death and the Regeneration of Life*, by Maurice Bloch and Jonathan Parry, published by Cambridge University Press, 1982. Copyright © 1982 by Cambridge University Press. Reprinted by permission of the author and Cambridge University Press.

22 "The 19th-Century Tlingit Potlatch: A New Perspective," by Sergei Kan, from *American Ethnologist*, Volume 13, No. 2, Issue May 1996, pp. 191–212. Copyright © 1996 by the American Anthropological Society. Reprinted by permission of the author and American Anthropological Society.

23 Extracts from *The Political Lives of Dead Bodies: Reburial and Postsocialist Change*, by Katherine Verdery, published by Columbia University Press. Copyright © 1999 by Columbia University Press. Reprinted with permission of the author and the publishers.

Every effort has been made to trace copyright holders and to obtain their permission for the use of copyright material. The publisher apologizes for any errors or omissions in the above list and would be grateful if notified of any corrections that should be incorporated in future reprints or editions of this book.

Death and Anthropology: An Introduction

Antonius C. G. M. Robben

Anthropologists, and in particular those from Western societies, stand in a peculiar relation to death. They have often had a brief personal brush with death at home – an aunt, a grandparent or a favorite cousin – but only become engrossed in the cultural complexities of death, mourning, and burial once in the field. This situation contains several dangers. The ethnographic experience overshadows their general understanding of death, misleads them into believing that their own culture has a much poorer death culture than that of their hosts, and may result in a distortive opposition between the ordinary, shallow, secular death culture of Western society and the intricate, profound, sacred death rituals elsewhere.

My understanding of death has been colored by the study of violent death and impaired mourning in Argentina during the 1970s and 1980s. Thousands of people were killed in those times of political turmoil, revolutionary fervor and authoritarian rule. Some died in armed combat or were executed by hit squads, but most were assassinated while held captive by the Argentine armed forces. The military did not give away death carelessly. Some interrogators offered their captives the choice between a quick death with a bullet if they cooperated and a slow death under torture if they refused to talk.

Captives regarded death therefore as a liberation from suffering instead of an end to life. Some perceived death even as a victory wrested from the absolute control of their captors. An unintentional death during excessive torture undermined the omnipotence of the interrogators and a suicide was seen as an act of empowerment. Under such extreme circumstances, it was not the mode of death (violent vs. natural, good vs. bad, planned vs. accidental) and the treatment of the body (clandestine cremation, secret burial, dumping at sea) but the mode of dying (shooting, strangling, drowning, electrocuting, poisoning) and the absence of a ceremonial treatment of the body that were of foremost concern to relatives, comrades, and friends.

My ethnographic experience may seem unusual within the anthropology of death, were it not that there was a strong interest in uncommon forms of death during the early days of anthropology. After all, James Frazer (1976) opened his monumental *The Golden Bough* with the ritual murder of the priestly king who resided at the sanctuary of the goddess Diana in Italy. This foundational interest in the anthropological study of death was matched by a similar interest in sociology by Emile Durkheim, and carried forward by the next generation of anthropologists, in particular Mauss, Hertz, Van Gennep, and Malinowski.

The anthropology of death led a rather dormant existence after this promising start, and has only revived since the 1970s with the publication of sophisticated ethnographies rather than the ambitious comparative efforts that characterized earlier anthropological scholarship. The result has been that there is only a small number of cross-cultural approaches but many excellent ethnographies, articles, and collections of essays.[1] The most prominent comparative efforts are Rosenblatt, Walsh, and Jackson (1976) on grief and mourning, Huntington and Metcalf (1979) on mortuary rituals, Bloch and Parry (1982a) on regeneration, Palgi and Abramovitch (1984) on theoretical approaches and thematic issues, Counts and Counts (1991a) on grief, Hallam and Hockey (2001) on material culture and remembrance, and Barley (1997) with a sweeping popularizing study about death culture.[2]

This volume aims to provide the readership with a good sense of the foundational texts in the anthropology of death, to delineate enduring research interests, and demonstrate the intellectual depth and breadth of the field in recent decades. The organizing principle is the trajectory from dying to afterlife, while paying close attention to the social and cultural consequences of death. The trajectory is organized into six parts which each comprise one main subfield of the anthropology of death: (I) *Conceptualizations of Death*; (II) *Death and Dying*; (III) *Uncommon Death*; (IV) *Grief and Mourning*; (V) *Mortuary Rituals*; and (VI) *Remembrance and Regeneration*.

Conceptualizations of Death

The inevitability of biological death challenged early generations of anthropologists to look for universal features in the diverse cultural responses to death, whereas later generations became absorbed in the practices themselves through meticulous ethnographies and sophisticated interpretations. The comparative dimension of recent anthropological studies is therefore implicit but seldom spelled out. Conceptualizing death is so daunting in the face of the tremendous variation of mortuary practices that anthropology has tended to generalize about death

more in interdisciplinary dialogues than in internal debates. A central theme of interdisciplinary inquiry has been the tension between the inevitability of death and the belief in spiritual immortality. The selection of texts in part I demonstrate how various disciplines, but especially psychology and psychoanalysis, have inspired anthropological thinking about death and immortality.

In the excerpt from his 1925 essay *Magic, Science, and Religion*, Bronislaw Malinowski challenges the idea by the psychologist Wilhelm Wundt that people are dominated by a fear of death. Malinowski indicates that this universal fear is complemented by an equally universal denial of death through a belief in immortality. These two attitudes translate into an ambivalent attachment of the living and the dead. Surviving relatives want to break and at the same time prolong their association with the deceased. Close relatives accompany the loved one during the dying process, care for the corpse, assume the social status of mourners, and display their grief in public. Mortuary rituals separate the living from the dead. The corpse is removed from the place of death, and undergoes some sort of transformation through burial, mummification, cremation or consumption, thus betraying the ambivalent relation between the living and the dead. The mourners are concerned about the dangers of the corpse and the contamination by death, but there reigns also a sublime sense of spirituality, hope, the sacred, and the otherworldly. Malinowski considers such religious imagination as a functional response to death because people loathe the idea of a final ending. They cling to a belief in a spiritual life after death by imagining the salvation of an eternal spirit from the visibly decaying corpse. Thus, religion gives people a comforting sense of immortality, while the mortuary practices restore the group that has been disturbed temporarily by the death of one of its members.

Half a century after Malinowski, the psychological anthropologist Ernest Becker continues to grapple with people's universal fear of death in the chapter *The Terror of Death* taken from his book *The Denial of Death* (1973). Inspired by psychoanalysis, Becker tries to show that the fear of death is one of the most important inner drives of human beings. He delineates two principal scientific viewpoints about the fear of death. The *healthy-minded argument* states that this fear is a social construction. Children raised in a sheltered environment by loving mothers will develop basic notions of trust and security. They cannot imagine separation or loss during infancy, and when older will accept death as a fact of life. Instead, the *morbidly minded argument* states that the fear of death is natural and universal. It is driven by people's instinct of self-preservation and their attempt to control life-threatening situations. This fear would be paralyzing if permanently conscious and is therefore repressed during early childhood through a complex internalization of contradictory feelings of love and rage towards their caretakers. Still, repression does not dissipate the fear of death but lodges it firmly in the unconscious. Becker concludes therefore that both arguments hold part of the truth. The first proves the strength of repressing a universal fear of death that is explained by the second.

Very much like Becker, the psychiatrist Robert Jay Lifton and Eric Olson postulate the universal fear of death in the chapter *Symbolic Immortality* from their book *Living and Dying* (1974), and like Malinowski, they consider the belief in immortality as its universal response. Lifton and Olson reconcile Freud's emphasis on the finality of biological death and the human need to believe otherwise with Jung's attention to people's search for meaning and immortality through religious symbolization. They find this symbolic immortality in five modes of expression. *Biological immortality* consists of extending life through one's offspring, family name, tribe or nation. Art, literature, and knowledge lead to *creative immortality*. *Theological immortality* refers to beliefs in resurrection, reincarnation, rebirth and a spiritual life after death. *Natural immortality* makes people part of an eternal universe and the interminable cycles of nature. Finally, *experiential immortality* concerns altered states of consciousness such as ecstasy, enlightenment, drug-induced highs, and collective effervescence. The fear of death impels people to procure these five modes of symbolic immortality to overcome their innate death anxiety, and live meaningful lives in the promise of a continuity with others. Society reaps the good works of these personal quests but may also suffer its conse-

quences when leaders pursue self-aggrandizing and megalomaniac projects through war, political repression, and economic exploitation. In the vein of Becker, Lifton and Olson, the sociologist Zygmunt Bauman has argued that people try to transcend the fear of death through culture and social organization. Culture is a defiant denial of death in the desire for meaning and immortality: "Without mortality, no history, no culture – no humanity" (Bauman 1992: 7).

Unlike the previous authors, the historian Philippe Ariès does not attempt to isolate any universals about death but focuses on the transitions in Western European death models. Ariès approaches this processual study of death in the excerpt from his book *The Hour of Our Death* (1987) through four psychological themes: (1) people's sense of the individual; (2) the defense of society against the unpredictable forces of nature; (3) the belief in life after death; and (4) the belief in the existence of evil. The particular manifestations and historical combinations of these four themes have led to five death models during the last millennium of European history.

The *tame death model* was dominant in the eleventh century and disappeared by the seventeenth century. Death was not a personal but a social affair in which family and community were present at the deathbed, wake, and funeral. Catholic mortuary rituals served to harness this unpredictable natural phenomenon through highly ordered procedures and provide the deceased with a peaceful repose till Judgment Day. In addition, these rituals repaired broken ties, and reaffirmed the continuity and solidarity of the community. Thus, death was ritualized and tamed. The *death of the self model* arose in the eleventh century among the elite and had replaced the tame death model entirely by the seventeenth century. This shift was due to changes in the first and third psychological themes, while the second and fourth remained the same. People began to regard themselves as individuals rather than members of a collectivity, developed notions about the separation of body and soul, emphasized the active role played by the immortal soul in the afterlife, and became increasingly afraid of the decaying corpse. By the late sixteenth century, people's notion about society's defense against nature began to change, and by the eighteenth century, nature was widely regarded as partaking both in life and death. This belief manifested itself in people's fear of being buried alive. Death was neither tame nor hidden, but savage and mysterious. This is the period during which the fear of death – regarded by Malinowski, Becker, Lifton and Olson as universal – arose according to Ariès. Ariès calls this the *remote and imminent death model* because death was distant yet could strike at any time.

All four psychological themes, and in particular people's awareness of themselves in relation to others, became affected between the eighteenth and twentieth century and gave rise to the *death of the other model*. People did not so much fear their own death but that of their relatives and the suffering of a final separation from loved ones. Death became sublime and even beautiful because it was no longer associated with guilt, hell, and evil but people could look forward to a reunion with family members already in heaven. The *invisible death model* became dominant in the twentieth century, however, without causing any substantial changes in the four themes. Death's medicalization distanced the community from the dying and the deceased. Individualism ruled, nature was conquered, social solidarity waned, and not the afterworld but family ties mattered. Western society surrounded death with so much shame, discomfort, and repulsion that Gorer (1965) even spoke of a pornography of death. Death became concealed in hospitals, nursing homes, and trailer parks. Yet, the fear of death remained, a fear corresponding more to people's social than biological death, as can be sensed each time the newspapers report about some lonely soul lying dead for months in a squalid rundown apartment.

In the early 1970s, Johannes Fabian (1973) took a reflexive look at the anthropological study of death in his essay "How Others Die: Reflections on the Anthropology of Death." He argued that the discipline contributed little to general debates about death because of a tendency towards parochialization, folklorization and exoticization. An obsessive concern for cultural variation, the folkloric isolation of death as a self-contained experience, and a fascination with exotic mortuary practices inhibited the formulation of statements that transcended local peculiarities.

Thus, anthropologists placed themselves outside major theoretical debates and maneuvered their discipline into a subsidiary role to other social sciencees, providing them with raw data about the alien "other" for the development of their theoretical and analytical models. Fabian wanted anthropology to focus on the social construction of death, and suggested three possible directions: (1) a processual, constitutive, practice-oriented view of cultural conceptions of death; (2) a dialectical model of the sociocultural reality of death paying attention to the construction of individual and social realities of death as intertwined yet separate processes; and (3) a communicative, intersubjective, language-centered approach to death and dying. These three approaches can be identified in the ethnographies and articles produced since the 1970s but the comparative agenda has remained largely empty. Be that as it may, the ethnographic harvest and interpretive finesse of the anthropology of death has been so rich that the field is thriving and is in a position to participate fully in interdisciplinary discussions and debates.

Death and Dying

There exists a great variation in cultural beliefs about death and dying. The idea of death as an irreversible event is strong in Western culture but many cultures have processual, cyclical or stage-like notions of death. Furthermore, cultures differ in the substantive ways to give meaning to such notions. The selections in part II focus on death as a predestined event, a developmental process, a natural cycle, and a clinical condition, but anthropologists have also written about death as a process of suffering (Mimica 1996) and as a cycle of reincarnation (Desjarlais 2000, 2003; Parry, chapter 21).

The people of Brittany, France, have a fatalistic worldview. Ellen Badone reveals in her article "Death Omens in a Breton Memorate" (1987) how the Bretons believe that death is foretold by omens (*intersignes*) such as bird calls, neighing horses, howling dogs, dreams, and visions.[3] Badone analyzes the omens of the fatal cycling accident of a young man hit by a drunken driver, interpreted four years after his death by his mother. The mother weaves a narrative of portents to the tragic death that helps her cope with her grief, attests to the existence of omens, and confirms the belief in a supernatural force which predestines people's lives. Omens can seldom be observed when old people are dying, but, so argues Badone, occur generally with unexpected deaths that require a framework of meaning and emotional comfort.

The Cheyenne consider death as a long process during which a person's development is reversed, according to Anne Straus in her article "The Meaning of Death in Northern Cheyenne Culture" (1978). The body disintegrates but the spirit-self and tribal identity survive and participate in Cheyenne society. The Creator (*Ma?heo?o*) provides animals and human beings alike with a life force, but endows people with the gifts of spirit (*mahta?sooma*) and breath/power (*omotone*). A child develops into a human being as the spirit achieves a balance between two "good" human parts and two "crazy" animal parts. Death is a process that begins when the spirit and later the breath/power leave the body. The body ceases to function, and spirit and breath/power unite into one spirit-self. Sometimes, a spirit returns to the inert body after having visited the land of the departed, and the Northern Cheyenne will therefore only bury their dead after four days. The life force remains in the corpse and will slowly sediment in the bones as the flesh disintegrates. The mourners weep for four days and come to accept the inevitable processes of life and death. The spirit-self will then reunite with the spirit-selves of all deceased Cheyennes, however, without taking leave from the community of the living because spirit-selves are animate, self-conscious entities with identities, names and kinship terms. These spirit-selves continue to partake in the Cheyenne community by giving advice to the living through their dreams.

Whereas the Cheyenne differentiate between animal and human death, the cattle-herders from Asturias in northern Spain interpret death as part of a natural lifecycle, as becomes clear from the excerpts of María Cátedra's ethnography *This World, Other Worlds: Sickness, Suicide, Death, and the Afterlife among the Vaqueiros de Alzada of Spain* (1992). Just as cattle can die prematurely through sickness or accident, so too can people. The natural cycle of life and death unfolds most clearly within the social cycle of the house. The ageing head of the household (*amo*) must decide on the most suitable heir to preserve the house and ensure his own immortality as one in an unbroken chain of keepers. The house bears heavily on the lives of the villagers, and *amos* have even committed suicide over its loss. One concrete problem is that the most industrious son and daughter-in-law may not be the best persons to nurse the *amo* as his health deteriorates. Generally, the balance weighs down on the side of the house. The *amo* retreats from public life into the house, and dies socially. Life begins to lose its *gracia*, its *joie de vivre*, its charm and pleasure, a condition bound to end in sickness and death.

Although an inevitable fact of nature, the Asturian cattle-herders are apprehensive about their mortality and try to master it through a taxonomy of modes of death. They differentiate among a good death, a bad death, and a tragic death in terms of the preceding circumstances and the emotional and social consequences for the relatives. The *good death* is fast, without suffering, and is accepted most readily by the relatives. The *bad death* involves a long, painful dying process exacting a heavy toll on both the sufferer and the family members. Finally, the *tragic death* takes place suddenly and strikes healthy human beings, often in the midst of their lives. These deaths are hard on the surviving relatives. Suicide is a tragic death that stands at the extreme opposite of natural death because it involves a violation of cultural norms and the agency of the deceased in his own demise.

The advance of Western technology in the area of organ transplants has placed a tremendous moral pressure on people to accept the idea that death is an event whose occurrence can be established with precision. Margaret Lock compares in her essay "Displacing Suffering: The Reconstruction of Death in North America and Japan" (1997) American and Japanese definitions of death, and reveals how distinct notions of personhood, the place of the medical profession in society, and cultural beliefs about identity can account for their differences.[4] North American physicians and the general public alike have always considered people to be dead when the heart stopped beating. The first successful heart transplant in 1967 required a medical definition of death to protect the legal rights of donors and physicians. The US 1981 Uniform Determination of Death Act established that someone was considered dead when an irreversible coma had set in and the person was effectively brain dead. Death as the final stage in a process of dying with elaborate social and cultural significance had become medicalized and turned into a biological event objectively measurable in terms of time and neurological activity. Culture retreated from the brain-dead organism and became confined to mortuary rituals and grief work.

The almost uniform acceptance by North American society of the brain death definition contrasts sharply with the situation in Japan. Brain death became first defined in 1974 but received nationwide criticism. The Japanese government instituted in 1989 a special committee to present an authoritative opinion. Even though a committee majority acceded that brain death was a human death and that the taking of organs was acceptable, a minority called for a national debate on the social and cultural dimensions of death. Many Japanese regarded brain death as unnatural. Margaret Lock argues that this public criticism should be understood within a much larger context of Japanese concerns about modernization, industrialization, and Westernization at the cost of Japanese values, traditions, and notions of death and self. Death is not seen as an event but as a process in which the soul must be ritually separated from the body. Furthermore, the body's integrity is important to prevent the spirit from suffering and allow the surviving relatives to show proper respect to the deceased (see also Suzuki, chapter 19). Thus, popular Japanese notions about processual death resisted clinical notions, and opened a public debate about the cultural construction of life and death not taking place in the USA.

Uncommon Death

Most anthropological studies on death are concerned with natural death, but a growing number of studies have retaken Durkheim's (1966) interest in suicide and Frazer's (1976) fascination with murder, sacrifice, and sorcery.[5] Marcel Mauss (1979:37–56)

expanded Durkheim's sociological explanation of suicide by adding that not only suicide but also death by suggestion was the result of collective beliefs.[6] Uncommon deaths must be studied together with natural deaths, as María Cátedra (chapter 8) has pointed out, because they are all influenced by the social context. Part III presents three selections about such forms of uncommon death, namely through witchcraft, live burial, and disappearance.

Evans-Pritchard's study *Witchcraft, Oracles and Magic among the Azande* (1968) provides a classic analysis of the cultural scenarios set in motion to deal with the disruptive consequences of witchcraft. He notices that the Azande of southern Sudan distinguished between natural and magical causes of death. Snake bites, a collapsing granary or the wound of a spear were recognized as natural causes of death. However, these natural causes did not stand on their own but were related to secondary causes, usually witchcraft. Witchcraft made the victim cross the snake's path, so both the witch and the snake killed the person. What happened when a person's death was attributed to witchcraft? First, the bereaved relatives consulted a poison oracle (*benge*) to establish the cause of death. A nobleman administered poison to a chicken, asked the oracle whether a particular person was a witch, and waited for the poison to take effect. If the chicken died, then poison was given to a second chicken to validate the first outcome. If the second chicken was spared, then the oracle had confirmed the suspicion of witchcraft and the surviving family would take revenge by magically killing the guilty witch or by demanding material compensation.

Ever since James Frazer wrote about the murder of the priestly king on the shores of lake Nemi, anthropologists have been fascinated by such uncommon deaths. Evans-Pritchard has reinterpreted Frazer's analysis of regicide among the Shilluk of southern Sudan (Evans-Pritchard 1969:66–86). He doubts whether Shilluk kings had ever been strangled to death when sick or senile, and rejects the view that enfeebled kings were murdered to avert a major disaster and prevent the suffering of the Shilluk people. Instead, he interprets the alleged regicide as a political legitimization of rebellion. Such rebellions were always made by a prince and thus helped to reunite the divided nation and strengthen the kingship. Whatever the truth about Shilluk regicide, Evans-Pritchard's student, Godfrey Lienhardt, pursued the study of similar uncommon deaths in the southern Sudan. The chapter from his ethnography *Divinity and Experience: The Religion of the Dinka* (1961) reads almost like a trial record in which incredulity rules. Lienhardt confesses that he did not witness any live burials, and feels therefore obliged to add account upon account to prove his argument.

Lienhardt describes the burial alive of fishing-spear masters among the Dinka, neighbors of the Shilluk. The burial (*dhor*) took place on the ageing master's request who asked his clansmen to dig a large grave near his home. Next, a bull was sacrificed. A platform of branches was raised in the pit on which the master would be lifted and to which a live ram was tied. The master began singing, and the clansmen joined in his joyful mood. Another platform was raised above the master's head, and the grave was closed with cattle dung. Finally, a bull and a calf were sacrificed on top of the heap, and the ritual ended with a feast in honor of the fishing-spear master. The crux of the burial was that the master did not die an involuntary but a deliberate death staged by the people to increase the clan's vitality, regeneration, and good fortune. The master was believed to carry the life of his people and therefore needed to be buried alive, because a natural death would expire the life force with him and would thus threaten the survival of his people. Lienhardt concludes that not the Western notion of personal immortality but the Dinka notion of collective immortality was at stake in these uncommon burials.

Whereas the Dinka celebrated the voluntary burial alive of the fishing-spear masters, the Argentine people have agonized over the involuntary burial alive of thousands of disappeared citizens during the last military dictatorship. My contribution (Robben 2000) to this reader, "State Terror in the Netherworld: Disappearance and Reburial in Argentina," describes how the Argentine military regime used the disappearance of political opponents as a terror tactics to intimidate their comrades-in-arms, paralyze family protest, and exploit the cultural belief in the relation of body and spirit. The Argentine military abducted tens of thousands of civilians, kept them in captivity for months on end, and finally assassinated most of them. Their remains were cremated or buried in mass graves. One of the most gruesome assassinations was carried out by the Navy which sedated its captives and dropped them from airplanes flying across the south Atlantic ocean. After misleading the Argentine people for several years about the real fate of the disappeared, the Argentine military discovered to their dismay the political and especially emotional force of people's need to bury and mourn their dead. Incessant human rights protests helped to topple the regime, and allowed for the exhumation, identification, and reburial of hundreds of disappeared Argentines. The reburials manifested the Argentine belief in a political life after death, a life which the military wanted to extinguish and the relatives were determined to resurrect. The uncommon and violent death of the disappeared contributed, therefore, directly to the survival of their spirit and their continuing influence on Argentine politics.

Grief and Mourning

Grief may be a universal emotion of bereavement, as psychologists such as Bowlby (1981) have noted, but its social expression in mourning is culturally specific. Loss is therefore the central concept in the selections gathered in part IV, and grief and mourning should be understood in relation to other losses that provoke personal and collective crises, as has been argued by Freud (1968). Mourning becomes then a social and cultural way to cope with any significant loss for which death is the ultimate metaphor.

Emile Durkheim has had a lasting influence on the anthropology of death by emphasizing that the individual grief experienced at the death of another human being is expressed collectively in culturally prescribed ways of mourning. Crying relates in the same way to grief as weeping and wailing relate to mourning. Mourning is not a spontaneous emotion but a collective obligation manifested in appeasement rites. In his classic work *The Elementary Forms of Religious Life*, Emile Durkheim (1995) draws upon ethnographic accounts of Australian aborigines to argue that the spontaneity of their wailing is deceptive, because all these expressions are clearly prescribed, controlled, and monitored by the community. Durkheim's explanation of such rites is that the death of an individual diminishes the group numerically and socially. Durkheim was fascinated by questions of social order and disintegration. This Hobbesian puzzle becomes particularly pressing in the case of death. Indifference to a death expresses a lack of moral and cultural unity, and an absence of social cohesion and solidarity. Instead, collective mourning helps to draw people closer together and invigorate the weakened social group. This social function of mourning rites is not limited to the death of individuals. Mourning is a general expression of loss for a social collectivity under threat, as is demonstrated by aboriginal rites for illness, famine, drought, and the desecration of religious symbols.

Radcliffe-Brown (1964) demonstrates in the excerpt from his ethnography *The Andaman Islanders* how weeping and embracing are collective performances rather than spontaneous personal expressions of sorrow or happiness. The Andamanese can cry on demand when required by society. Radcliffe-Brown even suggests that these cultural practices produce the emotions which they are obliged to express, and affirm the social attachments that hold society together. He delineates seven occasions of ceremonial weeping related to initiations, marriages, deaths, friendships, and peace-making. These rites are subdivided into two varieties: reciprocal or symmetrical rites (meeting of friends or relatives, peace-making ceremonies, communal mourning) and one-sided or asymmetrical rites (wailing over a corpse, weeping over initiated novices and newly-weds). The practice of embracing at reciprocal rites expresses the emotional attachment of two persons, while weeping provides relief from built-up tensions. This dual function becomes clear at the end of a mourning period when secluded mourners renew their social ties with the community. Weeping is a general response to loss, as shown not only in mortuary rituals but also in weddings and initiation ceremonies. Asymmetrical rites signify affective and collective attachments, and are expressed by embracing and weeping over the inert body, the novice or the newly-wed. In the case of death, weeping and em-

bracing manifest the social attachment of the living and the dead, enhance the social solidarity of the survivors, and mend the weakened social collectivity.

The separation of parents and children upon marriage is experienced as such a great loss in several cultures that an analogy is drawn with death. The sadness of a mother bidding farewell to her departing daughter turns the wedding metaphorically into a funeral. In the excerpts from his book *The Death Rituals of Rural Greece* (1982), Loring Danforth interprets this metaphoric relation through an analysis of Greek wedding songs and funeral laments.[7] There is strong social pressure on the bereaved to channel sorrow into culturally meaningful laments. Danforth demonstrates that there are remarkable similarities in content, structure, melody, and lyrics between wedding songs and death songs. The variation exists in the context, style, and tempo in which the songs are sung. The metaphoric relation between death and marriage appears also in similar symbolic relations between death and labor migration, the lifecycle of plants, the migration of birds, the flowing of water, and the shedding of tears. These connections among death, marriage and all other metaphors deny the finality of death, relativize separation, and mediate the too stark and too painful opposition of life and death. Grief is channeled into culturally significant laments led by distant relatives or talented outsiders. The exhumation of the dead, several years after the funeral, symbolizes the negation of death by a return of the ossified remains to their homes and families. Once again, the laments sung at the exhumation closely resemble wedding songs, and the dry bones are greeted, kissed, and honored as if they were newly-weds.

Renato Rosaldo reveals in the essay "Grief and a Headhunter's Rage" (1993) how the accidental death of his wife Michelle deepened his understanding of bereavement among the Ilongot of the Philippines. Bereaved Ilongot men used to engage in headhunting to dispel the rage embedded in their grief by severing and casting away the head of an unsuspecting victim. For the Ilongot, "grief, rage, and headhunting go together in a self-evident manner" (1984:178).[8] His wife's unfortunate fall to death while conducting fieldwork, provoked an unsuspected anger and rage in Rosaldo resembling that of bereaved Ilongot men. This personal reaction made him eventually shift his analysis from headhunting as a ritual manifestation of bereavement to headhunting as an expression of grief, rage, and emotional loss. A reinterpretation of the ethnographic record showed that headhunting was a common Ilongot response to a severe loss. Not only the death of a close relative, but also dramatic life transitions made young Ilongot men boil over with anger and eager to take a head.

Nancy Scheper-Hughes has taken the cultural construction of bereavement one step further by arguing that not only mourning but grief itself is a product of culture.[9] In the excerpts from her ethnography *Death Without Weeping: The Violence of Everyday Life in Brazil* (1992), she points out that mothers in a northeast Brazilian shanty town are aware of the structural causes of high infant mortality (poverty, malnutrition, poor health care) as well as the immediate causes (diarrhea, communicable diseases). Still, they endow babies with a life force, a will to live, whose strength will ultimately determine whether or not an infant survives. This belief makes mothers withhold food from weak, passive babies and give more food to strong, active babies. These Brazilian mothers accept the death of their weak infants stoically. Crying is even considered detrimental to the babies because the heavy tears on the thin angel wings burden their flight to heaven. Scheper-Hughes emphasizes that the maternal aloofness does not cover a deep sorrow, and the absence of a display of grief is not the repression of an inconsolable loss. The mother feels pity rather than grief for the baby.[10]

Mortuary Rituals

Mortuary rituals are a true cultural universal that show people's resistance to accepting biological death as a self-contained event, and their desire to prolong the departure from the dead through a process of phased transitions. The largest number of studies in the anthropology of death is on mortuary rituals, and many anthropologists still follow the structuralist paths cleared by Hertz and Van Gennep. Part V contains excerpts from their two most influential texts, an application of their approach to Japanese funerals, and an article about Amazonian endocannibalism demonstrating the intertwinement of mortuary ritual and grief.

A Contribution to the Study of the Collective Representation of Death by Robert Hertz (1960) endures as the single most influential text in the anthropology of death.[11] Hertz argues forcefully that the death of a human being is not exclusively a biological reality or confined to the individual sorrow of the bereaved relatives, but that death evokes moral and social obligations expressed in culturally determined funeral practices. Although Hertz restricts his analysis largely to the mortuary practices of South Asian tribal societies, he reveals a structure of great cross-cultural significance. In the excerpts included in this reader, Hertz isolates the key elements in the secondary burials among the Dayak of Kalimantan, Indonesia. He points out that the inert body, the deceased's soul, and the surviving relatives play changing roles during the time between death and secondary burial, a time which he subdivides into two periods. First, there is the intermediary period during which (1) the inert body is temporarily stored or buried, (2) the spirit or soul of the deceased remains near the corpse, and (3) the bereaved relatives are separated from society and enter into mourning. Clearly, death does not occur at one moment in time but is a drawn-out process. The dead person is still considered part of society, and his or her continued residence among the living obliges them to provide food, engage in conversation, and show respect as if he or she were still alive. In a comparable way, the deceased's spirit or soul does not depart for the land of the dead but wanders in the vicinity of the corpse and frequents the places where the deceased used to dwell. The bereaved relatives fear the soul's wrath for past wrongdoing, and are prone to appease the soul through sacrifices, taboos, and mourning. These circumstances make the mourners stand apart from society. They cannot participate in its daily routines, and wear distinctive clothing and ornaments.

The second and final period begins when the body has disintegrated sufficiently, the soul has detached from the deceased, and the mourners have properly expressed their grief and carried out their social obligations. Hertz (1960:54) sums up this second period as follows: "The final ceremony has three objects: to give burial to the remains of the deceased, to ensure the soul peace and access to the land of the dead, and finally to free the living from the obligations of mourning." In contrast to the temporary burial of the first period, the final burial is a collective affair through which the deceased joins the ancestors and the community bids him or her farewell. The surviving relatives can now end their mourning. They cleanse themselves ritually from the impurities of their extended proximity to death, change into new clothing, and reunite with the community.

Arnold van Gennep made an extremely important contribution to the anthropology of death by interpreting mortuary rituals as one among similar rites of passage: "The life of an individual in any society is a series of passages from one age to another and from one occupation to another" (1960:2–3). These transitions, such as birth, puberty, marriage, and death, are life crises and become therefore the subject of elaborate elevation rituals as a person rises from one status to the next. These rituals take place in what Durkheim (1995) has called sacred time, and Turner (1967) liminal time. The chapter from Van Gennep's book *the Rites of Passage* (1960) included here discusses funerals.

Mortuary transition or elevation rituals have three distinct phases. First, there is a relatively short preliminary phase characterized by a rite of separation that isolates the corpse and the mourners from society, and makes them wear special clothing and observe certain taboos. The rite of transition takes place during the second or liminal phase marking the passage from the land of the living to the afterworld. This phase has the most elaborate rituals because the journey is considered long and the deceased has to be equipped with food, clothing, weapons, protective amulets, means of transportation, and a guide to lead the way. Finally, there is the postliminal rite of incorporation to mark both the passage of the soul to the world of the dead and the return of the mourners to the bosom of society. The remains are buried in a cemetery, placed in a tree, cremated, or separated in any other way from their temporary stay. The bereaved relatives join for a meal, sing songs and celebrate the final passage of the deceased.

The mourning has come to an end, the social order is restored, and the flow of everyday life is picked up again.

Hikaru Suzuki refines the ideas of Hertz and Van Gennep by demonstrating that the form and content of modern Japanese mortuary rituals are the outcome of considerable negotiation between funeral professionals and bereaved relatives. In the excerpt from her ethnography *The Price of Death: The Funeral Industry in Contemporary Japan* (2000), she analyzes the preparations for the rite of separation, and demonstrates how professionals are in charge of the corpse, and direct the mourners towards certain ceremonies and expenses to conform with their social status. The rite of separation begins when bereaved relatives call a funeral company to take care of the deceased in the ceremonial trajectory from the place of death, by way of the home and the funeral auditorium, to the cemetery. A person is not considered dead in Japanese culture until the remains are cremated, so the deceased is welcomed home by the relatives before proceeding to the funeral auditorium. In the past, the closest family members would bathe the corpse to protect the deceased and the relatives from death pollution. This bathing ceremony fell into disuse but was reintroduced during the 1990s by a professional bathing service. The bathing ceremony ends with the closing of the coffin. After a wake by relatives and guests, a nightly vigil by a few close relatives, and a funeral ceremony the following morning, the rite of separation has concluded and the rite of transition can begin around the cremation of the deceased.

The structural approaches developed by Hertz and Van Gennep continue to be important for the anthropology of death because they offer analytical frameworks that can be applied to every mortuary ritual. Hikaru Suzuki has given this approach a new impulse by demonstrating that rites of passage are not static scripts but dynamic practices. Beth Conklin (1995) provides yet another way of looking at mortuary practices in her article "'Thus are our bodies, thus was our custom': Mortuary Cannibalism in an Amazonian Society." Although she does not analyze mortuary cannibalism as a rite of passage but focuses on grief, mourning, and attachment, I have, nevertheless, placed her contribution in this part because her approach gives new meaning to the work of Hertz and Van Gennep. She shows the complex entwinement and difficult separation of corpse, spirit, and the bereaved, and demonstrates that mortuary practices do not stand by themselves but encompass emotions, subjectivities, and life processes.[12]

The Brazilian public was shocked to learn in the early 1960s that the Wari' indians of western Amazonia ate their dead. The integrity of the body, the sacredness of the corpse, and the burial of the remains are so deep-seated in Western culture that such endocannibalism could only provoke horror. However, from the perspective of the Wari', not the eating of the dead but the Western custom of abandoning them to rot away in cold, uncaring soil was callous and heartless. Two notions of Wari' cosmology are fundamental to understand their mortuary cannibalism: (1) the body's blood and flesh are the seat of subjectivity, social identity and social relationships; and (2) there is a reciprocal relation between humans and animals. Social ties continue to embody the corpse upon biological death, while the deceased's spirit materializes into a white-lipped peccary. Rather than merciless, mortuary cannibalism was an expression of compassion for the bereaved relatives, helped severing the ties of living and dead, and contributed to the community's subsistence by effectuating the transformation of human into animal.

The death of a person resulted in the division of the bereaved relatives into two groups of mourners: close blood relatives and the spouse on the one hand, and in-laws on the other. The blood relatives gathered closely around the dead body, while calling out the deceased's kinship terms. The affines occupied themselves with organizing the funeral by preparing food and drinks, and eventually by consuming the corpse. The physical separation of the blood relatives from the corpse and its subsequent dismemberment were the most emotional moments of the funeral because the cutting implied the severing of the embodied social ties, resembled the butchering of game, and marked the spirit's departure. Not the blood relatives, but the affines consumed the roasted flesh and organs. This rite of transition dissipated grief by the consumption of the sociophysical body and its embodied identity and social ties, helped the

mourning process, resuscitated the Wari' spirit under water, and foreshadowed its incarnation into a peccary. This transformation from human into animal showed that the deceased cared for the surviving relatives by providing them with game for their subsistence. Ritual and loss ended as shamans talked to the spirits embodied in peccaries killed in the hunt, and thus gave comfort to the grieving relatives by communicating the deceased's well-being.

Remembrance and Regeneration

In many cultures, life does not end with biological death because of a belief in an eternal spirit, a surviving soul, a cycle of life and death, or notions of reincarnation and regeneration. Jonathan Parry (1982) analyzes in his essay "Sacrificial Death and the Necrophagous Ascetic" two opposite yet complementary approaches to life and death in Hinduism through a study of heads of household and Aghori ascetics in the holy city of Benares, India. Life and death constitute a zero-sum game in Hinduism because life can only be created by causing death, while death regenerates life. This interminable cycle is complemented by a fundamental homology between the human body and the cosmos, meaning that both are composed of the same five elements and ruled by the same laws. Sacrifice and rebirth of body, time, and cosmos are thus inextricably linked. Just as the cosmos will be devoured by fire and flood to enable its rebirth, so the deceased are cremated on the funeral pyre and their ashes scattered in the Ganges river to allow their rebirth. A "good" death is therefore a sacrificial act through cremation which regenerates the deceased, time, and the cosmos as if in an embodied big bang.

Unlike ordinary Hindus, Aghori ascetics try to escape death by skirting the cycle of reincarnations and by returning to the origins of the Hindu cosmos when there was only a void. The Aghori ascetics suspend time and become endowed with life-giving powers through ways that would be considered polluting to others, such as mortuary cannibalism, and living on cremation grounds. This intimate association with death frees them from life, and makes them deny a social order organized along the rigid cultural oppositions of purity and pollution, life and death, and high and low. Thus, ascetics return to the primordial cosmic unity beyond time and place. People believe that ascetics do not die but enter into a deep meditation. They achieve a state of non-duality and therefore escape the death–rebirth cycle. Their physiological functions may cease one day but their vital breath remains in the animate body. In sum, ordinary Hindus embrace death in order to regenerate life, while Aghori ascetics embrace death to defy life.

The northwest coast of North America has been a region of continuing anthropological interest since Franz Boas conducted fieldwork there. The potlatch – the competitive reciprocation of property among ranked position holders from different villages – has intrigued generations of scholars. Potlatches have been interpreted as rituals reaffirming group membership and its ranking of social statuses, as a social leveling mechanism redistributing property among neighboring tribes, as a ritual exchange system regulating intermarriages, and as a religious cultural complex (Kan 1986:192–193). Sergei Kan adds a new explanation by focusing on the potlatch as a memorial for the deceased and their ancestors.[13]

A death among the nineteenth-century matrilineal Tlingit was followed by a funeral, a reburial, and a memorial potlatch. Sergei Kan (1986) describes in the excerpt from his article "The 19th-Century Tlingit Potlatch: A New Perspective" how the memorial potlatch was an occasion to rebury the remains in a new grave house, allow the deceased's ghost to depart for the afterworld, and mark the end of mourning. The memorial potlatch also served to compensate the paternal/affinal kin for their services, and especially to evoke the memory of the ancestors. The four-day potlatch was preceded by a month of preliminary rites in which guests were feasted with dances, songs and masked performances. Before presenting the gifts to the guests, orations and songs were delivered by each individual host to express his or her relation to the deceased. What began as the remembrance of the deceased, soon evolved into a memorial ritual for all matrilineal ancestors. All deceased relatives were named in public, and offerings were made to commemorate the matriclan's dead members. The potlatch emphasized the corporate identity of the dead, united the deceased with his or her forebears, and allowed each living clan member to remourn, remember, honor, and bestow his or her relatives with food, gifts and love, thus guaranteeing their immortality and the well-being of the living.

Katherine Verdery (1999) demonstrates in the excerpt from her book *The Political Lives of Dead Bodies: Reburial and Postsocialist Change* how long-buried corpses can acquire new public meanings under changing political circumstances.[14] Post-socialist Eastern Europe witnessed a political regeneration of the biographies of deceased public figures, whether these be kings, politicians, bishops or artists. The repatriation and reburial of such public figures appealed to many different audiences and political groups which each sensed a deep affinity with the deceased. The importance of the many political, religious, ideological, generational or historical meanings of the public figure became enhanced by the aura surrounding the dead body, and the affect and emotion it evoked. Death inspires an awe among the living which is materialized by the corpse. An anthropological analysis of the treatment and reburial of the dead becomes therefore a causeway into the politics of action, meaning, and emotion.

Future of the Anthropology of Death

What is the state of the anthropology of death today? In 1973, Johannes Fabian criticized anthropology for its parochialization, folklorization, and exoticization of death, and called upon the discipline to participate more centrally in leading contemporary debates and exploit anthropology's significant comparative and theoretical potential. Palgi and Abramovitch repeated this plea for cross-cultural analysis and theoretical engagement in their major 1984 review essay. Two decades later, this summons still awaits a sustained answer. Somehow, anthropologists recoil from making the sweeping generalizations common in sociology and psychology which, it must be said, operate only within the limited cultural universe of Western society. Anthropology's attention to cultural variation seems difficult to reconcile with the building of grand theories and the singling out of universal principles about death because there is always the unexpected cultural twist undermining such theoretical endeavors. Still, the broader theoretical and empirical relevance of the anthropology of death is shown overwhelmingly in the rich contributions collected in this reader, and I believe that the field can develop further into at least six directions, namely critique, comparison, self-reflexivity, objectification, death-centeredness, and dialogue.

The ethnographic critique of grand social theories and conceptual reductionism has been an enduring value but also a continuing liability of anthropology. The emphasis on the cultural aspects of social life has given short shrift to a search for more universal characteristics. The anthropology of death should engage more directly with disciplines such as sociology, psychology, and medicine which claim to have uncovered general principles of death, dying, grief, and mourning. Becker (chapter 2) and Scheper-Hughes (chapter 16) provide two examples of how to enrich other disciplines with the anthropological sensitivity to cultural variation in human conduct and cognition. The human conception of death consists of many cultural edifices with numerous nooks and crannies yet with a limited number of foundations, some of which have been delineated outside anthropology.

Comparison, either between or within cultures and societies, is one of the core missions of anthropology, but it remains still underdeveloped in the study of death. The comparative approaches of Hertz (chapter 17) and van Gennep (chapter 18) may count on wide acceptance in anthropology but hardly anything as daring has been attempted since then. Furthermore, the present inattention to comparison also exists within ethnographic work. There is a tendency to either focus on normal death or on uncommon death, but there is seldom an integrated approach studying the entire variation of modes of death within a larger cultural scheme. Cátedra (chapter 8) and Parry (chapter 21) show how fruitful and rewarding this approach can be.

Self-reflexivity has been a narrative style and epistemological approach in anthropology since the 1970s. How often do deaths in the personal sphere or in the field remain unreported? We can only wonder how Malinowski's understanding of Tro-

briand mourning and mortuary practices was affected by the death of his mother. The entries during the last month of his rather abruptly ending diary are suffused with profound sorrow and great mood swings: "Overcome with grief, I sobbed. Then deep sadness, and fatigue. I feel so strong and healthy now – and all this is so pointless. I know that if I lost my eyesight or my health now, I could easily commit suicide" (Malinowski 1967:292). Rosaldo's (chapter 15) reinterpretation of Ilongot grief in the light of his personal sorrow is pointing the way to more self-reflexive ethnographies in the anthropology of death.

The objectification of death in material culture was a major concern of anthropologists at the turn of the nineteenth century, but following generations lost interest. Kan (chapter 22) draws attention to the importance of material culture in his ethnography of memorial potlatches, and so do Hallam and Hockey (2001) for Western culture. Western societies may have rather poor mortuary rituals, but they have a rich but understudied death culture ranging from art, cinema and literature to commemorations, cemeteries, memorials and oral culture.

Paradoxically, much work in the anthropology of death is life centered instead of death centered. Death is regarded as a disturbance of the social order, a laceration of the social body, and a gap in social and family networks. Nadia Seremetakis has called for more attention to the content of death itself, and praises the work of Ariès (chapter 4) who demonstrated the relative autonomy of death rituals in a changing historical context. Seremetakis encourages anthropologists "to treat death rites as an arena of social contestation, a space where heterogeneous and antagonistic cultural codes and social interests meet and tangle . . . [and to] analyze death rituals as integrities with their own temporal rhythms, transformations, and levels of engagement with and disengagement from the social order" (1991:15). Lock (chapter 9) provides another example of a death-centered approach. Studies about euthanasia, the hospice movement (Hockey 1990), genocide (Hinton 2002a), AIDS (Farmer 2003), species death through nuclear, chemical or biological weapons (Lifton 1967), and the search for immortality through cloning and cryonics are promising areas for further research.

Finally, the anthropology of death should enter more forcefully into a dialogue with various subdisciplines, such as the anthropology of violence, religion, the body and the senses, and with medical, psychological and political anthropology, to mention the most obvious ones. Verdery (chapter 23) and my own essay (chapter 12) are examples of such dialogue with political and psychological anthropology.

NOTES

1   The most important anthropological collections are Bloch and Parry (1982b); Bohannan (1967); Cederroth, Corlin, and Lindström (1988); Counts and Counts (1991b); Hinton (2002a, 2002b); Humphreys and King (1981); Platt and Persico (1992); Reynolds and Waugh (1977).

2   Without in any way trying to be exhaustive, there are also a number of publications in other disciplines of particular interest to anthropologists, such as in sociology (Bauman 1992; Elias 1985; Kamerman 1988; Riley 1983; Seale 1998; Walter 1999), psychology (Archer 1999; Cook and Oltjenbruns 1989; Kastenbaum and Costa 1977; Nadeau 1998; Parkes 1996; Stroebe, Hansson, Stroebe, and Schut 2001), history (Ariès 1974, 1987; Guthke 1999; Kselman 1993; Merridale 2000; Mosse 1990), religious studies (Bowker 1991), thanatology (Aiken 1994; Core, Nabe and Core 2000), and comparative literature (Holst-Warhaft 2000).

3   See also Badone (1989).

4   See also Lock (2001).

5   The rapidly growing field of the anthropology of violence (see e.g. Scheper-Hughes and Bourgois 2003) is providing a unique confluency of research opportunities with the anthropology of death.

6   Eastwell (1982) has confirmed the existence of death by suggestion.

7   See also Alexiou (1974) and Seremetakis (1991).

8   Renato Rosaldo had tried to understand Ilongot headhunting from a historical perspective (Rosaldo 1980), while Michelle Rosaldo took resort to symbolic and psychological anthropology (Rosaldo, M. 1980).

9   The sociologist Walter (1999) makes a similar argument.

10 The interpretation of Scheper-Hughes is highly controversial because it goes against the grain of well-established psychological theory about bereavement.

Psychologists would diagnose the maternal response to infant death as denial or impaired mourning.

11 Huntington and Metcalf (1979) regard their book as an elaboration of the seminal work by Hertz.

12 See also Conklin (2001:157–177).

13 See also Kan (1989) and Simeone (1991).

14 See also Gal (1991).

BIBLIOGRAPHY

Aiken, Lewis R., 1994 *Dying, Death, and Bereavement*. 3rd edn. Boston: Allyn and Bacon.

Alexiou, Margaret, 1974 *The Ritual Lament in Greek Tradition*. Cambridge: Cambridge University Press.

Archer, John, 1999 *The Nature of Grief: The Evolution and Psychology of Reactions to Loss*. London: Routledge.

Ariès, Philippe, 1974, *Western Attitudes toward Death: From the Middle Ages to the Present*. Baltimore: Johns Hopkins University Press.

Ariès, Philippe, 1987 [1977] *The Hour of Our Death*. London: Penguin.

Badone, Ellen, 1987 Death Omens in a Breton Memorate. *Folklore* 98:99–104.

Badone, Ellen, 1989 *The Appointed Hour: Death, Worldview, and Social Change in Brittany*. Berkeley: University of California Press.

Barley, Nigel, 1997 *Dancing on the Grave: Encounters with Death*. London: Abacus.

Bauman, Zygmunt, 1992 *Mortality, Immortality and Other Life Strategies*. Cambridge: Polity Press.

Becker, Ernest, 1973 *The Denial of Death*. New York: The Free Press.

Bloch, Maurice and Jonathan Parry, 1982a Introduction: Death and the Regeneration of Life. *In Death and the Regeneration of Life*. Maurice Bloch and Jonathan Parry, eds. pp.1–44. Cambridge: Cambridge University Press.

Bloch, Maurice and Jonathan Parry, eds., 1982b *Death and the Regeneration of Life*. Cambridge: Cambridge University Press.

Bohannan, Paul, ed., 1967 *African Homicide and Suicide*. New York: Atheneum.

Bowker, John, 1991 *The Meanings of Death*. Cambridge: Cambridge University Press.

Bowlby, John, 1981 *Attachment and Loss*. 3 vols. Harmondsworth: Penguin.

Cátedra, María, 1992 *This World, Other Worlds: Sickness, Suicide, Death, and the Afterlife among the Vaqueiros de Alzada of Spain*. Chicago: University of Chicago Press.

Cederroth, S., C. Corlin, and J. Lindström, eds., 1988 *On the Meaning of Death: Essays on Mortuary Rituals and*

Eschatological Beliefs. Stockholm, Sweden: Almqvist and Wiksell International.

Conklin, Beth A., 1995 "Thus are our bodies, thus was our custom": Mortuary Cannibalism in an Amazonian Society. *American Ethnologist* 22(1): 75–101.

Conklin, Beth A., 2001 *Consuming Grief: Compassionate Cannibalism in an Amazonian Society*. Austin: University of Texas Press.

Cook, Alicia Skinner and Kevin Ann Oltjenbruns, 1989 *Dying and Grieving: Life Span and Family Perspectives*. New York: Holt, Rinehart, and Winston.

Core, Charles A., Clyde M. Nabe, and Donna M. Core, 2000 *Death and Dying, Life and Living*. 3rd edn. Belmont, CA: Wadsworth/Thomson Learning.

Counts, David R. and Dorothy A. Counts, 1991a Conclusions: Coping with the Final Tragedy. *In Coping with the Final Tragedy: Cultural Variation in Dying and Grieving*. David R. Counts and Dorothy A. Counts, eds. pp. 277–291. Amityville, NY: Baywood Publishing Company.

Counts, David R. and Dorothy A. Counts, eds., 1991b *Coping with the Final Tragedy: Cultural Variation in Dying and Grieving*. Amityville, NY: Baywood Publishing Company.

Danforth, Loring M., 1982 *The Death Rituals of Rural Greece*. Princeton: Princeton University Press.

Desjarlais, Robert, 2000 Echoes of a Yolmo Buddhist's Life, in Death. *Cultural Anthropology* 15 (2):260–293.

Desjarlais, Robert, 2003 *Sensory Biographies: Lives and Deaths among Nepal's Yolmo Buddhists*. Berkeley: University of California Press.

Durkheim, Emile, 1966 [1897] *Suicide: A Study in Sociology*. New York: The Free Press.

Durkheim, Emile, 1995 [1912] *The Elementary Forms of Religious Life*. Karen E. Fields, trans. New York: The Free Press.

Eastwell, Harry D., 1982 Voodoo Death and the Mechanism for Dispatch of the Dying in East Arnhem, Australia. *American Anthropologist* 84(1):5–18.

Elias, Norbert, 1985 *The Loneliness of the Dying*. Oxford: Basil Blackwell.

Evans-Pritchard, E. E., 1968 [1937] *Witchcraft, Oracles and Magic among the Azande*. Oxford: Clarendon Press.

Evans-Pritchard, E. E., 1969 *Essays in Social Anthropology*. London: Faber and Faber.

Fabian, Johannes, 1973 How Others Die: Reflections on the Anthropology of Death. *In Death in American Experience*. Arien Mack, ed. pp. 177–201. New York: Schocken.

Farmer, Paul, 2003 *Pathologies of Power: Health, Human Rights, and the New War on the Poor*. Berkeley: University of California Press.

Frazer, James G., 1976 [1890] *The Golden Bough: A Study in Magic and Religion*, vol. 1. London: Macmillan Press.

Freud, Sigmund, 1968 [1917] Mourning and Melancholia. *In The Standard Edition of the Complete Psychological Works of Sigmund Freud*. James Strachey, ed. vol. 14:243–258. London: Hogarth Press.

Gal, Susan, 1991 Bartók's Funeral: Representations of Europe in Hungarian Political Rhetoric. *American Ethnologist* 18(3):440–458.

Gorer, Geoffrey, 1965 *Death, Grief, and Mourning*. Garden City: Doubleday and Company.

Guthke, Karl S., 1999 *The Gender of Death: A Cultural History in Art and Literature*. Cambridge: Cambridge University Press.

Hallam, Elizabeth and Jenny Hockey, 2001 *Death, Memory and Material Culture*. Oxford: Berg.

Hertz, Robert, 1960 *Death and the Right Hand*. London: Cohen and West.

Hinton, Alexander Laban, ed., 2002a *Genocide: An Anthropological Reader*. Malden, MA: Blackwell Publishers.

Hinton, Alexander Laban, ed., 2002b *Annihilating Difference: The Anthropology of Genocide*. Berkeley: University of California Press.

Hockey, Jenny, 1990 *Experiences of Death: An Anthropological Account*. Edinburgh: Edinburgh University Press.

Holst-Warhaft, Gail, 2000 *The Cue for Passion: Grief and Its Political Uses*. Cambridge, MA: Harvard University Press.

Humphreys, S. C., and Helen King, eds., 1981 *Mortality and Immortality: The Anthropology and Archaeology of Death*. London: Academic Press.

Huntington, Richard, and Peter Metcalf, 1979 *Celebrations of Death: The Anthropology of Mortuary Ritual*. Cambridge: Cambridge University Press.

Kamerman, Jack B., 1988 *Death in the Midst of Life: Social and Cultural Influences on Death, Grief, and Mourning*. Englewood Cliffs, NJ: Prentice Hall.

Kan, Sergei, 1986 The 19th-Century Tlingit Potlatch: A New Perspective. *American Ethnologist* 13(2):191–212.

Kan, Sergei, 1989 *Symbolic Immortality: The Tlingit Potlatch of the Nineteenth Century*. Washington: Smithsonian Institution Press.

Kastenbaum, Robert, and Paul T. Costa, 1977 Psychological Perspectives on Death. *Annual Review of Psychology* 28:225–249.

Kselman, Thomas A., 1993 *Death and the Afterlife in Modern France*. Princeton: Princeton University Press.

Lienhardt, Godfrey, 1961 *Divinity and Experience: The Religion of the Dinka*. Oxford: Clarendon Press.

Lifton, Robert Jay, 1967 *Death in Life: Survivors of Hiroshima*. New York: Random House.

Lifton, Robert Jay and Eric Olson, 1974 *Living and Dying*. London: Wildwood House.

Lock, Margaret, 1997 Displacing Suffering: The Recon-struction of Death in North America and Japan. *In Social Suffering*. Arthur, Kleinman, Veena Das, and Margaret Lock, eds. pp. 207–244. Berkeley: University of California Press.

Lock, Margaret, 2001 *Twice Dead: Organ Transplants and the Reinvention of Death*. Berkeley: University of California Press.

Malinowski, Bronislaw, 1954 [1925] *Magic, Science and Religion*. Garden City, NY: Doubleday & Company.

Malinowski, Bronislaw, 1967 *A Diary in the Strict Sense of the Term*. London: Routledge and Kegan Paul.

Mauss, Marcel, 1979 *Sociology and Psychology: Essays*. London: Routledge & Kegan Paul.

Merridale, Catherine, 2000 *Night of Stone: Death and Memory in Twentieth-Century Russia*. New York: Viking.

Mimica, Jadran, 1996 On Dying and Suffering in Iqwaye Existence. *In Things as They Are: New Directions in Phenomenological Anthropology*. Michael Jackson, ed. pp. 213–237. Bloomington: Indiana University Press.

Mosse, George L., 1990 *Fallen Soldiers: Reshaping the Memory of the World Wars*. New York: Oxford University Press.

Nadeau, Janice Winchester, 1998 *Families Making Sense of Death*. Thousand Oaks, CA: Sage Publications.

Palgi, Phyllis and Henry Abramovitch, 1984 Death: A Cross-Cultural Perspective. *Annual Review of Anthropology* 13:385–417.

Parkes, Colin Murray, 1996 *Bereavement: Studies of Grief in Adult Life*. 3rd edn. London: Routledge.

Parry, Jonathan, 1982 Sacrificial Death and the Necrophagous Ascetic. *In Death and the Regeneration of Life*. Maurice Bloch and Jonathan Parry, eds. pp. 74–110. Cambridge: Cambridge University Press.

Platt, Larry A. and V. Ricardo Persico, eds., 1992 *Grief in Cross-Cultural Perspective: A Case Book*. New York: Garland Publishing.

Radcliffe-Brown, A. R., 1964 [1912] *The Andaman Islanders*. New York: The Free Press.

Reynolds, Frank E. and Erale H. Waugh, eds., 1977 *Religious Encounters with Death: Insights from the History and Anthropology of Religions*. University Park: Pennsylvania State University Press.

Riley, John W., 1983 Dying and the Meanings of Death: Sociological Inquiries. *Annual Review of Sociology* 9:191–216.

Robben, Antonius C. G. M., 2000 State Terror in the Netherworld: Disappearance and Reburial in Argentina. *In Death Squad: The Anthropology of State Terror*. Jeffrey A. Sluka, ed. pp. 91–113. Philadelphia: University of Pennsylvania Press.

Rosaldo, Michelle Z., 1980 *Knowledge and Passion: Ilongot Notions of Self and Social Life*. Cambridge: Cambridge University Press.

Rosaldo, Renato, 1980 *Ilongot Headhunting, 1883–1974: A Study in Society and History*. Stanford, CA: Stanford University Press.

Rosaldo, Renato, 1993 Introduction: Grief and a Headhunter's Rage. *In Culture and Truth: The Remaking of Social Analysis*, pp. 1–21. Boston: Beacon Press.

Rosenblatt, Paul C., R. Patricia Walsh, and Douglas A. Jackson, 1976 *Grief and Mourning in a Cross-Cultural Perspective*. New Haven: HRAF Press.

Scheper-Hughes, Nancy, 1992 *Death Without Weeping: The Violence of Everyday Life in Brazil*. Berkeley: University of California Press.

Scheper-Hughes, Nancy and Philippe Bourgois, eds., 2003 *Violence in War and Peace: An Anthology*. Malden, MA: Blackwell Publishers.

Seale, Clive, 1998 *Constructing Death: The Sociology of Dying and Bereavement*. Cambridge: Cambridge University Press.

Seremetakis, C. Nadia, 1991 *The Last Word: Women, Death, and Divination in Inner Mani*. Chicago: University of Chicago Press.

Simeone, William E., 1991 The Northern Athabaskan Potlatch: The Objectification of Grief. *In Coping with the Final Tragedy: Cultural Variation in Dying and Grieving*. David R. Counts and Dorothy A. Counts, eds. pp. 157–167. Amityville, NY: Baywood Publishing Company.

Straus, Anne S., 1978 The Meaning of Death in Northern Cheyenne Culture. *Plains Anthropologist* 23(79):1–6.

Stroebe, Margaret S., Robert O. Hansson, Wolfgang Stroebe, and Henk Schut, eds., 2001 *Handbook of Bereavement Research: Consequences, Coping, Care*. Washington, DC: American Psychological Association Press.

Suzuki, Hikaru, 2000 *The Price of Death: The Funeral Industry in Contemporary Japan*. Stanford, CA: Stanford University Press.

Turner, Victor, 1967, Betwixt and Between: The Liminal Period in *Rites de Passage*. In *The Forest of Symbols: Aspects of Ndembu Ritual*. pp. 93–111. Ithaca, NY: Cornell University Press.

Van Gennep, Arnold, 1960 [1909] *The Rites of Passage*. Chicago: University of Chicago Press.

Verdery, Katherine, 1999 *The Political Lives of Dead Bodies: Reburial and Postsocialist Change*. New York: Columbia University Press.

Walter, Tony, 1999 *On Bereavement: The Culture of Grief*. Buckingham, England: Open University Press.

Part I

Conceptualizations of Death

1

Magic, Science and Religion

Bronislaw Malinowski

Death and the Reintegration of the Group

Of all sources of religion, the supreme and final crisis of life – death – is of the greatest importance. Death is the gateway to the other world in more than the literal sense. According to most theories of early religion, a great deal, if not all, of religious inspiration has been derived from it – and in this orthodox views are on the whole correct. Man has to live his life in the shadow of death, and he who clings to life and enjoys its fullness must dread the menace of its end. And he who is faced by death turns to the promise of life. Death and its denial – Immortality – have always formed, as they form today, the most poignant theme of man's forebodings. The extreme complexity of man's emotional reactions to life finds necessarily its counterpart in his attitude to death. Only what in life has been spread over a long space and manifested in a succession of experiences and events is here at its end condensed into one crisis which provokes a violent and complex outburst of religious manifestations.

Even among the most primitive peoples, the attitude towards death is infinitely more complex and, I may add, more akin to our own, than is usually assumed. It is often stated by anthropologists that the dominant feeling of the survivors is that of horror at the corpse and of fear of the ghost. This twin attitude is even made by no less an authority than Wilhelm Wundt the very nucleus of all religious belief and practice. Yet this assertion is only a half-truth, which means no truth at all. The emotions are extremely complex and even contradictory; the dominant elements, love of the dead and loathing of the corpse, passionate attachment to the personality still lingering about the body and a shattering fear of the gruesome thing that has been left over, these two elements seem to mingle and play into each other. This is reflected in the spontaneous behavior and in the ritual proceedings at death. In the tending of the corpse, in the modes of its disposal, in the post-funerary and commemorative ceremonies, the nearest relatives, the mother mourning for her son, the widow for her husband, the child for the parent, always show some horror and fear mingled with

From Bronislaw Malinowski, "Magic, Science and Religion," in *Magic, Science and Religion*, ed. James Needham (Macmillan: 1925; repr. Garden City, NY: Doubleday, 1954).

pious love, but never do the negative elements appear alone or even dominant.

The mortuary proceedings show a striking similarity throughout the world. As death approaches, the nearest relatives in any case, sometimes the whole community, forgather by the dying man, and dying, the most private act which a man can perform, is transformed into a public, tribal event. As a rule, a certain differentiation takes place at once, some of the relatives watching near the corpse, others making preparations for the pending end and its consequences, others again performing perhaps some religious acts at a sacred spot. Thus in certain parts of Melanesia the real kinsmen must keep at a distance and only relatives by marriage perform the mortuary services, while in some tribes of Australia the reverse order is observed.

As soon as death has occurred, the body is washed, anointed and adorned, sometimes the bodily apertures are filled, the arms and legs tied together. Then it is exposed to the view of all, and the most important phase, the immediate mourning begins. Those who have witnessed death and its sequel among savages and who can compare these events with their counterpart among other uncivilized peoples must be struck by the fundamental similarity of the proceedings. There is always a more or less conventionalized and dramatized outburst of grief and wailing in sorrow, which often passes among savages into bodily lacerations and the tearing of hair. This is always done in a public display and is associated with visible signs of mourning, such as black or white daubs on the body, shaven or disheveled hair, strange or torn garments.

The immediate mourning goes on round the corpse. This, far from being shunned or dreaded, is usually the center of pious attention. Often there are ritual forms of fondling or attestations of reverence. The body is sometimes kept on the knees of seated persons, stroked and embraced. At the same time these acts are usually considered both dangerous and repugnant, duties to be fulfilled at some cost to the performer. After a time the corpse has to be disposed of. Inhumation with an open or closed grave; exposure in caves or on platforms, in hollow trees or on the ground in some wild desert place; burning or setting adrift in canoes – these are the usual forms of disposal.

This brings us to perhaps the most important point, the two-fold contradictory tendency, on the one hand to preserve the body, to keep its form intact, or to retain parts of it; on the other hand the desire to be done with it, to put it out of the way, to annihilate it completely. Mummification and burning are the two extreme expressions of this two-fold tendency. It is impossible to regard mummification or burning or any intermediate form as determined by mere accident of belief, as a historical feature of some culture or other which has gained its universality by the mechanism of spread and contact only. For in these customs is clearly expressed the fundamental attitude of mind of the surviving relative, friend or lover, the longing for all that remains of the dead person and the disgust and fear of the dreadful transformation wrought by death.

One extreme and interesting variety in which this double-edged attitude is expressed in a gruesome manner is sarco-cannibalism, a custom of partaking in piety of the flesh of the dead person. It is done with extreme repugnance and dread and usually followed by a violent vomiting fit. At the same time it is felt to be a supreme act of reverence, love, and devotion. In fact it is considered such a sacred duty that among the Melanesians of New Guinea, where I have studied and witnessed it, it is still performed in secret, although severely penalized by the white Government. The smearing of the body with the fat of the dead, prevalent in Australia and Papuasia is, perhaps, but a variety of this custom.

In all such rites, there is a desire to maintain the tie and the parallel tendency to break the bond. Thus the funerary rites are considered as unclean and soiling, the contact with the corpse as defiling and dangerous, and the performers have to wash, cleanse their body, remove all traces of contact, and perform ritual lustrations. Yet the mortuary ritual compels man to overcome the repugnance, to conquer his fears, to make piety and attachment triumphant, and with it the belief in a future life, in the survival of the spirit.

And here we touch on one of the most important functions of religious cult. In the foregoing analysis I have laid stress on the direct emotional forces created by contact with death and with the corpse, for they primarily and most powerfully determine the behavior of the survivors. But connected with these emotions and born out of them, there is the idea of the spirit, the belief in the new life into which the departed has entered. And here we return to the problem of animism with which we began our survey of primitive religious facts. What is the substance of a spirit, and what is the psychological origin of this belief?

The savage is intensely afraid of death, probably as the result of some deep-seated instincts common to man and animals. He does not want to realize it as an end, he cannot face the idea of complete cessation, of annihilation. The idea of spirit and of spiritual existence is near at hand, furnished by such experiences as are discovered and described by Tylor. Grasping at it, man reaches the comforting belief in spiritual continuity and in the life after death. Yet this belief does not remain unchallenged in the complex, double-edged play of hope and fear which sets in always in the face of death. To the comforting voice of hope, to the intense desire of immortality, to the difficulty, in one's own case, almost the impossibility, of facing annihilation there are opposed powerful and terrible forebodings. The testimony of the senses, the gruesome decomposition of the corpse, the visible disappearance of the personality – certain apparently instinctive suggestions of fear and horror seem to threaten man at all stages of culture with some idea of annihilation, with some hidden fears and forebodings. And here into this play of emotional forces, into this supreme dilemma of life and final death, religion steps in, selecting the positive creed, the comforting view, the culturally valuable belief in immortality, in the spirit independent of the body, and in the continuance of life after death. In the various ceremonies at death, in commemoration and communion with the departed, and worship of ancestral ghosts, religion gives body and form to the saving beliefs.

Thus the belief in immortality is the result of a deep emotional revelation, standardized by religion, rather than a primitive philosophic doctrine. Man's conviction of continued life is one of the supreme gifts of religion, which judges and selects the better of the two alternatives suggested by self-preservation – the hope of continued life and the fear of annihila-

tion. The belief in spirits is the result of the belief in immortality. The substance of which the spirits are made is the full-blooded passion and desire for life, rather than the shadowy stuff which haunts his dreams and illusions. Religion saves man from a surrender to death and destruction, and in doing this it merely makes use of the observations of dreams, shadows, and visions. The real nucleus of animism lies in the deepest emotional fact of human nature, the desire for life.

Thus the rites of mourning, the ritual behavior immediately after death, can be taken as pattern of the religious act, while the belief in immortality, in the continuity of life and in the nether world, can be taken as the prototype of an act of faith. Here, as in the religious ceremonies previously described, we find self-contained acts, the aim of which is achieved in their very performance. The ritual despair, the obsequies, the acts of mourning, express the emotion of the bereaved and the loss of the whole group. They endorse and they duplicate the natural feelings of the survivors; they create a social event out of a natural fact. Yet, though in the acts of mourning, in the mimic despair of wailing, in the treatment of the corpse and in its disposal, nothing ulterior is achieved, these acts fulfill an important function and possess a considerable value for primitive culture.

What is this function? The initiation ceremonies we have found fulfill theirs in sacralizing tradition; the food cults, sacrament and sacrifice bring man into communion with providence, with the beneficent forces of plenty; totemism standardizes man's practical, useful attitude of selective interest towards his surroundings. If the view here taken of the biological function of religion is true, some such similar role must also be played by the whole mortuary ritual.

The death of a man or woman in a primitive group, consisting of a limited number of individuals, is an event of no mean importance. The nearest relatives and friends are disturbed to the depth of their emotional life. A small community bereft of a member, especially if he be important, is severely mutilated. The whole event breaks the normal course of life and shakes the moral foundations of society. The strong tendency on which we have insisted in the above description: to give way to fear and horror, to abandon the corpse, to run away from the village, to destroy all the belongings of the dead one – all these impulses exist, and if given way to would be extremely dangerous, disintegrating the group, destroying the material foundations of primitive culture. Death in a primitive society is, therefore, much more than the removal of a member. By setting in motion one part of the deep forces of the instinct of self-preservation, it threatens the very cohesion and solidarity of the group, and upon this depends the organization of that society, its tradition, and finally the whole culture. For if primitive man yielded always to the disintegrating impulses of his reaction to death, the continuity of tradition and the existence of material civilization would be made impossible.

We have seen already how religion, by sacralizing and thus standardizing the other set of impulses, bestows on man the gift of mental integrity. Exactly the same function it fulfills also with regard to the whole group. The ceremonial of death which ties the survivors to the body and rivets them to the place of death, the beliefs in the existence of the spirit, in its beneficent influences or malevolent intentions, in the duties of a series of commemorative or sacrificial ceremonies – in all this religion counteracts the centrifugal forces of fear, dismay, demoralization, and provides the most powerful means of reintegration of the group's shaken solidarity and of the re-establishment of its morale.

In short, religion here assures the victory of tradition and culture over the mere negative response of thwarted instinct.

2

The Terror of Death

Ernest Becker

Is it not for us to confess that in our civilized attitude towards death we are once more living psychologically beyond our means, and must reform and give truth its due? Would it not be better to give death the place in actuality and in our thoughts which properly belongs to it, and to yield a little more prominence to that unconscious attitude towards death which we have hitherto so carefully suppressed? This hardly seems indeed a greater achievement, but rather a backward step . . . but it has the merit of taking somewhat more into account the true state of affairs.

SIGMUND FREUD[1]

The first thing we have to do with heroism is to lay bare its underside, show what gives human heroics its specific nature and impetus. Here we introduce directly one of the great rediscoveries of modern thought: that of all things that move man, one of the principal ones is his terror of death. After Darwin the problem of death as an evolutionary one came to the fore, and many thinkers immediately saw that it was a major psychological problem for man.[2] They also very quickly saw what real heroism was about, as Shaler wrote just at the turn of the century:[3] heroism is first and foremost a reflex of the terror of death. We admire most the courage to face death; we give such valor our highest and most constant adoration; it moves us deeply in our hearts because we have doubts about how brave we ourselves would be. When we see a man bravely facing his own extinction we rehearse the greatest victory we can imagine. And so the hero has been the center of human honor and acclaim since probably the beginning of specifically human evolution. But even before that our primate ancestors deferred to others who were extrapowerful and courageous and ignored those who were cowardly. Man has elevated animal courage into a cult.

Anthropological and historical research also began, in the nineteenth century, to put together a picture of the heroic since primitive and ancient times. The hero was the man who could go into the spirit world, the world of the dead, and return alive. He had his descendants in the mystery cults of

From Ernest Becker, "The Terror of Death," in *The Denial of Death* (New York: The Free Press, 1973).

the Eastern Mediterranean, which were cults of death and resurrection. The divine hero of each of these cults was one who had come back from the dead. And as we know today from the research into ancient myths and rituals, Christianity itself was a competitor with the mystery cults and won out – among other reasons – because it, too, featured a healer with supernatural powers who had risen from the dead. The great triumph of Easter is the joyful shout "Christ has risen!", an echo of the same joy that the devotees of the mystery cults enacted at their ceremonies of the victory over death. These cults, as G. Stanley Hall so aptly put it, were an attempt to attain "an immunity bath" from the greatest evil: death and the dread of it.[4] All historical religions addressed themselves to this same problem of how to bear the end of life. Religions like Hinduism and Buddhism performed the ingenious trick of pretending not to want to be reborn, which is a sort of negative magic: claiming not to want what you really want most.[5] When philosophy took over from religion it also took over religion's central problem, and death became the real "muse of philosophy" from its beginnings in Greece right through Heidegger and modern existentialism.[6]

We already have volumes of work and thought on the subject, from religion and philosophy and – since Darwin – from science itself. The problem is how to make sense out of it; the accumulation of research and opinion on the fear of death is already too large to be dealt with and summarized in any simple way. The revival of interest in death, in the last few decades, has alone already piled up a formidable literature, and this literature does not point in any single direction.

The "Healthy-Minded" Argument

There are "healthy-minded" persons who maintain that fear of death is not a natural thing for man, that we are not born with it. An increasing number of careful studies on how the actual fear of death develops in the child[7] agree fairly well that the child has no knowledge of death until about the age of three to five. How could he? It is too abstract an idea, too removed from his experience. He lives in a world that is full of living, acting things, responding to him,

amusing him, feeding him. He doesn't know what it means for life to disappear forever, nor theorize where it would go. Only gradually does he recognize that there is a thing called death that takes some people away forever; very reluctantly he comes to admit that it sooner or later takes everyone away, but this gradual realization of the inevitability of death can take up until the ninth or tenth year.

If the child has no knowledge of an abstract idea like absolute negation, he does have his own anxieties. He is absolutely dependent on the mother, experiences loneliness when she is absent, frustration when he is deprived of gratification, irritation at hunger and discomfort, and so on. If he were abandoned to himself his world would drop away, and his organism must sense this at some level; we call this the anxiety of object-loss. Isn't this anxiety, then, a natural, organismic fear of annihilation? Again, there are many who look at this as a very relative matter. They believe that if the mother has done her job in a warm and dependable way, the child's natural anxieties and guilts will develop in a moderate way, and he will be able to place them firmly under the control of his developing personality.[8] The child who has good maternal experiences will develop a sense of basic security and will not be subject to morbid fears of losing support, of being annihilated, or the like.[9] As he grows up to understand death rationally by the age of nine or ten, he will accept it as part of his world view, but the idea will not poison his self-confident attitude toward life. The psychiatrist Rheingold says categorically that annihilation anxiety is not part of the child's natural experience but is engendered in him by bad experiences with a depriving mother.[10] This theory puts the whole burden of anxiety onto the child's nurture and not his nature. Another psychiatrist, in a less extreme vein, sees the fear of death as greatly heightened by the child's experiences with his parents, by their hostile denial of his life impulses, and, more generally, by the antagonism of society to human freedom and self-expansiveness.[11]

As we will see later on, this view is very popular today in the widespread movement toward unrepressed living, the urge to a new freedom for natural biological urges, a new attitude of pride and joy in the body, the abandonment of shame, guilt, and self-hatred. From this point of view, fear of death is something that society creates and at the same time uses against the person to keep him in submission; the psychiatrist Moloney talked about it as a "culture mechanism," and Marcuse as an "ideology."[12] Norman O. Brown, in a vastly influential book that we shall discuss at some length, went so far as to say that there could be a birth and development of the child in a "second innocence" that would be free of the fear of death because it would not deny natural vitality and would leave the child fully open to physical living.[13]

It is easy to see that, from this point of view, those who have bad early experiences will be most morbidly fixated on the anxiety of death; and if by chance they grow up to be philosophers they will probably make the idea a central dictum of their thought – as did Schopenhauer, who both hated his mother and went on to pronounce death the "muse of philosophy." If you have a "sour" character structure or especially tragic experiences, then you are bound to be pessimistic. One psychologist remarked to me that the whole idea of the fear of death was an import by existentialists and Protestant theologians who had been scarred by their European experiences or who carried around the extra weight of a Calvinist and Lutheran heritage of life-denial. Even the distinguished psychologist Gardner Murphy seems to lean to this school and urges us to study *the person* who exhibits the fear of death, who places anxiety in the center of his thought; and Murphy asks why the living of life in love and joy cannot also be regarded as real and basic.[14]

The "Morbidly-Minded" Argument

The "healthy-minded" argument just discussed is one side of the picture of the accumulated research and opinion on the problem of the fear of death, but there is another side. A large body of people would agree with these observations on early experience and would admit that experiences may heighten natural anxieties and later fears, but these people would also claim very strongly that nevertheless the fear of death is natural and is present in everyone, that it is the basic fear that influences all others, a fear from which no one is immune, no matter how disguised it may be.

William James spoke very early for this school, and with his usual colorful realism he called death "the worm at the core" of man's pretensions to happiness.[15] No less a student of human nature than Max Scheler thought that all men must have some kind of certain intuition of this "worm at the core," whether they admitted it or not.[16] Countless other authorities – some of whom we shall parade in the following pages – belong to this school: students of the stature of Freud, many of his close circle, and serious researchers who are not psychoanalysts. What are we to make of a dispute in which there are two distinct camps, both studded with distinguished authorities? Jacques Choron goes so far as to say that it is questionable whether it will ever be possible to decide whether the fear of death is or is not the basic anxiety.[17] In matters like this, then, the most that one can do is to take sides, to give an opinion based on the authorities that seem to him most compelling, and to present some of the compelling arguments.

I frankly side with this second school – in fact, this whole book is a network of arguments based on the universality of the fear of death, or "terror" as I prefer to call it, in order to convey how all-consuming it is when we look it full in the face. The first document that I want to present and linger on is a paper written by the noted psychoanalyst Gregory Zilboorg; it is an especially penetrating essay that – for succinctness and scope – has not been much improved upon, even though it appeared several decades ago.[18] Zilboorg says that most people think death fear is absent because it rarely shows its true face; but he argues that underneath all appearances fear of death is universally present:

> For behind the sense of insecurity in the face of danger, behind the sense of discouragement and depression, there always lurks the basic fear of death, a fear which undergoes most complex elaborations and manifests itself in many indirect ways. . . . No one is free of the fear of death . . . The anxiety neuroses, the various phobic states, even a considerable number of depressive suicidal states and many schizophrenias amply demonstrate the ever-present fear of death which becomes woven into the major conflicts of the given psychopathological conditions. . . . We may take for granted that the fear of death is always present in our mental functioning.[19]

Hadn't James said the same thing earlier, in his own way?

> Let sanguine healthy-mindedness do its best with its strange power of living in the moment and ignoring and forgetting, still the evil background is really there to be thought of, and the skull will grin in at the banquet.[20]

The difference in these two statements is not so much in the imagery and style as in the fact that Zilboorg's comes almost a half-century later and is based on that much more real clinical work, not only on philosophical speculation or personal intuition. But it also continues the straight line of development from James and the post-Darwinians who saw the fear of death as a biological and evolutionary problem. Here I think he is on very sound ground, and I especially like the way he puts the case. Zilboorg points out that this fear is actually an expression of the instinct of self-preservation, which functions as a constant drive to maintain life and to master the dangers that threaten life:

> Such constant expenditure of psychological energy on the business of preserving life would be impossible if the fear of death were not as constant. The very term "self-preservation" implies an effort against some force of disintegration; the affective aspect of this is fear, fear of death.[21]

In other words, the fear of death must be present behind all our normal functioning, in order for the organism to be armed toward self-preservation. But the fear of death cannot be present constantly in one's mental functioning, else the organism could not function. Zilboorg continues:

> If this fear were as constantly conscious, we should be unable to function normally. It must be properly repressed to keep us living with any modicum of comfort. We know very well that to repress means more than to put away and to forget that which was put away and the place where we put it. It means also to maintain a constant psychological effort to keep the lid on and inwardly never relax our watchfulness.[22]

And so we can understand what seems like an impossible paradox: the ever-present fear of death in the normal biological functioning of our instinct of self-preservation, as well as our utter obliviousness to this fear in our conscious life:

> Therefore in normal times we move about actually without ever believing in our own death, as if we fully believed in our own corporeal immortality. We are intent on mastering death. . . . A man will say, of course, that he knows he will die some day, but he does not really care. He is having a good time with living, and he does not think about death and does not care to bother about it – but this is a purely intellectual, verbal admission. The affect of fear is repressed.[23]

The argument from biology and evolution is basic and has to be taken seriously; I don't see how it can be left out of any discussion. Animals in order to survive have had to be protected by fear-responses, in relation not only to other animals but to nature itself. They had to see the real relationship of their limited powers to the dangerous world in which they were immersed. Reality and fear go together naturally. As the human infant is in an even more exposed and helpless situation, it is foolish to assume that the fear response of animals would have disappeared in such a weak and highly sensitive species. It is more reasonable to think that it was instead heightened, as some of the early Darwinians thought: early men who were most afraid were those who were most realistic about their situation in nature, and they passed on to their offspring a realism that had a high survival value.[24] The result was the emergence of man as we know him: a hyperanxious animal who constantly invents reasons for anxiety even where there are none.

The argument from psychoanalysis is less speculative and has to be taken even more seriously. It showed us something about the child's inner world that we had never realized: namely, that it was more filled with terror, the more the child was different from other animals. We could say that fear is programmed into the lower animals by ready-made instincts; but an animal who has no instincts has no programmed fears. Man's fears are fashioned out of the ways in which he perceives the world. Now, what is unique about the child's perception of the world? For one thing, the extreme confusion of cause-and-effect relationships; for another, extreme unreality about the limits of his own powers. The child lives in a situation of utter dependence; and when his needs are met it must seem to him that he has magical powers, real omnipotence. If he experiences pain, hunger, or discomfort, all he has to do is to scream and he is relieved and lulled by gentle, loving sounds. He is a magician and a telepath who has only to mumble and to imagine and the world turns to his desires.

But now the penalty for such perceptions. In a magical world where things cause other things to happen just by a mere thought or a look of displeasure, anything can happen to anyone. When the child experiences inevitable and real frustrations from his parents, he directs hate and destructive feelings toward them; and he has no way of knowing that malevolent feelings cannot be fulfilled by the same magic as were his other wishes. Psychoanalysts believe that this confusion is a main cause of guilt and helplessness in the child. In his very fine essay Wahl summed up this paradox:

> the socialization processes for all children are painful and frustrating, and hence no child escapes forming hostile death wishes toward his socializers. Therefore, none escape the fear of personal death in either direct or symbolic form. Repression is usually . . . immediate and effective. [25]

The child is too weak to take responsibility for all this destructive feeling, and he can't control the magical execution of his desires. This is what we mean by an immature ego: the child doesn't have the sure ability to organize his perceptions and his relationship to the world; he can't control his own activity; and he doesn't have sure command over the acts of others. He thus has no real control over the magical cause-and-effect that he senses, either inside himself or outside in nature and in others: his destructive wishes could explode, his parents' wishes likewise. The forces of nature are confused, externally and internally; and for a weak ego this fact makes for quantities of exaggerated potential power and added terror. The result is that the child – at least some of the time – lives with an inner sense of chaos that other animals are immune to. [26]

Ironically, even when the child makes out real cause-and-effect relationships they become a burden to him because he overgeneralizes them. One such generalization is what the psychoanalysts call the "talion principle." The child crushes insects, sees the cat eat a mouse and make it vanish, joins with the family to make a pet rabbit disappear into their interiors, and so on. He comes to know something about the power relations of the world but can't give them relative value: the parents could eat him and make him vanish, and he could likewise eat them; when the father gets a fierce glow in his eyes as he clubs a rat, the watching child might also expect to be clubbed – especially if he has been thinking bad magical thoughts.

I don't want to seem to make an exact picture of processes that are still unclear to us or to make out that all children live in the same world and have the same problems; also, I wouldn't want to make the child's world seem more lurid than it really is most of the time; but I think it is important to show the painful contradictions that must be present in it at least some of the time and to show how fantastic a world it surely is for the first few years of the child's life. Perhaps then we could understand better why Zilboorg said that the fear of death "undergoes most complex elaborations and manifests itself in many indirect ways." Or, as Wahl so perfectly put it, death is a *complex symbol* and not any particular, sharply defined thing to the child:

> the child's concept of death is not a single thing, but it is rather a composite of mutually contradictory paradoxes . . . death itself is not only a state, but a complex symbol, the significance of which will vary from one person to another and from one culture to another. [27]

We could understand, too, why children have their recurrent nightmares, their universal phobias of insects and mean dogs. In their tortured interiors radiate complex symbols of many inadmissible realities – terror of the world, the horror of one's own wishes, the fear of vengeance by the parents, the disappearance of things, one's lack of control over anything, really. It is too much for any animal to take, but the child has to take it, and so he wakes up screaming with almost punctual regularity during the period when his weak ego is in the process of consolidating things.

The "Disappearance" of the Fear of Death

Yet, the nightmares become more and more widely spaced, and some children have more than others: we are back again to the beginning of our discussion, to those who do not believe that the fear of death is normal, who think that it is a neurotic exaggeration that draws on bad early experiences. Otherwise, they say, how do you explain that so many people – the vast majority – seem to survive the flurry of childhood nightmares and go on to live a healthy, more-or-less optimistic life, untroubled by death? As Montaigne said, the peasant has a profound indifference and a patience toward death and the sinister side of life; and if we say that this is because of his stupidity, then "let's all learn from stupidity."[28] Today, when we know more than Montaigne, we would say "let's all learn from repression" – but the moral would have just as much weight: repression takes care of the complex symbol of death for most people.

But its disappearance doesn't mean that the fear was never there. The argument of those who believe in the universality of the innate terror of death rests its case mostly on what we know about how effective repression is. The argument can probably never be cleanly decided: if you claim that a concept is not present because it is repressed, you can't lose; it is not a fair game, intellectually, because you always hold the trump card. This type of argument makes psychoanalysis seem unscientific to many people, the fact is that its proponents can claim that someone denies one of their concepts because he represses his consciousness of its truth.

But repression is not a magical word for winning arguments; it is a real phenomenon, and we have been able to study many of its workings. This study gives it legitimacy as a scientific concept and makes it a more-or-less dependable ally in our argument. For one thing, there is a growing body of research trying to get at the consciousness of death denied by repression that uses psychological tests such as measuring galvanic skin responses; it strongly suggests that underneath the most bland exterior lurks the universal anxiety, the "worm at the core."[29]

For another thing, there is nothing like shocks in the real world to jar loose repressions. Recently psychiatrists reported an increase in anxiety neuroses in children as a result of the earth tremors in Southern California. For these children the discovery that life really includes cataclysmic danger was too much for their still-imperfect denial systems – hence open outbursts of anxiety. With adults we see this manifestation of anxiety in the face of impending catastrophe where it takes the form of panic. Recently several people suffered broken limbs and other injuries after forcing open their airplane's safety door during take-off and jumping from the wing to the ground; the incident was triggered by the backfire of an engine. Obviously underneath these harmless noises other things are rumbling in the creature.

But even more important is how repression works: it is not simply a negative force opposing life energies; it lives on life energies and uses them creatively. I mean that fears are naturally absorbed by expansive organismic striving. Nature seems to have built into organisms an innate healthy-mindedness; it expresses itself in self-delight, in the pleasure of unfolding one's capacities into the world, in the incorporation of things in that world, and in feeding on its limitless experiences. This is a lot of very positive experience, and when a powerful organism moves with it, it gives contentment. As Santayana once put it: a lion must feel more secure that God is on his side than a gazelle. On the most elemental level the organism works actively against its own fragility by seeking to expand and perpetuate itself in living experience; instead of shrinking, it moves toward more life. Also, it does one thing at a time, avoiding needless distractions from all-absorbing activity; in this way, it would seem, fear of death can be carefully ignored or actually absorbed in the life-expanding processes. Occasionally we seem to see such a vital organism on the human level: I am thinking of the portrait of *Zorba the Greek* drawn by Nikos Kazantzakis. Zorba was an ideal of the nonchalant victory of all-absorbing daily passion over timidity and death, and he purged others in his life-affirming flame. But Kazantzakis himself was no Zorba – which is partly why the character of Zorba rang a bit false – nor are most other men. Still, everyone enjoys a working amount of basic narcissism, even though it is not a lion's. The child who is well nourished and loved develops, as we said, a sense of magical omnipotence, a sense of his own indestructibility, a feeling of proven power and secure support. He can imagine himself, deep down, to be eternal. We might say that his repression of the idea of his own death is made easy for him because he is fortified against it in his very narcissistic vitality. This type of character probably helped Freud to say that the unconscious does not know death. Anyway, we know that basic narcissism is increased when one's childhood experiences have been securely life-supporting and warmly enhancing to the sense of self, to the feeling of being really special, truly Number One in creation. The result is that some people have more of what the psychoanalyst Leon J. Saul has aptly called "Inner Sustainment."[30] It is a sense of bodily confidence in the face of experience that sees the person more easily through severe life crises and even sharp personality changes; it almost seems to take the place of the directive instincts of lower animals. One can't help thinking of Freud again, who had more inner sustainment than most men, thanks to his mother and favorable early environment; he knew the confidence and courage that it gave to a man, and he himself faced up to life and to a fatal cancer with a Stoic heroism. Again we have evidence that the complex symbol of fear of death would be very variable in its intensity; it would be, as Wahl concluded, "profoundly dependent upon the nature and the vicissitudes of the developmental process."[31]

But I want to be careful not to make too much of natural vitality and inner sustainment. As we will see in Chapter Six, even the unusually favored Freud suffered his whole life from phobias and from death-anxiety; and he came to fully perceive the world under the aspect of natural terror. I don't believe that the complex symbol of death is ever absent, no matter how much vitality and inner sustainment a person has. Even more, if we say that these powers make repression easy and natural, we are only saying the half of it. Actually, they get their very power from repression. Psychiatrists argue that the fear of death varies in intensity depending on the developmental process, and I think that one import-

ant reason for this variability is that the fear is transmuted in that process. If the child has had a very favorable upbringing, it only serves all the better to hide the fear of death. After all, repression is made possible by the natural identification of the child with the powers of his parents. If he has been well cared for, identification comes easily and solidly, and his parents' powerful triumph over death automatically becomes his. What is more natural to banish one's fears than to live on delegated powers? And what does the whole growing-up period signify, if not the giving over of one's life-project? I am going to be talking about these things all the way through this book and do not want to develop them in this introductory discussion. What we will see is that man cuts out for himself a manageable world: he throws himself into action uncritically, unthinkingly. He accepts the cultural programming that turns his nose where he is supposed to look; he doesn't bite the world off in one piece as a giant would, but in small manageable pieces, as a beaver does. He uses all kinds of techniques, which we call the "character defenses": he learns not to expose himself, not to stand out; he learns to embed himself in other-power, both of concrete persons and of things and cultural commands; the result is that he comes to exist in the imagined infallibility of the world around him. He doesn't have to have fears when his feet are solidly mired and his life mapped out in a ready-made maze. All he has to do is to plunge ahead in a compulsive style of drivenness in the "ways of the world" that the child learns and in which he lives later as a kind of grim equanimity – the "strange power of living in the moment and ignoring and forgetting" – as James put it. This is the deeper reason that Montaigne's peasant isn't troubled until the very end, when the Angel of Death, who has always been sitting on his shoulder, extends his wing. Or at least until he is prematurely startled into dumb awareness, like the "Husbands" in John Cassavetes' fine film. At times like this, when the awareness dawns that has always been blotted out by frenetic, ready-made activity, we see the transmutation of repression redistilled, so to speak, and the fear of death emerges in pure essence. This is why people have psychotic breaks when repression no longer works, when the forward momentum of activity is no longer possible. Besides, the peasant mentality is far less romantic than Montaigne would have us believe. The peasant's equanimity is usually immersed in a style of life that has elements of real madness, and so it protects him: an undercurrent of constant hate and bitterness expressed in feuding, bullying, bickering and family quarrels, the petty mentality, the self-deprecation, the superstition, the obsessive control of daily life by a strict authoritarianism, and so on. As the title of a recent essay by Joseph Lopreato has it: "How would you like to be a peasant?"

We will also touch upon another large dimension in which the complex symbol of death is transmuted and transcended by man – belief in immortality, the extension of one's being into eternity. Right now we can conclude that there are many ways that repression works to calm the anxious human animal, so that he need not be anxious at all.

I think we have reconciled our two divergent positions on the fear of death. The "environmental" and the "innate" positions are both part of the same picture; they merge naturally into one another; it all depends from which angle you approach the picture: from the side of the disguises and transmutations of the fear of death or from the side of its apparent absence. I admit with a sense of scientific uneasiness that whatever angle you use, you don't get at the actual fear of death; and so I reluctantly agree with Choron that the argument can probably never be cleanly "won." Nevertheless something very important emerges: there are different images of man that he can draw and choose from.

On the one hand, we see a human animal who is partly dead to the world, who is most "dignified" when he shows a certain obliviousness to his fate, when he allows himself to be driven through life; who is most "free" when he lives in secure dependency on powers around him, when he is least in possession of himself. On the other hand, we get an image of a human animal who is overly sensitive to the world, who cannot shut it out, who is thrown back on his own meagre powers, and who seems least free to move and act, least in possession of himself, and most undignified. Whichever image we choose to identify with depends in large part upon ourselves. Let us then explore and develop these images further to see what they reveal to us.

NOTES

1 S. Freud, "Thoughts for the Times on War and Death," 1915, *Collected Papers*, vol. 4 (New York: Basic Books, 1959), pp. 316–17.

2 Cf., for example, A. L. Cochrane, "Elie Metschnikoff and His Theory of an '*Instinct de la Mort*,'" *International Journal of Psychoanalysis* 1934, 15:265–70; G. Stanley Hall, "Thanatophobia and Immortality," *American Journal of Psychology*, 1915, 26:550–613.

3 N. S. Shaler, *The Individual: A Study of Life and Death* (New York: Appleton, 1900).

4 Hall, "Thanatophobia," p. 562.

5 Cf., Alan Harrington, *The Immortalist* (New York: Random House, 1969), p. 82.

6 See Jacques Choron's excellent study: *Death and Western Thought* (New York: Collier Books, 1963).

7 See H. Feifel, ed., *The Meaning of Death* (New York: McGraw-Hill, 1959), Chapter 6; G. Rochlin, *Griefs and Discontents* (Boston: Little, Brown, 1967), p. 67.

8 J. Bowlby, *Maternal Care and Mental Health* (Geneva: World Health Organization, 1952), p. 11.

9 Cf. Walter Tietz, "School Phobia and the Fear of Death," *Mental Hygiene*, 1970, 54:565–8.

10 J. C. Rheingold, *The Mother, Anxiety and Death: The Catastrophic Death Complex* (Boston: Little, Brown, 1967).

11 A. J. Levin, "The Fiction of the Death Instinct," *Psychiatric Quarterly*, 1951, 25:257–81.

12 J. C. Moloney, *The Magic Cloak: A Contribution to the Psychology of Authoritarianism* (Wakefield, Mass.: Montrose Press, 1949), p. 217; H. Marcuse, "The Ideology of Death," in Feifel, *Meaning of Death*, Chapter 5.

13 LAD, p. 270.

14 G. Murphy, "Discussion," in Feifel, *The Meaning of Death*, p. 320.

15 W. James, *Varieties of Religious Experience: A study in Human Nature*, 1902 (New York: Mentor Edition, 1958) p. 121.

16 Choron, *Death*, p. 17.

17 *Ibid.*, p. 272.

18 G. Zilboorg "Fear of Death," *Psychoanalytic Quarterly*, 1943, 12: 465–75. See Eissler's nice technical distinction between the anxiety of death and the terror of it, in his book of essays loaded with subtle discussion: K. R. Eissler, *The Psychiatrist and the Dying Patient* (New York: International Universities Press, 1955), p. 277.

19 Zilboorg "Fear of Death," pp. 465–7.

20 James, *Varieties*, p. 121.

21 Zilboorg, "Fear of Death," p. 467. Or, we might more precisely say, with Eissler, fear of annihilation, which is extended by the ego into the consciousness of death. See *The Psychiatrist and the Dying Patient*, p. 267.

22 *Ibid*.

23 *Ibid*., pp. 468–71 *passim*.

24 Cf. Shaler, *The Individual*.

25 C. W. Wahl, "The Fear of Death," in Feifel, pp. 24–5.

26 Cf. Moloney, *The Magic Cloak*, p. 117.

27 Wahl, "Fear of Death," pp. 25–6.

28 In Choron, *Death*, p. 100.

29 Cf., for example, I. E. Alexander *et al.*, "Is Death a Matter of Indifference?" *Journal of Psychology*, 1957, 43:277–83; I. M. Greenberg and I. E. Alexander, "Some Correlates of Thoughts and Feelings Concerning Death," *Hillside Hospital Journal*, 1962, no. 2:120–6; S. I. Golding *et al.*, "Anxiety and Two Cognitive Forms of Resistance to the Idea of Death," *Psychological Reports*, 1966, 18: 359–64.

30 L. J. Saul, "Inner Sustainment," *Psycholoanalytic Quarterly*, 1970, 39:215–22.

31 Wahl, "Fear of Death," p. 26.

3

Symbolic Immortality

Robert Jay Lifton and Eric Olson

The idea of immortality is the answer to a profound human question or, really, the answer to two such questions. The first question is, What happens to a person after death? The second is, How can a person live without overwhelming anxiety in the face of the certainty of death? Behind both questions lies the human aspiration to live forever.

It is possible to look at all of human history as a record of man's diverse answers to these questions of immortality. Religions and empires have been founded, wars fought, and untold millions of people killed on behalf of conflicting notions of the path to immortal life. And the concern about immortality, as well as the debate about what it means, continues in our own time.

Freud said that the aim of life is death. By this he meant to convey at least two distinct ideas. The first implication of this concept is the idea of the death instinct as an innate tendency toward return to an inanimate state.

Instincts are modes of energy that lead to certain forms of life-preserving behavior. Therefore, the concept of an instinct that leads to death is something of a contradiction in terms. As we have suggested previously, however, Freud's idea of a death instinct did contain an important element of truth that should be preserved: that death is psychically present from the beginning of life. We wish to preserve this Freudian insight about the psychological significance of death. But we believe that this influence of death on psychological life is due to the importance of symbolization in mental activity rather than to what Freud called a death instinct.

What we call experience can occur only insofar as our minds are able to give form to our perceptions. This form structures and orders sensory data. "Seeing" and "recognizing" are thus very closely related, because inner psychic structures create meaning and the possibility for recognition. The inner forms in our minds are images and symbols which can be either very clear and distinct or rather vague and cloudy. The most general psychic organization of these inner images and symbols takes place around the polarities of connection-separation, movement-stasis, and integrity-disintegration. The extreme form of separation, stasis, and disintegra-

From Robert Jay Lifton and Eric Olson, "Symbolic Immortality," in *Living and Dying* (London: Wildwood House, 1974).

tion is death, and imagery that relates to these is psychologically extremely powerful.

The second implication of Freud's concept of the death instinct is that "every organism wants to die in its own fashion." In that spirit, recent psychiatric investigators speak of the "appropriate" death, by which they mean a readiness to die because a full life has reached completion. But this sense is often inseparable from despair – the feeling that one no longer has sufficient purpose to go on living.

These problems have been dealt with chiefly in literature, philosophy, and theology – disciplines outside the realm of science. Only recently have psychologists become concerned with them. The scientific world view has generally been limited to questions of the "means" of life, rather than confronting problems of ultimate value. The purposes of human life and the question of what lies beyond it – these are precisely the issues that science has considered inappropriate to its proper concerns. Because science has great prestige in our society, scientists' avoidance of issues of value has a profound influence on our culture and our lives.

Psychology has been partly within the scientific tradition in this sense and partly outside it. Most academic psychologists have been more interested in psychological *mechanisms* (such as how people learn) than in questions of ethical *goals* (such as what it is people should learn). On this point Freud was a great rebel, because he was concerned with alleviating psychological misery. To achieve that end, he believed people should be educated to accept reality, and he was convinced that the scientific truths discovered by psychology would lead to the abolition of man's spiritual illusions.

Chief among humanity's illusions, in Freud's view, was religion. He saw the spiritual comfort given by religion as a false support used by people who had not outgrown childish dependence on parents. Maturity, according to Freud, would consist in facing squarely the hard realities of life, and death, and not searching after false hopes.

Freud saw the idea of immortality as supreme among civilization's false hopes. He said that this illusion derives from clinging to the pretense that one will not die, and that it serves to compensate for the reality of death which is too hard to accept. Freud believed that by pinning its hopes on an illusion – the illusion that death is not total and final – civilization undermines its only real hope: the rational pursuit of the truth.

When, in his later writings, Freud attacked religion as an illusion, he aroused almost as much controversy and contempt as he had in his earlier emphasis on the importance of sexuality. Freud insisted that death is *final* and means the total annihilation of the organism. He believed that doctrines of the immortality of the soul derive from a childlike refusal to accept the finality of death.

In the early 1900s, Carl Jung, initially one of Freud's followers, began to take psychology in a very different direction. Jung had done extensive study of world religions and mythology and was impressed by the discovery that myths from all parts of the world and in every age have contained beliefs about life after death. Jung felt that the long history of mythology must reveal deep truths about the nature of the human mind that psychology was ignoring. These truths Jung called "archetypes" – universal psychic images which he believed arose from the deepest level of the unconscious. Jung argued that humankind's relatively recent stress upon narrow materialistic science could bring about the loss of the vital truths displayed in dreams and myths. To ignore these universal archetypal truths would result in the impoverishment of psychic life.

Jung described the psychic vitality of "primitive" peoples who live in tune with archetypal truth. And he observed the positive effects of belief in myths for persons nearing death. He said that when man's conscious thinking is in harmony with the deep truths of the unconscious revealed in mythology, then fear of death is no longer overwhelming. Life can then be lived to the fullest until the end. Therefore, Jung, in contrast to Freud, encouraged belief in religious teachings because he thought such belief was, in his words, "hygienic" – necessary for healthy living. He wrote:

> When I live in a house that I know will fall about my head within the next two weeks, all my vital functions will be impaired by this thought, but if, on the contrary, I feel myself to be safe, I can dwell there in a normal comfortable way.

Jung was convinced that the unconscious part of the mind has a timeless quality and that belief in eternal life is consistent with the timelessness of the unconscious. To achieve psychological wholeness, in his view, requires that one become more in touch with this part of the unconscious in daily living. In his autobiography, published posthumously, Jung wrote:

> If we understand and feel that here in this life we already have a link with the infinite, desires and attitudes change.

We can learn something important from both Freud and Jung. But neither, in our opinion, had a totally satisfactory view.

Freud stressed what is biologically true about death: its absolute destruction of the organism. He was also aware of man's great capacity for self-delusion. Though he knew that confronting death could heighten the vitality of living, he did not grasp the symbolic significance of images of immortality. In this he under-estimated the human need for images of connection beyond the life span of each individual. This need is not itself delusional, nor need it necessarily result in delusions. Freud was bound to a conception of psychic activity that we think fails to do justice to the characteristically human tendency continually to create and re-create images and inner forms. We speak here of symbolization as a process rather than the creation of specific symbols. What we have referred to as the psychoformative process encompasses this overall tendency, and its complexity is such that it cannot be reduced to the idea of the sexual or death instinct. The important question, then, is how and when symbolization can become rich enough to sustain full vital life.

Here, Jung made a real contribution. He took religious imagery very seriously and appreciated its significance in man's search for meaning and the effort to express it. The problem with Jung's position is that he did not always distinguish between man's need for symbolization around immortality and the literal existence of an afterlife. We agree with Jung that the scientific tradition as reflected in Freud's insistence on seeing religious symbols as mere delusion misses the point of such symbols.

But Jung's refusal to distinguish between symbolic meaning and literal reference undermines and distorts both religion and science.

In the seventeenth century, a French philosopher named Blaise Pascal proposed what he called a "wager." If there is no afterlife, and one doesn't believe, then one has lost nothing, Pascal argued. But if there really is such a thing, and one fails to gain admission through lack of belief, then all is lost. Therefore, Pascal argued, since there is everything to be gained by believing, and nothing to lose, one should make the wager and decide to believe in the afterlife. Jung's position is a bit like Pascal's wager. Moreover, Jungian symbols tend to have a fixed quality, so that there is little connection between what Jung calls archetypal symbols and ongoing history.

Our own view of symbolic immortality draws from both Freud and Jung. We would stress not only the finality of death, but also the human need for a sense of historical connection beyond individual life. We [. . .] need to develop concepts, imagery, and symbols adequate to give a sense of significance to experience. This psychological process of creating meaningful images is at the heart of what we will now call *symbolic immortality*.

We can see the sense of symbolic immortality as reflecting man's relatedness to all that comes before him and all that follows him. This relatedness is expressed in the many kinds of symbolization that enable one to participate in ongoing life without denying the reality of death. Without this unending sense of attachment to aims and principles beyond the self, the everyday formative process we have been discussing – as well as the capacity to feel at home in the world – cannot be sustained. When people believe in such cultural projects and expressions, they feel a sense of attachment to human flow, to both their biology and their history. They feel a *sense of immortality* which enables active, vital life to go on.

This sense of immortality is expressed in five modes or categories: biological, creative, theological, natural, and experiential.

Biological immortality is perhaps the most obvious mode. It means simply that a person lives on through (and in) his sons and daughters and their sons and daughters in an endless chain. In addition to generational continuity, this mode also symbolizes the reproductive cells as they are passed along from parent to child.

The biological mode of immortality has been greatly emphasized in East Asia, especially in China and Japan, where the failure to have offspring implies lack of respect for ancestors. But the idea of a continuing family and a "family name" protected from blemish is important in all cultures. The act of writing a will to insure the transmission of inherited wealth to one's descendants reflects this concern for the preservation of one's posterity.

This mode is never purely biological. It is experienced emotionally and symbolically and transcends one's own biological family to include one's tribe, organization, people, nation, or even species. Similarly, the sense of biological continuity becomes intermingled with cultural continuity as each generation passes along its traditions to the next.

We can speak of a kind of "biosocial immortality" that occurs through the continuity of one's family and other important social groupings. Historically this mode has been a mixed blessing. It has encouraged cooperation with those beyond one's immediate family (one's people), but has also led through chauvinism to the killing of those whom one views as "different." Nevertheless, there has been a significant trend among large numbers of people throughout the world to view all of humanity as a single species sharing a common destiny. Unfortunately, that beginning recognition has hardly touched ideological and nationalistic antagonisms.

A second mode is that of human "works," or the *creative* mode. One may feel a sense of immortality in this mode through teaching, art-making, repairing, construction, writing, healing, inventing, or through lasting influences of any kind on other human beings – influences that one feels can enter into a general human flow beyond the self. In professions like science or art that have a long heritage, one is frequently aware of the historical sources of one's own work and the tradition that one's own contribution is maintaining.

In such service professions as medicine or education, one has a sense that one's direct influence on patients or students is transmitted to more distant persons not seen or known. When efforts at healing or teaching seem unsuccessful, one may feel a profound despair originating in the perception that one's efforts are not making any lasting difference. This despair itself reveals a deep human need to have an enduring effect – to leave a trace.

Ordinarily, when one's work is progressing well, there is little conscious concern with its immortalizing effect. But when the products of creative effort do not seem sufficient to embody one's sense of self, then the question (previously unconscious) of the value and meaning of one's life and work begins to become a conscious concern.

The Christian tradition has distinguished between "work" and "works." "Work" in this sense has referred to mundane, often unsatisfying toil which regenerates neither the worker nor his community. "Works" imply contributions of lasting value to the larger community; these contributions are made in part through one's "vocation."

Entering a vocation was originally dependent upon feeling oneself "called" to do some particular kind of work, and the word vocation still suggests something beyond just a job. It implies that one feels in one's work connections and commitments beyond the self. At some level of consciousness, such actions are perceived to involve the lasting extension of the valued elements of one's own life into the lives of others. Through such doctrines as karma, service, and duty, other religions have expressed similar ideas.

The *theological* mode of immortality is the one most readily suggested by the word immortality. For, historically, it has been through religion and religious institutions that people have most self-consciously expressed the aspiration of conquering death and living forever. Different religions give the assurance of immortality in different ways, but concern with the problem of the meaning of life in the face of death is common to all religious traditions. No religion is based on the premise that human life is eternally *insignificant*. Thus, Buddha, Moses, Christ, and Muhammad, through various combinations of moral attainment and revelation, transcended individual death and left behind teachings through which their followers could do the same.

The danger with religious images of immortality is that they can quickly lose their symbolic quality and result in the assertion that people don't really die. For centuries, great religious teachers have attacked institutionalized "religion" as the real stumbling block to authentic spiritual attainment. Such images as heaven, hell, reincarnation, and the resurrection of the body are often understood in the same sense as scientific observations of nature. Thus, the concept of the "immortal soul" – a part of man that escapes death – was seen by Freud as a characteristic example of the human capacity for self-delusion through religion.

We believe Freud was justified in his attack upon literalized doctrines that deny death. But Freud did not appreciate that religious symbols of life after death or life beyond death can mean something other than literal images of angels living serenely in a blissful heaven or, negatively, damned souls condemned to eternal suffering in the fires of hell. The image of immortality can connect with the experience of spiritual death and rebirth which may occur many times during one's earthly existence. Spiritual rebirth in this sense may be interpreted as a dying to profane or vulgar existence and a regenerated life on a more intense and meaningful plane, an experience that gives rise to profound and revitalizing hope. The Jewish religion has emphasized rebirth as something that happens to the whole people or nation. Christianity has focused more on individual spiritual attainment and salvation.

Imagery of rebirth is found in the Hindu and Buddhist as well as the Jewish and Christian religions. And whenever such imagery is present, the danger of its being literalized is always present, too. But central to all these traditions, and more compatible with our own psychoformative position, is the conception of transcending death through spiritual attainment that connects one with eternal principles.

Thus the idea of being "chosen by God," experiencing the grace of God, or, in Eastern religions, removing the veil of ordinary existence – all these images speak symbolically of a changed experience of time and of death somehow losing its sting. Whether through prayer, worship, contemplation, or meditation, all religions have taught methods of reorienting oneself in relation to time and death. This reorientation is often spoken of as a spiritual rebirth that

must be preceded by a death of the old self. This is expressed in the Christian tradition in the words "He who finds his life will lose it, and he who loses his life for my sake will find it," a paradoxical image suggesting both death and rebirth.

A fourth mode is the sense of immortality achieved through continuity with *nature*. "From dust you come and to dust you shall return" is an Old Testament injunction against pride, as well as an expression of confidence that the earth itself does not die. Whatever happens to man, the trees, mountains, seas, and rivers endure. Partly for this reason, we constantly go back to nature, however briefly, for spiritual refreshment and revitalization.

In traditional Japanese culture, nature has been seen as a divine embodiment of the gods of mountain, valley, rain, wind, field, and stream. The delicate beauty of Japanese gardens is an expression of this cultural legacy. In India, the gods are always pictured as residing amidst lush mountains and valleys – nature being the ideal spiritual home. Americans, too, have had an intense concern with the "great outdoors," a concern originally demonstrated by the importance of the great frontier – that ever expanding horizon of the earthly realm of man.

The image of nature as the great frontier still exists in our journeys to the moon and aspirations beyond. (These journeys and aspirations, being human, become corrupted by the competitive insistence of a single nation upon being the first there – in effect, upon claiming an immortalizing advantage for this priority.) An avid interest in outdoor sports of all kinds and a growing preoccupation with ecology witness the continuing importance of being in touch with a surviving natural habitat. The concern with ecology has arisen from the very real possibility of the destruction of the environment, and also from the continuing importance of nature for our imaginations. In this sense, the enduring rhythms of nature have a significance that is undiminished, and perhaps intensified, for those city-dwellers to whom they are no longer visible.

A fifth mode of immortality, which we call *experiential transcendence*, is a bit different from the others in that it depends solely on a psychological state. This state is the experience of illumination or rapture attained as time seems to disappear. The term transcendence – meaning "going beyond" – refers to the feeling of being beyond the limits and confines of ordinary daily life. Moments of transcendence have an ecstatic quality, and the word "ecstasy" means "to stand outside of" – to be outside of oneself. In this sense, moments of experiential transcendence are moments of being beyond prosaic life, and beyond death.

Experiential transcendence is similar to the spiritual reorientation which we spoke of as religious rebirth. But such psychological experience may also be found in music, dance, battle, athletics, mechanical flight, contemplation of the past, artistic or intellectual creation, sexual love, childbirth, comradeship, and the feeling of working together with others in common cause. This experience can occur in relation to any of the other four modes (biological, creative, theological, natural) and, in fact, may be essential in order to integrate any of them into one's life. However it occurs, experiential transcendence involves a sense of timelessness, of which Jung spoke. There does seem to be a universal psychic potential and even need for occasional suspension of ordinary awareness of time.

The state of experiential transcendence may be brought on with the aid of drugs, starvation, physical exhaustion, or lack of sleep. However induced, this state is felt as involving extraordinary psychological unity, intensity of sensual awareness, and unexpressible illumination and insight. After such an experience, life is not quite the same. In fact, it is the result of such experiences – the sense of "new life" – that is often valued more than the experiences themselves.

Transcendent experiences result in a reordering of the dominant symbols and images by which one lives. The result can be a new tone of vitality in living, a new sense of commitment to one's projects, or the abandoning of one's old projects and commitments in favor of a totally new style of life. The reordering can also lead to greater ethical integrity and more courageous moral actions. Experiences of this kind can be of greater or lesser intensity. But even such relatively less intense and more common occurrences as exertion on a tennis court or in a sprint, a moment of insight or quietude, or gentle sensual touching can involve an altered sense of time and a feeling of expanded life space.

Over the centuries, men have frequently used drugs in pursuit of these experiences. In recent years drugs have been increasingly used, often in combination with music, to achieve various kinds of "highs." Many people in describing such "trips" have emphasized the importance of the setting in which the drug is taken, the person with whom one shares the experience (the "guide"), and the expectations that one brings to the experience. All these refer to the symbolic context or set of images present in the mind prior to and during the use of the drug. This, in turn, suggests that drugs *by themselves* do not bring about spiritual reorientation. Large numbers of people are finding forms of spiritual discipline, such as meditation, which can offer similar experiences without recourse to drugs.

The "highs" which some people experience with drugs (or alcohol) are obtained by other people in different ways. William James long ago remarked that getting drunk was the poor man's substitute for what the rich get from going to the symphony. Whether that is precisely true or no, we might wonder what he would say now about the more modern combination of listening stoned to the Stones. In any case it is interesting that the use of marijuana has come to be termed getting "stoned" – almost in the way getting drunk is sometimes referred to as being "plastered." In each case the image is of becoming desensitized, even inanimate – but in a very special way that is thought of as highly pleasurable and beyond pain. Although alcohol is primarily a depressant and marijuana characteristically intensifies perception, both can result in either heightened sensitivity or the reverse, depending upon the setting and the expectations that one brings to their use.

Those who would connect the use of drugs with the experience of transcendence (as we are doing here) are nevertheless compelled to recognize the addiction and deterioration which can also result. The deaths of Janis Joplin and Jimi Hendrix, for example, suggest the way in which drug use may involve the user in destructive experiences, even death trips.

When reordering and renewal give way to exclusive reliance upon the chemical influence of the drug, habituation and addiction can be said to occur. No longer having access to liberating images, the "old self" remains in a state of symbolic death. Use of the drug then becomes more desperate, and the breakdown of inner integrity becomes increasingly associated with the death imagery of separation, disintegration, and stasis. The anxiety associated with these impels the user to return even more desperately to the drug in a pathetic downward spiral. There are many people whose relationship to drugs is a mixture of these extremes, containing elements of symbolic reordering and rebirth as well as habituation and anxiety.

The quest for experiential transcendence is usually related not only to the search for the new, but also to the unfolding of that which is oldest and deepest in the self. Rebirth and new life are recurrent images in all religious traditions; the Christian spiritual message is, in fact, referred to as "good news." The experience of addiction, not only to drugs but to anything else as well, is a desperate search for novelty (always a new high) with continually less experience that is actually new. Thus, addiction comes to be the experience that nothing is new – a nullification of the life imagery of movement. It becomes instead a deathlike numbness from which recovery is difficult.

The process of therapy in psychiatry involves a symbolic reordering analogous to that which occurs in experiential transcendence. When therapy is successful, a patient feels a widening of the space in which he lives. It is as if the narrow images through which he has seen reality have been reorganized so that the past appears more coherent and the future more inviting. Death imagery is reconceived, and life imagery of connection, integrity, and movement becomes dominant.

In many societies experiential transcendence is encouraged through fiestas, festivals, holidays, and celebrations which help people to break free of the restraints of routine and to sing, dance, drink, laugh, and love in a spirit of excess. Such celebrations radically interrupt ordinary daily life and allow participants to forget time and responsibility. The occasions for these celebrations are often religious holy days which derive from society's myth of its own beginnings. The celebration is a kind of birthday in which the society's birth is commemorated and its people's lives renewed.

Experiential transcendence is thus a key to the sense of immortality in any mode. For what lies at the heart of experiential transcendence – reorientation of time – is necessary to the other modes as well if they are in fact to connect with a sense of the eternal. Experiential transcendence involves entry into what has been called "mythic time," in which the perception of death is minimized and the threat of extinction is no longer foreboding. One feels oneself alive in a "continuous present" in which ancient past and distant future are contained.

We spoke earlier of the innate death imagery of separation, disintegration, and stasis. The five modes of symbolic immortality provide avenues through which the death anxiety associated with these images can be mastered. By achieving significant relation to these modes, one's life assumes qualities of continuity and the life imagery of connection, movement, and integrity is affirmed. We can speak of the need to master death anxiety as basic to the human condition, and we can see the modes of symbolic immortality as providing paths for this mastery.

It is possible to think of human life at every moment as moving between two poles: imagery of total severance (death imagery) and imagery of continuity (symbolic immortality). Both are present in a kind of balance; neither is able totally to abolish the other. Death imagery makes the quest for symbolic immortality more urgent and provides a stimulus for creative effort of all kinds. Images of continuity and immortality make the certainty of death less threatening. Feeling moments of experiential transcendence or a strong sense of relation to one of the other modes of symbolic immortality enables one to affirm the continuity of life without denying death. Much of the time these matters are not part of conscious awareness, although they underlie and support the tone and quality of one's awareness. At crisis points and times of transition, however, they become very conscious issues.

Periods of historical dislocation are characterized by lack of confidence in a society's institutions. But institutions – family, church, government, work, schools – are themselves structures through which to facilitate the sharing of images of immortalizing connectedness. In times like our own when these institutions are in flux, the task for each individual of maintaining a sense of immortality becomes vastly more difficult.

Death anxiety becomes overwhelming when one has to confront it in isolation. Societies and social institutions – when people believe in them – are able to aid in mastering death anxiety by generating shared images of continuity beyond the life of each single person. The capacity to live with death is generated by available social forms as well as by forms made available by one's own life.

Suicide is therefore never a purely private matter. When a person takes his own life, not only does he demonstrate his own failure to master death anxiety; he reveals a social failure as well. The society has not managed to share with him its symbols of continuity. In committing suicide a person makes a once-and-for-all total effort to master death anxiety.

Paradoxically, suicide can be an attempt to assert symbolic integrity: It is a way of holding to certain principles, of actively defining one's life boundaries, and of affirming value. This is not to say that suicide does not result from despair. But to live with despair is one thing; to perform the final act of ending one's life is another. Suicide can be seen as a kind of false mastery: One commits suicide when one is unable to live with the knowledge of death or envision a viable connection beyond it.

That suicide cannot be understood solely as an act of valueless despair is shown by the traditional Japanese practice of hara-kiri. In this act of ritual sui-cide, dying with dignity overcomes the humiliation of defeat. In accordance with the samurai code, suicide is an honorable act through which one can maintain the purity and immortality of one's name and country and, in the act of dying, reassert immortalizing principles. Yukio Mishima, the great Japanese novelist, attempted to revive that tradition and to convey in his recent suicide the message that contemporary Japan is losing its national essence. Though many found his act of ritual suicide absurd, it had a profound impact on Japanese society.

What about other kinds of suicide? Certainly not everyone who commits suicide lives by so demanding a code as that of the samurai. Nevertheless, a person who voluntarily ends his life is asserting in a positive way – although through a negative act – that under certain conditions life is not endurable. The act of suicide thus presumes the presence of some standards as to what a livable life would be. Under extreme conditions, such as Nazi extermination camps, suicide could become an assertion of freedom (to take one's own life rather than to wait to be killed) and even an inspiration for rebellion. For this to happen, suicide must be associated with a vision of life renewal beyond the death-dominated moment.

Suicide can rarely be the source of such renewal. More characteristically, it is the ultimate failure to master that which can never be completely mastered: death itself. But destructive and self-destructive acts are less likely to be resorted to when one feels oneself to be animated by a sense of immortality.

4

The Hour of Our Death

Philippe Ariès

In the preface, I explained how I was gradually led to select certain kinds of documentation: literary, liturgical, testamentary, epigraphic, and iconographic. I did not study these documents separately or in any particular order. I studied them simultaneously, in the light of a question that arose in the course of my first explorations. My hypothesis, which had already been proposed by Edgar Morin, was that there was a relationship between man's attitude toward death and his awareness of self, of his degree of existence, or simply of his individuality. This is the thread that has guided me through a dense and confusing mass of documents; this is the idea that has determined the itinerary that I have followed to the end. It is in terms of these questions that the information contained in the documents has taken on a form and a meaning, a continuity and a logic. This has been the key that has helped me to decipher facts otherwise unintelligible or unrelated.

In *Essais sur l'historie de la mort*, I held to this system of analysis and interpretation. I have also used it in the general organization of the present work. It has inspired the titles of three of the five parts: "The

Tame Death," "The Death of the Self," and "The Death of the Other." These titles were also suggested by Vladimir Jankélévitch in his book on death.

But my research for that gave me a greater familiarity with the facts, which slightly altered my original hypothesis, raised other questions, and opened up other perspectives. Awareness of one's self or one's destiny was no longer the only possible point of departure. Other systems of analysis and interpretation appeared along the way, systems that were just as important as the one I had chosen to guide me and that would have served just as well to give some order to the formless mass of documentation. I have allowed them to take shape in my text as I discovered them in the documents, while I continued my research and reflection. I hope that the reader has noticed them in passing.

Today, at the end of this seemingly endless itinerary, the assumptions I started out with are no longer exclusive. Having abandoned my preconceived ideas along the way, I turn and cast my eye over this thousand-year landscape like an astronaut looking down at the distant earth. This vast space seems to

From Philippe Ariès, *The Hour of Our Death* (London: Penguin, 1987 [1977]).

me to be organized around the simple variations of four psychological themes. The first is the one that guided my investigation, *awareness of the individual*. The others are: the *defense of society against untamed nature*, *belief in an afterlife*, and *belief in the existence of evil*.

By way of conclusion I shall try to show how the various models defined in the course of this book (the tame death, the death of the self, remote and imminent death, the death of the other, and the invisible death) can be explained in terms of variations on these four themes.

The Tame Death

All four themes appear in the first model of the tame death, and all are of equal importance in defining it.

Death is not a purely individual act, any more than life is. Like every great milestone in life, death is celebrated by a ceremony that is always more or less solemn and whose purpose is to express the individual's solidarity with his family and community.

The three most important moments of this ceremony are the dying man's acceptance of his active role, the scene of the farewells, and the scene of mourning. The rites in the bedroom or those of the oldest liturgy express the conviction that the life of a man is not an individual destiny but a link in an unbroken chain, the biological continuation of a family or a line that begins with Adam and includes the whole human race.

One kind of solidarity subordinated the individual to the past and future of the species. Another kind made him an integral part of his community. This community was gathered around the bed where he lay; later, in its rites of mourning, it expressed the anxiety caused by the passage of death. The community was weakened by the loss of one of its members. It expressed the danger it felt; it had to recover its strength and unity by means of ceremonies the last of which always had the quality of a holiday, even a joyous one. Thus, death was not a personal drama but an ordeal for the community, which was responsible for maintaining the continuity of the race.

If the community feared the passage of death and felt the need to recover itself, this was not only because it was weakened by the loss of one of its members. It was also because death – the death of an individual or the repeated deaths caused by an epidemic – opened a breach in the defense system erected against the savagery of nature.

From the earliest times man has refused to accept either sex or death as crude facts of nature. The necessity of organizing work and maintaining order and morality in order to have a peaceful life in common led society to protect itself from the violent and unpredictable forces of nature. These included both external nature, with its intemperate seasons and sudden accidents, and the internal world of the human psyche, which resembles nature in its suddenness and irregularity; the world of the ecstasy of love and the agony of death. A state of equilibrium was achieved and maintained by means of a conscious strategy to contain and channel the unknown and formidable forces of nature. Death and sex were the weak points in the defense system, because here there was no clear break in continuity between culture and nature. So these activities had to be carefully controlled. The ritualization of death is a special aspect of the total strategy of man against nature, a strategy of prohibitions and concessions. This is why death has not been permitted its natural extravagance but has been imprisoned in ceremony, transformed into spectacle. This is also why it could not be a solitary adventure but had to be a public phenomenon involving the whole community.

The fact that life has an end is not overlooked, but this end never coincides with physical death. It depends on the unknown state of the beyond, the solidity or ephemerality of survival, the persistence of memory, the erosion of fame, and the intervention of supernatural beings. Between the moment of death and the end of survival there is an interval that Christianity, like the other religions of salvation, has extended to eternity. But in the popular mind the idea of infinite immortality is less important than the idea of an extension. In our first model, the afterlife is essentially a period of waiting characterized by peace and repose. In this state the dead wait, according to the promise of the Church, for what will be the true end of life, the glorious resurrection and the life of the world to come.

The dead live a diminished life in which the most desirable state is sleep, the sleep of the future blessed who have taken the precaution of being buried near the saints. Their sleep may be troubled owing to their own past impiety, the stupidity or treachery of survivors, or the mysterious laws of nature. In this case they cannot rest; they wander and return. The living do not mind being close to the dead in churches, parks, and markets, provided they remain asleep. But it is impossible to forbid these returns; so they must be regulated, channeled. Society permits the dead to return only on certain days set aside by custom, such as carnivals; then it can control their presence and ward off its effects. The Latin Christianity of the early Middle Ages reduced the ancient risk of their return by installing them among the living, at the center of public life. The gray ghosts of paganism became the peaceful recumbent figures, whose sleep was likely to remain untroubled thanks to the protection of the Church and the saints; later, thanks to the Masses and prayers said in their behalf.

This conception of life after death as a state of repose or peaceful sleep lasted much longer than one might believe. It is surely one of the most tenacious forms of the old attitude toward death.

Death may be tamed, divested of the blind violence of natural forces, and ritualized, but it is never experienced as a neutral phenomenon. It always remains a misfortune, a *mal-heur*. It is remarkable that in the old Romance languages physical pain, psychological suffering, grief, crime, punishment, and the reverses of fortune were all expressed by the same word, derived from *malum*, either alone or in combination with other words: in French, *malheur, maladie, malchance, le malin* (misfortune, illness, mishap, the devil). It was not until later that an attempt was made to distinguish the various meanings. In the beginning there was only one evil that had various aspects: suffering, sin, and death. Christianity explained all of these aspects at once by the doctrine of original sin. There is probably no other myth that has such profound roots in the collective unconscious. It expressed a universal sense of the constant presence of evil. Resignation was not, therefore, submission to a benevolent nature, or a biological necessity, as it is today, as it was no doubt among the Epicureans or Stoics; rather it is the recognition of an evil inseparable from man.

The Death of the Self

Such is the original situation, as defined by the relationship of our four themes. Later, as one or more of these fundamental elements varied, the situation changed.

The second model, the death of the self, is obtained quite simply by a shift of the sense of destiny toward the individual.

We recall that the model was originally limited to an elite of rich, educated, and powerful persons in the eleventh century, and still earlier to the isolated, organized, and exemplary world of monks and canons. It was in this milieu that the traditional relationship between self and other was first overthrown, and the sense of one's own identity prevailed over submission to the collective destiny. Everyone became separated from the community and the species by his growing awareness of himself. The individual insisted on assembling the molecules of his own biography, but only the spark of death enabled him to fuse them into a whole. A life thus unified acquired an autonomy that placed it apart; its relations with others and with society were transformed. Friends came to be possessed like objects, while inanimate objects were desired like living beings. No doubt the balance sheet of the biography should have been closed at the formidable hour of death, but soon it was carried beyond, under the pressure of a desire to be more – something death could not touch. These determined men colonized the beyond like some new continent, by means of Masses and pious endowments. The chief instrument of their enterprise, their guarantee of continuity between this world and the next, was the will. The will served both to justify the love of earth and to make an investment in heaven, thanks to the transition of a good death.

Individualism triumphed in an age of conversions, spectacular penitences, and prodigious patronage, but also of profitable businesses; an age of unprecedented and immediate pleasures and of immoderate love of life.

So much for awareness of the individual. It was inevitable that such an exaltation of the individual, even if it was more empirical than doctrinal, would cause some changes in the third theme, the nature of the afterlife. The passion for being oneself and for being more than was manifested during a single lifetime spread by contagion to the afterlife. The strong individual of the later Middle Ages could not be satisfied with the peaceful but passive conception of *requies*. He ceased to be the surviving but subdued *homo totus*. He split into two parts: a body that experienced pleasure or pain and an immortal soul that was released by death. The body disappeared, pending a resurrection that was accepted as a dogma but never really assimilated at the popular level. However, the idea of an immortal soul, the seat of individuality, which had long been cultivated in the world of clergymen, gradually spread, from the eleventh to the seventeenth century, until eventually it gained almost universal acceptance. This new eschatology caused the word *death* to be replaced by trite circumlocutions such as "he gave up the ghost" or "God has his soul."

This fully conscious soul was no longer content to sleep the sleep of expectation like the *homo totus* of old – or like the poor. Its immortal existence, or rather its immortal activity, expressed the individual's desire to assert his creative identity in this world and the next, his refusal to let it dissolve into some biological or social anonymity. It was a transformation of the nature of human existence that may well explain the cultural advance of the Latin West at this time.

So the model of the death of the self differs from the older model of the tame death with respect to two of our themes, that of the individual and that of the afterlife. The second and fourth parameters, on the other hand, have hardly moved. Their relative immobility protected the model from too sudden a change. It gave it a centuries-old stability that can be deceptive and that can give the impression that things had not changed at all.

Our fourth theme, belief in evil, remained virtually unchanged. It was necessary to the economy of the will and to the maintenance of a love of life that was based partly on an awareness of its fragility. It is obviously an essential element of permanence.

The second, defense against nature, might have been affected by the changes in the sense of the individual and of the afterlife. It was certainly threatened, but its equilibrium was restored.

The desire to assert one's identity and to come to terms with the pleasures of life gave a new and formidable importance to the hour of death mentioned in the *Ave Maria*, a prayer for a good death that dates from the end of this period. This could very well have upset the relationship of the dying man to his survivors or to society, making death pathetic, as in the romantic era, or solitary, like the death of the hermit, and abolishing the calming ritual that men had created as a defense against natural death. Death might then have become wild and terrifying, because of the force of emotion and the fear of hell. But this did not happen, because a new and totally opposite ceremony took the place of what had been threatened by individualism and its agonies.

The deathbed scene, which had once been the most important part of the ceremony, persisted, sometimes with just a touch more pathos, until the seventeenth and eighteenth centuries, when the pathetic element declined under the influence of an attitude of mingled acceptance and indifference. A series of ceremonies was inserted between death and burial: the funeral procession, which became ecclesiastical in character, and the service at the church in the presence of the body, which was the work of the urban reform movement of the late Middle Ages and the mendicant orders. Death was not abandoned to nature, from which the ancients had claimed it in order to tame it. On the contrary, death was more concealed than ever, for the new rites also included a fact that may seem negligible but that is highly significant. The face of the cadaver, which had been exposed to the eyes of the community and which continued to be for a long time in Mediterranean countries and still is today in Byzantine cultures, was covered by the successive masks of the sewn shroud, the coffin, and the catafalque or representation. After the fourteenth century, the material covering of the deceased became a theatrical monument such as was erected for the decor of mystery plays or for grand entrances.

The phenomenon of the concealment of the body and face of the deceased is contemporaneous with the attempts we find in the macabre arts to represent the underground decay of bodies, the underside of life, which was all the more bitter because this life was so well loved. This interest was transitory, but the concealment of the body was permanent. The features of the deceased, once calmly accepted, were henceforth covered because they might be upsetting, that is, frightening. The defense against untamed nature was invaded by a new fear, but this fear was immediately overcome by the taboo to which it gave rise. Once the body was conjured away by the catafalque or representation, the old familiarity with death was restored and everything returned to normal.

The definitive concealment of the body and the prolonged use of the will are the two most significant elements of the model of the death of the self. The first balances the second, maintaining the traditional order of death against the pathos and nostalgia of the individualism illustrated by the will.

Remote and Imminent Death

This model of the death of the self, with all that it preserved in the way of traditional defenses and a sense of evil, influenced customs until the eighteenth century. However, profound changes were beginning to take place by the end of the sixteenth century, to some extent in actual customs and conscious ideas, but more especially in the secret world of the imagination. These changes, although barely perceptible, are very important. A vast transformation of sensibility was under way. The beginning of a reversal – a remote and imperfect adumbration of the great reversal of today – was starting to appear in representations of death.

Where death had once been immediate, familiar, and tame, it gradually began to be surreptitious, violent, and savage. Already, as we have seen, the old familiarity had been maintained only by means of the artifices of the later Middle Ages: more solemn rites and the camouflage of the body under the representation.

In the modern era, death, by its very remoteness, has become fascinating; has aroused the same strange curiosity, the same fantasies, the same perverse deviations and eroticism, which is why this model of death is called "remote and imminent death."

What was stirring in the depths of the collective unconscious is something that had hardly moved at all for thousands of years, our second theme, the

defense against nature. Death, once tame, was now preparing its return to the savage state. It was a discontinuous movement, made up of violent jolts, long imperceptible advances, and real or apparent retreats.

At first sight it may seem surprising that this period of returning savagery was also characterized by the rise of rationalism, the rise of science and technology, and by faith in progress and its triumph over nature.

But it was at this time that the barriers patiently maintained for thousands of years in order to contain nature gave way at two points that are similar and often confused: love and death. Beyond a certain threshold, pain and pleasure, agony and orgasm are one, as illustrated by the myth of the erection of the hanged man. These emotions associated with the edge of the abyss inspire desire and fear. An early manifestation of the great modern fear of death now appears for the first time: the fear of being buried alive, which implies the conviction that there is an impure and reversible state that partakes of both life and death.

This fear might have developed and spread and, combined with other effects of the civilization of the Enlightenment, given birth (over a century ahead of time) to our culture. This is not the first time that the late eighteenth century seems to lead directly into the twentieth. But instead, something happened that could not have been foreseen and that restored the actual chronology.

The Death of the Other

If the momentum really did carry from the eighteenth to the twentieth century, it hardly seems that way to the unsophisticated observer. The continuity exists on deeper levels, but only rarely does it show above the surface. This is because in the nineteenth century, which saw the triumph of the industrial and agricultural techniques born of the scientific thought of the previous period, romanticism (the word is convenient) gave birth to a sensibility characterized by passions without limit or reason. A revolution in feeling seized the West and shook it to its foundation. All four of our themes were transformed.

The determining factor was the change in the first theme, the sense of the individual. Up to now this theme had alternated between two extremes: the sense of a universal and common destiny and the sense of a personal and specific biography. In the nineteenth century both of these declined in favor of a third sense, formerly confused with the first two: the sense of the other. But this was not just any other. Affectivity, formerly diffuse, was henceforth concentrated on a few rare beings whose disappearance could no longer be tolerated and caused a dramatic crisis: the death of the other. It was a revolution in feeling that was just as important to history as the related revolutions in ideas, politics, industry, socioeconomic conditions, or demography.

An original type of sensibility now came to dominate all others, a type that is well expressed by the English word *privacy*. It found its place in the nuclear family, remodeled by its new function of absolute affectivity. The family replaced both the traditional community and the individual of the late Middle Ages and early modern times. Privacy is distinguished both from individualism and from the sense of community, and expresses a mode of relating to others that is quite specific and original.

Under these conditions, the death of the self had lost its meaning. The fear of death, born of the fantasies of the seventeenth and eighteenth centuries, was transferred from the self to the other, the loved one.

The death of the other aroused a pathos that had once been repressed. The ceremonies of the bedroom or of mourning, which had once been used as a barrier to counteract excess emotion – or indifference – were deritualized and presented as the spontaneous expression of the grief of the survivors. But what the survivors mourned was no longer the fact of dying but the physical separation from the deceased. On the contrary, death now ceased to be sad. It was exalted as a moment to be desired. Untamed nature invaded the stronghold of culture, where it encountered humanized nature and merged with it in the compromise of "beauty." Death was no longer familiar and tame, as in traditional societies, but neither was it absolutely wild. It had become moving and beautiful like nature, like the immensity of nature, the sea or the moors. The compromise of

beauty was the last obstacle invented to channel an immoderate emotion that had swept away the old barriers. It was an obstacle that was also a concession, for it restored to this phenomenon that people had tried to diminish an extraordinary glamour.

But death could not have appeared in the guise of the highest beauty if it had not ceased to be associated with evil. The ancient and intimate relationship between death and physical illness, psychic pain, and sin was beginning to break down. Our fourth theme, the belief in evil, which had long been stationary, was preparing to withdraw, and the first stronghold it deserted was the heart and the mind of man, which was believed to be its original and impregnable seat. What a revolution in thought! It is a phenomenon as important as the return of untamed nature within the human psyche, and indeed, the two are related; it is as if evil and nature had changed places.

The first barrier that fell in the eighteenth century – perhaps as early as the seventeenth in England – was belief in hell and in the connection between death and sin or spiritual punishment. (The necessity of physical illness was not yet questioned.) Scholarly thought and theology raised the problem as early as the eighteenth century. By the beginning of the nineteenth century, the debate in Catholic and Puritan cultures was over; belief in hell had disappeared. It was no longer conceivable that the dear departed could run such a risk. At most, among Catholics, there still existed a method of purification: time in purgatory, shortened by the pious solicitude of survivors. No sense of guilt, no fear of the beyond remained to counteract the fascination of death, transformed into the highest beauty.

If hell is gone, heaven has changed too; this is our third theme, the afterlife. We have followed the slow transition from the sleep of the *homo totus* to the glory of the immortal soul. The nineteenth century saw the triumph of another image of the beyond. The next world becomes the scene of the reunion of those whom death has separated but who have never accepted this separation: a re-creation of the affections of earth, purged of their dross, assured of eternity. It is the paradise of Christians or the astral world of spiritualists and psychics. But it is also the world of the memories of nonbelievers and freethinkers who deny the reality of a life after death.

In the piety of their love, they preserve the memories of their departed with an intensity equal to the realistic afterlife of Christians or psychics. The difference in doctrine between these two groups may be great, but it becomes negligible in the practice of what may be called the cult of the dead. They have all built the same castle, in the image of earthly homes, where they will be reunited – in dream or in reality, who knows? – with those whom they have never ceased to love.

The Invisible Death

In the nineteenth century the psychological landscape was completely transformed. Neither the nature of the four themes nor the relationships among them were the same. The situation that resulted did not last more than a century and a half. But the model of death that came next, our model, which I have called the invisible death, does not challenge the underlying tendency or the structural character of the changes of the nineteenth century. It continues them, even if it seems to contradict them in its most spectacular effects. It is as if beyond a certain threshold, these tendencies produced the opposite effects.

Our contemporary model of death is still determined by the sense of privacy, but it has become more rigorous, more demanding. It is often said that the sense of privacy is declining. This is because today we demand the perfection of the absolute; we tolerate none of the compromises that romantic society still accepted beneath its rhetoric – or beneath its hypocrisy, as we would say. Intimacy must be either total or nonexistent. There is no middle ground between success and failure. It is possible that our attitude toward life is dominated by the certainty of failure. On the other hand, our attitude toward death is defined by the impossible hypothesis of success. That is why it makes no sense.

The modern attitude toward death is an extension of the affectivity of the nineteenth century. The last inspiration of this inventive affectivity was to protect the dying or the invalid from his own emotions by concealing the seriousness of his condition until the end. When the dying man discovered the pious game, he lent himself to it so as not to disappoint

the other's solicitude. The dying man's relations with those around him were now determined by a respect for this loving lie.

In order for the dying man, his entourage, and the society that observed them to consent to this situation, the protection of the patient had to outweigh the joys of a last communion with him. Let us not forget that in the nineteenth century, death, by virtue of its beauty, had become an occasion for the most perfect union between the one leaving and those remaining behind. The last communion with God and/or with others was the great privilege of the dying. For centuries there was no question of depriving them of this privilege. But when the lie was maintained to the end, it eliminated this communion and its joys. Even when it was reciprocal and conspiratorial, the lie destroyed the spontaneity and pathos of the last moments.

Actually, the intimacy of these final exchanges had already been poisoned, first by the ugliness of disease, and later by the transfer to the hospital. Death became dirty, and then it became medicalized. The horror and fascination of death had fixed themselves for a moment on the apparent death and had then been sublimated by the beauty of the Last Communion. But the horror returned, without the fascination, in the repellent form of the serious illness and the care it required.

When the last of the traditional defenses against death and sex gave way, the medical profession could have taken over the role of the community. It did so in the case of sex, as is attested by the medical literature on masturbation. It tried to do so in the case of death by isolating it in the scientific laboratory and the hospital, from which the emotions would be banished. Under these conditions it was better to communicate silently in the complicity of a mutual lie.

It is obvious that the sense of the individual and his identity, what we mean when we speak of "possessing one's own death," has been overcome by the solicitude of the family.

But how are we to explain the abdication of the community? How has the community come to reverse its role and to forbid the mourning which it was responsible for imposing until the twentieth century? The answer is that the community feels less and less involved in the death of one of its members. First, because it no longer thinks it necessary to defend itself against a nature which has been domesticated once and for all by the advance of technology, especially medical technology. Next, because it no longer has a sufficient sense of solidarity; it has actually abandoned responsibility for the organization of collective life. The community in the traditional sense of the word no longer exists. It has been replaced by an enormous mass of atomized individuals.

But if this disappearance explains one abdication, it does not explain the powerful resurgence of other prohibitions. This vast and formless mass that we call society is, as we know, maintained and motivated by a new system of constraints and controls. It is also subject to irresistible movements that put it in a state of crisis and impose a transitory unity of aggression or denial. One of these movements has unified mass society against death. More precisely, it has led society to be ashamed of death, more ashamed than afraid, to behave as if death did not exist. If the sense of the other, which is a form of the sense of the self taken to its logical conclusion, is the first cause of the present state of death, then shame – and the resulting taboo – is the second.

But this shame is a direct consequence of the definitive retreat of evil. As early as the eighteenth century, man had begun to reduce the power of the devil, to question his reality. Hell was abandoned, at least in the case of relatives and dear friends, the only people who counted. Along with hell went sin and all the varieties of spiritual and moral evil. They were no longer regarded as part of human nature but as social problems that could be eliminated by a good system of supervision and punishment. The general advance of science, morality, and organization would lead quite easily to happiness. But in the middle of the nineteenth century, there was still the obstacle of physical illness and death. There was no question of eliminating that. The romantics circumvented or assimilated it. They beautified death, the gateway to an anthropomorphic beyond. They preserved its immemorial association with illness, pain, and agony; these things aroused pity rather than distaste. The trouble began with distaste: Before people thought of abolishing

physical illness, they ceased to tolerate its sight, sounds, and smells.

Medicine reduced pain; it even succeeded in eliminating it altogether. The goal glimpsed in the eighteenth century had almost been reached. Evil was no longer part of human nature, as the religions, especially Christianity, believed. It still existed, of course, but outside of man, in certain marginal spaces that morality and politics had not yet colonized, in certain deviant behaviors such as war, crime, and nonconformity, which had not yet been corrected but which would one day be eliminated by society just as illness and pain had been eliminated by medicine.

But if there is no more evil, what do we do about death? To this question modern society offers two answers.

The first is a massive admission of defeat. We ignore the existence of a scandal that we have been unable to prevent; we act as if it did not exist, and thus mercilessly force the bereaved to say nothing. A heavy silence has fallen over the subject of death. When this silence is broken, as it sometimes is in America today, it is to reduce death to the insignificance of an ordinary event that is mentioned with feigned indifference. Either way, the result is the same: Neither the individual nor the community is strong enough to recognize the existence of death.

And yet this attitude has not annihilated death or the fear of death. On the contrary, it has allowed the old savagery to creep back under the mask of medical technology. The death of the patient in the hospital, covered with tubes, is becoming a popular image, more terrifying than the *transi* or skeleton of macabre rhetoric. There seems to be a correlation between the "evacuation" of death, the last refuge of evil, and the return of this same death, no longer tame. This should not surprise us. The belief in evil was necessary to the taming of death; the disappearance of the belief has restored death to its savage state.

A small elite of anthropologists, psychologists, and sociologists has been struck by this contradiction. They propose not so much to "evacuate" death as to humanize it. They acknowledge the necessity of death, but they want it to be accepted and no longer shameful. Although they may consult the ancient wisdom, there is no question of turning back or of rediscovering the evil that has been abolished. They propose to reconcile death with happiness. Death must simply become the discreet but dignified exit of a peaceful person from a helpful society that is not torn, not even overly upset by the idea of a biological transition without significance, without pain or suffering, and ultimately without fear.

5

How Others Die: Reflections on the Anthropology of Death

Johannes Fabian

Mes larmes ne la ressusciteront pas.
C'est pourquoi je pleure.

Anonymous French epitaph

Death *seems to be a harsh victory of the species over the definite* individual *and to contradict their unity. But the particular individual is only a* particular species being, *and as such mortal.*

Karl Marx

I

In recent years, anthropologists were consulted — and often gave profuse advice — on such vital American problems as war with exotic societies, or aid to exotic societies; rural and urban poverty; the intricacies of ethnic identity; ecology and the use of drugs; marriage, divorce and promiscuity; or simply the future of the species. In many instances, societal interests, expressed in patterns of funding for research, were quickly translated into conceptualizations and theories and have in some cases given rise to subdisciplines and professional alliances of the secret society type. Department chairmen, having to sell their discipline to tightfisted university administrators, proudly point to rising enrollment figures. Often, and probably correctly, this is interpreted as a shift from introductory philosophy, literature and history to anthropology as a provider of a *Weltbild* to undergraduate freshmen.

Why is it, then, that in recent years anthropologists have had little to say about death? With few — and rather doubtful — exceptions, we cannot report on any major ground-breaking work.[1] Therefore it seems that, at this point, the anthropologist's contribution toward understanding death in modern soci-

From Johannes Fabian, "How Others Die: Reflections on the Anthropology of Death," in *Death in American Experience*, ed. Arien Mack (New York: Schocken, 1973).

ety can only be made in a roundabout way, as a self-searching examination of an aspect in the discipline's history, a history which, of course, is situated in the social and cultural context of the society or societies which produce anthropology.

A negative question (Why do anthropologists *not* speak about death?) has its logical pitfalls. Imagination simply offers too many reasons when one tries to account for the absence of things. But the question may set an historical trap which might be even more dangerous. Students of death in contemporary society appear to agree on the fact that modern man "suppresses" thinking about death.[2] It is tempting to see in anthropology an accomplice of presumed societal interests in suppressing death. The possibility cannot be ruled out since it has been demonstrated for other issues and areas such as colonialism, racial discrimination and the control of the poor (although there remain founded claims to the contrary). But to transpose attempts at understanding to the level of ethical-moral accusations (and confessions) is the worst kind of obfuscation that can be perpetrated on any intellectual enterprise, since it can only create self-righteousness, not self-understanding.

Hope for clarification and critical examination would seem to lie in our ability to relate our negative rhetorical question to positive barriers to communication, to practical impediments and normative prohibitions. It will be the contention of this paper that, while some of these may be understood as direct reflexes of a present social context, others – and more important ones – will have to be sought in the intellectual history of the discipline and in the history of the use to which anthropological findings have been put in other contexts, notably in philosophical, psychological and sociological approaches to death in modern society.

II

Our attempt to understand that development will be guided by the following thesis: Much like the concept of culture, approaches to death in anthropology have undergone a process of parochialization. Parochialization has had the effect of eliminating a transcendental and universal conception of the problem. "Death" (in the singular) has ceased to be a problem

of anthropological inquiry; there are only deaths and forms of death-related behavior.

In his essay on "Matthew Arnold, E. B. Tylor, and the Uses of Invention," George W. Stocking revealed – and debunked – one of anthropology's favorite myths: that Tylor with his definition of culture (in 1871) became the father of modern anthropology in the sense that he provided the discipline with its relativist and strictly scientific foundations. He is supposed to have brought the study of culture out of a haze of humanist appreciation of human achievements into the light of non-evaluative, systematic investigations of man's cultural products. But Stocking maintains:

> Far from defining its modern anthropological meaning, he simply took the contemporary humanist idea of culture and fitted it into the framework of progressive social evolutionism.[3]

The humanist idea of culture and the notion of social evolutionism are the reference points between which we have to place the origins of a transformation of anthropological inquiry into death. J. G. Frazer clearly combined them when he wrote in one of the introductory chapters to his *The Belief in Immortality*:[4]

> The problem of death has very naturally exercised the minds of men in all ages. Unlike so many problems which interest only a few solitary thinkers, this concerns us all alike.

But from a humanist "us" he imperceptibly switches to an evolutionist "they":

> Some of their solutions of the problem, though dressed out in all the beauty of exquisite language and poetic imagery, singularly resemble the rude guesses of savages.

For Tylor and Frazer alike, evolutionism remained a frame of self-identification, a means of locating one's own society at the peak of human intellectual development. In a seemingly paradoxical way this resulted in steering anthropological inquiry away from universal problems of human existence to concern with particular products of evolution. For Frazer the "problem of death" became a matter of studying particular savage customs, leading him to embark on one of his *tours de force* around the ethnographic globe.[5]

A further step in the parochialization of anthropological inquiry can be recognized in the position Franz Boas developed in violent opposition to evolutionism (and therefore inevitably accepting many of its tenets). Boas shared with Tylor and Frazer a view of the importance of "customs" in the study of culture and human thought, but he was concerned with their "tyranny" rather than their curiosity value. As Stocking notes, this in fact led to an identification of culture with folklore, a profound change in concept.[6] Once the anthropological concept of culture had lost its universal (albeit elitist) character, it was clear that the discipline simply no longer had a theoretical plane on which to face challenges such as the problem of death. Anthropologists had ceased to answer for humanity; their investigations had left the field of tension which is created when particular phenomena are related to universal concepts or processes (be it the 18th century's Natural Law, the *Geist* of the romantics, the natural laws of evolution, or even the Universal History of the diffusionists). Having lost a universal frame of inquiry, questions having to do with the nature and meaning of death had to be implanted (if not buried, if the pun be permitted) in various parochial "units" of research which came to replace that frame. In fact, Hertz's classical study, "Contribution à une étude sur la représentation collective de la mort" (see note 21), conceived in the line of Durkheim's powerful attempt to base a universal theory of knowledge on a parochial conception of the social nature of man, has remained the last generally significant contribution to guide social anthropological research (and even that one has been largely outside the horizon of Anglo-American anthropology until its recent reception in a translation).

To be sure, classical authors of modern anthropology continued to assert convictions of their predecessors. Echoing Tylor and Frazer, B. Malinowski admits that these "orthodox views" of the experience of death as the core of primitive religiosity "are on the whole correct." There is at least a core of an earlier universalism preserved when he states:

> Even among the most primitive peoples, the attitude towards death is infinitely more complex and, I may add, more akin to our own, than is usually assumed.

But all this must be seen in the perspective of his own theoretical progress beyond "orthodox views." Malinowski was among those who advanced a parochialization of anthropological inquiry by first isolating religion from intellectual life in general:

> Thus the belief in immortality is the result of a deep emotional revelation, standardized by religion, rather than a primitive philosophic doctrine.

That was a radical departure from Tylor's views. Secondly, there is Malinowski's idea of religious ceremonies addressed to the experience of death as "self-contained acts, the aim of which is achieved in their very performance," which, lastly, led him to define the scope of anthropological inquiry in a way that has remained exemplary:

> The ceremonial of death which ties the survivors to the body and rivets them to the place of death, the beliefs in the existence of the spirit, in its beneficent influences or malevolent intention, in the duties of a series of commemorative or sacrificial ceremonies – in all this religion counteracts the centrifugal forces of fear, dismay, demoralization, and provides the most powerful means of reintegration of the group's shaken solidarity and of the re-establishment of its morale.[7]

Later criticism and quite important modifications[8] notwithstanding, this encapsulation of the experience of death in self-contained acts, performed for the sake of a self-containing social unit, had the intellectually disastrous effect of opening to anthropology an easy escape from the "supreme dilemma of life and final death" (Malinowski).⌈The argument is this: Beyond all differences in theoretical and methodological inclination, social-cultural anthropologists may be presumed to be students of human behavior inasmuch as it is determined by cultural orientations (among other things). Death as an event is the termination of individual behavior. Therefore there cannot be an anthropological study of death, but only of behavior toward death as it affects those who survive.⌋It must be a study of "how others die" in more than one sense: examining the reactions of survivors and interpreting these reactions through ceremonies, ritual practices, ideological rationalizations – in short, as "folklore." Whether this is intended or not, death-related behavior will then be placed at a safe distance from the core of one's own society.[9]

I hasten to emphasize that this is not the whole story, although it describes the most influential orientations[10] in the discipline. We should give recognition to dissenting views[11] and examine the possibilities of an anthropology of death which faces, rather than escapes from, the "supreme dilemma." But first we must consider yet another context in which anthropological inquiry into death appears to have been forced into the position of a spectator of, rather than participant in, social reality. We should at least note that in this context we are unable to do justice to a more profound theoretical issue concerning an epistemological conception of "the other." It is raised by Donald T. Campbell in his discussion of the foundations of behaviorist versus introspective psychology. Similarly, our cursory sketch of the parochialization and folklorization of anthropological inquiry should not give the impression that the notion of "primitive" otherness has always and necessarily had a stultifying effect. On the contrary, in the tradition of the Enlightenment *philosophes*, anthropologists such as Lévi-Strauss (see section V of this paper) and Diamond have employed it in a critical fashion. As Diamond argued, "the authentic historian [which is what he thinks an anthropologist must be]. . . . approaches other societies in other times with the confidence that his humanity is equal to the task of registering *differences*. And that, though not the only element, is the *critical* one in all human communication."[12]

III

In one form of the Roman games (the *munera*), alien and exotic people were put to death by other exotic people or animals. Similarly, fascination with the curious, the violent, and the exotic seems to be the arena assigned to the use of anthropological studies of death by analysts of contemporary personality and society. Among the many examples that could be

adduced to support that observation. I should like to point to Talcott Parsons. In his essay, "Theoretical Development of the Sociology of Religion" (first published in 1944), as well as in *The Social System*, it is the problem of death which causes him to turn to Malinowski's "classic analysis" of Trobriand funeral rites, and to W. L. Warner, E. E. Evans-Pritchard and C. Kluckhohn and their studies of death in relation to witchcraft. The point is that here the issue of death is not one among many occasions to turn to anthropology but, with few exceptions, the only one.[13]

While our metaphorical allusion to the Roman games[14] captures much of the rationale for appealing to anthropological studies of death-folklore, we should not overlook a number of theoretical reasons which led investigators of death in modern society to assume the role of spectators of the "primitive." Most importantly, the turn from the "us" to the "they" was taken by anthropologists themselves, as we tried to show in the preceding section. In part it was dictated by their basic evolutionary perspective, by that imperceptible transformation of culture into folklore, and by all sorts of murky mixtures of racism and colonialism which, often unconsciously, imposed themselves on seemingly objective analyses. But these tendencies appear to have been reinforced and codified when philosophers, psychologists and sociologists put ethnographic reports to use in their own approaches to death. "Primitive" reactions to death may then be consulted for the purpose of illuminating ontogenetic development with parallels from man's early history.[15] Or, more frequently, we will find attempts to identify contemporary reactions to death, especially those that appear irrational, overly ritual and picturesque, as survivals of "archaic" forms. However, essentially the same connection may be made for an inverse argument: that what is wrong with modern man's relation to death is the absence or suppression of these ancient ways of coping with its threat. Usually without critical examination, these "primitive" reactions to death are placed in the domain of religion (which in turn is taken to constitute a self-contained aspect of human activity) and this makes it possible to replace the general evolutionist perspective with a view of "secularization," religious devolution, as an intrinsic component of modernity. Primitive and folkloric death-customs may then be located in a nostalgic past – which is yet another way of relegating reactions to death to "the others," or at least the other that has survived in us . . .

Werner Fuchs published a study entitled *Images of Death in Modern Society*[16] in which he offers a tantalizing combination of astute criticism and simple acceptance of the very syndrome we are trying to describe. His point of departure is an observation which, I am sure, must be rather disconcerting to modern social-scientific students of death. Upon closer examination, it turns out that sociologists and psychologists who make "suppression" of death the cardinal topic of their analyses (here he refers to Fulton and Gorer) are in fact arguing very much like Christian theologians who lament modern man's apparent indifference to death. The suppression hypothesis, Fuchs argues, is an interpretation supported more by interests in preserving the vanishing influence of religious institutions than by empirical facts (pp. 7–14). In his own approach he dissociates himself from such conservative culture-criticism for which death has become the "last trump" (p. 8) against secular, industrial society. On the one hand he rejects the idea of death as a constant; on biological as well as social grounds it can be shown that man's increasing power over nature has made such a notion obsolete. On the other hand he takes it upon himself to demonstrate that modern man does not simply suppress his reactions to death. He may submit to death as a fact, but he has preserved many of the ancient ways, symbolic and ritual, of coping with that experience. This is the point where he is compelled to turn to anthropological studies of primitive death-lore in order to create a background and contrast for his views of the genesis of modern images (pp. 26–50). There is no need for us to criticize extensively his use of anthropological concepts and findings, for he himself anticipates objections when he admits to the analogous and abstract nature of his arguments (e.g., pp. 26 f., 50 f.). It suffices to point out some of those assertions which we take to confirm our thesis that anthropological studies of death have been, by and large, assigned the role of providing the exotic "other" to the sociologist's "we."

First we find, as expected, the "folklorization" of primitive culture in a formulation worth quoting at length:

> It stands to reason that in primitive societies such ideas [of death] will not be found as opinions and attitudes but always closely linked to the institutional field in which death is symbolized. Images of death in primitive societies can hardly be identified as relatively independent intellectualizations [*als Geistiges*] but only in and with social institutions in which the group attempts to socialize death. (p. 38)

Secondly, Fuchs is compelled – by his assumption that emerging modern images are determined by notions of a "natural" and "peaceful" death – to project into primitive reactions the violence we would expect to be associated with the exotic spectacle of dying: primitive man related to nature not by mastering it, but through "magical" interpretation (pp. 46 ff.); the helplessness and oppressive nature of primitive socialization in turn resulted in violence (p. 47). The mere frequency of violent death must have led to a kind of confusion between dying and killing (pp. 48 ff.). Death is experienced as interaction and hence can be induced by social agents (e.g., in the forms of Voodoo death and similar phenomena, p. 49). It would be easy to show that speculations of that kind are not at all borne out by what present anthropology and prehistoric archeology tell us about the ecological adaptations of "primitive" man or the role of violence and the history of warfare. In any case, Fuchs' argument must be read backwards. Primitive reactions to death are bound to be seen as magic-exotic and violent because they serve as points of departure in a series of developments toward "rational" (natural and peaceful) images of death.

Appeals to anthropological findings in this study and in many comparable ones have little more than projective value. They express more about the spectators than about those who are being watched.

IV

It appears that progress in understanding will depend on our ability to free the notion of death from its encapsulation in behavior, custom and folklore and to restore the experience of the termination of individual life to its full problematic status. This would call for an anthropology for which social reality and subjective participation in that reality are irreducible conceptual poles of inquiry. One would have to reject the use of anthropological research for the sole purpose of illustrating "socializations" of death, especially all those utilizations of ethnography in which the *analytical* notion of socialization is transformed into *programmatic* socialization, i.e., into support for contemporary recipes for coping with death.[17] To pose social and individual reality as irreducible conceptual poles implies that the thrust of anthropological inquiry must be directed toward "mediations" between them. Above all, it entails an epistemological orientation which approaches conceptualizations and institutionalizations of death experience as *processes*, as productive "constructions of reality" rather than disembodied schemes of logic or social control.

Without trying to suggest systematic connections where there are none, we shall explore a number of intellectual contexts in which we see the potential for such processual approaches. First, however, we shall take up the case of modern prehistoric archeology since it may help us to determine more exactly what we are looking for.

More than twenty years ago, Edgar Morin began his *anthropologie de la mort* by observing that research in the process of hominization has been guided by two important kinds of evidence: the use of tools, and the burial of the dead (Morin, *op. cit.*, pp. 19 ff.). In the decades that followed, our image of early man has undergone considerable change. The timespan allotted to the process of hominization has been enormously expanded and at the same time former generic distinctions, often based on the scantiest evidence, have become blurred. Today, "Neanderthal" man, at first codified as the *Urmensch* in evolutionary scientific classification and popular iconography, turns out to be a much closer relative of modern man than we ever expected. Nevertheless, evidence for burials has lost little of its theoretical importance. It may no longer be invoked as "proof" for achieved hominization since such a notion has become meaningless, but it has retained its crucial role as a phenomenon involved in hominization as a process. Thus in a recent analysis of

Mousterian and Upper Paleolithic materials, Sally R. Binford sees in burials evidence for "new forms of social organization," "leading to the appearance of fully modern man."[18]

Of course, prehistoric archeology has been and will be under severe limitations due to the precarious nature of preserved evidence, no matter how much progress is made in the quantitative analysis of even the tiniest bits of data. Edgar Morin rightly cautioned against the "platitudes" which might be derived from a suggestive association of tool use and burial rites, i.e., of technology and symbolic activity. There is little use, he argues, in declaring that the tool humanizes nature and that notions of an afterlife humanize death, as long as the "human" remains a concept suspended in thin air. Rather, one should start with the assumption that "death, as does the tool, affirms the individual; it prolongs it in time as the tool extends it in space; (and the assumption) that it, too, strains to adapt man to the world and, by virtue of that, expresses the same lack of adaptation of man to the world, and the same conquering potential of man in relationship to the world" (*op. cit.*, p. 20). It is easy to see that modern prehistoric research with its fixation on linear "adaptation" would react uneasily to so paradoxical a proposition. Yet it is because Morin accepts the epistemological frame we sketched earlier that his evaluation of prehistoric evidence does not take the folkloric turn. Notions of death and afterlife are not merely seen as customary expressions of man's functional conquest of death. Death, he maintains, "is assimilated to life" and filled with "metaphors of life" and ritual action based on and elaborating these metaphors, is action which "modifies the normal order of life" and reveals in the prehistoric and ethnological material a "realistic consciousness of death" (*op. cit.*, p. 22).

There is no sign that these propositions were taken up in the theoretical development of prehistoric research on burial customs. On the contrary, one can observe an increasing functionalization of burial evidence, making it more and more derivative of socio-economic relationships (while preserving its methodological importance).[19] All this amounts to a theoretical "socialization" of death in man's early history. The theoretical counter-part of such functionalization, by the way, seems to be an almost phobic avoidance of "catastrophism," i.e., of the violent, sudden termination of certain societies or cultural traditions as an explanation for discontinuities in the archeological record. While contemporary society seriously contemplates (and inflicts) societal death in war, in the nuclear threat and in the doom of ecological catastrophe, the New Archeologists appear to picture man's early history as continuous adaptation and growth within which individual as well as societal death is entirely subordinate to processes of social differentiation and ultimately to the law of selection. "Death as the servant of life" is a notion which places neoevolutionary theory in a curious vicinity to evolutionary theology, old (as in Smyth's *Death and Evolution*) and new (as in Teilhard de Chardin's all-embracing visions). If these observations are correct, then they suggest an interesting counterpoint to a tendency noted earlier. Whereas analysts of contemporary man and society project exotic, and often violent images of death into the human past, students of that human past offer naturalistic, adaptive and systematic explanations which are in contrast to the erratic and violent preoccupations of contemporary society. With this, the general contention of this paper – that the historical development of anthropological inquiry into death has had a self-cancelling effect – acquires yet another dimension.

Our interpretation would of course be unfair and outright wrong if we should leave the impression that nothing was gained in the course of that history. "Folklorization" and functionalization of primitive culture have produced an impressive number of detailed reports on human reactions to death. Evidence for variation as well as for the persistence of certain general themes should make it once and forever impossible to revert to anemic, abstract notions of a gradual evolution "away from death." Nevertheless there remains the task of placing the problem of death back into the context of a "we," of its universal significance as well as its particular expressions, of its unmitigated threat as well as its achieved domestications. To achieve that transposition it will not suffice to revive the *Totentanz* motif of death as the great equalizer. Rather, we

shall have to explore and develop the avenues which the discipline provides for breaching the gaps created by self-inflicted parochialization and imposed exoticism.

V

From the vantage point from which this essay is being written – contemporary anthropology in its more "humanist" and historical-critical orientations – there appear several theoretical confluents with a potential for leading an anthropology of death beyond its present confines. None of them is without predecessors in the history of the social sciences; their innovative power at the present time rests with the challenge they can bring against those entrenched tendencies we have tried to characterize.

The first example I find is Lévi-Strauss' radical structuralism. He, more than anyone else among the leading figures in current anthropology, has prepared the way back from a folklorized ethnography of death into investigations of its universal significance. To cite but one statement of his:

> When an exotic custom fascinates us in spite of (or on account of) its apparent singularity, it is generally because it presents us with a distorted reflection of a familiar image, which we confusedly recognize as such without yet managing to identify it.[20]

Written in a tradition which had produced one of the classical studies of the problem,[21] Lévi-Strauss' *The Savage Mind* addresses itself to the issue of death in three contexts: the elementary contrast of life and death as expressed in the symbolic use of color-contrasts (pp. 64 f.), the role of names in marking an individual's position in a community consisting of living *and* dead (pp. 191 ff.), and the significance of material reminders of the dead in providing "contact with pure historicity" (p. 242; see also pp. 236 ff.). Far from being relegated to the function of opening comforting, self-contained ritual escapes, death-related customs are in this system analyzed as crucial evidence for the constitution of the "savage mind" (which, it will be remembered, is studied not as a defective but as a pure form of the human mind).

In each case death is seen as the *mediator* between the living and the dead and is given a seminal role in the construction of those systems of classification which govern man's natural, social and historical universes. The existentialist critic may resent the intellectualist and seemingly abstract character of that notion of death. But it is one which restores the universal significance of primitive conceptions of death (many of which Lévi-Strauss sees realized in his own society, cf. pp. 200 f., 238 f.). His investigations are addressed to all of humanity, and especially the chapter on names, bearing the intriguing title "The individual as a species" (Ch. 7, pp. 191–216) could be read as a commentary to Marx's enigmatic statement with which we prefaced this paper.

Objections have been raised against Lévi-Straussian structuralism in general and, implicitly or explicitly, against the analyses we alluded to. Some concern his empirical basis, others the epistemological foundations of his thought and yet others his ways with "structuralism." We share many of them and we are inclined to express them with more conviction the closer they relate to our own areas of competence. Yet it takes a task like the present one to recognize the power and potential which the structuralist trend in anthropology (at least in its original intentions) might have for undoing the parochialization of inquiry and the folklorization of culture we perceived as major obstacles to a non-trivial anthropology of death. For what it is worth, we may add a quotation from Lévi-Strauss which contains the startling proposition that anthropology is *nothing but* the study of death:

> The world began without the human race and it will end without it ... Man has never – save only when he reproduces himself – done other than cheerfully dismantle million upon million of structures and reduce their elements to a state in which they can no longer be reintegrated ... "Entropology," not anthropology, should be the word for the discipline that devotes itself to the study of this process of disintegration in its most highly evolved forms.[22]

We can credit Lévi-Strauss with vindicating the logical nature of human reactions to death or, conversely, with vindicating death as the supreme mediator of those oppositions and contradictions by means of which the human mind constructs its universes.[23]

Put in slightly different terms, we may say that structuralism provides for a possibility of viewing human experience of death as the core of a language, of a universal code. This is a far cry from previous fixations on exotic customs. Yet there remains a legitimate and fruitful concern in the anthropological tradition – the search for the *specific* message, the "what" that may be expressed in the language of death.

This brings us to the question of the "meaning" of culturally defined reactions to death. We should note at once that this problem, too, is by no means a new one and that consequently one would have to work through much accumulated rubble in order to get at its more productive and promising formulations. For one thing, search for meaning has at times been inseparable from a search for "functions" seen either as directed action or as measurable effects of action. Culturally specific forms of reacting towards death were then interpreted as implementations of beliefs in souls, in immortality, or in supernatural powers. Or they were perceived as ritual redress of crises inflicted on the group, as an oblique way of exercising control over the living (in the complex of "ancestor worship"), or simply as means of providing mental hygiene, individual and social, in the face of events which cannot be coped with through direct rational and instrumental action.

This is perhaps the best place to point to the important work of an anthropologist continuing a tradition to which we paid little attention in this paper: the conceptualization of death as a rite of passage. Victor W. Turner, in his study of Ndembu ritual,[24] shares our contention that a gap between a "we" and an exotic "they" is a prime obstacle to understanding (pp. 3, 6), and that rituals ought to be approached as language, or as a "semantic," as he puts it (p. 10). The wider conclusions he draws from his analysis should be sufficient to dispel an impression which our admittedly somewhat anti-ritualist critique of the anthropology of death may have left with the non-initiated reader.

Paraphrasing a statement which Geertz makes about religion, we may stipulate that a cultural reaction to death

> is sociologically interesting not because, as vulgar positivism would have it . . . , it describes the social order (which, insofar as it does, it does not only very obliquely but very incompletely), but because . . . it shapes it.[25]

The essay from which this quotation is taken remained in many respects in the frame it attempted to break (and probably had to in order to have this effect), but it has been crucial in preparing the discipline for a formidable task: to discern in the exotic and the folkloric that which reveals, in Morin's formulation, a "realistic consciousness of death."

There are various directions in which further inquiry may proceed. Common to all of them are the following basic orientations:

(a) A processual, constitutive view of culture and, consequently, of cultural conceptions of, and reactions to, death. "Primitive," no less but also no more than modern ways of coping with death can be realistic only to the extent that they can be shown to constitute *praxis*, active transformation and elaborations of concepts which are open, so to speak, at both ends: toward the crude experience of the termination of life and toward the impact of those sublime formulations which give meaning to that event. Recently Roy Wagner proposed a view of processual, innovative metaphorization as an approach to culture and found the following formulation immediately relevant to our problem:

> The ultimate dogma, known to all cultures, is that of mortality, the inevitability of personal death, and it follows that the most powerful innovative constructs will be those which achieve their force against this kind of human limitation. Hence it is that ghosts, gods, and other religious creations are so often represented as being omnipotent, omniscient, and immortal. Insofar as these beings are constituted as innovations upon a universal state of man, they are of necessity represented anthropomorphically, as metaphorical people who share man's active, causational capacity but not his mortality or his other limitations. Most effectively they take the form of innovations upon living human

beings, and achieve their metaphoric status through acts of impersonation, the metaphorization of social role, whereby a person is "extended" into the role of a ghost or deity. Man's life-course can be seen as the ultimate social role, which subsumes all others, and it is at this level of generality, that of man as a whole being, that religious impersonation as a form of innovation takes place.[26]

(b) A dialectical model of socio-cultural reality. This is implied in the criterion of "openness." Realistic conceptions of death could not be formed if the social world were seen as a self-contained domain. For a social conception of death to emerge, the event of individual death must be recognized as an inalienable mediator, not only in the Lévi-Straussian logical sense, but also in the phenomenological sense according to which subjectivity remains an irreducible pole in the construction of a social world. We may illustrate this position with a quote from Alfred Schütz in which he states

> that the whole system of relevances which governs us within the natural attitude is founded upon the basic experience of each of us: I know that I shall die and I fear to die . . . It is the primordial anticipation from which all the others originate. From the fundamental anxiety spring the many interrelated systems of hopes and fears, of wants and satisfactions, of chances and risks which incite man within the natural attitude to attempt the mastery of the world, to overcome obstacles, to draft projects, and to realize them.[27]

Schütz' phenomenology of the social world has been applied by Ilona H. Fabian to an analysis entitled *The Concept of Time in Zulu Myth and Ritual* (unpublished M.A. thesis, University of Chicago, 1969). There it is argued that conceptualizations of, and relationships with, the dead are crucial in the formation of a person's as well as a society's historical consciousness. The "I," the "we" and the ancestors are all seen to be involved in a constant process of mythical formulation and ritual action, resulting in an interpretation of "ancestor worship" bearing little resemblance to entrenched magico-religious or sociologistic explanations.

(c) A communicative approach to ethnographic reality. This, again, should be understood both in the struc-

turalist sense which holds that all of culture is a system of communication (and that death, being a seminal "distinctive contrast," is a prime datum of communication), and in the sense that any study of "others" is possible only on the basis of an inter-subjective context. As far as anthropological research is concerned, that context can usually not be presumed to exist but must be constituted in the process of producing ethnographic knowledge. As I have argued elsewhere,[28] this leads methodologically to a preoccupation with "language-centered" approaches. But more importantly, by including the ethnographic "other" in a communicative "we," it makes possible and necessary a critical, self-reflective anthropology. After all, attempts to breach the gap between the "we" and the "they" would probably end in egocentric delusions if they could be achieved by a simple act of good will, or a theoretical dictate. Redirecting the program for an anthropology of death from the stance we found to be dominant in its tradition to the problem of "how we die" does not rid us of the labors of careful ethnographic observation, comparison and analysis. However, it burdens these labors with the knowledge that, in working out an anthropology of death, we strive toward a realistic consciousness of death – ours.

VI

If our assessment of past and present developments is at least moderately accurate, we should be able to derive some rules for the interpretation of anthropological literature on death.

1. Ethnographic data cannot simply be adduced for the purpose of "explaining" antecedent forms of present attitudes, or to account for exotic survivals in present attitudes, or generally to support an evolutionary view of the history of death-related behavior. The reason is that a great deal of that ethnography has been selected, shaped, and interpreted precisely in terms of these research interests. There is at least the danger that one explanation (that of contemporary attitudes toward death) may be supported by something that poses as evidence (ethnography of "primitive" attitudes) but is in fact another explanation. *Mutatis mutandis*, the same rule applies when ethnographic support is sought for explanations of ontogenetic developments,

such as the role of ideas of death in the process of individuation, especially when this is done to retranslate ontogenetic notions into schemes of history. Critical anthropology can offer nothing to support the thesis that the history of attitudes toward death has been one of increasing individualization and personalization. All this does not mean that ethnographic data cannot ever be subject to historical interpretations (be they historical in the traditional sense or be they processual-systematic in terms of a theory of evolution), but to determine their applicability calls for a degree of competence the average user of anthropological lore does not have. For any serious analyst of modern society, anthropology should be anything but a source of facile illustrations.

2. To touch on a more specific point, it cannot *a priori* be assumed that the "primitive's" reaction to death, because of his deep roots in a relatively small and well defined society, are any more specific and "meaningful" than those of modern man. Sensitive, critical ethnography may come to the surprising conclusion that "everything that touches upon death is equivocal, ambiguous"[29] – as we should expect it would be if there is some validity to the conception of death as a mediator of knowledge and meaning. How else could anticipations of death in thought and experience become the sources of innovative thought?

3. Furthermore, one should not turn to anthropology if he is looking for proof that primitive man's life was much more under the influence of his beliefs in an afterlife and in the dead. To assess that influence one would have to specify its nature. Anthropologist-*cum*-psychologist Roger Bastide, for instance, points out that African traditional religion *externalizes* its dead and therefore can live with them, whereas Western society *internalizes* the dead in the form of obsessions and compulsive behavior. He comes to the surprising conclusion that

> If the structure of African cultures is that of a dialog [between the living and the dead] – then the structure of Western society is that of a monolog, but the monolog of the dead.[30]

4. Similarly, ethnographic evidence cannot easily be appealed to in support of culture-critical allegations that modern man, and modern man only, "suppresses" death because his secularized society does not give him mythical and ritual outlets for his reactions. Again, notions of primitive ritualism and of the all-pervasive sacredness of primitive man's world must at least be suspected of having been codified in reaction to the same economic and religious changes to which analysts of contemporary society link modern images of death (after all modern anthropology originated in that society).

5. Generally, one may predict that the "use" of ethnography to support schemes of evolution or devolution should become more and more difficult the closer the outside analyst gets to contemporary anthropology (hence the heavy reliance on early ethnography exemplified in the study by Fuchs quoted above).

This brings us to one last observation. As we see it, there simply is no way of getting directly at "the others." Anthropologists and other analysts of modern reactions to death must find or construct a meta-level of interpretation if they are to share their findings. In the late nineteenth century, this may have been the idea of a natural science of man in search of universal laws of progress to be verified by ethnographic "data" whose "objective" otherness was not seriously doubted. Today we seem to be left with the task of constructing a social hermeneutic, an interpretation of social reality (no matter whether it is "primitive" or "modern") which conceives of itself as part of the processes it attempts to understand. Lévi-Strauss was right: the anthropology of death is a form of dying, or of conquering death – which, in the end, may be the same.

NOTES

1 A cursory check of four major professional journals revealed that between 1960 and 1970 only nine "death-related" papers were published, and the majority of these dealt only with the purely ceremonial aspects of death. Concerning major monographs, the situation is not much better. The few that appeared within the last decade or so (Warner, Goody, Gorer, Douglass) have been widely recognized but cannot claim a trend-setting influence. Let me note, however, that Goody's study contains a wealth of information and suggestions which make it valuable beyond its declared limits.

2 To point to but one prominent example, see R. L. Fulton and Gilbert Geis, "Death and Social Values," in *Death and Identity*, edited by R. L. Fulton (New York, 1965), pp. 67–75.

3 George W. Stocking, *Race, Culture and Evolution* (New York, 1968), p. 87.

4 James George Frazer, *The Belief in Immortality and the Worship of the Dead*, Vol. I (London, 1913), pp. 3, 31 ff.

5 It is interesting to note that 19th century evolutionism could become a conceptual vehicle for a theologian in his search for a "positive" meaning of death. In the light of the theories of Darwin and Weismann, death is discovered as the "servant of life" (Newman Smyth, *The Place of Death in Evolution*, New York, 1897, p. 14), a "secondary event" in the course of life whose necessity is nothing but a form of adaptation following the law of natural selection (*ibid.*, p. 27). Echoing our epigram from Marx, Smyth states "that the duration of life for the individual members of different species seems to have been determined upon the principle of utility, for the preservation of the species" (*ibid.*, p. 33).

6 "Boas' equation of folklore and culture had implications for the idea of the 'culture' of civilized men. Just as folklore at the primitive level tended to be seen as encompassing culture, so also the culture of more advanced peoples was now largely seen as folklore" (Stocking, *op. cit.*, pp. 225 ff.).

7 Bronislaw Malinowski, *Magic, Science and Religion* (Garden City, NY 1954), pp. 47, 51, 52. In support of my contention that this view became paradigmatic, see David G. Mandelbaum, "Social Uses of Funeral Rites," in *The Meaning of Death*, H. Feifel, ed. (New York, 1959), pp. 189–217.

8 Notably by Meyer Fortes, *Oedipus and Job in West African Religion* (Cambridge, 1959).

9 A classical and extreme formulation of that position may be found in A. L. Kroeber, "Disposal of the Dead," *American Anthropologist*, 29 (1927), pp. 308–15, in which he classes mortuary practices with such peripheral phenomena as "fashion."

10 Attesting to that power is, for instance, Clyde Kluckhohn's essay "Conceptions of Death among the Southwestern Indians," in *Culture and Behavior*, R. Kluckhohn, ed. (New York, 1962), pp. 134–49, which begins with a sensitive formulation of the problem, looks to Boas for guidance, and ends with a Malinowskian statement. A more recent example may be found in the conclusion of William A. Douglass' study of funerary ritual in a Basque village, *Death in Murelaga* (Seattle, 1969).

11 The classical reference for such dissent has become Clifford Geertz, "Ritual and Social Change: A Javanese Example," *American Anthropologist*, 59 (1957), pp. 32–54.

12 Donald T. Campbell, "A Phenomenology of the Other One: Corrigible, Hypothetical, and Critical," in *Human Action: Conceptual and Empirical Issues*, Theodore Mischel, ed. (New York, 1969), pp. 41–69; Stanley Diamond (ed.), *Primitive Views of the World* (New York, 1964), p. xv.

13 Talcott Parsons, *Essays in Sociological Theory*, rev. edn. (Glencoe, Ill., 1963), pp. 204 f., and *The Social System* (Glencoe, 1951), pp. 304, 311. Other references in the latter to Malinowski (pp. 328, 469) and to R. Firth (p. 33) are again in the context of magic, i.e., exotic behavior, while only G. P. Murdock on kinship (pp. 154, 170) and A. Kroeber on culture growth (pp. 336, 488) appear to be recognized on predominantly theoretical grounds.

14 A recent interpretation of the Roman *munera* suggests, however, that the link may be more than just a metaphorical one. With the connivance of Roman intellectuals these games were presented to a people "who had lost the habit of forging its own history and was now content to participate, in their Sunday's best, in a parody. . . . the weapons of the gladiators and the techniques of combat borrowed successively from defeated peoples served as the fossilized image of the Roman conquest." (Roland Auguet, *Cruauté et Civilisation: Les Jeux Romains* (Paris, 1970), pp. 238 ff.)

15 To name a few examples from otherwise highly perceptive philosophical treatments, Plessner writes: "The empty forms of time, space, self, and death have in common the fact that they presuppose a detaching act of objectivization; they can be attained only by the type of human being who has become conscious of his individuation. By contrast, children and primitive peoples meet death, and indeed the phenomenon of disappearance as such, unselfconsciously and without wonder." (Helmuth Plessner, "On the Relation of Time to Death," in *Man and Time* (Papers from the Eranos Yearbooks, Bollingen Series xxx-3), edited by Joseph Campbell (New York, 1957), pp. 233–63). The idea is implicit in the way Morin juxtaposes Piaget's work on children and Leenhardt's findings in Melanesia (Edgar Morin, *L'homme et la Mort*, rev. edn. (Paris, 1970), p. 31), or when Choron puts "primitives" into the company of animals (Jacques Choron, *Death and Modern Man* (New York, 1972), Appendix 2).

16 Werner Fuchs, *Todesbilder in der modernen Gesellschaft* (Frankfurt, 1969).

17 This transformation was observed and made a point of critique in a comment of Alvin Gouldner's: "Over and against man's animal mortality, Parsons designs a 'social system' that, with its battery of defenses and equilibrating devices, need never run down. What Parsons has done is to assign to the self-maintaining social system an immortality transcending and compensatory for man's perishability. It is thus that Parsons' social system extrudes all embodied mortal beings and, indeed almost any kind of perishable 'matter,' and the system is instead constructed of 'role players' or roles and statuses that transcend and outlive men. Much of Parsons' theoretical effort, then, is, I suspect, an effort to combat death. But it does entail a denial not only of the death of individuals, but also of the death of society and, particularly, American society." Alvin W. Gouldner, *The Coming Crisis of Western Sociology* (New York, 1970), pp. 433 ff. One does not have to share Gouldner's position (especially not his contention that Parsons is the chief villain in the story) to see some of the deeper practical reasons for assigning to anthropological findings on death the theoretical value we found to be exemplified in Parsons' *The Social System*.

18 Sally R. Binford, "A Structural Comparison of Disposal of the Dead in the Mousterian and the Upper Paleolithic," *Southwestern Journal of Anthropology*, 24 (1968), pp. 139–54. This paper should be consulted for a review of earlier, mostly French, literature on the importance of burial evidence in prehistoric research.

19 This trend, as well as the theoretical and methodological sophistication which can be brought to it, is exemplified in a recent collection of papers edited by James A. Brown (*Approaches to the Social Dimensions of Mortuary Practices, Memoirs of the Society for American Archeology No. 25*; published as *American Antiquity*, 36, no. 3 (1971), part 2), especially in the contribution by Lewis R. Binford. The latter contains an interesting critique of Kroeber's paper (1927) which we cited as typical of the folklorization of burial customs (note 9).

20 Claude Lévi-Strauss, *The Savage Mind* (Chicago, 1966), pp. 238 ff.

21 Robert Hertz, "Contribution à une étude sur la représentation collective de la mort," *L'année Sociologique*, 10 (1905–6), pp. 48–137.

22 Claude Lévi-Strauss, *Tristes Tropiques* (New York, 1967), p. 397.

23 Some of the intellectual origins of that position should be sought in Hegel's philosophy of death; see Morin, *op. cit.*, pp. 262 ff.

24 Victor W. Turner, *The Ritual Process* (Chicago, 1969).

25 Clifford Geertz, "Religion as a Cultural System," in *Anthropological Approaches to the Study of Religion*, edited by Michael Banton (London, 1966), pp. 1–46. The material cited appears on pp. 35 ff.

26 Roy Wagner, *Habu* (MS scheduled for publication in 1972, Chicago), p. xx.

27 Alfred Schütz, *Collected Papers I*, edited by M. Natanson (The Hague, 1967), p. 228.

28 Johannes Fabian, "Language, History and Anthropology," *Philosophy of the Social Sciences*, 1, pp. 19–47.

29 J. Theuws, "Le styx ambigu," *Problèmes Sociaux Congolais*, 81 (1968), p. 33. For Theuws' attempt to place conceptions of, and reactions to, death into a wider context, see also "Naître et mourir dans le rituel Luba," *Zaire*, 14 (1960), pp. 115–73.

30 Roger Bastide, "Religions africaines et structures des civilisations," *Présence Africaine*, 66 (1968), p. 104. This and other quotations used in the concluding section are selected for the suggestiveness of formulations, not as proofs for our position. Furthermore, I should like to express my acute awareness of the fact that this paper does not really take up the challenge of alternate views of death expressed, for instance, in the great traditions of China, India, and the Near East. Even anthropologists have, by and large, not dared to relegate them to a "primitive" status. This essay, then, is critical *within* one tradition of thought but perhaps not sufficiently critical *of* it. Given the magnitude of even the limited task of an immanent criticism, I can only hope for indulgence.

Part II

Death and Dying

6

Death Omens in a Breton Memorate

Ellen Badone

Since the publication of Anatole Le Braz's *La Légende de la Mort chez les Bretons Armoricains* in 1893, Brittany has been renowned as a region rich in folklore related to death. The present discussion, based on fieldwork recently conducted in Brittany, will be concerned with only one aspect of the Breton death-related discourse. This is the category of precursors of death or *intersignes*.

Narratives concerning *intersignes* may be classified etically as memorates. They are unstructured personal narratives dealing with supernatural events interpreted as portents of death. Often related in the first person, they are considered to be true and deal with experiences lived through by the speaker or some close associate. As memorates, *intersigne* narratives provide particularly useful material for the study of folk belief.[1]

As van Gennep points out,[2] *intersigne* is a local Breton term for omen which first appears in the publications of folklorists working in Brittany during the late nineteenth century. The word *intersigne* literally means 'sign between.' These are signs which bridge two time dimensions, the present and the future, and two levels of reality, the natural and the supernatural. *Intersignes* are associated with a worldview in which there are no rigidly defined boundaries between these domains. In *intersigne* narratives, the supernatural expresses itself through the medium of natural phenomena: the actions of birds, dogs and horses, or noises heard in the night. Many people in rural Brittany are predisposed to recognize 'natural' signs in the surrounding environment, such as weather prognosticators. The observation that gulls are flying towards the coast, for example, is interpreted as a sign of good weather. Thus, it is not surprising that supernatural signs are also noted: a dog howling is a supernatural indicator of a forthcoming death. *Intersignes* differ from weather signs, however, in that they relate to more profound issues: death, grief and loss.

A number of different types of event are emically recognized as *intersignes*. The most common of these is the call of the 'death bird' in the neighbourhood of a person who is about to die. This bird, known in Breton as *Labous an Ankou*, is sometimes, but not exclusively, identified as the owl. Other birds whose continued appearance around a house is considered an omen of death include crows and magpies. Additional types of

From Ellen Badone, "Death Omens in a Breton Memorate," *Folklore*, 98 (1987), pp. 99–104.

intersigne include premonitory dreams and waking visions of funeral processions, seen well in advance of an actual death and funeral in the community. The classic *intersigne*, collected by Le Braz at the turn of the century and still observed today, is the sound of squeaking wheels along the roadway outside one's home. This is the *Karrigell an Ankou* or the wheelbarrow of the *Ankou* – death personified in Breton tradition – coming to carry away the soul of the dying.[3] It should be noted that many of the phenomena recognized as *intersignes* are not restricted to Breton folklore. The howling dog and the call of the owl, for example, are standard omens in many folk traditions, as even a cursory glance of the *Motif-Index of Folk Literature* demonstrates.

In the analysis of *intersigne* narratives the question arises of whether the signs observed are interpreted as *intersignes* before or after the fact of a death. In certain narratives, the *intersigne* appears as the cue which changes the status of the dying person. By those who have observed the *intersigne*, he is no longer viewed as a sick person who may recover. Rather, he is considered to belong in the liminal state of those for whom there will be no return, 'betwixt and between' the social categories of the living and the dead. In other cases, however, it is afterwards, and especially in the context of the narration of the experience, that the signs achieve their full significance, as Honko's 1964 study would suggest. The narrator, recounting what he or she observed before a death, traces a pattern which lends meaning and coherence to an otherwise inexplicable and tragic event.

In describing experiences with *intersignes*, the narrator both reconstructs and interprets his or her personal history. This process will become evident in the analysis of the following text, recorded during fieldwork. The speaker, Marie, is a middle-aged woman who lives with her alcoholic husband and her sister who runs a small rural café in interior Brittany. As Marie relates, she had two sons, one normal and one who developed psychiatric problems after his period of obligatory military service. In her narrative, Marie describes the *intersignes* experienced by each member of her immediate family, prior to the cycling accident in which her healthy son was killed, four years earlier.

Marie's narrative has two significant features. The death in question is an accidental death, and in addition, it is the death of a young person. Thus it is doubly shocking and tragic. Whereas the elderly are expected to die and are therefore not mourned to excess, the death of a young person falls into the category of deaths locally considered to be '*triste*'. As an accidental death, Marie's son's death is a source of special anxiety. It appears senseless, unnecessary, revolting. As his mother explains, he was knocked off his bicycle by a drunken driver. Through her narrative, Marie engages in a process akin to Lévi-Strauss' mythical thought, seeking to overcome contradictions by generating connections among seemingly unrelated events.[4] This process enables Marie to reconcile the apparent meaninglessness of her son's death with her desire for an ordered, meaningful vision of reality. She achieves this reconciliation by framing her son's death in the context of a predestined pattern beyond human control.

The narrative which follows has been translated from the French. My own comments and those of an acquaintance of the narrator, present during the interview, are interspersed with Marie's account.

> *Marie: Oui, bon.* My son was working at Carhaix, he, he is the one who died there. He was killed by a car. He was riding along the side of the road, like that, and then a driver who was drunk drove right into him. Right into him, like that. He was lifted up on the hood of the car, and then he fell back on the road. It was his skull that was . . . the bone was fractured. Yes, he died immediately.
>
> *My comment:* Because of a drunk driver!
>
> *Marie:* Yes, one who was going to see his wife in the hospital, because she had just given birth. So, you see, he had celebrated the event after work with his friends, he'd bought them all drinks.

Parenthetically, although these details were not included deliberately as a dramatic device, one might note the poetic irony in this linkage between birth and death. The narrative continues:

> *Marie:* So, my son was working at Carhaix, and one day he was home here. He was about to leave, he was standing on the doorstep. There, where I live, on the doorstep. And when he was going to put his

suitcase in the car, we heard a bird, who cried, twice, in the night, like that. Over there, by the poplars. We heard it twice, like that, twice.

Acquaintance: And you don't know what sort of a cry it was?

Marie: Oh, dismal cries. Twice it cried.

Acquaintance: And you don't know if it was a white bird? Was it an owl?

Marie: Oh, I don't know, since it was night-time. It was night-time, and me, I had always heard the old people say, before, that that was the death bird. *Labous an Ankou*, that's what we used to call it, *Labous an Ankou*. I mentioned that to my son: 'Do you think that's what it is?' I asked him. 'I don't know. The old people used to say so,' he replied, like that. But I didn't want to make him afraid, so I just left it at that, because, just at that moment, he was going to leave. Because, if I had told him too many things about it, he would have been afraid.

So, I just said one or two words, and then I stopped talking about it. *Bon*, that was that. My son went and worked, and after work he used to train to take part in cycling races. And, I don't know how many months later, three or four months later, perhaps, he was killed. But, my sister now, she was in Alsace. She was working in a hotel there at that moment, you see. And she had dreamed that she had seen my son in an ambulance, here. In her dream, she saw the courtyard here and my son in the ambulance. She wasn't even here at home. She was working in a hotel in Alsace and she dreamt that. She woke up with a start, like that, and she said to herself, 'Oh, perhaps he's going to have an accident,' because he was a cyclist. But the time passed, and it didn't come about right away. *Afterwards*, we found out that she had had that dream.

Here it is evident that the dream's premonitory quality was recognized after the death occurred.

Marie: And my mother, too. My mother had a dream too. That he had been killed.

My comment: That her grandson had been killed?

Marie: Yes, she told me so. I was in the chicken coop.

This inclusion of 'unnecessary' details is a characteristic feature of *intersigne* narratives, and of memorates in general.[5] Marie not only considers it important to relate the fact that her mother had told her about the dream, but also to describe the circumstances surrounding its narration. Such details

situate the incident in her mind and reinforce her memory of having discussed the premonitory dream well in advance of her son's accident. However, again, it is after the fact, in Marie's personal reconstruction of the events leading up to her son's death, that her mother's dream assumes its full significance as a precursor. The narrative continues:

Marie: She told me: 'I dreamt that Rémy had been killed.' She told me that. So, we had all heard something, or dreamed. And my husband heard the sound of hammering.

My comment: What was that?

Marie: Yes, before the death, too. And he told me. *He was made to feel it*, you see. It's bizarre, isn't it? *He was made to feel it*.

Marie's repeated comment, 'He was made to feel it,' is extremely significant. Her exact words were: '*On lui avait fait sentir*.' The impersonal subject and the passive voice implicitly raise the question: who or what made her husband sense their son's death in advance? I would suggest that the *intersigne* is an integral part of a worldview based on the concept of fate or *la destinée*. When discussing death or the choice of a marriage partner, many informants expressed the view that there is nothing one can do to exert control over these areas of life. Each person has his or her own destiny and, try as one might, it is impossible to deviate from this predetermined path. It is *écrit d'avance* – written in advance – that one will marry a certain person or die at a particular place and time. This idea of destiny is not conceived of so much in terms of the Christian concept of God's will as in terms of an ordering force in the universe, a force which bears no direct connection to Roman Catholic dogma. As another, strongly anticlerical informant explained, after describing a number of *intersignes* she had experienced:

It's because of that that I believe that there must be a Master. I don't know if it's *Le Bon Dieu* or another, but I think there must be a Master who forewarns us.

Thus, *intersignes* are interpreted as proof that there is a larger force which predetermines and controls the events in human lives. According to this fatalistic worldview, the future constitutes an objective reality, elements of which can be known in the present through the medium of the *intersigne*. Logically, if all the major crises in life are 'written in advance,' it is not surprising that some people are forewarned. It is 'given to them' – by the 'Master' – to know beforehand. As Marie says of her husband: '*On lui avait fait sentir* – He was made to feel it.'

Marie continues to relate the circumstances associated with the hammering noise heard by her husband in the night:

> *Marie*: 'I heard something,' he told me. 'I heard something, and I don't know what it is. I'm worried. I think I heard something.' He thought it must have been the neighbour behind, hammering in the electric fence pickets for his cows, since it was during the night. He thought it was that. But no-one knew what it was, the sound of hammering, no-one knew. When my son was dead, afterwards, then we found out. Because we couldn't get the coffin out of the room. No-one could have known. We had to knock down a bit of the wall at the door to get the coffin out of the room. And, you see, no-one knew that the wall would have to be knocked down. And it was that, the sign, it was that.
>
> *My comment*: He heard the same noise?
>
> *Marie*: Yes, the sound of hammering, yes. We knocked it down with the hammer too. And that, that's true!

Marie's insistence on the truth of this event is typical. Whereas certain categories of death-lore, including most legends dealing with ghosts, are considered improbable – 'the things ignorant people talked about in the old days' – *intersignes* are believed. Marie continues:

> *Marie*: And then, before, a long time before, there was a man who was sick, there in the village. I don't know how long before – one year, or two. There was a dog who came and howled at my door. And me, I believe in that sort of thing, eh? Crying and howling at my door. And I hadn't forgotten [at the time of her son's death]. I hadn't forgotten. I said to myself [when the dog came]: 'Oh, he's come to the wrong door, ha!' Because it was the other man who was ill. Yes, he was sick, and he died almost immediately after that. 'He was howling at the wrong door, ha!' I said to myself then. Because I believe in those things. *Non, non, non!* He wasn't mistaken.

> And another day, there was a magpie that came and tapped on my windowpane, too. And me, I believe in those things. And all that, I believe had a relationship with the death of my son.

Here Marie explicitly sets her son's death in the context of the predetermined pattern provided by the repeated occurrences of *intersignes*. Beginning at least one and possibly two years before the death of her son, with the dog howling at her door, this pattern of *intersignes* reaches a peak of intensity three or four months prior to the accident.

In the case of her son, as Marie observes:

> *Marie*: We heard all that, all that was heard beforehand. And for the death of my mother two years ago, we didn't hear a thing. Because she was an elderly person, you see, and everyone has to die, as you well know. She was an elderly person.
>
> *My comment*: That was more normal?
>
> *Marie*: Yes, and my son, you see, because of the fact that it was a young person, we were made to feel it. *On nous a fait sentir*.

This statement and other materials collected during fieldwork suggest that *intersigne* narratives are more often associated with accidental deaths, unexpected deaths or '*triste*' deaths of the kind described in this text than with 'normal,' peaceful deaths resulting from old age. This is because the contradictions inherent in '*triste*' deaths are more acute than in other types of death: youth and death are concepts which it is not easy to reconcile. Therefore there is a greater need to situate *triste* deaths in the type of explanatory framework provided by the *intersigne* narrative.

Marie continues:

> *Marie*: *Ma*, those things are true, those things that I've just told you. Yes, they're true. So, therefore, there is something supernatural, above us, don't you believe? Because, all that, it's bizarre, all the same! And yet, it's true. And me, I had heard the old people recount all that sort of thing before too. But now I believe, because we all heard something.

Here again the idea is expressed that *intersignes* provide evidence for the existence of some vaguely defined supernatural force 'above us' which directs our lives. In addition, Marie reaffirms the veracity of her experience, explicitly contrasting her present attitude of belief with her own former scepticism. Her comment, 'But now I believe, because we all heard something,' corroborates Honko's observation that 'In general, informants react critically to supernatural experiences. They want to consider true only that which they themselves saw or which some acquaintance experienced.'[6]

Marie's narrative is a particularly complete and coherent example of its type. It is unusual to be told an *intersigne* narrative involving so many different signs appearing to so many individuals in connection with the same death. It seems likely that the need to reconstitute a meaningful representation of reality was expecially great in this case, not only because of the young man's age and the accidental nature of his death, but also because Marie harbours a deeply felt sense of injustice that it was her healthy, 'good' son who was taken, while her mentally handicapped, 'bad' son had been left alive. As she states in connection with her mother's dream before the accident which killed Rémy, the healthy son:

> *Marie*: Me, I thought, because my mother had definitely dreamt about Rémy. Because my son, the other son, was sick in hospital with a nervous breakdown. The son you just met here. I believed that maybe he would die. And I had got that idea in my head, like this, 'maybe something will happen to him.' But I never imagined that anything would happen to the healthy one.

This last quotation illustrates another characteristic feature of *intersigne* narratives. Often when the sign is first observed it is incorrectly interpreted as an *intersigne* for someone considered likely to die. As the narrative progresses, it is discovered that, by an ironic twist of fate, another totally unexpected and more tragic death occurs, while the 'likely candidate' either does not die, or the relative importance of his death is minimized. The inclusion of details concerning the mistaken interpretation of an *intersigne* lends a shock value to such narratives which is aesthetically satisfying for Breton listeners on two

levels. First, it evokes a thrill of surprise and fear which is, in moderation, pleasurable. On a deeper level, however, the mistaken identification of the person about to die dramatically demonstrates the reality of fate as an uncontrollable and ultimately unknowable force.

Intersigne narratives are 'good stories' because they validate the fatalistic worldview shared by narrator and listeners. These narratives concretize the folk belief that the future exists as an objective reality and that one cannot, therefore, alter the pattern of one's life. Just at the moment when one seems to have glimpsed a fragment of this pattern, one finds that, ironically, the supernatural has reserved the right to its secrets. Although certain clues may be provided about how the future will unfold, mere human minds cannot always penetrate destiny's deeper logic.

The *intersigne* narrative discussed in this paper represents a reconstruction or ordering of past events which generates meaning and pattern where they are not otherwise apparent. It does so by appealing to specific natural phenomena and to dreams, through which the supernatural speaks. The howling dog, the hammering noise in the night and the premonitory dreams – observed prior to the tragedy – are as Lévi-Strauss would say, the 'remains of events' which are fitted together after the fact, to build up structures of significance.[7] It is in the telling and re-telling of events that the narrator attempts to bridge the gap between her desire to find a reason and the inherent unreason of her loss.

NOTES

1   Lauri Honko, 'Memorates and the Study of Folk Belief,' *Journal of the Folklore Institute* 1 (1964), 5–19; C. W. von Sydow, *Selected Papers on Folklore* (Copenhagen, 1948).

2   Arnold van Gennep, *Manuel de Folklore Français Contemporain*, Tome Premier, II (Paris: Picard, 1946), p. 661.

3   Anatole Le Braz, *La Légende de la Mort chez les Bretons Armoricains* (Paris: Champion 1928 [1st edn 1893]), p. 114.

4 Claude Lévi-Strauss, 'The Science of the Concrete,' in *The Savage Mind* (Chicago: University of Chicago Press, 1966), pp. 1–34.

5 See Honko, as in n. 1.

6 Honko, p. 10.

7 Lévi-Strauss, p. 22.

7

The Meaning of Death in Northern Cheyenne Culture

Anne S. Straus

Human death is distinguished from other death in Northern Cheyenne culture, human life from other life; and the meaning of human death must be considered in its relationship to the meaning of human life. Human-ness is tied to physical life, but selfhood and tribal identity are not: human death terminates physical life while self and Cheyenne-ness persist.

Human life is understood here as a "journey on the surface of the earth" (as represented in figure 7.1 below). The developing fetus has not yet begun the journey and is described as "someone coming to join us". Intercourse is understood as necessary but not sufficient for conception: conception is tripartite, male and female contributions of blood and substance are required, but the animating life principle comes from the Creator, *Ma?heo?o. Ma?heo?'s* blessing is tenuous and especially insecure during fetal life. Spontaneous abortions are believed to be caused by amoral or un-Cheyenne-like behavior of either parent which leads *Ma?heo?o* to "call the child back", withdrawing the blessing of life. A child is considered to be "close to the spirit", likely to be "called back" for the first twelve years of his life, but especially during this very early period. The death of

a newborn infant or a fetus is the source of great family strife, the relatives of each parent blaming the other parent for the death.

In the first months of life, the fetus is not considered to be fully living: the creation of life is a process, not an event. Traditionally, a fetus aborted in this early time would be treated like the placenta of a newborn, potentially lifeful, potentially human, but not yet realized, and it is hung on a branch of a tree beside a river to dry and ultimately to be eaten by carnivorous birds (and perhaps also to call forth its twin; the original 'second twin' developing in a river from the thrown-away placenta of the first). The older fetus, in particular the fetus which has manifest its life principle by beginning to move within the womb, is buried as if it were a newborn infant. At the moment of birth, the infant has life, but is not yet human: it has *Ma?heo?o's* first blessing only.

Ma?heo?o blesses all living things in this way. His special blessing to human beings is the gift of breath/power (*omotome*) and the associated spiritual potential (*mahta?sooma*). Omotome, meaning breath/air and also word, is inspired in the child when the "plug has

From Anne S. Straus, "The Meaning of Death in Northern Cheyenne Culture," *Plains Anthropologist*, 23, 79 (1978): 1–6.

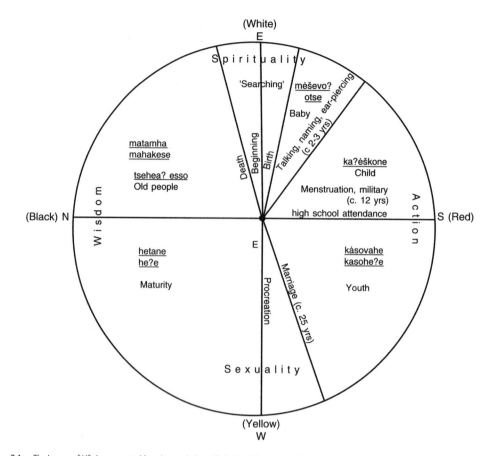

Figure 7.1 The Journey of Life is represented here in association with the Four Directions and the four earth colors; east is taken as the orienting direction and thus is found at the top

been removed", the mucus loosened in the infant's throat, and the child inhales his first breath of air. With his first breath he draws in his consciousness and his ability to communicate verbally, and thus his only access to power in a world where he is otherwise weak and ignorant (cf. Straus 1978: Chapter VI). In the exercise of his *omotome* and under the direction of his parents, especially during the first twelve years of his life, the human being develops his *mahta?sooma* or spiritual balance. When the *mahta?sooma* is differentiated into its four parts, two of them "good" (representing the ordered cultural existence of man), two of them "crazy" (representing his unordered, animal heritage), the individual will demonstrate in his behavior that he "knows the difference", that is, comprehends the moral order within which he must live. Only at this point is the

individual considered to be responsible for his own behavior as a functioning self, a full participant in the tribal community, a person. It is at this point as well that the individual's behavior may be classified by other adults, a fundamental classification being that based on the "good" and "crazy" potential present in everyone, and the extent to which each directs the behavior of the person in question. Personhood, full participation in the tribal society, then, is not ensured by birth: it is possible for a child never to become a person. Personhood is the result of a long process of development.

The origin of death like the origin of life is explained in sacred traditions. During his instruction within the Sacred Mountain, Bear Butte, the culture hero Sweet Medicine chose to be like a plant rather than like a rock which exists forever, and thus imposed death upon all human beings. Birth and death are closely associated here, as are the beginning and the end of the "journey of life": the very old like the very young are described as "close to the spirit". Reincarnation is a common though vague notion among contemporary Northern Cheyenne: Sweet Medicine himself was said to have lived four lifetimes; infants born with scars or with teeth, and those who cry until they are given a particular name are thought to be reincarnations of tribal ancestors; and all twins are considered to be reincarnations of the original twin spirits.

The demise, like the creation, of the human person is a process. The *mahta?-sooma*, last to develop is the first to leave the body, its loss resulting in behavioral and cognitive changes. The *omotome* departs next, bringing loss of senses, consciousness and ultimately, breathing. As the individual literally ex-spires, the *omotome* joins the *mahta?sooma* as the spirit self of the Above World. An individual who is strangled (traditionally a woman's way of suicide) traps his *omotome* inside his body and thus never makes the transition from living to spirit self.

The life principle, first gift of *Ma?heo?o*, once diffused throughout the body, becomes localized in the skeleton as the flesh rots away or is eaten, and remains there dormant until the bones begin to crumble into dust/earth. (In the old days, reburial of the disarticulated bones might occur at this time.) The skeletons of deceased human beings (*se?ote*) are known to move about on their own, playing handgame, which they taught to the Cheyennes, or frightening the living: they are animate (and animate in gender [cf. Straus and Brightman, 1977]) but unable to communicate verbally with the living. It was possible for such skeletons to become revivified through a sweat lodge ceremony, and there are many popular stories about dissembling human beings who are really skeletons, encountered by Cheyennes alone at night. One informant compared the revivification of such skeletons to the life cycle of the snake which he said sheds its flesh in the winter, becoming a mere skeleton, but returns to new body and full life each spring.

The process of death may be reversed. Occasionally a spirit which has travelled to *seana*, land of the departed, has returned to the body (often with the help of a powerful medicine person) which then "comes back" to full life. Individuals who have "come back" can recall visiting with those long dead and being in a beautiful place. Such experiences occur within the first four days after apparent death, so burial does not take place earlier than four days after apparent death. The spiritself may leave the human body temporarily without death, as in sleep and unconsciousness (both of which are named in Cheyenne by words related to that for "die": *na?eotse* (= becoming or almost unconscious/dead) sleep; and *na?a*, unconscious or dead. This equation causes an interesting confusion in Cheyenne-English between "passed out" and "passed away", which are used as identical phrases).

The moment of death, then, is difficult to discern: death is a long process. Clues to the immanence of death include the wandering about of the external *mahta?sooma* or shadow-image of the individual. One informant reported a typical experience of seeing the shadow-image of a particular woman walking along the Tongue River road one night when she was known to be in the Buffet Bar in Ashland. That same woman died later in the evening in a car wreck on Highway 212. Such a separation of image from body is taken as evidence of personal disintegration. The individual who sees his own shadow-image should also expect his own death: hence the special power of the mirror as an offensive weapon in oldtime warfare and the present-day anxiety concerning photographic images. Radical behavior change is also taken as evidence of illness, as is loss of hearing, which presumably indicates the failing physical powers of the *omotome*.

Continuity of the non-physical or spirit self after death is clear: "You die, but your spirit takes over", explained one young informant. The spirit-self is animate, even when separate from the body: it has self-awareness, it perceives its own death, separates from the body, and moves on to another place. It continues in its awareness of and participation in the Cheyenne community, both as a dream visitor and as a memory carried in a name. Young people especially encounter grandparents in dreams, and these deceased elders advise them about the direction of their lives. Spirits of the dead, called *heamavo?estaneo?0*, Above People (*seana* being above the surface of the earth), in general warn, advise, direct, and give power to living human beings: they are relatives and are addressed by kinship terms and/or appropriate respect terms for older and more powerful people; they have a place in the continuing tribal community and their behavior appropriately reflects that place. They have identities and names, and must grant permission for their names to be given to a new person, just as is the case among the living. They are conscious of the moral order within which they continue to function: they know how to behave in the Cheyenne Way. They are no longer alive and they are no longer human; but they are indeed persons, full participants in the tribal society.

Seana, at the end of the long fork of the Milky Way, is by far the most common destiny of Cheyennes after death; but it is not the only one. Medicine people, specially powerful on earth, may travel a special path after death. They are properly buried with their heads facing Bear Butte, (*noaha-vose*) and are said to go there after death. Within the sacred mountain, these medicine people may become *nesemoono*, personal spirits, who continue to guide and instruct their people, assuming a variety of incarnations on the surface of the earth. As *nesemoono* or *heama-vo?estaneo?o*, medicine people, like most Cheyennes continue to exist after death and to exist as fully functioning members of the tribal community. They are differentiated from other *heama-vo?estaneo?o* primarily on the basis of their greater power, just as in life medicine people are distinguished from others. The interaction of *nesemoono* with living human Cheyennes is patterned according to the norms for conduct between those of greater and lesser power (cf. Straus 1976: Chapter 5).

Some Cheyennes in death as in life are exiled from the tribal community, isolated from all that is meaningful to them. Those whose behavior in life was irredeemably evil, who sinned and had not been redeemed by ceremonial pledge of their relatives, travel the short fork of the Milky Way or "suicide road" and are lost. Some may fall back to earth and become reincarnated as were-animals befitting the animal-like, a-moral manner in which they conducted their lives on the surface of the earth. There are stories, for example, about does which enchant and entice solitary hunters in the hills at night,

causing them to become hopelessly lost and confused. Their mode of seduction is to appear as beautiful women, irresistable to the hunter who pursues them relentlessly. Perhaps such deer are the incarnations of women who had been sinfully "loose" during their life on the surface of the earth. Male "devils" as they are called, are reported frequently at night on the "divide" between Lame Deer and Ashland: a person driving a car may be hailed by a man asking for a ride only to find when he stops that the 'man' has green eyes and cloven hoofs. Such "devils" invariably incite their victims to unruly and unCheyenne-like behavior. Then there are the owls. Owls are widely recognized as heralds of death, and owls will haunt and bother people walking alone on the reservation at night (particularly terrifying is the noise of the flapping wings as the owl pursues you closely). Owls are in some sense seen as inherently evil: there may well be some connection between owls and the spirits of those who behaved in evil ways but are now deceased, perhaps even with murderers, the arch-sinners among traditional Cheyennes. The best way to cope with the curse of the owl is to kill it. Eventually all such were-animals die or are killed, thus ultimately purging both *seana* and the living Cheyenne community of evil beings.

Those who die a "bad death" may also become isolated from the tribal community. The most common "bad death" is death by violent accident. Accidents, particularly violent accidents, disturb the spiritual balance of the individual and may result in the loss of good spirits. With its two "crazy spirits" then dominant at the moment of death, the self may never regain sufficient integration to make it "over there" and may be condemned to earthbound wanderings and non-participant(!) observation of tribal life. Spirits of those who have been obsessed, unmodulated in life, perhaps as the result of a malicious curse, are likewise off-center and may fail to find the way. Moreover, it is important for the departing spirit to "rest upon its journey", its resting place being its own body: if that body is mutilated or otherwise unrecognizable, it may not be able to "find its home" and may exhaust itself to nothingness in its search. Hence, personal belongings and identifying paints are part of the traditional burial practice to mark and distinguish a particular body, and soldiers will risk their lives to recover the corpses of their fellows.

A "good death" is a tribal death, one which serves a tribal purpose and exemplifies tribal values; a "good death" contributes to the tribal solidarity and provides for the security of the self within the tribal community. From conception, a Cheyenne is a tribal being. His substance is Cheyenne substance, and his heart, the center of his physical being and locus of his person motivation, is a Cheyenne heart (the Cheyenne name for themselves, *tsetsehestahase*, means those who are hearted alike). Each individual is defined as special, unique: each has his own powers and his own problems. Individuals are encouraged freely to develop their own talents and interests and are taught not to interfere with the free development and expression of others. Yet this encouragement of individuality obtains only within the context of tribal membership which ensures, ultimately, that individualism serves a tribal purpose and supports a tribal identity. Without tribal membership, there is no freedom, there is only "being lost". The community is defined as prerequisite to, not limiting of, individual direction within it.

One's death should be as valuable a contribution to the tribe as one's life. In the days of warfare and still today in times of war, the best death was to die in battle, in defense of your community and your place within it. "If you died a natural death, your name was forgotten: if you died fighting, it was remembered" (Stands-in-Timber, 1969: 69). The old people are respected for their wisdom and their spiritual powers, for their special place in the life-system of creation. It is understood as "natural" that they should depend upon those younger than them for food and physical strength, as it is that others should depend upon them for advice and instruction. But physical debilitation is not good: it helps no one. "When a man gets old, he teeth are gone. I am afraid (of that time), I wish to die (before it comes)" (song of the Kit Fox Society). The suicide warrior was common in pre-reservation days, choosing to die a valuable, positive death instead of withering meaninglessly into nothing. The reservation period has had its suicide warriors as well, most famous among whom are Head Swift and Crazy Mule, whose names exemplify the importance of a death which is a meaningful, tribal death.

Loneliness is considered to be the universal condition of mankind, the inescapable consequences of *Ma?heo?o's* gift of human consciousness. "No two people on the face of this earth are alike in any one thing except for their loneliness" observes the controversial Northern Cheyenne author, Hyemeyohsts Storm (1972: 7). Isolation and loneliness are central themes in the major tribal rituals as well as in day to day interaction among contemporary Northern Cheyennes. This becomes particularly evident among those who are drinking, and whose expression is thus somewhat less guarded: the fears confided in these situations invariably include fear of loneliness and isolation from those important to him. Exile is considered to be the ultimate punishment for deviance: it is the worst possible condition for human or other persons; it imposes constant loneliness. The deepest and most acute loneliness is occasioned by the death of a relative or close friend. The anguish is sometimes so great, according to one informant, that the bereaved may expire of his loneliness, literally drowning his heart in the build up of fluid/tears around it. For those who remain, open contact with the departed is irrevocably lost: subsequent contact is dependent upon the will of the *heama-vo?estaneo?o*. The departing spirit, caught up in human loneliness during his four days' search for the Milky Way is said often to visit those closest to him and to beg them to accompany him. One informant spoke of her cousin's efforts to entice her to join him on his journey to *seana*, for example. Once "over there", however, the spirit is free of that loneliness and is no more a threat to the living. Many of the prayers for the recently deceased are focussed on helping him make it "over there".

The exquisite pain of loss through death is said to be the hardest thing a human being must face in the arduous journey on the surface of the earth: grief and the expression of grief are to be expected at such times. But the weeping must end in four days. If it continues longer, the mourners "may be given something else to cry about". They must realize that life is hard and that the departed has been liberated from a struggle. Death is a release, and reunion with those already departed is the great reward at the end of the journey. The place made ready for them by Sweet Medicine is a beautiful place, and it is one step closer to the Creator from whom all things came and to whom all things will return.

Cheyennes do not so much fear their own deaths as they do the deaths of others who will leave them, making them lonely. In facing one's own death, the possibility of dying in a bad way, of not finding the way, and thus of isolation and loneliness is the deepest concern. What Cheyennes fear most about death – their own as well as others' – is the loneliness associated with it. They do not fear the loss of 'productive self' (cf. Schulz, 1976) presumably primary for Americans in general, for normally it is not lost. They fear what they already know to be inevitable, – the loneliness which is at once their unique power and their universal problem as human beings.

Death is defined as transformation, not termination, of selfhood for those who have lived in the Cheyenne Way: deceased Cheyennes continue to participate in the tribal society as *heama-vo?estaneo?o* and *nesemoono*. Death is understood as a process, not an event; and the process of death may be reversed. Death should be expected, even courted: it should not be accidental. Isolation, not anihilation, is the greatest fear associated with death in the Northern Cheyenne community.

REFERENCES

Schulz, Carol, 1976 *Death anxiety and the Structuring of a death concerns cognitive domain*. Paper given at the American Anthropological Association meetings, Washington, DC.

Stands-in-Timber, John, 1967 *Cheyenne memories*. New Haven, Yale University Press.

Storm, Hyemeyohsts, 1972 *Seven arrows*. New York, Harper and Row.

Straus, Anne S., 1976 Being human in the Cheyenne way. Ph.D. thesis University of Chicago.

Straus, Anne S. and Brightman, Robert, 1977 *The implacable raspberry* (on Algonquin gender and its semantic motivation). Paper given at the Anthropology Seminar, University of Chicago, October 1977. Available on request from the authors at the University of Chicago.

8

Kinds of Death and the House

María Cátedra

Vaqueiros distinguish between three different kinds of death: "good death," "bad death," and "tragic death." By examining what they mean by these distinctions, I will outline the conceptual aspects of the phenomenon of death, treating its organizational aspects later. These distinctions, naturally, involve concepts and values specific to the culture of the *brañas*.

The positive and negative aspects of "good" and "bad" deaths do not refer only to the moment of death itself but also to the circumstances that precede it. A "good death," among other things, is rapid while a "bad death" may mean weeks, months, or even years of slow agony. For that reason, a good death is also known as a "sudden death" [*repentina*] while a bad death might be classed as a "death of chronic illness" or a "slow death" [*accidentada*]. In all the definitions of good death, there are two additional constants: the absence of pain and the absence of an awareness of dying. A good death that fulfills these three conditions is known as a "happy death" [*muerte feliz*], or even a "nice death" or "pretty death" [*muerte bonita, muerte guapa*]. This is the way all Vaqueiros, irrespective of age, want to die. The happy death comes peacefully during sleep when the dying person is not aware of it.

> A happy death is what would happen if I went to bed now and was stiff the next morning. It's not being aware . . . and not knowing about anything. It's not thinking about anything, just going to bed and not waking up, without suffering at all. It's what I would want. (Man, age 38)

In contrast, a bad death involves sickness with pain and an awareness of the imminence of a death without cure. A long, drawn-out agony precedes this kind of death.

> Bad death is that of some people who suffer, God save us, a lot of pain. Some more and some less, everybody dislikes pain and suffering. The more you have to be in bed, the more you suffer and dwell on death and think about those who remain. (Woman, age 62)

A bad death, then, comes from any long illness, especially cancer. A good death will have had no

From María Cátedra, *This World, Other Worlds: Sickness, Suicide, Death, and the Afterlife among the Vaqueiros de Alzada of Spain*, tr. W. A. Christian, Jr. (Chicago: University of Chicago Press, 1992).

symptoms, and that is why a heart attack is one of the more preferred types of death. This kind of death allows one to work and lead a normal life until the last moment – another aspect of a good death. A bad death is not only painful for the person who is dying but also for the household, those who must care for the sick person and see the suffering. The foreknowledge of one's own death, or the observation of a painful death in others, produces "apprehension":

If the Divine Lord prohibited dying when you know you're dying, I think it would be better, eh? When you realize it you get an apprehension, you see that you're dying and you die. You're dying with a disease for years and years, suffering there, seeing that you don't get any better and that you have to die. You are a burden for the family and those who are around you, and you lie there thinking, "Well, now I have to die." A bad death was that of X from F, who would spend all day going "Ay, ay, ay!" She must have had cancer, and she couldn't stand it; it was painful to hear her. (Man, age 65)

A good death ideally takes place when a person has completed the life cycle, in old age. It should occur in a "natural" way, without illness or violence, so that a person is unaware of it and feels no pain. Death of old age, also called "natural death," is a subcategory of the good death. It differs from the happy death in that the latter may occur at any age while the former takes place at around eighty years. Those who die "old" do not have a specific illness; they simply "terminate," which means they eat less and less and their blood ends or runs out [se agota]. People who die that way have a tranquil and soft conclusion; it is said that they "died like birds." Sometimes they lead normal lives, even doing work appropriate to their age up to the last moment. It is thought that this ending closes the cycle of a full life.

The man from C house died completely healthy, but he ran out of blood. And the grandmother here was the same; all she had was rheumatism, and she began to decline, eating little and kind of faded away, until she didn't have any strength left. She was eating less, and getting thinner, and declining with less strength, because the blood comes to an end, until they end up like a bird. (Woman, age 66)

This kind of death represents for humans the continuation of the general cycle of nature. Plants and animals share with humans some elements of this final process. Compare, for example, the following observations on the cycle of plant and animal life with the preceding statements about the natural death of humans:

December is known as the dead month because it's the last one of the year; it's the month that the blood declines. The grasses decline and the sap goes all the way down. It's something, I think, that's the same in humans; humans grow until they are thirty years old, and then they slowly get smaller. The grasses and plants grow in the spring until the end of autumn, then they are flattened by the wind or bad weather; they dry out. It's like dying; they lose their sap, their blood, and they have less strength. (Man, age 79)

A good cow gets sold when it is fifteen, sixteen, or seventeen years old. It may last until it's twenty-two or twenty-three, depending on its mouth – if its teeth aren't so worn down that it can't graze and eat. That's the main reason cows give out. Their teeth wear down and fall out; they waste away, getting thinner; they can't ruminate and they die. But no one waits until they die. When the cow gets old you to dispose of it, because the same happens to them as with people – rheumatism, etc., until they pass away. Me, they won't throw me out until God or the devil calls, but the cow, since it's useful you sell it, but not for much, since by then it's hard to fatten. (Man, age 65)

The death that forms the sharpest contrast with natural death is known as the "tragic death" [muerte desgraciada]. In natural death, one dies from intrinsic and entirely predictable causes; the tragic death is caused by external agents or accidents. First and foremost, tragic deaths occur in mortal accidents in the course of the traditional activities of the braña, but they also include more modern deaths in automobile accidents. Those who die in these ways are said to die tragically [de/por desgracia] or by accident. Another kind of death is known as "violent death," a form of tragic death that includes all deaths caused by humans, both murder and suicide.

Someone dies tragically who goes to hitch up the cart to the cows and gets caught and trampled. Or if a tree falls on him, or a landslide, like the one that fell on those here. Tragic death is when you fall from a roof, or a stone falls on you, or you fall off a cliff, or you're run over by a cart, or a car hits you and flattens you, since you end up pretty tragic. There are a lot of accidents. . . . No, hanging yourself is not an accident. That's more like a crime; that's violent death.

Tragic death shares some of the features both of the good death and of the bad death. It is usually quick like the happy death and consequently it is often without pain or an awareness of dying. But it is not always instantaneous; the moribund may have the long agony of the bad death. Although many Vaqueiros prefer a tragic death to a painful illness, they do not prefer it for those around them, for a tragic death is always a disagreeable surprise for those who remain. It can happen to persons of any age; in fact, the active population is especially susceptible to it. Furthermore, this kind of death involves the courts or a police investigation, an autopsy, and other legal problems. So Vaqueiros are ambivalent about this kind of death.

An accident is not a good death, woman. Well, it's a rapid death – but what if you barely stay alive? You could smash your hands or a leg, and God knows how long you'd be dragging around. *Hombre*, if you don't feel anything, then there's nothing quicker than an accident, because you die instantly. Nobody wants it, because it's a surprise for those who remain. Because it's a rapid death, but not for the family. (Woman, age 19)

The contrast between death of old age and tragic death is made clear in the following quotation. Death of old age is expected and inevitable, the conclusion of a natural process. Tragic death interrupts this process unexpectedly and prematurely. The subject came up when a cow was injured and had to be slaughtered.

The animal is destined to die. But this animal, like a person, shouldn't have died yet. It should have lasted a few years more, or however many it would have lasted; it's a pity. The cow, like a person, dies one way or another; you have to take it to the fair to be sold. But it makes you sadder when it's lost tragically, like that day. And with people it's the same. You have an apprehension when you lose a family member tragically. But it's

very different when they've fallen ill or come to an advanced age and then die, because that way you knew they had to die. But when you lose a person by accident, tragically, who was young, or middle-aged, *Ay Dios!* It's a different pain, a different feeling, a different sadness than when you get to the right age, you're old, and you die. (Man, age 67)

This same "apprehension" is felt when one merely talks about death. Any middle-aged Vaqueiro reacts to the subject with worry, distress, *aburrimiento*, or bitterness, when noting the inevitability of death. It also leads them to think about the futility of life, the selfishness of everyday life, the contrast between pleasure and entertainment, and the obligatory ending that must occur sooner or later. Often Vaqueiros prefer not to think or talk about this matter.

Death worries everybody. Just thinking about it. Because one never dies without having thought about it. But just to think that no matter how long a life is, it won't be more than a hundred years. So that all that work, all that slaving and all that loving . . . and then to think "I have to die." You almost get depressed [*te aburre*] thinking about it, eh? You almost get demoralized, and it's like you don't feel like working anymore. But we shouldn't be so bad or so selfish for the little time we have to live. Of course, sometimes it's not fun, but there are always moments of pleasure, good times at fiestas and fairs, of going from one thing to another . . . and then, nothing! Everybody dies. (Man, age 40)

If they told me I was going to die tomorrow, I wouldn't be afraid; I'd be sad. The sadness of going away forever and not coming back. Death. Here we are four days on loan. That's what the whole world is if you stop to think about it. But one can't talk about this, eh? I don't want to talk about it. (Woman, age 47)

When people get old, they often lose their fear of death. Thus certain elderly persons lose all awareness of their coming death; they are said "not to feel it." Others resign themselves to it or even accept the idea. And finally there are those in severe pain who "ask for death." The quotes that follow provide examples of these three ways of facing one's death.

There is a saying that when we get to be old we are like children, and it's true. In terms of the way of thinking and awareness. Old P, I think, is someone who doesn't even know he's going to die. He's already half sleep-walking, doesn't know when he's hot or when he's cold. He has no feeling in his body. He's shivering from the cold and doesn't realize it. That fellow doesn't feel death.

No, I've been counting on it. Can't you see that I'm tired of life ... it's not like you who are very young, and you haven't yet enjoyed anything in the world. Life is that way. I've seen everyone in this village die. And I'm still here. I don't know for how long – not long. And if I don't want to die, well, I have to die. Death comes and you have to *pelear*, eh? You have to die. As my mother would say – she was in fine shape, died when she was seventy-five. She went out of this house to go down the hill and she got tired. And we had to go get her and put her in bed, and then the woman she ... I don't remember what I said to her, and she said to me, "If I have to die, then I'll have to die." (Man, age 84)

You see some people with a lot of pain, and worn out, and they say, "The sooner I die the better." They are afraid because they have those pains. Someone who is very bad off asks for death, of course. A lot of them do! And they say, "Suffocate me, finish me off, I'll forgive you if you stop my suffering."

In the worst cases of bad death, both the person who is dying and those who are witnessing the suffering desire a quick ending. Life ceases to have meaning in some circumstances. Here one of these cases is compared with a case of tragic death.

When somebody old dies, you feel confused. On the one hand it makes you sad, but on the other you are wanting death [for an older person]. Because when one is that way, nothing helps, and one can't enjoy the world at all. If you're going to be in bed all day and in pain, then what are you doing in the world? But a young person is different. Poor E [who died after an accident], what he went through! So young and healthy. Look, he was the same age as I am now. Think about if I died now. And he just went into a coma, and there was nothing that could be done. (Woman, age 18)

It should be clear by now that death is not only a universal biological fact but also a complex cultural event. The Vaqueiros use language to express their perception of similarities and differences among the different ways of dying. By giving these different ways names, they give a certain order to an inherently chaotic human phenomenon. They are able to classify death, even if in arbitrary and subjective ways. The local taxonomy of death could be represented as shown in table 8.1.

Following the local procedure of expressing general distinctions by citing specific cases, I will conclude this introduction with three descriptions. Each shows the ethnographic context for the different ways of dying. I hope they bring color and spontaneity to the more formal exposition above.

A. Good Death (Happy)

Three years ago on Maundy Thursday, over in N [*aldea*] a woman died suddenly. She was from X house in M [*braña*], and she had gone down with her grandchildren to mass, by burro. That was something! If she had fallen off the burro on the way they would have said that the burro killed her. Anyway, down in N we were all in X's place [a bar/store]. I was standing up, getting things from the counter, and the woman was sitting on a bench. And she began to get purple, and stick out her arms and lean against a chair, and go over backwards, and the people went to grab her. And *ala!* She up and died in J's arms, just like that, without saying a word, she died. They called the priest, who must have been in his house, and she was still breathing and moving. And the priest said, "We have to get a mattress." J went upstairs and got a foam mattress, and they laid her down on it. By then she wasn't moving at all. And he said. "This woman's not right here among all these people. Why don't we take her upstairs?" And everyone carried her upstairs, and they sent word to her house that she had died. She wasn't aware of anything. And that day they took her up to the house. Yes, dear, she didn't suffer at all. That is a happy death.

Table 8.1 Death

Good Death		Bad Death	Tragic Death	
Happy or sudden	Of old age or natural	Slow or chronic illness	Accidental or by misfortune	Violent

B. Bad Death

"Bring me my clothes to lay me out in them, now! I don't have a reason to be here anymore," she would say. Her illness lasted four months. Sometimes she would say, "No, instead of suffering like this, it would be better if the devils took me." When she would say silly things, P would say to her, "Hush, you don't know what you are saying, don't say that." And she'd say, "I'm crazy, I know it, I'm crazy. You're not going to remember me; you complain a lot. If you had to stand what I stood, you wouldn't last so long!" She said, "If you'd only give me something to choke me, or if you'd choke me yourself . . ." And she offered a mass of one thousand pesetas to the Santo de los Dolores so that God would take her as soon as possible. You could see that she wasn't getting better; she realized that. She said, "*Ay Dios*, dear, if I die today I won't have to suffer tomorrow." She thought she had cancer and that we didn't want to tell her. She knew she was going to die, because she said, "Ah, ah, ah, don't go, don't go." "What do you have grandmother?" "Can, can, can." At the end she spoke badly, until we realized that she was saying what we didn't want to say – "cancer." When she was going to die, she had three or four blood blisters on her feet and on her body. And when they broke we looked at her, and she said, very faintly, "What is it?" That's all she said. And I said, "Nothing! Just a little blood." And she said, "Nothing . . . go and lay me out," very quietly. She could hear well. She got the blisters from being in bed so long. I don't know if it was that night or the next day that she died. It smelled of blood and pus. What she suffered! She had a very bad death.

C. Tragic Death (by Misfortune)

With my father it was by misfortune. We were together cutting a tree down by the river. And as I told you, for the felling of a tree, we had attached a rope high up, to pull for the direction of the fall. And when I saw the tree was falling I called to him, and he ran full speed in the direction of the fall. A branch caught him on the head and felled him on the spot. He died there. All you could see was that he gritted his teeth, his mouth and nothing else! It slayed him instantly. He was dead, but he could not be brought home because of the law. Some neighbors counseled me to take him home, others not, because someone could report it, denounce it, and they would take everything we had.

The judge from T came here and men from B [a nearby *braña*] volunteered as guards as well, two of them, day and night, almost twenty-four hours until the judge came. It was winter, but they made a fire, since there was wood. He wasn't even sixty years old; fifty-six, I think. The doctors of N, when they performed the autopsy, said, "What a shame! What a chest this man has!" I saw him die right in front of me. Thank goodness there was a man from B nearby. I called him, and I cut the branch and he lifted him up. We looked to see if there was any hope, but no. I was pretty afraid when he died. When the tree fell that got him, he must have suffered a lot, but if you think about it, it was something sudden, maybe a second. Because those who die with a lot of pain, maybe over a number of days, they suffer a lot.

In the following chapters I will discuss at greater length natural death and violent death, the two poles of the categories the Vaqueiros have established.

[. . .]

The different values accorded to death apply both to the Vaqueiros who die and to their survivors. A good death is one that is hardly felt at all, rapid and without pain; a bad death supposes a long illness or a slow and painful agony together with a consciousness of the approaching end. For those who attend the dying person, the good death is discreet; they say "it's almost not death," and it happens while the Vaqueiro is still participating in the collective work of the house. A bad death becomes a heavy burden for those who remain, adding to their other work and forcing them to share in the suffering and impotence.

While it might seem at first that the Vaqueiros refuse to accept death, these descriptive categories in fact involve a rejection of sickness and pain, and raise the problem of the selectivity of death. Vaqueiros consider the age of the person who dies very significant. They complain of the injustice involved when persons die who have not yet completed their life cycle, who have not worked and taken pleasure as they should have, those who still enjoy the *gracia* of living. When such persons die, even in the most benign cases of happy death or mortal accident, members of the group experience "surprise," "worry," and *descobertura* – a sense of loss and absence, which is not only affective but also economic for the people of the house of the deceased. By the same token, one hears muted criticism of those who, when they are very old and have amply fulfilled their life's cycle, "do not feel death" or "do not know that they have to die." When these persons die, survivors feel serenity and also a certain relief. Vaqueiro attitudes toward death thus depend on the context in which the death occurs.

My analysis of natural death and violent death brings out the contrast between these two different ways of dying. Death of old age means the continuation of the cycle of nature on a human level. Old Vaqueiros "dry up" like the grass of the meadows in winter, "finish up" like the animals of the Vaqueiro stable, "die like birds." Birds exemplify a sweet and quiet end, one that is barely noticeable and in accord with in the laws of the universe. Some Vaqueiros achieve this ideal: death finds them gathering wood, on a quiet walk, or shopping in the *aldea*. Without a period of sickness and suffering (these people are said to die "healthy"), death results from a physical exhaustion or emptying in which the dying person never loses his or her social personality. Those who are with them accept the fact of death with tranquillity.

The house is the context for death in the *braña*. This family enterprise provides the frame for death as it does for life, the last recourse even of those who had to abandon it so that it might survive. With each change of generation, the house, along with its old *amo*, suffers a crisis that the various legal dispositions governing the transmission of the property attempt to overcome.

The transmission of the house presents a dilemma for the Vaqueiro who is going to die. On the one hand, the house, through its continuity, offers the only possibility for immortality. The old *amo* who in his day received the house from "those who went before" and "who sweated" there, who raised a family there, wants the house "to go on" with "those who come afterwards." The duty to increase the house, or at least transmit it without loss to the next generation in an orderly succession, involves a lesson of humility – the recognition of one's own transience in relation to the permanence of the institution. Human beings die but the house survives. The old *amos* thus are linked in the collective but

anonymous chain that built the house. The fact that the house survives even when there are no bonds of kinship, when transmission from father to son is not possible, demonstrates the importance of the house. Perhaps even more significant, when the old *amo* must choose one of his children as the heir, he thereby virtually disinherits the others, doing a kind of violence to his own blood, especially when he must take into account, among other things, the aptitude of the preferred child to continue the house in spite of his own personal preferences. When the two roles of the elderly Vaqueiro, *amo* and parent, come into conflict, the dilemma is usually resolved in favor of the *amo*. Being a "good parent," that is, favoring all of one's children equally, is inconsistent with being a "good *amo*" and choosing the child best suited for the house. If an *amo* vacillates in making this choice or he refuses to make it altogether, he will be criticized severely by the Vaqueiro community.

The house holds other more practical and subjective interests for the elderly Vaqueiro. Traditionally the system of inheritance provided a way for the *amo* to ensure himself a peaceful old age, providing for care in sickness and company in death. From this point of view, the house is a property that one offers to those who might be interested, children or *heredeiros*. At times, when relations are strained and especially when the property is small, the old *amos* have to offer the heirs something more than the tenuous promise of preferring them in a will. The solution in such cases may be the deeding of the property or, more recently, the ceding of control, now made possible by the old-age subsidy. This subsidy demonstrates the endemic insecurity, both economic and affective, of the elderly, together with the efforts and legal ingenuity of the culture in protecting them. Until the old-age subsidy was instituted, the legal title to the house was the principal weapon of the elderly, together with control over the profits the house produced, in order to ensure dignity in old age.

The dying Vaqueiro must negotiate between two contradictory desires: the perpetuation of the house and personal care. The various cultural solutions aim at maintaining a difficult equilibrium between the moral obligation to continue a house and the peremptory necessity for personal security. But all solutions are inevitably partial: by placing the emphasis on one aspect or another, certain conflicts are resolved but others are created. One of the most frequent conflicts of this sort is the deterioration of relations between the older and younger couple within the house. The latter often resent their lack of independence and participation in family decisions, because they are doing most of the work of the house.

Today ceding control of the *mando* is perhaps the most viable attempt at solving the dilemma. In this respect the old-age subsidy also helps the young. Ceding control allows for an effective and gradual succession of one generation by another, compared with the definitive and drastic changeover of death or the deeding of the title. In such a situation, there is a possibility of combining the experience of years with the strength and vitality of the young. This method does not always work. At times there are clashes and conflicts between the two generations because of their differing ways of administering the house, and especially because of their differing ways of thinking about it. The old *amo* has a "faith" and an "affection" for his home that the young *amo* does not always share. The greater possibilities of emigration and work available outside the *braña* now make the traditional hope of becoming an *amo* less attractive. In local terminology, becoming an *amo* is now sometimes seen as becoming the "slave" of one's house.

Ceding control is also the first stage in the transition to death. The diminishing of responsibility and work coincide with a change in diet and the gradual loss of *gracia*. Learning to die is a process like learning to live. The child who is born in the *braña* stays in the house at least until he goes to school, a time that marks his formal entry in the outside world. He gradually begins to become interested in extrafamilial relations and creates his own kind of bonds to others. In old age a reverse process occurs in which there is an increasing disinterest in social life, eating and working, fiestas and entertainment, relations with neighbors, and interchanges with friends. At a certain point, children and the elderly coincide in their reclusion in the house. As Vaqueiros say, "You are a child twice." The elderly and children perform similar services in the house and develop a bond of friendship and solidarity.

Gracia signifies a pleasure in living, both everyday and social: traveling, seeing friends, going to the market, and playing cards. This social expansiveness is represented by metaphors of body expansion and lightness. Conversely, the loss of *gracia* means shrinkage and heaviness. Losing *gracia* is not just a matter of age, since there are some old people who have quite a lot of *gracia*. The main cause of the diminution of *gracia* is the increasing heaviness of blood. Blood is a metonymic sign for life; the absence of movement in blood or human beings is the characteristic trait of death.

Vaqueiros are able to maintain their *gracia* as long as they "defend themselves," that is, as long as they can can contribute is some way to the work of the house, maintain an appetite, get around the *braña*, or care for children. The old-age subsidy today helps the elderly to maintain *gracia* because it allows them to be economically independent, preventing them from becoming a burden on the house. Other Vaqueiros hold in high esteem the elderly who, in spite of their age, "defend" themselves with dignity; they praise those willing to do the small tasks they are able to perform. The loss of *gracia* signifies the entry into a phase of defenselessness that culminates in death.

Once the old Vaqueiro has taken to bed, he or she has reached the maximum separation in the process of reclusion. Nevertheless, it is at this point that a final and intense sociability forms around the sick person. Members of the household provide the three basic aspects of care: food, hygiene, and company. The rest of the community also participates in the process of sickness, helping in the work of the house in various ways, watching over the sleep of the sick person, and especially visiting. The same thing occurs when a Vaqueiro mother gives birth; the presents that she receives from relatives, friends, and neighbors are virtually the same. Like the mother who has just given birth, the sick person has urges for certain foods, which are generously supplied by the members of the house and by visitors. Like the young mother's, the sick person's diet is composed of unusual foods, fiesta fare rather than the everyday food of the *braña*. The similarity of ritual in both transitions suggests that death and birth have many points in common. The group that welcomes the newborn and celebrates the woman who has brought a new life into existence also thanks the person who leaves the group, wishing her or him well on the final journey. The people of the *braña* who gather around the sick person help to maintain his or her interest in life and contribute to his or her nourishment. At the same time, the *braña* neighbors monitor the condition of the sick person, making sure that the family fulfills its obligations.

Representatives of the outside world – the doctor, the priest, and the notary public also appear at the house at the time of death. The visits of these specialists tend to occur when the house is full of people. This is particularly true of the priest, whose arrival brings out the *braña* residents to participate in the religious ritual. Grave illness or death is the only formal occasion on which the intimacy of Vaqueiro home is opened to the outside. Normally the Vaqueiros go to the doctor and the notary in town, and see the priest at mass in the *aldea*. The respective jurisdictions of these professionals – over the body, legal status, and the soul – define the Vaqueiros and provide official recognition of their deaths.

If death from old age may be seen as the culmination of a natural process, suicide involves a sharp and drastic interruption of this process. Suicide is in some sense the most "cultural" way of death because it occurs according to the will of the Vaqueiro. Culture not only provides a set of norms for dying but also the possibility of violating these norms in certain circumstances. The examination of the motives that lead to suicide shows the existence of conflict in the Vaqueiro society as well as a system of values about life and death – when and why it is worth living, and when and why it is worth ending one's life. I will summarize these circumstances below.

Many suicides are considered "normal" by the group, and many persons who commit suicide are not considered sick in any way. What is more, suicide, although it may be considered a mistake, is not regarded as a sin or a crime. In the proper circumstances, anyone may do it.

Suicide is something that gets into the head from thinking wrong. I'm not sure, dearie, what I would do, I'm not sure. It is a mistake, of course, it has to be a mistake.

It seems to me to be something done backwards. That you should die when God wants it, and not before. Of course, when they're in pain, I don't know, since it never happened to me.

Among the circumstances leading to suicide may be a desire to avoid the punishment of the law. Vaqueiros generally agree that death in the *braña* is preferable to life in jail. They consider suicide a reasonable expiation or corrective for a crime or wrong decision. In the case of the attempted homicide, additional factors included an implicit fear of a serious economic loss for the house, the advanced age of the man, and the probability of his receiving a life sentence. In the face of the law and the courts, the Vaqueiro, as we have seen, feels impotent and defenseless.

A similar feeling of defenselessness results from prolonged sickness. When there is no hope that the person will get better and a bad death is expected, suicide is considered a "logical" solution. The Vaqueiros regard suicide as humanly reasonable in cases of chronic or painful illness because they live in a society where the use of painkillers traditionally has not been an option. Those around the suicide may even look on this act as ethical and moral, because the illness of a member of the house, especially when the treatment is long and costly, can lead to the loss of the household savings and the amassing of substantial debts. The possibility of suffering, combined with the possibility of making others suffer, thus can be more unbearable than the idea of death.

Suicide usually has its meaning or its motives in the house. Those suicides that result from family or marital disputes show up the conflicts and inequalities in the system of inheritance and its corresponding distribution of roles in the house. In such cases, much of the responsibility for the suicide is attributed to the surviving members of the household, but in a way so subtle and diffuse that, while it serves as a warning to the guilty, it does not threaten their daily relations with the community. Given that all of the houses are organized in the same way, these diffuse accusations serve as negative models, behavior to avoid, and allow for a collective recognition of guilt in which all Vaqueiros participate.

Within the house, certain persons appear more susceptible to suicide. The transmission of the property brings the *amo* security in old age and guarantees that he will be treated acceptably, for he can choose the child he prefers as heir and, by threatening to change the will, blackmail him or her into behaving well. But the other inhabitants of the house are "defenseless" when involved in the household tensions. Among the "disinherited" persons are the women, who very rarely are *amas*. Those women most likely to commit suicide are twenty-one to thirty years old, the age at which the "newcomer" women are adjusting to their new houses and to the difficult roles of daughter-in-law, wife, and mother.

The young woman faces a sharp change from the preceding period, *la mocedad* (approximately ages fourteen to twenty), which most women remember as one of the happiest times of their lives. *La mocedad* is a time of courtship, characterized by frequent attendance at dances, fairs, and diversions. It is a critical period in that the choice a woman makes will determine her entire future. It is necessary to weigh the candidates carefully. A good match would be a *mayorazo* with a good house that is easy to work in and has few relatives, but if the girl waits too long to find her mate, she runs the risk of remaining single or wasting her time. Hence in her late twenties, when she is in danger of becoming an old maid [*moza vieja*], a Vaqueiro woman will become less choosy. Marriage means the end of diversions and the beginning of a period of hard work, many obligations, and few rights. Many mature women lamented to me their choice of mates; they vividly remember their sorrow at leaving their own home and their conflicts with their mothers-in-law and sisters-in-law in the new house. Even after many years of residence in the new house, when they speak of "my" house, they refer to the house in which they were born, in contrast to "this" house, the one in which they now live.

The high suicide rate for women in their twenties must be understood in this context. But it is significant that few people spontaneously mentioned local cases of suicide of this sort, although they often admitted that this age is full of unpleasantness and "life problems." I think this avoidance of the subject has two sides. The first is that these are the suicides the people find most intolerable: they involve the disappearance of young persons "in their prime of life," for reasons for which all Vaqueiro feel a little guilty. By the same token, the suicides of older persons – mothers-in-law rather than daughters-in-law, for example – which are viewed as less morally unjust, are spoken of more frequently. In several cases, the suicides of young women were ascribed to "nerves," even though it was recognized that there were conflicts in the house. It seems that many women of this age have "the nerves," something I noticed myself. Once this condition is diagnosed, the behavior of the other members of the house toward the "newcomer" tends to improve.

A second reason why people were reluctant to mention female suicides is the lack of salience of women in the culture. According to Soto Vázquez, female Vaqueiros commit suicide almost as frequently as males (49 cases compared to 62). But in the cases of suicides mentioned to me, only nine women were mentioned compared with thirty men. It seems that the suicides of women are less frequently noticed and remembered than the suicides of *amos* because of the woman's weak juridical status in the house. As regards status, women, especially those who have not had children, resemble the bachelor uncle or any of the other "old people of the house." The distinction between women and *amos* becomes clear as well in the amount of publicity and number of attendees at their respective funerals and postmortem rituals. Note that in case 14 cited above, which involved an *ama*, the man of the house complained before committing suicide that "nobody paid him any attention," and that "he was nobody in the house." In the legal sense, all women who are not *amas* are "nobody" in the house, at least until they have children; even then, their rights depend on their sons.

Although conflicts in the houses principally affect women, some men find the role of *amo* unbearable. Because they are responsible for the prosperity and perpetuation of the house, a serious economic blunder that "does the house in [*acaba con la casa*]," or an error in foresight that leaves the house without a successor, can lead to much remorse and personal anguish. Both situations imply that the *amo* has made a mistake: either he does not know how to run the house or he has not exercised enough authority within the household. Being an *amo* demands an assertive personality. Given the difficulties of the Vaqueiro environment and the conflictive social organization of the household and the *braña*, the *amo* must sometimes be tough and aggressive. He must know how to defend himself in the family and in the *braña*, where some houses take advantage of the weakness of others in order to expand (at times in the crudest ways – by moving boundary markers or appropriating disputed fields). The role of the *amo*, with its implicit responsibility for the direction and decisions that affect the house, is the opposite of that of the bachelor uncle, who must work and obey. Some people are not at ease in their respective positions; for them, suicide is one way out.

Attributing a suicide to mental illness allows people to avoid the issue of responsibility. Mentally retarded persons who commit suicide are also thought not to have any responsibility for their actions. It is thought that because both the mentally ill and the mentally retarded do not follow the normal rules of reasoning, any incident may lead them to kill themselves. The Vaqueiros do distinguish a less serious and more transitory kind of mental problem: "suffering from nerves." As I have indicated, this may be an expression of conflict between the individual and the household. It is taken as a warning of the need for a change in behavior by the rest of the household lest the sick person have a "spell of craziness," an "attack," or a "bad hour." In these cases it is thought that certain physiological causes – violent blood and the bursting of the nerves in the head – can initiate the process of self-destruction if others do not avoid flare-ups and arguments as much as possible.

These spells or strains [*ramos*] that lead to suicide are believed to be "inherited," since they are transmitted in the house like other qualities or defects – the art of cooking, devoutness, studiousness, or thievery – although they affect some individuals more than others. The factor of "inheritance" implies a shift from the scrutiny of individual motives and social situations to that of the history of the house and its members. Vaqueiros intuitively relate personal disorders to the diachronic process of the family system as it unfolds within the confines of the house. Family precedents, repeated suicides in

the same house or even in the same *braña*, pose with a certain starkness the eternal truth that we are all products of the past and models for the future, or, in local terms, that "there are things that go beyond persons."

Indeed, "inheritance" seems to have certain deterministic aspects that turns it into "destiny," which in the *braña* is thought to be directed by God. Suicide is thus a moral expiation, a settling of accounts with the heavenly court, either for one's own debts or for those of prior members of the house. Possession of the house thereby supposes not only certain material objects but also these old faults, which can be redeemed only by obeying the Ten Commandments. I will treat religion at length in a later chapter, but I note here that the loss of life in itself is considered sufficient punishment for the person who commits suicide and further expiation in the "other world" is not expected. After death, suicides are distinguished from those who have died naturally only by certain acts carried out by the civil and religious authorities; the Vaqueiros consider these acts efforts to discourage others from doing the same thing. Here is how the Vaqueiros describe these differences:

> And you know that they can't put those who commit suicide in the church either. That's right; the persons who commit suicide, hang themselves, or shoot themselves or things like that, they aren't put in the church. You know that they take dead bodies to the church. Well, I went to X to the burial, and they didn't put it in the church. He hanged himself in a cherry tree there by the house. They say that such persons find themselves *arrepentidos*.
> With them it's different. Sometimes they have to go to the cemetery and so autopsy, and open their heads. I've never seen that and I hope to God I never do, because it's bad to see it, but they have to lift up the lid on the brains.

In addition to the specific motives given as causes for suicide, local explanations often point to a process called *aburrimiento*, a concept I generally have left untranslated. The situations that this term refers to include all of those that may lead Vaqueiros to end their lives: the people of the *braña se aburren* because of sickness, because they cannot defend themselves, when they see "the bad things in the houses," or see "everything going wrong"; because there are people "who pick on them" in the house when they are old, because of the "problems of life" when they are young, and because of loneliness, lack of money, debts, and even "the nerves." All of these negative aspects of Vaqueiro life produce, individually or in combination, a state of mind that begins with the loss of *gracia*, disinterest in life, and culminates with an abhorrence of life.

That's it – they see that they are *aburríos* of life. No, they're not wrong in the head, no, I think they see that they are *aburríos, aburríos*.

They see that they are *aburríos* of life. They see they are *aburridos* and so they say, "So, I'll do this to end it." *Ay Dios!* They have to be in a bad way, a bad way in order to do it.

Life is *gracia* – interest in things, activity, and struggle; *aburrimiento* means being tired, irked, and loathing life. It is associated with the state of *arrepentimiento*, an express renunciation of living. The Vaqueiro *arrepentido* finds death is the only solution.

No, the one who does it is considerably *arrepentío*. *Arrepentío* is when one is worn out, *aburrío*, when one is not able to go out to another town, or do anything else, when one thinks about it, when one is oppressed by the idea of it, when it seems that it is the best solution, when one finds oneself forced to do it.

When that happens, it'll be because they are *arrepentíos*; they don't have another solution, and they find themselves alone, and they *se aburren* and they come to that. *Hombre*, I feel they don't have any other choice because in order for them to hang themselves they have to be really *arrepentíos*.

Aburrimiento is evidence of the stress, conflicts, and inequalities of the inheritance system. But in some way the violence is inevitable. The family system here and everywhere is always arbitrary; it solves some problems and it creates others. If the loss of *gracia* follows a gradual and natural process of disinterest and disillusion with life, *aburrimiento* implies that this process is hastened. Although physically alive, the *arrepentidos*, once they have lost *gracia*, can be considered as socially and cognitively dead. So suicides properly hurry on their own death. Living,

in certain circumstances, makes no sense. Death is a flight from pain and human suffering.

Well, they are people who are cowards, who *se arrepienten*, who give up. Seeing myself in this situation. . . . Because you have to have *valor* for that . . . you have to be *arrepentío*.

I don't know what they think. They think, "Perhaps if I end my life, I'll end my suffering, I won't suffer anymore." Leaving is a way of getting out of the way.

In the next chapters I will examine where the Vaqueiros go when they "leave."

[. . .]

Perhaps the reader will agree by now that the process of death is broader than has been traditionally conceived. The relation of death with pain, age, and suffering seems to be critical for understanding the death process coherently. Where the boundaries of this process lie must be determined for a given culture. Death is no simple and obvious fact; it is a complex mass of beliefs, emotions, and activities that differ from one society to another are added to the organic event. Sickness and suicide are as integral to the process of death as mortuary ritual and the conditions of afterlife.

Death cannot be separated from its social context. It primarily affects the house in which it occurs, but certain deaths have more important social meaning than others, especially those of the old *amos*. Their deaths signify a relay of generations, the transmission of property, the periodic crisis critical for the survival of the institution and the human beings that people it. The permanence of the house requires that the old *amo* be considered a usufructuary, one link in an immortal chain. The ideology of the house affects the different personalities of those who live there, whether that of the father who should be in charge or those of other members who must be silent and obey. The natural death of the old *amo*, attended by a well-chosen heir with a family, is evidence of success in worldly terms, a guarantee of continuity.

Conversely, violent death, particularly suicide due to domestic problems, points up the negative aspects of the Vaqueiro way of passing houses. The house solves some problems but creates others that, in extreme cases and with certain kinds of people, are resolved in suicide. It is impossible, of course, to predict which individuals will commit suicide, but it is not at all difficult to figure out what kinds of people are most likely to do it. Most vulnerable to suicide, aside from the *amos* who find it impossible to fulfill their roles adequately, are the women and those who do not inherit. They are locally characterized as "defenseless" within the system of houses.

Studying natural death without considering violent death, or vice versa, would be partial and insufficient. The former shows how the house is organized, the relation of the individual to the collectivity, the structural norms, the ordinary procedures, and the ordered relations; the latter identifies problems in human relations, structural tensions, flaws in communication, and endemic family conflicts. The two kinds of death provide different perspectives on the institution of the house. Yet one frequently finds these ways of dying examined in isolation, providing an excessively dark and negative or unnaturally idylic and happy view of the community studied, the one permeated by violence and aggressivity, the other by solidarity and mutual aid. One wants to ask, "Does everybody die this way?"

The house is not isolated in its sorrow but is supported by the wider Vaqueiro community. At a certain point, death becomes a collective affair, both in requiring a house to live up to its responsibilities and in supplying it with its due. First the sick person, then the dead person, becomes the center of the community. Significantly, the attentions are similar (a visit and presents) for those who are born and those who are dying. Elaborate interchanges are organized between those of the house, those from the *braña*, and those from the outside. The doors of the house are open (and so is its pantry) more or less according to the different degrees of social interaction and geographical proximity. In the funeral process all levels of social relation are present and explicitly distinguished.

This collective organization can be seen in the group of specialists who appear to make the arrangements after death (those who shroud, pray, cook, cut the bread, make the coffin). Their help is evidence not only of solidarity but also of necessity, for there are no commercial alternatives in the *brañas*. In addition to these specialists, there are other, less visible helpers – those who cut the dead person's hay or carry the body down the mountainside. In addition to the specialists who appear at death, there are those who came before (nurse-practitioners and midwives, healers and bonesetters, prayer persons and diviners) and those who come after (spirits and *ánimas*, and again prayer persons and diviners). All comprise a generous response to precise ecological conditions, but they are much more: links between nature and the Vaqueiros, the sick and the healthy, the living and the dead, and the saints and humans.

The house continues to have fundamental value after death. The dead belong to the house as do the emigrants. When a house is inherited, all of its dead come along with it. Eternal rest, the payment of pending debts, and the immobility of the dead are transacted by means of the house. The continuity of the relation between the living and the dead is a result of their mutual dependence as well as their mutual identity: what remains of the dead in us and what the dead have taken away that is ours.

The social context is just one aspect of the process of death. The ideological aspect – how it is defined, evaluated, and predicted – helps us to understand it in different ways. A natural death is considered to be the human equivalent of death in nature, hence the frequent comparisons of this kind of death with the state of meadows in winter, with old cows, and especially with birds, metaphors for the environment that point to the lack of violence or rupture in this kind of dying. The old Vaqueiros who die naturally do so without illness. They die from old age, when their blood, the sap of their life, wears out. They disappear without causing trouble for the survivors, even helping out with small tasks, "defending themselves until the very end."

An unfortunate death is one in which the natural process is interrupted by external causes or human agents. Death by suicide is perhaps the least "natural" and most "cultural" way of death: it implies a social cause in the majority of the cases, such as legal or familial problems, or a physical cause, such as disease, which has grave social consequences – pain and suffering for the severely ill and for those who care for them. Suicide shows up the Vaqueiros' lack of defenses, which, for whatever reason, have led them to interrupt the normal process of life.

For me the most interesting aspect of death lies in its cultural definition: the Vaqueiros do not automatically disappear at physical death but continue on a long passage that began in life with the physical, social, legal, and intellectual decline of the Vaqueiro, or, in local terms, with the loss of *gracia*. Different persons lose *gracia* in different ways: some lose it gently and slowly (those who die natural deaths), others lose it swiftly and sharply (those who die violent deaths). Loss of *gracia* has physical causes (the change of speed of the blood) and social concomitants (changes of diet and a reduction in activity, work, and responsibility). A consequence of this process is the handing over of control in the house. This transfer of legal responsibility is repeated in the social sphere by a reduction of social activity and the gradual restriction of the radius of interaction from the region of the *braña* to the house. Finally, as the intellectual faculties decline, people can lose their awareness of life and death.

The factors that contribute to the maintenance of *gracia* are good health, ("a good stomach"), interest in work and activity, economic independence, the intensity of family and friendship relations, acceptable mental health, and so on. Obversely, a painful and chronic illness, personal insecurity, becoming a burden on others, and not being able to take care of oneself all lead to *aburrimiento* lack of interest in living, or to *arrepentimiento*, the express renunciation of life. Life is *gracia*, a pleasure in things, activity, and a struggle; *aburrimiento* means tiredness, impotence, and passivity. With *aburrimiento*, death is preferable to life.

One learns how to die just as one learns how to live. The child born in the *braña* stays in the house at first, only gradually venturing out to get involved in social relations beyond the family and outside the *braña*. In death this process is reversed; there is a gradual disengagement from social life, from fiestas and entertainment, from relations with friends and neighbors, and from work and eating. *Gracia*, as Pitt-Rivers (1989) suggests, is a gift from the gods, but so, too, is *desgracia*, misfortune. From this point of view, suicide is not the strange, aberrant, unnatural act it is usually considered to be, but rather a decision

that any Vaqueiro might come to in certain circumstances, the end result of a coherent process.

Indeed, it might be said that some Vaqueiros, although physically alive, are socially and cognitively dead when they have lost their *gracia*. The loss of *gracia* is not just a psychological state but also a cultural category imposed on the individual with given symptoms. This is precisely what the belief in the spirits of the living implies. A spirit is evidence of the existence of death in life or the continuance of life after death. The spirit of the living is the cultural self that has died, divorced from the physical self that is still alive. In other words, people can begin to belong to the world of the dead before clinical death. It is possible that many of the suicides, those who are "accelerating" their deaths, belong to this class of the living dead when they lose their grace.

There is plenty of behavioral evidence for the duality of spirits. Spirits do not, as is frequently supposed, come in one uniform model; rather, they come in many types, and these types change, ranging from animals to divine beings. Anthropological literature may portray spirits as aggressive (one wants to ask, are all of them so?) or may emphasize their nature as judges and benefactors. These oversimplifications may be due to a synchronic approach that leaves out the different kinds of spirits (both living and dead), the different "ages" of the spirits (the recent, the longer gone) that change over time, and their various situations (they may be in good or bad places).

After a process of domestication, thanks to the light of the candles that family members provide to illuminate its trip, the spirit metamorphoses from a night bird into a day bird, a symbol of the divine. At the end of this long journal, the spirits become *Ánimas*; they become immobile and command a cult from the living like that of the saints. We find the same fluctuation in the continuum of specialists who talk with the dead and the saints – from spiritists to the shamanlike *ánimas* to the prayer persons. These intermediaries try to maintain a difficult equilibrium between the *braña* and the outside, and between this world and other worlds.

As I have shown, the Vaqueiros express their perceptions of the different categories of existence by means of metaphorical associations with the animals around them. From the living person to saint, from the *amo* of the house to the *amo* of the sky or heaven, there is a series of transitions, an elaborate gradient of the different possibilities of being. Perhaps the most interesting aspect of this vision of the cosmos is that there is no quantum leap, no sharp division between the living and the dead, between human beings and divine beings. Ethnographic descriptions of other peoples remark on similarities between the humans and God, how we resemble those we venerate. The Vaqueiros, with their belief in spirits and *Ánimas*, extend this similarity farther. For them, divine beings are human beings, too. I wonder whether we have a general tendency to reify unnecessarily the boundaries of popular categories, perhaps overconditioned by the traditional subdivisions of the discipline and our penchant for closed mental compartments. Where does religion begin and social structure end? Are the *Ánimas* supernatural beings or the distant kin of the Vaqueiros? What are the similarities and differences between apparitions of saints and apparitions of neighbors? This last question itself merits another study. Such a study might well be informed by the Vaqueiro notion that holiness is not an absolute but rather a relative state, a state that presupposes an apprenticeship, a period of domestication like the apprenticeship necessary in the life of society for the living and in the afterlife for the dead.

REFERENCE

Pitt-Rivers, J., 1989. Postscript to Honour and Grace: The Place of Grace in Anthropology. Unpublished MS.

9

Displacing Suffering: The Reconstruction of Death in North America and Japan

Margaret Lock

We all labor against our own cure;
for death is the cure of all diseases.

Sir Thomas Browne, 1605–1682, "Urn Burial"

The boundaries which divide Life and Death are at best shadowy and vague. Who shall say where
the one ends, and where the other begins?

Edgar Allan Poe, "Premature Burial"

One vivid memory I retain from World War II is of an iron lung, massive and scary, that stood outside the hospital ward where I was taken after the family house was destroyed by a rocket fallen short of its London target. The iron lung was used, we kids knew all too well, for severe cases of polio, the infectious disease causing the greatest havoc at that time – scarlet fever and diphtheria having been brought largely under control, and tuberculosis confined (although only for the next forty years) to the "working classes" living in cities such as London, Birmingham, and Glasgow. Tales about the iron lung and who had died encased inside it circulated amongst us as we traded our shrapnel collections.

Together with the nightly air raids, this contraption signaled that death lurked close by, and we made sick jokes about the technologies of both war and medicine to hide our terror.

The history of technology has usually been transmitted as a heroic tale about the conquest of the enemy, whether it be human or the natural world – a narrative of progress, and of the betterment of humanity in general. Of course, this dominant ideology has, for the past century at least, been accompanied by a counter discourse replete with ambivalence and warnings about the consequences of technology gone wild. In novels by Mary Wollstonecraft Shelley, Charles Dickens, and Kurt

From Margaret Lock, "Displacing Suffering: The Reconstruction of Death in North America and Jahan," in *Social Suffering*, ed. Arthur Kleinman, Veena Das, and Margaret Lock (Berkeley: University of California Press, 1997).

Vonnegut, among many others, we read of the havoc and misery that technology can create. The humanities and social sciences have also sounded regular warnings: Jacques Ellul claimed, for example, that "Technique has become *autonomous*; it has fashioned an omnivorous world which obeys its own laws and which has renounced all tradition,"[1] a sentiment echoed by John Kenneth Galbraith, Rene DuBos, and Martin Heidegger, each from their very different vantage points. Autonomy in the Kantian tradition is, of course, associated with the notion of free will, of an individual no longer subject to externally created laws. As Langdon Winner has pointed out, the very idea of an autonomous technology raises an "unsettling irony, for the expected relationship of subject and object is exactly reversed."[2] We humans have apparently lost out to the monster, but nevertheless rush eagerly ahead creating new devices. Like Shiva in Hindu iconography, Bryan Pfaffenberger suggests, technology, as seen through a modernist lens at least, is both creator and destroyer, an agent of future promise and of culture's destruction.[3]

It has generally been assumed that the major driving force behind the creation of technologies is to meet universal human needs. Herbert Marcuse was one who accepted this position, and, although he was concerned about the way in which the products of technological progress could be subverted under the name of rationality for ideological purposes, he nevertheless emphasized that mastery of nature could, if properly applied, be associated with freedom and autonomy.[4] Jürgen Habermas, building in part on Marcuse, insisted that an apparent consensus created around the supposed rationality of technological progress veils the interests of powerful elites and removes debate from the public sphere.[5] Activities associated with technology are far from autonomous; on the contrary, they are intimately associated with the social and political order. Nevertheless, for both Marcuse and Habermas, since the creation of technology is a rational endeavor designed to meet universal human needs, there is nothing inherently questionable about the endeavor, provided that one goes about it in the right way.

G. Basalla and M. Sahlins take more radical positions, ones with which most anthropologists would agree; they stress that, aside from the fundamental requisites for sustaining life, it is culture and not nature that defines necessity. Necessity is not, after all, the mother of invention in any predetermined way; rather, human technology is a "material manifestation of the various ways men and women throughout time have chosen to define and pursue existence."[6] Technology is thus an integral part of the history of human aspirations and "the plethora of made things are a product of human minds replete with fantasies, longings, wants, and desires."[7] To simply link technology with power is to leave tacit the dominant modernist ideology of progress as an inherently rational pursuit to which culture makes no contribution.

It is easy to assume that among the many forms of technology those related to medicine exist, by definition, to meet basic human needs, in particular to reduce suffering and avert premature death. It is not surprising, perhaps, that aside from a concern about runaway expenditure and unwanted side effects on the body, there has been, until recently, relatively little resistance, in principle, to the development and application of medical technology. Despite the fact that the interests of powerful elites are often directly involved with the creation, manufacture, distribution, and application of medical technology,[8] the assumption that techniques that allow us to penetrate with increasing facility into the recesses of the body, together with those that supposedly relieve pain and prolong life, are inevitably for the good usually holds sway.

Over the past two decades it has become increasingly clear that biomedical technologies are by no means autonomous and, moreover, that the characterization of suffering, being culturally constructed, has a profound influence on their development, associated discourse, and application. It is in connection with the application of reproductive technologies, neonatal intensive care, genetic engineering, organ transplantation, and dying that contested domains have become most evident. That dispute has emerged around these dramatic manipulations should come as no surprise, for their application necessarily involves debate about tacit knowledge of what constitutes life and death.

In North America particularly, efforts to reduce suffering have habitually focused on control and repair of individual bodies. The social origins of suffering and distress, including poverty and discrimination, even if fleetingly recognized, are set aside, while effort is expanded in controlling disease and averting death through biomedical manipulations.[9] Disputes with respect to biomedical technology usually revolve around the question of individual rights, autonomy, and justice. Activists have focused on abuse of individual patients by powerful elites, but very few commentators have stepped back and asked why, for example, infertility, menopause, and aging should be conceptualized as diseases, or why we struggle to save extremely premature infants but show little concern about the reasons for their premature birth or the social consequences of their continued existence.

This essay will focus on disputes in North America and Japan that are associated with the transplantation of major organs, together with the required redefinition of death necessary to implement this technology. Were it not for the development of the iron lung, an ostensibly autonomous, supremely utilitarian piece of technology, and its successor, the artificial respirator or ventilator, by means of which many people who can no longer breathe independently are kept alive, there would be no debate today about the reduction of suffering and the "saving" of lives through transplant technology. The artificial respirator clearly meets a basic need, but the uses to which it is put today have implications that reach far beyond the simple function of sustaining breathing on a temporary basis. Transplant technology, involving the removal of body fluids or parts from one person, and their insertion into a second person designated as needy, could never be mistaken for a value free endeavor – from its inception, at the very minimum, altruism was inevitably implicated.[10] Once certain patients on the artificial ventilator were harnessed to the heroic and showy technology of organ transplants, it became apparent, particularly to those involved in medical practice, that there was some urgency to clarify exactly what is meant by biological death.

It would seem that there can be very little room for ideological posturing in connection with defining death – most of us raised in the contemporary West believe, I suspect, that death is a rather easily definable point of no return about which there can be little argument. Japan, like North America, is in theory a predominantly secular society, and is similarly driven by principles of rational order and scientific progress, principles that are evident in many aspects of the health-care systems on both sides of the Pacific. However, in Japan the possibility of tinkering with death has opened up the floodgates of a concern that reaches far beyond the demise of individuals, whereas in North America, by contrast, death was quietly redefined in 1968 by an elite group of Harvard physicians, and further modified in 1981 so that the concept of "whole-brain death" is now recognized in the Uniform Determination of Death Act as equivalent to the end of life. There was a brief period in the late 1960s when public concern about these changes was evident, but today, in the great majority of North American hospitals, brain death is accepted as the end of life, and the "harvesting" of organs from brain dead bodies has become routinized.

This contrast between North America and Japan invites comparison of the different forms the search takes in late modernity for the relief of suffering and the creation of a just and moral order, together with an examination of the relationship this search has to the production and application of scientific and technological knowledge. It is now apparent in most corners of the world, except perhaps in the heart of Leviathan, that science, in particular biomedicine, has come to be thought of by many as one form of neo-imperialism. In an era of struggles to create and recreate cultural identities and establish the grounds of cultural difference, the self-conscious possession of scientific knowledge, or, alternatively, its repudiation as inauthentic or culturally inappropriate, is explicitly made use of as an ideological tool to establish local power bases and authority. The production and circulation of technologies are, therefore, not only far from autonomous but, on the contrary, incite and foster culturally infused political activity. Suffering becomes grist for the mill of ideological dispute, and individual misery either disappears from sight or else is appropriated in the interests of dominant others.

Remaking Death

After the development of artificial respirators, attempts were made to clarify precisely what constitutes death in several international forums. In both a 1966 CIBA symposium held in London and a 1968 World Medical Association conference held in Sydney, delegates worked under the assumption that what they were participating in was an unprecedented response to new medical technologies that made it necessary for the first time to "define" death.[11] However, in an article entitled "Back from the Grave," Martin Pernick has shown that concern about establishing the time of death is not new but rather is the latest round in an ongoing historical debate, repeatedly revitalized in the wake of new medical discoveries.[12] Pernick cited a 1940 article in *Scientific American* as a relatively recent example of this concern, in which it was stated that "frequent" errors in diagnosing death remained the cause of cases of premature burial,[13] and concluded that it is not simply responses to specific medical discoveries that have shaped the content of debates about death, but that professional interests and cultural values are inevitably implicated, precluding the possibility of arriving at a rational, universally acceptable definition.

Phillipe Ariès, writing about the history of death in the *longue durée*, claims that for at least a millennium there existed in Europe, until the thirteenth century, what he terms "tamed death." A familiarity with death associated with neither fear nor despair, "halfway between passive resignation and mystical trust," was, Ariès claims, characteristic of the time.[14] Destiny was revealed through death, and the dying person participated in a public ceremony in which "his own personality was not annihilated but put to sleep."[15] Ariès suggests that from medieval times on, death gradually became more individualized; an awareness of personal mortality and of failure associated with death was apparent in medieval European iconography. After the Enlightenment, Ariès detects another shift in *mentalité* in which death "became challenged and furtively pushed out of the world of familiar things." Interest shifted to the death of the other – to the "loved one" – and our own deaths became asocial and unnameable.

Ariès has been criticized, quite rightly I believe, for downplaying the individual "torment and pain" that must always have accompanied many deaths, and for giving undue emphasis to its social significance.[16] Ariès was, after all, primarily interested in the cultural representation of death, rather than in everyday experiences, individual or collective. Zygmunt Bauman has commented that, in principle at least, death was "tame" prior to the Age of Reason because it posed no challenge to the social order. Being preordained, the end of the life cycle and also eminently social, there was no need to fight death. For Bauman, shared knowledge about death, which he believes is incited by a universal awareness of mortality, provides the driving force for cultural creativity, a push for transcendence – "culture is about expanding temporal and spatial boundaries of being, with a view to dismantling them altogether . . . the first activity of culture relates to *survival* – pushing back the moment of death, extending the life-span."[17] Bauman suggests that the knowledge and fact of mortality drives the cultural construction of the idea of immortality – "mortality is ours without asking – but immortality is something we must build ourselves. Immortality is not a mere absence of death; it is *defiance* and denial of death."[18] Thus, the construction of immortality is, in Bauman's estimation, the major source of life's meaning in all societies, resulting in the transformation of biological death, "a fact of nature," into a cultural artifact, which in turn "offers the primary building material for social institutions and behavioral patterns crucial to the reproduction of societies in their distinctive forms."[19]

A contemporary scientific approach to death has, in theory, by painting itself into the cold corner where culture is no longer deemed relevant, done away with all meaning, save that a corpse indicates biological failure. Moreover, as is well known, from at least the time of Descartes, the living body gradually came to be understood in medicine as a kind of "animated corpse," since dissection was the primary means of aggregating facts about human biology.[20] Thus, mortality was medicalized in order to combat death and disease. Today death is "measurable" and legally recognizable as an absence of neuronal functioning or, alternatively, of respiration and a heartbeat. Having apparently been stripped of culture, death can no longer transcend biology to act as a touchstone for coming to terms with mortality. Instead, it is simply understood, in medicine at least, as biological failure, a waste:

> Death is primarily regarded as an illness or an aberration rather than something that is natural [and] the physician is supposed both to certify death and state its cause.... These certificates also illustrate the belief that although human beings die from many causes at once, it is always possible to isolate a single and precipitate cause of death. ... Death is conceptualized as an ailment that is amenable to intervention.[21]

Narratives such as that of Ariès about a progression from a socially meaningful, preordained death to one where individual dying became the focus, and then to a vision of death as something to be conquered, are told from the vantage point of the *grand reçit* – as though cultures are monolithic, seamless wholes, and as though a neat cleavage exists between culture, a human creation, and nature, subject to timeless biological law. Ruth Richardson, in *Death, Dissection and the Destitute*, shows how in nineteenth-century England the "life strategies" of the common folk by no means coincided with the aspirations of those scientists who employed professional body snatchers to obtain corpses for dissection and autopsy. People went to great lengths to try to prevent the robbing of graves, anatomical dissection, and the commodification of corpses. For most citizens dissection was considered not only demeaning but literally cruel, and even in the medical literature there was much debate as to whether or not clinical detachment should be equated with inhumanity, although perhaps a "necessary inhumanity."[22] In *Middlemarch*, George Eliot has the townsfolk talk disparagingly and fearfully about Lydgate the "modern" doctor and his fascination with dissection.

The body in death *may* have been stripped of social and individual significance in the minds of pathologically oriented medical professionals but, for the majority of ordinary people living in nineteenth-century Europe, at least, death retained a meaning that transcended the physical demise of an individual. In theory, in the late twentieth century, by partici-

pating in the medicalization and sanitization of death – by virtually confining it to hospitals – we have capitulated to the view that death is essentially a biological event. This very capitulation is, of course, contingent upon a culturally created dominant ideology that understands the physical body as precultural, an aggregation of natural facts amenable to rational experiment and manipulation. Culture is left to deal, often rather peremptorily, with only the final disposal of the body, and the work of grief. Moreover, many writers confirm that we no longer know how to behave around those who are dying – the very process smells of failure and induces panic. Of course, a major paradox is evident because contemporary mass media is laden with images of violent deaths that leave nothing hidden or sanitized, but such garish endings belong to the other, not to ourselves, and perhaps actually facilitate the anesthetization of our own mortality. Nevertheless, there are now many signs of increasing public dispute about the confinement of death, and about the all-out battle to defeat it. As Martin Pernick points out, "Today, perhaps for the first time, public criticism involves both a fear of being wrongly declared dead, and a fear of being wrongly declared alive."[23]

Making Death Useful

In America the first major step in the most recent remaking of death was taken by an ad hoc committee of the Harvard Medical School in 1968. It is significant that this was accomplished shortly after the world's first heart transplant took place in South Africa in 1967. The group of physicians who comprised the committee declared unilaterally that individuals in a state of "irreversible coma," and diagnosed as having "brain death syndrome," could be declared dead.[24] Prior to this time, it was accepted simply by convention that death could only be medically established once the heart had stopped beating, but confusion arose when artificial respirators were brought into routine use, because they allow the heart to remain beating after integrated brain function has ceased. The committee gave two reasons for establishing a clear definition of death: 1) that "increased burdens" on patients, families, and hospital resources were caused by "improvements in resuscitative and support measures," and 2) that "obsolete criteria for the definition of death can lead to controversy in obtaining organs for transplantation."[25] Thus, reaching a medical consensus about a definition of brain death as the end of life was clearly linked from the outset to a demand for human organs. These debates captured some passing media and public attention.[26]

During the early 1970s, the concept of "brain death syndrome" was challenged in the courts. In one landmark case in Virginia in 1972 the jury ruled against the donor's family, who claimed that the transplant surgeons had been responsible for the death of their relative. Other court cases followed including several involving homicide victims, but none resulted in the prosecution of a doctor.[27] At the same time, a debate about medical practice was under way in the medical world itself as to which tests, if any, could be relied upon to confirm an individual doctor's opinion about brain death, and secondly as to who would act as "gatekeepers" to protect physicians from malpractice suits.[28] A Uniform Determination of Death Act was eventually declared in 1981, after extensive debate among the members of a President's Commission especially set up for that purpose. This Act was immediately supported by the American Medical Association and the American Bar Association, and was subsequently adopted over a number of years by the majority of state legislatures.

The President's Commission, in opposition to the position taken by a number of individual physicians, philosophers, and theologians (who were writing mostly in professional journals, rather than for the media), opted to further rationalize and update what they characterized as "obsolete" diagnostic criteria and to enshrine a definition of death in law, something that thus far had not been the situation.[29] The Commission recommended that a concept of "whole-brain death," equated with an "irreversible loss of all brain function," be adopted. This condition was carefully distinguished in the report from a "persistent vegetative state," as exemplified by patients such as Karen Ann Quinlan and Nancy Beth Cruzan, whose brain stems continued to function despite an irreversible loss of higher brain function. The earlier definition of "irreversible coma" left

room for doubt as to whether patients such as these could be taken for dead, and the concept of whole-brain death sought specifically to clarify this point. Thus, physicians, in constructing a "uniform" death, deliberately set out to protect themselves against malpractice, while at the same time ensuring a source of organs for transplants from legally defined dead bodies.

Despite this effort, a number of publications appeared shortly after the Act was passed in which medical professionals, philosophers, and social scientists pointed out the numerous ways in which the wording of the Act is ambiguous. In particular, two criteria remain acceptable for the determination of death: irreversible cessation of circulatory and respiratory functions *or* irreversible cessation of all functions of the entire brain, including the brain stem. The philosopher David Lamb, in summarizing this controversy, suggests that ambiguity is present because the Commission wished to avoid a radical departure, a "paradigm shift," from what had been conventionally recognized as death prior to the invention of the artificial ventilator, while at the same time meeting the pragmatics demanded by the necessity of a legal definition.[30] One of the problems the Commission faced was to transform the *process* of dying into a clearly definable *event* – to establish death as a point in time. Pressure to remove organs as expediently as possible made the transformation of death into a recognizable, scientifically determinable event absolutely essential. As Roy Selby and Marilyn Selby had noted just prior to the Commission, "dying must never be confused with death."[31] Despite the apparent routinization of brain death as a diagnosis, and efforts to create uniformity in the determination of death, considerable doubt and debate continues to this day as to whether we are on an ethical slippery slope, and as to what actually constitutes death.[32] Thus, we remain, in Kuhn's terms, in a paradigm crisis, striving for commensurability but unable to achieve it.

This relatively quiet remaking of death has been masked throughout by a focus on the heroics of medicine and the prolongation of life. Two impending deaths are, of course, involved – that of the donor and that of the recipient – but the public imagination has been fired in North America by the idea of the "gift" of life. The life and death of the patient from whom organs will be "harvested" is left unmarked except as "donor" (although the use of anencephalic babies temporarily swayed this priority).[33] The media usually focuses our attention on the life that will be "saved," and particularly on the moments during and immediately after surgery when the proclamation of success is made; survival rates beyond the first few weeks fail to make more than serendipitous news coverage, and very few people indeed know about the prognosis for transplant patients, long-term outcomes, or about their "quality of life" after surgery.

Between 1982 and 1992, the number of transplants performed in the United States tripled, and it is estimated that over thirty-five thousand Americans are currently living with a donated organ in their body.[34] Transplants of all kinds, many of them repeat attempts after rejection, are routinized procedures; the "cutting edge" of transplant technology is concerned with "cluster" transplants, brain tissue implants, and the paring down of large organs for use in infants and children. The current drive to "maximize" the availability of organs is grounded in the utilitarian assumption that organs must be made available for the greatest good of all and includes a major debate about whether the buying and selling of organs should be established. Discussion is focused on organ procurement, including what type of contract with potential donors and their families is most appropriate for making them more readily available;[35] whether adoption of a market model for obtaining organs is appropriate;[36] and whether the body should be understood as a form of property.[37]

It is evident, therefore, that whatever discussion takes place about the remaking of death in North America is being carried out after the fact of the routinization of organ transplants from brain dead donors, and is colored by the pressures that a perceived escalating "shortage" of organs adds to the debate. Moreover, public consciousness, molded by the media, is focused almost without exception on the heroics of transplants and the "saving" of life, a situation that Ivan Illich has characterized as a fetishization of life.[38] The health "fad," particularly evident in the United States,

requiring constant personal vigilance and body control, together with the imbibing of medications (such as hormone replacement therapy) purported, among other claims, to extend life, are other facets of this fetishization.[39]

In contrast to debates about death prior to the introduction of the artificial respirator, the issue today is infinitely more complex, because there are now *two* deaths inextricably linked through the coincidental failure of their body parts. It is not unreasonable to assume that public concern about the death of the donor should have been powerful enough to limit the rather rapid routinization of major organ transplants; current biomedical ethics in North America, and to a lesser extent in Europe, are, after all, grounded in respect for autonomous individuals and their welfare. These values inevitably become somewhat unraveled at the seams with two patients and their competing rights to consider, and one might expect to see some evidence in the media of this conflict of interest, perhaps even a national debate similar to the one about abortion. Clearly this has not happened. Organ donors, as a class of people, are praised for their generosity and altruism – for the "gift of life" – but as individuals their deaths remain essentially unnoticed. *Apparently* we equate lack of brain function with the end of life, and we trust the medical profession in their judgment as to when exactly this takes place. Perhaps this situation should come as no surprise in a rational, secular society where it makes little sense to dwell on the misfortune of "neomorts," to use Willard Gaylin's graphic neologism;[40] perhaps it is simply more "healthy" to think of individuals "living" on in others, and to recognize transplants as a life saving technology – a device that not only sidesteps the failure of death, but seemingly vanquishes it.

In 1991, more than two thousand people were on the waiting list for heart transplants in the United States, and the number of donors has decreased in recent years. One transplant surgeon has talked of the "alarming number of patients who die waiting,"[41] a situation described as a "public health crisis."[42] But by no means does everyone understand this crisis in the same way. Leon Kass, for example, characterized the problem very differently in a recent article on the selling of organs:

Now, embarked on the journey, we cannot go back. Yet we are increasingly troubled by the growing awareness that there is neither a natural nor a rational place to stop. Precedent justifies extension, so does rational calculation: we are in a warm bath that warms up so imperceptibly that we don't know when to scream.[43]

Few cultural commentators are as explicit as Kass, but doubts, although rarely publicly discussed, apparently extend well beyond critics situated within the medical world, as was clearly also the case in the nineteenth century. Renée Fox's assessment of a Gallup Poll taken in 1985, for example, is that "many respondents . . . expressed anxiety about the possibility that if they signed a donor card physicians might prematurely take steps to pronounce them dead, to surgically excise their organs, or even to hasten their death."[44] Another smaller survey revealed that the willingness of people who perceive themselves to be on the margins of society (in particular blacks) to become donors is lower than among the middle classes.[45] This finding has a macabre irony to it, since, from the point of view of surgeons, the "best" organs come from those who die in traffic accidents, gunshot wounds, knifings, and so on, among whom the numbers of young blacks and Hispanics are very high.

A recent study from Scandinavia shows that among an age-stratified, random sample of 1950 Swedish individuals, nearly 70 percent showed some discomfort about autopsy and organ donation. People reported, for example, that they were ill at ease at the thought of cutting up a dead body, and many were concerned that the patient might not be dead at the time of organ removal.[46] Not only is the public cautious, but several studies have shown that, in North America at least, many nurses and other medical staff are conflicted when it comes to identifying donors and approaching their families to obtain consent.[47] The fact that we cannot bring ourselves to simply talk of "death" but refer consistently to "brain death" clearly suggests that life is still present in the minds of most people;[48] continued usage of the term brain death is in itself an example of the ambiguity and uncertainty involved. These researchers have also pointed out that newspaper and televi-sion accounts regularly report that patients who have been declared brain dead later "die" when "life-support" measures are removed, and health professionals, they claim, regularly use terminology "that implies such patients die twice."[49]

The Slippery Slope of Personhood

The President's Commission that culminated in the Death Act stated clearly that for death to be diagnosed all brain function must have ceased, including the reflexes controlled by the brain stem. At this point there is a lack of "neurological integration," and what is left is "no longer a functional or *organic* unity, but merely a *mechanical* complex.[50] Richard Zaner has pointed out that, for whole-brain advocates, "it is the biological organism (or, more specifically, the physiological/anatomical nervous system) which is definitive for life and death, not the *person* whose organism (or nervous system) it is."[51] Zaner and the majority of the contributors to the book *Death: Beyond Whole Brain Criteria* believe that the Commission put the cart before the horse by trying to develop a concept of death out of a set of standardized medical tests while evading the central issue of *who* had died. In order for there to be a uniform statutory definition of human death there must first be, according to Zaner, a general consensus over what constitutes "personhood" or "personal identity."[52] The Commission, recognizing that no such consensus exists, pointed out that the issue has been debated for centuries, and explicitly sought to circumvent the problem by making a biological argument in which rationally conceived operational criteria and medical tests provide the answer. The response of Edward Bartlett and Stuart Youngner was that neither operational criteria nor valid tests can be decided upon unless a working definition is first established – namely a concept of what it *means* to die.[53] Such a definition has to be "societal," not biological they argued, since a permanent loss of "personhood" should be of central concern, rather than the demise of the body physical. With this in mind, Zaner concluded that "at the very least . . . the central issues inherent to any definition of death must be kept rigorously open."[54]

Definitions grounded in the idea of a loss of personhood have been characterized as "ontological" and contrasted with what are taken to be narrowly defined scientific definitions based on the state of brain function.[55] Lamb, a philosopher, is concerned that those who argue for a redefinition based on ontological criteria are in actuality appealing to the idea that a loss of higher brain function is equivalent to death. He points out that such arguments are concerned only with criteria that describe "the minimum necessary qualities for personhood, defined in terms of psychological abilities," and he asserts that a Cartesian dualism is present in such arguments, which assume the ethical cutoff point to be the moment when the "ghost" leaves the machine.[56]

Karen Gervais criticized Lamb in turn for placing too much reliance on a biological definition; Lamb, she states, understands death as "a fact awaiting discovery," and she characterizes the ontological approach, in contrast, as based in ethical reflection.[57] Lamb has countered this rebuttal by claiming that whole-brain death is an "ethically superior formulation" because "in matters of life and death, objective testable criteria concerning presence or absence of vital functions are more reliable than indeterminate assessments concerning the quality of residual life, or speculations regarding personhood, or utilitarian requirements for transplant organs."[58] Lamb is clearly concerned that overriding interests about the supposed crisis precipitated by an "organ shortage" will seize the day and send us on our way down the slippery slope to redefining death in response to perceived needs. He adds that a whole-brain death formulation does not dispute the loss of all capacity for integrated mental activity, but because the "essence" of personal identity is an elusive concept, which in any case resides in a different logical space than the cessation of vital functions, it is certainly not one on which doctors should rely in making decisions about death. Personal identity, after all, does not have any specific anatomical location, insists Lamb, but is a quality akin to "spirit," "will," or "soul," with religious, legal, and political associations. Loss of personhood or moral integrity are cultural conceptions and are, therefore, subject to a wide range of interpretation and open to easy ma-

nipulation and abuse where pragmatism and utilitarianism hold sway. Norman Fost, arguing along similar lines, has asserted that the problem with utilitarian justifications for redefining death, exemplified by the recently enacted Uniform Determination of Death, is that constant redefinition is invited whenever utility requires it, creating "not only instability, but the perception and possibility that unwanted persons can be defined out of existence [whenever] it serves the greater good."[59]

Given this climate, Lamb and other supporters of whole-brain death believe it is imperative to search out "precise" measurement of neurological functioning because they are suspicious of a culturally produced, psychologically driven interpretation of life, and see less of an opening for abuse when using a tightly defined, biologically based definition (provided in practice there is an under diagnosis of death whenever there is doubt). This argument assumes, of course, not only that death is measurable, but also that such measurements are accurate and unfailingly replicable. A recent survey conducted among 195 physicians and nurses produced some disquieting results. Youngner and colleagues remind us that the concept of whole-brain death was initially accepted because it was assumed that "in the hands of competent physicians" a diagnosis of irreversible loss of all brain function is clinically practical and completely reliable. However, they found that only 35 percent of survey respondents both knew the whole brain criteria for death and were able to apply it correctly.[60] One fifth of these respondents were directly involved in making diagnoses about death at that time. Moreover, when asked to give their personal opinions about concepts of death and then apply them to hypothetical cases, 58 percent of the respondents did not use a concept of death consistently, and furthermore personal concepts varied widely among health-care professionals.[61]

Because of possible conflict of interest, neurosurgeons and neurologists are today expected to do nothing more than suggest to the families of their patients, once brain death has been declared, that they might think about donation of organs. Transplant surgeons and physicians, for their part, may not enter the scene until after brain death has been declared on two separate occasions. This ruling, not applied when transplants were first performed, seems eminently sensible, but it means that involved medical specialists know little of each other's interests and concerns in the application of these technologies. Of more importance, perhaps, it ensures that the failure of death is rapidly transformed, the bereaved family willing, into a celebration of immortality.

Striving for Consensus: The Japanese Debate

There are some remarkable differences at the present time between Japan and North America with respect to organ transplants: whereas, for example, in America nearly two thousand heart transplants took place in 1990, in Japan there were none. It is obvious that this difference cannot be explained by a lack of technology or skills, or by a shortage of economic resources on the part of the Japanese. So, cultural differences *must* be at work. Initially, my inclination was to ask what it is about Japanese and *not* North American culture, experience, and social organization that could account for this discrepancy. What widely shared knowledge do the Japanese possess that makes them resistant to the technologically aided extension of human life? This approach seemed particularly pertinent because Japan utilizes and exports more complex medical technology than any other nation in the world.[62] Is this cultural difference to be found at the level of attitudes towards the mastery of nature or, more specifically, to a concern about tinkering with the bodies of the dying and the dead? Is Japan perhaps not as secular and rational, not as "modern" as its outward appearance leads us to believe? Alternatively, is it perhaps due to cultural influences on the actual production of scientific discourse about death and dying in Japan? Or is the difference due largely to the way in which the power and interests of doctors are played out, and the form of institutionalization that medicine takes in Japan? Or is it some combination of the above?

It is relatively easy to take off from this point, embracing an implicit assumption that there is something inherently odd about not striving to "save" lives in a secular society with neither economic nor technological constraints; to set out, therefore, to

scrutinize the relics of tradition, survivals from an archaic past lurking in Japanese late modernity that account for this anomaly. But such an approach violates the majority of interpretations given by Japanese on this subject, many of whom flatly deny that culture, that is, the "culture of tradition" is involved and argue instead for a more pragmatic explanation in which politics and power relations among the professions, and between the medical world and the public, are implicated.[63] Equally important, by focusing on Japan as the anomaly, North American assumptions about the good and just society remain unproblematized and thus, implicitly, the norm for the contemporary world, something that also concerns many Japanese participants as they argue their version of the brain death debate.

Shortly after the world's first heart transplant was conducted in South Africa, several attempts were made in other locations to carry out the same procedure, including Sapporo, Hokkaido in 1968. As in other parts of the world, the Sapporo procedure initially produced an accolade from the media, and was heralded as a dramatic medical triumph. However, several months later, the physician in charge, Dr. Wada, was arraigned on a murder charge and only acquitted after six years of wrangling. The majority of Japanese believe in retrospect that the patient whose heart was removed was not brain dead, and that the recipient, who died two and a half months after the operation, was not sufficiently in need of a new heart to have undergone the procedure in the first place.[64] As part of the ongoing national debate about brain death, discussion of the case was formally reopened in 1991, and the chairman of the Japanese Medical Association, testifying before a government committee, reported that twenty-three years ago, right after the removal of the supposedly ineffective heart from the recipient patient, it had been tampered with, indicating that the involved doctors may have tried to exaggerate the degree of its deterioration.[65] The case is now considered in retrospect as a barbarous piece of medical experimentation carried out by a doctor who received a good portion of his training in America and is, moreover, described as self-aggrandizing.

There have been a good number of other cases in connection with organ transplants where the Japanese medical profession has not shown up in a good light. One, for example, involved a highly controversial kidney/pancreas transplant at Tsukuba University in which organs were removed from a young mentally retarded woman diagnosed as brain dead, but neither she nor her parents had given permission for her to be a donor.[66]

Contested Definitions of Death

The first definition of brain death in Japan was formulated by the Japan Electroencephaly Association in 1974. Probably in response to the much publicized case of the mentally retarded patient, the Life Ethics Problem Study Parliamentarians League, composed of twenty-eight Diet members and forty-five other professionals, was established in 1985, and after one year endorsed the need for legislation about brain death.[67] In the same year, the Ministry of Health and Welfare set up a Brain Death Advisory Council, the final report of which contained the definition of brain death made use of in Japan today.[68] This report is explicit, however, that "death cannot be judged by brain death." Nevertheless, the diagnosis is frequently applied, not as a signal to turn off the respirator, but to prepare relatives for an impending death.[69]

The report spurred other involved groups to make pronouncements about their positions. In January 1988, after two years of meetings by a working group, the directors of the Japanese Medical Association voted unanimously to accept brain death as the termination of human life. Despite this decision, there remains a lack of agreement among the representatives of medical specialties and also among individual physicians who are deeply divided on the issue. The politically outspoken Japan Association of Psychiatrists and Neurologists (some of the sixty-nine hundred members of whom are responsible for making brain death diagnoses) fear that if brain death is equated with death, the handicapped, mentally impaired, and disadvantaged will be at risk of being diagnosed prematurely in a greedy desire to get at their organs. In their 1988 report they state that a major problem is with the difficulty in deciding when brain function is irreversibly lost.[70]

Some physicians have joined members of the public to form the highly visible Patients' Rights Committee, whose interests range well beyond the question of brain death. Under the leadership of the flamboyant Dr. Honda from the prestigious department of internal medicine at Tokyo University, they have recently filed several lawsuits charging murder when organs have been removed from brain dead patients, one of which was in connection with the Tsukuba University case described above. The Public Prosecutor's Office has not thus far reached a decision in connection with any of these cases, but has thrown two of them out of court, stating that there is no public consensus in Japan as to how to define death.[71] Eric Feldman believes that because, after almost seven years, complaints made by the Patients' Rights Committee remain unresolved, hesitation on the part of doctors to forge ahead with transplanation is reinforced.[72]

As a result of the unresolved debate, copiously documented by the media, the government felt compelled in late 1989 to set up a Special Cabinet Committee on Brain Death and Organ Transplants in order to bring about closure. This committee, composed of fifteen members from various walks of life, was charged to make a report to the Prime Minister by 1991, and its very formation signaled to the public that the government was ready to support a move to legalize brain death as the termination of life. The group was so deeply divided that for a while it appeared that it would never produce anything more than an interim report, but in January 1992 a final report was forthcoming. In principle the members should have reached consensus, but this they could not achieve. The majority position is that brain death is equivalent to human death, that organ transplants from brain dead donors are acceptable, and that the current definition of brain death as formulated by the Ministry of Health is appropriate. The minority position made it clear that they wished to have the social and cultural aspects of the problem fully debated; in their opinion the discussion thus far had been largely confined to "scientific" information, which they believed to be inadequate.[73] The public was kept fully apprised of just who appeared before the committee. It was evident that many of those who testified, including certain scientists and doctors, argued against the acceptance of brain death, but nevertheless the majority of the committee eventually moved to support its approval.[74]

Throughout, the Japan Federation of Bar Associations (Nichibenren) has maintained its position against the acceptance of brain death as the termination of life. It has expressed concern for the "sanctity of life," and about possible medical "experimentation." The Federation has also pointed out that there may be unforeseen consequences in connection with inheritance claims, and a lack of public consensus on the issue was noted by them.[75] The day following the announcement of the Cabinet Committee report, the Ministry of Justice, the National Police Agency, and the Public Prosecutor's Office all reiterated their continued resistance to brain death.[76]

The Patients' Rights Committee, lawyers, the police, several television producers, and many authors of newspaper articles and books on the subject of brain death, and even a number of medical professionals appear to be publicly contesting the authority of transplant surgeons. What they usually cite as their principal cause for concern is a lack of trust in the medical teams who will make decisions about cases of brain death; they believe that in the rush to retrieve organs the process of dying will be curtailed or even misdiagnosed. The opposition is explicitly opposed to the secrecy and arrogance of some members of the medical profession, and points out that patients and their families are vulnerable to exploitation.

Certain of these same opponents of brain death are pushing for informed consent, together with a frank disclosure and discussion of diagnoses with patients, neither of which activities are by any means routinely established in Japan. This contest, therefore, although at one level a debate about the accuracy and replicability of scientific decision-making, is also a challenge to the hegemony of invested authority, exerted in what is characterized by several of the challengers as a traditionally Japanese way, whereby subjects are rendered passive and expected to comply with medical regimen without question.

One of the national newspapers, Asahi Shinbun, recently described the medical world as "irritated"

with government dithering, and doctors sense that their international reputations as outstanding surgeons are fading. At the annual meeting of the Japanese Medical Association held in Kyoto in 1990, which I attended, two plenary sessions and several smaller panels were given over to brain death and organ transplants. The principal paper givers were physicians who had lived and worked for some time in the United States and who had practiced transplant surgery while there. Aside from the scientific part of their presentations, every one of them strongly asserted that Japanese medicine is suffering because of the national uproar over brain death. They all showed slides of themselves standing, usually in surgical garb, side by side with American transplant surgeons together with happy, lively patients who had recently received organ transplants. These presentations were one of the few occasions, until very recently, when attention was focused on the situation of patients whose lives might be prolonged, however temporarily, by transplant procedures.[77]

Reaching Public Consensus

Taking place in concert with government, professional, and media discussion is the most persistent search for a national consensus (kokuminteki gôi) among the Japanese public that has taken place to date on any subject. There were at least ten national surveys about brain death and organ transplants between 1983 and 1992. Over the years the number of people who recognize brain death has increased from 29 percent to nearly 50 percent. In all of the surveys, a paradox is evident, however: many people approve of organ transplants from brain dead patients although they themselves do not accept brain death as the end of life. It seems that the Japanese public is willing to allow transplants to take place, even though they personally would not be comfortable with participating in such a procedure.

The results of opinion polls are usually used by those who are against brain death to support their arguments, since it has been frequently reiterated that public consensus must be reached before brain death can be nationally recognized. Nevertheless, one is left with the feeling, voiced by many members of the Japanese public, that the whole exercise of repeatedly surveying the nation is essentially a farce, and that the idea of trying to achieve a simple consensus on such an inflammatory subject is essentially without meaning.

Cultivating the Natural

Clearly, the Japanese public's mistrust of physicians contributes to the brain death "problem," but why has *this* issue more than any of the other pressing problems in connection with biomedical technology captured the attention of the nation for nearly thirty years? Discussions about informed consent, euthanasia, and the new reproductive technologies appear in the media with increasing frequency today, but not nearly to the same extent as the topic of brain death and organ transplants, debate about which can become exceedingly vituperative.[78]

A perusal of the over five hundred articles, books, and newspaper editorials published on brain death and organ transplants since 1986 reveals that brain death is reported to be too "unnatural" (*fushizen*) to be called "death," for example,[79] or that it is "contrary to basic human feelings." The idea of "controlling" death is also described as going against nature.[80] Organ transplants are characterized in one book as *egetsu nai* (a powerful vernacular expression indicating that something is foul, ugly, or revolting) and *chi ma mire* (bloody).[81] Arguments against the institutionalization of organ transplants requiring a brain dead donor appear, therefore, to raise major concerns about interfering with the natural order. However, for the most part these concerns remain articulated only as emotion-laden adjectives or else by indirect allusions to the "cold," over-rational "West."

Contemporary Japanese attitudes towards scientific knowledge and its associated technology are difficult to pin down because of their intimate connection to a widespread ambivalence about the process of Japanese modernization. Moreover, Japanese attitudes towards modernization cannot be understood in isolation from ever changing interpretations, produced both inside and outside the country, about the relationship of Japan to the West. The form that current debate takes about body technologies in Japan, therefore – the feasibility of tinkering with

the margins between culture and nature, and the very definition of those margins – reflect more general concerns about modernization, postmodernization, and "Westernization."

In Japan throughout the late nineteenth century, the eager quest for Western science and technology "was grounded in [a] sense of cultural certitude";[82] an awareness that the "core" or the bass note (*koso*) of Japanese culture would remain unaffected. Technology, self-consciously aligned with the other, was placed in opposition to culture in this discourse, and epitomized by the platitudes *wakon yōsai* (Japanese spirit and Western technology) and *tōyō dōtoku, seiyō gijutsu* (Eastern morality, Western technology). Tetsuo Najita and others have shown how this confidence in the endurance of "traditional" culture was gradually eroded. Early this century and again after World War II internal tension erupted over Japan's increasing technological sophistication and internationalization.[83] Fears about an imminent collapse of the nation's cultural heritage became commonplace, and one reaction was a reassertion of cultural essentialism.[84]

For many Japanese, the specter of Westernized individualism, utilitarianism, and super-rationalism triggers emotional responses that push them towards a rhetoric of difference, even as they buck at its inherently nationalistic underpinnings. This is the discursive background against which the brain death debate is taking place. Appellations such as "tradition" and "religion" smack of superstition and premodern sentimentality to a large number of people, but Japan is repeatedly described by internal commentators and outside observers alike as having undergone a unique form of modernization and hence of being quintessentially different.

Those who have doubts about the introduction of new technologies have to struggle very hard, therefore, to find a suitable language with which to articulate their discomfort. Criticizing a "Western," "scientific," interventionist approach to nature makes one vulnerable to accusations of Japanese essentialism and antirationalism. Equally difficult to voice is criticism of the epistemological grounds on which a scientific determination of death is constructed, for this smacks of antirationalism. Criticizing the unethical behavior of the Japanese press and activities of Japanese doctors as lacking standardization and quality control is rather easily justified and, almost everyone agrees, is a valid critical stance. Thus, the issue is politicized, but the possible contribution of culture to the argument is usually ignored or explicitly rejected.[85]

Those who choose to make a cultural argument about redefining death usually defend the status quo on the grounds that as a nation the Japanese do not like "unnatural" things, and posit an essential difference from the "West," leading to very dangerous territory. However, one or two attempts have been made to create a more nuanced argument based on the structure of Japanese social relationships. Masahiro Morioka suggests, for example, that rather than focusing on the standardization of brain death, as does so much of the literature, attention should be shifted to the brain dead person at the center of a nexus of characteristically Japanese human relations both familial and medical. He deliberately seeks to redefine the problem as social rather than clinical.[86] The anthropologist E. Namihira analyzes Japanese attitudes towards the dead body to account for resistance to brain death and organ transplants – an argument that highlights the cultural construction of nature, but one to which the majority of Japanese intellectuals with whom I have talked have reacted with a good deal of resistance.[87]

The entire commentary about tampering with definitions of death is, therefore, complex, emotional, and fraught with ideological pitfalls because debate cannot be divorced from other pressing issues of national import. A tension between technology as both creator and destroyer of culture is evident. Not surprisingly, negotiating a moral high ground has thus far proved impossible, not least when people try to shelter behind scientific justifications for their arguments.

Discourse on Social Death

In Japan biological death is usually understood as a process, not as a point in time.[88] Moreover, a distinction is made by many commentators between biological and social death, believed to take place some time after the demise of the physical body. Although few commentators talk explicitly about a

Confucian-derived belief in the ancestors, its influence on the brain death debate is apparent. Preliminary interviews I conducted with fifty Japanese informants, men and women, made it clear that the fate of the body after biological death, together with a concern about the recently dead, may contribute to a reluctance both to donate and to receive organs. Everyone interviewed stated that they no longer believe in the elaborate prewar ancestor system, integral to the extended family. Nevertheless, over half of the respondents indicated that they carry out regular, often daily rituals in their homes and at the graves of their deceased parents and grandparents. Most pointed out that family and social obligations require that the bodies and memories of deceased family members be treated with respect.

A 1981 survey showed that the majority of Japanese (between 60 and 70 percent) believe that when and where one is born and dies is determined by destiny, and that this should not be changed by human intervention.[89] Appropriate separation of the soul from the body at the moment of death is central to the Japanese belief about dying;[90] in a recent survey, 40 percent responded that they believe in the continued existence after death of *reikon* (soul/spirit).[91] This same survey showed that among young people between the ages of sixteen and twenty-nine, belief in the survival of the soul is particularly prevalent.[92]

From an analysis of the very moving narratives provided by relatives of victims of the Japan Air Lines crash in the mountains of Gunma prefecture in 1985, Namihira concluded that the spirit of the deceased is often anthropomorphized and is believed to experience the same feelings as the living. Hence, relatives have an obligation to make the spirit "happy" and "comfortable." People were in agreement that it is important for a dead body to be brought home, and that a corpse should be complete (*gotai manzoku*), otherwise the spirit will suffer and may cause harm to the living. Namihira cites the results of a 1983 questionnaire by a committee set up to encourage the donation of bodies for medical research: Of 690 respondents, 66 percent stated that cutting into dead bodies is repulsive and/or cruel, and also shows a lack of respect for the dead. Against these figures, the numbers of people agreeing to autopsies has steadily increased in recent years,[93] as has the number of people willing to go abroad to obtain organ transplants[94] as well as those willing to recognize brain death as the end of life. Clearly, the population is deeply divided about attitudes towards the dying and the recently dead, and many would, in any case, probably state one thing in response to a survey and actually do another when confronted with personal suffering.

In Japan the boundary between the social and the natural was never very rigidly defined – the ancestors were immortalized as entities who continue to act in the everyday world, but eventually become part of an animized natural order, forming a vital bridge between the spiritual, social, and natural domains. Despite the Confucian origins of the ancestors, the philosopher Akira Omine links the type of animism with which the ancestors are associated to Shinto, the indigenous religion of Japan, which represents, he believes, "quirky local beliefs cherished in our peculiarly unspiritual island country and incomprehensible to most of the world."[95] Shinto, associated with the Emperor and with nationalism, has an exceedingly delicate status among large numbers of liberal minded Japanese today. Omine goes on to claim that although animism affects attitudes about the dead, it "simply lacks the depth of vision to address a challenge like that of redefining the boundary between life and death."[96] It seems that Omine, in common with many of his intellectual colleagues, would like to keep formalized religious belief (but not necessarily spirituality) out of the brain death discussion.

Comments such as those of Omine make it evident that everyday discourse and practices about social death produce considerable anxiety among certain Japanese who wish their nation to be understood as eminently rational, in particular because such discourse is grist for the mill of commentators (both inside and outside Japan) who hope to signal that "tradition" and the "old moral order," including the ancestors who signify continuity above all else, is intact and functioning in the Japan of late modernity.

When it comes to discussing organ transplantation, many people point out that formalized gift giving remains central to ongoing relationships of reciprocity in Japan, and continues to contribute to the moral order. The idea of receiving an organ that had been anonymously donated would be very difficult for many to accept without incurring an enormous sense of guilt and without violating a sense of what is correct behavior.[97] In addition, a few people with whom I have talked have clearly been physically repulsed by the very idea of organ transplantation. For them, transfer of body parts among unrelated people extends beyond the bounds of what is "natural" and entails a completely unacceptable mixing of self and other. Certain scientists also see things this way, for transplant technology has explicitly been described by an eminent Japanese immunologist as the conjoining of the "self" and "nonself."[98] A similar, rather special, manifestation of this concern was demonstrated around the dying Emperor Shôwa, who received many blood transfusions during the last year of his life, all of which had to be supplied by family members. It should be noted that there is little or no opposition to organ transplants from living, related donors, suggesting that it is an inappropriate mixing of self and other beyond the "natural" bounds of the family that causes discomfort.

Although abortion is acceptable to most Japanese citizens, and is usually characterized as an unfortunate but necessary intervention at times, use of fetal tissue for research and transplants is not permitted. Fetuses are thought of by most people as living and conceptually inseparable from the body of the pregnant woman. However, since a fetus has no independent social or moral standing it is not fully human. Many Japanese are nevertheless concerned about mistreatment of fetal tissue, although its status is less problematic than that of a brain dead individual. Concern is evident about the traumatic death of a fetus, especially on the part of Japanese women, and lucrative Buddhist-based rituals are enacted all over Japan to appease the souls of aborted fetuses.[99] Thus, traumatic and sudden death, together with the mixing of self and other, both before birth and later in the life cycle, are culturally sensitive and contested events in Japan. However, the politics of solid organ transplants, coupled with a pervasive concern about respect for the deceased, means that the brain death debate takes center stage, whereas abortion continues to be accepted quite simply as an unfortunate but unavoidable part of human life.

Late Modernity, Cultural Identity, and the Other

It is striking that the culture and values of the "West" are scrutinized in the brain death debate in Japan. We hear and read much about Christianity (but nothing of Judaism), about rationality and the brain as the center of the body, about altruism, individualism, and even selfishness – all values associated with the "West." But, despite a call to move beyond a discussion of scientific decision-making, as noted above, Japanese values are not often examined explicitly. It has been suggested by some that if the original heart transplant, the Wada case, had not flared up into a legal battle, the entire brain death debate may never have surfaced, and the medical world would simply have gone ahead unilaterally as they did in North America. Others strongly disagree with this position, although many believe that brain death will be made legally acceptable in Japan fairly soon and that the search for a national consensus is simply a placatory exercise before those in power go ahead to institutionalize organ transplants; indeed, a private members bill has recently been submitted for consideration to the Diet.

Thoughtful people recognize that while brain death is obviously a sensitive topic, the definition of death, although clearly the nub of the debate, has a metaphorical significance that triggers a cascade of ideological repercussions reaching far beyond the medical world. The present dilemma for progressive thinkers in Japan is how to dispose of the remnants of patriarchal and patronage thinking – the reactionary part of the Confucian heritage – without drawing on a language that single-mindedly pursues the entrenchment of the "Western" values of individual autonomy and rights. It is in this context that the argument about brain death is taking place, and, as in the West, it is an overwhelmingly secular argument in which representatives of religious organizations are, for the most part, remarkably absent.[100] At its most abstract level, the current angst is a manifestation of the ceaseless, restless, contradictory debate about Japan and the West, a debate that has proceeded unabated for something approaching two hundred

years, in which the "West" has come to be associated with ideas having universal application, whereas Japanese ideas are linked to uniqueness. As one pediatrician has recently put it, "Why should we mindlessly imitate Westerners? We would only be turning ourselves into white Westerners with Asian faces."[101]

Although a certain amount of genuine passion is aroused over the fate of those individuals whose lives are directly involved, little is heard from patients and their families, whether they be potential donors or receivers. Recently, however, a woman whose daughter will soon require a liver transplant, when interviewed by *Newsweek* for its Japanese edition, complained, "Why do we have to suffer just because we have the misfortune to be Japanese?"[102] Since the beginning of 1994, the year in which an international conference on organ transplantation was deliberately staged in Japan by surgeons keen to break through the current impasse, the fate of those patients not able to receive transplants, together with those who have gone abroad to obtain organs, has started to capture the imaginations of the media and the Japanese public. An extraordinarily moving art exhibition, at which pictures created by Japanese children who had received organs were exhibited beside accounts of their medical histories, was held in Kyoto in conjunction with the transplant conference.

Thus far, the debate has not been about individual human suffering, but rather a manifestation of the struggle by citizens and activists from a whole range of political persuasions about moral order in contemporary Japan. Those who recognize brain death as the end of life usually accept a modernist ideology of technologically driven progress in the relief of human suffering, while many (but not all) of those against embrace an argument about the essentialist difference of Japan and exhibit concerns about a perceived loss of moral order. Very slowly and painfully forced, it seems to me as I interview and observe Japanese who are dealing directly with this problem in ethics committees, citizens groups, and so on, by a genuine concern about the suffering of individuals, a middle ground is emerging. Nevertheless, extremists on both sides remain highly vocal and influential. Those arguing for a modulated position usually start with case studies rather than from abstract propositions, or from the simple assumption that biomedical technology is intrinsically good. Some people arguing for a middle ground actively seek to avoid the silencing of individual suffering in the name of nationalism, or professional or governmental interest, but these voices are only just becoming audible, and are not great in number as yet. It is notable, however, that even in modulated discussion grounded in everyday experience, the split between those for and against the acceptance of brain death remains strikingly evident. Even when the suffering of potential recipients is clearly recognized this does not mean that involved Japanese will necessarily agree that transplants are an unequivocal good. When I asked one pediatrician, often visible in the media, who deals with dying children every day, why she remains adamantly opposed to the introduction of organ transplants from brain dead donors, she acknowledged that Buddhism, although of no apparent consequence in her daily life, is probably an influence since she believes deeply that death is in some way preordained and that we humans should not play God. Although Buddhist related, the sentiments of this pediatrician may not be very far removed from those of people living in other parts of the world today, but when contextualized in the current debate about death in Japan they reveal the extent to which "needs" and "suffering" and our responses to those marked as "suffering" and "needy" remain shaped by culturally derived values.

The talk today in the United States is of "rewarded gifting" and "organ wastage," signs of the urgent need to procure more and more organs in a steady move towards the large-scale commodification of human parts. In our haste in North America we talk little about the flow of organs from the poor to the rich, from the Third World to the First World, and even less of possible atrocities, despite documentation of such by Amnesty International. Leon Kass has described this process as a "coarsening of sensibilities and attitudes" and adds that " . . . there is a sad irony in our biomedical project, accurately anticipated in Aldous Huxley's Brave New World: We expend enormous energy and vast sums of money to preserve and prolong bodily life, but in the process our embodied life is stripped of its gravity and much of its dignity. This is, in a word, progress as tragedy."[103] We also keep death firmly under wraps

and, despite evidence of societal disagreement and misunderstanding about the new death we have created, refuse to debate this issue in public. Perhaps we can learn directly from the Japanese case on this point, if nothing else, and begin to recognize once again that mortality is not merely biological demise. In striving to make the brain dead immortal by stating that they live on in others as donated organs, we in fact collapse the very culture/nature distinction that made the yardstick for justifying brain death in the first place. Surely such a contradiction deserves debate.

The monster is amongst us, and we need more courage than Frankenstein exhibited if we are to use technology to relieve suffering in an equitable manner; a first step is to recognize how easily suffering can be used in the service of ideological and political ends. On both sides of the Pacific, if debate about technology and the body is reduced to a confirmation or otherwise of scientific accuracy, or to a discussion of political interest, or even, for that matter, to one of ethical correctness, we will consistently lose sight of the necessity to step further back so that more difficult questions can be posed. Prominent among them is a consideration of the relationship of tacit, culturally shaped knowledge to the production of scientific knowledge and its practices, together with the associated contests, within and among societies, about legitimization of such knowledge as truth. Most important, of course, is the effect of such discussion on the recognition of suffering and what, if any, condition should be assigned as beyond the realm of cultural intervention.

NOTES

1 Jacques Ellul, *The Technological Society*, trans. John Wilkinson (New York: Alfred A. Knopf, 1964).

2 Langdon Winner, *Autonomous Technology: Technics-out-of-Control as a Theme in Political Thought* (Cambridge, Mass.: The MIT Press, 1977), 16.

3 Bryan Pfaffenberger, "Social Anthropology of Technology," *Annual Review of Anthropology* 21 (1992): 495.

4 Herbert Marcuse, *One-Dimensional Man: Studies in the Ideology of Advanced Industrial Society* (Boston, Mass.: Beacon Press, 1964).

5   Jürgen Habermas, *Toward a Rational Society* (Boston, Mass.: Beacon Press, 1970).

6   G. Basalla, *The Evolution of Technology* (Cambridge: Cambridge University Press, 1988), 14.

7   *Ibid.*, 14.

8   Andrew Kimbrell, *The Human Body Shop: The Engineering and Marketing of Life* (San Francisco, Calif.: Harper San Francisco, 1993). Margaret Lock, *Encounters With Aging: Mythologies of Menopause in Japan and North America* (Berkeley, Calif.: University of California Press, 1993), 341 ff.

9   Arthur Kleinman, *The Illness Narratives: Suffering, Healing and the Human Condition* (New York: Basic Books, 1988). Mary-Jo DelVecchio Good, Paul E. Brodwin, Byron J. Good, and Arthur Kleinman, eds., *Pain as Human Experience: An Anthropological Perspective* (Berkeley, Calif.: University of California Press, 1992).

10 Renée C. Fox and Judith P. Swazey, *Spare Parts: Organ Replacement in American Society* (New York: Oxford University Press, 1992).

11 L. A. Rado, "Death Redefined: Social and Cultural Influences on Legislation," *Journal of Communication* 31 (1981): 41–7.

12 Martin Pernick, "Back from the Grave: Recurring Controversies Over Defining and Diagnosing Death in History," in Richard Zaner, ed., *Death: Beyond Whole-Brain Criteria* (Dordrecht: Kluwer Academic Publishers, 1988), 17.

13 *Ibid.*

14 Phillipe Ariés, *Western Attitudes Towards Death: From the Middle Ages to the Present*, trans. Patricia M. Ranum (Baltimore, Md.: The Johns Hopkins University Press, 1974), 103.

15 *Ibid.*, 104.

16 Norbert Elias, *The Loneliness of the Dying*, trans. Edmund Jephcott (Oxford: Basil Blackwell Ltd., 1985).

17 Zygmunt Bauman, *Mortality, Immortality and Other Life Strategies* (Stanford, Calif.: Stanford University Press, 1992), 5.

18 *Ibid.*, 7.

19 *Ibid.*, 9.

20 Drew Leder, *The Absent Body* (Chicago, Ill.: The University of Chicago Press, 1990).

21 Lindsay Prior, *The Social Organization of Death: Medical Discourse and Social Practices in Belfast* (London: Macmillan, 1989), 32, 33.

22 Ruth Richardson, *Death, Dissection and the Destitute* (London: Penguin, 1988), 31.

23 Pernick, "Back from the Grave: Recurring Controversies Over Defining and Diagnosing Death in History," 58.

24 Ad Hoc Committee of the Harvard Medical School to Examine the Definition of Death, "A Definition of Irreversible Coma," *Journal of the American Medical Association* 205 (1968): 337–40.

25 *Ibid.*, 337.

26 See, for example, "When is Death?," *Time*, 16 August 1968.

27 R. Simmons *et al.*, *Gift of Life: The Effect of Organ Transplantation on Individual, Family, and Societal Dynamics* (New Brunswick, NJ: Transaction Books, 1987).

28 Peter Black, "Brain Death," *The New England Journal of Medicine* 229 (1978): 338–44.

29 George J. Annas, "Brain Death and Organ Donation: You Can Have One Without the Other," *Hastings Center Report* 18 (1988): 621.

30 David Lamb, *Death, Brain Death and Ethics* (London: Croom Helm, 1985), 23.

31 Roy Selby and Marilyn Selby, "Status of the Legal Definition of Death," *Neurosurgery* 5 (1979): 535.

32 Paul Byrne and Richard Nilges, "The Brain Stem in Brain Death: A Critical Review," *Issues in Law and Medicine* 9 (1993): 3–21. Robert Veatch, "The Impending Collapse of the Whole-Brain Definition of Death," *Hastings Center Report* 23 (1993): 18–24.

33 Margaret Lock, "Deadly Disputes: The Remaking of Death in Japan and North America," in Francis Zimmermann and Beatrice Pfleiderer, eds., *Medicine and Social Criticism* (Cambridge: Cambridge University Press, forthcoming).

34 J. M. Prottas, *The Most Useful Gift: Altruism and the Public Policy of Organ Transplants* (San Francisco, Calif.: Jossey-Bass, 1994).

35 M. Somerville, "Access to Organs for Transplantation: Overcoming Rejection," *Canadian Medical Association Journal* 132 (1985): 113–17.

36 Prottas, *The Most Useful Gift: Altruism and the Public Policy of Organ Transplants*. J. R. Williams, "Human Organ Sales," *Annals of the Royal College of Physicians and Surgeons of Canada* 18 (1985): 401–4.

37 L. B. Andrews, "My Body, My Property," *Hastings Center Report* 16 (1986): 28–38.

38 Ivan Illich, *In the Mirror of the Past: Lectures and Addresses 1978–1990* (New York: Marion Boyars Publishers Ltd., 1992), 224.

39 Robert Crawford, "Healthism and the Medicalization of Everyday Life," *International Journal of Health*

Services 10 (1980): 365–88. Lock, *Encounters With Aging: Mythologies of Menopause in Japan and North America*.

40 Willard Gaylin, "Harvesting the Dead," *Harpers Magazine* 52 (1974): 23–30.

41 T. G. Peters, "Life or Death: The Issue of Payment in Cadaveric Organ Donation," *Journal of the American Medical Association* 265 (13 March 1991): 1302.

42 T. Randall, "Too Few Human Organs for Transplantation, Too Many in Need . . . and the Gap Widens," *Journal of the American Medical Association* 265 (13 March 1991): 1223.

43 Leon Kass, "Organs for Sale? Propriety, Property, and the Price of Progress," *The Public Interest*, April 1992, 84.

44 Renée C. Fox and Judith P. Swazey, *Spare Parts: Organ Replacement in American Society* (New York: Oxford University Press, 1993), 57.

45 J. F. Childress, "Ethical Criteria for Procuring and Distributing Organs for Transplantation," in J. F. Blumstein and F. A. Sloan, eds., *Organ Transplantation Policy: Issues and Prospects* (Durham, N.C.: Duke University Press, 1989), 87–113.

46 Margareta Sanner, "A Comparison of Public Attitudes Toward Autopsy, Organ Donation and Anatomic Dissection," *JAMA* 271 (1994): 284–8.

47 Arthur L. Caplan, "Professional Arrogance and Public Misunderstanding," *Hastings Center Report* 18 (1988): 34–7. J. M. Prottas and H. L. Batten, "Health Professionals and Hospital Administrators in Organ Procurement: Attitudes, Reservations, and their Resolutions," *American Journal of Public Health* 78 (1988): 642–45. S. J. Youngner, M. Allen, E. T. Bartlett *et al.*, "Psychosocial and Ethical Implications of Organ Retrieval," *New England Journal of Medicine* 313 (1 August 1985): 321–4.

48 Youngner, Allen, Bartlett *et al.*, "Psychosocial and Ethical Implications of Organ Retrieval."

49 S. J. Youngner, S. Landefeld, C. J. Coulton *et al.*, "'Brain Death' and Organ Retrieval: A Cross-Sectional Survey of Knowledge and Concepts among Health-Care Professionals," *Journal of the American Medical Association* 261 (1989): 2205–10.

50 J. L. Bernat *et al.*, "On the Definition and Criterion of Death," *Annals of Internal Medicine* 94 (1981): 391.

51 Richard M. Zaner, "Introduction," in Richard Zaner, ed., *Death: Beyond Whole-Brain Criteria* (Dordrecht: Kluwer Academic Publishers, 1988), 7.

52 *Ibid.*, 5.

53 Edward T. Bartlett and Stuart J. Youngner, "Human Death and the Destruction of the Neocortex," in Zaner, ed., *Death: Beyond Whole-Brain Criteria*, 199–216.

54 Zaner, "Introduction," in Zaner, ed., *Death: Beyond Whole-Brain Criteria*, 13.

55 Karen G. Gervais, *Redefining Death* (New Haven, Conn.: Yale University Press, 1987).

56 David Lamb, *Organ Transplants and Ethics* (London: Routledge, 1990).

57 Gervais, *Redefining Death*, 155.

58 Lamb, *Death, Brain Death and Ethics*.

59 Norman Fost, "Organs from Anencephalic Infants: An Idea Whose Time Has Not Yet Come," *Hastings Center Report* 18 (1988): 7.

60 Youngner, Landefeld, Coulton *et al.*, "'Brain Death' and Organ Retrieval," 2208.

61 *Ibid.*, 2209.

62 Naoki Ikegami, "Health Technology Development in Japan," *International Journal of Technology Assessment in Health Care* 4 (1989): 239–54.

63 Jiro Nudeshima, *Nôshi, zôkiishoku to nihon shakai* (Brain Death, Organ Transplants and Japanese Society) (Tokyo: Kôbundô, 1991).

64 Masaharu Gôto, "Body and Soul: Organ Transplants," *Look Japan* 38 (1992): 32–3.

65 "Cover-up suspected in first heart transplant," *Mainichi Shinbun*, 31 March 1991.

66 "Organs removed from woman without consent," *Mainichi Daily News*, 24 December 1984.

67 Eric A. Feldman, "Over My Dead Body: The Enigma and Economics of Death in Japan," in Naoko Ikegami and John C. Campbell, eds., *Containing Health Care Costs in Japan* (Ann Arbor, Mich.: University of Michigan Press, 1995).

68 Kôseishô, "Kôseishô kenkyuhan ni yoru nôshi no hantei kijun" (Brain death determination criteria of the Ministry of Health and Welfare) (Tokyo: Kôseishô, 1985).

69 Gen Ohi, Tomonori Hasegawa, Hiroyuki Kumano, Ichiro Kai, Nobuyuki Takenaga, Yoshio Taguchi, Hiroshi Saito, and Tsunamasa Ino, "Why are cadaveric renal transplants so hard to find in Japan? An analysis of economic and attitudinal aspects," *Health Policy* 6 (1986): 269–78.

70 "Silence on Heart Transplant," *Asahi Shinbun*, 2 April 1991. Masaya Yamanchi, "Transplantation in Japan," *British Medical Journal* 301 (1990): 507.

71 Taro Nakayama, *Nôshi to Zôki Ishoku* (Brain Death and Organ Transplants) (Tokyo: Saimaru Shippansha, 1989).

72 Feldman, "Over My Dead Body: The Enigma and Economics of Death in Japan."

73 Kantô Chiku Kôchôkai, "Rinji nôshi oyobi zôkiishoku chôsa kai," Tokyo, 1992. Yomiuri Shinbun, "Noshi ishoku yônin o saigo tôshin" (Final report approves of brain death, organ transplants), 23 January 1992.

74 "'Nôshi Ishoku' michisuji nao futômei" (Brain Death and Transplants: The Way is Still Not Clear), Nihon Keizai Shinbun, 23 January 1992.

75 "Giron fûjûbun to hihan no kenkai" (Insufficient debate is the critical opinion), Asahi Shinbun, 17 October 1991.

76 "'Nôshi wa hito no shi,' tôshin" (Brain death is death, says report), Asahi Shinbun, 23 January 1992.

77 See also Shumon Miura, "Attitudes Towards Death," Japan Echo 18 (1991): 67. "Zoki ishoku no saizensen" (The frontline in transplants), Newsweek Nihon Han (Japanese edn), 25 February 1993.

78 Takeshi Umehara and Michi Nakajima, "Soredeme nôshi wa shi dewa nai" (Still Brain Death is Not Death), Bungeishunju (March 1992): 302–12.

79 Kôshichirô Hirosawa, "Tachiba kara mita nôshi to shinzô ishoku" (Brain death and heart transplants from the point of view of a circulatory system specialist), in Takeshi Umehara, ed., Nôshi to zôki-ishoku (Brain Death and Organ Transplants) (Tokyo: Asahi Shinbunsha, 1992).

80 Toyô Watanabe, Ima naze shi ka (Why Death Now?) (Tokyo: Niki Shuppan, 1988). Takeshi Umehara, ed., "Hajime ni" (Introduction), in 'Nôshi' to zôki-ishoku (Brain Death and Organ Transplants) (Tokyo: Asahi Shinbunsha, 1992), 1–7.

81 Eiko Fukumoto, Seibutsugaku jidai sei to shi (Life and Death in the Era of Biological Sciences) (Tokyo: Gijitsu to Ninjen sha, 1989).

82 Tetsuo Najita, "On Culture and Technology in Postmodern Japan," in M. Miyoshi and H. D. Harootunian, eds., Postmodernism and Japan (Durham, NC: Duke University Press, 1989), 3–20.

83 Najita, "On Culture and Technology in Postmodern Japan," in Miyoshi and Harootunian, eds., Postmodernism and Japan.

84 H. D. Harootunian, "Visible Discourse/Invisible Ideologies," in Miyoshi and Harootunian, eds., Postmodernism and Japan, 63–92.

85 M. Nakajima, Mienai shi: Nôshi to zôki ishoku (Invisible Death: Brain Death and Organ Transplants) (Tokyo: Bungei Shunju, 1985). Nudeshima, Nôshi, zôkiishoku to nihon shakai.

86 Masahiro Morioka, Nôshi no Hito (Brain Dead People) (Tokyo: Fukutake Shoten, 1991).

87 E. Namihira, Nôshi, Zôki Ishoku, gan Kokuchi (Brain Death, Organ Transplants, Truth-Telling about Cancer) (Tokyo: Fukubu Shoten, 1988).

88 Tôru Uozumi, "Nôshi mondai ni kansuru shiken to teian" (My opinion and proposals on the brain death issue), in Takeshi Umehara, ed., Nôshi to zôki-ishoku (Brain Death and Organ Transplants) (Tokyo: Asahi Shinbunsha, 1992). Koshichirô Hirosawa, "Tachiba kara mita nôshi to shinzô ishoku" (Brain death and heart transplants from the point of view of a circulatory system specialist), in Takeshi Umehara, ed., Nôshi to zôki-ishoku (Brain Death and Organ Transplants). Yoshihiko Komatsu, "Sentaki gijutsu to nôshironsô no shikaku" (The blind spot in advanced technology and brain death debates), Gendai Shisô 21 (1993): 198–212.

89 Kumiko Maruyama, Hayashi Fumi, and Kamisaka Hisashi, "A Multivariate Analysis of Japanese Attitudes Toward Life and Death," Behaviormetrika 10 (1981): 37–48.

90 Fleur Woss, "When Blossoms Fall: Japanese Attitudes Towards Death and the Other-World: Opinion Polls 1953–1987," in R. Goodman and K. Refsing, eds., Ideology and Practice in Modern Japan (London: Routledge, 1992), 72–100.

91 Shôwa 61 nenpan yoron chôsa nenkan (Yearbook of Opinion Polls), "Kokoro no jidai. Zenkoku yoron chôsa" (The era of heart. Opinion poll by the Mainichi publishing house for the whole of Japan), in Naikaku Sôri Daijin Kanbô Kôhôshitsu, ed. (Tokyo: Mainichi Shinbunsha, 1987), 508–10.

92 Shôwa 54 nenpan yoron chôsa nenkan (Yearbook of Opinion Polls), "Zenkoku kenmin ishiki chôsa" (Research on the consciousness of the Japanese prefectural populations), in Naikaku Sôri Daijin Kanbô Kôhôshitsu, ed. (Tokyo: NHK hôsô yoron chôsasho, 1979), 585–91.

93 Monbushô, Kaibôtai shûshû sû to kontai hiritsu (Total Number of Bodies Accumulated for Autopsy and Percentage of Anatomical Gifts) (Tokyo: Monbushô Igaku Kyôikuka Shirabe, 1993).

94 Hiroshi Takaji, "Nôshi to zôki ishoku ni kansuru daii no shinpojûmu" (The First Symposium in Connection with Brain Death and Organ Transplants), in Nagoya Bengoshi Kai, eds., Nôshi to zôki ishoku miezarushî o mochimete (Tokyo: Roppo shuppansha, 1991).

95 Akira Omine, "Right and Wrong in the Brain-Death Debate," Japan Echo 18 (1991): 69.

96   *Ibid.*

97   Emiko Ohnuki-Tierney, "Brain Death and Organ Transplantation: Culture Bases of Medical-Technology," *Current Anthropology* 35 (1994): 233–54.

98   Tomio Tada, *Meneki no Imi ron* (The Meaning of Immunity) (Tokyo: Seidosha, 1993).

99   William LaFleur, *Liquid Life: Abortion and Buddhism in Japan* (Princeton, NJ: Princeton University Press, 1992).

100   Carl Becker, *Breaking the Circle: Death and the Afterlife in Buddhism* (Carbondale, Ill.: Southern Illinois University Press, 1993).

101   "Zoki ishoku no saizensen" (The frontline in transplants), *Newsweek Nihon Han* (Japanese edn.), 25 February 1993.

102   *Ibid.*

103   Kass, "Organs for Sale? Propriety, Property, and the Price of Progress."

Part III

Uncommon Death

10

Witchcraft, Oracles and Magic among the Azande

E. E. Evans-Pritchard

[. . .]

Death is due to witchcraft and must be avenged. All other practices connected with witchcraft are epitomized in the action of vengeance. In our present context it will be sufficient to point out that in pre-European days vengeance was either executed directly, sometimes by the slaughter of a witch, and sometimes by acceptance of compensation, or by means of lethal magic. Witches were very seldom slain, for it was only when a man committed a second or third murder, or murdered an important person, that a prince permitted his execution. Under British rule the magical method alone is employed.

Vengeance seems to have been less a result of anger and hatred than the fulfilment of a pious duty and a source of profit. I have never heard that to-day the kin of a dead man, once they have exacted vengeance, show any rancour towards the family of the man whom their magic has struck down, nor that in the past there was any prolonged hostility between the kin of the dead and the kin of the witch who had paid compensation for his murder. To-day if a man kills a person by witchcraft the crime is his sole responsibility and his kin are not associated with his guilt. In the past they assisted him to pay compensation, not in virtue of collective responsibility, but in virtue of social obligations to a kinsman. His relatives-in-law and his blood-brothers also contributed towards the payment. As soon as a witch is to-day slain by magic, or in the past had been speared to death or had paid compensation, the affair is closed. Moreover, it is an issue between the kin of the dead and the kin of the witch and other people are not concerned with it. They have the same social links with both parties.

It is extremely difficult to-day to obtain information about victims of vengeance-magic. Azande themselves do not know about them unless they are members of a murdered man's closest kin. One notices that his kinsmen are no longer observing taboos of mourning and one knows by this that their magic has performed its task, but it is useless to inquire from them who was its victim because they will not tell you. It is their private affair and is a secret between them and their prince who must be informed of the action of their magic since it is necessary for his poison oracle to confirm their poison oracle before they are permitted to end their mourning. Besides, it is a verdict of the poison

From E. E. Evans–Pritchard, *Witchcraft, Oracles and Magic among the Azande* (Oxford: Clarendon, 1968 [1937]).

oracle and one must not disclose its revelations about such matters.

If other people were acquainted with the names of those who have fallen victims to avenging magic the whole procedure of vengeance would be exposed as futile. For it may be observed here, though the point will more readily be understood later, that if it were known that the death of a man X had been avenged upon a witch Y then the whole procedure would be reduced to an absurdity because the death of Y is also avenged by his kinsmen upon a witch Z. Some Azande have indeed explained to me their doubts about the honesty of the princes who control the oracles, and a few have seen that the present-day system is fallacious. At any rate, its fallaciousness is veiled so long as everybody concerned keeps silence about the victims of their vengeance-magic. In the past things were different, for then a person accused by the prince's oracles of having killed another by witchcraft either paid immediate compensation or was killed. In either case the matter was closed because the man who had paid compensation had no means of proving that he was not a witch, and if he were killed at the prince's orders his death could not be avenged. Nor was an autopsy permitted on his corpse to discover whether it contained witchcraft-substance.

When I have challenged Azande to defend their system of vengeance they have generally said that a prince whose oracles declare that Y has died from the magic of X's kinsmen will not place the name of Z before his oracles to discover whether he died from the magic of Y's kinsmen. When Y's kinsmen ask their prince to place Z's name before his poison oracle he will decline to do so and will tell them that he knows Y to have died in expiation of a crime and that his death cannot therefore be avenged. A few Azande explained the present system by saying that perhaps vengeance-magic and witchcraft participate in causing death. The part of the vengeance-magic explains the termination of mourning of one family and the part of witchcraft explains the initiation of vengeance by another family, i.e. they seek to explain a contradiction in their beliefs in the mystical idiom of the beliefs themselves. But I have only been offered this explanation as a general and theoretical possibility in reply to my objections. Since the names of victims of vengeance are kept

secret the contradiction is not apparent, for it would only be evident if all deaths were taken into consideration and not any one particular death. So long therefore as they are able to conform to custom and maintain family honour Azande are not interested in the broader aspects of vengeance in general. They saw the objection when I raised it but they were not incommoded by it.

For Azande do not discuss problems of witchcraft among themselves nor pool their information about vengeance. So little do they generalize about witchcraft that I found they were seldom able to say which lineages in their neighbourhood were witches. The reason for this is given in later chapters.

Princes must be aware of the contradiction because they know the outcome of every death in their provinces. When I asked Prince Gangura how he accepted the death of a man both as the action of vengeance-magic and of witchcraft he smiled and admitted that all was not well with the present-day system. Some princes said that they did not allow a man to be avenged if they knew he had died from vengeance-magic, but I think they were lying. One cannot know for certain, for even if a prince were to tell the kin of a dead man that he had died from vengeance-magic and might not be avenged he would tell them in secret and they would keep his words a secret. They would pretend to their neighbours that they were avenging their kinsman and after some months would hang up the barkcloth of mourning as a sign that vengeance was accomplished, for they would not wish people to know that their kinsman was a witch.

Consequently if the kinsmen of A avenge his death by magic on B and then learn that B's kinsmen have ceased mourning in sign of having accomplished vengeance also, they believe that this second vengeance is a pretence. Contradiction is thereby avoided.

[. . .]

V

Zande belief in witchcraft in no way contradicts empirical knowledge of cause and effect. The world known to the senses is just as real to them as it is to us. We must not be deceived by their way of expressing causation and imagine that because they say a man was killed by witchcraft they entirely neglect the secondary causes that, as we judge them, were the true causes of his death. They are foreshortening the chain of events, and in a particular social situation are selecting the cause that is socially relevant and neglecting the rest. If a man is killed by a spear in war, or by a wild beast in hunting, or by the bite of a snake, or form sickness, the reaction is the same and it is not directed in different modes of expression by the different modes of death. In every case witchcraft is the socially relevant cause, since it is the only one which allows intervention and determines social behaviour. If a buffalo kills a man you can do nothing about it as far as the buffalo is concerned. But, though surely enough the buffalo has killed him, it would not have killed him if it had not been for the operation of witchcraft at the same time, and witchcraft is a social fact, a person. In a number of co-operating causes this single one is selected and spoken of as the cause of death because it is the ideological pivot around which swings the lengthy social procedure from death to vengeance.

Belief in death from natural causes and belief in death from witchcraft are not mutually exclusive. On the contrary, they supplement one another, the one accounting for what the other does not account for. Besides, death is not only a natural fact but also a social fact. It is not simply that the heart ceases to beat and the lungs to pump air in an organism, but it is also the destruction of a member of a family and kin, of a community and tribe. Death leads to consultation of oracles, magic rites, and revenge. Among the causes of death witchcraft is the only one that has any significance for social behaviour. The attribution of misfortune to witchcraft does not exclude what we call its real causes but is superimposed on them and gives to social events their moral value.

As a matter of fact Zande thought expresses the notion of natural and mystical causation quite clearly by using a hunting metaphor to define their relations. Azande always say of witchcraft that it is the *umbaga* or second spear. When Azande kill game there is a division of meat between the man who first speared the animal and the man who plunged a second spear into it. These two are considered to have killed the beast and the owner of the second spear is called the *umbaga*. Hence if a man is killed by an elephant Azande say that the elephant is the first spear and that witchcraft is the second spear and that together they killed the man. If a man spears another in war the slayer is the first spear and witchcraft is the second spear and together they killed him.

VI

Since Azande recognize plurality of causes, and it is the social situation that indicates the relevant one, we can understand why the doctrine of witchcraft is not used to explain every failure and misfortune. It sometimes happens that the social situation demands a common-sense, and not a mystical, judgement of cause. Thus, if you tell a lie, or commit adultery, or steal, or deceive your prince, and are found out, you cannot elude punishment by saying that you were bewitched. Zande doctrine declares emphatically 'Witchcraft does not make a person tell lies'; 'Witchcraft does not make a person commit adultery'; 'Witchcraft does not put adultery into a man. "Witchcraft" is in yourself (you alone are responsible), that is, your penis becomes erect. It sees the hair of a man's wife and it rises and becomes erect because the only "witchcraft" is, itself' ("witchcraft" is here used metaphorically); 'Witchcraft does not make a person steal'; 'Witchcraft does not make a person disloyal.' Only on one occasion have I heard a Zande plead that he was bewitched when he had committed an offence and this was when he lied to me, and even on this occasion everybody present laughed at him and told him that witchcraft does not make people tell lies.

If a man murders another tribesman with knife or spear he is put to death. It is not necessary in such a case to seek a witch, for an objective towards which vengeance may be directed is already present. If, on the other hand, it is a member of another tribe who has speared a man his relatives, or his prince, will take steps to discover the witch responsible for the event.

It would be treason to say that a man put to death on the orders of his king for an offence against authority was killed by witchcraft. If a man were to consult the oracles to discover the witch responsible for the death of a relative who had been put to death at the orders of his king he would run the risk of being put to death himself. For here the social situation excludes the notion of witchcraft as on other occasions it pays no attention to natural agents and emphasizes only witchcraft. Also, if a man were killed in vengeance because the oracles said that he was a witch and had murdered another man with his witchcraft then his relatives could not say that he had been killed by witchcraft. Zande doctrine lays it down that he died at the hand of avengers because he was a homicide. If a man were to have expressed the view that his kinsman had been killed by witchcraft and to have acted upon his opinion by consulting the poison oracle, he might have been punished for ridiculing the king's poison oracle, for it was the poison oracle of the king that had given official confirmation of the man's guilt, and it was the king himself who had permitted vengeance to take its course.

In the instances given in the preceding paragraphs it is the natural cause and not the mystical cause that is selected as the socially significant one. In these situations witchcraft is irrelevant and, if not totally excluded, is not indicated as the principal factor in causation. As in our own society a scientific theory of causation, if not excluded, is deemed irrelevant in questions of moral and legal responsibility, so in Zande society the doctrine of witchcraft, if not excluded, is deemed irrelevant in the same situations. We accept scientific explanations of the causes of disease, and even of the causes of insanity, but we deny them in crime and sin because here they militate against law and morals which are axiomatic. The Zande accepts a mystical explanation of the causes of misfortune, sickness, and death, but he does not allow this explanation if it conflicts with social exigencies expressed in law and morals.

For witchcraft is not indicated as a cause for failure when a taboo has been broken. If a child becomes sick, and it is known that its father and mother have had sexual relations before it was weaned, the cause of death is already indicated by breach of a ritual prohibition and the question of witchcraft does not arise. If a man develops leprosy and there is a history of incest in his case then incest is the cause of leprosy and not witchcraft. In these cases, however, a curious situation arises because

when the child or the leper dies it is necessary to avenge their deaths and the Zande sees no difficulty in explaining what appears to us to be most illogical behaviour. He does so on the same principles as when a man has been killed by a wild beast, and he invokes the same metaphor of 'second spear'. In the cases mentioned above there are really three causes of a person's death. There is the illness from which he dies, leprosy in the case of the man, perhaps some fever in the case of the child. These sicknesses are not in themselves products of witchcraft, for they exist in their own right just as a buffalo or a granary exist in their own right. Then there is the breach of a taboo, in the one case of weaning, in the other case of incest. The child, and the man, developed fever, and leprosy, because a taboo was broken. The breach of a taboo was the cause of their sickness, but the sickness would not have killed them if witchcraft had not also been operative. If witchcraft had not been present as 'second spear' they would have developed fever and leprosy just the same, but they would not have died from them. In these instances there are two socially significant causes, breach of taboo and witchcraft, both of which are relative to different social processes, and each is emphasized by different people.

But where there has been a breach of taboo and death is not involved witchcraft will not be evoked as a cause of failure. If a man eats a forbidden food after he has made powerful punitive magic he may die, and in this case the cause of his death is known beforehand, since it is contained in the conditions of the situation in which he died even if witchcraft was also operative. But it does not follow that he will die. What does inevitably follow is that the medicine he has made will cease to operate against the person for whom it is intended and will have to be destroyed lest it turn against the magician who sent it forth. The failure of the medicine to achieve its purpose is due to breach of a taboo and not to witchcraft. If a man has had sexual relations with his wife and on the next day approaches the poison oracle it will not reveal the truth and its oracular efficacy will be permanently undermined. If he had not broken a taboo it would have been said that witchcraft had caused the oracle to lie, but the condition of the person who had attended the seance provides a reason for its failure to speak the truth without having to bring in the notion of witchcraft as an agent. No one will admit that he has broken a taboo before consulting the poison oracle, but when an oracle lies every one is prepared to admit that a taboo may have been broken by some one.

Similarly, when a potter's creations break in firing witchcraft is not the only possible cause of the calamity. Inexperience and bad workmanship may also be reasons for failure, or the potter may himself have had sexual relations on the preceding night. The potter himself will attribute his failure to witchcraft, but others may not be of the same opinion.

Not even all deaths are invariably and unanimously attributed to witchcraft or to the breach of some taboo. The deaths of babies from certain diseases are attributed vaguely to the Supreme Being. Also, if a man falls suddenly and violently sick and dies, his relatives may be sure that a sorcerer has made magic against him and that it is not a witch who has killed him. A breach of the obligations of blood-brotherhood may sweep away whole groups of kin, and when one after another of brothers and cousins die it is the blood and not witchcraft to which their deaths are attributed by outsiders, though the relatives of the dead will seek to avenge them on witches. When a very old man dies unrelated people say that he has died of old age, but they do not say this in the presence of kinsmen, who declare that witchcraft is responsible for his death.

It is also thought that adultery may cause misfortune, though it is only one participating factor, and witchcraft is also believed to be present. Thus is it said that a man may be killed in warfare or in a hunting accident as a result of his wife's infidelities. Therefore, before going to war or on a large-scale hunting expedition a man might ask his wife to divulge the names of her lovers.

[. . .]

I am aware that my account of Zande magic suffers from lack of co-ordination. So does Zande magic. Magical rites do not form an interrelated system, and there is no nexus between one rite and another. Each is an isolated activity, so that they cannot all be described in an ordered account. Any description of them must appear somewhat haphazard. Indeed, by treating them all together in Part IV I have given

them a unity by abstraction that they do not possess in reality.

This lack of co-ordination between magical rites contrasts with the general coherence and interdependence of Zande beliefs in other fields. Those I have described in this book are difficult for Europeans to understand. Witchcraft is a notion so foreign to us that it is hard for us to appreciate Zande convictions about its reality. Let it be remembered that it is no less hard for Azande to appreciate our ignorance and disbelief about the subject. I once heard a Zande say about us: 'Perhaps in their country people are not murdered by witches, but here they are.'

Throughout I have emphasized the coherency of Zande beliefs when they are considered together and are interpreted in terms of situations and social relationships. I have tried to show also the plasticity of beliefs as functions of situations. They are not indivisible ideational structures but are loose associations of notions. When a writer brings them together in a book and presents them as a conceptual system their insufficiencies and contradictions are at once apparent. In real life they do not function as a whole but in bits. A man in one situation utilizes what in the beliefs are convenient to him and pays no attention to other elements which he might use in different situations. Hence a single event may evoke a number of different and contradictory beliefs among different persons.

I hope that I have persuaded the reader of one thing, namely, the intellectual consistency of Zande notions. They only appear inconsistent when ranged like lifeless museum objects. When we see how an individual uses them we may say that they are mystical but we cannot say that his use of them is illogical or even that it is uncritical. I had no difficulty in using Zande notions as Azande themselves use them. Once the idiom is learnt the rest is easy, for in Zandeland one mystical idea follows on another as reasonably as one common-sense idea follows on another in our own society.

It is in connexion with death that Zande belief in witchcraft, oracles, and magic is most coherent and is most intelligible to us. Therefore, though I have before briefly described the interplay of these notions at death it is fitting to give a slightly fuller account in conclusion, for it is death that answers the riddle of mystical beliefs.

It is not my intention to give a detailed description of Zande funeral ceremonies and vengeance. I shall not even attempt to recount the elaborate magical rites by which vengeance is accomplished. These will find a place in another volume. Here I give the barest outline of what happens from the time a man falls sick to the time his death is avenged.

It is with death and its premonitions that Azande most frequently and feelingly associate witchcraft, and it is only with regard to death that witchcraft evokes violent retaliation. It is likewise in connexion with death that greatest attention is paid to oracles and magical rites. Witchcraft, oracles, and magic attain their height of significance, as procedures and ideologies, at death.

When a man falls sick his kinsmen direct their activities along two lines. They attack witchcraft by oracles, public warnings, approaches to the witch, making of magic, removal of the invalid to the bush, and dances of witch-doctors. They attack the disease by administration of drugs, usually summoning a leech who is also a witch-doctor, in serious sickness.

A leech attends a man till all hope of his recovery is abandoned. His relations gather and weep around him. As soon as he is dead they wail, and the relatives-in-law dig the grave. Before burial the dead man's kin cut off a piece of barkcloth and wipe his lips with it and cut off a piece of his finger-nail. These substances are necessary to make vengeance-magic. Sometimes earth from the first sod dug when the grave is being prepared is added to them.

On the day following burial steps are taken towards vengeance. The elder kinsmen of the dead man consult the poison oracle. In theory they ask it first whether the dead man has died as a result of some crime he has committed. But in practice, except on rare occasions when his kinsmen know that he has committed adultery or some other crime, and that the injured man has made lethal magic, this step is omitted. Not that a Zande would admit its omission. He would say that if this question were not directly put to the oracle it is contained in those questions that follow, for the oracle would not announce that their magic would be successful unless

the dead man were innocent of crime and were a victim of witchcraft.

In practice, therefore, they first ask it to choose the man who will undertake to act as avenger. His duties are to dispatch magic on the tracks of the witch under the direction of a magician who owns it, and to observe the onerous taboos that enable it to achieve its purpose. If the kin of the dead man wish to make certain of avenging him they insist on placing only the names of adults as candidates for this office, but usually senior men are anxious to avoid the ascetic routine it imposes and propose the name of a lad who is too young to feel the hardship of sex taboos and yet old enough to realize the seriousness of food taboos, and of sufficient character to observe them. They ask the oracle whether the magic will be successful in its quest if a certain boy observes the taboos. If the oracle says that it will be unsuccessful they place before it the name of another man or boy. When it has chosen a name they ask as a corroborative verdict whether the boy will die during his observance of the taboos. He might die as a result of breaking a taboo or because the man they wish to avenge was slain in expiation of a crime. If the oracle declares that the boy will survive vengeance is assured.

They then ask the poison oracle to choose a magician to provide vengeance-magic. They put before it the name of a magician and ask it whether vengeance will be accomplished if his medicine is used. If the oracle rejects one name they propose to it another.

Having chosen a boy to observe the taboos and a magician to provide the medicines, they proceed to prosecute vengeance. I will not describe the various types of medicines employed nor the rites that dispatch them on their errand. It is not expected that they will immediately accomplish their purpose. Indeed, if people in the vicinity die shortly after the rites have been performed the kinsmen do not suppose that they are victims of their magic.

From time to time the kinsmen make presents of beer to the magician to stir up the medicines, because Azande think that they go out on their mission and, not having discovered the guilty man, return to their hiding-place. They have to be sent forth afresh on their quest by further rites. This may happen many times before vengeance has been accomplished, perhaps two years after magic has first been made, and usually not before six months afterwards. Although the taboos are only incumbent on a single boy in so far as the virtue of the magic is concerned, all near kinsmen and the spouse of the dead must respect irksome prohibitions to a greater or lesser degree, for a variety of reasons, and all are anxious to end their fast. Nevertheless, everything must be done in good order and without haste. From time to time they ask the poison oracle whether the medicines are being diligent in their search and for further assurance of ultimate success.

In the past medicine of vengeance was placed on the dead man's grave, but it is said that people interfered with it there, either removing it and plunging it into a marsh to deprive it of power, or spoiling it by bringing it into contact with some impure substance, like elephant's flesh. To-day they often continue to place some medicines on the grave but they also hide others in the bush, generally in the cavity of a tree. There they are safe from contamination by ill-disposed persons.

Several months after magic has been made some one dies in the vicinity and they inquire of the poison oracle whether this man is their victim. They do not, as a rule, inquire about persons who have died several miles away from the homestead of the deceased. If the oracle tells them that the magic has not yet struck they wait till another neighbour dies and consult it again. In course of time the oracle declares that the death of a man in the neighbourhood is due to their magic and that this man is the victim whom they have slain to avenge their kinsman.

They then ask the oracle whether the slain man is the only witch who killed their kinsman or whether there is another witch who assisted in the murder. If there is another witch they wait till he also is slain, but if the oracle tells them that the man who recently died was alone responsible they go to their prince

and present him with the wings of the fowl that died in declaration of the witch's guilt. The prince consults his own poison oracle, and if it states that the oracle of his subjects has deceived them they will have to await other deaths in their neighbourhood and seek to establish that one of them was caused by their magic.

When the oracle of the prince agrees with the oracle of the kinsmen vengeance is accomplished. The wings of the fowls that have died in acknowledgement of their victory are hung up, with the barkcloth and sleeping-mat of the boy who has observed taboos, on a tree at the side of a frequented path in public notification that the kinsmen have done their duty.

The owner of the medicine is now summoned and is asked to recall it. When his fee has been paid he cooks an antidote for the boy who has borne the burden of taboos, the kinsmen of the dead, and the widow; and he destroys the medicine, for it has accomplished its task. He destroys it so that it can do no further harm. Those who are close kinsmen of the dead man may now live unrestricted lives.

Thus death evokes the notion of witchcraft; oracles are consulted to determine the course of vengeance; magic is made to attain it; oracles decide when magic has executed vengeance; and its magical task being ended, the medicine is destroyed.

Azande say that in the past, before Europeans conquered their country, their customs were different. Provincials used the methods I have just described, but men who regularly attended court did not make magic. On the death of a kinsman they consulted their poison oracles and presented to their prince the name of a witch accused by them. If the prince's oracle agreed with their oracles they exacted compensation of a woman and twenty spears from the witch or slew him. In those days death evoked the notion of witchcraft; oracles denounced the witch; compensation was exacted or vengeance executed.

11

Burial Alive

Godfrey Lienhardt

I

If any literate foreigner has seen the full mortuary ceremonies of a master of the fishing-spear, he has not, to my knowledge, described them. It is unfortunate, therefore, that our knowledge of these centrally important ceremonies must depend upon hearsay evidence,[1] even though it may be derived from Dinka who claim first-hand knowledge of the subject. There can be no doubt, however, that the ceremonies we now describe did, and perhaps do, actually occur; for although the ceremonies are now known to be officially forbidden, Dinka admit to having seen or heard of them, when they do not think it imprudent to admit to interest in a custom known to be illegal, and felt to be repugnant to foreigners whose knowledge of its meaning is superficial. During my stay in Dinkaland, but in another part of the country, one successful case attracted attention at a high official level, and in the discussions which followed the abortive ceremony already mentioned those who tried to probe the intention of the participants were clearly aware, up to a point, of the general procedures which ought to accompany the full ceremonial burial of a master of the fishing-spear. During the course of these discussions I was told the names of several masters of the fishing-spear who had been put in the grave alive in comparatively recent times. Since the mystery which surrounds the custom gives rise to many misunderstandings which are to the disadvantage of the Dinka, I do not consider it a breach of confidence to represent the situation as it was represented to me, omitting only names and places which would identify the actors. In view of the ethnographical and theoretical interest of the ceremonies, I have added reports from others to the little evidence which I was able to collect, in face of the reticence induced partly by official prohibition of these practices.

The burial of a master of the fishing-spear with full honour is called *dhor beny ke pir*, or *thiok (beny) ke pir*, or sometimes *beny aci lo thoc*. The *dhor*[2] of the first expression is a technical term of Dinka religion for which I can find no certain equivalent in English. Its object may be either a clan-divinity (*ok alo yanh wa dhor* means 'we are going to *dhor* the clan-divinity of my father') or a master of the fishing-spear, and I do not think that it is used outside these contexts. When

From Godfrey Lienhardt, "Burial Alive," in *Divinity and Experience: The Religion of the Dinka* (Oxford: Clarendon, 1961).

used of the clan-divinity, it has the sense of serving, or giving homage to, the divinity, at a 'feast' with sacrifice and hymns of the kind we have described. People *dhor* the clan-divinity so that it may augment their strength, and in doing so satisfy a demand which it makes upon them. Similarly, as will appear, in placing their master of the fishing-spear in the grave while he yet lives, they think to augment their vitality and also, normally, to gratify his own desire. With these elements of the meaning of *dhor* in mind, we may perhaps translate *dhor beny ke pir* as 'to bury a master while he lives', which is its practical significance in ordinary Dinka usage. This also is the literal meaning of the second expression commonly used of the ceremony, *thiok ke pir*. The third, *beny aci lo thoc*,[3] means literally 'the master has gone to sit up' or 'the master has gone to his seat'. *Thoc* is to sit erect, and it is also something upon which one can sit erect, such as a saddle. Its implication here is that the subject is not lying prone in death as are the corpses of ordinary men, but is in some way propped up. It may be in fact that masters of the fishing-spear do recline when they are placed in the grave alive; but the expression used contradicts the impression of inert recumbence which is made by any mere corpse, and which is conveyed by the usual Dinka word *toc* which applies equally to the lying down of a corpse and the lying in sleep of the living. Similarly, the ceremonies now described contradict the customary configuration of ideas surrounding the deaths of ordinary men and women.

The following is a text typical of the accounts which Dinka friends may give of what happens at the deaths of masters of the fishing-spear. The author did not claim to have witnessed such a ceremony, though he said that he knew of one which had been held in a tribe adjacent to his own. I have changed proper names, but the lineages actually mentioned were known to me.

> When a master of the fishing-spear has fallen sick and is becoming weak, he will call all his people and tell them to bring his whole camp (tribe or subtribe) to his home to bury him whilst he lives. His people will obey him and quickly come, for if they delay and the master of the fishing-spear dies before they reach him, they will be most miserable.

> They will come and drive their cattle-pegs into the ground by the side of the home of the master of the fishing-spear who is to be buried alive. When they have arrived, the master will talk to his people and tell them what they are to do with him. When his talk with the older people is finished, he will tell them to send the young men for *akoc (Cordia rothii)* branches, and the young men will be quickly sent to fetch *akoc*.

> When they return, they clear a patch of ground so that nothing harmful remains in it;[4] and when they have prepared the ground they dig a grave and put the branches of *akoc* in it to make a platform. Then they will cut into strips the skin of a bull previously sacrificed, and make it like an *angareeb*[5] on the frame they have prepared. And they will take a living ram and tether it at the bottom of the hole (grave) at the side of the platform. They then lift up the master of the fishing-spear, and put him into the earth while he yet lives.

> And he will not be afraid of death; he will be put in the earth while singing his songs. Nobody among his people will wail or cry because their man has died. They will be joyful because their master of the fishing-spear will give them life (*wei*) so that they shall live untroubled by any evil.

> When they have placed the master of the fishing-spear on the platform on the ground, they make another platform above it, also with strips of hide, and put a gourd of milk in the earth with him. Then when all is completed, the young men and old men, girls, women and children, will all take cattle-dung and fling it upon the grave, until the grave is completely covered over with a heap of dung. For the grave of a master of the fishing-spear is not to be covered with earth. And they will sacrifice another bull and a cow-in-calf.

> After this is finished, they cover the top of the grave with dungashes, and make a feast for the master of the fishing-spear. After another month, they will make beer and porridge, and kill two bulls, and remove the fence of *awar* grass with which the homestead of the master has been surrounded after the burial. And they will dance and sacrifice to all divinities so that they will be pleased with men.

The two texts which follow were dictated by a friend who claimed that, as a youth, he had been present at the ceremonies he here describes. His evidence, with proper names, was most circumstantial, and I have changed those names which might make the particular area recognizable; it was far from the country of the man who provided the text already quoted.

I first saw a master of the fishing-spear called Deng Deng buried alive in the land of the Majok tribe across the river. I was only a boy. The master's own home was called Malek, in the subtribe Magol, and he was the master of the fishing-spear of that subtribe. His clan was called Pakedang. They are few now but they are very strong in invocation, so that in my country we sometimes call them 'witches of the fishing-spear'.[6] There are other masters of the fishing-spear in that subtribe, but there are none to equal them.

The master of the fishing-spear Deng Deng was becoming very old, and when his years were finished and he was very old indeed, so that he could not see well and all his teeth had fallen out, he told his lineage that he wished to be buried alive, and that they should go and tell the people of the country and see if they agreed.

They prepared the ground for his burial at a very ancient cattle-camp site called Malwal, which was also hard by the homestead of Deng Deng and near his cattle-byre.[7] So it was at his very own original home [panden nhom, literally 'the head of his home']. The clan which cleared and dug the ground was Padiangbar; it is that clan which buries a master of the fishing-spear alive in my country.[8]

They dug a very big hole on the highest point of the cattle-camp site, in the middle of the cattle. Next to it were two bulls, a big white one and a red one. They were the whole beasts of the clan-divinities Mon Grass and Flesh. When the hole had been dug, they made two platforms [frameworks] of akoc wood, which had been fetched by the young men of Padiangbar from far away in the forest, as much as a day's journey distant.

They worked for three days, and the old man was still above the ground. They honoured the bulls with songs for two days, speaking invocations each day in the morning and the evening. Then the masters of the fishing-spear of Pakedang, along with those of Paketoi and Pagong,[9] slit the throats of the bulls at about 10 o'clock. Deng Deng's mother was the daughter of a woman of Paketoi and his mother's father was of the clan Pagong. So they were all there together, to join together his father's and his maternal uncle's families (bi panerden mat kek pan e wun).

Deng Deng made invocations over the bulls, and the horns of the first bull, the white one, sank forwards to the ground. When the bull had been killed, they took its skin and cut it into strips, and made a bed from it on the framework. And every day they made a feast (cam yai) and danced inside the cattle-byre during the daytime, and outside at night. And men slept in the byre with other men's wives, and everyone agreed to this [literally 'and there was no bad word'].

They then placed a war-shield, made from the hide of a bull of the clan-divinity which had been killed in the past, on top of the bed. It was a war-shield which had for long been kept in the byre, and which the people had anointed with butter every spring and autumn, during the 'dividing months'.[10] They placed Deng Deng on the shield and lowered him into the grave.

The red (brown) bull remained. When Deng Deng had been lowered into the hole, they made a platform over him, and so arranged it that the top of the platform was level with the surface of the ground. They sang hymns, and after the singing was finished they made an enclosure of dhot wood around the grave. The enclosure was about twice the area of the surface of the grave, and of such a height that a man could just see over it if he tried. Then they took cattle-dung and partly covered over the top of the grave, leaving part uncovered so that his voice could be heard. From his grave, Deng Deng called the older men together outside the enclosure, and all the women and children, even his own wives, were sent away.

The author of the text was therefore also sent away; but according to him, when the old master of the fishing-spear had finished speaking to the old men, they returned to the rest and reported to them what he had said. The text continues:

Deng Deng had died at the time of the harvest. He said that in the following dry season, in the month of Akanythii,[11] his tribe would fight with a neighbouring tribe, and that he was distressed because his people were not brave enough in war.

Two months later, this fight took place, and eight of his people were killed and two from the neighbouring tribe. That neighbouring tribe soundly beat his tribe and drove them off as far as Agar Dinka country. Eventually, the Government forces came and prevented thefts of cattle. But even then that neighbouring tribe made a feast near the river in the face of the dry-season pastures of his own tribe, which had been so harried that they could do nothing about it.

He added:

> While the master of the fishing-spear still speaks, they do not cover the grave with dung. But when he no longer replies when they address him, they heap up the dung over him. And when it has all sunk in, they make a shrine.[12] Some people may then say 'The master of the fishing-spear has died', but they will usually say 'The master has been taken into the earth'. And nobody will say 'Alas, he is dead!' They will say 'It is very good.'

The same informant told me of the following case which he clearly preferred not to discuss at length as it had occurred much more recently. He spoke as follows:

> Two masters of the fishing-spear known to you today are the sons of that master of the fishing-spear I saw buried. He was the master of the fishing-spear with supremacy in the whole tribe of Kwek, and was a man of the clan Pagong who are the chief masters of the fishing-spear in that tribe.

There follows a description which does not significantly differ from that previously given, and in which again it is made clear that the master of the fishing-spear was very old, though not sick, and asked that he might be buried. The site chosen was again an old cattle-camp site adjoining his homestead. The following part of this text adds something to what has already been described:

> All the people of his tribe came, and the cattle were tethered around. They made an enclosure, but this time they did not dance. The young men were sent away when he was in the grave. The older men later

reported that he had spoken to them in this way: 'I am going to see (deal with) in the earth the Powers of sickness which kill people and cattle. And I am still displeased with my son Moror because we quarrelled. I have nothing bad in my heart towards other people.' After three months, there was no more cattle-plague, and after three months also his son Moror died. His father had fetched him (*aci wun lo dhiec*).

The indication of the ground-plan of such a ceremony is given in figure 11.1

I include this simple plan because it represents what Dinka themselves drew in the dust to explain such a ceremony, and thus includes, one may suppose, a Dinka view of what is essential. The new gourd, to hold water for aspersions and the split sacred cucumbers for drawing over the backs and chests of the sick, was strongly marked in the plan. The sacred spears, for consecration and reconsecration, are placed round the shrine. At least four beasts are required. The bull-calf is tethered during invocations, and then returned to the herd, where it becomes the new 'bull of the clan-divinity'. The bull of the clan-divinity is sacrificed, and provides the strips of hide for the burial-platform. The cow-calf is tethered during the invocations, and is then returned to the herd, to become later the dam of a new 'bull of the clan-divinity', of which the bull-calf will be the sire. Beasts for sacrifice to the clan-divinity should be bred of consecrated stock, though this is not always possible, at least in routine sacrifices. The white ram was specifically stated to be the offering of the women, and those who provided the plan mentioned also that butter would be brought in gourds for anointing the horns and the testicles of the sacrificial victim.

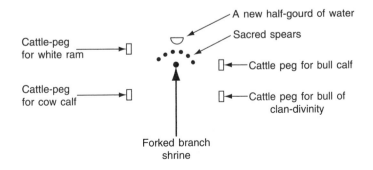

A new half-gourd of water

Sacred spears

Cattle-peg for white ram

Cattle peg for bull calf

Cattle-peg for cow calf

Cattle peg for bull of clan-divinity

Forked branch shrine

Figure 11.1

These accounts are typical of what one hears of the burial of masters of the fishing-spear in Western Dinkaland. I add to them some conclusions drawn from the inquiry into a suspected case of burial alive to which I have already referred, and which (if indeed it really was intended) was unsuccessful owing to official intervention. In the course of this inquiry it became apparent that certain activities were associated, in the minds of most of those present, with ceremonial burial. Naturally, since most of those who had attended the preliminaries of the trampling of the calf (already described) were implicated in the accusation that they intended to bury their chief alive, they were anxious to testify that their ceremony was intended only to strengthen the old man, and was therefore innocent in the eyes of the Government's law. The statements they made, however, reveal what for them would have been considered significant in suggesting that burial alive was intended. One emphasized that the old master of the fishing-spear was 'not an important master of the fishing-spear', rather minimizing his standing, because it is known that not everyone who is technically a master of the fishing-spear has sufficient standing to be treated in this manner. Others emphasized the frequency with which, in the ceremonies and in the preliminaries to them, people spoke of 'strengthening' the old man, and not of burying him. The son of the master of the fishing-spear said that his father had never told him that he wished to be buried, and it was in this case clear throughout the evidence and the reactions of those present to it that the desires of the master of the fishing-spear were considered relevant to the interpretation of the ceremony. Everyone seemed to take it for granted that such a burial would normally take place only at the initial instigation of the master of the fishing-spear concerned, and not against his will. The old master of the fishing-spear himself said that he had called his people to strengthen, and not to bury, him. One piece of evidence of innocence of intention which was strongly urged was that the young men of the camp had not been sent to cut the *akoc* wood from which the platform for the grave is made, and that when the people were making their sacrifice there was no *akoc* in the homestead. Further, the cattle had not been tethered outside around the home of the

sick old man and, as his son insisted, there were several beasts in the cattle-byre. It is clear from this that the tethering of cattle outside around the place of burial is considered an important feature of the ceremony. The manner in which the calf was killed was said to be a quite normal procedure for the death of a beast sacrificed for the recovery of a master of the fishing-spear, as was the fact that some of the young men had brought gourds of milk for libations. But, it was pointed out, the young men were also drinking milk, whereas when a master of the fishing-spear was buried alive milk was not drunk, it was 'respected' (*thek*). Also, it was suggested, the sacrifice was not large enough for a burial alive, and the ceremony had not been mooted sufficiently long beforehand to make it possible for all those members of the sick man's clan who would have come to be informed. Only two days' preparation had been made. One man said also that if a burial of a master of the fishing-spear had been about to take place, all lineages in the subtribe would have produced beasts for sacrifice, that the young men would have gone into the woods and there slaughtered bulls and goats and left them for the birds to eat, and for Powers of sickness. Strangers, moreover, had been made welcome at the ceremony, but in a burial alive they would not have been encouraged to come near. It would also have been expected that the spear of an enemy should be taken and bent in the dust.

Some of this evidence was questioned by the Dinka elders who inquired into the case. It was pointed out, as a significant feature, that the young warriors and women of the whole subtribe were about the homestead, or near by in the cattle-camp, and that if only the strengthening ceremony had been intended the closer kin of the master of the fishing-spear would have been the only ones concerned. It was maintained that the trampling to death of the calf *was* a feature which suggested something more than the ordinary sacrificial act, and that, most importantly, some of the warriors were carrying warshields. There was some disagreement about the situations in which it would be expected that the victim should be trampled to death (*kacic*), some saying that this would really be done in the forest, in order to free people from a serious pestilence, or as a preparation for war. We have remarked already upon the close connexion between religion and war among the Dinka. It was largely on these grounds, and on what was considered to be the untrustworthiness of some of the evidence of those accused – that, for example, though the cattle had not been tethered in the homestead, they had been brought to a cattle-camp near by – that the investigators decided that those who took part in the ceremony had a case to answer.

There are some differences between the substance of these accounts from Western Dinkaland, and what has been reported from other parts. Since evidence is unavoidably slender, I quote at length from the fullest published accounts of what happens at a burial alive, those of Professor and Mrs. Seligman, Major G. W. Titherington, and Ibrahim Eff. Bedri. The following is the information collected by Professor and Mrs. Seligman, whose visits to Dinkaland were made in 1909–10 and 1911–12. Professor and Mrs. Seligman write:[13]

In 1922 we found that Byordit [a rainmaker or master of the fishing-spear of a section of the Bor Dinka] was dead. Fear of the Government led to unwillingness to speak of the manner of his passing, but we understood that after he had several times requested that he might be killed his couch was at last placed in the midst of a cattle-hearth, i.e. upon a mass of dried and burnt dung, and his people danced round him until so much dust was raised that in a few hours the old man – a chronic bronchitic – was dead.

The rain-maker of the Niel tribe was also one of our informants; he told us that his father and paternal uncle had both been killed in the traditional manner, the Niel custom being to strangle their *bañ* in his own house, having first prepared his grave. They then wash the corpse and kill a bullock in front of the house, skinning it immediately and making a couch (*angareeb*) of its skin, which is placed in the grave and the body laid upon it; a cell should then be built over the couch so that the earth does not come in contact with the body. The Niel take every care to guard their *bañ* from accidental death, for should he die suddenly as a result of an accident some sickness would surely occur, even though his son or a close blood relative would immediately succeed him. If it was thought that the *bañ* was seriously ill, he would be killed, even though he were quite young, for it would be a dangerous matter if he were to die of an illness, since as our informant pointed out, this would prevent any of his sons (i.e. presumably any relative) from becoming *bañ* in their turn. Actually this had never happened.

An Agar Dinka gave the following account of the slaying of their rainmaker. A wide grave is dug, and a couch is placed in it, upon which the rainmaker lies on his right side with a skin under his head. He is surrounded by his friends and relatives, including his younger children, but his elder children are not allowed near the grave, at any rate towards the end, lest in their despair they should injure themselves. The *bañ* lies upon his couch without food or drink for many hours, generally for more than a day. From time to time he speaks to his people, recalling the past history of the tribe, how he has ruled and advised them, and instructing them how to act in the future. At last he tells them he has finished, and bids them cover him up; earth is thrown into the grave and he is soon suffocated.

Captain J. M. Stubbs, writing of the Reik, informs us that the *bañ bith* is laid on a bier in a roofed-in cell built in the grave, and that his neck, elbows and knees are broken; sometimes he is first strangled with a cow-rope. According to another account, the *bañ* eats a little millet, drinks milk, and throws the remainder to the east, praying and affirming that he is going to his fathers but that the food he leaves to his children. A cow-rope is placed around his neck, his elbows and knees are broken, and one of the sacred spears is placed in his hand, which he is helped to raise. His son takes the spear, and the *bañ* is strangled. It appears that this is done in semi-privacy; then the drums beat, the people gather, and the grave is filled in. A shelter is built over it, which when it falls to pieces is not rebuilt, though the ground around is kept cleared lest bush fires should sweep across the tomb. It seems that certain species of trees are expected to grow on or near the grave, and there may be some connection between this and the initiation of sacrifice at the grave. Concerning the Bor, Archdeacon Shaw informs us that a rain-maker is buried in a *lwak* (cattle-byre) which continues to be used, the grave being fenced off with short poles. He is said to take the food of the community with him into the grave, so when the next season arrives a hole is dug at the side of the byre so that the food may come out again. This will ensure good crops, abundance of termites and other food. Dr. Tucker writes of the Cic that when the *bañ bith* is buried, milk is poured into his right hand, millet placed in his left and the hands closed over their contents, thus ensuring plenty until the new *bañ bith* is installed.

We believe that all tribes sprinkle milk on the graves of their rain-makers, and it is probable that all place some property in the grave, while perhaps some bury a bullock or a cow with their rainmaker.

I was not able to confirm the presence of any idea that the master of the fishing-spear took the food of the community with him into the grave, though undoubtedly most people say that he is buried with milk and perhaps with a beast, sometimes an ox and sometimes a ram. It is thought, among the Western Dinka, that the sick master of the fishing-spear may take some affliction of the community away with him into the grave. There is one famous case in Western Dinkaland of a renowned master of the fishing-spear who entered the grave clutching in his hand a tsetse fly, and thereby removed the scourge of tsetse from his people. It may now happen also that a living beast is buried *in place of* a master of the fishing-spear. Shortly after the abortive ceremony already mentioned, it was reported that a burial alive was intended in a village of the same district. Police descended upon the village to find a new grave containing only a ram. Other discrepancies between my own accounts and those of Professor and Mrs. Seligman from other parts of Dinkaland are left for comment until other accounts have been considered, and a minimal measure of agreement between them all can be reached.

The account of 'Burial Alive among Dinka of Bahr-el-Ghazal Province' published in 1925 by G. W. T. (Major G. W. Titherington),[14] then a Sudan Political Officer in that Province, agrees substantially with that I myself was told. He says, however, that the custom was originally confined to the clans of Pagong and Parum, from whom it was copied by Payi. The various lineages represented among the people of a master of the fishing-spear are said to bring beasts to slaughter at the feast for his burial. Major Titherington also says that the burial takes place in a cattle-byre, which continues to be used as before until it falls into disrepair, when earth is taken from the grave and used to make a mound-shrine. There is no mention of strangulation or of other violence done to the master of the fishing-spear in Major Titherington's note, and it is made clear that his manner of meeting his death is voluntarily chosen by him. From the grave he eventually raises a spear to indicate that he wishes the grave to be filled in. Again, a platform is built over him, and he rests upon a 'pillow' under this platform, which is covered with grass. An ox, buried alive with him at the other end of this vast grave, is said to die in eight days, and he himself is covered in ten days unless he has given a sign that he wishes this to be done earlier. Major Titherington mentions that, once in the grave, the master of the fishing-spear does not usually come out again, but that he has heard of one successful case of change of mind.

Finally, though in this book not much attention has been paid to the Northern Dinka whom I never visited, we cannot omit the accounts of the deaths of their masters of the fishing-spear which Ibrahim Eff. Bedri has given. They have to be considered in relation to ceremonies for the installation of a master of the fishing-spear which, among the Northern Dinka, seem to be elaborate. These Dinka, in closer contact with the Shilluk than any of the others we have discussed, may have a development of ceremonial influenced by, but not modelled upon, that of the Shilluk kingship. In one article,[15] Ibrahim Eff. Bedri states briefly that generally the 'famous' rain-makers, when they become old or sick, should be killed in some way. Suffocation, he says, is the most common way. He continues:

> Aiyong Dit, the famous Rain Maker of Danjol, was built into his barn with his first wife and favourite bull, and left to die of starvation.
>
> Another way to kill a Beny Riem is to hold him standing, cover the whole body with thick cow butter, and vigorously stretch his legs, fingers, arms and privates and press the testicles. Then they break all the joints. Some people say they are broken before the death but others say after.
>
> The question why the privates are stretched and the testicles pressed, is always an annoying one, and is simply answered by a shrug with a prompt 'I don't know.'

In a longer account[16] Bedri writes that 'When the elders of a section decide to kill their *Beny Rem*, or when he himself has made the request, all the warriors who were initiated by him are summoned.'[17] They are said to dance and sing in his honour, and finally to suffocate him. The treatment described in the last quotation is then given. The account continues:

> He is buried secretly by night usually in the bed of a khor or in the forest so that nobody else may know his grave.[18] He is buried in a deep hole sitting on a bed made of *inderab*[19] stakes, and with stakes at his back bound with hide to keep him upright. His *mendyor* spear[20] is put in his hand pointing in the direction of the enemies of the tribe. The body is then covered with *Leyie* grass from the river bank, and the grave is filled in.
>
> If an enemy interferes with the grave or the position of the body he brings misfortune to the section.

Further, it is said that all but children fast from the time of the master's death until his burial, that before the sunrise following his death people leave the village or the cattle-camp and stay in the sun until midday, that food which is cooked on fire is thrown away and all the fires in the village are put out, and that the grass around the village or cattle-camp is burnt and people return to their homes through the smoke. A sheep is sacrificed and thrown to the birds. On the third day, another sheep is killed and half of it boiled and eaten by those who have assisted in the burial, while half is thrown into the forest for the dead man. Meat, water, and charcoal from the cooking are thrown on the grave 'in order to release people from the spiritual keeping of the dead *Beny Rem* into which they had been symbolically delivered by placing a necklace of ostrich-egg beads round his neck at his installation'. At the first harvest after his death there is a big sacrifice attended by all the people of his section who dance and drink beer:

> On the last day the heads of the sons of the *Beny Rem* are shaved and this signifies the end of the period of mourning, which is observed by his family only and not by the whole section. If for any reason the *Beny Rem* dies in another way, e.g. accidental drowning, a sheep is suffocated and buried with him in the same grave, and the rites are conducted in the same way.
>
> It is not always necessary to kill a *Beny Rem* and it is generally sufficient if a sheep is killed and buried with him, but this ceremonial killing is essential in the case of a *Beny Nial* and there are always people accompanying him for this purpose.

By *Beny Rem* and *Beny Nial* Ibrahim Eff. Bedri refers to a distinction something like that we have already made between minor and major masters of the fishing-spear. In Northern Dinkaland, however, this distinction seems to be formally made by ceremonial action, in a way which I never encountered among the Western Dinka. It is said that the ordinary *Beny Rem* is the spiritual leader of a tribe, while a *Beny Nial* is an outstanding *Beny Rem* who seems to have a wider following. The ordinary *Beny Rem* is installed after sacrifice, from the bones of which a shrine is made, while the fire upon which the flesh is roasted is used for starting a special sacred fire in the new master's home. There are then other ceremonies which may be summarized as follows. The *Beny Rem* sits on a bed of *ambatch* (a very light wood which is of considerable ceremonial importance among the neighbouring Shilluk). He is washed by the elders, who then place special strings of ostrich egg-shell beads round his neck, and a circlet of roan antelope-hide round his head, and anoint him with butter. He then sits on an untrimmed bull-hide, and all those who had any right to his office cut bits from the hide, thereby renouncing their rights and reducing the hide to the usual, trimmed, oval shape. Other ceremonies expressive of promising allegiance are performed, and finally the sacred spear associated with the clan-divinity is placed in the master's hand. The warriors parade before him and he is sprinkled with blood and water. He then travels from village to village of his tribe with a few elders, carrying pieces of wood anointed with butter, which seem to represent life and fertility for his people. At each village the women come out to meet the *Beny Rem* 'and those without children touch the pieces of wood with their hands and then their stomachs and kiss their hands as a good omen for becoming pregnant'. This again is a much richer and more explicit ceremonial than I have found elsewhere among the Dinka, though to a large extent it simply presents overtly what the master of the fishing-spear means to the Dinka as, in a more latent way, that meaning may be found among the Western Dinka.

The installation of the *Beny Nial*, who is automatically destined for burial alive, is thus described:[21]

A Dindyor member who is deemed of exceptional character and shows interest in his people's affairs, is carried (in order to evince their feelings) in an *ambach* bed on the shoulders of elders who run with him towards the four directions singing, while the chorus repeats '*beny aci jaj, beny aci riak kany*' (The Chief has been carried, the Chief destroys things). I do not know whether they mean their own or their enemies' things. Such a *Beny Riem* must not be left to die a natural death, otherwise some evil, such as famine, will fall on the country.

Elsewhere, Bedri writes: 'The people . . . lower the ambach bed and before it reaches the ground the *Beny Rem* jumps from it as though returning to life again.'

2

The information assembled above indicates that there is some variety in the practice described for different parts of Dinkaland, but that, except for the elaborate ceremonies of the Northern Dinka which I have not found elsewhere, these varieties can scarcely be ordered on a regional basis. Details from ceremonies described for one part are repeated in another, while considerable differences may appear in different accounts of the ceremonies performed in one area. It is safe for one who knows the Dinka to say that nothing in any of the accounts given above would surprise Dinka anywhere, even though it might not be part of their actual practice. A characteristically Dinka symbolism is integral to all.

The fundamental principle, clear in all accounts, is that certain masters of the fishing-spear must not or should not be seen to enter upon physical death and the debility which precedes it in the same way as ordinary men or domestic animals. Their deaths are to be, or are to appear, deliberate, and they are to be the occasion of a form of public celebration. It is with this point that we may start a consideration of the material presented above.

First, it is necessary to make clear that the ceremonies described in no way prevent the ultimate recognition of the ageing and physical death of those for whom they are performed. This death is recognized; but it is the public experience of it, for the survivors, which is deliberately modified by the

performance of these ceremonies. It is clear also that this is the Dinka intention in performing the rites. They do not think that they have made their masters of the fishing-spear personally immortal by burying them before they have become corpses or, in some accounts, by anticipating their deaths by ritual killing. The expressions used for the deaths of masters of the fishing-spear are euphemisms for an event which is fully admitted. In my experience they are not even inevitably used, though a Dinka would prefer to say gently 'The master has gone to the earth' or 'The master has gone to sit', rather than 'The master has died', particularly at the time of death. These euphemisms replace the involuntary and passive connotations of the ordinary verb for 'to die' (*thou*) by expressions suggesting a positive act. Similarly (though this point is not specifically made in any of the accounts) when we hear that the people 'bury their master of the fishing-spear' it is as an alternative to 'letting him die'. In other words, the deliberately contrived death, though recognized as death, enables them to avoid admitting in this case the involuntary death which is the lot of ordinary men and beasts. Further, it is not the master of the fishing-spear who 'kills' himself, though he requests or receives a special form of death. The action to avoid, for him, the mere deprival of life which death represents for ordinary Dinka, is action taken by his people. And, as we see in most of the accounts given, their intention is not primarily to undertake the special ceremonies for *his* sake, but for their own.

If we regard the ceremonies so far described in this way, we do not need to make much of the variations which seem to contradict each other with regard to the part played, in the ceremony, by the master of the fishing-spear's own volition. It *is* possible for the Dinka to conceive of the burial of a master of the fishing-spear alive against his will, though it must be said that, in the case of the Western Dinka, I have never heard that this has been done within the limits of what might be considered real historical tradition. The account which these Dinka will give of the custom almost invariably begins with the request of the old master of the fishing-spear himself, and his securing of the agreement of his people. There is, however, a story which tells of the burial of one master of the fishing-spear against his will, and I doubt if it would surprise any Dinka. It is told as follows among the Agar Dinka:

Jokom was a person of long ago. Long ago he thought that he would build a cattle-byre with people, with some people standing and then others standing on their heads and other people on their backs. And he built for two days and the cattle-byre collapsed. And his son called Macot thought about this, and acted craftily, and spoke with the people of his father's camp, and said 'The camp of my father is being finished [killed]. Better that we bury my father alive.' The people of the camp agreed.

A clan called Pabuong brought out a *mangok* (blue-grey) bull to bury their master Jokom. Jokom did not know they were going to bury him alive, even when they had dug the earth out. When they had finished digging, they brought out the bull and deceived the master of the fishing-spear into coming to the grave. When he came, they seized him and pushed him in, and pushed the bull in with him, and covered the grave with wood and covered it with earth and then cleared the ground around it.

They stayed there by the grave for about five days and after that the master of the fishing-spear and the bull died. And while they yet lived, the bull bellowed and the master answered it.

His son Macot remained. When people fought with spears he took a rod and went between the people and spoke, that the fighting might end, and people were afraid [to continue]. And if a man had been killed Macot said that compensation must be paid [rather than revenge taken] and people listened to him because they feared his word.

The cruel master of the fishing-spear who 'tried to build a cattle-byre with living people' figures in the lore of many Dinka;[22] and in this story his death against his will is clearly intended to follow from his cruelty. Even here, however, though he does not consult his people, his son must. We do not have to go further than a consideration of the communal labour involved, however, to conclude that in such ceremonies the will of the people of the master of the fishing-spear is what is primarily significant for the Dinka. Their purpose, in burying the master alive, is served whatever may be his intentions in the situation, though it is usually supposed that he takes the initiative, and this is expected of him.

We have earlier discussed the Dinka belief that the master of the fishing-spear 'carries the life' of his people. It appears from the account of Ibrahim Eff. Bedri that, among the Northern Dinka, this belief is symbolically represented by the ostrich shell beads, which stand for his people, which a master keeps in his possession. Among the Western Dinka, at least, it is this belief which is invoked when one asks why it is necessary to bury a master of the fishing-spear alive. If he 'dies' like ordinary men, the 'life' of his people which is in his keeping goes with him. It may be that the frequent references to strangulation and suffocation which we find in other accounts relate also to this belief; for, as we have shown, for the Dinka 'life', *wei*, is recognized particularly in breath, and these forms of killing involve, above all, the retention within him of the master's breath. He is not, in our idiom, allowed to 'breathe his last' or 'expire'. This situation should not be interpreted too materialistically or literally. The Dinka know, as we have said, that the master dies. What they represent in contriving the death which they give him is the conservation of the 'life' which they themselves think they receive from him, and not the conservation of his own personal life. The latter, indeed, is finally taken away from him by his people so that they may seem to divide it from the public 'life' which is in his keeping, and which must not depart from them with his death.

The action by which this separation is achieved is clearly shown in some of the accounts which we have given. In my own discussions with the Western Dinka, one feature of their reaction to the death of a master of the fishing-spear was very marked; it was that people should not mourn, but rather should be joyful. It is conceded to the man's close kin – those for whom his own personality has been most significant – that they may indeed break down under the strain imposed, by custom, upon them, in having to control the expression of the sadness they may feel. It is said also, by some, that the closest kin may observe some of the customs of mourning. This is clearly felt to be a concession to their sense of personal bereavement, a recognition by the Dinka indeed of the artifice by which, in a collective act of will and control of sentiment, they repudiate the contradiction in experience which the inevitability of personal death would otherwise here represent. For the rest of the master's people (and even for the close kin in that they are also his people) the human symbolic action involved in the 'artificial' burial must be seen to transform the experience of a leader's death into a concentrated public experience of vitality and, in the Dinka world, aggressiveness. It is sometimes said that the cattle of his people, bellowing because they have not been milked, alone mourn his death with their cries; but also, since the crying of cattle heavy with milk is one of the most joyful sounds a Dinka can wish to hear, their cries simultaneously call to mind the plenty with which the master of the fishing-spear has always in life been ideally associated – the fecundity of cattle and the watered pastures upon which they depend. To confirm this impression, and re-create the whole configuration of experience which, in a previous chapter we have seen to be associated with the master of the fishing-spear, we find in some accounts that the materials necessary for the burial have riverain associations, or are connected with the dry-season pastures which represent for the Dinka much of the 'life' which they hope to ensure for themselves. In some accounts the fence round a grave is made with *awar* grass, the grass of the riverain pastures which appears and gives sustenance to the cattle before others in a protracted dry season, as we have earlier described. It is also, it will be remembered, the grass from beneath which the prototype of spear-masters, Aiwel Longar, watered his cattle in a time of famine and drought. In another account (p. 302) it is said that *dhot* wood is required. This again is associated with the dry-season pastures, and, it may be remembered, is the tree with branches of which sacrificial victims are covered as they lie in state immediately after death. Finally, it is fairly consistently stated that the wood from which the framework of the platform on which the master reclines is made is *akoc* (*Cordia rothii*), a wood which is renowned for its sappy moistness, and which, in putting forth its leaves before other trees, is associated with moisture and persistence through the most arid and difficult period of the dry season.

If the burial is thus associated by a wide range of associations with a social triumph over death and the factors which bring death in Dinkaland, this association is reinforced by the militant display

which the ceremony involves. Fighting was for the Dinka often a condition of survival, and it still has something of the value attached to it which must have made it a serious necessity in the time of their complete autonomy. One of the functions of masters of the fishing-spear was to open and close age-sets; and though the age-sets seem never to have had in themselves specific regimental functions, their pride and reputation were and are still connected with their military prowess. Consequently, a renowned master of the fishing-spear was himself at the centre of the military organization of his people, and the inspiration of the most active fighting men. So, though every public sacrifice involves warlike display, at the burial of a master of the fishing-spear the fighting power of his people is particularly emphasized. Members of groups other than those rallied by the ceremony are in danger if they approach it; the young men are fully armed for war; and the cattle are tethered during the day, not taken out in their separate herding groups which are weak in the face of attack.

In other ways also the ceremony emphasizes the unity, and equivalence, of those taking part. The lineages represented in the community should all contribute victims to the feast; and, very characteristically of Dinka thought, it is specifically said in one text that the master's maternal kin are 'put together' with his paternal kin. His daughters and their families also bring their offerings to the grave at his burial. He is recognized as 'the maternal uncle of the camp' (*nar wut*), which such a leader is often called. A further indication of the solidarity which such a ceremony ideally creates is the statement, in one of the texts, that after the burial men and women may sleep promiscuously together. I do not know if in fact this happens; but that it should be thought to do so is significant, not only in its similarity to orgiastic behaviour at critical periods elsewhere, but in that such an abandonment of personal rights which would normally be strongly asserted is a measure of the common interests and equivalence of members of the community.

In his death, then, the Dinka master of the fishing-spear is made to represent to his people the survival with which masters of the fishing-spear are associated in myth and present-day ritual. Nor, in one sense, are the Dinka deceiving themselves in maintaining that the death of an old master of the fishing-spear produces a renewal of life in his people. His burial ceremonies do create a militant self-consciousness, as we have seen. The masters of the fishing-spear who are the principal repositories of their tribal and subtribal traditions, are said to recall these traditions when they lie in the grave. They cannot die like ordinary men, for the traditions and beliefs which they embody, reaching back to the myth of Aiwel, live on. Notions of individual personal immortality mean little to non-Christian Dinka, but the assertion of collective immortality means much, and it is this which they make in the funeral ceremonies of their religious leaders.

NOTES

1 Similar doubt surrounds the manner of the deaths of the kings of the Shilluk, which has considerable bearing on theories of 'divine kingship' which we have borne in mind in the presentation of our account of the deaths of masters of the fishing-spear.

2 A similar word also means 'to be tired of', but I do not think the meanings are related.

3 Though *toc* means 'to rest'.

4 That is, they clean the ground and remove any thornbushes.

5 This is the bedstead of the Northern Sudan, made of strips of hide or rope laced across a wooden framework.

6 In view of what we have earlier suggested, that there is on the whole a correspondence between religious reputation and political influence, which depends partly on the size of the spear-master clan, it is interesting to see here that their small numbers seen in relation to their religious reputation at once evokes the notion of something unnatural – witchcraft.

7 This refers to a wet-season camping site, many of which are very near permanent villages.

8 It is in this area particularly that the clan Padiangbar are regarded as having something of the strength of a spear-master clan (see pp. 145–6). Structurally, therefore, their role in the situation of the death of masters of the fishing-spear may be seen to have something in common with the reported role off the *ororo*, the demoted members of the royal clan of the Shilluk, at

the death of the Shilluk king. See, for example, C. G. and B. Z. Seligman, 1932, pp. 49–50.

9 I have retained the real clan-name here and in the case of Padiangbar.

10 That is at the times between the seasons, when the Dinka move to and from the dry-season pastures.

11 This is the height of the dry season.

12 It is not clear whether this is actually on the site of burial, or near by. I have never seen or heard of a shrine of this type (the mud shrine) separated from a homestead.

13 G. G. and B. Z. Seligman, 1932, pp. 196–8.

14 G. W. T., 'Burial Alive among Dinka of the Bahr-al-Ghazal Province', *S. N. & R.*, vol. viii, 1925, p. 196.

15 Ibrahim Eff. Bedri, 1939.

16 Ibrahim Eff. Bedri, 1948.

17 The *beny rem* or *beny riem* is described as a master of the fishing-spear who has been formally and ceremonially installed, as leader of his tribe or subtribe. I was not told of such formal installations among the Dinka I visited.

18 Professor Evans-Pritchard was told by a Dinka that the master of the fishing-spear was buried secretly so that his grave should not be found. I did not hear of this.

19 This is the *akoc* wood mentioned earlier.

20 Among the Northern Dinka, those who claim descent from Aiwel Longar are called *mendyor* (pl. *dindyor*). This relates to the *wendyor* of the Western Dinka (pp. 108–9) but is clearly a much more important term among the Northern Dinka than among the Western.

21 Ibrahim Eff. Bedri, 1939, p. 130.

22 P. P. Howell, 1948, reports that, according to some legends, it was thus that the 'pyramid' of Aiwel Longar at Puom was built.

REFERENCES

Bedri, Ibrahim Eff. 1939. Notes on Dinka Religious Beliefs in Their Hereditary Chiefs and Rainmakers. *S. N. & R.*

——— 1948. More Notes on the Padarg Dinka. *S. N. & R.* 29: 44.

Howell, P. P. 1948. "Pyramids" in the Upper Nile Region. *Man* 52–53.

Seligman, C. G. and B. Z. 1932. *Pagan Tribes of the Nilotic Sudan*.

12

State Terror in the Netherworld: Disappearance and Reburial in Argentina

Antonius C. G. M. Robben

The funeral procession advanced slowly through the Jewish cemetery of La Tablada, a town on the outskirts of Buenos Aires. The old rabbi, together with the father of the deceased and four escorts, pulled the iron cart with its coffin in measured paces to each new crossroad. A halt. A glance to the left. A glance to the right. The front wheel of the bier spun round and round its axis, resisting the resolute hand of the rabbi. Another halt, more glances. The procession progressed from one juncture to another as if to mark the stages of a life climbing to the final resting place where death and reconciliation meet at last.

When the procession arrived at its destination, the coffin was lifted off the cart and placed on two crooked beams that rested across the pit. Ropes were pulled under the coffin, beams were removed, and the casket was lowered into the grave. The father appeared stoic during the entire ceremony from synagogue to burial, while the mother of the deceased cried inconsolably. The lawyer Emilio Mignone spoke a eulogy in the name of various human rights groups. He had not known Marcelo Gelman when he was alive, he said, but he remem-bered well the day his mother announced his disappearance. Mignone had known so many others who shared Marcelo's ideals and who had also disappeared, like his own daughter Monica.

Marcelo Gelman was a twenty-year-old journalist when he disappeared with his nineteen-year-old pregnant wife María Claudia Iruretagoyena on 24 August 1976. Marcelo was abducted by a task force of the Army Intelligence Service, most likely for being the son of Juan Gelman, a high-ranking member of the Montoneros guerrilla organization.[1] At dawn on 14 October, a corporal of the coast guard observed how several men were throwing large objects into the river San Fernando. He notified his superiors. The river was dragged for hours until eight oil drums were found. Each drum contained a corpse in an advanced state of putrefaction. The bodies of six men and two women were recovered. Most of them had been killed by a gun shot to the head. Fingerprints were taken, but no positive identification was made. The eight bodies were buried by the coast guard as unidentified corpses on 21 October 1976. The remains were finally exhumed and

From Antonius C. G. M. Robben, "State Terror in the Netherworld: Disappearance and Reburial in Argentina," in *Death Squad: The Anthropology of State Terror*, ed. Jeffrey A. Sluka (Philadelphia: University of Pennsylvania Press, 2000).

identified in October 1989. Marcelo Gelman was one of them, but his wife María Claudia still remains missing (Cohen Salama 1992:233–42).[2]

As the first flowers showered on the grave, one person shouted, "Comrade Marcelo! Present!" Numerous people raised a clenched fist in communist salute. One person yelled, "Only with blood can spilled blood be paid!" More flowers fell on the grave. The sobs of the bystanders grew louder. Juan Gelman, Marcelo's father, removed a tear from his right eye, turned around slowly and walked away with his ex-wife, Berta Schubaroff.

On 1 October 1989, three months before the funeral of Marcelo Gelman, another reburial had occurred. After resting for 112 years at the Catholic cemetery of Southampton, Brigadier General Juan Manuel de Rosas was placed in his family's tomb at the Recoleta cemetery in the heart of Buenos Aires. The event was of great historical significance. Rosas had fled Argentina on board a British vessel in 1852 after his defeat at the battle of Caseros. Ever since, he had been depicted as the tyrant whose twenty-four-year rule was known simply as "the terror." In the 1930s, a movement of historical revisionism arose that emphasized Rosas's patriotism and claimed that official history had misrepresented him. A public call for the repatriation of the remains of Rosas was made in 1934. The political spirit of Rosas was reinvigorated, and nineteenth-century animosities between Unitarists and Federalists became fomented again in the confrontation of liberals and nationalists.[3] Rosas's name also became linked to the ten-year populist government of Juan Domingo Perón during the mid-twentieth century as liberal opponents condemned his government as "the second tyranny."[4] A congressional debate about Rosas's remains was held in the mid-1970s. Repatriation was approved but not carried out because of the political violence preceding the 1976 coup d'état. The 1989 reburial of Rosas by the Peronist president Carlos Menem was therefore full of historic reference.

Symbolizing national reconciliation, the funeral procession with the remains of Rosas was escorted by two groups of horsemen representing the Federalist and Unitarist armies that had fought one another during the nineteenth-century civil wars. Descend-

ants of Rosas and those of several of his onetime enemies Paz, Viamonte, Lavalle, and Urquiza were present at the interment at the Recoleta national cemetery.[5] "Today we bury more than one hundred years of black legend, of darkness, of history written with inaccuracies," so spoke the priest Alberto Ezcurra in his homily (La Nación, 2 October 1989). President Carlos Menem had said the preceding day that "Nobody, absolutely nobody has the legitimate right to continue to arrest our development because of bygone events, for history cannot be a heavy load, an insupportable burden, a painful memory or a petty opinion. History must be a chain of union, stronger than frustration, than war, than death" (La Prensa, 1 October 1989).[6] According to Menem, the political repatriation of Rosas served to close the wounds of the past that had continued to fester in the Argentine nation for more than a century. However, it was clear to everyone in Argentina that Menem's more pressing political objective was to relegate the fresh memories of the 1976–82 dirty war to history. One week after Rosas's reburial, president Menem pardoned 277 military officers and former guerrillas, among whom was Juan Gelman, Marcelo's father. Former president Raúl Alfonsín expressed his doubts about Menem's success at bringing about a national reconciliation: "One cannot decree the amnesia of an entire society because every time anyone tried to sweep the past under the carpet, the past returned with a vengeance" (La Nación, 10 October 1989).[7]

Despite the different circumstances surrounding the funerals of Juan Manuel de Rosas and Marcelo Gelman – the glory and honor bestowed upon the first and the controversy surrounding the exhumation of the last – both public ceremonies reveal the central importance of human remains and their reburial in Argentine political culture. Their importance arises from the belief in the influence of the dead on the world of the living, and the obligation to bury comrades-in-arms with full honors. These two political reasons add to a general human care for the dead and the emotional need for mourning. This cultural complex was exploited by the military junta in their dirty war against the guerrilla insurgency and left-wing sectors of Argentine society. State terror in Argentina between 1976 and 1982 was as much inflicted on the dead as on the living. The bodies of the victims of military repression were incinerated, dumped at sea, or buried in mass graves by counterinsurgency task forces. Between 10,000 and 30,000 people disappeared during the seven-year military rule. This paper analyzes the ongoing anxiety about the spirit of the enemy dead, the acts of resistance by relatives of the disappeared, and the concealment and funerary obstruction of the victims of Argentina's dirty war as means to extend state terror into the hereafter.

Disappearance as Terror

Torture and disappearance are not the cruel realities of war, and the targeting of tens of thousands of civilians of the political left was not inevitable. Counterinsurgency is also possible with the help of military courts and due process. A confidential 1980 status report by the American embassy in Buenos Aires to the State Department in Washington said about the junta's preference for disappearances: "Disappearance is still the standard tactic for the Argentine security forces in dealing with captured terrorists. The military's commitment to this method is profoundly rooted in elements that range from effectiveness through expediency to cultural bias. We doubt whether international sanctions and opprobrium will, in themselves, cause the government to change the tactic and grant captured terrorists due process" (quoted in Guest 1990: 430).

The rationale of turning disappearance into the principal repressive tactic was revealed in a rare interview with the Supreme Court of the Armed Forces. Upon my provocative question why the junta had not executed the guerrillas publicly, instead of making them disappear, a brigadier general answered while the other judges nodded in agreement: "If one would have done what you have asked then there would have been immediate revenge, not only on the executioner or those who presided over the trial but also on their families. That is to say, the terror had also infused terror among the armed forces, and they responded with terror. This is the tremendous problem, the tremendous tragedy of this war" (interview, 20 December 1989).

Argentine society became terror-stricken. The terror was intended to debilitate people politically and emotionally without them ever fathoming the magnitude of the force that hit them. The armed forces had divided the country into five large zones, each subdivided into subzones. The subzones were divided into areas, and the areas might be further subdivided into subareas. The areas and subareas were the operational territories of the task forces (*grupos de tarea*). The special task forces stood generally under the command of the army or the navy. The air force participated to a far lesser extent in the repressive apparatus. The regular forces did not participate in the actual abductions, although army units might seal off a neighborhood and provide logistical support. The disappearances were generally carried out by small task forces of five or six men, under the command of a lieutenant, who pertained to the various intelligence services of the armed forces. Typically, they would first ask for a "green light" from the local police station to prevent the police from responding to distress calls from any concerned neighbor. Next, the assault gang would force its way into a home under the cover of darkness, threaten and beat the inhabitants into submission, blindfold their victim, and leave in unmarked private cars (CONADEP 1986:11–13; Mittelbach 1986).

The special task forces would take the abducted persons to the 365 secret detention centers, which were usually located in Argentina's police stations. Only one-quarter of the centers were situated at military installations. The abducted were never publicly acknowledged as detainees or prisoners once they disappeared into these so-called "pits" (*pozos*) or "black holes" (*chupaderos*). Some were released into exile, but most of them were assassinated. The corpses were cremated or interred clandestinely as unidentified bodies in municipal cemeteries. They were also abandoned at roadsides, thrown in rivers, and even flung from planes at sea under sedation (García 1995:461–70; Verbitsky 1995).

The disappearance of guerrillas sowed great uncertainty among the revolutionary organizations. They were severely hampered in their operations when they did not know whether their combatants were dead or alive, had defected or deserted, were held up in traffic, or were being tortured for information about surprise attacks and upcoming meetings. It also allowed intelligence officers to take the disappeared detainees on missions to identify their comrades at border posts, railway stations, airports, and bus stops. Some pointed out complete strangers so that a comrade could leave unnoticed. They hoped that the innocence of the unsuspected victim would soon be discovered, and that his torture would end.

The Argentine military leaders believed furthermore that historical judgment could be decisively influenced if there was no body to mourn, dead to commemorate, or epitaph to read. The disappearance of the corpses was motivated by a strategic concern about the political future of the armed forces. Eventually the military would have to hand power to a democratic government, and they knew that without a corpus delicti future criminal prosecution would be impossible.

The disappearance were also ordered to prevent the mobilization of international public opinion. A lesson was learned from the adverse reactions to the mass arrests during Pinochet's first years in power, and from the public execution of convicted members of the ETA during the Franco dictatorship.

However, it was not just the fear of international protests, operational advantages, or historical judgment that made the military choose disappearance as their principal method of repression. The disappearances were directed at the core of Argentine society. They converted the torture of detainees into the anguish of friends, colleagues, relatives, and family members. Disappearances had, and continue to have, very complex effects. People knew that torture was a common practice in Argentina among the security forces. Since many relatives were present at the abductions – 60 percent of the disappeared were detained in the home – they feared that the abducted were being tortured (CONADEP 1986:11). Yet, they were helpless because the authorities denied having them in custody. Tormenting thoughts about the suffering of the disappeared person haunted those left behind. The term "home front" seldom had a more sinister double meaning.

Unlike the public display and dismemberment of enemy corpses in nineteenth-century Argentina, the disappearances of the 1970s had their greatest effect within the homes of their victims. Michel Foucault has described how the spectacle of torture in eighteenth-century France served to assert the power of the king. The public confession and dismemberment of criminals demonstrated to the people that the law was the will of the divine ruler, and that anyone who violated that law was an enemy of the sovereign and had to be punished by the sword. However, despite this awesome display of force, it also showed spectators the limits of power. "A body effaced, reduced to dust and thrown to the winds, a body destroyed piece by piece by the infinite power of the sovereign constituted not only the ideal, but the real limit of punishment" (Foucault 1979:50). The sovereign's power did not reach beyond the dust of the assassin, making it finite and therefore, according to Foucault, vulnerable.

The disappearances in Argentina were so terrifying exactly because they were not public but intensely private. Violent death was taken away from the eye and control of the people, confined to the secrecy of the detention centers, and spread through society. Fear of the military did not diminish as it was taken out of the public arena but it increased, through the conversion from public into secret into private. The continued absence of the disappeared son, daughter, husband, or wife etched a silhouette in the homes of surviving family members that had lasting political and psychological effects (see APDH 1987; ICIHI 1986; Kordan et al. 1988). The disappearances absorbed the political consciousness of the relatives into a desperate search (see Hagelin 1984; Herrera 1987). The social problems of Argentine society that had impelled people to become politically active dwarfed in comparison to the disappearance of loved ones. The initial paralysis made place for political protest. In a convoluted way, the repressive attempt to silence the political opposition in Argentina had the reverse effect. Human rights organizations emerged during the military dictatorship that dedicated all their political energy to public protest.

Even though many relatives had a premonition that the disappeared had been killed, it was difficult to reconcile oneself with such fatality. There was no body to grieve over, and the mourning process was intertwined with guilt feelings. Mourning meant abandoning the disappeared and surrendering to the conditions created by the military junta. This suffering dispersed in all directions of people's existence. The victimized relatives felt guilty about their suffering, and had to justify their public protests, while the victimizers claimed innocence in the absence of a corpse. Victory and omnipotence were instilled as defeat and fear. Disappearance extended war and torture into civil society and the hereafter.

The strategy of obliterating all physical traces of the disappeared continued with different means after the guerrilla insurgency had been defeated and the overall military repression of Argentine society began to lessen. Two official attempts were made to have the disappeared pronounced dead in absence of a corpse. The military junta issued a law in September 1979 that declared all persons presumed dead who had disappeared between 6 November 1974 and 6 September 1979. They hoped that this decree would end the insistent appeals by human rights organizations. After their 1982 defeat in the Falklands/Malvinas War, the ruling military junta was forced to step down and hand power to the interim government of General Reynoldo Bignone. This interim government published a final report in April 1983 about the 1976–1982 dictatorship and declared once again all disappeared as presumed dead (San Martino de Dromi 1988:343, 360; Somos, 1983, no. 346, p. 15).

At the same time, General Bignone secretly ordered the destruction of all documentation related to persons who had been detained during the 1976–1982 dictatorship, thus preventing the verification of the presumption of death made in their official report. When Raúl Alfonsín assumed power in December 1983, he installed a commission to inquire into the whereabouts of the disappeared. This commission stated in a letter to Alfonsín that its task was "hindered by an essential lack of documentary information regarding the specific operational orders of the repression, the identification of those arrested, prosecuted, sentenced, freed or killed, and the places where they were held or should have been given a decent burial" (CONADEP 1986:264).

I have now given tactical, strategic, legal, and political reasons for making the corpses of political

detainees disappear, but what is the cultural significance? What is the cultural bias, referred to in the 1980 report of the American embassy in Buenos Aires, that made the Argentine military prefer the practice of disappearance? And why did the military continue to conceal the disappeared after the dirty war had ended? The French anthropologist Robert Hertz (1960:83) has said that "It is the action of society on the body that gives full reality to the imagined drama of the soul" or, in the rephrasing of Huntington and Metcalf (1979:14), "the fate of the body is a model for the fate of the soul." Thus, a study of how Argentine culture has conceived of the spirit of deceased political opponents can reveal why disappearance became the preferred repressive tactic. How have enemy corpses been treated in other violent domestic conflicts in Argentina?

Reburial at Recoleta National Cemetery

The abuse of the corpses of political opponents is not a recent practice in Argentina. Defeat and terror in nineteenth-century Argentina were intimately tied to the destination of the corpse. Decapitation and the display of their heads on public squares became the fate of many commanders. It was an extreme humiliation that defiled the personal honor of the fallen leader, and damaged the collective honor of his family and political following. The beheading and subsequent exhibition of the trophy were particularly dishonorable because they placed the victim on the level of the native American Indians who often befell the same fate in Argentina. It also symbolized the political dismemberment of the fallen leader from his supporters, and the power of the new rulers. The importance of honor, charisma, and clientalism in these times made decapitation, rather than execution, imprisonment, or exile, the preferred practice of victory. Godoy Cruz, for instance, exhibited the head of the Federalist leader Felipe Alvarez to "serve as a warning to those who have been led astray by his example" (quoted in Halperín Donghi 1975:380). The Chilean caudillo Carrera, who had taken refuge in Argentina, was eventually captured on 31 August 1821 and executed four days later after a summary trial. His head and right arm were sent on display to Mendoza, and his left arm to

San Juan (CGE 1974:283). Felipe Alvarez and Francisco Ramírez were decapitated in the same year. The latter's head was placed in an iron cage and put on display in a church in Santa Fé (Rock 1987:97).

The flight of a party of ragged cavalrymen in 1841 with the decaying body of General Lavalle to prevent it from falling into the hands of General Oribe's enemy troops has become legendary. Ernesto Sábato described their getaway in his novel *On Heroes and Tombs* as follows: "Thirty-five leagues to go still. Three days' march at full gallop, with the corpse that stinks and distills the liquids of putrefaction, with sharpshooters in the rear guard covering their retreat, comrades who perhaps have little by little been decimated, run through with lances, or had their throats slit. From Jujuy to Huacalera: twenty-four leagues. Only thirty-five leagues to go now, they tell themselves. Only four or five days' march, with God's help" (Sábato 1990:472). As the days pass and the stench becomes unbearable, the men decide to remove the bloated flesh, and preserve the general's bones and heart. It would take two full decades before the remains of General Lavalle were repatriated and reburied with national honor at Recoleta cemetery (Frias 1884).

There was a widespread conviction in the nineteenth century, grounded in the Catholic belief that the soul survives after death, that human remains carried a spiritual power that could affect the world of the living. The belief in this spiritual force (*virtus*) can be traced back to medieval times when the remains of saints became relics for the believers (Angenendt 1994:155–8; Snoek 1995:11–20). Just as saints were believed to heal medieval worshippers because their relics contained a life force, so the remains of slain commanders in nineteenth-century Argentina continued to provide strength to their comrades and inflict harm on their enemies. The mutilation of enemy corpses was regarded as a way to disperse, although not to destroy, the spiritual force of the deceased.[8]

This same fear of the spirit of the dead can also be found in the terrible curse placed on Juan Manuel de Rosas by José Mármol from his exile in Montevideo on 25 May 1843: "Not even the dust from your bones will America have" (Mármol 1894:58). A similar belief is expressed by Sarmiento about Facundo Quiroga, a caudillo who together with Rosas was vilified in Sarmiento's literary indictment *Civilization and Barbarism*. Sarmiento went so far as to evoke the spirit of Facundo Quiroga to reveal the ills of the Argentine nation: "Terrible shadow of Facundo! I am going to conjure you up so that, shaking the blood-stained dust from your ashes, you will arise to explain to us the secret life an internal convulsions that tear at the entrails of a noble people! You possess the secret! Reveal it to us! . . . Facundo has not died; he is alive in the popular traditions, in the Argentine politics and revolutions; in Rosas, his heir, his alter ego: his soul has passed to this other mold, more finished and perfect" (Sarmiento 1986:7–8). The belief that the spirit of a dead person could pass into a living person turned the corpse into an object of contestation, and its ultimate destination became a matter of great political significance. Sarmiento's fear about the continued influence of Facundo's spirit on Argentine political life seemed to come true. One year after his assassination in 1835 at Barranco Yaco, Facundo's remains were exhumed from the cemetery of Córdoba at the express order of Rosas. The bones were cleansed, disinfected, perfumed, and reburied in Buenos Aires (*Buenos Aires Nos Cuenta*, no. 5, pp. 20–2).[9] What had been despised could now be revered and honored. The same spiritual force that used to be feared was now believed to be beneficial to the nation. At Recoleta cemetery Facundo joined the many military commanders who had fought in the nineteenth-century civil wars. The remains of other illustrious Argentines who died in places such as Washington, Paris, Montevideo, and Santiago de Chile – many of them in exile and some others by accident – were also exhumed and reburied at Recoleta. In this way, the cemetery became eventually the pantheon of the nation, and the life force of those buried there continued to infuse Argentine society.

Just as Durkheim has said that society worshipped itself in religion, so the Argentine nation seemed to represent and celebrate itself at the Recoleta cemetery. To be reburied at Recoleta meant to achieve immortality in the eyes of the Argentine people. This immortality was achieved by the ceremonial reburial and, as a consequence, by the continued presence of the reburied person's ossified remains and eternal spirit in the public place. Their life force became embodied in the people who visited the grave, while its political effects were determined by the strength of conviction of their ideological adherents.

At first sight, Recoleta seems very much like a late eighteenth-century Parisian cemetery. "[The memorials] were to be 'a source of emulation for posterity' to inspire visitors to the cemetery to equal or excel the deeds or accomplishments of their predecessors. The cemetery, then, was to become a school of virtue" (Etlin 1984:43). Yet, Recoleta turns into a disturbing source of incessant political conflict when understood within the context of the place of the dead in the world of the living. Mortal enemies are buried next to one another, and victims rest in the same cemetery as their assassins. Facundo is buried there together with his slayers. Rosas rests there, and so do Sarmiento, Mármol, and many other adversaries he had forced into exile. Their reburial at Recoleta did not represent their reconciliation in death but the reinvigoration of their ideas. These ceremonial reburials encouraged political adversaries to believe that the ideological battles of the past had not yet been decided and that their opposed political spirits still resonated among the Argentine people. Recoleta cemetery became in this way as much a source as a metaphor of continued political strife in Argentina.

Repatriation and Reburial in the Twentieth Century

The Argentine political obsession with corpses and their spirits continued well into the twentieth century, albeit different in form and meaning. Beheading became replaced by disappearance as the practice of terror and intimidation inflicted on political opponents and surviving relatives. The disappearance of the body of Evita Duarte de Perón, one of the most prominent and charismatic figures in twentieth-century Argentine politics, illustrates the preoccupation with the dead body in Argentine political culture.[10] Her embalmed body was missing for more than a decade and its bizarre wanderings can be compared to those of General Lavalle in the nineteenth century.

Evita died on 26 July 1952. For two weeks, an estimated 65,000 mourners a day passed by her body

in state at the headquarters of the labor union confederation CGT in Buenos Aires. After months of dedicated work, the body was preserved in a perfect state by a Spanish embalmer. A 1955 coup d'état ended the official Evita cult and the glorification of Perón. Their names were removed from buildings, streets, squares, and public works. Evita's embalmed body was taken from the trade union headquarters under protest of its embalmer, Doctor Ara. Lieutenant Colonel Moore Koenig, who was in charge of the operation, responds in the fictionalized account *Santa Evita* by Eloy Martínez: "You know very well what is at stake ... It is not the cadaver of that woman but the destiny of Argentina. Or both, which to many people seems the same. Look how the dead and useless body of Eva Duarte has become confused with the country ... [By] embalming it, you moved history from its place. You left history inside. You realize that whoever has this woman, has the country in its fist?" (Martínez 1995:34).

It would take more than two decades before the corpse of Eva Perón came to rest in a tomb at Recoleta cemetery. The officers entrusted in 1955 with the disappearance of the body were at a loss about what to do. At this point, fact and fiction become entwined in a complex tangle. However, it can be documented from several sources that the mummified body was shipped out of the country in 1957. Eloy Martínez tells the uncorroborated story that a number of identical coffins, all but one containing wax casts of the real body, were sent to different places in the world to conceal the true whereabouts of Evita's remains.

In 1970, a commando force of Montoneros guerrillas first kidnapped and later executed General Aramburu. Aramburu had been responsible for the overthrow of Perón in 1955. His summary execution was perceived by many Peronists as a deed of justice. The disappearance and profanation of Evita's body were among the list of charges. One year later, a public notary handed President Lanusse a letter written by General Aramburu in 1957 stating that Evita's corpse had been buried secretly in Milan. Supposedly, the body was first flown to Buenos Aires for examination, and then returned to Perón, who was living in exile in Madrid at the time. The embalmed body remained in his house for several years. Purportedly, the spiritist López Rega burned candles and spoke incantations as María Estela, Perón's third wife, lay atop the coffin to receive Evita's spiritual energy. The nineteenth-century belief in the life force of human remains continued unshaken in occultist circles, and was even embraced by the future head of state.

Perón returned to Argentina in 1973 to head the government as president with his wife as vice president. Perón died in 1974 and was succeeded by María Estela Martínez de Perón. In mid-October 1974, a Montoneros task force kidnapped the body of General Aramburu from the Recoleta cemetery as ransom for Evita's embalmed corpse, which had remained in Perón's Spanish residence. Aramburu's coffin was returned a few hours after Evita's body was repatriated on 17 November 1974 (Gillespie 1982:183). Perón's widow, María Estela, placed Evita next to the embalmed body of Perón at her presidential residence in Olivos. When the military overthrew María Estela Martínez de Perón in March 1976, they handed Evita's body to her two sisters, who reburied her at the family tomb at Recoleta cemetery (Anderson 1993:121; Martínez 1995; Page 1983:344, 424–5, 500; *Somos*, 1984, no. 415, pp. 46–9; Taylor 1979: 69–71).

The strange journey of Evita's body has the quality of a phantasmagorical story, were it not that the documented wanderings of the embalmed body and the disputes over its resting place reveal the continued importance of human remains and their burial in Argentine political culture. The 1934 and 1975 attempts to retrieve the remains of Juan Manuel de Rosas from Great Britain provide additional proof of the importance of the body, the spirit, and their reburial in Argentine political culture.[11]

The political right considered the repatriation of the remains of Rosas in 1934 as an appeal to authoritarian rule. These fervent Rosistas were convinced that world capitalism and parliamentary democracy were in a major crisis. Fascism would replace these outdated systems in the entire world. Just as Rosas had pacified the country after decades of civil war, so a new strong leader would protect Argentina against the threat of communism. As one of the proponents of repatriation said in 1934, "It has been exactly one hundred years since we gave birth to this same

illness, and it was precisely the iron hand of Rosas which ended the dissolute anarchy" (Manuel Gálvez, quoted in Barletta and Amézola 1992:26–7). The opponents of repatriation feared the reincarnation of Rosas's political spirit in his right-wing heirs: "The most serious is not to bring the ashes, but to bring his spirit. . . . Bringing his remains would not mean anything, if it would not imply giving amnesty to a tyrant. The Argentine people must know that to give him amnesty is to make way for his imitators. History is not only a science concerned with texts, but history is also the spirit of times in the heart of generations. To bring his remains is to awaken the spirit that gave them life" (Ricardo Rojas, quoted in Barletta and Amézola 1992:30–1). The repatriation of Rosas's remains was debated with great intensity in the Argentine press but never became official policy.

The issue of repatriation arose again four decades later, but the political discourse changed. Whereas the 1934 debate evolved around the rehabilitation of Rosas and his political ideas, the 1973–1974 congressional debates were embedded in a general discourse about the similarities between Perón and Rosas. Both leaders had been forced into exile, had protected the sovereignty of Argentina against imperialist incursions, and had ruled with the support of the popular masses. Just as in the mid-1950s, the opponents of repatriation continued to denounce Perón as the "second tyrant" who thrived on mob rule and a hostile attitude toward the United States. The Rosista historian José María Rosa rebutted that "The hatred towards Rosas . . . is the best homage to his memory, because it demonstrates that his political ideas are still current" (quoted in Barletta and Amézola 1992:45). The repatriation of Rosas's remains was approved by Congress in October 1974 and authorized by the government of María Estela de Perón in June 1975. The diplomatic efforts by the Argentine embassy in Great Britain were suspended three months later because of the spiraling political violence in Argentina (Barletta and Amézola 1992:40–1).

The twentieth-century belief in the survival after death of political ideas evoked by the presence of human remains is a continuation of the nineteenth-century religious conviction that enemy corpses may possess a vengeful spiritual force, but there is a noticeable shift in meaning. In the nineteenth century, there was a belief in the spirit as a supernatural energy – a soul or *virtus* – which could pass between organic substances. In the twentieth century, the spirit becomes a metaphor for the ideas associated with the remains of the deceased. Notwithstanding this reinterpretation of the spirit, the cultural focus and political rituals that surround it have remained remarkably similar. Victors in both centuries believe that reburial would turn the enemy dead into martyrs and invigorate their spirit, so they resorted to mutilation and disappearance as repressive practices.

This treatment of enemy corpses betrays the continued cultural belief in a relation between body and spirit, and the great significance of a proper funeral. If reburial symbolizes the transition of the soul from the land of the living to the land of the dead ancestors, as Hertz (1960:78–81) has argued, then the unceremonial burial of the hidden corpses of tens of thousands of Argentines implies that the spirits of the deceased must be still wandering through the misty passage between life and death. The great efforts that went into reburying Juan Lavalle, Juan Manuel de Rosas, Evita Perón, and many other illustrious Argentines at Recoleta cemetery provide a cultural explanation why surviving relatives searched for the remains of the victims of Argentine state terror in the 1970s.

Contested Exhumations and Revolutionary Protest

The first evidence of the mass executions that had occurred during the dirty war surfacd in late October 1982, only months after the Falklands/Malvinas War. Eighty-eight unmarked graves with an estimated four hundred unidentified bodies were found at the park cemetery of Grand Bourg near Buenos Aires. The gruesome discovery was made during the exhumation of the skeletal remains of the union leader Miguel Angel Sosa, who had disappeared in 1976. On the evening of 25 May 1976, his naked body was found floating in the Reconquista River. It showed obvious signs of torture. The police established Sosa's identity, did not notify his relatives, and buried him as an unidentified corpse. The 1982 exhumation was made at the request of relatives

who had been tipped off in 1981 by an employee of the ministry of the interior (Cohen Salama 1992:60–62; *Somos*, 1982, no. 319, p. 11). The effect of the discovery on the Argentine public was devastating. There was both disbelief and anger. Soon, more mass graves were opened and the bullet-ridden skulls were exhibited on the edge of their makeshift graves in what was called a "horror show." The display of piles of bones and perforated skulls revealed to the stunned Argentines the horrors of the military regime as well as their own mortality and the chance that they could have very well met the same fate.

The Madres de Plaza de Mayo, a human rights organization consisting of hundreds of mothers of the disappeared, believed in October 1982 that the exhumations would give the disappeared a name and an identity.[12] At last, the hastily interred bodies would be wrested from anonymity and given a proper burial. As new mass graves continued to be opened, but the identification of the victims failed to be made because of improperly performed exhumations that destroyed crucial evidence, the Madres began to raise questions about the sense of these disinterments. Its president, Hebe de Bonafini, expressed in January 1984 the conviction that "there is sufficient proof to send a great number of those guilty of this horror to prison," but she had doubts about the political will to prosecute them (*Humor*, 1982, no. 92, p. 47; *Somos*, 1984, no. 382, p. 20). The Madres' faith in the justice system declined further when the Alfonsín government decided that the nine commanders of the three military juntas of 1976–1982 were to be tried under martial law by the Supreme Court of the Armed Forces. The Madres continued their rounds around the Plaza de Mayo on Thursday afternoons at 3:30 as they had been doing since April 1977.[13] They placed white scarves on their heads, walked arm in arm, and talked to the sympathizers who continued to join their thirty-minute protest.

Sometime during the second half of 1984, the Madres de Plaza de Mayo began to formulate their opposition to the exhumations, and this was the principal cause of their separation into two independent organizations in 1986.[14] Reflecting on the intense soul-searching in 1984 about which position to take on the exhumations, Hebe de Bonafini has said: "It cost us weeks and weeks of meetings at which there were many tears and much despair, because the profound Catholic formation of our people creates almost a need to have a dead body, a burial, and a Mass" (*Madres*, 1987, no. 37, p. 10).[15] Despite the anguish, the de Bonafini group decided to keep the wounds inflicted by the disappearances open to resist a national process of forgetting. "It has been eleven years of suffering, eleven years that have not been relieved in any sense. Many want the wound to dry so that we will forget. We want it to continue bleeding, because this is the only way that one continues to have strength to fight . . . But, above all, it is necessary that this wound bleeds so that the assassins will be condemned, as they deserve, and that what has happened will not happen again. This is the commitment in the defense of life which the Madres have taken upon themselves" (*Madres*, 1987, no. 29, p. 1).

In December 1984, the de Bonafini group condemned the exhumations as a government scheme to have them accept the presumption of death of all disappeared. The Madres demanded that first the assassins had to be identified before any further exhumations were to be carried out (*Madres*, 1984, no. 1, p. 2). Their position was strengthened by a parcel received on 13 November 1984 by Mrs. Rubinstein, whose daughter Patricia had disappeared on 7 February 1977. An accompanying letter from the so-called Condor Legion read: "Dear Madam: As the culmination of the incessant search for your daughter Patricia, we have decided to send you only part of what remains of her, but which shall undoubtedly satisfy your yearning to reunite earlier with your dear daughter than foreseen by Jehovah" (*Madres*, 1984, no. 1, p. 15). A forensic examination determined that the bones belonged to a man between twenty and forty years of age. In the eyes of the Madres, the perpetrators were using the fate of the disappeared as a bargaining chip. If a deal could be struck that would end all legal prosecution and public protests, then they would be willing to reveal the makeshift resting places of the disappeared.

A new argument against forensic investigations arose in 1986. The de Bonafini group protested against proposed legislation to impose a statute of limitations on the ongoing depositions against mili-

tary officers accused of human rights violations. They argued that since an exhumation only determined the cause of death, but did not identify the executioner, any future prosecution would become impossible because of a ten-year statute of limitations. Only by providing a legal status to disappearance, comparable to a kidnapping, could legal action be taken against the guilty without any time restrictions (*Madres*, 1986, no. 19, p. 16). By mid-1986, belief in the prosecution of the hundreds of military officers accused of serious violations was declining rapidly. The government had prepared legislation to impose a final date on the presentation of court depositions (*ley de Punto Final*), while the outcome of the trial against the nine junta members had not satisfied the Madres. Their ideas about forensic investigations had changed from personal hope to legal justice, and ended in disillusionment and defiance. Their opposition to the exhumations turned from a legal into a political argument.

The leading figures of the de Bonafini group were of course well aware of the psychological toll of the enduring uncertainty and had a team of psychotherapists at hand to provide assistance. The Madres never opposed individual exhumations when asked for by relatives, but they remained firmly against the opening of mass graves and the performance of unsolicited identifications. They realized that the recuperation of the remains would allow relatives to grieve for their dead, but they regarded the deliberate setting in motion of this mourning process as a sinister ploy to achieve resignation and depoliticization among the surviving relatives. Mourning would break the solidarity of the Madres and produce a reconciliatory attitude. Continued political protest weighed more heavily than individual relief because anxiety was the hinge of memory and oblivion.

Since 1988, the issue of exhumations fell in the background of attention, with the exception of late 1989 when the remains of Marcelo Gelman were being exhumed. "We know that they are exhuming cadavers. We are against these exhumations because we don't want our children to die. Our children cannot be enclosed in tombs, because they are free and revolutionary" (Hebe de Bonafini, *Página 12*, 22 December 1989). The inhibition of mourning is supposed to transform the continued anguish into a fight for the ideals of their disappeared sons and daughters. The Madres want to keep the disappeared alive by leaving their remains unidentified in mass graves, and divulge their ideals instead. "They have interred their bodies it doesn't matter where, but their spirit, their solidarity, and their love for the people can never be buried and forgotten" (Hebe de Bonafini, *Madres*, 1989, no. 58, p. 11). Reburial would confine them to the world of the dead, instead of allowing their spirit to influence the dealings of the living, very much as friend and foe believed that the spirit of Evita, Facundo, and Rosas could influence the affairs of the world.

The position of the Madres of the de Bonafini group is remarkable. They did not only go against the cultural grain of Argentine society with its profound Catholic formation, as they themselves realized very well, but they also radically changed the political significance of reburials and the spiritual meaning of the human remains. Body, spirit, and funeral were dissociated. The ossified remains lost their meaning, and so did their reburial. The spirit as metaphor for political ideas was exalted as the only thing worthy of survival in the embodiment of kindred political spirits.

In 1988, as most military officers accused of gross human rights violations had become immune to prosecution as a result of the June 1987 Due Obedience Law (*ley de Obediencia Debida*), the de Bonafini group started on a path of ideological radicalization that made them embrace the political project attributed to the disappeared. They denounced the political system as corrupt and ethically bankrupt, and talked about the need to form grassroots organizations in factories, schools, universities, and poor neighborhoods because "there will be no liberation without revolution. Our children took this road. Today the Madres follow it. Tomorrow it will be the entire population. In order not to forget, not to forgive, not to succumb and to fight for victory" (Hebe de Bonafini, *Madres*, 1988, no. 43, p. 16). By late 1988, the idea arose that the Madres have to "socialize their maternity" (*Madres*, 1988, no. 48, p. 17) and adopt the suffering of all victims of political violence in the world. "When we understood that our children were not going to appear, we socialized

motherhood and felt that we are the mothers of everybody, that all are our children" (Hebe de Bonafini, *Madres*, 1989, no. 53, p. 17). Pressing social problems such as widespread poverty, declining social services, high unemployment, poor benefits for the aged, government corruption, police brutality, and the privatization of state companies have become a political platform to pursue the revolutionary ideals of their disappeared children.

The development of the arguments against exhumation and reburial demonstrates a continuous refinement of the understanding of the consequences of state terror and its many ramifications in the political life of the Argentines. In the eyes of the Madres de Plaza de Mayo, reburials become synonymous with spiritual and physical death. Reburials destroy the living memory of the disappeared, and inter them in an enclosed remembrance. The Madres fear that the disappeared will be forgotten, and that they will be relegated to an increasingly more distant past, to the time of the dictatorship and the dirty war. Instead, they try to keep the spirit of their disappeared children alive by reincarnating their political ideals. This position led the Madres to condemn the exhumation of Marcelo Gelman: "With these tactics they implement the obliteration and reconciliation demanded by the assassins, the Church and a few Montoneros. These tactics are repudiated by the people" (*Sur*, 7 January 1990). The de Bonafini group of Madres condemns the very exhumations that could give them an answer to their original plea about the whereabouts of the disappeared.

Reburial and Reconciliation

The relatives of exhumed and identified missing persons have generally felt a great sense of relief at finally being able to reunite with the remains of their loved ones. Berta Schubaroff expressed this sentiment at seeing her son's remains in the following way: "I felt that I was emotional because I found my son. I kissed him again. I kissed all his bones, touched him, caressed him. But the emotion confounded with the pain, because once I found him, he turned out to be dead. So I cried the death of my son, and those thirteen years of search vanished. I can't relate anymore to this period" (quoted in Cohen Salama 1992:249). Juan Gelman confessed to similar sentiments a few weeks later: "I feel that I have been able to rescue him from the fog" (quoted in Cohen Salama 1992:250). But what did he rescue from the fog? His son's remains or his spirit? The remembrance of the political assassination or his son's ideals? Was Juan Gelman talking about the fog that drifts between the land of the living and the land of the dead? Or was he referring to similar state terror practices during World War II, in particular the 1941 *Nacht und Nebel* (night and fog) decree with which General Keitel ordered the disappearance of the Jews on the eastern front? A similar historical spirit may have persuaded Berta Schubaroff to bury her son in a Jewish cemetery out of vindication, even though she never practiced the Jewish faith. She had become conscious of her Jewish heritage when she learnt that her son's tormentors had treated him as a "shit Jew" (*judío de mierda*), and she therefore wanted to demonstrate her forgotten identity openly through a Jewish reburial (Cohen Salama 1992:250).

The feelings of Marcelo Gelman's parents, their sense of having rescued their son in medias res, and the detachment from the thirteen-year search experienced upon caressing the bones, are feared by the de Bonafini group of Madres. Most human rights organizations, however, have become convinced of the judicial, historical, political, and psychological importance of forensic investigations. Exhumations provide evidence for legal prosecution, give historical proof of the human rights violations committed by the military, and can provide forensic evidence about disappeared women who gave birth in captivity. Exhumations also make reburials possible that allow surviving relatives to begin a process of mourning. Reburials rehabilitate the disappeared because the public ceremony gives a deference to the deceased which had been denied by the military, precisely because they believed that they were subversive of society and thus undeserving of its public respect.

Robert Hertz has argued that reburials serve three general purposes: "to give burial to the remains of the deceased, to ensure the soul peace and access to the land of the dead, and finally to free the living from the obligations of mourning" (Hertz 1960:54). These purposes seem to have been served in Argentina as much for the nineteenth-century generals and statesmen who came to rest at Recoleta cemetery as for the nearly two hundred disappeared who were exhumed, identified, and finally reburied. The torn fabric of society is restored by funerary rituals, the deceased are reconciled with their forebears, and their souls come to rest in sacred ground, only to be recaptured periodically in commemorations. However, the violent death suffered by the disappeared and their political role in Argentine history accord them a special position that continues to infuse society with potential conflict. Reburials turn from rituals of remembrance into acts of restoration for their comrades-in-faith, and into acts of defiance and public provocation for their political opponents. It is this political significance which caused the persistent efforts to repatriate Juan Manuel de Rosas and rebury him at Recoleta cemetery, and which gave political meaning to the reburial of Marcelo Gelman at La Tablada Jewish cemetery. The fight about the remains of victims of violence thus becomes a struggle about the survival of their political spirit and the reconstruction of their legacy to Argentine history and society.

The belief in the eternity of the spirit, the imperishability of the bones, and the human need to mourn the dead are indeed as deeply engrained in Argentine society as they are in most cultures. The political practice of obstructing funerary rituals prevents people from coming to terms with their dead and from reconciling eventually with their opponents. This continued effort to hold the surviving relatives hostage to their anguish led one group of the Madres de Plaza de Mayo to forego all claims to the human remains – instead of clinging to the desperate hope to ever recover them – and to appropriate the political ideals of the disappeared. Political animosities have thus become further entrenched, and continue to kindle the memory of past humiliations and injustices. State terror will only come to an end when the perpetrators of violence acknowledge their common humanity with their victims – the living as well as the dead – and by returning the dead for proper reburial.

NOTES

1   Juan Gelman was until 1978 a leading member of the Montoneros guerrilla organization. He left Buenos Aires in 1975 after receiving death threats from the Argentine Anticommunist Alliance (AAA), a right-wing paramilitary organization run from the ministry of social welfare headed by López Rega, the right hand of Perón's widow María Estela Martínez de Perón.

2   María Claudia Iruretagoyena was seven months pregnant when she was abducted, and she was still seen alive on October 7, about one week after her husband Marcelo had already been killed. Her mother-in-law Berta Schubaroff became a member of the Grandmothers of the Plaza de Mayo (Abuelas de Plaza de Mayo), and continued to search for a surviving grandchild.

3   In the nineteenth century, the Unitarists pursued a strong central government under the hegemony of the port city of Buenos Aires. They wanted to continue to enrich themselves with the profitable foreign trade, and the import and export tax revenues. The Federalists desired a federal government which would give greater political autonomy to the provinces, and protect the rudimentary local industries against foreign imports. Rosas championed the Federalist cause, but his ouster in 1852 reestablished the dominance of Buenos Aires. In the twentieth century, the Unitarist ideas lived on in liberal politicians who wanted to open the Argentine economy to foreign investment, while the Federalist ideas were embraced by protectionist nationalists.

4   An official decree from 14 August 1956 ordered the publication of a "black book about the second tyranny" that would divulge to the Argentine people the corruption and misgovernment of Perón. This book outlines in detail the historical analogies between Rosas and Perón (Comisión de Afirmación 1987:25–34).

5   Rosas died in 1877 and entered the clause in his testament that his remains could only be reburied in Argentina if a 1857 sentence would be revoked that had declared him to be a traitor to the country (*Buenos Aires Nos Cuenta*, no. 13, p. 107; Martínez 1978:115–27).

6   The reburial of Rosas had been carefully orchestrated. Three weeks before the historic event, on 11 September, Menem had attended the commemoration in the province of San Juan of the 101st anniversary of the death of Domingo Sarmiento. Sarmiento and Rosas had been archrivals for decades. Rosas had forced Sarmiento into exile for championing the Unitarist cause, while Sarmiento had reviled the Federalist Rosas in his memorable denouncement *Civilization and Barbarism* (Sarmiento 1986).

7   The pardoned officers consisted of military commanders who had been indicted for human rights violations, junta members convicted for waging the 1982 Falklands/Malvinas War, and the leaders of several military mutinies in 1986 and 1987. The members of the 1976–1982 military juntas who had been convicted for their repressive regime and the disappearances of the 1970s remained in prison, but were pardoned in December 1990.

8   It is plausible to assume that the desecration of the corpse was also related to the Catholic belief in Purgatory and the survival of the soul after death. The mutilated were believed to suffer horribly as they were cleansed of their earthly sins. Natalie Zemon Davis comes to the same doctrinal explanation in her interpretation of the mutilation of corpses by Catholic crowds during the sixteenth-century religious wars against the Huguenots in France. Protestant crowds were particularly keen on torturing Catholic priests, but were indifferent to the corpse, possibly because "the souls of the dead experience immediately Christ's presence or the torments of the damned, and thus the dead body is no longer so dangerous or important an object to the living" (Davis 1975:179). On the other hand, the exhumation, mutilation, and public display of the mummified remains of priests, nuns, and saints during the Spanish civil war was an iconoclastic attack by the Republican left on the conservative Church and the Nationalists (Lincoln 1989: 117–27). Mutilation must be distinguished from the medieval practice of multiplying saintly relics through dismemberment (*dismembratio*) (Snoek 1995:22–4).

9   In 1708, a small chapel was built at the present location of the cemetery for the order of the Holy Recollect (*Santa Recolección*). The barefoot friars who lived in reclusive meditation were called *recoletos*, and the church that was erected in 1732 was popularly called Recoleta. Deceased members of important families and brotherhoods were buried inside the church, while others were laid to rest in the adjoining holy ground.

10 The body of Juan Domingo Perón was also not left undisturbed. In July 1987, someone broke into Perón's tomb at Chacarita cemetery and stole the hands from the corpse, the very hands Perón used to raise in his characteristic pose during his speeches from

the balcony of the presidential palace as he received the cheers and chants of the Peronist masses.

11   Commissions to recover the remains of Rosas were also installed in 1917 and 1954, but these attempts did not reach congress (Barletta and Amézola 1992:50).

12   The following books provide historical background to the Madres de Plaza de Mayo: Bousquet (1984); Diago (1988); Fisher (1989); Guzman Bouvard (1994); Oria (1987); and Sánchez (1985).

13   The first protest was held on Saturday afternoon, 13 April 1977, but was moved initially to Friday and soon to Thursday afternoons. The city was deserted on Saturdays, and Friday was believed to be an unlucky day (Simpson and Bennett 1985:157–8).

14   The group that split itself off from the main organization called itself the Linea Fundadora (Founding Line) because several of its members belonged to the original group of fourteen women who began the public protest in 1977. They cooperated with the CONADEP investigation and supported the exhumations. The main group, which continued under the name Madres de Plaza de Mayo, condemned any cooperation with the government as a political concession and opposed the exhumations.

15   Elena Nicoletti, a member of the psychological team of the Madres, has argued that the Madres have rejected all mortuary rituals of Western culture because these rites cannot initiate a genuine mourning process in the absence of any certainty about the fate of the disappeared (Nicoletti 1988:116).

BIBLIOGRAPHY

Andersen, Martin Edwin, 1993 *Dossier Secreto: Argentina's Desaparecidos and the Myth of the "Dirty War."* Boulder, Colo.: Westview Press.

Angenendt, Arnold, 1994 *Heilige und Reliquien: Die Geschichte ihres Kultes von frühen Christentum bis zur Gegenwart.* Munich: Beck Verlag.

APDH, 1987 *La Desaparición: Crimen Contra la Humanidad.* Buenos Aires: Asamblea Permanente por los Derechos Humanos.

Barletta, Ana María, and Gonzalo de Amézola, 1992 "Repatriación: Modelo para armar. Tres fechas en la repatriación de los restos de Juan Manuel de Rosas (1934–1974–1989)." *Estudios e Investigaciones*, 12, pp. 7–61. La Plata: Universidad Nacional de la Plata.

Bousquet, Jean-Pierre, 1984 *Las Locas de la Plaza de Mayo.* Córdoba: Fundación para la Democracia en Argentina.

CGE (Comando General del Ejército), 1974 *Política Seguida con el Aborigen* (1820–1852). Buenos Aires: Círculo Militar.

Cohen Salama, Mauricio, 1992 *Tumbas anónimas.* Buenos Aires: Catálogos.

Comisión de Afirmación de la Revolución Libertadora, 1987 *Libro Negro de la Segunda Tiranía.* Fourth edition. Buenos Aires.

CONADEP, 1986 *Nunca Más: The Report of the Argentine National Commission on the Disappeared.* New York: Farrar, Straus and Giroux.

Davis, Natalie Zemon, 1975 *Society and Culture in Early Modern France.* Stanford: Stanford University Press.

Diago, Alejandro, 1988 *Conversando con las Madres de Plaza de Mayo: Hebe de Bonafini, Memória y Esperanza.* Buenos Aires: Ediciones Dialectica.

Etlin, Richard A., 1984 *The Architecture of Death: The Transformation of the Cemetery in Eighteenth-Century Paris.* Cambridge: MIT Press.

Fisher, Jo, 1989 *Mothers of the Disappeared.* Boston: South End Press.

Foucault, Michel, 1979 *Discipline and Punish: The Birth of the Prison.* New York: Vintage Books.

Frias, Félix, 1884 *Escritos y Discursos.* Vol. 3. Buenos Aires: Imprenta y Libreria de Mayo.

García, Prudencio, 1995 *El Drama de la Autonomía Militar: Argentina Bajo las Juntas Militares.* Madrid: Alianza Editores.

Gillespie, Richard, 1982 *Soldiers of Perón: Argentina's Montoneros.* Oxford: Clarendon Press.

Guest, Iain, 1990 *Behind the Disappearances: Argentina's Dirty War Against Human Rights and the United Nations.* Philadelphia: University of Pennsylvania Press.

Guzman Bouvard, Marguerite, 1994 *Revolutionizing Motherhood: The Mothers of the Plaza de Mayo.* Wilmington, Del.: Scholarly Resources.

Hagelin, Ragnar, 1984 *Mi Hija Dagmar.* Buenos Aires: Sudamericana/Planeta.

Halperín Donghi, Tulio, 1975 *Politics, Economics and Society in Argentina in the Revolutionary Period.* Cambridge: Cambridge University Press.

Herrera, Matilde, 1987 *José.* Buenos Aires: Editorial Contrapunto.

Hertz, Robert, 1960 *Death and the Right Hand.* Aberdeen: Cohen and West.

Huntington, Richard, and Peter Metcalf, 1979 *Celebrations of Death: The Anthropology of Mortuary Ritual.* Cambridge: Cambridge University Press.

ICIHI (Independent Commission on International Humanitarian Issues), 1986 *Disappeared!* London: Zed Books.

Kordan, Diana R., Lucila I. Edelman, D. M. Lagos, *et al.*, 1988 *Psychological Effects of Political Repression.* Buenos Aires: Sudamericana/Planeta.

Lincoln, Bruce, 1989 *Discourse and the Construction of Society: Comparative Studies of Myth, Ritual, and Classification.* New York: Oxford University Press.

Mármol, José, 1894 *Obra Poéticas y Dramáticas.* Paris: Bouret.

Martínez, Tomás Eloy, 1995 *Santa Evita.* Buenos Aires: Planeta.

—— 1978 *Lugar Común la Muerte.* Caracas: Monte Avila Editores.

Mittelbach, Federico, 1986 *Informe sobre Desaparecidos.* Buenos Aires: Ediciones de la Urraca.

Nicoletti, Elena, 1988 "Missing People: Defect of Signifying Ritual and Clinical Consequences." In *Psychological Effects of Political Repression.* D. Kordon *et al.*, eds. Buenos Aires: Sudamericana/Planeta.

Oria, Piera Paola, 1987 *De la Casa a la Plaza.* Buenos Aires: Editorial Nueva America.

Page, Joseph A., 1983 *Perón: A Biography.* New York: Random House.

Rock, David, 1987 *Argentina, 1516–1987: From Spanish Colonization to Alfonsín.* Berkeley: University of California Press.

Sábato, Ernesto, 1990 *On Heroes and Tombs.* London: Jonathan Cape. (First published 1961).

Sánchez, Matilde, 1985 *Histórias de Vida: Hebe de Bonafini.* Buenos Aires: Fraterna/Del Nuevo Extremo.

San Martino de Dromi, María Laura, 1988 *Historia política Argentina (1955–1988).* Buenos Aires: Editorial Astrea de Alfredo y Ricardo Depalma.

Sarmiento, Domingo F., 1986 *Facundo o Civilización y Barbarie.* Buenos Aires: Biblioteca Ayacucho y Hyspamérica Ediciones Argentina S.A. (First published 1845).

Simpson, John, and Jana Bennett, 1985 *The Disappeared and the Mothers of the Plaza: The Story of the 11,000 Argentinians Who Vanished.* New York: St. Martin's Press.

Snoek, G. J. C., 1995 *Medieval Piety from Relics to the Eucharist: A Process of Mutual Interaction.* Leiden: E. J. Brill.

Taylor, J. M., 1979 *Eva Perón: The Myths of a Woman.* Chicago: University of Chicago Press.

Verbitsky, Horacio, 1995 *El Vuelo.* Buenos Aires: Planeta.

Newspapers and Periodicals

Buenos Aires Nos Cuenta

Humor

La Nación

La Prensa

Madres de Plaza de Mayo

Página 12

Somos

Sur

Part IV

Grief and Mourning

13

The Andaman Islanders

A. R. Radcliffe-Brown

[. . .]

The marriage ceremony and the peace-making dance both afford examples of the custom which the Andamanese have of weeping together under certain circumstances. The principal occasions of this ceremonial weeping are as follows: (1) when two friends or relatives meet after having been for some time parted, they embrace each other and weep together; (2) at the peace-making ceremony the two parties of former enemies weep together, embracing each other; (3) at the end of the period of mourning the friends of the mourners (who have not themselves been mourning) weep with the latter; (4) after a death the relatives and friends embrace the corpse and weep over it; (5) when the bones of a dead man or woman are recovered from the grave they are wept over; (6) on the occasion of a marriage the relatives of each weep over the bride and bridegroom; (7) at various stages of the initiation ceremonies the female relatives of a youth or girl weep over him or her.

First of all it is necessary to note that not in any of the above-mentioned instances is the weeping simply a spontaneous expression of feeling. It is always a rite the proper performance of which is demanded by custom. (As mentioned in an earlier chapter, the Andamanese are able to sit down and shed tears at will.) Nor can we explain the weeping as being an expression of sorrow. It is true that some of the occasions are such as to produce sorrowful feelings (4 and 5, for example), but there are others on which there would seem to be no reason for sorrow but rather for joy. The Andamanese do weep from sorrow and spontaneously. A child cries when he is scolded or hurt; a widow weeps thinking of her recently dead husband. Men rarely weep spontaneously for any reason, though they shed tears abundantly when taking part in the rite. The weeping on the occasions enumerated is therefore not a spontaneous expression of individual emotion but is an example of what I have called ceremonial customs. In certain circumstances men and women are required by custom to embrace one another and weep, and if they neglected to do so it would be an offence condemned by all right-thinking persons.

According to the postulate of method laid down at the beginning of the chapter we have to seek such an explanation of this custom as will account for all the different occasions on which the rite is performed,

From A. R. Radcliffe-Brown, *The Andaman Islanders* (New York: The Free Press, 1964 [1922]).

since we must assume that one and the same rite has the same meaning in whatever circumstances it may take place. It must be noted, however, that there are two varieties of the rite. In the first three instances enumerated above the rite is reciprocal, i.e. two persons or two distinct groups of persons weep together and embrace each other, both parties to the rite being active. In the other four instances it is one-sided; a person or group of persons weeps over another person (or the relics of a person) who has only a passive part in the ceremony. Any explanation, to be satisfactory, must take account of the difference between these two varieties.

I would explain the rite as being an expression of that feeling of attachment between persons which is of such importance in the almost domestic life of the Andaman society. In other words the purpose of the rite is to affirm the existence of a social bond between two or more persons.

There are two elements in the ceremony, the embrace and the weeping. We have already seen that the embrace is an expression, in the Andamans as elsewhere, of the feeling of attachment, i.e. the feeling of which love, friendship, affection are varieties. Turning to the second element of the ceremony, we are accustomed to think of weeping as more particularly an expression of sorrow. We are familiar, however, with tears of joy, and I have myself observed tears that were the result neither of joy nor of sorrow but of a sudden overwhelming feeling of affection. I believe that we may describe weeping as being a means by which the mind obtains relief from a condition of emotional tension, and that it is because such conditions of tension are most common in feelings of grief and pain that weeping comes to be associated with painful feelings. It is impossible here to discuss this subject, and I am therefore compelled to assume without proof this proposition on which my explanation of the rite is based.[1] My own conclusion, based on careful observation, is that in this rite the weeping is an expression of what has been called the tender emotion.[2] Without doubt, on some of the occasions of the rite, as when weeping over a dead friend, the participants are suffering a painful emotion, but this is evidently not so on all occasions. It is true, however, as I shall show, that on every occasion of the rite there is a condition of emotional tension due to the sudden calling into activity of the sentiment of personal attachment.

When two friends or relatives meet after having been separated, the social relation between them that has been interrupted is about to be renewed. This social relation implies or depends upon the existence of a specific bond of solidarity between them. The weeping rite (together with the subsequent exchange of presents) is the affirmation of this bond. The rite, which, it must be remembered, is obligatory, compels the two participants to act as though they felt certain emotions, and thereby does, to some extent, produce those emotions in them. When the two friends meet their first feeling seems to be one of shyness mingled with pleasure at seeing each other again. This is according to the statements of the natives as well as my own observation. Now this shyness (the Andamanese use the same word as they do for "shame") is itself a condition of emotional tension, which has to be relieved in some way. The embrace awakens to full activity that feeling of affection or friendship that has been dormant and which it is the business of the rite to renew. The weeping gives relief to the emotional tension just noted, and also reinforces the effect of the embrace. This it does owing to the fact that a strong feeling of personal attachment is always produced when two persons join together in sharing and simultaneously expressing one and the same emotion.[3] The little ceremony thus serves to dispel the initial feeling of shyness and to reinstate the condition of intimacy and affection that existed before the separation.

In the peace-making ceremony the purpose of the whole rite is to abolish a condition of enmity and replace it by one of friendship. The once friendly relations between the two groups have been interrupted by a longer or shorter period of antagonism. We have seen that the effect of the dance is to dispel the wrath of the one group by giving it free expression. The weeping that follows is the renewal of the friendship. The rite is here exactly parallel to that on the meeting of two friends, except that not two individuals but two groups are concerned, and that owing to the number of persons involved the emotional condition is one of much greater intensity.[4] Here therefore also we see that the rite is an affirmation of solidarity or social union, in this instance between the groups, and that the rule is in its nature such as to make the participants feel that they are bound to each other by ties of friendship.

We now come to a more difficult example of the rite, that at the end of mourning. It will be shown later in the chapter that during the period of mourning the mourners are cut off from the ordinary life of the community. By reason of the ties that still bind them to the dead person they are placed, as it were, outside the society and the bonds that unite them to their group are temporarily loosened. At the end of the mourning period they re-enter the society and take up once more their place in the social life. Their return to the community is the occasion on which they and their friends weep together. In this instance also, therefore, the rite may be explained as having for its purpose the renewal of the social relations that have been interrupted. This explanation will seem more convincing when we have considered in detail the customs of mourning. If it be accepted, then it may be seen that in the first three instances of the rite of weeping (those in which the action is reciprocal) we have conditions in which social relations that have been interrupted are about to be renewed, and the rite serves as a ceremony of aggregation.

Let us now consider the second variety of the rite, and first of all its meaning as part of the ceremony of marriage. By marriage the social bonds that have to that time united the bride and bridegroom to their respective relatives, particularly their female relatives such as mother, mother's sister, father's sister and adopted mother, are modified. The unmarried youth or girl is in a position of dependence upon his or her older relatives, and by the marriage this dependence is partly abolished. Whereas the principal duties of the bride were formerly those towards her mother and older female relatives, henceforth her chief duties in life will be towards her husband. The position of the bridegroom is similar, and it must be noted that his social relations with his male relatives are less affected by his marriage than those with his female relatives. Yet, though the ties that have bound the bride and bridegroom to their relatives are about to be modified or partially destroyed by the new ties of marriage with its new duties and rights they will still continue to exist in a weakened and changed condition. The rite of weeping is the expression of this. It serves to make real (by feeling), in those taking part in it, the presence of the social ties that are being modified.

When the mother of the bride or bridegroom weeps at a marriage she feels that her son or daughter is being taken from her care. She has the sorrow of a partial separation and she consoles herself by expressing in the rite her continued feeling of tenderness and affection towards him in the new condition that he is entering upon. For her the chief result of the rite is to make her feel that her child is still an object of her affection, still bound to her by close ties, in spite of the fact that he or she is being taken from her care.

Exactly the same explanation holds with regard to the weeping at the initiation ceremonies. By these ceremonies the youth (or girl) is gradually withdrawn from a condition of dependence on his mother and older female relatives and is made an independent member of the community. The initiation is a long process that is only completed by marriage. At every stage of the lengthy ceremonies therefore, the social ties that unite the initiate to these relatives are modified or weakened, and the rite of weeping is the means by which the significance of the change is impressed upon those taking part in it. For the mother the weeping expresses her resignation at her necessary loss, and acts as a consolation by making her feel that her son is still hers, though now being withdrawn from her care. For the boy the rite has a different meaning. He realises that he is no longer merely a child, dependent upon his mother, but is now entering upon manhood. His former feelings towards his mother must be modified. That he is being separated from her is, for him, the most important aspect of the matter, and therefore while she weeps he must give no sign of tenderness in return but must sit passive and silent. So also in the marriage ceremony, the rite serves to impress upon the young man and woman that they are, by reason of the new ties that they are forming with one another, severing their ties with their families.

When a person dies the social bonds that unite him to the survivors are profoundly modified. They are not in an instant utterly destroyed, as we shall see better when we deal with the funeral and mourning customs, for the friends and relatives still feel towards the dead person that affection in which they held him when alive, and this has now become a source of deep grief. It is this affection still binding them to him that they express in the rite of weeping over the corpse. Here rite and natural expression of emotion coincide, but it must be noted that the weeping is obligatory, a matter of duty. In this instance, then, the rite is similar to that at marriage and initiation. The man is by death cut off from the society to which he belonged, and from association with his friends, but the latter still feel towards him that attachment that bound them together while he lived, and it is this attachment that they express when they embrace the lifeless corpse and weep over it.

There remains only one more instance of the rite to be considered. When the period of mourning for a dead person is over and the bones are recovered the modification in the relations between the dead and the living, which begins at death, and is, as we shall see, carried out by the mourning customs and ceremonies, is finally accomplished. The dead person is now entirely cut off from the world of the living, save that his bones are to be treasured as relics and amulets. The weeping over the bones must be taken, I think, as a rite of aggregation whereby the bones as representative of the dead person (all that is left of him) are received back into the society henceforth to fill a special place in the social life. It really constitutes a renewal of social relations with the dead person, after a period during which all active social relations have been interrupted owing to the danger in all contact between the living and the dead. By the rite the affection that was once felt towards the dead person is revived and is now directed to the skeletal relics of the man or woman that once was their object. If this explanation seem unsatisfactory, I would ask the reader to suspend his judgment until the funeral customs of the Andamans have been discussed, and then to return to this point.

The proffered explanation of the rite of weeping should now be plain. I regard it as being the affirmation of a bond of social solidarity between those taking part in it, and as producing in them a realisation of that bond by arousing the sentiment of attachment. In some instances the rite therefore serves to renew social relations when they have been interrupted, and in such instances the rite is reciprocal. In others it serves to show the continued existence of the social bond when it is being weakened or modified, as by marriage, initiation or death. In all instances we may say that the purpose of the rite is to bring about a new state of the affective dispositions that regulate the conduct of persons to one another, either by reviving sentiments that have lain dormant, or producing a recognition of a change in the condition of personal relations.

The study of these simple ceremonies has shown us several things of importance. (1) In every instance the ceremony is the expression of an affective state of mind shared by two or more persons. Thus the weeping rite expresses feelings of solidarity, the exchange of presents expresses good-will. (2) But the ceremonies are not spontaneous expressions of feeling; they are all customary actions to which the sentiment of obligation attaches, which it is the duty of persons to perform on certain definite occasions. It is the duty of everyone in a community to give presents at a wedding; it is the duty of relatives to weep together when they meet. (3) In every instance the ceremony is to be explained by reference to fundamental laws regulating the affective life of human beings. It is not our business here to analyse these phenomena but only to satisfy ourselves that they are real. That weeping is an outlet for emotional excitement, that the free expression of aggressive feelings causes them to die out instead of smouldering on, that an embrace is an expression of feelings of attachment between persons: these are the psychological generalisations upon which are based the explanations given above of various ceremonies of the Andamanese. (4) Finally, we have seen that each of the ceremonies serves to renew or to modify in the minds of those taking part in it some one or more of the social sentiments. The peace-making ceremony is a method by which feelings of enmity are exchanged for feelings of friendship. The marriage rite serves to arouse in the minds of the marrying pair a sense of their obligations as married folk, and to bring about in the minds of the witnesses a change of feeling towards the young people such as should properly accompany their change of social status. The weeping and exchange of presents when friends come together is a means of renewing their feelings of attachment to one another. The weeping at marriage, at initiation, and on the occasion of a death is a reaction of defence or compensation when feelings of solidarity are attacked by a partial breaking of the social ties that bind persons to one another.

NOTES

1   In a few words the psycho-physical theory here assumed is that weeping is a substitute for motor activity when the kinetic system of the body (motor centres, thyroid, suprarenals, etc.) is stimulated but no effective action in direct response to the stimulus is possible at the moment. When a sentiment is stimulated and action to which it might lead is frustrated, the resultant emotional state is usually painful, and hence weeping is commonly associated with painful states.

2   McDougall, *Social Psychology*.

3   Active sympathy, the habitual sharing of joyful and painful emotions, is of the utmost importance in the formation of sentiments of personal attachment.

4   It is a commonplace of psychology that a collective emotion, i.e. one felt and expressed at the same moment by a number of persons, is felt much more intensely than an unshared emotion of the same kind.

REFERENCE

McDougall, William 1908. *An Introduction to Social Psychology*. London: Methuen.

14

Metaphors of Mediation in Greek Funeral Laments

Loring M. Danforth

The funeral laments of rural Greece are generally classified as *miroloyia*.[1] In Potamia they are also referred to as *nekratika traghoudhia*, meaning death songs. The most important defining characteristics of these laments are their performance by women at death rituals and their association with the expression of intense grief and sorrow. Greek funeral laments are part of a longstanding oral tradition in which the literary concept of one authentic or correct version of a song does not exist. These laments are composed, performed, and transmitted orally. The degree to which each performance is an original creation or composition varies greatly from one region of Greece to another, and, within any region, from one performer to another.[2]

In Potamia, although several women have the ability to compose very original laments, the vast majority of laments sung are well known to most women. In such cases the variation that exists involves the complexity and the degree of elaboration with which traditional themes are presented. In addition, each time a lament is sung, the proper names, kin terms, and descriptive phrases that fit

the circumstances of the deceased are inserted in the appropriate places. Thus the formulaic phrase "an old man, a kind father" (*enas yerondas ky enas kalos pateras*) may replace "a youth, a handsome young man" (*enas nioutsikos ky enas kalos levendis*). Similarly, any appropriate proper name or kin term can substitute for "my mother" in the verse "My mother is weeping for me with tears and with pain." Finally, certain laments or themes are only appropriate for certain categories of people. A lament suitable for a young girl who has died would not be sung at the funeral of an elderly widow.

Throughout rural Greece, it is the older women who maintain the tradition of singing laments at funerals, memorial services, and exhumations. Given the rapid rate of urbanization and modernization in Greece, it is not surprising that most younger women do not know laments, do not approve of them, and anticipate that they will not be sung at death rites for which they will be responsible in the future. These young women, who belong to an emerging village middle class with aspirations for a more modern and sophisticated way of life,

From Loring M. Danforth, "Metaphors of Mediation in Greek Funeral Laments," in *The Death Rituals of Rural Greece* (Princeton: Princeton University Press, 1982).

regard the singing of laments as a source of embarrassment, indicative of rural backwardness and superstition.[3]

Wives, daughters, mothers, and sisters of the deceased, those who are most moved by his death, do not usually lead the singing of laments, because they are too overcome by grief. They spend much of their time crying, sobbing, and calling out to the deceased. The singing is led by women who are less directly touched by the death, more distant relatives of the deceased or women who are not related to him at all. In Potamia these women are not professional mourners in any sense. They are not paid, nor are they even specifically invited to attend a funeral. They are usually women who have become good singers and have learned many laments because they have had much experience with death. Often the women who lead the singing are themselves in mourning and through their singing express their own grief for their own dead.

After the singing of each verse of a lament there is a break during which women whose grief is most intense cry, sob, shout personal messages to the deceased, or talk emotionally about the recent death. When the women who lead the singing begin the next verse they interrupt these cries and shouts. Then those who are most upset pick up the verse and rejoin the singing. In extreme cases, when the close relatives of the deceased continue to cry and shout and do not resume the lament, they may be angrily instructed to do so by other women. For example, at a funeral in Potamia where the widow of the deceased was wildly hugging and kissing her dead husband, her sister, in an attempt to restrain and calm her, spoke to her sharply: "Don't shout like that! Sit down and cry and sing!"

The women of Potamia generally agree that the singing of laments is preferable to wild shouting and wailing as a means of expressing grief at death rituals. Many women believe that such shouting is physically harmful and may cause illness. It is also likely that during this period of uncontrolled shouting the bereaved relative of the deceased may say something inappropriate and embarrassing. She may, for example, reveal information concerning private family matters which would provoke undesirable gossip.[4]

By contrast the singing of laments eliminates the possibility of revealing embarrassing information, since these laments constitute a public language, a cultural code, for the expression of grief. They provide the bereaved with a set of shared symbols, what Lévi-Strauss (1963:199) has called a social myth, which enables them not only to organize their experience of death in a culturally meaningful way but also to articulate it in a socially approved manner. Women singing laments are communicating in a symbolic language and in the context of a public performance. The goal of a structural analysis of Greek funeral laments is to learn this language in order to understand what is being said about death.

One of the most striking features of Greek funeral laments is the close resemblance they bear to the songs that are sung at weddings throughout rural Greece. In Potamia these wedding songs are called *nifika traghoudhia* or *nifiatika traghoudhia*, literally bridal songs. The classification of songs as *miroloyia* or as *nifika traghoudhia* depends on the context in which they are performed. These two categories of songs resemble each other with regard to their musical form, their narrative structure, and their iconography. So close is this resemblance that many songs can be sung at both death rites and weddings. Of such a song it is said: "You can sing it as a funeral lament, and you can also sing it as a wedding song" (*To les miroloyi, to les ke nifiko*). The lyrics and the basic melody of these songs are the same whether they are performed at death rites or at weddings, but the manner in which the melody is sung varies according to the occasion. When these songs are sung at weddings, the style is more forceful, vigorous, and joyful; the melody more elaborate, with trills and light melismatic phrases. At death rites the style is more somber and restrained; the melody flatter and less elaborate.[5]

This relationship between funeral laments and wedding songs is but one aspect of a larger correspondence or analogy between death rites and marriage rites which is to be found in Greek culture. To members of American and Western European cultures the parallel suggested here between marriage and death may at first glance appear startling, since the structural similarities between these rites are largely masked by a cultural emphasis on the differences between them. What two occasions could be more different than the joyful celebration of life that is a wedding and the sad commemoration of death that is a funeral? What could contrast more sharply than the white dress of the bride and the black dress of the widow; the former gaining a husband, the latter losing one? Although it is important to bear in mind the logical opposition that exists between these two episodes in the life cycle, it is equally important to understand the no less significant parallels.

Van Gennep and Hertz have both pointed to the similarities that exist between funerals and weddings in cultures throughout the world. Both death and marriage are marked by elaborate rites of passage in which separation is an important theme. The analogy between death and marriage is well developed in ritual and folk song throughout the Balkans (Muslea) and particularly so in the long tradition of Greek funeral laments (Alexiou 1974, Alexiou and Dronke 1971).

In Potamia, as in most villages of mainland Greece, a bride leaves her home and family of origin at marriage in order to live with her new husband in his father's home. For this reason a woman's wedding, like her funeral, is for her parents and her other close relatives a sad occasion at which her departure evokes the expression of grief.[6] The emotional power of this separation and the psychological distance it introduces between mother and daughter are great, whether the daughter is moving only a few hundred yards away, to the other side of her village, or whether she is leaving her village, and Greece as well, for the United States or Australia. It is therefore not at all surprising that the same songs are sung at both funerals and weddings, that these two rites of passage exhibit many other important similarities, or that the metaphor of death as marriage figures so prominently in Greek folk songs.

The following laments, sung at both funerals and weddings, suggest many of the parallels that exist between these two rites of passage.

10

Κάτσε, Νίκο μ', ἀκόμ'ἀπόψ',
κι αὔριο πρωι νὰ φύγης.
— Τώρα σὲ χάμποσην ὥρα
δ χωρισμὸς βαρὺς θὰ γίν'.
Θὰ χωρίσ' ἀπ' τὴνἀγάπη μ'.
Θὰ χωρίσ' ἀπ' τὸ Δημήτρη μ'.
Θὰ χωρίσ' ἀπ' τὰ ἐγγόνια μ'.

"Stay here, Nikos, just for tonight,
and leave tomorrow morning!"
"In a short time
the painful separation will take place.
I will be separated from my wife.
I will be separated from Dhimitris.
I will be separated from my grandchildren."

In the context of death rites this lament presents Nikos, the deceased, as if he were still alive, anticipating his death and his separation from his wife, his son Dhimitris, and his grandchildren. It is sung at the house of the deceased shortly before the arrival of the village priest just prior to the funeral service. The "painful separation" refers specifically to the imminent removal of Nikos' body from the house. In the context of marriage rites this lament is sung when the groom and his party arrive at the house of the bride to take her to the church for the wedding service. It is at this point that the expression of grief at the departure of the bride is most intense. The name of the bride replaces the name of the deceased in the first line, while "my mother," "my father," and "my brothers and sisters" are inserted in the final lines.

11

Κάτου στὸ Δάφνο ποταμό,
καὶ στὰ δασιὰ τριαντάφυλλα,
ν-ἐκεῖ λαλοῦν τρεῖς πέρδικες.
Καὶ μιὰ πέρδικα δὲ λαλεῖ.
— Γιατί, πέρδικα μ', δὲ λαλεῖς;
— Τί νὰ λαλήσω;Τί νὰ πῶ;
Ν-ἄφησα τὴ μανούλα μου
δίχως καμιὰ παρηγοριά.

Μὴν κλαῖς, μανούλα μου γλυκιά,
καὶ μὴν παραπονιέσαι.
Ἡ τύχη μας τὸ ἔγραψε,
μάνα μ', νὰ χωριστοῦμε.
Σύρι, μάνα μ', στὸ σπίτι μας,
σύρι καὶ στὸ καλό μας.

Down by the river Dhafnos,
by the dense rose bushes,
there three partridges are singing.
But one partridge isn't singing.
"My little partridge, why aren't you singing?"
"Why should I sing? What should I say?
I abandoned my mother
without any solace.
Don't cry, my sweet mother.
Don't have a heavy heart.
Our fate has written
that we must be parted.
Go home, mother.
Farewell!"

This lament, which was sung during the exhumation of Eleni described in Chapter 1, emphasizes the unavoidable nature of the separation that takes place at death. It also suggests the complete break in communication which occurs when the deceased crosses the boundary (suggested perhaps by the river) separating the living from the dead. The deceased is portrayed here as feeling guilty since her death has caused her mother pain. In the context of marriage rites this lament is sung while the bride, the silent partridge, stands, surrounded by her female relatives and friends, awaiting the arrival of the groom to take her away.

12

Ἕνας νέος κι ἕνας καλὸς λεβέντης
μαῦρον τάϊζε καὶ μαῦρον μον' ταΐζει
στὰ ψηλὰ βουνά, ψηλὰ στὶς κρύες βρύσες.
– Τρώει ὁ μαῦρος μου τὸ δροσερὸ χορτάρι.
Πιε κρύο νερὸ ἀπὸ τὶς κρύες βρύσες.
Κι αὔριο τὸ πρωί, κι αὔριο τὸ μεσημέρι,
δρόμον ἔχομε κι ἕνα βαρὺ ποτάμι.
Πῶς νὰ διάβομε πέρ' ἀπὸ τὸ ποτάμι;
Ν-ὅλοι πέρασαν πέρ' ἀπὸ τὸ ποτάμι.
Μόν' ὁ νηούτσικος δὲ μπόρεσε νὰ περάοη.
Πίσω γύρισε πολὺ μακριὰ στὰ ξένα.

A brave and handsome young man
was feeding his black horse
high in the mountains at cold springs.
"My horse is eating the cool grass.
He is drinking the cold spring water.
Tomorrow morning, tomorrow at noon,
we have a long journey in front of us, and
     a wide river to cross.
How will we cross over to the other side
     of the river?"
Everyone crossed over to the other side of the river.
Only the young man was unable to cross.
He turned back; he returned to that foreign land.

When performed at a funeral this lament employs the images of a long journey and the crossing of a river to represent death. The presentation is somewhat unusual in that the journey is not a departure from home, nor is it the deceased who crosses the river, as one might expect. The journey is a return home, while the deceased is permanently "on the other side of the river," "in a foreign land" (sta xena). What is emphasized here is the impossibility of overcoming the separation introduced by death. The river, which symbolizes this separation, is literally referred to as "heavy" (vari), as is the separation itself in lament 10, line 4. This suggests the power, the emotional or psychological "weight," which this irreversible separation connotes. At a wedding this lament is sung as the groom and his party make their way from the groom's home to that of the bride. It refers to the separation of the groom from his childhood and his status as a single man.

In addition to the parallels between marriage rites and death rites suggested by the existence of songs that are both funeral laments and wedding songs, there are also a great many similarities between the ritual details of weddings and funerals as they are performed in rural Greece. Both are rites of passage that begin with the formal dressing of the central character in the ritual drama, the deceased in the case of the funeral and the bride in the case of the wedding. The relationship between the clothing associated with funerals and the clothing associated with weddings is indicated by an old woman's joking reference to the clothes she had prepared for her funeral as her "dowry." Both sets of clothing accompany a woman through an important rite of passage.

The departure of the bride from her home after the arrival of the groom is analogous to the departure of the deceased from his home after the arrival of the priest. In both cases the principal character in the ritual drama is escorted by relatives and friends from the home to the church in a procession. Wedding processions in Potamia are led by two young men holding large white candles. They are followed by several people carrying baskets full of small packages of candy to be distributed after the wedding. Then come the bride and groom, and their relatives. This procession corresponds quite closely to the funeral procession, composed as it is of acolytes with their staffs, women carrying baskets of *koliva*, the coffin with the body of the deceased, and the bereaved kin. At the conclusion of the wedding service, which, like the funeral, takes place in the center of the village church, all those present, led by the close relatives of the bride and groom, file by the newly married couple, greet them with a kiss, and present them with a gift of money, much as they do at the conclusion of the funeral service. The procession from the church to the house of the groom and the rites of incorporation which take place there correspond to the procession from the church to the graveyard and the rites of burial.

The analogy between marriage and death is even clearer, and is explicitly articulated, at the funeral of an unmarried person. On such occasions people say, "We celebrate the funeral like a wedding" (*Tin kidhia tin kanoume sa ghamo*). In effect, the funeral of an unmarried person becomes his wedding. On such occasions funeral laments that are also wedding songs are particularly appropriate.

[. . .]

Just as a man at death is said to take "the black earth" as his wife, so a woman at death is said to take Haros (Politis 1978:224), or less frequently Hades (Passow 1972:265), as her husband. More often Hades, rather than being a personification of death,

is simply the name for the underworld, where the marriage takes place (Alexiou and Dronke 1971:846). In these laments the husband is portrayed as an unknown and feared stranger who has snatched the young bride away from her home. The image of marrying a personification of death is also found in the Orthodox funeral service, shorn, however, of its associations with classical mythology. God is asked, "Why were we given up to decay? And why *to death united in wedlock*?" (*sinezefhthimen to thanato*). The answer is simply that it is written. It is the will of God (Vaporis 1977:109).[7]

As we have seen, death is in many important respects both like and unlike marriage. This paradoxical relationship of simultaneous opposition and identity, difference and likeness, is the essence of metaphor. To assert through ritual and song that a funeral is a wedding is to establish a metaphoric relationship between the two rites of passage. This association, like all powerful metaphors, involves the "encapsulation of paradox" (Herzfeld 1979:285). It provides a "perspective by incongruity" (Burke 1954:89–96 and 1964:94–9). It is an "appropriately ill-formed utterance" (Basso 1976:116).

By asserting similarity where there exists difference, by demonstrating identity where there exists opposition, metaphors force us to see things in a different light. They establish relationships between things that were thought to be unrelated. The power of metaphors lies in their ability to change the way we view our world. A metaphor makes something that had been vague more concrete, more sharply defined, and it does so in a specific way, for a particular purpose. According to Fernandez (1971:58) the study of metaphor is the study of "the ways in which men are aided in conveying inchoate psychological experiences by appealing to a range of more easily observable and concrete events in other domains of their lives."

Life	Marriage	Death
Alive (+)	Alive (+)	Not alive (−)
Not separated (+)	Separated (−)	Separated (−)

Figure 14.1

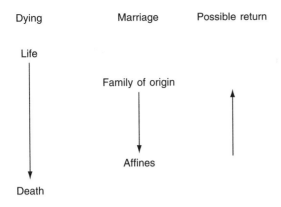

Dying   Marriage   Possible return

Life

                 Family of origin

                 Affines

Death

Figure 14.2

Death is perhaps the most "inchoate" experience men confront. As such it would seem to be a particularly suitable subject for metaphor. The metaphoric assertion that death is marriage (and its corollaries, that a funeral is a wedding and that the grave is the home of one's affines) is an attempt to make death more familiar. More importantly, however, the metaphor of death as marriage "moves" death closer to life. It makes death a part of life by identifying it with an experience from life. In doing so it denies the finality and the "otherness" of death. It creates the fiction that death is not the end of life, not a total negation of life.

The metaphor of death as marriage is ultimately an attempt to mediate the opposition between life and death. It attempts to do this by establishing marriage as a mediating term and then asserting that death is marriage, that death is not what it really is, a polar term in the opposition between life and death, but that it is the mediating term. The metaphor of death as marriage "moves" death from the opposite of life to the mediator between life and death, from the antithesis of life to a synthesis of life and death.

Marriage is a most appropriate metaphor to mediate the opposition between life and death because of the paradoxical relationship of similarity and difference which it holds with respect to death. Like death marriage involves departure and separation. However, the departure that takes place at marriage is not as extreme as that which occurs at death. At marriage one does not depart from life, from this world. One simply departs from one's home and family of origin. After marriage, as after death, one is apart; but after marriage, as is not the case after death, one is still alive. Marriage therefore is a kind of half death, a partial death. Figure 14.1 illustrates the position of marriage as a mediator between life and death.

The opposition between life and death can never actually be mediated. The mediation of marriage is only metaphoric. However, the metaphor of marriage introduces or generates a new opposition, the opposition between one's home and family of origin, on one hand, and the home of one's affines, on the other. This opposition is weaker than that between life and death because it can actually be mediated. A return from the home of one's affines to one's family of origin is literally possible, even though one cannot return permanently without seriously interrupting the accepted course of one's life cycle. The process by which an extreme opposition is mediated metaphorically and replaced by a weaker opposition that can actually be mediated is represented in figure 14.2.

The analysis of the relationship between the funeral and the exhumation presented in Chapter 3 revealed that the return of the deceased from the grave to his home and family, which is ritually attempted at the exhumation, is a negative transformation of his departure from home and family to the grave, which occurs at death. However, this attempt to bring the deceased back to the world of the living is thwarted by the process of decomposition, which transforms a living person into dry bones. The analysis here of the relationship between the funeral and the wedding demonstrates that both rites involve a departure, from home and family to the earth at death, and from home and family of origin to the home of one's affines at marriage. In both cases this movement is portrayed as extremely undesirable, as a movement from good to bad.

Each of the three rites of passage under consideration, the wedding, the funeral, and the exhumation, is an episode in the life cycle of the individual. As such each rite is a "metaphoric transformation" of the other (Leach 1976:25). Having examined two of the three possible relationships between these rites (the relationship between funeral and exhumation and the relationship between funeral and wedding), we now turn to a consideration of the third: the relationship between wedding and exhumation.

An exhumation is similar to a wedding in several respects. This is particularly true when the person whose remains are exhumed never married. The greeting of the skull at the exhumation by kissing it and placing money on it corresponds remarkably to the greeting the bride and groom receive at the conclusion of the wedding ceremony, when those present greet the newly married couple with a kiss and pin money to their chests. The parallel between exhumation and marriage is also indicated by the wrapping of Eleni's exhumed skull in a kerchief she had embroidered as part of her dowry. Just prior to her exhumation, as people gathered at her house before setting out for the graveyard, several of Eleni's relatives made comments that further em-phasized the relationship between her exhumation and her wedding, a wedding that never took place. One of Eleni's sisters said that she planned to place a large sum of money on Eleni's skull (money to be used to build a gate for the graveyard in Eleni's memory) because she would have bought her an expensive gift at her wedding. Eleni's mother com-plained that more relatives had not come from other villages, adding that if it had been Eleni's wedding more people would certainly have come.

The analogy between exhumation and wedding is also suggested by the fact that the movement in both rites of passage is one of emergence. When the remains of a widow's husband are exhumed, she comes out into society (*vyeni exo stin kinonia*). Simi-larly, when a woman marries, it is said that she will go out into society (*tha vyi stin kinonia*), or that her husband will take her out into society (*tha tin vgali exo stin kinonia*).[8] Thus just as a woman at marriage emerges into society from the confinement associ-ated with being single, so a widow at the exhumation of her husband's remains re-emerges into society from the confinement of widowhood.

The metaphoric relationship between exhumation and wedding is suggested even more forcefully by the fact that of the sixteen laments sung at Eleni's exhum-ation, ten were either songs that could be sung at weddings or else versions that had been slightly modified or transformed to render them appropriate

for exhumations. Of the seven laments sung at Eleni's exhumation that were presented all except one (lament 6) are wedding songs or transformations of them.

In the following discussion of the laments sung at Eleni's exhumation the texts as recorded at the exhumation are presented on the left, while the versions of them that would be sung at a wedding are presented on the right.

Lament 5 (Exhumation)	5A (Wedding)
Τώρα κίνησα, τώρα θὰ φύγω ἀπ᾽ τὴ μαύρη γῆς κι ἀπ᾽ τ᾽ ἀραχνιασμένη.	Τώρα κίνησα, τώρα θὰ φύγω ἀπ᾽ τὸ σπίτι μου κι ἀπ᾽ τὰ γλυκά μ᾽ ἀδέρφια. Ν-ὅλοι μὲ διώχνουν κι ὅλοι μὲ λένε:– Φεύγα. Ν-ὡς κι ἡ μάνα μου μὲ διώχνει, δὲ μὲ θέλει. Κι ὁ πατέρας μου, κι αὐτὸς μοῦ λέει:–Φεύγα. Φεύγω κλαίγοντας καὶ παραπονεμένη.
Now I have set out. Now I am about to depart from the black and cobwebbed earth.	Now I have set out. Now I am about to depart from my home and from my dear brothers and sisters. Everyone is driving me away; everyone is telling me to leave. Even my mother is driving me away. She doesn't want me. And my father too, even he tells me to leave. I am leaving with tears and with a heavy heart.[9]

Lament 5, sung as Eleni's skull was being un-covered, describes her departure from the earth, a "black," negatively valued place. Lament 5A, which has a melody and a narrative structure very similar to those of lament 5, but which is sung at a wedding rather than at an exhumation, describes the departure of the bride from her home and family of origin. This is obviously a departure from a cherished, positively valued place. Musically and structurally parallel, these songs contrast sharply with respect to content, with respect to the direction of movement. One is a negative transformation of the other.

Lament
7 (Exhumation)   7A (Wedding)

—Πέρδικα,   —Πέρδικα,
περδικούλα μου,   περδικούλα μου,
μὲ ποιὸν ἐμάλωνες   μὲ ποιὸν ἐμάλωνες
ἐψές;   ἐψές;
—Μὲ τὴ μανούλα   —Μὲ τὴ μανούλα
μάλωνα,   μάλωνα.
καὶ μὲ τὸ κάρο   Ἀιώξες με, μάνα μ',
δέρνομαν.   ᾽διώξες με.
Ν' ἄφ'σες με, κάρε μ',   Θαρρεῖς θὰ πάνω καὶ
ν' ἄφ'σες με,   θὰ 'ρθῶ,
νὰ πάω στὴ μανούλα   θὰ κάνω
μου,   χρόνους ἑκατό.
νὰ τὴ δῶ.   Ἐγὼ πίσω δὲν
    ἔρχομαι.

"My partridge, my little   "My partridge, my little
partridge,   partridge,
with whom were you   with whom were you
arguing yesterday?"   arguing yesterday?"
"I was arguing with my   "I was arguing with my
mother.   mother.
I was struggling with   You are driving me away,
Haros.   mother. You are driving me
Let me go, Haros! Let me   away.
go!   You think I will go away and
So that I can go to my   come back again,
mother,   but I will stay away one
so that I can see her again."   hundred years.
    I will never return."

Lament
9 (Exhumation)   9A (Wedding)

—Πέρδικα, περδικούλα   —Πέρδικα, περδικούλα
μου,   μου,
γιὰ ποῦ   γιὰ ποῦ βραδιάστηκες
βραδιάστηκες ἐψές;   ἐψές;
—᾽Εψὲς ἤμαν στὴ   —᾽Εψὲς ἤμαν
μαύρη γῆς.   στὴ μάνα μου,
Ἀπόψ' ἦρθα   προψὲς στὴν
στὴ μάνα μου,   ἀδερφή μου.
ν-ῆρθα καὶ στὸν   Κι ἀπόψ'
πατέρα μου,   ἦρθα στὴν ἀφεντιά σ',
καὶ στὰ καλὰ   ν-ῆρθα στ'
'δερφούλια μου.   ἀρχοντικό μας.

"My partridge, my little   "My partridge, my little
partridge,   partridge,
where did you sleep last   where did you sleep last
night?"   night?"
"Last night I slept in the   "Last night I was with my
black earth,   mother,
but tonight I have come to   the night before last with my
my mother.   sister,
I have come to my   but tonight I have come to
father   you, mother-in-law,
and to my dear brothers   I have come to our fine
and sisters."   house."

In lament 7 the deceased expresses a desire to escape from the grasp of Haros and to return to her home and her mother. Lament 7A, sung when the groom comes to take the bride to church, portrays an argument between the bride and her mother after which the bride departs, never to return. In lament 7 Haros tries to hold back the person whose remains are being exhumed from the grave, while in lament 7A the bride's mother drives the bride away from her home. The opposition between Haros and the mother, restraint and rejection, grave and home, could not be more vivid.

These two songs again illustrate the parodoxical relationship of similarity and difference, identity and opposition, which is the essence of metaphor and which characterizes the relationship between the wedding and the exhumation. Lament 9A is sung after the wedding at the door of the house of the groom and his parents, as the mother of the groom greets her new daughter-in-law. The bride responds to her mother-in-law's question with politeness and deference (indicated by the euphemistic reference to her fine new home and the form of address employed – i afendia s'). The movement described here, from home and family of origin to the home of the groom, is an unhappy, negatively valued departure. Lament 9, musically and structurally parallel, describes a diametrically opposed movement, a desired return from the grave to home and family of origin.

In the context of an exhumation, the marriage metaphor asserts that an exhumation is a wedding, but it establishes several analogies between the two rites which appear particularly incongruous, paradoxical, and ill-formed. Furthermore, they contra-

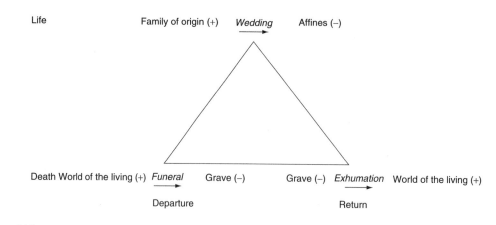

Figure 14.3

dict the analogies established by the same metaphor used in the context of funeral rites.

The funeral-as-wedding metaphor establishes an analogy between a departure from the world of the living for the grave, on one hand, and a departure from one's home and family of origin for the home of one's affines, on the other. The world of the living is like one's home and family of origin (both positively valued), and the grave is like the home of one's affines (both negatively valued). The appropriateness of this metaphor seems clear. The exhumation-as-wedding metaphor, however, establishes an analogy between a return from the grave to the world of the living, on one hand, and a departure from one's home and family of origin for the home of one's affines, on the other. This metaphor asserts paradoxically that the grave is like one's home and family of origin, and the world of the living is like the home of one's affines. Thus the exhumation-as-wedding metaphor seems to contradict the funeral-as-wedding metaphor.[10]

This apparent contradiction recalls the relationship of opposition between the exhumation and the funeral discussed in Chapter 3. The exhumation seems to reverse the movement brought about by the funeral. However, this reversal proves to be illusory, since it is only the dry, white bones of the deceased that return from the earth and not the deceased himself. The exhumation in fact continues the departure that was initiated by the funeral; it does not reverse it.

In effect, the laments sung during Eleni's exhumation assert that the exhumation is a return at the same time as they deny it. Although the lyrics of the laments describe a return, both their musical and narrative structure reveal that what is really taking place is a wedding-like departure. The exhumation-as-wedding metaphor transforms a return into a departure. It asserts that the world of the living to which the deceased appears to have returned is really the home of his affines, that is, the underworld or the grave. It also asserts that the mother to whom the deceased appears to have returned is really his mother-in-law, the heavy tombstone. Thus this metaphor captures the paradoxical nature of the exhumation and conveys to those who perform it the message that the exhumation is not a resurrection. It is a confirmation, not a negation, of death.

The relationships between these three rites of passage, as well as the different movements they bring about, are illustrated in figure 14.3. This diagram, modeled after Lévi-Strauss' "culinary triangle" (Lévi-Strauss 1966 and Leach 1970:15–33), demonstrates how the relationships between three terms in a semantic field can be expressed as a double opposition. Here the relationships between wedding, funeral, and exhumation are expressed in terms of the opposition between life and death and the opposition between departure and return. The metaphor of marriage, a rite of passage of the living, is applied to two rites of passage of the dead. This is an attempt to render the inchoate experience of death more accessible and to mediate the opposition between life and death by transforming an experience of the dead into an experience of the living.

Another important image in Greek funeral laments is that of *xenitia*, a term that refers to foreign or distant lands and the loneliness of living a life of exile there. In addition to being a prominent image in laments, *xenitia* is also very much a psychological and social reality in many parts of Greece at the present time. For years Greeks have left their homes to settle abroad in the United States, Canada, Australia, and more recently Germany, in search of a better standard of living for themselves and their families. Virtually everyone in Potamia has a child, sibling, or cousin who is living abroad. *Xenitia* is a recurrent theme in the conversations of the residents of Potamia. Parents discuss the difficulty of not having their children nearby. They often express the fear that one of their children might die in *xenitia*, or that they themselves might die at home alone with all their relatives far away. *Xenitia*, then, like marriage and death, involves a painful departure and a difficult separation from the social network of family, friends, and fellow villagers.

Many songs that can be sung at both weddings and death rituals are songs about *xenitia*. These songs are also sung at family gatherings when close relatives are absent or when someone present is about to depart. Lament 4 is an example of such a song. Here the person living in *xenitia* may represent either the deceased or the bride or groom, depending on the context in which the song is performed. In another version of this song the main character announces that he has married in *xenitia* and will never return home. The departure of a child, particularly a daughter, for *xenitia* at marriage is especially feared.

2 On oral composition and transmission generally see Lord (1971). For an application of Lord's ideas to modern Greek folk poetry see Beaton (1980). On authorial originality and creativity see Caraveli-Chaves (1980) and Herzfeld (1981b).

3 For additional views of the changing social context of Greek funeral laments see Alexiou (1974:50–1) and Caraveli-Chaves (1980:130–1).

4 This is an example of the type of exposure involving violation and loss of reputation discussed by Herzfeld (1979:293–4). Compare also the exposure of the sins of the deceased at the exhumation of his undecomposed remains.

5 For further discussion of the relationship between *miroloyia* and wedding songs see Alexiou (1974: 120–2), Alexiou and Dronke (1971), and Herzfeld (1981a).

6 In discussions of marriage here and elsewhere the perspective of the bride is adopted because it is from this perspective (in a society where residence after marriage is patrilocal) that the analogy between death and marriage is clearest.

7 In both ancient and modern Greece the field of dream interpretation provides another context in which to explore the relationship between marriage and death. To dream of one is generally believed to foretell the other. See Lawson (1910:553–4) and Alexiou and Dronke (1971:837–8) for evidence concerning ancient Greece, and Pazinis (nd) for information about dream interpretation in modern Greek culture. Note also the dream seen by Eleni's mother just before her daughter's death (chapter 1).

8 The last two examples are from Hirschon (1978:71 and 78). On the emergence of women into public roles associated with the ritual therapy of the Anastenaria see Danforth (1979).

9 Note the similarity between lament 5A and lament 3, which was also sung at Eleni's exhumation.

10 This discussion demonstrates, as Herzfeld (1981b:130) points out, that "symbols do not stand for fixed equivalences, but for contextually comprehensible analogies."

NOTES

1 The most thorough study of Greek funeral laments is Margaret Alexiou's *The Ritual Lament in Greek Tradition* (1974). See Herzfeld (1981a) for a discussion of the position of *miroloyia* in a taxonomy of rural Greek performative genres.

REFERENCES

Alexiou, Margaret, 1974 *The Ritual Lament in Greek Tradition*. Cambridge: University Press.

Alexiou, Margaret, and Peter Dronke, 1971 The Lament of Jephtha's Daughter: Themes, Traditions, Originality. *Studi medievali* 12(2):819–63.

Basso, Keith, 1976 'Wise Words' of the Western Apache: Metaphor and Semantic Theory. In *Meaning in Anthropology*, ed. K. Basso and H. Selby, pp. 93–121. Albuquerque: University of New Mexico Press.

Beaton, Roderick, 1980 *Folk Poetry of Modern Greece*. Cambridge: University Press.

Burke, Kenneth, 1954 *Permanence and Change: An Anatomy of Purpose*. Indianapolis: Bobbs-Merrill.

—— 1964 *Perspectives by Incongruity*. Ed. Stanley Hyman. Bloomington: Indiana University Press.

Caraveli-Chaves, Anna, 1980 Bridge Between Worlds: The Greek Women's Lament as Communicative Event. *Journal of American Folklore* 93:129–57.

Danforth, Loring 1979 The Role of Dance in the Ritual Therapy of the Anastenaria. *Byzantine and Modern Greek Studies* 5: 141–63.

Fernandez, James, 1971 Persuasions and Performances: Of the Beast in Every Body . . . and the Metaphors of Every Man. In *Myth, Symbol, and Culture*, ed. C. Geertz, pp. 39–60. New York: W. W. Norton & Co.

Herzfeld, Michael, 1979 Exploring a Metaphor of Exposure. *Journal of American Folklore* 92:285–301.

—— 1981a Performative Categories and Symbols of Passage in Rural Greece. *Journal of American Folklore* 94:44–57.

—— 1981b An Indigenous Theory of Meaning and its Elicitation in Performative Context. *Semiotica* 34:113–41.

Hirschon, Renée, 1978 Open Body/Closed Space: The Transformation of Female Sexuality. In *Defining Females*, ed. Shirley Ardener, pp. 66–88. New York: John Wiley & Sons.

Lawson, John C., 1910 *Modern Greek Folklore and Ancient Greek Religion*. Cambridge: University Press.

Leach, Edmund, 1970 *Claude Lévi-Strauss*. New York: The Viking Press.

—— 1976 *Culture and Communication*. Cambridge: Cambridge University Press.

Lévi-Strauss, Claude, 1963 *Structural Anthropology*. New York: Basic Books.

—— 1966 The Culinary Triangle. *New Society* (London) 166:937–40.

Lord, Albert, 1971 *The Singer of Tales*. New York: Ath"
eum.

Passow, Arnoldus, 1972 *Popularia carmina Graeciae recentioris*. Athens: Tegopoulos-Nikas. (1st edn. 1860).

Pazinis, Goustavos nd *O alanthastos oneirokritis*. New York: Atlantis.

Politis, N. G., 1978 *Eklogai apo ta tragoudia tou ellinikou laou*. Athens: Vayionakis.

Vaporis, N. M., 1977 *An Orthodox Prayer Book*. Brookline, Mass.: Holy Cross Orthodox Press.

15

Grief and a Headhunter's Rage

Renato Rosaldo

If you ask an older Ilongot man of northern Luzon, Philippines, why he cuts off human heads, his answer is brief, and one on which no anthropologist can readily elaborate: He says that rage, born of grief, impels him to kill his fellow human beings. He claims that he needs a place "to carry his anger." The act of severing and tossing away the victim's head enables him, he says, to vent and, he hopes, throw away the anger of his bereavement. Although the anthropologist's job is to make other cultures intelligible, more questions fail to reveal any further explanation of this man's pithy statement. To him, grief, rage, and headhunting go together in a self-evident manner. Either you understand it or you don't. And, in fact, for the longest time I simply did not.

In what follows, I want to talk about how to talk about the cultural force of emotions.[1] The *emotional force* of a death, for example, derives less from an abstract brute fact than from a particular intimate relation's permanent rupture. It refers to the kinds of feelings one experiences on learning, for example, that the child just run over by a car is one's own and not a stranger's. Rather than speaking of death in general, one must consider the subject's position within a field of social relations in order to grasp one's emotional experience.[2]

My effort to show the force of a simple statement taken literally goes against anthropology's classic norms, which prefer to explicate culture through the gradual thickening of symbolic webs of meaning. By and large, cultural analysts use not *force* but such terms as *thick description, multi-vocality, polysemy, richness,* and *texture*. The notion of force, among other things, opens to question the common anthropological assumption that the greatest human import resides in the densest forest of symbols and that analytical detail, or "cultural depth," equals enhanced explanation of a culture, or "cultural elaboration." Do people always in fact describe most thickly what matters most to them?

The Rage in Ilongot Grief

Let me pause a moment to introduce the Ilongots, among whom my wife, Michelle Rosaldo, and I lived

From Renato Rosaldo, "Introduction: Grief and a Headhunter's Rage," in *Culture and Truth: The Remaking of Social Analysis* (Boston: Beacon Press; London: Taylor & Francis, 1993 [1989]).

and conducted field research for thirty months (1967–69, 1974). They number about 3,500 and reside in an upland area some 90 miles northeast of Manila, Philippines.[3] They subsist by hunting deer and wild pig and by cultivating rain-fed gardens (swiddens) with rice, sweet potatoes, manioc, and vegetables. Their (bilateral) kin relations are reckoned through men and women. After marriage, parents and their married daughters live in the same or adjacent households. The largest unit within the society, a largely territorial descent group called the *bertan*, becomes manifest primarily in the context of feuding. For themselves, their neighbors, and their ethnographers, headhunting stands out as the Ilongots' most salient cultural practice.

When Ilongots told me, as they often did, how the rage in bereavement could impel men to headhunt, I brushed aside their one-line accounts as too simple, thin, opaque, implausible, stereotypical, or otherwise unsatisfying. Probably I naively equated grief with sadness. Certainly no personal experience allowed me to imagine the powerful rage Ilongots claimed to find in bereavement. My own inability to conceive the force of anger in grief led me to seek out another level of analysis that could provide a deeper explanation for older men's desire to headhunt.

Not until some fourteen years after first recording the terse Ilongot statement about grief and a headhunter's rage did I begin to grasp its overwhelming force. For years I thought that more verbal elaboration (which was not forthcoming) or another analytical level (which remained elusive) could better explain older men's motives for headhunting. Only after being repositioned through a devastating loss of my own could I better grasp that Ilongot older men mean precisely what they say when they describe the anger in bereavement as the source of their desire to cut off human heads. Taken at face value and granted its full weight, their statement reveals much about what compels these older men to headhunt.

In my efforts to find a "deeper" explanation for headhunting, I explored exchange theory, perhaps because it had informed so many classic ethnographies. One day in 1974, I explained the anthropologist's exchange model to an older Ilongot man named Insan. What did he think, I asked, of the idea that headhunting resulted from the way that one death

(the beheaded victim's) canceled another (the next of kin). He looked puzzled, so I went on to say that the victim of a beheading was exchanged for the death of one's own kin, thereby balancing the books, so to speak. Insan reflected a moment and replied that he imagined somebody could think such a thing (a safe bet, since I just had), but that he and other Ilongots did not think any such thing. Nor was there any indirect evidence for my exchange theory in ritual, boast, song, or casual conversation.[4]

In retrospect, then, these efforts to impose exchange theory on one aspect of Ilongot behavior appear feeble. Suppose I had discovered what I sought? Although the notion of balancing the ledger does have a certain elegant coherence, one wonders how such bookish dogma could inspire any man to take another man's life at the risk of his own.

My life experience had not as yet provided the means to imagine the rage that can come with devastating loss. Nor could I, therefore, fully appreciate the acute problem of meaning that Ilongots faced in 1974. Shortly after Ferdinand Marcos declared martial law in 1972, rumors that firing squads had become the new punishment for headhunting reached the Ilongot hills. The men therefore decided to call a moratorium on taking heads. In past epochs, when headhunting had become impossible, Ilongots had allowed their rage to dissipate, as best it could, in the course of everyday life. In 1974, they had another option; they began to consider conversion to evangelical Christianity as a means of coping with their grief. Accepting the new religion, people said, implied abandoning their old ways, including headhunting. It also made coping with bereavement less agonizing because they could believe that the deceased had departed for a better world. No longer did they have to confront the awful finality of death.

The force of the dilemma faced by the Ilongots eluded me at the time. Even when I correctly recorded their statements about grieving and the need to throw away their anger, I simply did not grasp the weight of their words. In 1974, for example, while Michelle Rosaldo and I were living among the Ilongots, a six-month-old baby died, probably of pneumonia. That afternoon we visited the father and found him terribly stricken. "He was sobbing and staring through glazed and bloodshot eyes at the cotton blanket covering his baby."[5] The man suffered intensely, for this was the seventh child he had lost. Just a few years before, three of his children had died, one after the other, in a matter of days. At the time, the situation was murky as people present talked both about evangelical Christianity (the possible renunciation of taking heads) and their grudges against lowlanders (the contemplation of headhunting forays into the surrounding valleys).

Through subsequent days and weeks, the man's grief moved him in a way I had not anticipated. Shortly after the baby's death, the father converted to evangelical Christianity. Altogether too quick on the inference, I immediately concluded that the man believed that the new religion could somehow prevent further deaths in his family. When I spoke my mind to an Ilongot friend, he snapped at me, saying that "I had missed the point: what the man in fact sought in the new religion was not the denial of our inevitable deaths but a means of coping with his grief. With the advent of martial law, headhunting was out of the question as a means of venting his wrath and thereby lessening his grief. Were he to remain in his Ilongot way of life, the pain of his sorrow would simply be too much to bear."[6] My description from 1980 now seems so apt that I wonder how I could have written the words and nonetheless failed to appreciate the force of the grieving man's desire to vent his rage.

Another representative anecdote makes my failure to imagine the rage possible in Ilongot bereavement all the more remarkable. On this occasion, Michelle Rosaldo and I were urged by Ilongot friends to play the tape of a headhunting celebration we had witnessed some five years before. No sooner had we turned on the tape and heard the boast of a man who had died in the intervening years than did people abruptly tell us to shut off the recorder. Michelle Rosaldo reported on the tense conversation that ensued:

As Insan braced himself to speak, the room again became almost uncannily electric. Backs straightened and my anger turned to nervousness and something more like fear as I saw that Insan's eyes were red. Tukbaw, Renato's Ilongot "brother," then broke into

what was a brittle silence, saying he could make things clear. He told us that it hurt to listen to a headhunting celebration when people knew that there would never be another. As he put it: "The song pulls at us, drags our hearts, it makes us think of our dead uncle." And again: "It would be better if I had accepted God, but I still am an Ilongot at heart; and when I hear the song, my heart aches as it does when I must look upon unfinished bachelors whom I know that I will never lead to take a head." Then Wagat, Tukbaw's wife, said with her eyes that all my questions gave her pain, and told me: "Leave off now, isn't that enough? Even I, a woman, cannot stand the way it feels inside my heart."[7]

From my present position, it is evident that the tape recording of the dead man's boast evoked powerful feelings of bereavement, particularly rage and the impulse to headhunt. At the time I could only feel apprehensive and diffusely sense the force of the emotions experienced by Insan, Tukbaw, Wagat, and the others present.

The dilemma for the Ilongots grew out of a set of cultural practices that, when blocked, were agonizing to live with. The cessation of headhunting called for painful adjustments to other modes of coping with the rage they found in bereavement. One could compare their dilemma with the notion that the failure to perform rituals can create anxiety.[8] In the Ilongot case, the cultural notion that throwing away a human head also casts away the anger creates a problem of meaning when the headhunting ritual cannot be performed. Indeed, Max Weber's classic problem of meaning in *The Protestant Ethic and the Spirit of Capitalism* is precisely of this kind.[9] On a logical plane, the Calvinist doctrine of predestination seems flawless: God has chosen the elect, but his decision can never be known by mortals. Among those whose ultimate concern is salvation, the doctrine of predestination is as easy to grasp conceptually as it is impossible to endure in everyday life (unless one happens to be a "religious virtuoso"). For Calvinists and Ilongots alike, the problem of meaning resides in practice, not theory. The dilemma for both groups involves the practical matter of how to live with one's beliefs, rather than the logical puzzlement produced by abstruse doctrine.

How I Found the Rage in Grief

One burden of this introduction concerns the claim that it took some fourteen years for me to grasp what Ilongots had told me about grief, rage, and head-hunting. During all those years I was not yet in a position to comprehend the force of anger possible in bereavement, and now I am. Introducing myself into this account requires a certain hesitation both because of the discipline's taboo and because of its increasingly frequent violation by essays laced with trendy amalgams of continental philosophy and auto-biographical snippets. If classic ethnography's vice was the slippage from the ideal of detachment to actual indifference, that of present-day reflexivity is the tendency for the self-absorbed Self to lose sight altogether of the culturally different Other. Despite the risks involved, as the ethnographer I must enter the discussion at this point to elucidate certain issues of method.

The key concept in what follows is that of the positioned (and repositioned) subject.[10] In routine interpretive procedure, according to the method-ology of hermeneutics, one can say that ethnograph-ers reposition themselves as they go about understanding other cultures. Ethnographers begin research with a set of questions, revise them throughout the course of inquiry, and in the end emerge with different questions than they started with. One's surprise at the answer to a question, in other words, requires one to revise the question until lessening surprises or diminishing returns indi-cate a stopping point. This interpretive approach has been most influentially articulated within anthropol-ogy by Clifford Geertz.[11]

Interpretive method usually rests on the axiom that gifted ethnographers learn their trade by pre-paring themselves as broadly as possible. To follow the meandering course of ethnographic inquiry, field-workers require wide-ranging theoretical cap-acities and finely tuned sensibilities. After all, one cannot predict beforehand what one will encounter in the field. One influential anthropologist, Clyde Kluckhohn, even went so far as to recommend a double initiation: first, the ordeal of psychoanalysis, and then that of fieldwork. All too often, however, this view is extended until certain prerequisites of field research appear to guarantee an authoritative ethnography. Eclectic book knowledge and a range of life experiences, along with edifying reading and self-awareness, supposedly vanquish the twin vices of ignorance and insensitivity.

Although the doctrine of preparation, knowledge, and sensibility contains much to admire, one should work to undermine the false comfort that it can convey. At what point can people say that they have completed their learning or their life experience? The problem with taking this mode of preparing the ethnographer too much to heart is that it can lend a false air of security, an authoritative claim to certi-tude and finality that our analyses cannot have. All interpretations are provisional; they are made by positioned subjects who are prepared to know cer-tain things and not others. Even when knowledge-able, sensitive, fluent in the language, and able to move easily in an alien cultural world, good ethnog-raphers still have their limits, and their analyses always are incomplete. Thus, I began to fathom the force of what Ilongots had been telling me about their losses through my own loss, and not through any systematic preparation for field research.

My preparation for understanding serious loss began in 1970 with the death of my brother, shortly after his twenty-seventh birthday. By experiencing this ordeal with my mother and father, I gained a measure of insight into the trauma of a parent's losing a child. This insight informed my account, partially described earlier, of an Ilongot man's reac-tions to the death of his seventh child. At the same time, my bereavement was so much less than that of my parents that I could not then imagine the over-whelming force of rage possible in such grief. My former position is probably similar to that of many in the discipline. One should recognize that ethno-graphic knowledge tends to have the strengths and limitations given by the relative youth of field-workers who, for the most part, have not suffered serious losses and could have, for example, no per-sonal knowledge of how devastating the loss of a long-term partner can be for the survivor.

In 1981 Michelle Rosaldo and I began field re-search among the Ifugaos of northern Luzon, Philip-pines. On October 11 of that year, she was walking along a trail with two Ifugao companions when she lost her footing and fell to her death some 65 feet down a sheer precipice into a swollen river below. Immediately on finding her body I became enraged. How could she abandon me? How could she have been so stupid as to fall? I tried to cry. I sobbed, but rage blocked the tears. Less than a month later I described this moment in my journal: "I felt like in a nightmare, the whole world around me expanding and contracting, visually and viscerally heaving. Going down I find a group of men, maybe seven or eight, standing still, silent, and I heave and sob, but no tears." An earlier experience, on the fourth anniversary of my brother's death, had taught me to recognize heaving sobs without tears as a form of anger. This anger, in a number of forms, has swept over me on many occasions since then, lasting hours and even days at a time. Such feelings can be aroused by rituals, but more often they emerge from unexpected reminders (not unlike the Ilongots' unnerving encounter with their dead uncle's voice on the tape recorder).

Lest there be any misunderstanding, bereavement should not be reduced to anger, neither for myself nor for anyone else.[12] Powerful visceral emotional states swept over me, at times separately and at other times together. I experienced the deep cutting pain of sorrow almost beyond endurance, the cadaverous cold of realizing the finality of death, the trembling beginning in my abdomen and spreading through my body, the mournful keening that started without my willing, and frequent tearful sobbing. My present purpose of revising earlier understandings of Ilongot headhunting, and not a general view of bereavement, thus focuses on anger rather than on other emotions in grief.

Writings in English especially need to emphasize the rage in grief. Although grief therapists routinely encourage awareness of anger among the bereaved, upper-middle-class Anglo-American culture tends to ignore the rage devastating losses can bring. Paradoxically, this culture's conventional wisdom usually denies the anger in grief at the same time that therapists encourage members of the invisible community of the bereaved to talk in detail about how angry their losses make them feel. My brother's death in combination with what I learned about anger from Ilongots (for them, an emotional state

more publicly celebrated than denied) allowed me immediately to recognize the experience of rage.[13]

Ilongot anger and my own overlap, rather like two circles, partially overlaid and partially separate. They are not identical. Alongside striking similarities, significant differences in tone, cultural form, and human consequences distinguish the "anger" animating our respective ways of grieving. My vivid fantasies, for example, about a life insurance agent who refused to recognize Michelle's death as job-related did not lead me to kill him, cut off his head, and celebrate afterward. In so speaking, I am illustrating the discipline's methodological caution against the reckless attribution of one's own categories and experiences to members of another culture. Such warnings against facile notions of universal human nature can, however, be carried too far and harden into the equally pernicious doctrine that, my own group aside, everything human is alien to me. One hopes to achieve a balance between recognizing wide-ranging human differences and the modest truism that any two human groups must have certain things in common.

Only a week before completing the initial draft of an earlier version of this introduction, I rediscovered my journal entry, written some six weeks after Michelle's death, in which I made a vow to myself about how I would return to writing anthropology, if I ever did so, "by writing Grief and a Headhunter's Rage ..." My journal went on to reflect more broadly on death, rage, and headhunting by speaking of my "wish for the Ilongot solution; they are much more in touch with reality than Christians. So, I need a place to carry my anger – and can we say a solution of the imagination is better than theirs? And can we condemn them when we napalm villages? Is our rationale so much sounder than theirs?" All this was written in despair and rage.

Not until some fifteen months after Michelle's death was I again able to begin writing anthropology. Writing the initial version of "Grief and a Headhunter's Rage" was in fact cathartic, though perhaps not in the way one would imagine. Rather than following after the completed composition, the catharsis occurred beforehand. When the initial version of this introduction was most acutely on my mind, during the month before actually beginning to write, I felt diffusely depressed and ill with a fever. Then one day an almost literal fog lifted and words began to flow. It seemed less as if I were doing the writing than that the words were writing themselves through me.

My use of personal experience serves as a vehicle for making the quality and intensity of the rage in Ilongot grief more readily accessible to readers than certain more detached modes of composition. At the same time, by invoking personal experience as an analytical category one risks easy dismissal. Unsympathetic readers could reduce this introduction to an act of mourning or a mere report on my discovery of the anger possible in bereavement. Frankly, this introduction is both and more. An act of mourning, a personal report, *and* a critical analysis of anthropological method, it simultaneously encompasses a number of distinguishable processes, no one of which cancels out the others. Similarly, I argue in what follows that ritual in general and Ilongot headhunting in particular form the intersection of multiple coexisting social processes. Aside from revising the ethnographic record, the paramount claim made here concerns how my own mourning and consequent reflection on Ilongot bereavement, rage, and headhunting raise methodological issues of general concern in anthropology and the human sciences.

Death in Anthropology

Anthropology favors interpretations that equate analytical "depth" with cultural "elaboration." Many studies focus on visibly bounded arenas where one can observe formal and repetitive events, such as ceremonies, rituals, and games. Similarly, studies of word play are more likely to focus on jokes as programmed monologues than on the less scripted, more free-wheeling improvised interchanges of witty banter. Most ethnographers prefer to study events that have definite locations in space with marked centers and outer edges. Temporally, they have middles and endings. Historically, they appear to repeat identical structures by seemingly doing things today as they were done yesterday. Their qualities of fixed definition liberate such events from the untidiness of everyday life so that they can be "read" like articles, books, or, as we now say, *texts*.

Guided by their emphasis on self-contained entities, ethnographies written in accord with classic norms consider death under the rubric of ritual rather than bereavement. Indeed, the subtitles of even recent ethnographies on death make the emphasis on ritual explicit. William Douglas's *Death in Murelaga* is subtitled *Funerary Ritual in a Spanish Basque Village;* Richard Huntington and Peter Metcalf's *Celebrations of Death* is subtitled *The Anthropology of Mortuary Ritual;* Peter Metcalf's *A Borneo Journey into Death* is subtitled *Berawan Eschatology from Its Rituals.*[14] Ritual itself is defined by its formality and routine; under such descriptions, it more nearly resembles a recipe, a fixed program, or a book of etiquette than an open-ended human process.

Ethnographies that in this manner eliminate intense emotions not only distort their descriptions but also remove potentially key variables from their explanations. When anthropologist William Douglas, for example, announces his project in *Death in Murelaga*, he explains that his objective is to use death and funerary ritual "as a heuristic device with which to approach the study of rural Basque society."[15] In other words, the primary object of study is social structure, not death, and certainly not bereavement. The author begins his analysis by saying, "Death is not always fortuitous or unpredictable."[16] He goes on to describe how an old woman, ailing with the infirmities of her age, welcomed her death. The description largely ignores the perspective of the most bereaved survivors, and instead vacillates between those of the old woman and a detached observer.

Undeniably, certain people do live a full life and suffer so greatly in their decrepitude that they embrace the relief death can bring. Yet the problem with making an ethnography's major case study focus on "a very easy death"[17] (I use Simone de Beauvoir's title with irony, as she did) is not only its lack of representativeness but also that it makes death in general appear as routine for the survivors as this particular one apparently was for the deceased. Were the old woman's sons and daughters untouched by her death? The case study shows less about how people cope with death than about how death can be made to appear routine, thereby fitting neatly into the author's view of funerary ritual as a mechanical programmed unfolding of prescribed acts. "To the Basque," says Douglas, "ritual is order and order is ritual."[18]

Douglas captures only one extreme in the range of possible deaths. Putting the accent on the routine aspects of ritual conveniently conceals the agony of such unexpected early deaths as parents losing a grown child or a mother dying in childbirth. Concealed in such descriptions are the agonies of the survivors who muddle through shifting, powerful emotional states. Although Douglas acknowledges the distinction between the bereaved members of the deceased's domestic group and the more public ritualistic group, he writes his account primarily from the viewpoint of the latter. He masks the emotional force of bereavement by reducing funerary ritual to orderly routine.

Surely, human beings mourn both in ritual settings *and* in the informal settings of everyday life. Consider the evidence that willy-nilly spills over the edges in Godfrey Wilson's classic anthropological account of "conventions of burial" among the Nyakyusa of South Africa:

> That some at least of those who attend a Nyakyusa burial are moved by grief it is easy to establish. I have heard people talking regretfully in ordinary conversation of a man's death; I have seen a man whose sister had just died walk over alone towards her grave and weep quietly by himself without any parade of grief; and I have heard of a man killing himself because of his grief for a dead son.[19]

Note that all the instances Wilson witnesses or hears about happen outside the circumscribed sphere of formal ritual. People converse among themselves, walk alone and silently weep, or more impulsively commit suicide. The work of grieving, probably universally, occurs both within obligatory ritual acts and in more everyday settings where people find themselves alone or with close kin.

In Nyakyusa burial ceremonies, powerful emotional states also become present in the ritual itself, which is more than a series of obligatory acts. Men say they dance the passions of their bereavement, which includes a complex mix of anger, fear, and grief:

"This war dance (*ukukina*)," said an old man, "is mourning, we are mourning the dead man. We dance because there is war in our hearts. A passion of grief and fear exasperates us (*ilyyojo likutusila*)." . . . *Elyojo* means a passion or grief, anger or fear; *ukusila* means to annoy or exasperate beyond endurance. In explaining *ukusila* one man put it like this: "If a man continually insults me then he exasperates me (*ukusila*) so that I want to fight him." Death is a fearful and grievous event that exasperates those men nearly concerned and makes them want to fight.[20]

Descriptions of the dance and subsequent quarrels, even killings, provide ample evidence of the emotional intensity involved. The articulate testimony by Wilson's informants makes it obvious that even the most intense sentiments can be studied by ethnographers.

Despite such exceptions as Wilson, the general rule seems to be that one should tidy things up as much as possible by wiping away the tears and ignoring the tantrums. Most anthropological studies of death eliminate emotions by assuming the position of the most detached observer.[21] Such studies usually conflate the ritual process with the process of mourning, equate ritual with the obligatory, and ignore the relation between ritual and everyday life. The bias that favors formal ritual risks assuming the answers to questions that most need to be asked. Do rituals, for example, always reveal cultural depth?

Most analysts who equate death with funerary ritual assume that rituals store encapsulated wisdom as if it were a microcosm of its encompassing cultural macrocosm. One recent study of death and mourning, for example, confidently begins by affirming that rituals embody "the collective wisdom of many cultures."[22] Yet this generalization surely requires case-by-case investigation against a broader range of alternative hypotheses.

At the polar extremes, rituals either display cultural depth or brim over with platitudes. In the former case, rituals indeed encapsulate a culture's wisdom; in the latter instance, they act as catalysts that precipitate processes whose unfolding occurs over subsequent months or even years. Many rituals, of course, do both by combining a measure of wisdom with a comparable dose of platitudes.

My own experience of bereavement and ritual fits the platitudes and catalyst model better than that of microcosmic deep culture. Even a careful analysis of the language and symbolic action during the two funerals for which I was a chief mourner would reveal precious little about the experience of bereavement.[23] This statement, of course, should not lead anyone to derive a universal from somebody else's personal knowledge. Instead, it should encourage ethnographers to ask whether a ritual's wisdom is deep or conventional, and whether its process is immediately transformative or but a single step in a lengthy series of ritual and everyday events.

In attempting to grasp the cultural force of rage and other powerful emotional states, both formal ritual and the informal practices of everyday life provide crucial insight. Thus, cultural descriptions should seek out force as well as thickness, and they should extend from well-defined rituals to myriad less circumscribed practices.

Grief, Rage, and Ilongot Headhunting

When applied to Ilongot headhunting, the view of ritual as a storehouse of collective wisdom aligns headhunting with expiatory sacrifice. The raiders call the spirits of the potential victims, bid their ritual farewells, and seek favorable omens along the trail. Ilongot men vividly recall the hunger and deprivation they endure over the days and even weeks it takes to move cautiously toward the place where they set up an ambush and await the first person who happens along. Once the raiders kill their victim, they toss away the head rather than keep it as a trophy. In tossing away the head, they claim by analogy to cast away their life burdens, including the rage in their grief.

Before a raid, men describe their state of being by saying that the burdens of life have made them heavy and entangled, like a tree with vines clinging to it. They say that a successfully completed raid makes them feel light of step and ruddy in complexion. The collective energy of the celebration with its song, music, and dance reportedly gives the participants a sense of well-being. The expiatory ritual process involves cleansing and catharsis.

The analysis just sketched regards ritual as a timeless, self-contained process. Without denying the insight in this approach, its limits must also be considered. Imagine, for example, exorcism rituals described as if they were complete in themselves, rather than being linked with larger processes unfolding before and after the ritual period. Through what processes does the afflicted person recover or continue to be afflicted after the ritual? What are the social consequences of recovery or its absence? Failure to consider such questions diminishes the force of such afflictions and therapies for which the formal ritual is but a phase. Still other questions apply to differently positioned subjects, including the person afflicted, the healer, and the audience. In all cases, the problem involves the delineation of processes that occur before and after, as well as during, the ritual moment.

Let us call the notion of a self-contained sphere of deep cultural activity the *microcosmic view*, and an alternative view *ritual as a busy intersection*. In the latter case, ritual appears as a place where a number of distinct social processes intersect. The crossroads simply provides a space for distinct trajectories to traverse, rather than containing them in complete encapsulated form. From this perspective, Ilongot headhunting stands at the confluence of three analytically separable processes.

The first process concerns whether or not it is an opportune time to raid. Historical conditions determine the possibilities of raiding, which range from frequent to likely to unlikely to impossible. These conditions include American colonial efforts at pacification, the Great Depression, World War II, revolutionary movements in the surrounding lowlands, feuding among Ilongot groups, and the declaration of martial law in 1972. Ilongots use the analogy of hunting to speak of such historical vicissitudes. Much as Ilongot huntsmen say they cannot know when game will cross their path or whether their arrows will strike the target, so certain historical forces that condition their existence remain beyond their control. My book *Ilongot Headhunting, 1883–1974* explores the impact of historical factors on Ilongot headhunting.

Second, young men coming of age undergo a protracted period of personal turmoil during which they desire nothing so much as to take a head. During this troubled period, they seek a life partner and contemplate the traumatic dislocation of leaving their families of origin and entering their new wife's household as a stranger. Young men weep, sing, and burst out in anger because of their fierce desire to take a head and wear the coveted red hornbill earrings that adorn the ears of men who already have, as Ilongots say, arrived (*tabi*). Volatile, envious, passionate (at least according to their own cultural stereotype of the young unmarried man [*buintaw*]), they constantly lust to take a head. Michelle and I began fieldwork among the Ilongots only a year after abandoning our unmarried youths; hence our ready empathy with youthful turbulence. Her book on Ilongot notions of self explores the passionate anger of young men as they come of age.

Third, older men are differently positioned than their younger counterparts. Because they have already beheaded somebody, they can wear the red hornbill earrings so coveted by youths. Their desire to headhunt grows less from chronic adolescent turmoil than from more intermittent acute agonies of loss. After the death of somebody to whom they are closely attached, older men often inflict on themselves vows of abstinence, not to be lifted until the day they participate in a successful headhunting raid. These deaths can cover a range of instances from literal death, whether through natural causes or beheading, to social death where, for example, a man's wife runs off with another man. In all cases, the rage born of devastating loss animates the older men's desire to raid. This anger at abandonment is irreducible in that nothing at a deeper level explains it. Although certain analysts argue against the dreaded last analysis, the linkage of grief, rage, and headhunting has no other known explanation.

My earlier understandings of Ilongot headhunting missed the fuller significance of how older men experience loss and rage. Older men prove critical in this context because they, not the youths, set the processes of headhunting in motion. Their rage is intermittent, whereas that of youths is continuous. In the equation of headhunting, older men are the variable and younger men are the constant. Culturally speaking, older men are endowed with knowledge and stamina that their juniors have not yet attained, hence they care for (*saysay*) and lead (*bukur*) the younger men when they raid.

In a preliminary survey of the literature on headhunting. I found that the lifting of mourning prohibitions frequently occurs after taking a head. The notion that youthful anger and older men's rage lead them to take heads is more plausible than such commonly reported "explanations" of headhunting as the need to acquire mystical "soul stuff" or personal names.[24] Because the discipline correctly rejects stereotypes of the "bloodthirsty savage," it must investigate how headhunters create an intense desire to decapitate their fellow humans. The human sciences must explore the cultural force of emotions with a view to delineating the passions that animate certain forms of human conduct.

Summary

The ethnographer, as a positioned subject, grasps certain human phenomena better than others. He or she occupies a position or structural location and observes with a particular angle of vision. Consider, for example, how age, gender, being an outsider, and association with a neo-colonial regime influence what the ethnographer learns. The notion of position also refers to how life experiences both enable and inhibit particular kinds of insight. In the case at hand, nothing in my own experience equipped me even to imagine the anger possible in bereavement until after Michelle Rosaldo's death in 1981. Only then was I in a position to grasp the force of what Ilongots had repeatedly told me about grief, rage, and headhunting. By the same token, so-called natives are also positioned subjects who have a distinctive mix of insight and blindness. Consider the structural positions of older versus younger Ilongot men, or the differing positions of chief mourners versus those less involved during a funeral. My discussion of anthropological writings on death often achieved its effects simply by shifting from the position of those least involved to that of the chief mourners.

Cultural depth does not always equal cultural elaboration. Think simply of the speaker who is filibustering. The language used can sound elaborate as it heaps word on word, but surely it is not deep.

Depth should be separated from the presence or absence of elaboration. By the same token, one-line explanations can be vacuous or pithy. The concept of force calls attention to an enduring intensity in human conduct that can occur with or without the dense elaboration conventionally associated with cultural depth. Although relatively without elaboration in speech, song, or ritual, the rage of older Ilongot men who have suffered devastating losses proves enormously consequential in that, foremost among other things, it leads them to behead their fellow humans. Thus, the notion of force involves both affective intensity and significant consequences that unfold over a long period of time.

Similarly, rituals do not always encapsulate deep cultural wisdom. At times they instead contain the wisdom of Polonius. Although certain rituals both reflect and create ultimate values, others simply bring people together and deliver a set of platitudes that enable them to go on with their lives. Rituals serve as vehicles for processes that occur both before and after the period of their performance. Funeral rituals, for example, do not "contain" all the complex processes of bereavement. Ritual and bereavement should not be collapsed into one another because they neither fully encapsulate nor fully explain one another. Instead, rituals are often but points along a number of longer processual trajectories; hence, my image of ritual as a crossroads where distinct life processes intersect.[25]

The notion of ritual as a busy intersection anticipates the critical assessment of the concept of culture developed in the following chapters. In contrast with the classic view, which posits culture as a self-contained whole made up of coherent patterns, culture can arguably be conceived as a more porous array of intersections where distinct processes crisscross from within and beyond its borders. Such heterogeneous processes often derive from differences of age, gender, class, race, and sexual orientation.

This book argues that a sea change in cultural studies has eroded once-dominant conceptions of truth and objectivity. The truth of objectivism – absolute, universal, and timeless – has lost its monopoly status. It now competes, on more nearly equal terms, with the truths of case studies that are em-

bedded in local contexts, shaped by local interests, and colored by local perceptions. The agenda for social analysis has shifted to include not only eternal verities and lawlike generalizations but also political processes, social changes, and human differences. Such terms as *objectivity, neutrality*, and *impartiality* refer to subject positions once endowed with great institutional authority, but they are arguably neither more nor less valid than those of more engaged, yet equally perceptive, knowledgeable social actors. Social analysis must now grapple with the realization that its objects of analysis are also analyzing subjects who critically interrogate ethnographers – their writings, their ethics, and their politics.

NOTES

An earlier version of this chapter appeared as "Grief and a Headhunter's Rage: On the Cultural Force of Emotions," in *Text, Play, and Story: The Construction and Reconstruction of Self and Society*, ed. Edward M. Bruner (Washington, DC: American Ethnological Society, 1984), pp. 178–95.

1   In contrasting Moroccan and Javanese forms of mysticism, Clifford Geertz found it necessary to distinguish the "force" of cultural patterning from its "scope" (Clifford Geertz, *Islam Observed* [New Haven, Conn.: Yale University Press, 1968]). He distinguished force from scope in this manner: "By 'force' I mean the thoroughness with which such a pattern is internalized in the personalities of the individuals who adopt it, its centrality or marginality in their lives" (p. 111). "By 'scope,' on the other hand, I mean the range of social contexts within which religious considerations are regarded as having more or less direct relevance" (p. 112). In his later works, Geertz developed the notion of scope more than that of force. Unlike Geertz, who emphasizes processes of internalization within individual personalities, my use of the term *force* stresses the concept of the positioned subject.

2   Anthropologists have long studied the vocabulary of the emotions in other cultures (see, e.g., Hildred Geertz, "The Vocabulary of Emotion: A Study of Javanese Socialization Processes," *Psychiatry* 22 (1959): 225–37). For a recent review essay on anthropological writings on emotions, see Catherine Lutz and Geoffrey M. White, "The Anthropology of Emotions," *Annual Review of Anthropology* 15 (1986): 405–36.

3   The two ethnographies on the Ilongots are Michelle Rosaldo, *Knowledge and Passion: Ilongot Notions of Self and Social Life* (New York: Cambridge University Press, 1980), and Renato Rosaldo, *Ilongot Headhunting, 1883–1974: A Study in Society and History* (Stanford, Calif.: Stanford University Press, 1980). Our field research among the Ilongots was financed by a National Science Foundation predoctoral fellowship, National Science Foundation Research Grants GS-1509 and GS-40788, and a Mellon Award for junior faculty from Stanford University. A Fulbright Grant financed a two-month stay in the Philippines during 1981.

4   Lest the hypothesis Insan rejected appear utterly implausible, one should mention that at least one group does link a version of exchange theory to headhunting. Peter Metcalf reports that, among the Berawan of Borneo, "Death has a chain reaction quality to it. There is a considerable anxiety that, unless something is done to break the chain, death will follow upon death. The logic of this is now plain: The unquiet soul kills, and so creates more unquiet souls" (Peter Metcalf, *A Borneo Journey into Death: Berawan Eschatology from Its Rituals* [Philadelphia: University of Pennsylvania Press, 1982], p. 127).

5   R. Rosaldo, *Ilongot Headhunting, 1883–1974*, p. 286.

6   *Ibid.*, p. 288.

7   M. Rosaldo, *Knowledge and Passion*, p. 33.

8   See A. R. Radcliffe-Brown, *Structure and Function in Primitive Society* (London: Cohen and West, Ltd., 1952), pp. 133–52. For a broader debate on the "functions" of ritual, see the essays by Bronislaw Malinowski, A. R. Radcliffe-Brown, and George C. Homans, in *Reader in Comparative Religion: An Anthropological Approach* (4th edn.), ed. William A. Lessa and Evon Z. Vogt (New York: Harper and Row, 1979), pp. 37–62.

9   Max Weber, *The Protestant Ethic and the Spirit of Capitalism* (New York: Charles Scribner's Sons, 1958).

10 A key antecedent to what I have called the "positioned subject" is Alfred Schutz, *Collected Papers*, vol. 1, *The Problem of Social Reality*, ed. and intro. Maurice Natanson (The Hague: Martinus Nijhoff, 1971). See also, e.g., Aaron Cicourel, *Method and Measurement in Sociology* (Glencoe, Ill.: The Free Press, 1964) and Gerald Berreman, *Behind Many Masks: Ethnography and Impression Management in a Himalayan Village*, Monograph no. 4 (Ithaca, NY: Society for Applied Anthropology, 1962). For an early anthropological article on how differently positioned subjects interpret the "same" culture in different ways, see John W. Bennett, "The Interpretation of Pueblo Culture," *Southwestern Journal of Anthropology* 2 (1946): 361–74.

11 Clifford Geertz, *The Interpretation of Cultures* (New York: Basic Books, 1974) and *Local Knowledge: Further Essays in Interpretive Anthropology* (New York: Basic Books, 1983).

12 Although anger appears so often in bereavement as to be virtually universal, certain notable exceptions do occur. Clifford Geertz, for example, depicts Javanese funerals as follows: "The mood of a Javanese funeral is not one of hysterical bereavement, unrestrained sobbing, or even of formalized cries of grief for the deceased's departure. Rather, it is a calm, undemonstrative, almost languid letting go, a brief ritualized relinquishment of a relationship no longer possible" (Geertz, *The Interpretation of Cultures*, p. 153). In cross-cultural perspective, the anger in grief presents itself in different degrees (including zero), in different forms, and with different consequences.

13 The Ilongot notion of anger (*liget*) is regarded as dangerous in its violent excesses, but also as life-enhancing in that, for example, it provides energy for work. See the extensive discussion in M. Rosaldo, *Knowledge and Passion*.

14 William Douglas, *Death in Murelaga: Funerary Ritual in a Spanish Basque Village* (Seattle: University of Washington Press, 1969); Richard Huntington and Peter Metcalf, *Celebrations of Death: The Anthropology of Mortuary Ritual* (New York: Cambridge University Press, 1979; Metcalf, *A Borneo Journey into Death*.

15 Douglas, *Death in Murelaga*, p. 209.

16 *Ibid.*, p. 19.

17 Simone de Beauvoir, *A Very Easy Death* (Harmondsworth, United Kingdom: Penguin Books, 1969).

18 Douglas, *Death in Murelaga*, p. 75.

19 Godfrey Wilson, *Nyakyusa Conventions of Burial* (Johannesburg: The University of Witwatersrand Press, 1939), pp. 22–3. (Reprinted from *Bantu Studies*.)

20 *Ibid.*, p. 13.

21 In his survey of works on death published during the 1960s, for example, Johannes Fabian found that the four major anthropological journals carried only nine papers on the topic, most of which "dealt only with the purely ceremonial aspects of death" (Johannes Fabian, "How Others Die – Reflections on the Anthropology of Death," in *Death in American Experience*, ed. A. Mack [New York: Schocken, 1973], p. 178).

22 Huntington and Metcalf, *Celebrations of Death*, p. 1.

23 Arguably, ritual works differently for those most afflicted by a particular death than for those least so.

Funerals may distance the former from overwhelming emotions whereas they may draw the latter closer to strongly felt sentiments (see T. J. Scheff, *Catharsis in Healing, Ritual, and Drama* [Berkeley: University of California Press, 1979]). Such issues can be investigated through the notion of the positioned subject.

24   For a discussion of cultural motives for headhunting, see Robert McKinley, "Human and Proud of It! A Structural Treatment of Headhunting Rites and the Social Definition of Enemies," in *Studies in Borneo Societies: Social Process and Anthropological Explanation*, ed. G. Appell (DeKalb, Ill.: Center for Southeast Asian Studies, Northern Illinois University, 1976), pp. 92–126; Rodney Needham, "Skulls and Causality," *Man* 11 (1976): 71–88; Michelle Rosaldo, "Skulls and Causality," *Man* 12 (1977): 168–70.

25   Pierre Bourdieu, *Outline of a Theory of Practice* (New York: Cambridge University Press, 1977), p. 1.

16

Death Without Weeping

Nancy Scheper-Hughes

Mortal Ills, Fated Deaths

Whereas doctors in the clinics and hospitals of Bom Jesus were unconcerned about properly diagnosing and recording the causes of infant and child deaths for the poor of Bom Jesus, Alto women readily shared with me their notions of the causes of childhood mortality. I posed the question in two ways. I asked a general question: "Why do so many babies die on the Alto do Cruzeiro?" Then in the course of recording personal reproductive histories, I asked each woman to tell me at length about the circumstances surrounding each child's death, including her perception of the baby's key symptoms, the various steps she took to remedy the illness, and her understanding of the cause of the death. The two questions elicited very different answers.

In response to the general question on the incidence and causes of high child mortality in the community, Alto women were quick to reply with blanket condemnations of the hostile environment in which they and their children were forced to live and die. They responded:

"Our children die because we are poor and hungry."

"They die because the water we drink is filthy with germs."

"They die because we cannot afford to keep shoes on their feet."

"They die because we get worthless medical care."

"They die of neglect. Often we have to leave them alone in the house when we go to work. So you wash them, feed them, give them a pacifier, close the door, and say a prayer to the Virgin hoping that they will still be alive when you get home. Yes, they die of neglect [à míngua] but it's not due to a lack of goodwill toward our children. The problem isn't one of *vontade* [willingness] but one of *poder* [power or ability]."

When asked what it is that infants need most to survive the first and most precarious year of life, Alto women invariably answered that it was *food*, pure and simple: "Can it be that mothers of ten, twelve, even sixteen children don't know what a child needs to survive? Of course we know! Rich people's children have proper food. Our children are

From Nancy Scheper–Hughes, *Death Without Weeping: The Violence of Everyday Life in Brazil* (Berkeley: University of California Press, 1992).

fed catch as catch can. Some days we have one ingredient for the baby's *mingau*, but we don't have the other. We may have the *farinha* but not the sugar. Or we have the sugar but not the powdered milk. And so we improvise. What else can we do?"

Another shook her head in perplexity: "I don't know why so many die. Some babies are born strong and healthy enough. Their stomachs when they are round and full give one such pleasure! But something is wrong with the food we give them. No matter how much we feed them, they lose their fat and turn into toothpicks. It makes one discouraged."

Still another could identify the exact problem and its remedy: "They die from the miserable *engano* [ruse] of *papa d'água*. Babies need food to live. Most older babies require at least two cans [four hundred grams each] of powdered milk a week. But people here can afford only one can, and so the babies are fed mostly on water. Soon their blood turns to water as well. Money would solve all our problems."

Many others agreed with her: "Here on the Alto there are a multitude of children who live in neglect, eating garbage that other people leave behind, sucking on banana skins and on orange peels. It's because their parents don't earn enough to feed them, and the only solution is to set the children out on the streets."

In short, Alto mothers gave highly politicized answers to the question of child mortality in general, ones that stressed the external constraints on the ability to care for their offspring. But when these same women were asked to explain why any of *their own* children died, their answers were more clinical, and the causes of death were seen as more proximate, sometimes as *internal* to the child. Often the dead infant was judged as lacking a vital life force, his or her own "will" to live. And not a single Alto mother stated that hunger was the cause of death for any of her own children, although many of the dead babies were described as having "wasted" or "withered" away, "shriveled up," or "shrunk to nothing." In response to what may have caused a particular infant to "waste away," Alto women often replied that the baby was born with a "fragile," "nervous," or "weak" constitution. Hunger, it seemed, only killed Alto children in the abstract. It

may kill *your* children (perhaps) but not any of mine. It may be that Alto mothers had to exercise a certain amount of denial because the alternative – the recognition that one's own child is slowly starving to death – is too painful or, given the role that mothers sometimes play in reducing food and liquid (see chapter 8), too rife with psychological conflict.

Alto women distinguished between child deaths viewed as "natural" (coming from God or from nature) and those suspected to be caused by sorcery, evil eye, and magical possession. They attributed most of their own children's deaths to natural causes, especially to communicable diseases. But the women also explained child deaths in terms of failures in proper nurturing, including disregard for the normal "lying-in" precautions for mother and newborn, mortal forms of neglect, and strong and passionate emotions. Table 16.1 gives a very condensed rendering of Alto mother's perceptions of the major pathogens affecting the lives of their offspring.

Alto mothers considered simple diarrhea the greatest single killer of their babies, carrying away 71 of the 255 children who died. But more "complex" and complicated forms of diarrhea were also implicated in the folk category *doença de criança*, "child sickness," and in some cases of *dentição* (teething illness), *gasto* (wasting illness), *susto* (fright sickness), and *fraqueza* (general weakness and debility). Were we to include all the folk pediatric diagnoses in which diarrhea was at least a secondary symptom, then as many as 189 of the 255 deaths, 74 percent of all infant and child deaths on the Alto, could be attributed to diarrhea. Mothers distinguished among many different subtypes (*qualidades*) of infant diarrhea (e.g., *intestino, quentura, barriga desmantelada*), based on color, consistency, smell, and force of the stools. Mothers saved the dirty nappies of their ailing babies to discuss the differential diagnoses with neighbors and elderly healing women of the Alto. In all, mothers recognized the severity of this disease in particular as a primary child-killer on the Alto. Among the other communicable diseases commonly cited by mothers were (in order of importance) measles, pneumonia and other respiratory ailments, infant jaundice, tetanus, fevers, whooping cough, smallpox, and other skin diseases and infections.

Table 16.1   Causes of infant/child deaths (Alto mothers' explanations)

Cause	Number
Diarrhea/vomiting	71
Measles, smallpox, pneumonia, and other infectious childhood diseases	41
Doença de criança (doomed child syndrome, various subtypes)	39
Fraqueza (weakness, wasting)	37
Pasmo, susto (fright, shock, and other malignant emotions)	14
Dentição (malignant teething)	13
Diseases of skin, liver, blood	13
De repente (sudden death)	9
Mal trato (conscious, if unintentional, neglect)	6
Resguardo quebrado (lying-in precautions broken, violated)	5
Castigo (punishment, divine retribution)	4
Cause unknown to mother	3

Note: $N = 255$ deaths.
Source: Anthropological interviews of Alto women.

Underlying and uniting these diverse etiological notions were the same structural principles that informed Alto people's beliefs about the "nervous" body. Here, once again, life was conceptualized as a *luta*, a power "struggle" between large and small, strong and weak. Infants were born both "weak" and "hot"; their tiny systems were easily overwhelmed. Poor infants were already compromised in the womb. Born (as the women said) of prematurely aged fathers whose blood was "sick and wasted" and whose semen was "tired" and of mothers whose breasts offered blood and infection instead of rich milk, it is little wonder that Alto babies were described as born "already thirsty and starving in the womb," as "bruised and discolored," their "tongues swollen in their mouths."

The babies of the rich were described as coming into the world fat and fair and "greedy" for life. They emerged from the womb with a lusty cry. The babies of the Alto, "poor things," came out of the womb "like wet little birds, barely chirping" and with a "nausea" for food. "Our babies," I was often told, were "born already *wanting* to die." Although few Alto mothers could give me the accurate birth weights of their offspring, their descriptions of "skinny," "wasted," "pale," "quiet" newborns, infants who came into the world with no *gosto* (taste) for life and no will to suckle, seemed very much the descriptions of preterm and low-birth-weight infants, babies all too aptly de-

scribed by Alto women as born already "disadvantaged."[1]

What mothers expectantly looked for in their newborn infants were qualities that showed a readiness for the uphill struggle that was life. And so Alto mothers expressed a preference for those babies who evidenced early on the physical, psychological, and social characteristics of fighters and survivors. Active, quick, responsive, and playful infants were much preferred to quiet, docile, inactive infants, infants described as "dull," "listless," and spiritless. Although differences in infant temperament were believed to be innate, in a precarious environment such as the Alto parasitic infection, malnutrition, and dehydration reproduced these same traits in a great many infants. A particularly lethal form of negative feedback sometimes resulted when Alto mothers gradually withdrew from listless infants whose "passivity" was the result of hunger itself.

Conversely, for an Alto mother to say proudly of a child that she or he suffered many "crises" during the first year of life but "conquered" or "endured" the struggle was a mother's fondest testimony to some hidden inner strength or drive within the child. And so fat, resilient babies were described as having *força*, an innate charismatic power and strength. Many frail infants easily succumbed to death from teething because the innate *força* of the teeth straining against the soft gums holding the teeth captive overwhelmed the little body, making the infant vulnerable to any of

181

several lethal and incurable child diseases. Perhaps the ethnopediatric illness *gasto* best captured the image of the beleaguered little body unable to resist powerful forces. In *gasto*, a fatal form of infant gastroenteritis, the infant's body offered no "resistance" and was quickly reduced to a hollow tube or sieve. Whatever went into the infant's mouth emerged directly in virulent bouts of vomiting and diarrhea. The infant was quickly "spent," "wasted," used up; her fight and her vital energy were gone.

[. . .]

Angel-Babies: The Velório de Anjinhos

If he died at this angelic age, the small child became an object of adoration. The mother rejoiced over the death of the angel . . . weeping with delight because the Lord had carried away her fifth child.

Gilberto Freyre (1986a:58)

From colonial Brazil to the present the death of an infant or a very young child was treated as a blessing among the popular classes, an event "to be accepted almost joyfully, at any rate without horror" (Freyre 1986b:144). The dead baby was an *anjinho*, a "little cherub," or an *inocente*, a "blameless creature" who died unregretted because his or her future happiness was assured. The bodies of the little angels were washed, their curls were prettily arranged, and they were dressed in sky blue or white shirts, with the cord of the Virgin tied around their waists. Their little hands folded in prayerful repose, their eyes left open and expectantly awaiting the Beatific Vision, angel-babies were covered with wild flowers, including floral wreaths on their heads. Little petition prayers and messages to the saints were tucked into their hands to be delivered to the Virgin on arrival. Even the poorest were arranged on wooden planks laden with flowers or in large, decorated cardboard boxes "of the kind used for men's shirts" (Freyre 1986b:388). The *velório de anjinho* was immortalized in Euclides da Cunha's classic, *Rebellion in the Backlands*: "The death of a child is a holiday. In the hut the poor parents' guitars twang joyfully amid the tears; the noisy, passionate samba is danced again and the quatrains of the poetic challengers loudly resound; while at one side, between two tallow candles,

wreathed in flowers, the dead infant is laid out, reflecting in its last smile, fixed in death, the supreme contentment of one who is going back to heaven and eternal bliss" (1944:113).

The festive celebration of angel wakes, derived from the Iberian Peninsula, has been noted throughout Latin America from the Andes of Peru to the pampas of Argentina to the tropical coastal regions of Brazil and Colombia (see Foster 1960:143–166; Schechter 1983, 1988; Belote and Belote 1984; Dominguez 1960; Lenz 1953). It is found among Amerindians, blacks, whites, and *criollos* and among the wealthy as well as the poor. Roger Bastide attributed the angel wake customs to the introduction of the "baroque" in Brazil, whereas Freyre (1986b:388) suggested that the Jesuits introduced *anjinho* beliefs to console native women for the alarming death rate of Indian children resulting from colonization.

All-night drinking, feasting, party games, courting rituals, special musical performances, and dances cross many culture areas in South America, where the infant wake may last for three or four consecutive days (Schechter 1983). Weeping is proscribed at the infant wake because a mother's tears make the angel-baby's path slippery and dampen its delicate wings (Nations and Rebhun 1988). Rather, the mother is expected to express her joy, as did the plantation mistress from Rio de Janeiro who exclaimed, "Oh, how happy I am! Oh, how happy I am! When I die and go to the gates of Heaven I shall not fail of admittance, for there will be five little children pressing toward me, pulling at my skirts, and saying, 'Oh, mother, do come in, do come in'" (Freyre 1986b:388). In rural Venezuela, the mother of the dead baby generally opens the dancing at her child's wake so that her angel may rise happily to the kingdom of heaven (Dominguez 1960:31).

The body of the dead infant was fetishized during traditional angel wakes in rural Latin America. The little corpse was sometimes taken out of the tiny coffin and handled like a doll or live baby. The corpse could be displayed like a saint, propped up on a home altar in between candlesticks and vases of sweet-smelling flowers. Or the dead child might be seated in a little chair, elevated on a small platform, set up inside an open box, tied to a ladder placed on top of the casket (to suggest the angel's ascent into heaven), or even tied to a swing suspended on ropes from the house beam. The infant's flight on the swing was said to symbolize the baby's transformation into an angel. The custom of leasing out angel-corpses to enliven local fiestas was described for the late nineteenth through the twentieth centuries in the Argentine pampas as well as in Venezuela, Chile, and Ecuador (see Ebelot 1943; Lillo 1942). In all, the traditional infant wake was a grand pretext for "unbridled merry-making," perhaps (some suggested) as a culturally institutionalized "defense" against grief and mourning in a context in which infant death was all too common.

But what of a situation where neither festive joy nor deep grief is present? My own startlingly different ethnographic observations of angel-babies and the *velório de anjinho* in Bom Jesus today lead me to another set of conclusions, which I must touch on as a prelude to my final discussion of mother love, attachment, grief, and moral thinking. In Bom Jesus today, where an angel-baby is sent to heaven on the average of one every other day, infant wakes are brief, rarely lasting more than a couple hours, and dispensed with a minimum of ceremony. The *velório* of an infant younger than one is at best perfunctory. There are no musical accompaniments, no songs, no prayers, no ritual performances of any kind. Neither food nor drink is offered the casual visitor, most of them curious neighborhood children. Household life simply goes on as usual around the infant in her or his little casket, which may be placed on the kitchen table or across one or two straight-backed kitchen chairs. The infant's grandmother or godmother is in charge, in addition to the older woman who specializes in preparing the body for burial. There is neither great joy nor grief expressed, and the infant is rarely the focus of conversation.

I recall one particularly poignant infant wake that took place in an Alto household in 1987 on the day following the celebration of the one-year-old birthday party and formal christening of another child of the household. Mariana, the middle-aged mother of the one-year-old *caçula*, had purchased christening clothes, a large decorative birthday cake with candles, soft drinks, a wine punch for the adults, balloons, and party favors. The frosted cake was the centerpiece, and Mariana was quite protective of it, frequently brushing away flies that gathered near it and more than once dusting away a persistent procession of little ants. A borrowed record player was turned up loud; samba and lambada music blasted into the main street of the Alto, and the dancing spilled outside of the tiny house. The fiesta lasted for the better part of that Sunday afternoon and early evening. The little birthday girl in her ruffled dress was the center of a great deal of praise and attention. Meanwhile, Mariana's oldest, sixteen-year-old daughter, herself the single mother of a four-month-old infant, sat out the festivities very much on the margins. Her boyfriend was nowhere in evidence. To engage and entertain the girl a bit, I asked if I might take a peek at her baby. She brought me into the back room where her infant, in an advanced stage of marasmic malnutrition, had been left to sleep through the party. She slept very deeply, indeed, for the next morning I was called back for her brief, understated wake and burial.

The young mother sat in the front room repairing a fishing net. The grandmother's only comment was the usual *moradora* words of consolation: "Man makes; God takes." The "snowball baby" in her white tunic, decoratively strewn with sweet forget-me-nots, took the place of the birthday cake as the centerpiece on the table in the front room. A few crumbs of cake and frosting left over from the day before were still on the table, and a couple of deflated pink balloons lolled about on the mud floor. The crepe paper decorations were still in place. The previous day's little birthday girl seemed confused by the muted and ambivalent sentiments so soon after her own animated party, and she was fussy and demanding, insisting to be lifted up to see her infant niece. Finally, Mariana carried the child over to the table and let her peek inside the little casket. "Baby, baby," said the toddler. "Yes," repeated her tired mother, "baby is sleeping," and as Mariana leaned over to adjust the infant in her little cardboard pauper's coffin, I saw her hand once again, almost instinctively, brush away a line of ants, but this time from the infant's frosted, white face.

Men are rarely present at a *velório de anjinho*. Female relatives, neighbor women, and children often mill about. Meanwhile, however, the women and young girls of the household often go about their regular housework. They wash clothes at the back of the house, sort beans in preparation for the main meal, and do piecework for the local hammock industry, while the children do homework, play checkers, cut out paper dolls, or read comic books on the floor.

The procession of the angels to the cemetery is formed on the spur of the moment from the children who happen to be present. No special clothes are worn. There may or may not be a small floral wreath carried in front of the ragtag little parade. Some adults, but never the infant's own mother, may follow the procession to the graveyard. On one occasion the father, godfather, and paternal grandfather attended the funeral of a firstborn child, and all were deeply and visibly affected. On another occasion the godfather (and uncle to the dead child) followed the children's procession at some distance while walking his bicycle. Although he came as far as the graveyard, before the baby was put into the grave, the godfather left to attend a previously scheduled soccer game.

The procession of the angels takes the main, and only paved, street of the Alto, but once at the foot of the hill it veers away from the main *praça* of town and bypasses the church of Nossa Senhora das Dores. The procession does not stop (as it once did) for the priest's blessing; consequently, the bells of Our Lady of Sorrows no longer toll for the death of each child of Bom Jesus da Mata. That way of counting the dead has gone the way of many other folk Catholic pieties, swept away by the reformist spirit of the Vatican Council and by the socialist philosophy of the new regime of liberation theology. And no priest accompanies the procession to the cemetery, where the body is disposed of casually and unceremonially. Children bury children in Bom Jesus da Mata today. Where once clergymen and religious sisters taught patience and resignation to child death and other domestic tragedies, which were said to reveal the imponderable workings of God's will, the new church participates in the public indifference and social embarrassment toward infant death, which exists only as a bloody breech, a rupture with, and a glaring contradiction to the hierarchy's prolife and pronatalist teachings. So instead

of the church *praça* in the dead center of Bom Jesus, the procession of the angels discreetly passes through the back streets of town, under the trestles of the railroad or across the tracks, through the open-air yam market, past the rural sugar workers syndicate building, just under the barred windows of the municipal jail, close to the edge of the new reform school for abandoned street children run by the FEBEM, and up the muddy trail to the municipal cemetery at the farthest edge of town. The children know the route by heart; most have been part of other processions to bury dead siblings or playmates' siblings. The procession shares the street with cars, trucks, donkeys, wagons, and carts. Most cars and trucks hurriedly whiz by, and the children have to run to the side of the road with their little charge.

At the cemetery Seu Valdimar, the disabled and often ill-tempered municipal gravedigger and an assistant lead the children to the common space where pauper children are buried. The temporary space is normally already waiting, and in a few minutes the coffin is placed in the grave and covered over, thereby leaving a small, fresh mound to mark the space. No prayers are recited, and no sign of the cross is made as the coffin goes into its shallow grave. Valdimar often chides the children for one reason or another. It may be that the coffin is larger than expected, and he will have to enlarge the grave. Or he may scold the children for not tacking closed the top of the coffin, although he surely knows well the customs of the region. "Didn't you have any nails, any tacks?" he asked the brother of one deceased child. "Soon the bugs will get to your little sister," he said unnecessarily. Other times Valdimar can be gentle with the children, in his own gruff way.

"Have you any flowers?" Valdimar once asked the older sister of a little toddler who had just been buried. "No," she shook her head sadly. "Well, hurry up and get some, then . . . I haven't all day." Permission granted, the children scampered off in opposite directions to pull up flowers from other fresh graves. "Not *that* many; be careful," yelled Valdimar. And the children returned to scatter the picked flowers on top of the little one's grave. That is normally the extent of the ceremony, except the washing off of muddy hands and feet in the public spigot on the way out.

If an adult is present, the children in the procession have the right to expect a treat on the way home. "*Picolé* [ices] *Picolé!*" the cry may go up, and the responsible adult will be pulled toward a little storefront shack. I have seen a grandfather gather the children into a small shop and carefully count out his few, wrinkled cruzados and negotiate quietly with the shopkeeper so that every child in the procession could have two pieces of hard candy. He himself carefully distributed the sweets, two by two to each child, a sad, gentle smile on his face.

I have tried to imagine, working slowly, intuitively, and unobtrusively with the people of the Alto and with women and children in particular, what meaning the angel-baby and the *velório de anjinho* has for them. At times it seems as if the dead infant were a "transitional object" for the women of the Alto, not only in the ritual, anthropological sense of a liminal being in between social statuses ("Neither here nor there," as one mother said of her dying infant) but in the psychoanalytic sense of a liminal, transitional "attachment" (as to a teddy bear or a "rubby" blanket), which, created out of the imagination, has a self-soothing quality (see Winnicott 1964:167–72). *Anjinhos* allow Alto mothers to "let go" of so many of their young children by allowing them to "hold on" to an idealized image of spirit-children populating the heavens, as close, really, as the stars can seem on a still night. All transitional objects ultimately foster autonomy and independence through the breaking or the breaking out of "impossible" attachments (as in infancy the "rubby blanket" or teddy bear substitutes for the "impossible" desire to have mother's breast available at will). Just so, for Alto women, *anjinhos* in heaven substitute for the impossible attachment to half-live babies in the hammock.

The shaping of the emotions and responses at child death is formed in early childhood as Alto children, mere babies themselves, are schooled in the normalization of child death as they are sooner or later delegated the role of their dead siblings' and playmates' pallbearers and undertakers. The average Alto girl between the ages of five and thirteen participates in two or more angel processions each year.

The average boy participates in at least one a year. One notes, in the reactions and fantasy play of Alto children, the awesome power of these early "primal scenes" in shaping, routinizing, and muting later adult responses to child death.

Many little girls on the Alto do Cruzeiro have no baby dolls to play with. Nor do they tend to fashion them out of available scrap materials, such as torn socks or the corn husks discarded on the main streets after *feira* in the harvest months of June and July. Nor do they fashion dolls and play furniture from the red clay that is commonly found not far from the banks of the local river. Alto girls prefer active games, circle dances, and pretend "talent shows" in which they can imitate the beautiful and seductive children's television star, Xuxa. Girls covet the cheap, plastic soccer balls that any of their older brothers are lucky enough to own. Playing with dolls and playing house are of little interest to Alto girls. I soon learned to bring costume jewelry, hair ribbons, play cosmetics, and small, battery-run video games as gifts for Alto girls and to leave at home the pretty little baby dolls, which elicited so little interest or curiosity. In a half dozen of the more prosperous Alto homes where the children have an abundance of toys, girls are given dolls as presents, but these are treated as display, rather than play, objects and are often kept in the original cellophane-covered boxes standing up on a shelf and are taken down for visitors to admire and are then carefully replaced.

I am tempted to suggest why Alto children are so uninterested in a form of play that is so common among little girls the world over. This lack of interest is born, perhaps, of an early and negative association between lifeless dolls in pretty cardboard boxes and lifeless siblings in decorated cardboard coffins. This possibility was brought home to me during a conversation with Xiquinha, the elderly praying woman of the Alto, who had been washing and dressing dead children for their angel wakes since she was seven and a half. In the following conversation, Xiquinha explained how she became a specialist in angel wakes at so tender an age.

"Whenever a baby died on the Rua dos Sapos, where I had been raised since I was a tiny child, a neighbor would call for me because I always enjoyed dressing the baby for its wake. The other little girls would run away; some didn't even like being in the procession of the angels. But not me; I adored it all. I would take the baby on my lap across my knees, and it was *just like a little doll for me to play with*. Little angel-bodies are different from [dead] big bodies. Angel-bodies stay soft and flexible, so you can handle them easily. I would wash it and put on its blue or white clothes and a veil for the little girls and, if their mother had one, a blue ribbon around their waist. All little angel-girls are dressed like little brides. White is the color of virgins, which all of them are. When an infant is stillborn, people call it an angel-*carobim* [i.e., possibly derived from cherubim] because it is untouched by this world. Blue is the color that the Virgin Mary loves best. So you want to have the little angels dressed that way when they arrive to greet the Virgin at the gates of heaven."

When my Brazilian informants tell me that they do not weep, that they are pleased to have a little *coração santa* in heaven looking after them, I am inclined to believe them and to take them at face value. In most cases the socialization experience has been adequate. Angel-baby beliefs not only "console" *moradores*, they shape and determine the way that death is experienced.

Once as my then-fifteen-year-old daughter, Jennifer, and I were on our way up the Alto to an angel wake near the very top of the hill, Jennifer burst into angry tears. She was to have been the "official" photographer at the wake because the mother of the baby was unable to pay for a professional photographer from the town. I had quite insensitively offered Jennifer's services without asking her permission. "I don't want to photograph a dead baby," she yelled at me, quite reasonably. I apologized and brought her inside Terezinha's house along the way to compose herself. Terezinha and her teenage daughter Rosália were quite concerned. Why was Jennifer so upset? Did she have "boyfriend troubles"? Rosália wanted to know. When I explained that she was upset about having to attend an infant wake, they stared at her unbelievingly. "Why?" they asked. "It's only a baby!"

On only one occasion out of the dozens of angel wakes and burials that I have witnessed over the years did a child express a subdued, yet nonethe-

less ravaged, grief. It was just as little Mercea's body was going into the dirt that her seven-year-old cousin, Leonardo, turned to me to say in an anxious aside: "Nancí, I don't want any more of mine to die." Ashamed, I put aside my camera and my dog-eared, rain-soaked notebook and allowed myself, too, to sit down on a low marble stone and rediscover and feel pain and grief for a moment: "I don't either, Leonardo. I don't either."

Grief Work: A Political Economy of the Emotions

Sorrow concealed, like an oven stopp'd,
Doth burn the heart to cinders where it is.
William Shakespeare, *Titus Andronicus*

And so when an infant dies on the Alto do Cruzeiro, few tears are shed, and women are likely to say that the death came as a blessing or a great relief. "I feel free" or "I feel unburdened" is what many say. This is not to suggest, however, that the women are "cold" and unfeeling, for very often the mother expresses pity (*pena*) for the dead child, saying, "*Faz pena* [what a shame], *menina*, to see them suffer and die." But pity is distinctly different from the sentiments of grief (*desgosto, nojo, luto*), sadness (*tristeza*), depression (*depressão, deprimida*), or bittersweet longing or yearning for a lost or dead loved one (*saudade*). And just as there is no immediate display of grief or mourning in many Alto mothers, I have found no evidence of "delayed" or "displaced" grief in the days, weeks, and months following the death of an infant, unless, perhaps, a new pregnancy can be seen as a symptom of displaced grief.

I made a point of visiting the homes of women who had recently lost an infant, both to offer support and observe their responses to death. What I found did not conform to the conventional biomedical wisdom concerning "normal" grieving following child death, a model of "human" behavior that is, in part, the creation of a few influential psychologists, among them John Bowlby (1961a, 1961b, 1980), Elisabeth Kübler-Ross (1969), and Robert Jay Lifton (1967, 1975, 1979).

Several days following the death and burial of her first baby, a three-month-old daughter named

Daniella, I visited the young mother, Anita, to see how she was getting along. She had been calm, composed, and dry-eyed during the wake and had gone back to work on the next day.

"Are you *triste* [sad]?" I asked.

"No, ma'am, not much; Mario says I'll soon have another."

"Did you cry?"

"Oh, no! It's not good to cry, for it will keep the baby from rising up to heaven."

"Did you sleep all right?"

"Oh, yes, I was very tired yesterday."

"Did you eat well?"

"No, I didn't," she said sadly. But then the resilient girl added, "There was nothing in the house to eat but *fubá* [cornmeal], and I *hate* fubá!" Then Anita went outside, humming along with a popular tune on the radio, to wash clothes. I stayed behind to chat with a few of her neighbors, who confirmed that one does not really miss a very young baby.

Sometimes, it is more obvious why grief at the death of an innocent "angel" is not forthcoming. When Dona Amor received word that her first and only grandson was born puny and weak to her adopted and mentally disabled teenage daughter, who had been seduced and raped by a pimp, the old woman hurriedly lit a candle to São Antônio, her patron saint. She begged the saint to carry off the day-old infant, born, she said, of a "race of beasts." Amor's prayers were answered later that same day. Laughing and clapping her hands, Amor told how she went to the local *casa funerária* to pick out the little coffin. She carried it to the hospital, where she washed and dressed the infant in his baptismal/burial clothes. Then jauntily, as if "it were a basket of fruit," Amor put the little casket on her head and started off across town to the municipal cemetery. When street children laughed to see Dona Amor balancing the little coffin on her head in a solitary procession, the old woman shooed them off, saying, "There is no shame in burying the dead." There was certainly no sorrow either.

Against these altogether normative responses to infant death on the Alto do Cruzeiro are the modern psychiatric theories of "healthy" versus "disordered" mourning, which constitute a hegemonic theory of the emotions. The psychologists and psych-

iatrists of mourning (see Freud 1957:244–5; Bowlby 1980; Lifton 1967) consider child death, and infant death in particular, to be among the most wrenching of all experiences of loss, especially for the mother who may not yet feel herself to be separate from the newborn. "Infant death is," Marshall Klaus remarked, "a kind of death to the self not dissimilar to the loss of a limb" (personal communication). Bowlby (1980:113–24) described the phases of *normal* mourning after the death of a young child as follows: numbing and shock, disbelief, anger, depression, disorganization, and reorganization.

Every major hospital today has clinical social workers and nurses who specialize in helping women (and men) to grieve the premature death of an infant. They distribute helpful booklets, such as "Newborn Death" (Johnson, Cunningham, Ewing, Hatcher, and Dannen 1982) to the bereaved parents. The advice offered is succinct and *very* direct. It counsels the parents to "see, hold, touch, and name your [dead] newborn" and stresses the importance of the mother's presence at a graveside service and burial (1). Weeping over the death is cast as a human right and a necessity: "We have finally come to realize that crying is a strength. . . . Remember, you have a right to cry when your baby dies. Allowing your tears to come, while talking to others, can help you move through your grief" (4). But the booklet cautions against taking to heart the "insensitive" comments of relatives and friends who may not know the "right" things to say. Those around may offer just the kind of advice and comfort that "you *don't* need": "Every parent will hear some well-meaning person say that you can have another baby. You'll get the 'don't cry' messages, and 'just forget about it' statements. Some people will act as if your baby never existed. Others will act as if you can be a *little* sad, but not as much as if your baby were older. It's as if they think the amount of sadness is somehow connected to the size of the dead person" (8).

If the inherent psychological conflicts produced by the loss of an infant or a very young child are not resolved, various pathologies are believed likely to occur, of which chronic mourning (similar to Freud's notion of melancholia) or its opposite, a "prolonged absence of conscious grieving" (Bowlby 1980:139), is common. The absence of grief or the "inability to mourn" was first identified by Helene Deutsch (1937) in her clinical practice with women, some of whom were evidently rather "merry" widows. The "denial" of an "appropriate" grief may last, Bowlby wrote, for years, decades, and even in some cases "for the rest of a person's life" (1980:139). The "disordered mourner" may feel relief and may be quite cheerful and seem well adjusted. Some may even report feelings of relief and euphoria following the death of a loved one. But such feelings are disallowed and pathologized. Lifton was direct: "To be unable to mourn is to be unable to enter into the great human cycle of death and rebirth; it is to be unable to 'live again'" (1975:vii). Those who cannot grieve are scarcely human. This is a weighty moralism, indeed.

It strikes me as no coincidence that so much of the psychological literature on disordered mourning concerns *female* patients who appear to be at a "high risk" of producing, according to the canons of psychotherapy, the wrong emotions in response to death, either too much or too little sadness. In the grief and mourning literature, as in the attachment and bonding literature, we are faced with a biomedical prescription concerning the womanly duty not only to marry and procreate but to *love* offspring and mourn the family's dead. Emotion work is frequently gendered work. And we may want to consider whether the psychological theories on maternal love, attachment, grief, and mourning are not a "rhetoric of control" (M. Rosaldo 1984) and a discourse on power "by other means."

Catherine Lutz (1988) recently pointed out in this regard that conventional biomedical theories of emotion represent an American "ethnopsychology" based on Western notions of mind and body, feeling and reason, nature and culture, self and other, male and female, and individual and society. Psychotherapy is concerned with fostering emotional expression; with "speaking truth" to the deeply repressed, hidden spaces of individual emotional life; and with overcoming the "cultural" constraints that produce distortions and defenses against knowing what one is *really* thinking and feeling.[5] There is a presumed binary split between public sentiments and private feelings, between what is cultural and what is "natural." Culture emerges as an artificial facade con-

cealing the dangerous intensity of hidden or unconscious human passions and desires. What is "real" and "authentic" is just what is most concealed from view.

Along this same binary divide, women and the female are associated with nature, body, and feeling, just as men and the male are associated with culture, mind, and reason. It is expected that women will be more emotionally responsive than men; consequently, society relegates more emotion work, including love work and grief work, to them. In the extensive psychological literature on grief and bereavement (see, for example, Glick, Weiss, and Parkes 1974:263–5; Scheff 1979), it is assumed that the sexes differ in emotionality. Men are said to cry less than women following the death of a family member and are less often depressed. Often they do not appear to be deeply moved or touched by death. But this is treated as appropriate gender behavior. There is no respected body of psychological research on the "inability of men to cry" comparable to the research on the "inability of mothers to love." And the clinical portraits of "failure to grieve" are almost exclusively concerned with the absence of "appropriate" emotionality in women following the death of a spouse or a child.

Bereavement customs worldwide (see Kligman 1988; Rosenblatt, Walsh, and Jackson 1976:26–7) commonly assign women to prolonged and ritualized grieving, both during the funeral services and long after they are over. It is widows who commonly cut their hair, cover themselves with ashes, mutilate their bodies, or shroud themselves in black for the remainder of their lives, while widowers walk freely, indistinguishable from "ordinary" men. This cross-cultural "specialization" of women in the division of emotional labor may be related to the generally lower status of women in the societies observed. Just as women may be coerced into feeding males before they themselves eat or into carrying the heaviest loads, they may be coerced into assuming the emotional burden for grief work. Just as plebeians were expected to weep openly on the death of their king, women are expected to show proper "deference" by weeping publicly for the death of kin.

Alternatively, the expectation that women will grieve for the dead may be an extension of the division of labor found in many traditional rural and peasant societies that delegates to older women specialists the task of washing and dressing the bodies of the dead, as they do, for example, in the two ethnographic instances that I know best: western Ireland and rural Northeast Brazil. In "Ballybran," Ireland, the old women who dress the dead are also expected to recite long and sorrowful ritualized laments; on the Alto do Cruzeiro the old women who dress the dead are expected to recite special mortuary prayers, but they do so only for dead adults. "Why pray for angelbabies who have no need of our prayers?" asked Xiquinha. "It's *their* job to pray for us!" Given the often "coerced" nature of pregnancy on the Alto do Cruzeiro – recall, for example, the sexual and reproductive life of Lordes, whose second husband sadistically "enjoyed" seeing her pregnant again and again – it is also possible that the refusal to grieve for the death of their infants is at times a gesture of defiance. It could be a way of saying, "You can make me pregnant, but you cannot make me love all of them . . . or *keep* all of them either."

Death Without Weeping

And so I maintain that Alto women generally face child death stoically, even with a kind of *belle indifférence* that is a culturally appropriate response. No one on the Alto do Cruzeiro criticizes a mother for not grieving for the death of a baby. No psychiatrist, pediatrician, or social worker visits the mother at home or tells her in the clinic what she is "supposed" to be feeling at a particular "phase" in her mourning. She is not told that crying is a healthy (and womanly) response to child death or that it is "natural" to feel bitter and resentful (which reduces anger to a manageable medical "symptom") or that she must "confront" her loss and get over her unhealthy emotional "numbness."

Poor Brazilians "work" on the self and emotions in a very different fashion. Instead of the mandate to mourn, the Alto mother is coached by those around her, men as well as women, in the art of resignation (*conformação*) and "holy indifference" to the vagaries of one's fate on earth and a hopefulness of a better life beyond. In this cultural milieu a deficit of emo-

tion is not viewed as unhealthy or problematic (as in the overly repressed Anglo-Saxon culture of the United States); rather, an excess is. To experience strong emotions and passions – of love and lust, envy and anger, ecstasy and joy, grief and longing – is for most Brazilians, rich as well as poor, urban as well as rural, the most "natural" and expected occurrence. It is what being human is all about. But if allowed to run riot, these emotions are understood as the harbingers of much misery and suffering. Excessive emotions can bring down large and powerful households as well as small and humble ones. They can ruin lives and livelihoods. They can destroy relationships. They can cause physical as well as mental sickness. The Brazilian folk ethnopsychology of emotion is based on a very different construction of the body, self, personhood, and society. One can, for example, contrast the once popular belief in American society that cancers were caused by the repressions of the inner self, by passion turned inward and feeding on itself (see Sontag 1979), with the popular belief in Brazilian culture that emotional outbursts can dissipate the individual, poison the blood, and cause tuberculosis or cancer.

The strong mandate *not* to express grief at the death of a baby, and most especially not to shed tears at the wake, is strongly reinforced by a *Nordestino* folk piety, a belief that for the brief hours that the infant is in the coffin, she is neither human child nor blessed little angel. She is something other: a spirit-child struggling to leave this world and find its way into the next. It must climb. The path is dark. A mother's tears can impede the way, make the road slippery so that the spirit-child will lose her footing, or the tears will fall on her wings and dampen them so that she cannot fly. Dona Amor told of a "silly" neighbor who was weeping freely for the death of her toddler when she was interrupted by the voice of her child calling to her from his coffin: "Mama, don't cry for me because my *mortália* is very heavy and wet with your tears." "You see," Amor said, "the child had to struggle even after death, and his mother was making it worse for him. The little one wasn't an angel yet because angels never speak. They are mute. But he was no longer a human child either. He was an *alma penanda* [wretched, wandering soul]."

"What is the fate of such a child?"

"Sometimes they are trapped in their graves. Sometimes when you pass by the cemetery, you can see little bubbles and foam pushing up from the ground where such infants are buried. And late at night you can even hear the sound of the lost souls of the child-spirits wailing."

In all, what is being created is an environment that teaches women to contain their affections and hold back their grief during the precarious first year of the child's life. The question remains, however, whether these cultural "conventions" actually succeed in producing the desired effects or whether the dry-eyed stoicism and nonchalant air of Alto mothers are merely "superficial" and skin-deep, covering up a "depth of sorrow," loss, and longing. Nations and Rebhun, for example, maintained that the lack of grief is mere facade: "The inner experience of grief may be hidden by the flat affect of impoverished Brazilians. This behavior is part of a culturally mandated norm of mourning behavior; rather than signify the *absence* of strong emotion at child and infant death, it reveals the *presence* of grief" (1988: 158).

What they wish to suggest, drawing inspiration from the writings of Robert J. Lifton and other psychologists of mourning, is that the "blankness" and "flat affect" that they observed in certain poor women of the Northeast "is the blankness of the shell-shocked" (160). They continued, "The loss is too great to bear, too great to speak of, too great to experience fully. . . . Their seeming indifference is a mask, a wall against the unbearable . . . While flamboyantly open about such emotions as happiness and sexual jealousy, they adopt a generally flat affect when discussing painful topics" (158).

Although I have no doubt (and have gone to great lengths to show) that the local culture is organized to defend women against the psychological ravagings of grief, I assume that the culture is quite successful in doing so and that we may take the women at their word when they say, "No, I felt no grief. The baby's death was a blessing." One need not speak of "masks" or "disguises" or engage in second-guessing on the basis of alien and imported psychological concepts of the self. Nations and Rebhun assumed a "divided self" that conforms to our Western ethnopsychiatry: a split between a public and a private self

and between a "true" and a "false" self-expression. Moreover, when they suggested that the "mothers' flat affect in response to infant deaths is due more to folk Catholic beliefs than to a lack of emotional attachment to infants" (141), they projected a very secular view of religious belief as a superficial feature of the interior life, rather than as a powerful force that penetrates and constitutes the person.

Until recently, most cultural and symbolic anthropologists tended to restrict their interest in emotions to occasions when they were contained within formal, public, collective, highly stylized, and "distanced" rites and rituals, such as in healing, spirit possession, initiation, and other life cycle events. They left the discussion of the more private, idiosyncratic feelings of individual, suffering subjects to psychoanalytic and biomedical anthropologists, who generally reduced them to a discourse on universal drives and instincts.[6] This division of labor, based on a false dichotomy between collective, "cultural" sentiments and individual, "natural" passions, leads to a stratigraphic model of human nature in which biology emerges as the base and culture as the mere veneer or patina, as the series of carnival masks and disguises alluded to previously.

But the view taken here is that emotions do not precede or stand outside of culture; they are part of culture and of strategic importance to our understanding of the ways in which people shape and are shaped by their world. Emotions are not reified things in and of themselves, subject to an internal, hydraulic mechanism regulating their buildup, control, and release. Catherine Lutz (1988) and Lila Abu-Lughod (1986), among others, understand emotions as "historical inventions" and as "rhetorical strategies" used by individuals to express themselves, to make claims on others, to promote or elicit certain kinds of behaviors, and so on. In other words, emotions are discourse; they are constructed and produced in language and in human interaction. They cannot be understood outside of the cultures that produce them. The most radical statement of this position is that without our cultures, we *simply would not know how to feel*.

In fieldwork, as in daily life, we often encounter radical difference, and we come up against things we do not like or with which we cannot immediately identify or empathize. These "discoveries" can make us supremely uncomfortable. As anthropologists with a commitment to cross-cultural understanding, we worry – as well we should – how our written materials will be read and received by those who have not experienced the pleasures (as well as the pains) of living with the complex people whose lives we are trying to describe. Consciously or unconsciously we may "screen out" or simply refuse to accept at face value what we see or what we are being told, as, for example, when Renato Rosaldo (1980) at first refused to believe that his Ilongot friends were capable of headhunting, as they insisted, for the simple, expressive "joy" of it as well as to "kill" the sadness and anger they felt. Rosaldo preferred to believe that there was a more "rational" and "instrumental" purpose behind Ilongot headhunting, such as avenging the death of a loved one. But his informants, after listening attentively to Rosaldo's explanation of the anthropologists' model of exchange theory, replied that "Ilongots simply did not think any such thing" at all (1983:180).

The temptation to second-guess our informants is particularly keen when their own explanations of their lives are "experience-distant" or counterintuitive to our own sociological or psychological understandings of human behavior. Sometimes, as in Rosaldo's case, it is because people's explanations may appear, as they did to him, "too simple, thin, opaque, implausible, stereotypic, or otherwise unsatisfying" (179). Similarly, Thomas Gregor, who investigated the "psychological impact" of infanticide among the Brazilian Amazonian Mehinaku Indians, found that he could not accept the villagers' claims that infanticide was easily accomplished and left no residue of guilt or blame: "We profoundly reject interring healthy children and therefore we assume that deep down the Mehinaku must feel the same way. Yet they claim otherwise. They institutionalize infanticide and assume that it is nearly painless: "The white man really feels for his infant. We do not. Infants are not precious to us" (1988:6).

These statements produced cognitive dissonance for Gregor, who began from the premise of a "universal human imperative requiring that children be protected and nurtured" (3). While aware of the danger of projecting his own moral repugnance

toward infanticide on the Amerindian villagers, Gregor found himself ultimately unable to "take Mehinaku opinion at face value" (6). The oft-repeated phrase "Infants are not precious to us," while emblematic of the "official" culture of Mehinaku infanticide, was covering a large reservoir of personal ambivalence and doubt. The Mehinaku mother, Gregor wrote, who brought an infant to term simply could not "be emotionally neutral about infanticide" (6) because she was subject to the same psychobiological feelings as the Western mother. And so Mehinaku cultural practices were interpreted as psychological "defenses" and "distancing devices": the rejected neonate was not referred to as a "baby" but rather as a *kanupa*, a "tabooed" or "forbidden" thing; the infanticidal act was accomplished very rapidly; and so forth. These led Gregor to conclude that, despite what the Indians told him, "Mehinaku infants are, in fact, precious to the villagers and infanticide is edged with moral and emotional ambivalence" (19). The burden of proof was, however, very thin, overinterpreted, and extremely circumstantial. It would not hold up in court. And it strikes me as indefensible to argue in a post hoc fashion that Mehinaku villagers *must* consider all their newborns precious because Western psychobiological theories tell us that all humans *are* this way.

Gregor's detailed descriptions of Mehinaku beliefs and practices toward their *kanupa* lead me to think that these women view and treat some of their neonates as prehumans, just as many women in the United States view and treat their fetuses. If we want to draw comparisons and analogies, it may be more appropriate to consider Mehinaku neonaticide as a form of "postpartum abortion." It seems to be practiced with similar intent and with a similar range of sentiments, explanations, and emotions. And just as Gregor would second-guess his informants' *real* feelings on the matter, some psychologists similarly dismiss the apparent psychological relief and the "indifference" of middle-class women who have had to abort a fetus as "denial" of their loss, grief, and deep moral ambivalence. With theories such as these, what is being "denied" are the disparate voices and moral sensibilities of women.

Renato Rosaldo, while later recovering from a profound personal loss in his own life, was moved to reflect (1983) on his initial refusal to "hear" what his Ilongot informants told him about "grief and the headhunter's rage." In rethinking Ilongot emotions in light of his own recent experience, Rosaldo came to accept that one could indeed feel a passionate, murderous, yet almost joyously self-affirming, rage in response to the death of a loved one. Or perhaps his own experience of grief was shaped by his Ilongot teachers, for fieldwork *is* transformative of the self. And so Rosaldo returned from his own mourning to challenge his anthropological colleagues to pay more attention to what their informants were telling them and to make room in their highly abstract theorizing for the often unanticipated "force" and intensity of emotions in human life.

NOTE

1   It has been well documented that preterm and low-birth-weight infants are at a considerably higher risk for mortality in the early months of life. F. C. Barros, C. G. Victoria, J. P. Vaughn, and A. M. B. Teixeira (1987) examined the causes of 215 infant deaths in a population-based cohort of 5,914 infants from southern Brazil: 87 percent of the deaths occurred in the first six months of life, and 53 percent of the infants who died were of low birth weight as compared to just 7.9 percent of the survivors.

REFERENCES

Abu-Lughod, Lila. 1986. *Veiled Sentiments: Honor and Poetry in a Bedouin Society*. Berkeley and Los Angeles: University of California Press.

Barros, F. C., C. G. Victoria, J. P. Vaughn, and A. M. B. Teixeira. 1987. "Infant Mortality in Southern Brazil." *Archives of Disease in Childhood* 62:487–90.

Belote, James, and Linda Belote. 1984. "Suffer the Little Children: Death, Autonomy, and Responsibility in a Changing Low Technology Environment." *Science, Technology and Human Values* 9 (4):35–48.

Bowlby, John. 1961a. "Childhood Mourning and Its Implications for Psychiatry." *Journal of American Psychiatry* 118:481–98.

——— 1961b. "Processes of Mourning." *International Journal of Psychoanalysis* 42:317–40.

——— 1980. *Loss: Sadness and Depression*. New York: Basic Books.

Da Cunha, Euclides. 1944. *Rebellion in the Backlands*. Chicago: University of Chicago Press. (Translation of 1904. *Os Sertões*. Rio de Janeiro: Livraria Francisco Alves.)

Deutsch, Helene. 1937. "Absence of Grief." *Psychoanalytic Quarterly* 6:12–22.

Dominguez, Luis Arturo. 1960. *Velorio de Angelito*. 2nd edn. Caracas: Ediciones del Ejecutivo del Estado Trujillo, Imprenta Oficial Estado Trujillo.

Ebelot, Alfredo. 1943. *La Pampa: Costumbres Argentinas*. Buenos Aires: Alfer and Vays.

Foster, George M. 1960. "The Ritual of Death in Spanish America." In *Culture and Conquest: America's Spanish Heritage*, 143–66. New York: Viking Fund.

Freud, Sigmund. 1957. "Mourning and Melancholia." In *The Standard Edition of the Complete Psychological Works of Sigmund Freud*, vol. 14, 243–58. London: Hogarth.

Freyre, Gilberto. 1945. *Brazil, an Interpretation*. New York: Knopf.

——— 1986a. *The Mansions and the Shanties: The Making of Modern Brazil*. Berkeley and Los Angeles: University of California Press. (Translation of 1936. *Sobrados e Macombos*. São Paulo: Companhia Editora Nacional.)

——— 1986b. *The Masters and the Slaves: A Study in the Development of Brazilian Civilization*. Berkeley and Los Angeles: University of California Press. (Translation of 1933. *Casa-Grande e Senzala*. Rio de Janeiro: Maia and Schmidt.)

Glick, Ira, Roster Weiss, and Murray Parkes. 1974. *The First Year of Bereavement*. New York: Wiley.

Gregor, Thomas. 1988. "Infants Are Not Precious to Us: The Psychological Impact of Infanticide Among the Mehinaku Indians." The 1988 Stirling Prize paper recipient, annual meeting of the American Anthropological Association, Phoenix, Arizona, November 16–20.

Johnson, J., M. J. Cunningham, S. Ewing, D. Hatcher, and C. Dannen. 1982. *Newborn Death*. Omaha: Centering Corp.

Kligman, Gail. 1988. *The Wedding of the Dead*. Berkeley and Los Angeles: University of California Press.

Kübler-Ross, Elisabeth. 1969. *On Death and Dying*. New York: Macmillan.

Lenz, Rodolfo. 1953. "Velorio de Angelito." In *Antología Ibérica Americana del Folklore*, ed. Félix Coluccio, 115–18. Buenos Aires: Guillermo Kraft.

Lifton, Robert Jay. 1967. *Death in Life*. New York: Touchstone.

——— 1975. "Preface." In *The Inability to Mourn*, by Alexander Mitscherlich and Margarete Mitscherlich, vii–xv. New York: Grove.

—— 1979. *The Broken Connection: On Death and the Continuity of Life.* New York: Simon and Schuster.

Lillo, Baldomero. 1942. "El Angelito." In *Relatos Populares*, 219–34. Santiago de Chile: Nascimento.

Lutz, Catherine. 1988. *Unnatural Emotions.* Chicago: University of Chicago Press.

—— 1990. "Emotion, Discourse, and the Politics of Everyday Life." In *Language and the Politics of Emotion*, ed. C. Lutz and L. Abu-Lughod, 1–23. Cambridge: Cambridge University Press.

Nations, Marilyn, and Linda-Anne Rebhun. 1988. "Angels with Wet Wings Can't Fly: Maternal Sentiment in Brazil and the Image of Neglect." *Culture, Medicine, and Psychiatry* 12:141–200.

Rosaldo, Michelle. 1984. "Toward an Anthropology of Self and Feeling." In *Culture Theory*, ed. Richard Shweder and Robert LeVine, 137–57. Cambridge: Cambridge University Press.

Rosaldo, Renato. 1980. *Ilongot Headhunting, 1883–1974: A Study in Society and History.* Stanford, Calif.: Stanford University Press.

—— 1983. "Grief and a Headhunter's Rage: On the Cultural Force of Emotion." In *Text, Play, and Story*, ed. Steven Plathner and Edward Bruner, 78–195. Washington, DC: American Ethnological Society.

—— 1989. *Culture and Truth: The Remaking of Social Analysis.* Boston: Beacon.

Rosenblatt, Paul, Patricia Walsh, and Douglas Jackson. 1976. *Grief and Mourning in Cross-Cultural Perspective.* New Haven, Conn.: HRAF Press.

Schecter, John. 1983. "Corona y Baile: Music in the Child's Wake of Ecuador and Hispanic America, Past and Present." *Revista de Músicia Latino America* 4(1):1–80.

—— 1988. *Velorio de Angelito / Baquiné / Wawa Velorio: The Emblematic Nature of the Transcultural, Yet Local, Latin American Child's Wake.* Latin American Studies Working Papers, no. 3. Santa Cruz: University of California.

Scheff, Thomas. 1979. *Catharsis in Healing, Ritual and Drama.* Berkeley and Los Angeles: University of California Press.

Sontag, Susan. 1979. *Illness as Metaphor.* New York: Farrar, Straus, and Giroux.

Winnicott, Donald Woods. 1964. *The Child, the Family, and the Outside World.* London: Penguin.

Part V

Mortuary Rituals

17

A Contribution to the Study of the Collective Representation of Death

Robert Hertz

We all believe we know what death is because it is a familiar event and one that arouses intense emotion. It seems both ridiculous and sacrilegious to question the value of this intimate knowledge and to wish to apply reason to a subject where only the heart is competent.

Yet questions arise in connection with death which cannot be answered by the heart because the heart is unaware of them. Even for the biologist death is not a simple and obvious fact; it is a problem to be scientifically investigated. But where a human being is concerned the physiological phenomena are not the whole of death. To the organic event is added a complex mass of beliefs, emotions and activities which give it its distinctive character. We see life vanish but we express this fact by the use of a special language: it is the soul, we say, which departs for another world where it will join its forefathers. The body of the deceased is not regarded like the carcass of some animal: specific care must be given to it and a correct burial; not merely for reasons of hygiene but out of moral obligation. Finally, with the occurrence of death a dismal period begins for the living during which special duties are imposed upon them.

Whatever their personal feelings may be, they have to show sorrow for a certain period, change the colour of their clothes and modify the pattern of their usual life. Thus death has a specific meaning for the social consciousness; it is the object of a collective representation. This representation is neither simple nor unchangeable: it calls for an analysis of its elements as well as a search for its origin. It is to this double study that we wish to contribute here.

In our own society the generally accepted opinion is that death occurs in one instant. The only purpose of the two or three days' delay between the demise and the burial is to allow material preparations to be made and to summon relatives and friends. No interval separates the life ahead from the one that has just ceased: no sooner has the last breath been exhaled than the soul appears before its judge and prepares to reap the reward for its good deeds or to expiate its sins. After this sudden catastrophe a more or less prolonged period of mourning begins. On certain dates, especially at the 'end of the year,' commemorative ceremonies are held in honour of the deceased. This conception of death, and this

From Robert Hertz, *Death and the Right Hand*, tr. Rodney and Claudia Needham (London: Cohen & West, 1960 [1907]).

particular pattern of events which constitute death and which follow it, are so familiar to us that we can hardly imagine that they are not necessary.

But the facts from many societies less advanced than our own do not fit into this framework. As Lafitau has already pointed out, 'In most primitive societies the dead bodies are only stored, so to speak, in the tomb where they are first placed. After a time they are given a new funeral and they receive the final funerary rites which are due to them.' This difference in custom is not, as we shall see, a mere accident; it brings to light the fact that death has not always been represented and felt as it is in our society.

In the following pages we shall try to establish the complex of beliefs relating to death and practices featuring a double burial. To achieve this aim we shall first use data gathered exclusively from Indonesian peoples, in particular the Dayak of Borneo, among whom this phenomenon takes a typical form. We shall then show, on the basis of sources relating to other ethnographic areas, that these are not merely local customs. In our account we shall follow the sequence of the events themselves, dealing first with the period between the death (in the usual sense of the word) and the final obsequies, and then with the concluding ceremony.

1.   The Intermediary Period

The ideas and practices occasioned by death can be classified under three headings, according to whether they concern the body of the deceased, his soul, or the survivors. This distinction does not by any means have an absolute value, but it does facilitate the presentation of the facts.

(a)   The body: provisional burial

Among peoples of the Malay archipelago who have not yet been too deeply influenced by foreign cultures it is the custom not to take the body at once to its final burial place; this move can only be made after a more or less long period of time during which the body is placed in a temporary shelter.

The general rule, among the Dayak, seems to have been to keep the bodies of chiefs and of wealthy people inside their own houses till the time of the final burial. The body is then put in a coffin the cracks of which are sealed with a resinous substance. The Dutch Government forbade this practice, at least in certain districts, for hygienic reasons; but quite different reasons besides that of foreign interference must have limited the extent of this kind of temporary burial. The living owe all kinds of care to the dead who reside among them. There is an uninterrupted wake which, as in Ireland or among our own farmers, entails much upheaval and great expenses, but for a much longer period. Furthermore, the presence of a corpse in the house imposes taboos on the inhabitants which are often severe: an inconvenience which is strongly felt because the Dayak longhouse is frequently the whole village in itself. It is for these reasons that the prolonged exposure of the body is nowadays exceptional.

As for those deceased who do not seem to deserve such heavy sacrifices, a shelter is provided by laying the coffin, after it has been exposed for a few days, either in a miniature wooden house raised on piles or, more often, on a kind of platform simply covered by a roof. This temporary burial place is sometimes in the immediate neighbourhood of the deceased person's house, but more often it is in a deserted place in the depth of the forest. Thus, if the deceased no longer has a place in the big house of the living, he at least possesses his own little house, one which is almost identical with those temporarily occupied by Dayak families when the cultivation of rice forces them to scatter over an area which is often very extensive.

This type of temporary burial, although apparently the most common one in the Malay archipelago, is not the only one that exists there; it may even be derived from a more ancient one which we find mentioned in several places: the exposure of the corpse, wrapped in bark, in the branches of a tree. On the other hand, instead of exposing the coffin to the atmosphere it is often preferred to bury it fairly deep, even though this means digging it up later. Whatever the variety of these customs, which often co-exist in one place and are substituted one for the other, the rite, in its essence, is constant; the body of the deceased, while awaiting the second burial, is temporarily deposited in a burial-place distinct from the final one; it is almost invariably isolated.

[. . .]

[L]et us conclude provisionally that the Indonesians attach a particular importance to the changes that occur in the corpse; their ideas in this matter prevent them from terminating the funeral rites at once and impose specific precautions and observances on the survivors.

So long as the final rite has not been celebrated the corpse is exposed to grave perils. It is a belief familiar to anthropologists and folklorists that the body is at certain times particularly exposed to the attacks of evil spirits and to all the harmful influences by which man is threatened; its diminished powers of resistance have to be reinforced by magical means. The period which follows death is particularly dangerous in this respect; that is why the corpse must be exorcised and be forearmed against demons. This preoccupation inspires, at least partly, the ablutions and various rites connected with the body immediately after death: such as, for instance, the custom of closing the eyes and other orifices of the body with coins or beads; it also imposes on the survivors the duty of keeping the deceased company during this dreaded period, to keep watch by his side and to beat gongs frequently in order to keep malignant spirits at bay. Thus the corpse, afflicted by a special infirmity, is an object of solicitude for the survivors at the same time as an object of fear.

(b)   The soul: its temporary stay on earth

In the same way as the body is not taken at once to its 'last resting-place', so the soul does not reach its final destination immediately after death. It must first undergo a kind of probation, during which it stays on earth in the proximity of the body, wandering in the forest or frequenting the places it inhabited while it was alive: it is only at the end of this period, at the time of the second funeral, and thanks to a special ceremony, that it will enter the land of the dead. This at least is the simplest form taken by this belief.

[. . .]

The stay of the soul among the living is somewhat illegitimate and clandestine. It lives, as it were, marginally in the two worlds: if it ventures into the after-world, it is treated there like an intruder; here on earth it is an importunate guest whose proximity is dreaded. As it has no resting place it is doomed to wander incessantly, waiting anxiously for the feast which will put an end to its restlessness. It is thus not surprising that during this period the soul should be considered as a malicious being: it finds the solitude into which it has been thrust hard to bear and tries to drag the living with it. Not yet having regular means of subsistence such as the dead are provided with, it has to pilfer from its relatives; in its present distress it remembers all the wrongs it has suffered during its life and seeks revenge. It watches its relatives' mourning sharply and if they do not properly fulfil their duties towards itself, if they do not actively prepare its release, it becomes irritated and inflicts diseases upon them, for death has endowed it with magical powers which enable it to put its bad intentions into practice. Whilst later, when it has its place among the dead, it will only visit its relatives when expressly invited, now it 'returns' of its own initiative through necessity or through malice, and its untimely appearance spreads terror.

This state of the soul, both pitiful and dangerous, during this confused period explains the complex attitude of the living in which pity and fear are mixed in variable proportions. They try to provide for the needs of the deceased and to ease his condition; but at the same time they remain on the defensive and refrain from contacts which they know to be harmful. When, the very next day after death, they have the soul led into the world of the dead, it is not known whether they are motivated by the hope of sparing the soul a painful wait, or by the desire to rid themselves as quickly as possible of its sinister presence; in fact both these preoccupations are mingled in their consciousness. These fears of the living can only end completely when the soul has lost the painful and disquieting character that it has after the death.

(c)   The living: mourning

Not only are the relatives of the deceased compelled to devote all kinds of care towards him during the intermediary period, not only are they the target of the spite and sometimes the attacks of the tormented soul, but they are moreover subjected to a whole set of prohibitions which constitute the mourning. Death, in fact, by striking the individual, has given him a new character; his body, which (except in certain abnormal cases) was in the realm of the ordinary, suddenly leaves it; it can no longer be touched without danger, it is an object of horror and dread. Now we know to what degree the religious or magical properties of things are regarded as contagious by 'primitives': the 'impure cloud' which, according to the Olo Ngaju, surrounds the deceased, pollutes everything it touches; i.e. not only the people and objects that have been in physical contact with the corpse, but also everything that is intimately connected, in the minds of the survivors, with the image of the deceased. His belongings may no longer be used for profane purposes; they must be destroyed or dedicated to the deceased, or at least stripped, by appropriate rites, of the harmful quality they have acquired. Similarly, the fruit trees that belonged to the deceased, and the streams where he used to fish, are the objects of a strict taboo; if the fruit and fish are taken they are used exclusively as provisions for the great funeral feast. The house of the deceased is impure for a more or less long period and the river on the bank of which it is built is tabooed.

As for the relatives of the deceased, they feel in themselves the blow that has struck one of them: a ban separates them from the rest of the community. They may not leave their village nor pay any visits; those most directly affected sometimes spend whole months confined to a corner of their house, sitting motionless and doing nothing. Neither may they receive visitors from outside, nor (should this be allowed) may they answer when they are questioned. They are forsaken, not only by men but also by the protective spirits: as long as their impurity lasts they cannot hope for any help from the powers above. The ban which is imposed on them affects their entire way of life. In consequence of the funerary contagion they are changed, and set apart from the rest of humanity; therefore they can no longer live the way others do. They may not share the diet nor follow the ways of dressing or adornment or of arranging the hair which are proper to individuals who are socially normal and which are the sign of this community to which (for a time) they no longer belong; hence the numerous taboos and special prescriptions to which people in mourning must conform.

Although the funeral pollution extends to all the relatives of the deceased and to all the inhabitants of the house where the death occurred, they are not all equally affected: thus the length of the mourning varies necessarily according to the degree of kinship. Among the Olo Ngaju, distant relatives are impure only for the few days immediately following the death; then, after a ceremony during which several hens are sacrificed, they may resume their ordinary life. But as for the closer relatives of the deceased, the particular condition which affects them is not dissipated so quickly or so easily; a long time must elapse before they can be completely freed of the ban that weighs upon them, a period which coincides precisely with the length of the temporary sepulture. During this period they must observe the taboos imposed on them by their state. A widower or a widow has no right to remarry, because the tie that binds the surviving spouse to the deceased will only be severed by the final ceremony. Indeed the close relatives, because they are as it were one with the deceased, share his condition, are included with him in the feelings which he inspires in the community, and are subject, like him, to a taboo during the whole interval between the death and the second funeral.

The facts do not always have the typical simplicity which we find, for instance, among the Olo Ngaju. The delay, often very long, necessitated by the preparations for the burial feast would prolong almost indefinitely the privations and hardships of mourning if the adoption of a fixed and relatively close date did not remedy this situation. It is very likely – though this fact cannot, it appears, be historically proved for the societies we are dealing with – that such a shortening of the mourning-period has occurred fairly frequently. Moreover, as Wilken has shown, the new date, set to mark the end of mourning instead of the final burial, need not have been chosen arbitrarily. Indeed, the state of the deceased during the intermediary period is not immutable: he undergoes changes which gradually weaken the dangerous character of the corpse and the soul and which compel the living, at certain dates, to hold special ceremonies. These dates, which at first constituted for the mourners merely stages towards liberation, have later become the time marking the end of their impurity. In this way compulsory mourning expires among the Olo Maanyan at the ceremony of the forty-ninth day and not, as among the Olo Ngaju, at the time of the final feast.

On the other hand, according to many sources, the lifting of the mourning-taboos coincides with the acquisition of a human head by the relatives of the decreased, and with the ceremony that takes place on the occasion of this happy event. But this custom too seems to be of an evolution whose principal stages we can determine. Among the Olo Ngaju the sacrifice of a human victim (whose head is cut off) is, as we shall see, one of the essential acts of the funeral feast. Sacrifice is indeed an indispensable condition for the conclusion of the mourning-period, but it is part of a complex whole and is bound up with the final burial. Among the Sea Dayak of Sarawak this rite assumes an autonomous character; certainly the *ulit* or taboo which constitutes the mourning ends completely only with the feast for the deceased. 'However, if in the meantime a human head has been acquired and celebrated in the village, the taboos are partially lifted and the wearing of ornaments is allowed again.' Should this procedure continue, and the practice of double burial be abandoned, a successful 'head-hunt', a partly fortuitous event and in any case external to the state of the deceased, will be enough to assure the release of the survivors.

Thus the long mourning of the relatives among these Indonesians seems to be bound up with ideas about the body and the soul of the deceased during the intermediary period; this mourning lasts normally till the second burial. Divergent customs in which this relationship is not apparent are due, we believe, to a later relaxation of the original custom.

The idea that the last funeral rites may not be celebrated immediately after death but only at the end of a certain period is not at all peculiar to the Indonesians nor to any one particular race; this is proved by the fact that the custom of temporary burial is extremely common.

Certainly the special forms which this custom takes are extremely varied; and it is very likely that ethnic and geographical reasons contribute to the predominance of a certain kind of temporary disposal of the body in a given cultural area, but that is a separate problem which we do not intend to discuss here. From our point of view there is a strict similarity between the exposure of the corpse in the branches of a tree, as is practised by tribes of Central Australia, or inside the house of the living, as is found among certain Papuans and among some Bantu tribes, or on a platform specially raised, as is usually done by the Polynesians and by many Indian tribes of North America, or lastly the temporary burial chiefly practised by South American Indians. All these various forms of temporary burial, which in a technical classification would probably have to appear under separate headings, are equivalent for us. They all have the same object, namely to offer the deceased a temporary residence until the natural disintegration of the body is completed and only the bones remain.

But certain funeral customs cannot, it seems, be reduced to this general type: the aim of embalmment is precisely to prevent the corruption of the flesh and the transformation of the body into a skeleton; cremation on the other hand forestalls the spontaneous alteration of the corpse with a rapid and almost complete destruction. We believe that these artificial ways of disposal do not differ essentially from the temporary ways that we have listed. The complete demonstration of this thesis would lead us too far from our subject; it must be enough for us merely to indicate here briefly the reasons which justify it in our eyes.

Let us first note that mummification is in certain cases a mere result of temporary exposure or burial, due to the desiccating qualities of the soil or of the air. Furthermore, even when the survivors do not intend to preserve the corpse artificially, they do not always abandon it completely during its decomposition. Since the transformation which it undergoes is painful and dangerous for itself as well as for those who surround it, steps are often taken to shorten the putrefaction, to diminish its intensity or to neutralize its sinister effects. A fire is kept burning beside the deceased in order to keep malign influences at bay, and also to warm the wandering soul and to exercise a soothing action upon the body, which is surrounded by scented smoke and smeared with aromatic ointments. The transition from these customs to the practice of smoking the corpse on a wickerwork frame or to a rudimentary embalmment is almost imperceptible. To pass from the spontaneous desiccation, which leaves only the bones, to the special form of desication which transforms the corpse into a mummy, it is enough for the survivors to have developed a desire to consign to the final grave a body as little changed as possible. In this the Egyptian funeral ritual agrees essentially with the beliefs and practices of the Indonesians: for seventy days, the embalmer fights the corruption which tries to invade the corpse; it is only at the end of this period that the body, having become imperishable, is taken to the grave, that the soul departs for the fields of Ialu and that the mourning of the survivors comes to an end. It seems legitimate therefore to consider mummification as a special case derived from temporary burial.

As for cremation, it is usually neither a final act, nor sufficient in itself; it calls for a later and complementary rite. In ancient Indian ritual, for instance, what is left of the body after it has been burnt must be carefully collected, as are the ashes, and deposited at the end of a certain period in a funeral monument, the cremation, and the burial of the burned bones, correspond respectively to the first and the second burial among the Indonesians. Evidently the very nature of the rite that is performed renders indeterminate the interval between the initial ceremony and the final one. This interval may be reduced to such an extent that both ceremonies form a single continuous whole, which does not, however, prevent the cremation being a preliminary operation and occupying, within the system of funeral rites, the same place as the temporary exposure. To this external similarity corresponds moreover a deeper resemblance: the immediate purpose of the temporary burial is, as well shall see, to give the bones time to dry completely. This transformation is not, in the eyes of the 'primitives', a mere physical disintegration; it changes the character of the corpse, turns it into a new body, and is, consequently, a necessary condition for the salvation of the soul. This is precisely the meaning of cremation: far from destroying the body of the deceased, it recreates it and makes it capable of entering a new life; it thus achieves the same result as the temporary exposure, but in a much faster way. The violent action of the fire spares the dead and the living the sorrows and dangers involved in the transformation of the corpse; or at least, it shortens that period considerably by accomplishing all at once the destruction of the flesh and the reduction of the body to immutable elements which in nature happens slowly and progressively. Thus there is a difference of duration and of means between cremation and the various modes of temporary sepulture, but not a difference of kind.

In all the rites studied so far, the soft parts of the corpse, where they are not preserved by artificial means, are purely and simply destroyed: they are looked upon as mere perishable and impure elements from which the bones must be separated; but more complex representations come to light in the practice known as endocannibalism, which consists in the ritual consumption of the deceased person's flesh by his relatives. This custom obviously does not have as exclusive aim the purification of the bones. It is not a refined cruelty like normal cannibalism, nor the fulfilment of a physical appetite; it is a sacred meal of which only certain definite groups of the tribe's members can partake and from which the women, among the Binbinga at least, are strictly excluded. By this rite the living incorporate into their own being the vitality and the special qualities residing in the flesh of the deceased; if this flesh were allowed to dissolve, the community would lose strength to which it is entitled. But, at the same time, endocannibalism spares the deceased the horror of a slow and vile decomposition, and allows his bones to reach their final state almost immediately. Furthermore, it secures for the flesh the most honourable of sepultures. In any case, the existence of this practice does not essentially alter the general type that we are trying to set up here, since after the consumption of the flesh the bones are gathered and kept by the relatives of the deceased for a certain period, at the end of which the final funeral is celebrated. During this period the soul is supposed to prowl around the bones and the sacred fire which is kept burning nearby, and silence is strictly imposed on close relatives of the deceased. Thus, endocannibalism, whatever its direct causes might be, takes its place among the various practices observed in order to lay bare the bones in the intermediary period between death and the last funeral rites.

[. . .]

We must beware of attributing to the various representations a generality and an explanatory value which they do not have. It would be arbitrary to elevate such and such a particular belief into a universal truth; to affirm for instance that the new body of the deceased is always formed by his volatised flesh. In fact, as we shall see, the bones are often thought to be the material support of the disincarnated soul. These opposed concepts agree in their essential point; in different ways they express a constant theme. Two complementary notions seem to compose this theme. The first is that death is not completed in one instantaneous act; it implies a lasting procedure which, at least in a great many instances, is considered terminated only when the dissolution of the body has ended. The second is that death is not a mere destruction but a transition: as it progresses so does the rebirth; while the old body falls to ruins, a new body takes shape, with which the soul – provided the necessary rites have been performed – will enter another existence, often superior to the previous one.

During this entire period when death is not yet completed, the deceased is treated as if he were still alive: food is brought to him, his relatives and friends keep him company and speak to him. He retains all his rights over his wife and guards them jealously. The widow is literally the wife of a person in whom death is present and continuous; thus she is considered during that period as impure and accursed and is condemned in a great many societies to the abject existence of an outcast; it is only at the time of the final ceremony that she can be freed and allowed by the kin of the deceased either to remarry or to return to her family. In the same way, the inheritance sometimes remains intact till the day the deceased has truly left this world. But the most instructive facts are those concerning the succession of kings and chiefs.

The custom of not proclaiming the successor to a chief until the final ceremony, a custom which we had already encountered in Timor, is reported from several peoples belonging to different ethnic groups. We may imagine the dangers of such an interregnum to the societies which are subjected to it. The death of a chief causes a deep disturbance in the social body which, especially if it is prolonged, has weighty consequences. It often seems that the blow which strikes the head of the community in the sacred person of the chief has the effect of suspending temporarily the moral and political laws and of setting free the passions which are normally kept in check by the social order. Thus we often encounter the custom of keeping the death of the chief secret during a period varying in length; those closest to the deceased are the only ones to know the truth, and they rule in his name; for others, the chief is merely ill. In Fiji, the secret is kept for a period varying between four and ten days; then, when the subjects, who begin to suspect something and who are impatient to be able legitimately to pillage and destroy, come to ask whether the chief has died, they are told that 'his body is decomposed by now'. It only remains for the disappointed visitors to go away; they have come too late and have missed their opportunity. The idea at work here, adds the author who reports these facts, is that so long as the decomposition is not sufficiently advanced, one is not really finished with the deceased, and his authority cannot be transmitted to his successor: the hand of the deceased can no longer hold the sceptre, but it has not yet let go. One must wait for the King to be entirely dead before one can cry: Long live the King! . . .

We have concentrated on demonstrating the relationship linking the condition of the soul and the period of mourning to the state of the corpse during the period preceding the final burial; but we do not maintain that the three terms are indissolubly tied together and cannot be found in isolation. This absolute assertion would be immediately contradicted by the facts; indeed it is hardly necessary to say that a belief in a temporary stay of the soul on earth and the institution of prolonged mourning are found in societies where no double burial has been reported. The end of the period of waiting is sometimes set conventionally: thus among certain Indian tribes of South America a rope is tied to the corpse, which is buried at once, and its extremity remains visible on the surface of the tomb; when this rope has vanished, as a result of rain or wear, it is an indication that the soul of the deceased, which was near the corpse until then, has finally left for the other world. But most often, when the deceased receives final burial without delay, it is the ideas relative to the passage of time itself which determine the end of the observances. The death will not be fully consummated, the soul will not leave the earth, the mourning of the living will not be ended till a certain period of time, considered complete, has elapsed; this period may be a month or a year; the coming of that day will then mark the close of the bad phase, the beginning of another life. Often it is the belief in the eminence and sanctity of a particular number which influences the choice: that is probably how we should explain the fact, so common among South American tribes, that the length of the soul's stay on earth or its journey to the other world is set at four days. Should we look upon these facts as detached and modified parts of the more complex whole that we have analysed? It is seldom possible to answer this question with certainty, but one would be tempted to answer in the affirmative if our view were accepted that there is a natural connection between the beliefs concerning the disintegration of the body, the fate of the soul, and the state of the survivors during that same period.

2. The Final Ceremony

The custom of a great feast connected with the final burial is general among the Indonesians; it is to be found under different names in most islands of the Malay Archipelago, from the Nicobars on the west to Halmahera on the east. This feast, which lasts for several days, sometimes even a month, is of extreme importance to the natives: it requires elaborate preparations and expenses which often reduce the family of the deceased to extreme poverty; many animals are sacrificed and eaten in banquets that often degenerate into huge orgies; invitations for this occasion are sent out to all the surrounding villages and they are never refused. In this way the feast tends to acquire a collective character; the expenses usually exceed the resources of a single family and, furthermore, such an interruption of normal life cannot be repeated often. Among the Olo Ngaju, the *tivah* is usually celebrated for several deceased persons at one time, the families concerned sharing the expenses. In other societies the feast is repeated at

regular intervals – every three years, for instance – and is celebrated in common for all those who have died in the meantime; it thus no longer directly concerns the family of a particular dead person, but the village as a whole. The final ceremony has three objects: to give burial to the remains of the deceased, to ensure the soul peace and access to the land of the dead, and finally to free the living from the obligations of mourning.

(a) The final burial

Among the Dayak of southeast Borneo, the final resting-place of the body is a small house, made entirely of ironwood, often finely carved, and raised on fairly high posts of the same material; such a monument is called *sandong*, and constitutes a family burial place which can hold a large number of people, and lasts many years. There are two kinds, which differ only in their contents and dimensions: the *sandong raung*, intended to hold coffins containing the dried remains of the deceased, and the *sandong tulang*, very much smaller, intended to hold only the bones wrapped in a cloth, or enclosed in an urn, and which have often been incinerated previously. There is no fixed place for this monument: often it is erected in the immediate neighbourhood of the house, inside the palisade which protects the village; often too it is erected fairly far away, on land specially reserved for the family.

These two types of final burial place are not peculiar to the southeastern Dayak; they are found among other tribes in Borneo itself and on other islands. We might perhaps be justified in relating these two types of burial to more primitive forms which are also found in the same ethnic family. The *sandong tulang* seems to be derived from a custom still in practice among the tribes of the interior of Borneo which consists in enclosing the remains of the deceased inside the trunk of an iron-wood tree which has been hollowed out for the purpose; and the *sandong raung* is probably only a modification of the custom, very common in the Malay Archipelago, by which all the coffins containing the bones are finally laid together in crevices in rocks or in underground caves.

These variations in the type of final burial place are however of secondary importance to us; the important thing is that in most cases it has a collective, at the very least familial, character; in this it contrasts clearly with the temporary burial in which, as we have seen, the corpse is usually isolated. The transfer of the remains, at the time of the final ceremony, is therefore not a mere change of place; it brings about a profound change in the condition of the deceased; it delivers him from the isolation in which he was plunged since his death, and reunites his body with those of his ancestors. This much emerges clearly from the study of the rites practised in the course of the second funeral.

The remains of the person or persons for whom the feast is to be celebrated are taken from their provisional sepulture and are brought back to the village, into the sumptuously decorated men's house, or into a house specially erected for the purpose; there they are laid on a sort of catafalque. But first an operation has to be performed which, according to one author, is the essential act of this feast: the bones are washed carefully. If, as sometimes happens, the bones are not completely bare, the flesh still clinging to them is detached. They are then put into a new wrapping, which is often precious. These rites are far from insignificant: by purifying the body, by giving the deceased a new attire, the living mark the end of one period and the beginning of another; they abolish a sinister past and give the deceased a new and glorified body with which to enter worthily the company of his ancestors.

But he does not depart without having been bid a solemn farewell and without the last days of his earthly existence being filled with pomp. As soon as the coffin is placed on the catafalque, among the Olo Ngaju, the widower or widow sits down very close to it and says to the deceased: 'You are with us for a while still, then you will go away to the pleasant place where our ancestors live.' They try to satisfy the deceased by displaying near his bones the sacred vases and most precious treasures belonging to the family, which he enjoyed during his life-time and which will assure him an opulent life in the other world.

[. . .]

(b)   The admittance of the soul to the land of the dead

Parallel to that which is done to the remains of the deceased, a funeral service is performed which changes the condition of the soul: namely, it puts

an end to its anxiety by solemnly introducing it into the society of the dead. It is an arduous task which requires powerful help, since the road that leads to the other world is strewn with perils of all kinds, and the soul will not reach the end of the journey unless it is led and protected by some powerful psycho-pomp, such as Tempon Telon of the Olo Ngaju. In order to guarantee this indispensable help to the soul, priests and priestesses, summoned by the family of the deceased, recite long incantations to the accompaniment of a drum.

[. . .]

By putting an end to the troubles of the soul, the final ceremony removes every cause that the soul has had since its death to be ill-disposed towards the living. It is still true, of course, that even after the great funeral feast the dead belong to another world, and that a too intimate contact with them is dangerous for the living. However, the souls generally leave their relatives alone once the latter have discharged their last duties towards them. In many cases, this negative position is not all: there are regular relations and an exchange of services between the community of the living and that of the dead. In certain Indonesian societies the appeased souls are actually worshipped, and they then settle near the domestic hearth in some consecrated object or in a statuette of the deceased which they animate: their presence, duly honoured, guarantees the prosperity of the living. Thus the act that re-unites the soul of the deceased to those of his ancestors sometimes confers on it the character of a tutelary divinity, and solemnly ensures its return to the heart of the family home.

(c)   The liberation of the living

The customs examined so far have dealt with the welfare of the deceased; any benefit to the living was merely incidental. But we find a series of no less important practices performed at the funeral feast, whose direct object is to end the mourning of the relatives of the deceased and to bring these back into communion with society.

On the first day of the *tivah*, after a banquet attended only by women, one of these prepares seven small parcels of rice for the souls of the dead, and seven others for the evil spirits; at the same time she pronounces a formula which clearly reveals the meaning of this act: 'I place here your food; by this I crush all resistance, all that is impure, all bad dreams, and I set an end to all tears.' This offering is the signal that the time has come for the living to part from the dead and to dispel the unease which has enveloped them during the mourning. It is only the first manifestation of a theme which will be taken up many times during the feast.

The living, especially the relatives of the deceased, occupy the central place in the song of the priestesses which leads the souls into the celestial city. During the entire time of the incantations, the priestesses carry the souls of the givers of the feast in their aprons, like small children; each time they ascend to heaven to ask the good spirits for help, they take their protégés with them. Also a kind of fascination draws the souls of the living towards the regions above: they have to be recalled by name if they are not to stay in the other world where they have followed the dead. But these spiritual journeys are not made in vain. The priestesses never fail to call the spirits' attention to the givers of the feast: 'Rise', they call to the most powerful among the spirits, 'squeeze the body of this man here to drive misfortune from him, remove the stench that petrifies like the thunderbolt, dispel the impure cloud of the deceased, repel the fate that degrades and that causes life to retreat.' It is not enough to 'kill the adversity' which oppressed the living. Tempon Telon must regenerate them and ensure their long life by sprinkling their body with revivifying water. He has also to give them 'the potent charms which secure wealth, success in commerce, and the lustre of glory'. Naturally, the priestesses simultaneously perform the acts which their song imposes on, or ascribes to, the celestial spirits; and these rites, both oral and manual, bring about a profound change in the living: delivered from the evil which possessed them, they return to normal life with a new fund of vital and social power.

But if the living are to be rid of their impurity a sacrifice is essential, preferably that which in the eyes of the Dayak and most Indonesians has irresistable efficacy: the sacrifice of a human victim whose head is cut off and afterwards kept. An entire day, at the time of the *tivah*, is devoted to this essential rite. The prisoners or slaves, who have previously been de-prived of their souls by a magical intervention, are chained to the sacrificial post; the male relatives of the deceased act collectively as sacrificers, dancing and leaping around the victim and striking him at random with their spears. The screams of pain are greeted with joyful shouts, because the more cruel the torture the happier the souls are in heaven. At last, when the victim falls to the ground he is solemnly decapitated in the midst of an intense joy; his blood is collected by a priestess who sprinkles it on the living 'to reconcile them with their deceased relative'; the head is either deposited with the bones of the deceased or attached to the top of a post erected near the *sandong*. The funeral sacrifice, without any doubt, is not meant simply to release the family of the deceased from the taboo; its functions are as complex as the aim of the feast of which it is the decisive act. The mystic fury of the sacrificers, while it desacralises the living, gives peace and beatitude to the soul of the deceased and (probably) regenerates his his body. The liberation of the mourners is only the most obvious among the changes brought about simultaneously by virtue of the sacrifice, that which interests the living most directly.

Every religious ceremony must be followed by practices which free the participants from the dangerous character they have acquired and which enable them to re-enter the profane world. The rites acquire a special importance at the time of the funeral feast, to the extent sometimes of constituting a second feast, distinct from the first one and succeeding it. The perils incurred during a ceremony like the *tivah* are in fact particularly intense. No doubt it has beneficial consequences and constitutes a kind of victory over misfortune; but on the other hand it touches the kingdom of death and compels the living to enter into relations with the forces of evil and with the residents of the other world. That is why the relatives of the deceased and also those who have taken part in the funeral proceedings are compelled to purify themselves. They bathe in the river, and to increase the effectiveness of this the blood of sacrificed animals is sometimes mixed with the water, and while they swim to the bank the priestesses, who follow them in boats, thrust aside evil influences from their bodies with the help of burning torches and sacred brooms. At last, if all the rites have been correctly observed, the living are washed clean of all pollution and freed of the deathly contagion.

[...]

We have seen that in Indonesia the feast that ends the funeral rites simultaneously releases the living from the obligation to mourn; this is a constant feature. The content of the rite may vary but the general meaning of it is fixed: the relatives of the deceased are unburdened of the dangerous character that misfortune has bestowed upon them, and they receive a 'new body', such as normal life demands; they part finally with death and with evil forces, in order to make their rightful re-entry into the world of the living.

The institution of secondary burial, whose meaning and generality we have tried to show, often undergoes a marked regression. In some societies unmistakable traces of the original custom subsist: the Dene, for instance, at a certain time after death open the sarcophagus holding the remains of the deceased and merely look at them without daring to run the risk and pollution entailed by contact with the corpse. After a meal has been offered to the souls the tomb is closed for ever. Among other peoples, the last rite consists in trampling on the grave, or in sealing it by the erection of a funeral monument. Only then does the deceased come into full possession of the place which up till that time he merely occupied. In other cases, even these survivals are not found: the only object of the feast is to terminate the funeral period, to put an end to the period of mourning, or to make final provision for the well-being of the disembodied soul. But these functions in turn are removed from the final ceremony or lose their importance. We have seen that there is a close solidarity between the body and the soul of the deceased: if the true funeral takes place immediately after death, one tends naturally to ensure the salvation of the soul from that moment on. On the other hand, the mourning has changed in nature; it is no longer a question of the survivors marking their participation in the present condition of the deceased, but of expressing a sorrow that is considered obligatory. Hence the duration of the mourning is no longer dependent on ideas about the deceased: it is entirely determined by causes of a domestic or social kind. Furthermore, special practices are no longer needed to liberate the relatives of the deceased; they regain their former position unaided at the end of the prescribed period. Thus impoverished, the final ceremony is now merely a simple anniversary service, whose only object is to pay last respects to the deceased and to commemorate his death.

3. Conclusion

It is impossible to interpret the body of facts that we have presented if we see in death a merely physical event. The horror inspired by the corpse does not spring from the simple observation of the changes that occur in the body. Proof that such a simplistic explanation is inadequate lies in the fact that in one and the same society the emotion aroused by death varies extremely in intensity according to the social status of the deceased, and may even in certain cases be entirely lacking. At the death of a chief, or of a man of high rank, a true panic sweeps over the group; the corpse is so powerfully contagious that among the Kaffir the entire kraal must be deserted at once and even enemies would not be willing to live there. On the contrary, the death of a stranger, a slave, or a child will go almost unnoticed; it will arouse no emotion, occasion no ritual. It is thus not as the extinction of an animal life that death occasions social beliefs, sentiments and rites.

Death does not confine itself to ending the visible bodily life of an individual; it also destroys the social being grafted upon the physical individual and to whom the collective consciousness attributed great dignity and importance. The society of which that individual was a member formed him by means of true rites of consecration, and has put to work energies proportionate to the social status of the deceased: his destruction is tantamount to a sacrilege, implying the intervention of powers of the same order but of a negative nature. God's handiwork can be undone only by himself or by Satan. This is why primitive peoples do not see death as a natural phenomenon: it is always due to the action of spiritual powers, either because the deceased has brought disaster upon himself by violating some taboo, or because an enemy has 'killed' him by means of spells or magical practices. The ethnographers who report this widespread belief see in it a gross and persistent error; but we ought rather to consider it as the naïve expression of a permanent social need. Indeed society imparts its own character of permanence to the individuals who compose it: because it feels itself immortal and wants to be so, it cannot normally believe that its members, above all those in whom it incarnates itself and with whom it identifies itself, should be fated to die. Their destruction can only be the consequence of a sinister plot. Of course, reality brutally contradicts this assumption, but the denial is always received with the same indignant amazement and despair. Such an attack must have an author upon whom the group may vent its anger. Sometimes the deceased himself is accused: 'What cause did you have, you ingrate, to forsake us?' And he is summoned to return. More often the near relatives are accused of culpable negligence or of witchcraft; the sorcerers must at all costs be discovered and executed; or, finally, curses are directed against the murderous spirits, as by the Naga, for instance, who threaten them with their spears and defy them to appear.

Thus, when a man dies, society loses in him much more than a unit; it is stricken in the very principle of its life, in the faith it has in itself. Consider the accounts by ethnographers of the scenes of furious despair which take place when death sets in or immediately after the expiry. Among the Warramunga, for instance, men and women throw themselves pell-mell on the dying person, in a compact mass, screaming and mutilating themselves atrociously. It seems that the entire community feels itself lost, or at least directly threatened by the presence of antagonistic forces: the very basis of its existence is shaken. As for the deceased, both victim and prisoner of evil powers, he is violently ejected from the society, dragging his closest relatives with him.

But this exclusion is not final. In the same way as the collective consciousness does not believe in the necessity of death, so it refuses to consider it irrevocable. Because it believes in itself a healthy society cannot admit that an individual who was part of its own substance, and on whom it has set its mark, shall be lost for ever. The last word must remain with life: the deceased will rise from the grip of death and will

return, in one form or another, to the peace of human association. This release and this reintegration constitute, as we have seen, one of the most solemn actions of collective life in the least advanced societies we can find. And when, closer to us, the Christian Church guarantees 'the resurrection and the life' to all those who have fully entered it, it only expresses, in a rejuvenated form, the promise that every religious society implicitly makes to its members.

Only what was elsewhere the achievement of the group itself, acting through special rites, here becomes the attribute of a divine being, of a Saviour who by his sacrificial death has triumphed over death and freed his disciples from it; resurrection, instead of being the consequence of a particular ceremony, is a consequence, postponed for an indeterminate period, of God's grace. Thus, at whatever stage of religious evolution we place ourselves, the notion of death is linked with that of resurrection; exclusion is always followed by a new integration.

Once the individual has surmounted death, he will not simply return to the life he has left; the separation has been too serious to be abolished so soon. He is reunited with those who, like himself and those before him, have left this world and gone to the ancestors. He enters this mythical society of souls which each society constructs in its own image. But the heavenly or subterranean city is not a mere replica of the earthly city. By recreating itself beyond death, society frees itself from external constraints and physical necessities which, here on earth, constantly hinder the flight of the collective desire. Precisely because the other world exists only in the mind, it is free of all limitations: it is – or can be – the realm of the ideal. There is no longer any reason why game should not be perpetually abundant in the 'happy hunting-grounds' of the other world, or why every day of the eternal life should not be a Sunday to the Englishman eager for psalms. Moreover, in some societies, the way in which earthly life ends is a kind of blemish; death spreads its shadow over this world, and the very victory that the soul has gained over death opens up for it an infinitely pure and more beautiful life. These notions, of course, do not appear at first in a clear-cut and precise form. It is especially when the religious society is differentiated from domestic or political social life that death seems to free the believer from the bodily and temporal calamities which kept him separated from God while on earth. Death enables him, regenerated, to enter the community of Saints, the invisible church which in heaven is worthy of being about the Lord from whom it proceeds. But the same conception is present, in a vague and concealed form, from the beginning of religious evolution: in rejoining his forefathers, the deceased is reborn transfigured and raised to a superior power and dignity. In other words, in the eyes of primitives, death is an initiation.

This statement is not a mere metaphor; if death, for the collective consciousness, is indeed the passage from the visible society to the invisible, it is also a step exactly analogous to that by which a youth is withdrawn from the company of women and introduced into that of adult men. This new integration, which gives the individual access to the sacred mysteries of the tribe, also implies a profound change in his personality, a renewal of his body and soul that gives him the religious and moral capacity he needs. The similarity of the two phenomena is so fundamental that this change is often brought about by the pretended death of the aspirant, followed by his resurrection into a superior life.

Death, as it is seen by the collective consciousness, should not be compared only with initiation. The close relationship that exists between funeral rites and rites of birth or marriage has often been noticed. Like death, these two events give rise to an important ceremony in which a certain anxiety is mixed with the joy. In all three cases, the mystical dangers incurred must be guarded against, and purificatory rites must be observed. The similarity of these practices expresses a basic analogy: marriage brings about a double change of status; on the one hand it withdraws the fiancée from her own clan or family in order to introduce her into the clan or family of the husband; and on the other hand, it transfers her from the class of young girls into that of married women. As for birth, it accomplishes, for the collective consciousness, the same transformation as death but the other way round. The individual leaves the invisible and mysterious world that his soul has inhabited, and he enters the society of the living. This transition from one group to another, whether real or imaginary, always supposes a profound renewal of the individual which is marked by such customs as the acquisition of a new name, the changing of clothes or of the way of life. This operation is considered to be full of risks because it involves a stirring to action of necessary but dangerous forces. The body of the new-born child is no less sacred than the corpse. The veil of the bride and that of the widow are of different colours, but they nonetheless have the same function, which is to isolate and set apart a redoubtable person.

Thus death is not originally conceived as a unique event without any analogue. In our civilisation, the life of an individual seems to go on in approximately the same way from birth to death; the successive stages of our social life are weakly marked and constantly allow the continuous thread of the individual life to be discerned. But less advanced societies, whose internal structure is clumsy and rigid, conceive the life of a man as a succession of heterogeneous and well-defined phases, to each of which corresponds a more or less organised social class. Consequently, each promotion of the individual implies the passage from one group to another: an exclusion, i.e. a death, and a new integration, i.e. a rebirth. Of course these two elements do not always appear on the same level: according to the nature of the change produced, it is sometimes the one and sometimes the other on which the collective attention is focused, and which determines the dominant character of the event; but both elements are in fact complementary. To the social consciousness, death is only a particular instance of a general phenomenon.

It is easy for us to understand now why death has long been looked upon as a transitory state of a certain duration. Every change of status in the individual, as he passes from one group to another, implies a deep change in society's mental attitude toward him, a change that is made gradually and requires time. The brute fact of physical death is not enough to consummate death in people's minds: the image of the recently deceased is still part of the system of things of this world, and looses itself from them only gradually by a series of internal partings. We cannot bring ourselves to consider the deceased as dead straight away: he is too much part of our substance, we have put too much of ourselves into him, and participation in the same social life creates ties which are not to be severed in one day. The 'factual evidence' is assailed by a contrary flood of memories and images, of desires and hopes. The evidence imposes itself only gradually and it is not until the end of this prolonged conflict that we give in and believe in the separation as something real. This painful psychological process expresses itself in the objective and mystical shape of the belief that the soul only gradually severs the ties binding it to this world: it finds a stable existence again only when the representation of the deceased has acquired a final and pacified character in the consciousness of the survivors. There is too deep an opposition between the persisting image of a familiar person who is like ourselves and the image of an ancestor, who is sometimes worshipped and always distant, for this second image to replace the former immediately. That is why the idea of an 'intermediary state between death and resurrection' imposes itself, a state in which the soul is thought to free itself from the impurity of death or from the sin attaching to it. Thus, if a certain period is necessary to banish the deceased from the land of the living, it is because society, disturbed by the shock, must gradually regain its balance; and because the double mental process of disintegration and of synthesis that the integration of an individual into a new world supposes, is accomplished in a molecular fashion, as it were, which requires time.

It seems that society cannot for long become conscious of itself and of the phenomena which constitute its life except in an indirect way, after it has been in a sense reflected in the material world. The infection which for a time takes possession of the body, shows in a perceptible form the temporary presence of evil spirits. The gradual destruction of the earthly body, which prolongs and completes the initial assault, expresses concretely the state of bewilderment and anguish of the community for so long as the exclusion of the deceased has not been completed. On the other hand, the reduction of the corpse to bones, which are more or less unchangeable and upon which death will have no further hold, seems to be the condition and the sign of the final deliverance. Now that the body is similar to those of its ancestors, there seems to be no longer any obstacle to the soul's entering their community. It has often been remarked, and rightly, that there is a close relationship between the representation of the body and that of the soul. This mental connection is necessary, not only because collective thought is primarily concrete and incapable of conceiving a purely spiritual existence, but above all because it has a profoundly stimulating and dramatic character. The group requires actions that will focus the attention of its members, orientate their imagination in a definite direction, and which will inspire the belief in everybody. The material on which the collective activity will act after the death, and which will be the object of the rites, is naturally the very body of the deceased. The integration of the deceased into the invisible society will not be effected unless his material remains are reunited with those of his forefathers. It is the action of society on the body that gives full reality to the imagined drama of the soul. Thus, if the physical phenomena which constitute or follow death do not in themselves determine the collective representations and emotions, they nevertheless help to give them the particular form that they present, and lend them a degree of material support. Society projects its own ways of thinking and feeling on to the world that surrounds it; and the world, in turn, fixes them, regulates them, and assigns them limits in time.

The hypothesis we have advanced above seems confirmed by the fact that in the very societies where the custom of secondary burial is predominant certain categories of people are purposely excluded from the normal funeral ritual.

This is the case, firstly, with children. The Olo Maanyan place a child less than seven years old in a coffin which will not be changed and which they carry to the family burial place the very day of the death. A sacrifice performed the next day suffices to enable the soul, purified, to enter the realm of the dead at once. The mourning of even the father and mother lasts only a week. But the most common practice among the Dayak and the Papuans seems to be to enclose the bodies of small children inside a tree or to hang them in branches. The concept underlying this custom is clearly revealed to us by the Dayak of Kutai: they believe that men come from the trees and must return there. That is why when a Bahau woman bears a premature child, or if she has been tormented by bad dreams during pregnancy, she can refuse the child by returning it to the tree that it has left either too early or in a worrying fashion. They obviously hope, as is explicitly stated of other peoples, that the soul will soon be reincarnated, perhaps in the womb of the same woman, and will this time make a more auspicious entry into this world. The deaths of children thus provoke only a very weak social reaction which is almost instantaneously completed. It is as though, for the collective consciousness, there were no real death in this case.

Indeed, since the children have not yet entered the visible society, there is no reason to exclude them from it slowly and painfully. As they have not really been separated from the world of spirits, they return there directly, without any sacred energies needing to be called upon, and without a period of painful transition appearing necessary. The death of a new-born child is, at most, an infra-social event; since society has not yet given anything of itself to the child, it is not affected by its disappearance and remains indifferent.

In various Australian tribes, old people who, because of their great age, are incapable of taking part in the totemic ceremonies, who have lost their aptitude for sacred functions, are buried immediately after death instead of being exposed on a platform till the complete desiccation of their bones, as are other members of the tribe. This is so because, due to the weakening of their faculties, they have ceased to participate in social life; their death merely consecrates an exclusion from society which has in fact already been completed, and which every one has had time to get used to.

Finally, the type of death also causes numerous exceptions to the normal ritual. All those who die a violent death or by an accident, women dying in childbirth, people killed by drowning or by lightning, and suicides, are often the object of special rites. Their bodies inspire the most intense horror and are got rid of precipitately; furthermore, their bones are not laid with those of other deceased members of the group who have died a normal death. Their unquiet and spiteful souls roam the earth for ever; or, if they emigrate to another world, they live in a separate village, sometimes even in a completely different area from that inhabited by other souls. It seems, in the most typical cases at least, that the transitory period extends indefinitely for these victims of a special malediction and that their death has no end.

In cases of this kind it is not weakness of the emotion felt by the group which opposes the performance of normal funeral rites, but on the contrary it is the extreme intensity and suddenness of this emotion. An analogy throws more light upon this phenomenon. We have seen that birth, like death, frees dangerous forces which make mother and child taboo for a while. Usually these forces gradually disperse and the mother can be freed. But if the event occurs in an unusual fashion – for instance, if twins are born – then, according to the illuminating expression of the Ba-Ronga, 'this birth is death', for it excludes from normal life those who seem fated to such a birth. It endows them with a sacred character of such strength that no rite will ever be able to efface it, and it throws the entire community into a state of terror and consternation. Similarly, the sinister way in which some individuals are torn from this world separates them for ever from their relatives: their exclusion is final and irremediable. For it is the last sight of the individual, as he was when death struck him down, which impresses itself most deeply on the memory of the living. This image, because of its uniqueness and its emotional content, can never be completely erased. So it is pointless to wait a certain period of time in order then to reunite the deceased with his ancestors; reunion being impossible, delay is senseless; death will be eternal, because society will always maintain towards these accursed individuals the attitude of exclusion that it adopted from the first.

The explanation we propose enables us therefore to understand at the same time why in a given society double burial rites are practised, and why in certain cases they are not.

Let us sum up briefly the results of our investigations. For the collective consciousness death is in normal circumstances a temporary exclusion of the individual from human society. This exclusion effects his passage from the visible society of the living into the invisible society of the dead. Mourning, at its origin, is the necessary participation of the living in the mortuary state of their relative, and lasts as long as this state itself. In the final analysis, death as a social phenomenon consists in a dual and painful process of mental disintegration and synthesis. It is only when this process is completed that society, its peace recovered, can triumph over death.

18

The Rites of Passage

Arnold van Gennep

Funerals

On first considering funeral ceremonies, one expects rites of separation to be their most prominent component, in contrast to rites of transition and rites of incorporation, which should be only slightly elaborated. A study of the data, however, reveals that the rites of separation are few in number and very simple, while the transition rites have a duration and complexity sometimes so great that they must be granted a sort of autonomy. Furthermore, those funeral rites which incorporate the deceased into the world of the dead are most extensively elaborated and assigned the greatest importance.

Once again I must be satisfied with a few brief suggestions. Everyone knows that funeral rites vary widely among different peoples and that further variations depend on the sex, age, and social position of the deceased. However, within the extraordinary multiplicity of detail certain dominant features may be discerned, and some of these I shall class together.

Funeral rites are further complicated when within a single people there are several contradictory or different conceptions of the afterworld which may become intermingled with one another, so that their confusion is reflected in the rites. Furthermore, man is often thought to be composed of several elements whose fate after death is not the same – body, vital force, breath-soul, shadow-soul, midget-soul, animal-soul, blood-soul, head-soul, etc. Some of these souls survive forever or for a time, others die. In the discussion that follows I shall abstract from all these variations, since they affect the formal complexity of rites of passage but not their internal structure.

Mourning, which I formerly saw simply as an aggregate of taboos and negative practices marking an isolation from society of those whom death, in its physical reality, had placed in a sacred, impure state,[1] now appears to me to be a more complex phenomenon. It is a transitional period for the survivors, and they enter it through rites of separation and emerge from it through rites of reintegration into society (rites of the lifting of mourning). In some cases, the transitional period of the living is a counterpart of the transitional period of the deceased,[2] and the

From Arnold van Gennep, *The Rites of Passage*, tr. Monika B. Vizedom and Gabrielle L. Caffee (Chicago: University of Chicago Press, 1960 [1909]).

termination of the first sometimes coincides with the termination of the second – that is, with the incorporation of the deceased into the world of the dead. Thus among the Habé of the Niger plateau "the period of widowhood corresponds, it is said, to the duration of the journey of the deceased's wandering soul up to the moment when it joins the divine ancestral spirits or is reincarnated."[3]

During mourning, the living mourners and the deceased constitute a special group, situated between the world of the living and the world of the dead, and how soon living individuals leave that group depends on the closeness of their relationship with the dead person. Mourning requirements are based on degrees of kinship and are systematized by each people according to their special way of calculating that kinship (patrilineally, matrilineally, bilaterally, etc.) It seems right that widowers and widows should belong to this special world for the longest time; they leave it only through appropriate rites and only at a moment when even a physical relationship (through pregnancy, for example) is no longer discernible. The rites which lift all the regulations (such as special dress) and prohibitions of mourning should be considered rites of reintegration into the life of society as a whole or of a restricted group; they are of the same order as the rites of reintegration for a novice.

During mourning, social life is suspended for all those affected by it, and the length of the period increases with the closeness of social ties to the deceased (e.g., for widows, relatives), and with a higher social standing of the dead person. If the dead man was a chief, the suspension affects the entire society. There is public mourning, the proclamation of holidays, and, following the death of certain petty kings of Africa, a "period of license." At this very moment (1908) in China, new political, economic, and administrative necessities tend to mitigate the considerable effects on the society of the Emperor's and Empress Regent's deaths.[4] Formerly, social life even in the households in China was completely suspended on such occasions for many months – a suspension which in our time would be simply catastrophic.

The transitional period in funeral rites is first marked physically by the more or less extended stay of the corpse or the coffin in the deceased's room (as during a wake), in the vestibule of his house, or elsewhere. But this stay is only an attenuated form of a whole series of rites whose importance and universality has already been pointed out by Lafitau. "Among most savage nations, the dead bodies are only in safekeeping in the sepulchre where they have initially been placed. After a certain time, new obsequies are given them, and what is due them is completed by further funeral duties."[5] Then he describes the rites of the Caribs: "They are convinced [that the dead] do not go to the land of souls until they are without flesh." The existence of a transitional period also interested Mikhailowski.[6] The chief rite of this period consists of either removing the flesh or waiting until it falls off by itself. On this idea are based, for instance, the ceremonies performed by the Betsileos of Madagascar, who have a first series of rites while waiting for the corpse to decompose in its abode (where its putrefaction is accelerated by a great fire) and then a second series for the burial of the skeleton.[7]

For others, the transition stage is sometimes subdivided into several parts, and, in the postliminal period, its extension is systematized in the form of commemorations (a week, two weeks, a month, forty days, a year, etc.) similar in nature to rites of the anniversary of a wedding, of birth, and sometimes of initiation.

Since funeral stages already have been closely studied for Indonesia,[8] I shall use instances from data pertaining to other regions. The ceremonies of the Todas are similar to the Indonesian rites.[9] They include cremation, preservation of the relics and burial of the ashes, and the erection of a circle of stones around them. The whole procedure lasts several months. The dead go to Amnodr, a subterranean world, and there they are called "Amatol"; the route is not the same for all the clans, and it is surrounded with obstacles. The "bad" fall from a thread which serves as a bridge into a stream on whose shores they live for a while, mingling with individuals from all sorts of tribes. The buffaloes also go to Amnodr. The Amatol walk a great deal there, and when they have worn their legs up to the knees they return to earth. Among the Ostyak of Salekhard,[10] the house is stripped of all its contents except the utensils of the deceased, who is dressed and placed in a dugout canoe. A shaman asks the deceased why he has died. He is taken to the burial place of his clan and deposited in the boat on the frozen ground, with his feet facing north, surrounded with all the things he will need in the next world. The deceased is thought to partake of a farewell meal eaten on the spot by the mourners, who then all leave. The female relatives make a doll in the image of the deceased, and they dress, wash, and feed it every day for two and a half years if the dead person was a man, or for two years if it was a woman.[11] Then the doll is placed on the tomb.

Mourning lasts five months for a man and four months for a woman. The dead go by a long and tortuous route toward the north, where the dark and cold land of the dead is located.[12] The length of the journey seems to coincide with the period during which the doll is kept. Thus there is a series of preliminary rites, a transitional period, and a final funeral when the dead person reaches his final abode.

The Northern Ostyaks place the land of the dead beyond the mouth of the Ob, in the Arctic Ocean;[13] it is illuminated only by the light of the moon. Not far from that world the road divides in three forks which lead to three entrances, one for the assassinated, the drowned, the suicides, etc., another for the other sinners, and a third for those who have lived a normal life. For the Irtysh Ostyak, the other world is in the sky. It is a lovely country reached by ascending ladders each three hundred to one thousand feet long, or by climbing up a chain; from it the gods, the sacred bears (totems perhaps),[14] and the dead sometimes come back to earth – or so say the ancient legends of the epics.[15] It seems to me that there must be a relationship between the length of time during which the dolls are kept and the supposed duration of the journey into the other world.

The funeral ceremonies of the Kol of India furnish a good example of a combination of known prophylactic rites with rites of passage.[16] Their order runs as follows: (1) Immediately after death the corpse is placed on the ground "so that the soul should more easily find its way to the home of the dead," which is under the earth. (2) The corpse is washed and painted yellow to chase away evil spirits who would stop the soul on its journey. (3) For the same purpose the assembled relatives and neighbors utter pitiable cries. (4) The corpse is placed on a scaffold with the feet facing forward so that the soul should not find the way back to the hut, and for the same reason the procesion travels by detours. (5) The cortege must not include either children or girls; the women cry; the men are silent. (6) Each man carries a piece of dry wood to throw on the pyre. (7) Rice and the tools of the deceased's sex are placed there, and in the mouth of the corpse there are rice cakes and silver coins for the journey, since the soul retains a shadow of the body. (8) The women leave, and the pyre is lighted;[17] the litter is also burned to prevent the deceased's return. (9) The men gather the calcified bones, place them in a pot, and bring the pot back to the deceased's house where it is hung from a post. (10) Grains of rice are strewn along the route, and food is placed in front of the door so that the deceased, should he return in spite of all precautions, will have something to eat without harming anyone. (11) All the deceased's utensils are carried far away, because they have become impure and because the deceased may be hidden in them. (12) The house is purified by a consecrated meal. (13) After a certain time the ceremony of "betrothal," or "union of the deceased with the population of the lower world," is performed. Marriage songs are sung, there is dancing, and the woman who carries the pot leaps with joy. (14) A marriage retinue with music, etc., goes to the village from which the deceased and his ancestors have originated. (15) The pot containing the bones of the deceased is deposited in a small ditch, above which a stone is erected. (16) On their return the participants must bathe. All those who have been mutilated or who have died because of a tiger or an accident remain evil spirits and cannot enter the land of the dead. That land is the home of the ancestors to which only persons who have been married can go. They return to the earth from time to time, and when they wish they are reincarnated in the first-born (this holds especially for grandfathers and great-grandfathers).[18]

This is not the place for a comparative description of worlds beyond the grave.[19] The most widespread idea is that of a world analogous to ours, but more pleasant, and of a society organized in the same way as it is here. Thus everyone re-enters again the categories of clan, age group, or occupation that he had on earth. It logically follows that the children who have not yet been incorporated into the society of the living cannot be classified in that of the dead. Thus, for Catholics, children who die without baptism forever remain in the transition zone, or limbo; the corpse of a semicivilized infant not yet named, circumcised or otherwise ritually recognized, is buried without the usual ceremonies, thrown away, or burned – especially if the people in question think that he did not yet possess a soul.

The journey to the other world and the entrance to it comprise a series of rites of passage whose details depend on the distance and topography of that world. First I should mention the Isles of the Dead to be found in the beliefs of ancient Egypt,[20] Assyro-Babylonia,[21] the Greeks in various times and regions (cf. Hades of Book XI of the *Odyssey*),[22] the Celts,[23] Polynesians,[24] Australians,[25] and others. These beliefs undoubtedly are the reason for the practice of giving the deceased a real or miniature boat and oars. Some peoples see the other world as a citadel surrounded by walls (such as Sheol, the underworld abode of the dead in Hebrew tradition which has bolted doors[26] or the Babylonian Aralu),[27] as a region with compartments (for instance, the Egyptian Duat), as situated on a high mountain (as do the Dyaks), or in the interior of a mountain (as in Hindu India).

What is important to us in these cases is that, since the deceased must make a voyage,[28] his survivors are careful to equip him with all the necessary material objects – such as clothing, food, arms, and tools – as well as those of a magico-religious nature – amulets, passwords, signs, etc. – which will assure him of a safe journey or crossing and a favorable reception, as they would a living traveler. Thus, in some particulars, these rites are identical with those discussed in chapter III. The Lapps, for instance, took care to kill a reindeer on the grave so that the deceased might ride it during the difficult journey to his final destination.[29] Some believed the journey lasted three weeks, while others said three years.

A great many similar customs could be mentioned. The passage is marked, for instance, by the ancient Greek rite of "the obol (coin) for Charon."[30] This rite has also been encountered in France, where the deceased was given the largest coin available, "so

that he would be better received in the other world."[31] The practice persists in modern Greece. Among the Slavs the money for the deceased is intended to pay the expenses of the trip, but among Japanese Buddhists it is given to the old woman who runs the ferry across the Sanzu; the Badaga use it for the passage over the thread of the dead. Moslems cannot cross the bridge formed by a sharpened sword unless they are pure or "good." In the Zend-Avesta dogs guard the bridge of Chinvat just as in the Rig-Veda Yama's dogs, who are spotted and have four eyes, guard the paths that lead to one of the ancient Hindu abodes beyond the grave, a sort of cavern, "a closed and covered enclosure" which is reached through a dark underworld.[32]

Sometimes special powers – magicians, evil spirits, deities – are charged with showing the dead the way, or with leading them in groups. (Those of ancient Greece are known as psychopompoi – guides of souls to the afterworld.) This role of Isis and of Hermes-Mercury is quite well known. Among the Muskwaki (commonly known as Fox) at the lifting of mourning the deceased is guided toward the prairies of the next world by a young warrior who takes the name of the deceased, gallops for several miles, makes a detour, and returns. He retains that name henceforth and is considered the adopted child of the relatives of the deceased.[33]

The Luiseno Indians of California have a dramatic ceremony which has the direct effect of sending the spirits of the dead away from the earth and "attaching," or fastening, them, as if by a physical bond, to the four sections of the sky and particularly to the Milky Way.[34]

Because of the familiar themes combined in the Haida's ideas about the next world, I shall describe them in some detail. The road to the afterworld leads to the banks of a sort of bay; on the other side of it is the land of souls, from which a self-propelled raft is sent by a soul to the deceased. When he has arrived on the other bank, the deceased begins the search for his wife, which takes a very long time, since the villages are scattered like those of the Haida and each dead person has only one wife assigned to him. When he is dying, a man indicates in which village he wants to live, and messengers are sent to guide him on his voyage. Each offering to the deceased multiplies for his use, and the funeral songs help the deceased to enter his village with his head held high. The dead send riches to their poor earthly relatives. In the land of the souls sacred dances are performed, and everyone amuses himself. Beyond that land lives a chief called Great Moving Cloud, who is responsible for the abundance of salmon. After some time in the land of souls the deceased equips a canoe, reassembles his belongings, and amid the lamentations of his companions goes away to a country called Xada. This is his second death, and he also goes through a third and a fourth. Upon his fifth death he returns to earth as a blue fly. Some think the four deaths occur only after several human reincarnations. There are different countries for the drowned, for those dead by violent means, for shamans, and so forth.

The funeral rites for a person who dies in the ordinary way are given below. The face of the deceased is painted, a sacred headdress is placed on his head, and he is seated on the bier, where he remains for four to six days. Special magical songs are sung, recited first by the members of the clan and then by those of the opposite clan. All sorts of food and drink and tobacco leaves are thrown into a "crying fire." These become multiplied many times and are taken by the deceased to the other world. Relatives put on the signs of mourning – they shave their heads and stain their faces with pitch. The coffin is carried out through a hole in the wall and is taken to the grave house, where only the deceased of the same clan can be placed.

For ten days the widow fasts, uses a rock in place of a pillow, and bathes daily without washing her face. Then she gathers some children of the opposite clan and serves them a meal. (The Haida are exogamous.) "This feast was called 'causing one's self to marry.' The object of it was that she might marry someone next time who had still more property, and that she herself and her new husband might have long lives and be lucky. Another informant added that the widow went through regulations much like those of a girl at puberty."[35] Briefly, while the purpose of the rites is to unite the corpse with those of members of his clan and to provide him with what he will need during his voyage and in his sojourn beyond the grave, these rites are at the same time prophylactic and animistic (the opening in the wall of the house, the coffin, the vault, etc., prevent a return of the deceased) or prophylactic and contagious (mourning, baths, etc.).

The funeral rites of ancient Egypt furnish a good example of a system of rites of passage whose purpose is incorporation into the world of the dead. Here I shall examine only the Osirian ritual,[36] whose fundamental idea is the identification of Osiris and the deceased on one hand, the sun and the deceased on the other. I think there must at first have been two separate rituals which were unified on the theme of death and rebirth. As Osiris the deceased is dismembered and then reconstituted; he is dead and is born again in the world of the dead, and so there are a series of resurrection rites. As Ra (the sun), the deceased dies each evening upon arrival at the edge of Hades. His mummy is thrown into a corner and abandoned; but the series of rites it undergoes during the night in the sun's barge, revives him little by little, and in the morning he is again alive and ready to resume his daily journey in the light, above the world of the living. These multiple rebirths of the sun ritual have been combined with the single reconstitution of the deceased upon his first arrival in Hades, according to the Osirian ritual, so that this reconstitution has come to take place daily. The performance of the converging rites is in accordance with the general idea that the sacred, the divine, the magical, and the pure are lost if they are not renewed in periodic rites.

The following is the syncretic pattern according to the *Book of What Is in Hades* and the *Book of the Doors*.[37] Different conceptions of Duat (Hades) were current in different periods and places, but through fusions and combinations the priests of Thebes developed a complete plan. Hades was "like an immense temple, very long, divided into a certain number of rooms separated by doors and having at each end an outside court and a pylon (gateway building) contiguous to both the inside world and the outside world."[38] In the first hour of the night, when the sun was dead, he received in his barge the souls which were "pure," that is, buried in accordance with the proper rites and provided with the necessary talismans, and the doors guarded by baboons and spirits were opened to him. The dead who did not go in the sun's bark had to vegetate eternally in the vestibule.[39]

According to the *Book of the Doors*, the doors were identical to those of fortresses and were guarded at the entrance and the exit by a god in the form of a mummy, at the bend by two uraei (cobras) emitting flames and nine mummy-gods; passage was obtained by an incantation.[40] The journey is described in the *Guide for the Traveller in the Other World*.[41] For details I refer the reader to the works cited, but I want to mention that each compartment was separated from the preceding one by doors whose opening had to be secured by ritual means. The names of the first three and of the last are unknown; the names of the fourth and the doors following it were "the one which hides the corridors," "the pillar of the gods," "the one adorned with swords," "the portal of Osiris," "the one which stands upright, motionless(?)," "the guardian of the flood," "the great one of beings, the begetter of forms," and "the one which incloses the gods of Hades." At the exit there was also a vestibule.

These "opening of the doors" had a counterpart in the ritual of daily worship – the opening of the doors of the naos (the part of the temple within the walls): the cord was broken, the seal was removed, and the bolts were slid.[42] Then came the dismemberment and reconstitution of the god, a rite which was also part of the funeral (opening the mouth,[43] etc.). The second opening of the naos reaffirmed the first. The god was washed with water and incense, dressed in sacred bands, and anointed with paint and perfumed oils. Then the statue was replaced in the naos and installed on the sand, just like the mummy and the statue of the deceased in the funerary ritual. The ritual closing of the naos which followed was the principal rite of departure from the sanctuary.[44]

Thus the divine worship had for its object the daily revival of Ra-Osiris, just as the funeral rites both (1) revived the deceased and made him a god by mummification and various rites, and (2) prevented a real and final death by a reconstitution and nocturnal rebirth.[45] There are, therefore, parallels among the funeral rites, the daily worship, the inauguration of a temple, and the ritual of enthronement.[46] The death and rebirth, simultaneously, of Ra, Osiris, the king, the priest, and every deceased man who was "pure"

certainly constitutes the most extreme case known to me of a dramatic representation of the death and rebirth theme. It should be added that birth into life on earth was in itself considered a rebirth.[47]

All these rites of rebirth prevented the deceased from dying again each day. The belief in such a possibility is found among many peoples, sometimes combined with the idea that after each death the deceased passes from one abode to another, as among the Haida. Among the Cheremiss, some groups believe that the deceased dies only once, but others – for example, the Cheremiss of Vyatka – say that a man may die seven times and pass from one world to another and that he is then changed into a fish.[48] The Cheremiss rites consist of feeding the deceased often at first and then periodically through "commemorations." The events of the afterlife explain in part the alimentary and sumptuary rites of the Vogul and the Ostyak, some of whom believe that the soul of the deceased lives for a time in the world under the sea or in the skies,[49] then diminishes little by little until it is only the size of a certain small insect or transforms itself into that insect, and then disappears altogether.[50] The doctrine of worlds superimposed on each other is widespread in Asia and existed in Mithraism. (There were seven planetary worlds and successive initiations.)

Like children who have not been baptized, named, or initiated, persons for whom funeral rites are not performed are condemned to a pitiable existence, since they are never able to enter the world of the dead or to become incorporated in the society established there. These are the most dangerous dead. They would like to be reincorporated into the world of the living, and since they cannot be, they behave like hostile strangers toward it. They lack the means of subsistence which the other dead find in their own world and consequently must obtain them at the expense of the living. Furthermore, these dead without hearth or home sometimes have an intense desire for vengeance. Thus funeral rites also have a long-range utility; they help to dispose of eternal enemies of the survivors. Persons included among the homeless dead vary among different peoples. In addition to those already mentioned, this category may include those bereft of family, the suicides, those dead on a journey, those struck by lightning, those dead through the violation of a taboo, and others. What I have said holds in general, but the same act does not have the same consequences among all peoples, and I want to reiterate that I do not claim an absolute universality or an absolute necessity for the pattern of rites of passage.

In this connection, I want to mention the diverse beliefs concerning the fate, in the next world, of persons who have committed suicide. Lasch isolated four categories: (1) Suicide is considered a normal act, and the fate of the person who has committed it is the same as that of the ordinary dead; in case of serious illness, mutilation, etc., suicide may even be a means of insuring that the soul is in good condition and not weakened or multilated, (2) Suicide is rewarded in the other world (suicide of the warrior, the widow, etc.). (3) The person who has committed suicide cannot be incorporated with the other dead and must wander between the world of the dead and that of the living. (4) Suicide is punished in the next world, and the individual must wander between the two worlds for the duration of the time he would normally have lived, or he is admitted only to a lower region of the world of the dead, or he is punished by tortures, etc. (as in hell).[51] Obviously the character of the funeral rites, those pertaining to prophylaxis and purification as well as rites of passage, differs with each one of the four categories.

The rites of passage are present also in rites of resurrection and reincarnation, for even if a soul has been separated from the living and incorporated into the world of the dead, it can also reverse the direction and reappear among us, either by itself or under the constraint of another person. The means are sometimes very simple. It may be sufficient for the soul to be reincarnated in a woman and to reappear in the form of a child. That is the case, for instance, among the Arunta of Australia, who think that souls lies in wait in stones, trees, etc., and that from there they leap into women who are young, fat, and desirable. The rites of reintegration into the world of the living which ensue are those that have been studied with reference to birth and naming.

The ceremonies of the Lushae tribes of Assam furnish a good example of the "eternal return."[52] The deceased is dressed in his best clothes and tied in a sitting position on a scaffold of bamboo, while next to him are placed the tools and weapons of his sex. A pig, a goat, and a dog are killed, and all the relatives, friends, and neighbors divide the meat; the deceased is also given food and drink. At nightfall he is placed in a grave dug right next to the house. His nearest relative says goodbye and asks him to prepare everything for those who will come and join him. The soul, accompanied by those of the pig, the goat, and the dog – without whom it would not find its way – goes dressed and equipped to the land of Mi-thi-hua, where life is hard and painful. But if the deceased has killed men or animals on the hunt, or if he has given feasts to the whole village, he goes to a pleasant country on the other side of the river, where he feasts continuously. Since women can neither fight nor hunt nor give feasts, they cannot go to this beautiful country unless their husbands take them there. After a certain time, the soul leaves one or the other of these regions and returns to earth in the form of a hornet. After another lapse of time it is transformed into water and evaporates in the form of dew, and, if a dewdrop falls on a man, that man will beget a child who will be a reincarnation of the deceased.[53] When the child is born, two chickens are killed, and the mother washes herself and the child. The child's soul spends the first seven days perched like a bird on the clothes or the bodies of his parents; for this reason they move as little as possible, and during this time the household god is appeased with sacrifices. All sorts of ceremonies follow, and during one of them the nearest maternal relative gives a name to the child – that is, the child is permanently incorporated into the clan.

Sometimes the souls of the dead are reincarnated directly into animals, vegetables, etc., especially into the totems. In that case there are rites incorporating the deceased into totemic species.

There is not always a special place beyond the grave for the dead. At least it frequently happens that their abode is in the environs of the house, the tomb (called "the isba of the dead" by the Votyak), or the cemetery (called "village of the dead" by the Mandan). In that case the burial is the real rite of incorporation in the world of the dead. This is very clear among the Cheremiss. Perhaps as a result of the Moslem influence of the Tatars, the Cheremiss also believe in a next world, analogous to the Ostyak heaven, which is reached by a pole forming a bridge over a cauldron, or by a ladder. The Mordvinian dead also have their abode in the tomb or the cemetery.[54] The bond with the living, and therefore the transition, lasts for a longer time in these instances, since, as has been pointed out, it is periodically renewed by the living, either by communal meals or by visits or by feeding the deceased (through a hole in the ground and in the coffin, with a reed, by depositing food on the tomb, etc.). But a moment always comes when this tie is broken, after being loosened bit by bit. The last commemoration or the last visit completes the rites of separation in relation to the deceased and the reconsolidation of the society or restricted group of the living.

The following is a list of rites of passage considered in isolation; I make no claim that it is complete, any more than other lists given in this volume.

Among rites of separation, some of which have already been reviewed, it is appropriate to include: the various procedures by which the corpse is transported outside; burning the tools, the house, the jewels, the deceased's possessions; putting to death the deceased's wives, slaves, or favorite animals; washings, anointings, and rites of purification in general; and taboos of all sorts. In addition, there are physical procedures of separation: a grave, a coffin, a cemetery, a wicker mat, places in the trees, or a pile of stones is built or used in a ritual manner; the closing of the coffin or the tomb is often a particularly solemn conclusion to the entire ceremony. There are periodic collective rites expelling souls from the house, the village, and the tribe's territory. There are struggles for the corpse, widespread in Africa, which correspond to the bride's abduction. Their true meaning seems not to have been understood up to now: it is that the living do not want to lose one of their members unless forced to do so, for the loss is a diminution of their social power. These struggles increase in violence with the higher social position of the deceased.[55] As for the destruction of the corpse itself (by cremation, premature putrefaction, etc.), its purpose is to separate the components, the various bodies and souls. Only very seldom do the remains (bones, ashes) constitute

the new body of the deceased in the afterlife, whatever Hertz may think on the matter.[56]

Among rites of incorporation I shall first mention the meals shared after funerals and at commemoration celebrations. Their purpose is to reunite all the surviving members of the group with each other, and sometimes also with the deceased, in the same way that a chain which has been broken by the disappearance of one of its links must be rejoined. Sometimes a meal of this sort also takes place when mourning is lifted. When the funerals are observed in two stages (provisional and permanent), there is usually a communion meal for the relatives at the end of the first, and the deceased is thought to partake of it. Finally, if the tribe, clan, or village is involved, convocation by drum, crier, or messenger gives the meal even more of the character of a collective ritual.

As for rites of incorporation into the other world, they are equivalent to those of hospitality, incorporation into the clan, adoption, and so forth. They are often alluded to in legends whose central theme is a descent to Hades or a journey to the land of the dead, and they are mentioned in the form of taboos: one must not eat with the dead, drink or eat anything produced in their country, allow oneself to be touched or embraced by them, accept gifts from them, and so forth. On the other hand, drinking with a dead person is an act of incorporation with him and the other dead, and it consequently enables one to travel among them without danger, as does the payment of a toll (coins, etc.). There are other special rites such as a club blow administered by the dead on a newcomer's head,[57] the Christian sacrament of extreme unction, or the custom of placing the deceased on the earth. Finally, the "dances of the dead" performed by certain American Indians, by the Nyanja of Africa,[58] by members of secret societies, and by other special magico-religious groups should perhaps be included in this category.

NOTES

1 Van Gennep, *Tabou et totémisme à Madagascar*, pp. 40, 58–77, 88, 100–3, 338–9, 342.
2 This is what George Alexander Wilken had already seen about Indonesia ("Uber das Haaropfer: Und

einige andere Trauergebräuche bei den Völken indo-
nesiens," *Revue coloniale internationale*, 1886 and
1887, see p. 254); he has been followed by Robert
Hertz, who generalizes his point ("Contribution à
une étude sur la représentation collective de la
mort," *Année sociologique*, X [1905–6], 82–3, 101,
105, 120). In reality, the duration of mourning
depends more often, as is stated below, on two
other factors.

3 Desplagnes, *Le plateau central nigérien*, p. 221; on
beliefs concerning the other world, see pp. 262–8.

4 [Both died in November, 1908. Van Gennep must be
referring to the considerable internal turmoil in
China due to economic and political reform and to
the often unsatisfactory relations with European
powers.]

5 Lafitau, *Mœurs des sauvages amériquains*, II, 444.

6 M. M. Mikhailowski, *Shamanstvo*, fasc. 1 (St. Peters-
burg, 1892), p. 13.

7 See reference in van Gennep, *Tabou et totémisme à
Madagascar*, chap. vi, pp. 277–8.

8 Hertz, "La représentation collective de la mort," pp.
50–66; a collection of detailed descriptions of the
world beyond the grave, journeys to reach it, etc.,
may be found in Kruijt, *Het Animisme in den Indischen
Archipel*, pp. 323–85, a work based on the theories
and points of view of Tylor, Wilken, and Le Tour-
neau.

9 See Rivers, *The Todas*, pp. 336–404; for a description
of Amnodr see pp. 397–400); for a description of
the rites, see also Thurston, *Ethnographic Notes in
Southern India*, pp. 145–6, 172–84.

10 I will keep the name given by the informant, al-
though the Ostyak of Salekhard are a mixture of
true Ostyaks and Samoyeds; see Arnold van Gennep,
"Origine et fortune du nom de peuple Ostiak," *Keleti
Szemle: Revue orientale pour les Études Ouralo-Altaïques*
(Budapest), II (1902), 13–22.

11 Gondatti, *Sledy iazychestva u inorodtsev Severo-Zapadnoi
Sibirii* ("Traces of Paganism among the Natives of
Northwest Asia") (Moscow, 1888), p. 43; he
states that the doll is kept for six months. If the
deceased was a man, the widow sleeps next to it;
among the Irtysh Ostyak, according to Patkanov (*Die
Irtysch-Ostiaken*, p. 146), the doll has in recent times
been replaced by the pillow and undergarments of
the deceased.

12 V. Bartenev, "Pogrebalnyia obychai Obdorskikh
Ostiakov" ("The Funeral Rites of the Ostyak of
Obdorsk [Salekhard]"), *Shivaia Starina*, V (1905),
478–92; Gondatti, p. 44.

13 I do not understand why Gondatti, followed by
Patkanov (*Die Irtysch-Ostiaken*, p. 146), later says of
this world that it is underground when it is underwater. Incidentally, there is no doubt that there was
some Christian infiltration into the beliefs of the
Vogul and the Ostyak (the devil, hell, punishment).

14 See my summary in the *Revue de l'histoire des religions*,
vol. XL (1899), of the monograph by N. Kharouzine,
*Le serment par l'ours et le culte de l'ours chez les Ostiak et
les Vogoul*.

15 Patkanov, *Die Irtysch-Ostiaken*, p. 146.

16 See Hahn, *Einführung in das Gebiet der Kolsmission*,
pp. 82–8.

17 If it is raining too hard, the corpse is buried according
to specific rites so that it may be disinterred after the
harvest and cremated; in this instance the ceremony
takes place in three stages.

18 I mention this document because it provides proof
for what has been said above (p. 52) about the rite in
which the newborn are placed on the ground (also
performed by the Kol; see Hahn, *Einführung in das
Gebiet der Kolsmission*, p. 72), as are corpses. Dieterich
(*Mutter Erde*, pp. 25–9) has collected parallels for the
latter practice, which he explains as "a return to the
bosom of Mother Earth"; it can be seen that here, at
least, this theory is not acceptable. I would like to
add that the Kol bury dead children but do not burn
them "because they do not have souls" (the Kol
acquire a soul only on their wedding day) and do
not have the right to go to the land of their ancestors,
the purpose of cremation being to give access to it.
Another of Dieterich's theories (*Mutter Erde*, pp. 21–
5) also collapses on this point.

19 See, among others, Tylor, *Primitive Culture*, ch. xiii.

20 On the subject of the fields and islands of Aaru, the
judgment and journey of the dead, see Gaston Maspéro, *Histoire ancienne des peuples de l'Orient classique*, I
(Paris: Hachette, 1895), 180ff., with bibliography.

21 *Ibid.*, pp. 574ff.

22 See, among others, Ervin Rohde, *Psyché* (2d edn.;
Tübingen: J. C. Mohr, 1898); Albrecht Dieterich,
Nekyia (Leipzig: B. C. Teubner, 1893); A. J. Reinach,
"Victor Bérard et l'Odyssée," *Les essais*, 1904, pp.
189–93.

23 K. Meyer, *The Voyage of Bran* (London, 1895).

24 Johannes Zemmrich, "Toteninseln und verwandte
geographische Mythen," *Internationales Archiv für Eth-
nographie*, Vol. IV (1891).

25 See Carl Strehlow and Leonhardi, *Dic Aranda und
Luritja-Stämme in Zentral Australia* (Frankfurt am
Main: Völker-Museum, 1907–8), I, 15; II, 6.

26 See Schwally, *Das Leben nach dem Tode: Nach dem Vorstellung die alter Israel in dem Judentus einschliesslich Volkglaubens in Zeitale Christi* (Giessen, 1892).

27 Maspéro, *Histoire ancienne*, I, 693ff.

28 Regarding the world of the dead according to Sabian beliefs, see Siouffi, *Étude sur la religion des Soubbas*, pp. 156–8; on the roads which lead there and join together, pp. 126–9; and on the corresponding funeral rites, pp. 120, 121 n., 124–6. The soul requires seventy-five days to make the journey, but mourning lasts only sixty days; the communal meal and the meal of commemoration are absolutely obligatory; the rite of the "last mouthful" provides the deceased in the other world with "something more than his ordinary ration, which is ordinarily insufficient."

29 N. Kharuzin, *Russkie Lopary* (Moscow, 1890), p. 157, and for more information of the same kind, Mikhailowski, *Shamanstvo*, pp. 19–24.

30 See Richard Andree, *Totenmünze* (2nd edn.; 1889), p. 24. Also *Mélusine, passim*.

31 J. B. Thiers, *Traité des superstitions* (Paris, 1667); for other French parallels, see Sebillot, *Le folk-lore de la France*, I, 419, where information can be found on the crossing of the sea (inside the earth) to reach hell.

32 See Oldenberg, *La réligion du Véda*, pp. 450–62; another abode is in the sky. Oldenberg is right in believing these two conceptions to be independent and juxtaposed on one another, but they are not elements in a dualistic system. This coexistence of different beliefs among a people is a frequent occurrence, and when there is localization of some dead in one of these worlds, and others in the other worlds, it is often on a social and magico-religious basis rather than on an ethical one.

33 Owen, *Folk-lore of the Musquakie Indians*, pp. 83–6.

34 Du Bois, *The Religion of the Luisenio Indians*, pp. 83–7.

35 J. R. Swanton, *Contributions to the Ethnology of the Haida* ("Publications of the Jesup North Pacific Expedition," V, Part I [Leiden, 1905]), 52–4; for Haida ideas of the afterlife see pp. 34–7.

36 Gaston Maspéro, *Études de mythologie et d'archéologie égyptienne*, vol. II: *Compte rendu de les hypogées royaux de Thèbes* (Paris: E. Leroux, 1893), 1–187; G. Jequier, *Le livre de ce qu'il y a dans l'Hadès: Version abregée publié d'après les papyrus de Berlin et de Leyde avec variations et traduction* (Paris: E. Bouillon, 1894); Alexandre Moret, *Le Rituel du culte divin journalier en Égypte*, and *La royauté pharaonique*.

37 This book was written to conciliate the solar theory with the Osirian theory not taken into account in the *Book of What Is in Hades*; see the summary of it given by Maspéro, *Les hypogées royaux de Thèbes*, pp. 163–79.

38 Jequier, *Le livre de ce qu'il ya dans l'Hadès*, p. 19.

39 *Ibid.*, pp. 20, 39–41; Maspéro, *Les hypogées royaux de Thèbes*, pp. 43–4; note the conversation between the god and cynocephalus (baboon) for the "opening of the doors."

40 *Ibid.*, Vol. II, pp. 166–8; on the door which opens on the place of judgment, see *Livre des morts* ("Book of the Dead"), ch. cxxv, I, ll. 52ff.

41 Maspéro, *ibid.*, vol. I. p. 384.

42 Moret, *Le rituel du culte divin journalier en Égypte*, pp. 35ff.

43 *Ibid.*, pp. 73–83, 87–9; Maspéro, "Le Rituel du sacrifice funéraire," *Les hypogées royaux de Thèbes*, pp. 289–318.

44 *Ibid.*, pp. 102–212.

45 Moret, *Le rituel du culte divin journalier en Egypte*, p. 226; cf. pp. 10–15 and pages noted above.

46 The compartments of Hades belong to at least two originally distinct systems. The final rebirth is secured on the twelfth hour, according to the Theban ritual, by the passage of the sacred barge, from tail to head, across the gigantic serpent "The life of the gods" – symbol, says Jequier, of the renewal due to the serpent's ability to change skins each year (*Le livre de ce qu'il y a dans l'Hadès*, pp. 132–3). But this does not explain the reason for the passage across the two bulls' heads (Maspéro, *Les hypogées royaux de Thèbes*, pp. 169–71); on the subject of the twelfth hour, see pp. 96–101.

47 *Ibid.*, I, 23 ff., 29. It should be noted that the purpose of mummification is precisely to make rebirth, the life beyond the grave, possible.

48 Ivan Nikolaevitch Smirnov, *Les populations finnoises des bassins de la Volga et de la Kama*, trans. Paul Boyer (Paris: E. Leroux, 1898), I, 138.

49 See above, p. 215, and the sources cited there.

50 Gondatti, *Sliédy iazytchestvra u inorodtsev Sièvero-Zapdnoï Sibirii*, p. 39.

51 R. Lasch, "Die Verbleibsorte der abgeschiedenen Seele der Selbstmörder," *Globus*, LXXVII (1900), 110–15.

52 Major Shakespear, "Typical Tribes and Castes," p. 225.

53 This is one of the very rare cases of reincarnation through the father.

54 See Smirnov, *Les populations finnoises*, I, 133–44, for the Cheremiss; pp. 357–76 for the Mordvinians.

55 For references, see Hertz, "La représentation collective de la mort," p. 128 n. 2.

56　*Ibid.*, p. 78; Hertz here presents a modification of Kleinpaul's theory, which is too absolute.

57　Haddon, *Cambridge Anthropological Expedition to Torres Straits*, V, 355; this same rite is among those performed at marriage.

58　See F. A. Werner, *The Natives of British Central Africa* (London: A. Constable, 1907), p. 229; R. Sutherland Rattray, *Some Folk-lore, Stories, and Songs in Chinyanja* (London: SPCK, 1907), p. 179.

19

The Phase of Negated Death

Hikaru Suzuki

My father-in-law was a retired vice president of one of the largest companies in Tokyo. Our family wanted to have a simple funeral [for him], but when the funeral company, which had conducted our mother's funeral three years earlier, arrived to discuss it, we were told that it is not proper to have a smaller funeral for our father than for our mother. The Buddhist temple priests nodded in agreement with the funeral professionals. As a result, we purchased a 2 million yen coffin for our father, a million yen more expensive than that of our mother, and had three priests instead of two. One can imagine [what funeral professionals will say] when our turn comes; they will explain [to our children], "for your grandfather's funeral your father purchased the most expensive coffin."

"The Halt of the Salt-Purification Rite in Funeral Ceremonies," *Asahi Shimbun*

Before the Rites of Separation

The handling of the deceased, whether transporting, dressing, or bathing, is the most important responsibility of funeral professionals. Near the end of my fieldwork at Moon Rise, a colleague told me about a funeral professional who had failed in this responsibility and was subsequently fired. My colleague told me that, while this funeral professional was transporting the deceased and his family from a hospital to the Moon Rise funeral hall, the back door of the company van had opened and the coffin had slid onto the street and fallen open; the deceased had landed face down on the pavement with an upturned coffin beside him. (Apparently the back door of the van had not been securely locked.) The family members were furious; enraged, they shouted at the professional that he had injured (*kizu wo tsuketa*) the deceased, who was almost hit (*hikareru tokoro datta*) by a car behind the van. The funeral professional knelt on the pavement, touching his forehead to the ground, and apologized to the family in a continuous kowtow. The family's ire did not dissipate, however, until the managers had apologized and offered to pay for the entire funeral.

From Hikaru Suzuki, "The Phase of Negated Death," in *The Price of Death: The Funeral Industry in Contemporary Japan* (Stanford: Stanford Unity Press, 2000).

What was manifested in this episode was the perception of the continued life of the deceased in the eyes of the family. Although dead in the medical or physical sense, the deceased was not yet acknowledged to be dead. Japanese believe that a person experiences death twice, once at the hospital and again at cremation. The pronouncement of death by a doctor does not complete the deceased's death; it is only after cremation that the finality of death is attained. As Ebersole points out in reference to the Izanami and Izanagi in Nihonshoki myth (where "Izanami's entry into Yomi and her 'death' are not viewed permanent until Izanagi breaks the taboo of entering the burial hall and view[ing] the corpse"), "the finality of death is a result of the actions of the living" (Ebersole 1989, 88).

Contemporary Japanese funeral ceremonies normally take two to three days. Several events occur before the funeral ceremony, starting with the announcement of death, followed by the transportation of the deceased, the consultation (uchiawase), the bathing ceremony (yukan), and the wake (tsuya). These performances of commercial funerals, however, have different meanings from those of community funerals. In community funerals, rituals of soshō (attempted resuscitation) were executed immediately after death. In contemporary funerals the period from death at a hospital to the end of a funeral ceremony can also be called a phase of sosei or "resurrection," but for a different reason. In community funerals the bereaved conducted a series of rituals to resuscitate the deceased by attempting to call back the spirit that had escaped from the body; in today's ceremony the living neither consider death a result of spirit ascendance nor attempt ritual resuscitation. The deceased is treated as if still alive, and death is delayed until the end of the funeral.

On the morning of November 29, 1994, the Moon Rise telephone rang at 10:00 a.m. The receptionist answered it. "It has happened" (hassei desu), she announced to the funeral staff in the room. At Moon Rise, the term "happen" (hassei) indicates that someone has died. She looked around to see who could take the call. It was another busy morning; recent deaths and funeral ceremonies in progress were all vying for attention. Most of the funeral staff were out of the office, at hospitals, at the homes of the deceased, and in the different rooms or halls of the auditorium. She put the call through to Tomi, who had been organizing another ceremony schedule.

Tomi reached for a notepad and a pencil. He opened his conversation with a sympathetic phrase that is used when hearing news of a death in a family. "I am very sorry for the loss of your family member" (konotabiwa makotoni goshūshō sama deshita). I noticed that the funeral staff spoke this sympathetic phrase only once during the initial conversation with the deceased's family. Tomi quickly switched to a businesslike manner and said, "I am sorry, but I need to ask you several questions concerning the deceased." He asked the person's name, gender, and age; the name of the chief mourner; the place where the person had died; the time of death; and the address and phone number of the person's home. Then he asked if the deceased was a Mutual-Aid Cooperative member (gojokai-kaiin); what religion and which sect the deceased belonged to; and what price of coffin the family desired. If the deceased had purchased a Mutual-Aid Cooperative (MAC) membership, there was a specific set of funeral materials provided according to the price of the MAC membership fee. If the deceased was a MAC member, the family could simply ask for the prepaid coffin. However, the items provided on the membership installment plan are usually the inexpensive ones, and it is common for the funeral staff to provide information about a higher-priced range of coffins. Funeral staff always end the conversation by reassuring the family that they are on their way. "Please feel at ease; we will be seeing you as soon as we can get ready," Tomi said and hung up the phone.

As soon as the phone call was completed, Tomi and Mitake, an assistant, began packing the necessary materials. First, they put the ¥100,000 coffin that the deceased's family had chosen into a company hearse. Because the deceased was a Buddhist belonging to a Jodoshinshū sect, they packed a Jodoshinshū coffin cover (kan-ooi) and the braided-string decoration that goes with the cover (sutachi). It is important to know what religion and sect the deceased belonged to; this determines the type of coffin cover and other funeral materials. Whether a sword (morigatana) is necessary or not also depends on the specific Buddhist sect. For instance, the Nichirenshoshū and Jodoshinshū sects do not require the sword. Also, for the Buddhist sects of Jodoshinshū, Shingonshū, Jōdoshū, Zenshū (Sōtō, Ohbaku, or Rinzaishū), Nichirenshū, and Tendaishū, coffin covers are made of thick silk in bright colors such as red, purple, or orange with gold and have large flower designs on them. In contrast, the Nichirenshoshū sect and Shintō use white and silver with diagonally striped designs. For Christians, the coffin cover is black velvet with a silver cross stitched on the front. Death garments differ for Buddhist and Shintō members as well.

Other objects that are packed include: dry ice cut into rectangular shapes; a box of stationery (tebunko), necessary during a wake and funeral ceremony; a pair of coffin stands (kandai); deodorants (bōshūzai); a chrysanthemum; a death robe (shinishōzoku); candles; a candle stand (rōsokutate); a vase; and incense (senkō). For Nichirenshoshū, Shintō, and Christians, the chrysanthemum is not necessary. Without much talk, the two men loaded these items quickly into the van. Moon Rise has three types of hearses. The one used most often is an ordinary white van that has been altered to leave room for a coffin and two passenger seats in the back. The minibus is larger than the van and has eight passenger seats as well as space for a coffin. The stretcher hearse is a black Cadillac that has been modified with a stretcher on the left and two passenger seats on the rear right. This hearse is used when the family members cannot decide on the price of the coffin at the time of the initial phone call, or when a family member specifically states that they do not want to put the deceased in a coffin until he or she is taken home, in which case the body is laid on the stretcher. All of these hearses have black lace curtains so that they can be immediately distinguished from other vans on the street. They are used specifically for transporting the dead from hospitals to their homes or to the funeral auditorium. Although these hearses could be used for transporting the body to the crematorium after the funeral, they are unpopular for that purpose. In fact, MAC members can use these hearses free of charge but rarely choose to do so, preferring the lavishly decorated golden hearse for the trip to the crematorium.

I joined Tomi in the van as soon as the coffin and other materials were loaded. Mitake led the way in another van. In most cases two funeral staff members work together at the initial stages of greeting the family of the deceased. Working in pairs speeds the encoffining; having two vans is convenient if the bereaved need a ride home or to the auditorium from the hospital. As usual, Mitake raced past other cars, speeding along, and we followed closely in the second van. It is customary for funeral staff to rush to hospitals whatever the traffic conditions; I noticed that police never stop them for speeding.

The hospital we went to that day was a modern, beautifully designed structure. From the outside it looked almost like a hotel. There was even a small gift shop on the first floor, unusual in Japan.[1] The hospital, Tomi told me, had been built recently by the city government and accepted only city officials and their family members. Tomi remarked that just by knowing the name of a hospital he could guess the approximate social status of the patients and their family. Companies often built hospitals for their workers, although private hospitals for the general public are also stratified by cost. Passing the entrance and parking spaces in front, we drove into the basement to the back door of the hospital, unloaded the coffin onto a hospital gurney, and headed to the room for the soul.[2] The room for the soul (reianshitsu, literally, the peaceful room for the soul) was on the top floor. In general, those who die are segregated immediately from other patients. In most hospitals, the room for the soul is located at the back or in the basement. Tomi explained that modern hospitals have relocated the room nearer to the sky than to the ground, in an attempt to change the common dark image of death. On our way there, we passed spacious tatami rooms where family and relatives could wait for the funeral staff. Pretty pastel-colored sofas and small tables lined the corridor. Sunlight and fresh air entered through tall windows. This hospital was distinctly different from most others, where the rooms of the deceased have few or no windows and smell of antiseptic.

Transporting the Deceased

The deceased had been laid on a bed across from the door. The body was covered with a comforter and the face with a white cloth. I could only see the long braided black hair. A young woman and a middle-aged man were standing in front of the body. (Later we learned that the man was the father and the woman the sister of the deceased.) A narrow piece of stained glass resembling a church window hung on the wall where the deceased lay. In one corner of the room on a table was a set of materials for burning incense sticks (shōkō). After bowing and introducing themselves, Tomi and Mitake confirmed that the man was the Mr. Yamaha who had called Moon Rise. The funeral staff explained that they would begin preparing for the departure. They rolled the table with the incense to the bed. Tomi lit a candle on the table and asked Yamaha and his daughter Sanae to burn incense. The father chose an incense stick, lit it with the candle flame, and placed it in the incense pot (kōro). He then pressed his hands together in front of his chest and bowed to the deceased. Sanae and each funeral staff member followed and offered incense. Since the medical staff had not already offered incense to the deceased, we waited for them to do so.

While waiting, Tomi asked the relatives if they would like to have a bathing ceremony for the deceased. He explained that although the body is wiped clean with antiseptics by nurses, a bathing ceremony provides a true bath for the deceased. "We use a real bathtub. Wouldn't you like to have her bathed for the last time in this life?" asked Tomi. Yamaha and Sanae looked at each other. "Will I be able to put makeup on Yoshiko one last time with my own hands?" Sanae asked. "Certainly," Tomi answered. When Sanae was assured that she could, the father said, "Please go ahead with that [bathing ceremony]" (sōshite kudasai). Tomi then asked if the father planned to have a wake at home or at the auditorium. The father said that he wanted to have both the wake and the funeral at the funeral auditorium, but wished to take Yoshiko home first. "My daughter Yoshiko was very sick for half a year and [during that time] she couldn't even come back home once," he explained. "I am sorry to hear that," Tomi said in a sympathetic tone. Their conversation stopped; the medical staff had finally arrived.

The medical staff burned incense for the deceased in the hierarchical order of doctors first, then senior nurses, and finally the younger nurses. When all the people who had cared for the dead woman had offered her incense, Tomi extinguished the candle and moved the table to its original position. Nurses and doctors bowed to Yamaha and left; there was no conversation between the medical staff and the family.

When they were alone again, Tomi asked the father's permission to begin the preparation of the body. "Yes, please," the father answered with a nod. Sometimes the family wants to help, but most of the time, as in the case of Yamaha and his daughter, they chose to watch the funeral staff perform their tasks.

The Buddhist death garments are laid out first; they are completely white and consist of a triangular head cloth (zukin), a pair of hand guards (tekkō), a robe (kyō-katabira), a pair of knee guards, a pair of Japanese-style socks (shiro-tabi), and beads (juzu). The comforter was removed from the corpse (the face cloth was not taken away at this time), revealing the body of Yoshiko in her yukata (Japanese gown, a thin kimono).

Tomi and Mitake shared the task of putting on the death garments. The hand guards and knee guards were easily placed, but putting on Japanese socks can be time-consuming because the big toes must fit into the division for them. Anchoring the beads between the fingers is often the most difficult part of the process. When the deceased has just passed away and rigor mortis has not set in, the hands laid on the chest easily fall apart. Sometimes hospital nurses have already tied the hands together with a cord, but in this case they had not. The funeral staff had to struggle to keep the hands and beads in place.[3] When all of death garments were in place, except for the head cloth,[4] Tomi gently removed the white cloth covering the face of Yoshiko, and she was ready to be encoffined.

The coffin, which had been left outside of the room on the stretcher, was brought in. The coffin stands were set on the floor, the coffin placed on them, and the lid removed. Tomi supported Yoshiko's neck and head while Mitake lifted her feet. Yoshiko was so light they were able to carry her easily to the coffin without any help. (The funeral staff sometimes ask family members or nurses for help if the body is particularly heavy.) When the deceased was encoffined, the funeral staff opened a fresh packet of a deodorant set, which contains four fragrance bags and a small perfume spray. The fragrance bags were placed at the top, left, and right and beneath the deceased, and the perfume was sprayed directly onto the interior of the coffin. The perfume is sufficiently powerful to be effective for the rest of the day. Next, the four rectangular dry ice blocks were placed directly on the deceased's body — one on the chest, two on the stomach, and one on the feet. Last, Yoshiko was covered with two blankets and the lid of the coffin was closed. When the bright orange coffin cover and the braided purple string were in place on the coffin, it was ready to leave.

The funeral staff lifted the coffin onto the gurney and rolled it to the elevator door while the rest of us followed. We all entered the elevator and got out at the basement where our van was parked; Tomi and Mitake loaded the coffin into the van. Sanae decided to come with us so she could remain with Yoshiko. Sanae sat in the back of the van beside the coffin. The father said he would drive his car and lead us to his house. With nurses sending us off at the back gate, we left the hospital.[5]

In more than half of the cases in which a person has died in a hospital, the funeral staff are asked to take the body home first. Often the deceased had expressed feelings of homesickness while hospitalized, or the family has missed the deceased and wants all the family members to be united one last time. While we were taking the body home, Sanae continued to sob with her arm on the coffin. The silence at the red traffic light emphasized the sound of her weeping. Tomi called to her and said, "Cheer up, Miss Yamaha, we will be home very soon." Sanae answered "Yes" (*hai*), quietly.

We arrived at the deceased's home, an apartment on the third floor of a newly built condominium. Tomi and Mitake helped Sanae out of the van. They then checked the width of the elevator and stairs. The elevator was too small to carry the coffin horizontally — a problem because the deceased must always be transported in a lying posture — so they could not use the elevator. Although the stairs were very narrow and steep, they were the only choice. "Customers are deities" (*okyakusama wa kamisama desu*), Tomi later told me. I responded, "You mean, the deceased are deities." "You got me on this one" (*ippon yarareta*) was his reply.

The coffin was carried with extreme care since striking the coffin in any way would be considered rude, inconsiderate, and immoral behavior on the part of the funeral staff. It was the beginning of winter, but perspiration was rolling down both the men's faces. After ten minutes of struggle on the stairs, they were able to safely negotiate the coffin into the apartment. The apartment was very clean. I noticed Tomi surveying the rooms while he was working.

Yoshiko was welcomed by family members and relatives who were waiting inside. "You are finally back," the women in the house sobbed as the coffin was set down in the room beside the kitchen. Mitake brought materials for burning incense from his van and prepared them for the family. One by one, each family member and relative burned a stick of incense. The window of the coffin was opened and the family began telling Yoshiko how much they missed her.

The family wanted to keep the deceased at home until other family members arrived. They said they would call us when they were ready to transport the deceased to the auditorium. We headed back to the auditorium to wait for their call. On the way back, Tomi told me that he once had to carry a deceased all the way up to the twentieth floor. "Japanese elevators in these condominiums are too narrow," he complained. "Do Americans have the custom of taking the deceased back to their home?" he asked me. When I said I hadn't heard of such a case, he commented with a little envy, "American funeral professionals must have an easier time than we do." The father called two hours later and was requested to prepare a photo of the deceased as well as his own seal (*inkan*).[6] The funeral staff returned to the family's home and collected the coffin to take to the auditorium; the family followed them in their car.

Moon Rise's Kokura Funeral Auditorium has five funeral halls (equipped with chairs) and six tatami rooms. Each hall and room has a name instead of a number to make it easy to find and avoid confusion. The Yamaha family was taken to the tatami room called the Moon Room (*tsuki-no-ma*) on the first floor. On the left-hand side of the room there was a funeral altar. Yoshiko's coffin was placed on a coffin stand in front of the altar, and the coffin cover was folded down so that the family could see Yoshiko's face through the coffin window.[7] When the family arrived, I added flowers to the vase in front of the altar. Yamaha was sitting alone near Yoshiko. It seemed that the rest of the family had left for a while to do errands. This was my first chance to talk to him. "I am so sorry about your daughter's death," I began. He nodded and told me that Yoshiko had become ill in June and within six months was much worse. "She passed away when none of us had time enough to care for her. It is often said that children who die earlier than their parents are bringing unhappiness to parents [oyafukō-mono], but I don't blame her. It really was not her fault." "Sickness is not a crime," I agreed. He continued telling me how much he regretted that he had not taken enough care of her; he seemed to feel that Yoshiko's death was his fault. I served him green tea, which he accepted with his head down. I left quietly.

Thirty minutes later I took freshly cooked rice and rice balls to the Yamaha family's room. This time Sanae was sitting alone near the coffin, looking at her dead sister and sobbing. She stopped crying when I entered the room. I set the rice bowl and rice balls on the small table. The room, saturated with mourning, was totally silent. Not knowing what exactly should be said, I told her that the auditorium prepares these foods for the deceased but that she was welcome to bring other items or food for her sister if she wished. She nodded and said, "Anything?" I said nothing made out of metal but anything that could be burned.[8] I asked her how old Yoshiko was. Sanae told me that Yoshiko was only 29. "She went so quickly, without enjoying her life," Sanae sobbed. There is a Japanese saying that those who are pretty and well liked die young (bijin-bakumei); I told Sanae that Yoshiko must have been such a person. "Yes, she was a good-natured person," Sanae replied. "She suffered so much at the end, but after she died her face became peaceful at last. Don't you think so?" She was looking at her sister through the coffin window. I agreed that Yoshiko looked peaceful. This was my first encounter with the death of someone around my age; the experience made me think about my own life, and the grief of the Yamaha family left a deep mark in my memory.

[. . .]

The Bathing Ceremony

Traditionally, the bathing ceremony (yukan) was performed to cleanse the impurity of the deceased and further safeguard both the deceased and the living from death pollution. The ritual was performed by close family members at home. The bathing ritual ceased after World War II, in part because of a decrease in deaths occurring in the home and an increase in hospital deaths, where nurses wipe the body with antiseptic.[9] Having introduced a commercialized bathing service in November 1994, Moon Rise now has a contract with a Bathing Service Company called CSC, and CSC reinstated the old custom as part of the contemporary funeral ceremony, for an additional charge of ¥50,000.

Hirata and Oka, who work for CSC and Moon Rise, met the Yamaha family after Tomi had finished his consultation. They bowed first and asked immediately who the chief mourner was. They both knelt in front of the deceased's father, and Oka sincerely stated the words of condolence (okuyami no kotoba) and followed them with a deep bow. She then apologized to the family members in advance that the bathing staff would be moving around the room constantly during the ceremony. She also asked which religion the deceased had belonged to so that she would not use the wrong type of death garments.

A clean fluffy futon was brought in and placed near the body. (All the necessary accoutrements are brought in the CSC vans.) A nylon sheet was laid in the middle of the tatami room and the tub was brought in. Next, the coffin was opened. A big bath towel was slipped beneath the body; Hirata grasped both sides of the towel and twisted the towel over the deceased's body to make a handle to lift the deceased. Hirata and Oka took hold of the towel and the deceased's neck and legs, lifted her, and laid her gently on the futon. This method of lifting the deceased was used throughout the ceremony.

The nightgown and some parts of the death garments that Tomi and Mitake had put on her at the hospital were removed. When Yoshiko was completely naked, a large white towel was laid on top of her, covering her body. Her hands and fingers were taken out of the pressed-together position. The bathing staff then began to massage the deceased's joints; by this time rigor mortis had begun to set in. The staff bent her arms, wrists, and hands into different positions to loosen the stiffness. Then they carried her to the bathtub in the towel. The body of the deceased is laid on a stretcher-cum-hammock that hangs inside the tub; this design allows water and soap to drain through while the deceased is being washed. On one side of the tub there are three rubber hoses connected to the van; two hoses provide hot and cold water, and the third vacuums out the used water after the ceremony is completed.

When Yoshiko was on the stretcher, Hirata explained that the traditional bathing ceremony was meant to cleanse the deceased of the impurities of this world before her soul's departure to Buddha-hood. Then he brought out a wooden bucket (oke) and a wooden ladle (shaku) with a long handle. Following the custom of the traditional bathing cere-mony, he added cold water to the hot water in the bucket to make the water warm (which is the oppos-ite of the usual way to make warm water). Hirata explained that the initial stage of the ceremony, "the splashing of water," would be performed by the family members, and he described to them how to do it. The person should stand in front of the de-ceased and hold the wooden bucket in the right hand and the wooden ladle in the left. Then the person should scoop the warm water out of the bucket in one movement and pour it on the deceased, beginning with the lower part of the body and working up to the heart. Hirata warned the Yamahas not to add more water to the ladle before emptying it completely. Returning a partially full ladle to the bucket is like calling back the soul to this life and would confuse the deceased (whose soul should travel toward Buddha-hood, not back toward life). The Yamahas rose and took turns performing as they had been instructed.

The splashing of water (particularly the way the water was mixed, the use of wooden bucket and ladle, and the prohibition against refilling the ladle before it was emptied) is closely connected to the concept of impurity in traditional funeral rituals.

Everything, from preparing the warm water to the materials used, was performed contrary to usual everyday practices. Hirata explained that non-ordin-ary behavior by the living indicated the irreversibility of the deceased's death so that the person would depart from this world. The performance of pouring water, during which a family member is not allowed to add water in the midst of the ritual act, also denotes that the deceased is forbidden from returning to or staying longer with the living. The bathing ritual was intended to make clear to the deceased the distinction and the boundary between this world and the world after. What lay behind this performance during community funerals had been fear that the malevolent spirit (onryō) would harm the living. However, in the commercialized bathing ceremony, the staff members put little emphasis on the concept of impurity, and the performance of the rituals is designed to bring the family members together and let them be part of the ceremony.

The remainder of the bathing service was very different from the traditional bathing ritual; there was no mention of impurity again by the bathing staff. After the family had taken turns wetting the body, Hirata asked them to sit down while the staff performed the rest of the ceremony. Oka began washing Yoshiko's toes with body soap and a fluffy bath sponge. During this time, Yoshiko's torso was kept covered with a white towel. Oka soaped her from her toes, up her legs and arms. Hirata sham-pooed her hair, and when that was finished, he helped Oka wash the chest, stomach, and abdomen. The front part of the body is uncovered by lifting the towel up toward the family. While Oka was soaping the body, Hirata kept his back toward the family, effectively blocking their view. The two worked in a coordinated rhythm, assisting each other in washing every part of Yoshiko's body. Hirata lifted the torso forward so that Oka could sponge her back.[10] When all of the body had been soaped, they rinsed off the lather with warm water from a shower head. Then they dried her with many bath towels. Yoshiko was lifted so that thick cotton could be put between the buttocks and legs. The towel covering her was ex-changed for a fresh large white one. Then Hirata asked Yamaha and Sanae to come forward to dry Yoshiko's face. Hirata handed a fresh towel to the father. This was for the sake of performance because the deceased had been dried completely by the bathing staff.

The deceased was carried back to the futon by means of the wrapped and twisted towel. The death robe had been spread neatly on the futon earlier; it was a simple matter to place the deceased on top of it. Yoshiko was then dressed in a new set of death garments: a white gown (*kyō-katabira*), knee guards, and Japanese-style socks (*shiro-tabi*). Those that had been used at the hospital were discarded. When the deceased was dressed, her hands were pressed together and a pair of hand guards (*tekkō*) and beads (*juzu*) were carefully attached.

Oka knelt on the tatami near Yoshiko's face. She removed the cotton from inside the nose, ears, and mouth where the hospital nurses had placed it. She used long, narrow pieces of fresh cotton for the nose and ears, and thicker, wider cotton for the mouth; this helps form aesthetically shaped cheeks and lips. Then Oka asked Sanae if she would like to apply the makeup. (Usually Oka applies the makeup, but in this case Tomi had passed on the information that the sister had requested to do so.) Sanae brought out her own makeup kit. While she applied foundation to the deceased, the aunt, Mariko, approached to observe the process. Sanae and Mariko began talking to the deceased: "You are so clean. I'm so glad you had a chance to take a bath; you couldn't take a bath for a long time, could you?" Their conversation drew everyone near. Soon family and relatives all commented to each other how fresh Yoshiko looked after her bath. Meanwhile, Sanae was asking the deceased her color preferences. "Yoshiko, do you prefer brown eye shadow? Is red lipstick O.K.?" As if Yoshiko had replied, Sanae went on, "Yes, I know you always liked bright red." As soon as Sanae completed the makeup, Mariko murmured, "You look so beautiful, as if you were a bride." The statement triggered the emotions of the entire family; they broke into sobs. The deceased had died young and never married.

Meanwhile, Hirata had been cleaning the tub and putting it back into the van. When he returned, he asked the father to help him lay Yoshiko in the coffin. When she was settled in the coffin, he began the last stage of the bathing ceremony – the decoration

around the deceased's face with white cotton and cloth. One pack of cotton, about the size of a big cushion, was used to make a frame for the face. Oka cut a flat rectangular sheet of cotton into four narrow rectangular pieces and handed them to Hirata, who carefully laid each piece around the deceased's face like a picture frame. The cotton was added in many layers to give depth. A triangular head cloth (*zukin*) was arranged on top of the deceased's head. Oka handed blocks of dry ice wrapped in white flannel cloth to Hirata, who placed them on the stomach. Two comforters, one white and gold and one pure white, were used to cover Yoshiko's body. At this point, the finale of the bathing ceremony, Hirata called the family members for the last performance: all family members held the coffin lid and shut the coffin. Hirata laid the coffin cover and the decoration string on the coffin but kept the window open for viewing. The small incense table that had been moved out of the way was put back in front of the coffin. The candle and incense were lit again. Hirata knelt down facing family and relatives and said, "We have concluded the bathing ceremony. I am sure the next few days are going to be very difficult for you. I hope you will all take care of your health. Thank you for your patience today." We bowed to the family while kneeling on the tatami floor. The family bowed back to us and said, "Thank you for all you have done." We bowed once again at the door. The whole bathing ceremony had taken about an hour and a half.

The reactions of the deceased's family during bathing ceremonies varied according to the age and gender of the deceased, as well as the cause of death. The atmosphere of the bathing ceremony described above was very emotional because Yoshiko was a young unmarried woman. She had much unfinished business and was pitied for the unfortunate illness that had struck her down so quickly.

In contrast, the bathing ceremony of Mori Rei, a woman in her nineties, was almost joyous. When we entered the room, the male family members stood up to go to the coffee shop in the auditorium. The son, Mori Teruo, a man in his late sixties who was the chief mourner, said to me with a smile, "I don't think I want to see my mother take a bath, and mother would be embarrassed, too," and left with the other male relatives. The women family members stayed and watched us with much curiosity. They chatted with each other and spoke to Rei from the beginning. One woman commented, "How lucky you are to have a bath for the last time." The other woman added, "How nice to be washed by such a young man and young women. I didn't think that young people did such things these days." No aspect of the bathing ceremony passed without comment from the women. When the bathtub was carried in and the shower was used to wash the deceased, the women came to admire the Western bathtub. "This is such a convenient thing, isn't it?" one woman said to the others, who all nodded in agreement. Before Hirata had a chance to announce the completion of the ceremony, the women were complimenting the deceased. "You look so fresh and young." "Rei looks so nice; now she is ready to meet her husband in heaven." The family seemed not only satisfied but pleased as well. The women told me during the ceremony that Rei had died quietly in her sleep. The reaction of the living naturally corresponded to the peaceful nature of this woman's death. Everyone was celebrating her death and her life.

One bathing ceremony that I remember clearly was for Tano Genzō, a man in his sixties. It took place at his home on a morning in early spring; the weather was still so cold that the boiler in the van took some time to heat the water. From the beginning, Hirata, Oka, and I all felt something was distinctly different about the reaction of this family. The atmosphere of the room was very heavy. It was not the silence that made me uneasy, but the way the family either stared at us or avoided our eyes while inspecting each other's faces as if they were trying to read each other's thoughts. As soon as we unclothed Tano Genzō, we saw a blue line on his neck, which looked like a scar. I assumed that the deceased had had an operation on his throat. While we were washing the deceased, the family did not speak to us, to each other, or to the deceased. There was an atmosphere of intense silence, ambivalence, and seriousness. When Oka and I went outside to the van for fresh towels, she commented that the atmosphere was extraordinary. "I don't understand this family," she whispered. "All families

react in some way, but these people are completely silent, as if they've been turned to stone" (ishimi-taini kataku natteru).

When the bathing was completed, male members of the family helped Hirata place the deceased into the coffin; so far no one had said a word. Then, as the bathing staff prepared to frame the deceased's face with cotton, the son, who was the chief mourner, approached and said something in a low voice that no one else in the room could hear. Hirata nodded and replied, "I will do so." After we had left, Hirata told us that the son had said, "Could you hide that scar?" Hirata had arranged the cotton around the face, and later the comforter, up to Tano's chin to hide his scar.

The second time the son spoke he asked if it was all right to put objects in the coffin. Interestingly, the first object they brought out was a Buddhist sutra. Often family members bring clothes, eye-glasses, and other objects that were used by the deceased in daily life or that were valuable to the deceased. But in this case many Buddhist objects were placed in the coffin. Hirata announced the end of the ceremony, and we bowed to the family and moved toward the door. At this point the family surprised me again: all of them came out of the house. The three of us got into the van and Hirata started the engine, then the van started to move. They were still standing in the cold rain. From inside the van we bowed at them while the car was moving forward. Then I saw the Tano family members bowing to us with their heads down low. I had never seen the bereaved bowing so low. I looked back from the moving van; they were still standing there.

"What is all this appreciation about? Weren't they bowing a bit too deeply?" I asked Hirata, who had been doing this job for three years. Hirata said that the deceased had committed suicide. According to him, when people hang themselves, they often bite their tongues. Their lips cannot be opened easily. That was exactly how Tano was that day. Oka had tried to put cotton in the mouth, but it had been shut tight. "The rigor mortis of the suicide victim occurs more rapidly than it does for people who die from other causes," Hirata added. The scar on Tano Genzō's neck was a mark from hanging. Hirata's explanation unraveled the mystery of the family's unusual behavior. "A suicide is still considered a very bad death in Japan," he said. "They must have been worried that we would treat the deceased with fear or refuse to perform the ceremony if the fact was revealed. The deep bows were the expression of their appreciation to us, that we did the job without causing the family to lose face."[11]

Although the size of the funeral is determined by deceased's social status, age, and gender, the atmosphere of the funeral corresponds to the cause of death and the deceased's personality. It was not difficult to tell if a death had been a "good death" or a "bad death" by the way families and relatives interacted with the funeral staff. The death of a young person is always traumatic, as are violent deaths whatever the age of the deceased, whereas anticipated deaths are more peaceful. Deceased who were well liked called forth strong feelings of grief. Such distinctions were amplified in the vigils and funerals.

The Wake at the Funeral Auditorium

The wake for the Yamaha family was scheduled for 7:00 p.m. on the same day the deceased was transported to the funeral auditorium. A few hours before the wake, Doi, the conductor hired by Moon Rise, arrived to meet the bereaved. He began by explaining the sequence of events and details about the wake and the funeral, such as where the bereaved would sit and what they would be expected to do. He finished by asking the family if they had any questions or problems so far. Yamaha and Mariko asked how large the monetary donation (*ofuse*) for the priest should be.[12] "That varies according to different temples, the rank of the deceased's posthumous name (*kaimyō*), and the number of attending priests," Doi replied. "In the case of my temple, which is Jōdoshū, I would enclose ¥100,000 for one priest." The higher the rank and the number of the priests, and the higher the rank of the posthumous name given, the larger the donation. Doi drew a picture of a donation envelope and wrote "contribution" on the upper portion and the name of the chief mourner below the ribbon. The father, who was also worried about his funeral speech as the chief mourner, asked what he was expected to say.

Opening his file, Doi took out copies of sample speeches and told Yamaha that he need only say a few words and thank the guests for coming in spite of their busy schedules. This meeting, which was a basic lesson on Japanese funerals, took about 40 minutes.

The Buddhist priest, from a Jōdoshinshū sect temple, arrived about fifteen minutes before seven. He was a young man in his late thirties. We bowed to him, and he lightly bowed back to the funeral professionals. A woman funeral assistant was there to take him to his waiting room, but instead he went directly to the tatami room where family and relatives had gathered for the wake. The family greeted the priest with a bow and began to talk to him about the deceased. Priests often do not have any knowledge of the deceased; the wake is the first time a priest is told about the cause of death and the deceased's life in general. Sometimes this may even be the first time the priest meets the family.[13] While the family was talking to the priest, Doi went into the room and introduced himself to the priest.

The guests arrived gradually. The first and most important obligation of a guest is to offer incense money to the deceased's family. In community rituals, incense money, or condolence money (*kōden*), was predominantly offered on the day of the funeral, but today those who cannot attend the funeral ceremony present their gifts at the wake. Incense money is enclosed in a special envelope with one's name on the lower portion in front and the amount of money on the back. The amount of money varies according to the giver's relationship to the deceased or to the bereaved (see table 19.1).

The gift of incense money necessitates a return gift (*kōden-gaeshi*). The exchange is a formal performance during which both sides present their gifts and then bow deeply. These exchanges are made even more solemn by elders who present their envelopes with both hands and use traditional incense money wrappers (*fukusa*) made out of dark-colored silk. This custom is fading, however. The younger generations, including people in their fifties and sixties, hand an unwrapped envelope of incense money directly to relatives or helpers who represent the bereaved family. I occasionally saw embarrassed guests, who had forgotten to inscribe their name on

Table 19.1   Incense Money Donations (in yen)

Donor's relationship to the deceased or the bereaved	Age of donor			
	20s	30s	40s	50s
Boss	¥ 5,000*	¥ 5,000	¥ 10,000	¥ 10,000
	6,100	7,000	8,600	7,760
Family member of boss	3,000	3,000	5,000	5,000
	3,800	3,900	5,200	5,000
Business colleague	3,000	5,000	5,000	5,000
	5,700	6,200	7,300	7,300
Family member of business colleague	3,000	3,000	5,000	5,000
	3,400	3,500	4,200	4,400
Younger business colleague	3,000	5,000	5,000	5,000
	4,600	6,000	7,700	6,500
Family member of younger business colleague	3,000	3,000	5,000	5,000
	3,600	3,200	4,200	8,000
Friend or acquaintance	5,000	5,000	5,000	5,000
	6,300	6,000	7,300	8,000
Brother or sister	10,000	10,000	50,000	50,000
	29,500	35,800	37,400	59,600
Grandparent	10,000	10,000	30,000	50,000
	21,000	26,300	32,300	40,100
Uncle or aunt	10,000	10,000	10,000	30,000
	13,000	17,600	18,600	29,400
Nephew or niece	10,000	10,000	10,000	30,000
	13,000	17,600	18,600	29,400

*The first figure is the amount cited most frequently by survey respondents; the second figure is the average of the figures cited by respondents. 110 yen = approximately one U.S. dollar.

Source: Survey by Shizuoka Newspapers in Shizuoka Prefecture, in *Shizuoka Ken no Kankon Sōsai* (*Weddings and funerals in Shizuoka*) (Shizuoka: Shizuoka Newspapers Press, 1995), 172.

the envelope, quickly writing their names on the spot.

It is not unusual for the funeral staff to help the deceased's families prepare a money offering to the priests, and also to assist guests with their incense envelopes. The coffee shop at the Moon Rise auditorium sells such basic funeral items as envelopes for incense money, rosaries (*juzu*), black neckties, black socks, and black stockings, because guests quite often forget to bring these items or wear inappropriate attire.

While representatives from Yamaha's family at the front desk were keeping track of incense money and giving return gifts, funeral assistants guided those guests who had finished the exchange to the tatami room. The room was becoming crowded, and an assistant had to ask people to move forward and add more cushions (*zabuton*). The guests were all seated neatly in two rows facing the coffin and the wake altar at the front of the room. The priest sat at the very front of the altar, and the family was seated in the front row on the right. Finally the wave of arriving guests subsided. It was time to begin.

Doi took a seat near the priest. He straightened his back and announced the beginning of the wake. He gave the deceased's name and age, the time of death, and the priest's rank and temple. Then he asked the priest to begin his sutra chanting. The priest began with the rhythmic "*nam-mu-a-mi-da-bu-tsu*" (Lord have mercy upon him/her), loudly at first, then more quietly at the end. After repeating the verse, he chanted the sutra text for twenty minutes. Unless one is a specialist in religion, it is difficult to understand even a word of what is being chanted. Many guests closed their eyes and lowered their heads until it was time for the incense offering (*shōkō*). It is not uncommon for people to fall asleep during the sutra chanting, and even to snore. Another participant quickly wakes the person.

When the priest had completed the major portion of the text, Doi announced the offering of incense. The offering began with the closest family members and continued until all of the guests had offered incense at the alter while the priest, sitting to the right, continued to chant. By 8:10 p.m. everyone had offered incense. The priest, who had been facing the altar, turned around to the family and guests. He announced that the prayers for the wake (*otsutome*) had been completed. He began to tell Buddhist stories (*hōwa*):

> There are two kinds of life in person. One is a physical life, and the other is the spiritual life. The world is alternating [*mu-jō-jissō*]; nothing stays the same and everything changes. All things change with a certain aim, namely, to achieve Buddhahood. Why do flowers bloom? Why do flowers fade away? Why do fruits ripen and fall? All lives exist for the sole purpose to become and to reach Buddhahood. The life of the physical body may stop at an early stage. But the spiritual life grows and develops without any limitations or bounds. The end of the physical life is not the final end. There is a life beyond in the world of Buddha [*jōbutsu*].

Unfortunately, the guests did not seem overly impressed with the priest's story; at least I did not notice anyone nodding in agreement. The message of the preaching was difficult to accept, even contradicting the emotions felt by a family that had lost a daughter so young. When the priest had completed his Buddhist exhortation, a funeral assistant served him a cup of tea. The priest pressed his hands together (*gasshō*), bowed, and drank a sip. Then he chatted with the chief mourner while sipping tea. Ten minutes later, the priest bowed once more to the family and left the room.

The priest's departure was the cue for other guests to leave. The vigil was about to begin. Family and relatives gathered around the table that had been prepared by a funeral assistant while guests were leaving. The Yamaha family asked Doi to join the vigil, but he courteously declined for the reason that he had to prepare for the funeral the following day.

The funeral assistant helped the family arrange two large plates of vegetarian sushi, nuts, other food items, plates, and cups. The assistant and the women of the family began serving sake and beer to the male family members and relatives. By 9:15 p.m., observing that the gathering was proceeding on its own, the funeral assistant also left.

The family spent a few more hours drinking and talking. At community funerals, wakes commonly served only vegetarian food (*shōjin*), no meat or alcohol. However, almost all the wakes I observed during my fieldwork served alcohol. Men drank, but few women did so. Drinking patterns at wakes and funerals varied according to the circumstances of the deceased's death and reflected a pattern in society at large. In the case of the Yamaha family, sipping sake was a way to share the sadness of losing a young daughter. For those who had lost an old grandmother, drinking was a way to celebrate her long life and peaceful death. For those who had lost loved ones in an accident or by suicide, gulping beer helped temporarily dull their grief. Drinking is not taboo at contemporary wakes or at funerals. On the contrary, it is an appropriate or even necessary gesture to demonstrate one's sympathy, pain, and sorrow over a particular death. Moon Rise's funeral auditorium has refrigerators stocked with beer beside each tatami room because drinking during a wake goes on until midnight and sometimes throughout the night.

The women in the Yamaha family retired before midnight, leaving the men drinking. After emptying a dozen large beer bottles and a dozen small sake bottles, male participants asked the funeral staff to call them cabs for the ride home. By midnight everyone had left except the two relatives who were staying overnight with Yoshiko in the tatami room.[14] Their bedding (futon, pillows, and blankets) was rented for this purpose.

Quite a few families do not have anyone stay with the deceased for the vigil. Elder funeral staff lamented about this to me. "Some families leave their deceased all alone. It's shameful." But in fact, the feeling of shame for not attending the deceased during the vigil is weakening. In community funerals, sitting or lying near the deceased's coffin or bedside throughout the night was essential. The deceased was at that time in a transitional period and had to be protected from the evil spirits (*akuryō*). For this reason, the family took turns keeping incense burning to ward off evil spirits and prevent them from entering the body. Today, however, funeral staff and funeral conductors are often asked the same questions by family members: Is it really necessary to stay with the deceased at night? Will anyone be at the auditorium for the night shift? Funeral professionals commonly state that it is not compulsory to stay with the deceased during the vigil and that there are three funeral professionals on the overnight shift. Upon hearing this, most families conclude that they do not need to remain because, as they put it, "The deceased is taken care of by the funeral staff." The funeral staff make sure the family understands that that they will not be in the deceased's room itself but in the night-shift room downstairs. A typical response to this is: "It's okay [*sorede kekkōdesu*], as long as someone is in the building." The bereaved, however, should not be solely blamed for this change in practice; even the funeral professionals themselves put out all incense and candles at night to avoid the risk of fire.

Why then did families cease to stay up with the deceased through the night? The change in this practice demonstrates that both the family and funeral professionals do not consider the deceased to be in a state of impurity. In this chapter I have described funerary performances after the announcement of death and prior to a funeral ceremony. What is explicit during this period is the absence of the perception of impurity, death pollution, and evil spirits. These concepts are irrelevant not only to professionals of Moon Rise but also to the bereaved. The reason the Yamaha family left two relatives with Yoshiko was not because she was in a dangerous transitional state but because "she will be lonely" (*hitoride kawaisō dakara*). Similarly, the funeral staff complained about the bereaved who did not stay with the dead, saying, "They are not fully showing respect to the deceased." On the one hand, if the living perceive the deceased to be alive, there is no impurity or danger of evil spirits to be dealt with. On the other hand, if funeral professionals view the deceased as alive but in a state of unconsciousness, then a family member should stay to assist the person just as would be done during a hospitalization. Both of these two commonly expressed rationales by the living and

professionals place the deceased, until the end of the funeral ceremonies, in a resuscitated state rather than in a biological or social transition phase. The belief in the "living-dead" explains why funeral professionals (who are engaged before cremation) display extreme respect and caution while treating the deceased's body.

NOTES

1   This is a direct result of the differences between health care in the United States and Japan. Japanese health care is socialistic; the government provides health care to all Japanese. Thus, city, prefectural, and public university hospitals have little money to spend on decor or patient conveniences.

2   The room for the soul in Japan and a morgue in America are different. The former is a single room (it varies in size) for one corpse, whereas in America the dead share one room.

3   Funeral staff do not use cord to tie the hands as the nurses do, although it would greatly facilitate arranging the beads between the deceased's pressed hands. Any action that makes it appear as if it causes pain for the deceased is strictly prohibited among funeral staff. The reason the funeral staff is prohibited from performing the same action that the medical staff is allowed to perform is a complex structure of perspective that illustrates the linguistic difference between "corpse" (*shitai*) and "a deceased's remains" (*itai*). The latter term implies the body of one's family, relative, or a close friend. It is a term that demonstrates respect to the deceased and the family. In contrast, the use of the word *shitai* implies a cadaver that has no relationship to anyone; it is a thing or an object. Thus, the "deceased's remains" need to be treated as if the person were still alive. The funeral industry must treat the deceased with extreme care so that the family does not believe the funeral staff have treated the deceased as a "corpse" and thus without respect.

4   The head cloth is not placed on the deceased's head until the encoffining.

5   Usually nurses send off the deceased from the hospital, but doctors are sometimes present. I was told by the funeral staff that the number of medical staff sending off the deceased depends on the number of gifts the deceased's family has given them during the period of hospitalization. The more gifts that were given, the more medical staff are willing to send him or her off.

6 A seal is a character-based stamp that is used as a signature. The person who is the chief mourner and is responsible for payment, in this case Yamaha, is required to provide his or her seal.

7 The coffin is never placed directly on the floor. The window on the coffin is made so that the two small doors on the coffin open outward. The window has a transparent plastic cover instead of glass so that it can be incinerated during cremation. Often the plastic cover became smeared with tears; part-time workers wipe off the plastic cover with cloths after the wake or on the morning of the funeral ceremony.

8 All these displayed foods are placed into the coffin after the funeral ceremony and incinerated with the deceased; they are to sustain the deceased on the journey to the other world.

9 According to statistics from the Kita-Kyūshū Department of Public Health, in 1992, 83.4 percent of all deaths occurred in hospitals, 1.9 percent in clinics, 0.1 percent in nursing homes, 11.9 percent at home, and the rest (2.7 percent) elsewhere.

10 The private parts of the body were given a more cursory cleansing to preserve the modesty of the deceased.

11 Uchiumi, who works at the coffee shop at the auditorium, told me a story that she remembers clearly. A couple of years earlier, the son of two famous doctors committed suicide. The son was carried directly to the Moon Rise Auditorium. His grandmother was the only attendant at the wake and the funeral. Nobody was invited or notified. On the blackboard of the funeral staff's office, where ordinarily the deceased's names are written, a sign said "Secret" and "Do not Disturb." Uchiumi said that the incident was concealed from the public because the son's parents were highly regarded doctors in the local area who feared their son's suicide would harm their reputations. Uchiumi explained to me, "Suicide destroys the family name. It is considered the most shameful way to die."

12 There is no set amount for the donation to the priest.

13 Many families who have moved away from the residence of their parents and ancestors do not belong to or have contact with a temple. Although each family needs a priest for the funeral and a place for the deceased's ashes, the family does not necessarily join the officiating priest's temple. Like the funeral services purchased from a company, the priests' services can be a single transaction.

14 For wakes at home, family members take turns staying up, but when a wake takes place at the auditorium, only one or two relatives remain in most cases.

REFERENCE

Ebersole, Gary L. 1989. *Ritual Poetry and the Politics of Death in Early Japan*. Princeton, NJ: Princeton University Press.

20

"Thus Are Our Bodies, Thus Was Our Custom": Mortuary Cannibalism in an Amazonian Society

Beth A. Conklin

The Wari'[1] (Pakaa Nova) are an indigenous population of about 1,500 people who live in the western Brazilian rain forest, in the state of Rondônia near the Bolivian border. Until the 1960s, they disposed of nearly all their dead by consuming substantial amounts of corpses' body substances. All Wari' elders living today took part in or witnessed mortuary cannibalism, and their recollections offer an opportunity to view cannibalism from the perspectives of those who participated in it. This article explores the question of why cannibalism was the preferred means for disposing of the dead, emphasizing indigenous interpretations of the logic and meanings of cannibalism.

From a cross-cultural perspective, Wari' customs appear unusual in several respects. In most other societies, mortuary cannibalism involved the consumption of only small amounts of a corpse's body substances, which typically were ingested by a dead person's consanguineal kin.[2] Among the Wari', however, the dead person's affines ideally consumed all of the roasted flesh, brains, heart, liver, and – sometimes – the ground bones. Cannibalism was the preferred treatment for all Wari' corpses, except in a few circumstances in which bodies were cremated.

The Wari' practiced both exocannibalism (the eating of enemies and social outsiders) and endocannibalism (the eating of members of one's own group) but considered the two forms of anthropophagy to have little in common. The eating of enemies, which will not be examined in detail here,[3] involved overt expressions of hostility: enemy body parts were abused and treated disrespectfully, and the freshly roasted flesh was eaten off the bone *ak karawa*, "like animal meat" (see Vilaça 1992:47–130). In contrast, the very different customs of mortuary cannibalism expressed honor and respect for the dead.

This article focuses on how mortuary cannibalism fit into Wari' experiences of grief and mourning. My approach traces themes emphasized by contemporary Wari' in reflecting on their past participation in cannibalistic funerals. The question "Why did you

From Beth A. Conklin, " 'Thus Are Our Bodies, Thus Was Our Custom': Mortuary Cannibalism in an Amazonian Society," *American Ethnologist*, 22, 1 (1995): 75–101.

eat the dead?" tended to draw a limited range of responses. The most common reply was "*Je' kwer-exi'*," "Thus was our custom."[4] This statement should be taken seriously; for many Wari', cannibalism was simply the norm; for reasons I discuss in this article, it was considered to be the most respectful way to treat a human body. Beyond this, when older people reflected on deeper, personal motives, they tended to link cannibalism to a process of achieving emotional detachment from memories of the dead: "When we ate the body, we did not think longingly [*koromikat*] about the dead much." Numerous middle-aged and elderly people – of both sexes and in various villages – independently offered the explanation that cannibalism altered memories and the emotions of grief in ways that helped them deal with the loss of a loved one. Elders were bemused and at times rather irritated by anthropologists' singular obsession with the eating of bodies, for they insisted that cannibalism cannot be understood apart from the entire complex of mortuary rites and mourning behaviors aimed at reshaping emotional and spiritual relations between the living and the dead.

To understand cannibalism's role in mourning, I propose to show that Wari' practices reflected two concepts of widespread salience in lowland South America: the idea of the human body as a locus of physically constituted social relationships and social identity, and ideas about human-nonhuman reciprocity. These concepts merged in a year-long series of traditional mourning rites that focused on actual and symbolic transformations of a dead person's body, from human to animal form. Cannibalism was a powerful element in a social process of mourning structured around images of ancestors' regeneration as animals with ongoing, life-supporting relations to their living relatives.

Wari' testimonies concerning the affective dimensions of cannibalism are unusual in the ethnographic literature, for we have few detailed accounts of cannibalism from the viewpoint of its practitioners. Most peoples who formerly practiced it no longer do so, leaving few individuals able or willing to speak to personal experiences of people-eating. Perhaps because of this, anthropological analyses of cannibalism have tended to focus mostly on the level of societal systems of meaning and symbolism. Cannibalism as

praxis is poorly understood. This is particularly striking in the case of mortuary cannibalism: although it is, by definition, a cultural response to a fellow group member's death, we know little about how the socially constituted symbols of mortuary cannibalism relate to emotions and fit into individuals' lived experiences of coming to terms with a relative's death. Wari' recollections offer insights into one people's experiences.

In the anthropology of anthropophagy, mortuary cannibalism has received rather short shrift. The ethnographic and ethnohistorical literatures are dominated by accounts of the exocannibalism of enemies, which has been reported more frequently, and described in more depth, than endo- or mortuary cannibalism. Concomitant with this predominant focus on enemy-eating, universalist theories of cannibalism have tended to interpret anthropophagy as a fundamentally antisocial act. Psychogenic theorists from Freud (1981[1913]) to Sagan (1974) have viewed all forms of people-eating as an expression of individuals' egocentric, oral-aggressive impulses. Recent social anthropological theories also have emphasized themes of antisociality. Lewis (1986:63–77) subsumed endo- and exocannibalism alike under a model in which consumption and ingestion reflect oral and genital aggression, and agonistic desires for dominance. Arens (1979) interpreted cannibalism as a universal symbol of barbarism, otherness, and inhumanity.

Mortuary cannibalism data have a special place in cannibalism studies, for the meanings associated with consuming one's fellows tend to be quite different from the motives for eating enemies. Mortuary cannibalism systems present the greatest potential challenge to interpretations of cannibalism as an antisocial act of aggression and domination, and the few ethnographic studies of mortuary cannibalism have tended to highlight its socially integrative dimensions. Analyses of several Melanesian systems have examined the role of mortuary cannibalism as part of the assemblage of cultural symbols and rituals whereby social groups defined and reconstituted themselves after a death (Gillison 1983; Lindenbaum 1979; Meigs 1984; Poole 1983). Sanday's (1986) cross-cultural analysis emphasized the semantic complexity of anthropophagy and showed that cannibalism may symbolize not only evil and chaos but also social order and the regeneration of life-giving cosmic forces.

Recent general theories of mortuary cannibalism have considered only a limited set of cultural motivations, however, and have focused exclusively on ethnographic data from a single region, Melanesia. The diverse Melanesian endocannibalism systems expressed a variety of cultural meanings, but they tended to share in two main ideas: the assumption that cannibalism primarily benefits those who consume human substance; and the notion of an economy of biosocial substance in which cannibalism serves as a means of acquiring body substances, vital energies, or personal attributes contained in the dead person's corpse and of transferring them to those who eat it. These concepts have been widely assumed to characterize all endocannibalism systems. In the two most recent anthropological syntheses of cannibalism theory, Sanday stated that "[e]ndocannibalism recycles and regenerates social forces that are believed to be physically constituted in bodily substances or bones" (1986:7) and Lewis asserted that "the ritual consumption of parts of the human body enables the consumer to acquire something of the body's vital energy" (1986:73). Neither interpretation applies to the Wari' case.

Although both endo- and exocannibalism were widely practiced in lowland South America well into the 20th century (Dole 1974; Métraux 1947:22–5), the Amazonian literature has received little attention in recent North American and British discourse on cannibalism, although it has been of longstanding interest among Brazilian and French anthropologists. Some Amazonian endocannibalism reflected concepts similar to the Melanesian theme of recycling dead people's energies or attributes (see, for example, Acosta Saignes 1961:161–2; Dole 1974:307; Erikson 1986:198; Reichel-Dolmatoff 1971:138–9), but many South American systems expressed quite different ideas, often involving notions of altering relations between body and spirit or between the living and the dead. Wari' informants universally denied that their consumption of either kin or enemies had anything to do with recycling substance, attributes, or energies from the dead to

those who ate them.[5] They consistently represented cannibalism not as a boon for the eaters of human flesh but as a service for those who did not eat: the deceased and their close kin.

Wari' mortuary customs reflect complex social and symbolic systems about which a great deal more can be said than is possible in this article. I refer interested readers to the works of other anthropologists who have studied Wari' society (Mason 1977; Von Graeve 1972, 1989) and the puzzle of Wari' anthropophagy (Meireles 1986; Vilaça 1989, 1992). Meireles has examined the role of cannibalism in defining self-other relations in the construction of Wari' personhood and emphasized the symbolism of fire as mediator of human-nonhuman relations. Vilaça presented symbolic-structuralist interpretations of both exo- and endocannibalism, with special attention to affinal relations, festivals, and origin myths related to anthropophagy. Her analysis has focused on Wari' conceptions of the social universe as structured around oppositions and reciprocal exchanges between predators and prey. Symbolic oppositions between the categories of Wari' ("we, people") and karawa ("animals") recur in Wari' ideology and rituals at multiple levels: humans vs. animals, Wari' vs. non-Wari', consanguines vs. affines, the living vs. the dead. Vilaça (1992:291) has emphasized that mortuary cannibalism symbolically associated the dead person with the category of prey and identified the living Wari' with the category of predators.

My analysis complements Vilaça's and Meireles's interpretations by situating cannibalism in relation to three other dimensions of Wari' experience: social processes of mourning, body concepts, and the regenerative imagery of ancestors' transformations into animals. To examine relationships among the social, symbolic, and ritual systems, I first describe the ethnographic context and mortuary rites and discuss why the Wari' case does not fit the major materialist and psychogenic models proposed to explain cannibalism elsewhere. I then examine social and psychological dimensions of Wari' body concepts to show why the corpse's destruction by cannibalism or cremation was considered essential. Finally, I explore Wari' ideas about human-animal relations that suggest an answer to the question of why the Wari' preferred cannibalism rather than cremation.

Ethnographic Context

The Wari' speak a language in the Chapakuran language family isolate. They entered permanent relations with Brazilian national society between 1956 and 1969, when the former national Indian agency, the SPI (Serviço de Proteção aos Índios), sponsored a series of pacification expeditions that terminated Wari' autonomy. The Wari' now reside in eight major villages in indigenous reserves along tributaries of the Mamoré and Madeira Rivers in the municipality of Guajará-Mirim, Rondônia. Prior to the contact they had no canoes and inhabited interfluvial (*terra firme*) areas of the rain forest, away from the larger rivers. Today, as in the past, subsistence depends on slash-and-burn farming, hunting, fishing, and foraging. Maize is the principal staple crop, and hunting is the most socially valued food-getting activity.

Precontact villages typically were comprised of about thirty people living in several nuclear family households. Contemporary Wari' communities are administered by FUNAI (Fundação Nacional do Índio), the Brazilian government Indian agency, whose policies of population concentration and sedentarization have disrupted traditional settlement patterns and social organization. Today's villages, of 80–400 people, are located at nontraditional sites near major rivers or roads accessible to transportation to town.

Wari' society is staunchly egalitarian, and social relations are characterized by a high degree of flexibility. Leadership is ephemeral; there are no "chiefs," and no formal positions of political authority above the household level. Mason (1977) categorized Wari' kinship terminology as a Crow/Omaha – type system. Wari' kin groups are ego-centered bilateral kindred; there are no lineages, and no internal segregation based on age grades or ceremonial activities. Precontact postmarital residence was flexible, with couples free to live near either spouse's bilateral kin after initial matrilocal bride service. Of central importance for understanding mortuary customs is the role of affinity as the strongest organizing principle in Wari' society. Alliances among families related by marriage[6] are important in food sharing, mutual aid, funeral duties and, in the past,

were one basis for war alliances. Wari' society is by no means conflict-free, but most decision making is consensual, and the general tenor of social relations emphasizes mutuality and reciprocity among kin, affines, and allies.

The precontact Wari' were divided into named, territorially based subgroups (Oro Nao', Oro Eo', Oro At, Oro Mon, Oro Waram, and Oro Waram-Xijein) that were the largest social units with which individuals identified. A subgroup's members were committed to peaceful coexistence and cooperation in warfare and emergencies. Amicable relations among the villages in a subgroup were affirmed and maintained by festival exchanges, including celebrations called *hüroroin* and *tamara* that are models for the human–nonhuman alliance exchanges represented in mortuary cannibalism.

After the first peaceful contacts with outsiders were established in the Rio Dois Irmãos area in 1956, government (SPI) agents and New Tribes missionaries witnessed several anthropophagous funerals. Most of the Wari' population entered contact in 1961–2. News of Wari' funerary cannibalism became public knowledge in early 1962, when an SPI agent sold his eyewitness account to a São Paulo newspaper (*Folha de São Paulo* 1962). In response, a competing paper sent journalists to the Rio Negro-Ocaia contact site, where they photographed dismemberment and roasting at a child's funeral (de Carvalho 1962). Brazilian anthropologists and SPI officials convinced the paper not to publish these photographs and attempted to use the ensuing publicity to call public attention to the tragic situation of the recently contacted Wari' (Cruzeiro 1962:123–5).

Contact with the pacification teams introduced devastating epidemics of measles, influenza, tuberculosis, and other cosmopolitan diseases. Within two or three years of contact, approximately 60 percent of the precontact population was dead. Chronically ill, psychologically traumatized, and unable to hunt or plant crops, the survivors became extremely dependent on outsiders for food and medical care. Missionaries and government agents manipulated this dependency to put an end to cannibalism by threatening to withhold food and medicines from those who continued to eat the dead. They insisted that corpses be buried instead. At each of the three major contact sites, Wari' initially resisted this forced change to burial.

The deadly epidemics, however, created another reason to abandon cannibalism: traditional illness concepts could not explain the unfamiliar maladies, and so people listened when missionaries told them that the new diseases were spread by eating infected corpses. Wari' began burying people who died of illness (the great majority of early postcontact deaths), but, for a while, they continued to cannibalize those whose deaths were attributed to accidents, sorcery, and other nondisease causes. Families carried corpses into the forest, to be roasted away from outsiders' eyes. However, these efforts at deception ultimately failed, and by the end of 1962 or early 1963, nearly everyone had abandoned cannibalism altogether. (The exception was a group of about thirty Oro Mon who lived autonomously until 1969.) Today, all Wari' follow Western customs of burying corpses in cemeteries in the forest.[7]

No anthropologist has witnessed Wari' anthropophagy, and many data presented here are based on retrospective reconstructions. My primary sources are the testimonies of numerous older Wari' who say that they participated in or observed mortuary cannibalism. During two years of medical anthropological field work in 1985–7, I interviewed all 198 families in the communities of Santo André, Ribeirao, Lage, Tanajura, and Rio Negro-Ocaia (85 percent of the total Wari' population). Interviews with adults of both sexes, aimed at collecting genealogies and mortality and morbidity histories, often led to discussions of personal experiences with relatives' deaths and funerals. I observed aspects of contemporary mourning behavior, including ritual wailing and the handling of a corpse, but no one died in a village where I was present, and I attended no burials or complete funerals. Santo André, a community of 190 people, was my principal residence, and I discussed issues treated in this article with all the elders and many middle-aged people there. The most detailed information and insights came from several key informants: three men and two women between ages 60 and 75, two men in their 50s, and a man and woman in their early 40s. Most Santo André residents are descendants of the precontact Rio Dois

Irmãos area population, and this article describes this group's practices, which differed only in minor details from other Wari' communities.

The Wari' do not conform to Arens' (1979) assertions that alleged cannibals seldom acknowledge eating anyone and that cannibalism is primarily a symbol of inhumanity and barbarism projected upon enemies, neighbors, and uncivilized "others." Wari' anthropophagy is not merely alleged by outsiders; Wari' themselves freely affirm practicing it in the past, even though they are aware that outsiders consider it barbaric. I found no one who denied that corpses customarily were cannibalized; numerous elders spoke openly of eating human flesh. Independent descriptions of particular funerals were internally consistent and corresponded to reports by New Tribes missionaries and SPI agents who observed cannibalism in the early postcontact period. By any reasonable standards for the documentation of past events not witnessed by an ethnographer, there is no question that the Wari' ate their dead.

Traditional Funerals

Today, as in the past, funerals generally take place in the house of a senior kinsman of the deceased.[8] The household's sleeping platform (or raised floor) is removed to permit mourners to crowd together under the palm-thatch roof. Two loosely defined groups have prescribed roles at funerals. The first is the iri' nari[9] ("true kin," or close sanguines and the spouse). Wari' define consanguinity in terms of shared blood and classify spouses as consanguines by virtue of sexual transfers of body fluids that create shared blood. Between spouses, it is said, "there is only one body" (xika pe' na kwere). Linked to the deceased by shared body substance, the iri' nari are the principal mourners. From the time of biological death until the body is disposed of, they remain nearest the corpse, holding it in their arms and crying.

The second group of mourners, nari paxi ("those who are like kin but are not truly related"), most properly consists of the dead person's own affines and affines of the deceased's close kin, but the term is extended to include all non-consanguines attending the funeral. Close affines are responsible for the work of funerals: female affines prepare maize *chicha* (a sweet, unfermented drink) and maize *pamonha* (dense, unleavened bread) to feed visitors, and male affines (ideally, the dead person's brothers-in-law or sons-in-law) serve as messengers summoning people to the funeral. They prepare and dispose of the corpse and funeral apparatus and look out for the welfare of emotionally distraught mourners.

In traditional funerals, the iri' nari sit together, apart from other mourners. In contemporary funerals, the spatial division is less marked, but close kin remain nearest the corpse. All mourners press close together around the body, leaning on each other's shoulders and wailing. Death wails are of several types, including wordless crying, the singing of kinship terms for the deceased, and a more structured keening called *aka pijim* ("to cry to speak"), in which mourners recount memories of the deceased, singing of shared experiences and the person's life history, deeds, and kindnesses. (On Amazonian ritual lament, see Briggs 1992; Graham 1986; Seeger 1987; Urban 1988, 1991.) From the moment of death until the funeral's end, everyone joins in a ceaseless, high-pitched keening that sends a haunting mantra of collective grief reverberating off the surrounding forest.

The dead person's humanity and social connections are repeatedly affirmed in funeral actions directed at the corpse itself, which is the constant focus of attention. Corpses are never left to lie alone. From the moment of death until the body is disposed of, grieving kin constantly cradle the corpse in their arms, hugging it, pressing their own bodies against it. Desire for physical contact can be so intense that, according to several Santo André residents, there was a funeral a few years ago where the corpse was in danger of being pulled apart by distraught kin struggling to embrace it. Finally, a senior kinsman enforced order by mandating that only one person at a time could hold the body.

Numerous funeral actions express mourners' self-identification with the dead person's physical state and desires to join the deceased in death. Any loss of consciousness, such as fainting, is considered a form of death. In one common funeral practice, close relatives "die" (*mi' pin*) by lying one on top of the other, in stacks of three or four people with the corpse on top. When someone faints from the suffocating press of bodies, he or she is pulled out of the pile and someone else joins the pile, in a process repeated again and again. In a 1986 funeral, people piled into the homemade coffin, embracing the corpse on top.

In traditional funerals, the male affine helpers constructed the ritual firewood bundle and roasting rack. Ideally, these were made of roofbeams, decorated with feathers and painted with red annatto (*urucú, Bixa orellana*). A beam was taken from each house in the dead person's village, leaving the thatched roofs sagging in visible expression of death's violation of the community's integrity. Funerals for infants were less elaborate; regular, undecorated firewood was used. When preparations were completed, the helpers lit the fire, spread clean mats on the ground, and dismembered the body, using a new bamboo arrow tip. Internal organs were removed first, and the heart and liver were wrapped in leaves to be roasted. Body parts considered inedible, including the hair, nails, genitals, intestines, and other entrails, were burned. The helpers then severed the head, removed the brains, cut the limbs at the joints, and placed the body parts on the roasting rack. Young children's body parts were wrapped in leaves in the manner used to roast small fish and soft foods.

Several elders recalled that the most emotionally difficult event in a funeral was the moment when the corpse was taken from its relatives' arms to be dismembered. As the body was cut, wailing and hysterical expressions of grief reached a fevered pitch. Up to this moment, funeral activities had been dominated by mourners' expressions of physical and affective attachments to the dead person's body. Dismemberment represented a radical alteration of the corpse and mourners' relations to it, a graphic severing of the attachments represented in the body. According to these elders, it was dismemberment, not cannibalism, that provoked the most intense emotional dissonance. Once the corpse had been cut, eating it was considered the most respectful possible treatment, for reasons discussed below.

The dead person's close consanguines (iri' nari) did not eat the corpse. Consumption of a close consanguine or spouse's flesh is strongly prohibited, because eating a close relative (with whom one shared body substance) would be tantamount to eating one's own flesh, or autocannibalism. It is believed to be fatal.[10]

The nari paxi, affines and other non-kin, were responsible for consuming the corpse; they are sometimes referred to as ko kao' ("those who ate"). In a married person's funeral, those who consumed the body typically included the dead person's spouse's siblings, spouse's parents, spouse's parents' siblings, and the deceased's children's spouses, as well as these individuals' own close consanguines. Unmarried people typically were eaten by their siblings' spouses, siblings' spouses' siblings, their parents' siblings' spouses, and these individuals' close kin. Thus, Wari' cannibalized members of the families from which their bilateral consanguines had taken marriage partners. Meireles (1986) noted that cannibalism restrictions generally coincided with incest prohibitions.

Cannibalism was a primary obligation of affinity. Adult men were obliged to eat their close affines; refusal to do so would have insulted the dead person's family. Women were not required to participate in cannibalism but did so at their own discretion.[11] Distinctions of generation, age, or gender were largely irrelevant; male and female adults and adolescents consumed corpses of all ages and both sexes. Men's and women's corpses were treated almost identically.

Roasting usually commenced in the late afternoon and eating usually began at dusk. The dead person's closest kin divided the well-roasted brains, heart, and liver into small pieces, placed the pieces on clean mats, and called the others to begin eating. The affines (nari paxi) did not descend greedily upon the flesh but hung back, crying and expressing reluctance to eat; only after repeated insistence by the dead person's close kin (iri' nari) did they accept the flesh. The iri' nari then prepared the other body parts by removing the flesh from the bones and dividing it into small pieces. They usually arranged these on a mat along with pieces of roasted maize bread (pamonha); in some funerals, they placed the flesh in a conical clay pot and handed pieces to the eaters, cradling the pot in their laps in the affectionate position used to hold someone's head in repose or during illness. In marked contrast to the aggressive,

disrespectful treatment of enemies' flesh in exocannibalism, funeral eaters did not touch the flesh with their hands but held it delicately on thin splinters like cocktail toothpicks. They are very slowly, alternately crying and eating. There appears to have been no special significance attached to ingesting particular body parts, and no pattern determining who ate which portions.

The ideal was to consume all of the flesh, heart, liver, and brains; in practice, the amount actually eaten depended on the degree of the corpse's decay. It is considered imperative that corpses not be disposed of (by cannibalism, cremation, or burial) until all important relatives have arrived at the funeral, seen the body, and participated in the wailing eulogies. The length of time before a body was roasted traditionally varied according to the dead person's age, status, and social ties: the older and more socially prominent the deceased, the longer the delay in roasting. Before the contact, when villages were scattered over a wide territory, most adults were not roasted until two or three days after death, when decay was well-advanced.

It was considered important to consume as much flesh as possible. When, however, flesh was too putrid to stomach — as it usually was in the case of adult corpses — the eaters forced themselves to swallow small pieces from various body parts, then cremated the rest. The ideal of total consumption was realized mainly in funerals for infants and young children who, having few social ties of their own, were roasted within a day or so of their deaths and eaten entirely. Complete consumption also appears to have occurred for some terminally ill elders whose relatives gathered and commenced wailing long before biological death. In most adult and adolescent funerals, however, most of the flesh probably was burned rather than eaten.

Consumption of the corpse continued until dawn, at which time any remaining flesh was cremated. Treatment of bones varied. Sometimes they were ground into meal, mixed with honey, and consumed. In other cases, especially in the Rio Dois Irmãos area, the bones were burned, pulverized, and buried. In all cases, the clay pots, mats, roasting rack, and funeral fire remains were burned, pounded to dust, and buried in situ by the male affine helpers. The helpers then swept the earth to eradicate all traces of the funeral and replaced the household sleeping platform over the spot where the ashes were buried.

The Question of Human Flesh as Food

Before examining what motivated Wari' mortuary cannibalism, it is useful to clarify what did not. The idea that institutionalized cannibalism may be motivated by needs for dietary protein was proposed by Harner (1977) to explain Aztec human sacrifice and has been elaborated by Harris (1977, 1985:199–234). Wari' practices involved the ingestion of significant quantitites of flesh and ground bones, and the adults who consumed them would have gained some nutrients, notably protein and calcium. Two factors nevertheless militate against a materialist interpretation of the Wari' system.

First, there is no reason to assume that the precontact population suffered significant food shortages. Wari' controlled a large territory with low population density and abundant game, fish, and Brazil nut resources. Elders assert that hunger was infrequent, although then, as now, there were days without meat or fish. Missionaries present at the first contacts observed no signs of malnutrition, and the assumption that the precontact Wari' did not suffer protein shortages is consistent with biomedical studies of similar groups. Although protein-scarcity hypotheses were hotly debated in Amazonian cultural ecology from the late 1960s through the early 1980s, researchers have never documented protein deficiency in relatively undisturbed native Amazonian populations living in circumstances similar to the precontact Wari'. On the contrary, studies have found adequate or more than adequate protein intake (Berlin and Markell 1977; Chagnon and Hames 1979; Dufour 1983; Milton 1984). My own data on household diets in two communities, and anthropometric assessments from four communities, indicate that contemporary Wari' diets are generally adequate, even with the depletion of game and fish near today's larger, more sedentary villages.

A second argument against nutritional motivations for Wari' cannibalism is that much potentially edible flesh was burned rather than eaten, with no attempt to preserve it for later consumption. Even in cannibalizing enemies, Wari' did not maximize protein acquisition: warriors usually took only the head and limbs, discarding the fleshy trunk. Clearly, social considerations took precedence over biological functionalism in shaping Wari' practices.

The Question of Hostility

Interpretations of cannibalism as an act of hostility are a staple of Western psychoanalytic theory (see Freud 1981 [1913]; Sagan 1974), and the fact that Wari' ate their affines raises the question of whether cannibalism expressed or mediated affinal tensions. Like Freudians, Wari' recognize that eating can express hostility, as it did in the aggressive consumption of enemy flesh. My informants, however, universally rejected the notion that mortuary customs expressed any form of overt, covert, or displaced hostility. They insisted that hostility has no place at funerals; individuals on bad terms with the deceased are barred from attending, as reportedly happened a few years ago when a man was ordered away on the grounds that "you did not love him, it is not good that you come here." In addition, Wari' emphasized that funeral "table manners" sharply differentiated affinal cannibalism from acts of eating that did express aggression. As discussed below, eating has multiple cultural connotations and can express respect for that which is eaten.

Sagan (1974:28) has dismissed the possibility of cannibalism as an act of respect or compassion for the deceased, asserting that such ideas are a mere facade for covert ambivalence, hostility, and sadistic urges rooted in resentments against the dead for having abandoned the living.[12] It is difficult to assess, retrospectively, the question of whether Wari' mortuary cannibalism expressed aggression or hostility, but Wari' practices and discourse on cannibalism offer little support for this interpretation. Affinal tensions appear no greater among the precontact Wari' than in many noncannibalistic societies. Wari' express few expectations of inherent affinal conflict; ideally, and to a large extent in practice, they treat affinity as a matter of amity and mutually beneficial reciprocity. Today, as in the past, most marriages are arranged or approved by the families involved, who are careful to establish and perpetuate ties only to families with whom they enjoy positive relations. Affines call each other by consanguineal kin terms (Vilaça 1989:41–45), exchange meat and fish frequently, and offer aid in emergencies. When conflicts among affines arise, there are cultural mechanisms for dealing with them, including ritual fights (*mixita*) and discussions between family heads.

Affinity and Exchange

Vilaça has emphasized the importance of mortuary cannibalism as a marker of Wari' affines' relations to one another: "The funeral rite . . . reveals, through the opposition between those who eat together [*comensais*] and those who do not [*não-comensais*], the opposition cognates/affines. In the interior of Wari' society, cannibalism constructs and identifies affinity" (1992:293).

Vilaça (1992:293) also observed that Wari' affinal cannibalism reflected a recurrent theme in South American mythology, identified by Lévi-Strauss in *The Raw and the Cooked* (1969): the characterization of affines (the "takers" of women) as real or potential cannibal prey. Besides the Wari', the Yanomami also practice affinal cannibalism, consuming their affines' ground bones (Albert 1985). Sixteenth-century Tupinambá exocannibalism involved another kind of affinal cannibalism: a war captive was married to a Tupinambá woman (making him an affine to her kin) before being killed and eaten (Staden 1928[1557]). In the cosmology of the Araweté of central Brazil (who bury their dead), cannibalism is seen as a transformative mechanism for creating affinal ties between humans and divinities: when Araweté die, the gods consume the human spirits (making them into beings like themselves), then rejuvenate and marry them (Viveiros de Castro 1992). Viveiros de Castro has observed that among the Araweté, Tupinambá, Yanomami, and Pakaa Nova (Wari'), cannibalism "links affines or transforms into affines those whom it links" (1992:259).[13]

Wari' affinal cannibalism might suggest a Lévi-Straussian model of exchanges of cooked meat (human flesh) for "raw" (virgin, fecund) women given in marriage (Lévi-Strauss 1969). As in many societies, eating is a Wari' metaphor for sexual

intercourse, and there are obvious parallels between affinal exchanges of human flesh in funerals and the frequent exchanges of meat (which men give to female affines) and fish (which women give to male affines) that mark affinity in everyday life. From a structuralist perspective, Wari' mortuary cannibalism resonates with exchanges of meat and marriage partners, but Wari' do not see it that way. Everyone with whom I raised this issue rejected an equation of cannibalism with exchanges of sexual partners or food; some found the suggestion insulting. Sexual and reproductive imagery has little place in Wari' mortuary practices, in marked contrast to its prominence in many other societies' mortuary rites (Bloch and Parry 1982), and in Melanesian endocannibalism practices linked to elaborate ideas about male and female body substances (see Gillison 1983; Poole 1983).

From an emic point of view, what was important in cannibalistic Wari' funerals was not the exchange of substance (human flesh) but the exchange of services. Disposal of the body is a primary obligation of affinity, a service performed out of respect for the dead person and his or her family. When asked why it was the affines who ate the corpse, Wari' elders invariably replied that the affines ate it because somebody had to eat it, and the dead person's consanguines (iri'nari) could not do so (because of the prohibition against eating the flesh of someone related to oneself by shared biological substance). In addition, a number of people asserted that one simply does not feel like eating anything when grieving intensely. Eating, particularly meat-eating, expresses happiness and social integration. Symbolic oppositions between sadness and oral activity (eating, drinking, singing, shouting) are numerous: adults eat little during close kin's illnesses, consume nothing at their funerals, and eat little while mourning. People considered it irrational to suggest eating flesh at a close relative's funeral.

By Wari' logic, these cultural assumptions definitively precluded cannibalism by consanguines. The task thus fell to affines, who were the only clearly defined social group that had close social ties to the dead person's family but did not share their intimate biological and affective ties to the deceased.[14] Affinal cannibalism was a matter of pragmatism.

It was also a matter of politics. Mortuary services are central in marking, strengthening, and reconstituting affinal ties after a death. Funerals draw extended families together as does no other event, and they are the most prominent occasion (aside from mixita fights) when affines act as discrete groups in complementary opposition to one another. In fulfilling mortuary obligations, including disposal of the corpse, Wari' families linked by marriage affirm continuing commitments that transcend the lifetime of any individual member.

If one accepts this indigenous view of the disposal of corpses (whether by burial, cannibalism, or cremation) as a service rendered to the family of the deceased, assigning this task to affines does not appear particularly unusual cross-culturally. In native Amazonian societies, affines perform burial and other funeral duties among the Cashinahua (Kensinger, in press), Canela (W. Crocker, in press), and Shavante (Maybury-Lewis 1974:281). Among the Mundurucú (Murphy 1960:72) and Kagwahiv (Kracke 1978:13), these tasks fall to members of the opposite moiety, the group from which the dead person's moiety takes marriage partners. Wari' mortuary cannibalism fit this pattern of delegating mortuary tasks to affines and reflected the associations between affinity and cannibalism found in other lowland South American societies' myths and cosmologies. But this does not explain why Wari' actually *ate* their affines, whereas other peoples with similar conceptual systems did not. In this article, the question to be addressed is not why the Wari' ate their affines, but why cannibalism was the preferred treatment for human corpses.

Eating as an Act of Respect

Pleasing the dead by consuming their bodies is a recurrent theme in Wari' discussions of mortuary cannibalism: the dead wanted to be eaten, or at least cremated, and not to have done either would have given offense. For dying individuals, the idea of being incorporated into fellow tribesmembers' bodies apparently had considerably more appeal than the alternative of being left to rot in the ground alone.[15] One man told of his great-aunt (FFZ) who, on her deathbed, summoned him and his father (normally

expected to cry rather than eat at her funeral) and asked them, as a favor, to join in consuming her body. In contrast to Western views of eating as an act of objectification and domination of the thing consumed, eating can express respect and sympathy in Wari' culture, especially in contrast to the alternative of burial. The ground is considered "dirty" and polluting. Adults who take pride in their bodies do not sit in the dirt, ritual objects must not touch the earth, and people avoid spilling food on the ground. These values influence attitudes towards burial in the earth, which informants often described as not only dirty, but also "wet" and "cold." Respectful treatment for human remains is dry and warm; the only traditional space for respectful burial was beneath household sleeping platforms, where small fires burned almost constantly, keeping the earth warm as well as dry. This is where funeral ashes were interred in the past and where placentae and miscarried fetuses continue to be buried. Before the contact, burial in the forest expressed dishonor and normally occurred in only one context: if a woman suffered multiple stillbirths or neonatal deaths, her family might request a male affine to bury her dead infant in an anthill or in wet earth beside a stream to discourage her future babies from dying and risking similarly unpleasant treatment.

In contrast to the disrespect manifest in burial, eating can be a sympathetic act, as shown in this story about the Maize Spirit (*Jaminain Mapak*) told by a Santo André man. The story explains why one should not leave maize lying on the ground:

> Long ago, a man was walking to his field carrying a basket of maize seeds to plant. A maize kernel fell to the ground on the path. The man did not see it and went on. The maize seed began to cry like a child. Another man came along and found it crying on the ground. He picked it up and *ate* it. In doing so, he *saved* it, showing that he felt sympathy [*xiram pa'*] for it. The man who ate the seed planted his field and it yielded great quantities of maize. The man who had left the seed on the ground planted his field, but nothing grew.

This parable demonstrates Wari' ideas that abandoning a spirit-being to lie on the forest floor connotes disrespect, whereas eating it expresses respect. Eating can be an act of compassion that pleases the thing consumed so that it bestows abundance on the eater.

Similar ideas about eating as an expression of respect for the eaten are evident in food taboos associated with *jami karawa*, animals whose spirits have human form (see Conklin 1989:336–50). Spirits never die, and when a hunter kills a jami karawa animal, its spirit assumes a new animal body. However, animal spirits cannot complete their transitions to new physical bodies as long as portions of their former bodies remain. To avoid provoking spirits' wrath, one must quickly roast and eat jami karawa. Animal spirits are offended by the killing and disrespectful treatment of their bodies, not by the eating of their flesh. On the contrary, eating demonstrates respect, especially in contrast to the alternative of abandoning uneaten body parts on or in the ground.

Several funeral customs expressed these values of honoring the dead by preventing their body substances from being lost to the earth. When corpses were cut, a close kinsman of the deceased sometimes lay face down, supporting the corpse on his back during the butchering, so that its fluids would spill onto his own body rather than onto the ground. Similarly, elders recalled that young children's corpses had much fat that dripped as they roasted; to prevent it from falling into the fire, a child's grieving parents and grandparents would catch the fat in a clay pot and smear it over their own heads and bodies as they cried. Mortuary cannibalism expressed similar compassion for the dead by saving their body substances from abandonment to the earth and, instead, incorporating them into a living person's body.

In the early postcontact period, many Wari' found the forced change to burial repulsive. One Santo André man told of his father's death, which occurred soon after outsiders had put an end to cannibalism. Unhappy with the prospect of being buried, the dying man requested that, as an approximation of traditional practices, his corpse be dismembered and the pieces placed in a large ceramic cooking pot to be buried by his affines. Even today, burial continues to be a source of covert dissatisfaction among some elders, who still view burial as a less loving way to treat a human body than cannibalism or cremation.

They consider the body's persistence problematic for close kin, whose attachments to the dead require attenuation and transformation.

Attachments to the Socially Constructed Body

Wari' view the human body as a primary nexus of kinship, personhood, and social relations. Kinship is defined as physically constituted in shared body substance (especially blood) that is created by parental contributions to conception and gestation and augmented by interpersonal exchanges of body fluids. As individuals mature, each major change in social status (at female puberty, male initiation, marriage, childbirth, enemy killings, and shamanic initiation) is believed to involve corresponding changes in blood and flesh induced by incorporating another individual's body substances (Conklin 1989:177–239). As in numerous other lowland South American societies, ideas about the physical bases of social relatedness reflect heightened recognition of individuals' interdependence as social actors (see J. Crocker 1977; da Matta 1979:105; Melatti 1979:65–8; Seeger et al. 1979; Turner 1980). Interpersonal attachments are conceived as shared physical substance that links individual body-selves in an organic unity transcending the boundaries of discrete physical forms.

Not only are kinship and social status physically constituted, but many cognitive and emotional processes are conceptualized as organic changes in the heart and blood, and behavior is considered to be rooted in the body (see Kensinger 1991 on similar concepts among the Cashinahua). This is reflected in the term *kwerexi'*, which means "body" or "flesh" but also means "custom," "habit," and "personality." A stock Wari' response to the ethnographer's plea to know "Why do you do that?" is a shrug and the phrase "*Je' kwerexi',*" "Thus is our custom," or, translated literally, "Thus are our bodies (or flesh)." Wari' consider spirits to have few personality qualities, and they account for individual behavioral differences mostly with reference to differences in body substance, not differences in mind or spirit. Peoples' habits, eccentricities, and personality quirks are explained with "His flesh is like that" (*Je' kwerekun*) or "That's the way her body is" (*Je' kwerekem*). The phrase is not merely metaphorical but reflects ideas of the physical body as a major locus of personal identity.

Westerners tend to assume that, with death, the loss of spirit or consciousness takes away most of a person's important qualities and leaves behind an empty, almost meaningless, body shell. In contrast, Wari' corpses are potent embodiments of identity, social relations, and interpersonal bonds. Body transformations were a primary symbolic focus in traditional mortuary rites that aimed to restructure relations between the dead and the living.

Detachment and Destruction

Gradual detachment from thinking about and remembering the dead is considered a desirable social goal, for prolonged sadness (*tomi xaxa*) is believed to endanger individual health and productivity. The negative psycho-emotional process of grieving is described with the verb *koromikat*, which refers to the negative experience of nostalgia: missing, remembering, and thinking longingly about a lost or distant object (usually a kinsperson, lover, or friend). Wari' emphasize vision and hearing as primary sources of knowledge and stimuli to memory. Because the sight of material objects evokes memories, they consider it essential to destroy or transform all tangible reminders of the dead. They burn a dead person's house and personal possessions and burn, discard, or give away crops planted by the deceased. Less-easily destroyed modern possessions, such as kettles, machetes, and shotguns, usually are given to nonrelatives. Neighbors often change their houses' appearance by altering doorways and paths, and close kin cut their hair. People traditionally have avoided using dead people's names or kin referents, although in speaking to outsiders they have recently relaxed name avoidances.

The cultural rationale for these practices reflects two concerns: banishing ghosts, and removing stimuli that evoke memories of the dead.[16] Vilaça has noted:

> According to the Wari', the destruction by fire of all reminders of the deceased is, in the first place, a protection against the sadness that is felt upon seeing

something that belonged to the deceased or that was touched, used or made by him; but it is also a way to avoid the coming of the ghost. [1992:228]

These dual concerns are consistent with the two primary objectives identified in cross-cultural analyses of death rites: to remove the deceased from the world of the living to the symbolic world of the dead, and to facilitate survivors' acceptance of the death and the consequent alteration of social life without the dead person (Bloch and Parry 1982:4). With regard to separating the dead from the living, the destruction of material traces is believed to lessen the tendency of ghosts (*jima*) to return to earth. Jima generally do not cause illness, but they do frighten people, and, in the days following a death, the jima of the recently deceased may try to carry kin away for companionship in death. Destroying possessions and altering appearances confuse jima so that, unable to find their former homes and companions, they return to the otherworld of the dead. Some people also suggested that the smoke surrounding roasting corpses obscured and confused the vision of jima who returned during their own funerals.

Banishing spirits, or liberating spirits from their physical bodies, has been cited as a motive for cannibalism in some other lowland South American societies (Albert 1985; Clastres 1974:316; Dole 1974:306; Ramos 1990: 196; Zerries 1960). Meireles asserted that the explanation for Wari' cannibalism was "based in the idea that the dead person's soul must be banished, at the risk of afflicting the living" (Meireles 1986:427). Vilaça (1992:233, 243, 262) has interpreted roasting as a dissociative mechanism required for spirits' liberation from their bodies and full transition to the afterlife.[17] This idea is clear in Wari' food taboos that require quick consumption of certain game animals to liberate the animal spirits from their bodies (Conklin 1989:345–346; Vilaça 1992:70), but it appears to be of limited relevance in explaining cannibalism. None of my informants spontaneously suggested that eating the dead liberated spirits or prevented their return. Rather, when asked if it had that effect, some agreed that it might. Others insisted that cannibalism had nothing to do with banishing spirits. As evidence, they cited the fact, which no one disputed, that the ghosts (jima) of people who are buried today do not return to wander the earth any more frequently than those who were cannibalized or cremated.

As Vilaça (1989:378) noted, the desire to dissociate body from spirit fails to explain the preference for cannibalism over cremation, except insofar as Wari' view the acts of cooking and eating as implicit in the act of making fire.[18] Because Wari' view cremation and cannibalism as equally effective in separating spirits from their bodies and from the world of the living, the preference for cannibalism must be explained in other terms.

Remembering and the Body

Wari' discussions of reasons for destroying corpses and possessions emphasized the need to remove reminders in order to help mourners stop dwelling on thoughts of the dead. In a cross-cultural study of grief and mourning, Rosenblatt et al. suggested that tie-breaking and "finalizing" acts (such as ghost fears, taboos on names of the dead, and destruction of personal property) facilitate survivors' transitions to new social roles:

> [I]n a long-term relationship such as marriage, innumerable behaviors appropriate to the relationship become associated with stimuli (sights, sounds, odors, textures) in the environment of the relationship. When death . . . makes it necessary to treat the relationship as ended and to develop new patterns of behavior, these stimuli inhibit the change, because they elicit old dispositions. To facilitate change, tie-breaking practices that eliminate or alter these stimuli seem to be of great value. [1976:67–8]

Battaglia has highlighted the cultural value ascribed to acts of "forgetting as a willed transformation of memory" (1991:3) in Melanesian mortuary rites that transform materially constituted aspects of the dead person's former social identity and replace them with new images. The importance that Wari' ascribe to the destruction of reminders and processual alteration of memories and images of the dead was evident in the ritual called ton ho' ("the sweeping"), practiced today in an attenuated form (see Vilaça 1992:227–9; for parallels among the Canela,

see Crocker and Crocker 1994:121). For several months after a death, senior Wari' consanguines, especially kin of the same sex as the deceased, make repeated trips to the forest to seek out all places associated with the dead person's memory: the place where a hunter made a blind to wait for deer, sites where a woman fished or felled a fruit tree, a favorite log where the dead person liked to sit. At each spot, the kinsperson cuts the vegetation in a wide circle, burns the brush, and sweeps over the burned circle. Elders said that, while doing this, they thought intensely about the dead person, recalling and honoring events of his or her life. Afterward, the burning and sweeping have definitively altered sentiments associated with each place so that "there is not much sadness there."

The imperative to destroy tangible elements traditionally extended to the corpse itself. Given the strength of Wari' ideas about the body's social construction and the physical bases of social relatedness, it is understandable that corpses are powerful reminders.[19] A number of individuals commented that today, when people are buried rather than eaten, their thoughts return again and again to images of the body lying under its mound of earth. A Santo André father who had recently buried a young son tried to explain this to me, saying:

> I don't know if you can understand this, because you have never had a child die. But for a parent, when your child dies, it is a very sad thing to put his body in the earth. It is cold in the earth. We keep remembering our child, lying there, cold. We remember and we are sad. In the old days when the others ate the body, we did not think about [koromikat] his body much. We did not think about our child so much, and we were not so sad.

The emotional potency of mourners' subjective attachments to the dead and their physical bodies is one of the keys to understanding Wari' cannibalism.[20]

In traditional funerals, mourners' dramatic manifestations of physical identification with the dead person's body were followed by a dramatic sundering of these bonds, beginning with the corpse's dismemberment. Cutting and roasting or cremating the body initiated a processal disassembling of physical objectifications of social identity and social relations. Although Wari' considered cannibalism and cremation equally effective ways of severing ties between human bodies and spirits, they considered cannibalism more effective in attenuating affective attachments. Cannibalism initiated and facilitated the construction of a new relationship between the living and the dead by evoking images of the dead person's regeneration in animal form, and human-animal reciprocity, in which endocannibalism was the mythic balance to human hunting.

Predation and Reciprocity

Wari' myth traces the origin of endocannibalism to the establishment of mutual predator-prey relations between hunters and animals. A story called *Pinom* is a variation of a widespread Amazonian mythic theme of the origins of cooking fire (see, for example, Lévi-Strauss 1969; Overing 1986; Wilbert and Simoneau 1990:111–33). (For analysis of the Wari' *Pinom* myth, see Meireles 1986; Vilaça 1989, 1992.) The Wari' version tells how mortuary cannibalism originated as the consequence of the theft of fire, which originally was possessed by an avaricious old woman who ate children raw. Violating Wari' principles of egalitarian sharing, this cannibal-crone let people temporarily use her fire only in exchange for large payments of firewood and fish. Without fire, Wari' could not farm, could not roast and eat maize or fish (most game animals did not yet exist), and had to subsist on raw forest fruits and hearts of palm.

Finally, two boys managed to outwit the old woman and steal her fire. They and the other Wari' escaped by climbing a liana into the sky, but the old woman pursued them. At the last moment, a piranha came to their rescue and cut the vine. The cannibal-crone fell into her own fire below, and from her burning body emerged the carnivores: jaguars, ocelots, and *orotapan* (an unidentified carnivore, probably wolf or fox). In Wari' cosmology, jaguars not only kill and eat humans but also transform themselves into other animal spirits that cause illness by capturing and eating human spirits. Other animals, including birds, monkeys, deer, and tapir, originated when the Wari' turned into animals in order to jump from the sky back to earth, and some

decided to remain animals. People and animals thus share a common origin. The myth highlights Wari' ideas about the balance of human-animal opposition: game animals came into existence, but people became prey for jaguars and animal spirit predators.

The origin of endocannibalism is attributed to parallel events in this myth's second part. The two boys turned into birds to carry the fire to earth, but a man named Pinom killed them and selfishly kept the fire to himself. Others could only watch hungrily while Pinom's family alone was able to cook food. Finally, a shaman tricked Pinom, captured the cooking fire, and shared it with everyone, thereby allowing the Wari': to become a hunting and farming society. Outwitted and enraged, Pinom told the Wari': "Now you will have to roast your children!"

This is interpreted as the mythic origin of endocannibalism, even though Pinom did not specify eating the dead, or affines' roles in it. Although most Wari' are now familiar with Christian concepts of sin and retribution, no one interpreted Pinom's dictum as a terrible punishment for human misdeeds. Instead, informants saw endocannibalism as a natural balance to humanity's acquisition of fire: the price for gaining fire to roast (and eat) animals was to be roasted (and eaten) oneself.

Reciprocity in relations between humans and animals is a common cross-cultural concept, especially among native American peoples whose survival depends on hunting and fishing. Sanday identified this idea as a recurrent theme in native North American myths about the origins of cannibalism and suggested that it reflected the following logic: "There is a reciprocal relationship between the eater and the eaten. Just as animals are hunted, so are humans; whoever wants to get food must become food" (1986:38–9). Notions of balanced, reciprocal, human-animal predation are central in Wari' cosmology and eschatology. Mortuary cannibalism reflected ideas of a human-nonhuman alliance predicated on reciprocal predation between living people and the spirits of animals and ancestors.

Afterlife and Alliance

In Wari' visions of the afterlife, the spirits of the dead reside under the waters of deep rivers and lakes. The ancestors appear as they did in life, but everyone is strong, beautiful, and free of deformity, disease, and infirmity. The ancestors' social world resembles pre-contact Wari' society, with villages, houses, fields, and intervillage festival exchanges. Life is easy and crops grow abundantly, but all food is vegetarian; there is no hunting or fishing because all animals have human forms underwater.

In this underworld, the Wari' ancestors are allied and intermarried with a neighboring indigenous group called "Water Spirits" (*jami kom*). The Water Spirits appear human, but they are not Wari' ancestors and have never lived on earth as ordinary people. Rather, they are primal forces that control human death, animal fertility, and destructive storms. Their leader is a giant with huge genitalia named Towira Towira (*towira* means "testicle"), who resembles the masters of animals and other mythic figures common in lowland South American cosmologies (see, for example, Reichel-Dolmatoff 1971:80–6; Zerries 1954). Towira Towira is master of the entire underworld; all its inhabitants, including Wari' ancestors, are called jami kom.

Wari' believe that when ancestral spirits emerge from the water, they assume the bodies of white-lipped peccaries (*Tayassu pecari*), a wild, pig-like animal that roams in large herds.[21] In everyday speech, *jami mijak*, "white-lipped peccary spirit," is one of the most common ways of referring to the dead. The nonancestral Water Spirits (Towira Towira's tribe) also can become white-lipped peccaries but more commonly appear as fish, especially as masses of small, easily killed fish that appear unpredictably in the flooded forest's shallow waters.

The Wari' cosmological system reflects a typically Amazonian view of cycles of reciprocal transformation and exchange between humans and animals (see, for example, Pollock 1992, in press; Reichel-Dolmatoff 1971). What is unusual about the Wari' case is that it links these ideas to an elaborate system of real cannibalism, framed in terms of symbolic and psychological rationales not previously examined in the mortuary cannibalism literature.

At the core of Wari' spiritual concerns is the idea of an alliance between Wari' society and the Water Spirits (comprised of both Wari' ancestors and Towira Towira's tribe). This is envisioned as a cyclic

festival exchange identical to the earthly hüroroin and tamara festivals that affirm and reproduce amicable relations among Wari' villages. These alliance-marking rituals are structured around dramatizations of antagonistic oppositions between a host village and visitors from another community. Hüroroin culminate in the hosts' symbolic killing of male visitors by inducing an unconscious state called *itam* that is explicitly equated with death by predation (hunting or warfare).[22] The hosts revive the visitors from this "death" with a warm water bath, symbol of birth and rebirth. Revival of the slain "prey" distinguishes this "killing" by itam from mere hunting or warfare. In a process parallel to shamanic initiation (in which an animal spirit kills and revives the initiate), the hüroroin festival's symbolic killing and revival create a bond between the killer and the killed, such that the two transcend their opposition and become allies. Role reversals are inherent in festival exchanges: the first party's visitor/prey usually later sponsor a festival at which the first party's host/killers become the visitor/prey who are "killed."

Wari' relations with the Water Spirits are conceived in identical terms, as festival exchanges in which the terrestrial and underwater societies alternate in the roles of predators (hosts) and prey (visitors), enacting a reciprocity reducible to an eminently egalitarian proposition: "We'll let you kill us if you let us kill you." The Water Spirits fulfill their side of this arrangement by visiting earth as white-lipped peccaries and fish that sing tamara songs, dance, and allow Wari' to kill and eat them.[23] Wari' reciprocate at the moment of biological death, when human spirits allow themselves to be killed by the Water Spirits. This occurs when a dying person's spirit (jami-) journeys to the underworld and becomes a guest at the hüroroin party that is always in progress there. The hosts, Towira Towira and his wife, offer maize beer. If the spirit accepts, it enters itam and "dies" underwater; on earth, the person's physical body dies. As in terrestrial alliance festivals, Towira Towira later bathes the spirit and resuscitates it. He then paints it with black *genipapo* dye (*Genipa americana*), marking the dead person's new identity as a Water Spirit.[24]

Each society benefits from this arrangement. Humans provide the Water Spirit society with new members who marry and bear children, enhancing the reproduction of Water Spirit society. The Water Spirits provide the living Wari' with life-sustaining animal food. For Wari', this exchange not only reproduces the primary human-nonhuman relations of their cosmology but also promises an enhancement of ecological resources important to their subsistence. White-lipped peccaries and fish are the only food animals encountered in dense concentrations in this environment; aside from the scarce and easily over-hunted tapir, they can yield the greatest quantities of animal food in return for the least expenditure of time and effort. Although they are relatively easy to kill when encountered, their appearance is highly unpredictable.[25] Given this combination of uncertainty and high potential productivity, it is not surprising that Wari' rituals focus on enhancing relations with peccaries and fish.

The mythic origin of the Wari' alliance with the Water Spirits is recounted in a story called *Orotapan*, which tells of how Wari', who used to be the Water Spirits' prey, became their allies instead. As allies, they gained the right to kill Water Spirits (as peccaries and fish) in return for submitting to being killed by them (at the time of biological death) and subsequently hunted, as peccaries, by the living. Three elements central to Wari' socio-ecological security originated in this myth: the festivals of intervillage alliance that ensure peace among neighbors, humans' postmortem transformations to peccaries (which ally the human and the nonhuman), and the songs that summon peccaries and fish to earth.

In the story of *Orotapan*, the power to hunt and eat the ancestors/Water Spirits (as peccaries and fish) is balanced by humans' destiny to become peccaries to be hunted and eaten. This is a reprise of themes from the myth of *Pinom*, in which the power to hunt and eat animals was balanced by the imperative for humans to become meat to be eaten, as corpses consumed in endocannibalism. Whereas the *Pinom* story emphasizes the primal balance between human and animal predation, the myth of *Orotapan* concerns the creation of cultural institutions that transform potentially antagonistic, antisocial, predator-prey relations into cooperative, security-enhancing alliances. The alliance festivals' symbolic predation substituted for the real killing and eating of humans

by animals in a precultural era. By accepting this human place in the universe, alternating between the position of eaters and the eaten, Wari' gained the animal spirits' powers of predation.

The power to summon their ancestral/Water Spirit allies to come to earth as animals is at the core of the sacred in Wari' life. In a precontact ritual that continues today in at least one community, villagers gather at night, before communal hunting or fishing expeditions, to sing the songs from the *Orotapan* myth that invite the Water Spirits to earth. People avoid speaking of this music's power; I learned of it only because, after the one occasion when I heard the spirit-summoning songs sung collectively, the peccaries appeared early the next morning for the first time in several months. The herd passed just outside the village, and nine white-lippeds were killed – three times as many as on any day in the previous two years at Santo André. The entire community ceased work to feast on this bounty of meat, a tangible embodiment of the human-nonhuman alliance.

Hunting the Ancestors

In contrast to Durkheimian views of death as a rupture in the social fabric to be mended, native Amazonian systems often treat death, not as discontinuity, but as essential for the continuation of social life (Viveiros de Castro 1992:255; see Graham 1995). The Wari' case offers a prime example of death treated as a creative moment, a productive context for extending and renegotiating social ties that regenerate the cycle of human-animal exchanges.

Human death is necessary to the reproduction of the peccaries and fish upon which Wari' subsistence and survival depend, and the perpetuation of Wari'–Water Spirit cooperation depends on the bonds of affection that link the recently deceased to their living kin. Only the recently dead, who still remember their terrestrial kin and are remembered by them, maintain active exchange relations with the living. The spirits of the recently dead send or lead the peccary herd to their living relatives' hunting territories, or send their allies, the fish. When ancestors appear as peccaries, they approach hunters who are their own kin and offer their bodies to be shot to feed their living relatives. Before butchering, a shaman is supposed to look at each peccary carcass to identify the human spirit inside. Today, people are lax about this; sometimes shamans are summoned to view peccaries, sometimes they are not. A peccary spirit usually is identified as being a close consanguine, or occasionally an affine, of the hunter who shot it.

Wari' see nothing odd about hunting their own relatives, as I learned from a conversation that took place the day after two white-lipped peccaries were slain. An elderly shaman was chatting with a young widower still saddened by his wife's death two years earlier. The shaman mentioned that he had talked to the roasting peccaries (who were killed by the deceased wife's patrilateral parallel cousin) and that one turned out to be the dead wife. "Is that so?" responded the young man. "Is it all right in the water?" "She's fine," the shaman replied. "With the peccaries, she took a peccary husband and has a peccary baby." "That's nice," was the widower's only comment.

Eavesdropping while eating fruit nearby, I nearby choked. "Hey!" I exclaimed. "Doesn't that make you sad? Aren't you sad that your wife's cousin killed her yesterday and that you ate her today?" The young man looked perplexed at my outburst, then replied, "No; why should I be sad? He just killed her body; she isn't angry. Her children are eating meat. It doesn't hurt her; she just will have another body. Why should I be sad? The ancestors are happy that we have meat to eat."

To Wari', the idea that some of the animals they eat are beloved kin is neither morbid nor repulsive, but a natural extension of familial food giving, a concrete manifestation of the ancestors' continuing concern for their families on earth. There are numerous stories of encounters with peccaries that were interpreted as gifts of food sent by specific ancestors. One man told me that in the 1970s, when his mother was dying, she told her family that she would send the peccaries three days after her death. True to promise, on the third night, the herd thundered into the village, stampeding under elevated houses, sending women and children screaming while men scrambled for their shotguns. Most deaths are not followed by

such immediate drama, but all peccary killings are potentially interpretable as visits from the ancestors. Each new death strengthens and reproduces the Water Spirits' ties to the world of the living.

Final Rites

The positive image of the ancestors' regeneration as animals was the central theme of the traditional sequence of mourning rites. The dead person's integration into Water Spirit society is seen as a gradual process: while the spirit is adjusting to life in the underworld, earthly survivors are adjusting to life without the deceased. The full realization of these processes traditionally was marked by a ritual hunt called hwet mao, meaning "the coming out" or "the reappearance." In the Rio Dois Irmãos area, it was last observed two decades ago.

Mourning is a period of attenuated sociality. Mourners withdraw from most productive activities and social interactions, do not sing, dance, or attend parties, and spend a great deal of time inside their houses. They farm, hunt, and fish less than usual, and, consequently, eat little meat. Hwet mao marked the transition back to full engagement in social life. When senior kin decided that it was time for mourning to end (typically about a month or two before the anniversary of the death), the family departed for an extended hunt deep in the forest. They killed as much game as possible and preserved it on a huge roasting rack over a smoky, slow-burning fire. It was considered especially important that certain animals present themselves to be killed as evidence of positive relations between the Wari' and their nonhuman allies. An encounter with the white-lipped peccaries could indicate that the deceased was fully integrated into life in the afterworld and, remembering loved ones on earth, had sent the herd to feed them.

At the full moon, the hunting party returned home carrying large baskets laden with game. The mourners painted their bodies for the first time since the death and made a ritual entrance into the village, ideally at the time of day when the deceased had died. Then, leaning over the baskets heaped with meat, they cried and sang kinship terms for the dead person one last time. After this final, public expression of sorrow and remembrance, an elder announced, "Sadness has ended; now happiness begins." Feasting and singing followed, initiating the return to normal social life. In feasting on game, the ex-mourners marked their acceptance of this death as part of the cycle of human-animal exchanges. Thus, the process that began with the funeral where the dead person's affines cannibalized the corpse concluded with consanguines and affines together eating the animal meat provided by the dead and their spirit allies.

Eating the Dead

Viewed in the context of the yearlong series of traditional mourning rites structured around the dead person's transition to white-lipped peccary, the roasting and eating of the corpse appears as a first, symbolic marker of this change. Consistent with Hertz's (1960[1907]:34, 58) insight that transformations of the corpse often parallel changes happening to the dead person's spirit, Wari' envisioned that at the moment when the cutting of the corpse commenced at the earthly funeral, Towira Towira began to bathe and resuscitate the spirit underwater. This resuscitation made the deceased into a Water Spirit who eventually would return to earth as a peccary. For terrestrial mourners, the corpse's dismemberment and roasting evoked this human-to-animal transformation.

"When we made the big fire and placed the body there, it was as if the dead person became a white-lipped peccary [ak ka mijak pin na]," explained a male elder of Santo André. Switching to Portuguese, he emphasized, "It appeared to be peccary [parece queixada]." As mourners watched a beloved relative's corpse being dismembered, roasted, and eaten, the sight must have graphically impressed upon them both the death's finality and the dead person's future identity as a peccary that would feed the living. Dismembering the body that is the focus of so many notions of personhood and relatedness made a dramatic symbolic statement about the dead person's divorce from human society, and imminent change from living meat eater to animal meat to be eaten. Cannibalism appears to have been the preferred method for disposing of the dead because

eating (as opposed to cremation) not only destroyed the corpse but also affirmed the dead individual's eventual regeneration as an immortal animal.

Cannibalism made a symbolic statement about the eaters as well as the eaten. At the same time that it evoked images of the dead as peccaries, numerous prior aspects of funeral rites and mourning behavior emphasized the humanity and social identity of the eaten, explicitly rejecting any equation of human flesh with animal flesh. Thus, when mourners roasted and ate human flesh, they themselves were cast as carnivores, identified with the animal powers of predation traced to the *Pinom* and *Orotapan* myths. Funeral decorations recalled these associations: firewood and roasting racks were adorned with feathers of vultures and scarlet macaws (Orotapan's sacred bird), and firewood was tied with "fire vine" (*makuri xe*), a liana associated with warfare and predatory powers linked to the Water Spirits and the jaguar-cannibal in the myth of *Pinom*.

Eating the dead identified Wari' society as a whole with the transcendent powers of their allies, the immortal Water Spirits. Cannibalism evoked and enacted the human position in this relationship, the alternation between the positions of meat-eater and meat to be eaten. Bloch (1992) has argued that a wide variety of religious and political rituals is structured around a quasi-universal dynamic: the transformation of individuals from prey/victims into hunter/killers. This theme, which is explicit in the origin myths of *Pinom* and *Orotapan*, was the central image underlying the traditional Wari' mortuary ritual sequence. The death rites moved living mourners from the position of being victims of the Water Spirit forces of death to becoming hunters of Water Spirits embodied as animals. At the same time, as was consistent with the egalitarian reciprocity that permeates Wari' social arrangements, the rites also enacted the reverse dynamic, marking humans' postmortem destiny to become animals, transformed from eaters into the eaten.

Mourning and Transformation

The image of the dead as peccaries dominates Wari' visions of death and the afterlife. The ancestors' return as peccaries is a powerful negation of death's finality. It promises not only reunion after death but also contacts during life through encounters with the herd that are the only interactions that ordinary people (nonshamans) have with their deceased kin. This is not just an abstract religious notion but a moving experience for the many individuals who have interpreted encounters with peccaries as visits from dead relatives.

Cannibalism represented a dramatic affirmation of this human-to-animal transformation, an affirmation of the interdependency of human mortality and animal fertility. Thematic links between death and regeneration are prominent in many societies' mortuary rites (Bloch and Parry 1982; Metcalf and Huntington 1991), and the psychological importance of ideas about the continuity of life after death is widely recognized (see Lifton 1979). The Wari' preference for cannibalism as a way to dispose of human corpses reflected the intersection between these psychological-spiritual concerns, cast in images of human spirits' regeneration as peccaries, and cultural concepts of the human body's social meanings. As a focus of social identity and psycho-emotional ties between the living and the dead, the dead person's body served as the primary locus for the playing out of transformations of mourners' memories, images, and emotions related to the deceased. Beginning with the corpse's dismemberment, roasting, and eating, and proceeding through the memory-altering "sweeping" ritual (ton ho') to the final hunt (hwet mao) and feast, the mourning rites posited a processual transmutation of socially projected images of the dead person's body. The rites aimed to move mourners from experiences of loss, embodied in images of the deceased as corpse, to acceptance of the death as part of a regenerative cycle, embodied in images of the deceased rejuvenated as an animal.

It is difficult to assess, retrospectively, the extent to which the ritual transformations that operated on the level of the culturally constructed person also operated on the level of the individual. However, contemporary Wari' emphases on cannibalism's psychological significance, as an act that facilitated mourners' detachment from all-consuming memories of the dead, and elders' expressions of emotional dissonance concerning burial, suggest that many

people found the body's destruction by cannibalism meaningful in personal experiences of grief and mourning. The eating of the dead was one powerful element in a social process of mourning understood to have eased the experience of coming to terms with a loved one's death. By casting the dead in the image of the animals they would become, cannibalism overlaid images of the deceased as corpse with new images of the deceased as an animal with ongoing relations to its living kin. It affirmed the transmutation of specific kinship ties between the living and the dead into a general enhancement of life-supporting relations between humans and animals. In essence, cannibalism was the dead person's first offering of self as food.

Conclusion

The explanation for Wari' mortuary cannibalism cannot be reduced to a single, simple function, for it reflected a complex amalgam of myth, eschatology, ideas about the human body, and social, psychological, and ecological concerns. Extending Lévi-Strauss's (1977:65) observation about myth, these are best understood as "an *interrelation* of several explanatory levels." As a central symbol in the rites of mourning, cannibalism presented a powerful, symbolic condensation of beliefs about life's continuity after death, affirmed in the ancestors' regeneration as animals. Mortuary cannibalism's symbolic potency derived from its evocation of multiple dimensions of the social and ecological relations in which Wari' perceive their security to be grounded. In the rites of mourning, human-nonhuman oppositions merged in what Sanday (1986:226) has called a "ritual of reconciliation" that transformed unpredictable ecological and social constraints into a meaningful conceptual order. Much anthropological discourse on cannibalism has tended to treat cultural-symbolic and ecological interpretations as mutually exclusive paradigms, but, explored in indigenous terms, the Wari' system is a symbiosis of social and ecological concerns that must be considered holistically. The material motivations associated with endocannibalism were not biological needs for protein from human flesh, but concerns with structuring cultural meanings in regard to human-animal relations that were essential, not just to subsistence but to the entire social order.

In contrast to views of anthropophagy as the ultimately antisocial act, the act of eating the dead affirmed and reproduced the bases of Wari' society. Endocannibalism was mythically linked to the origins of culture and the festival exchanges that transform potentially antagonistic relations into cooperative alliances between neighboring villages, and between humans and the nonhuman forces of death and animal fertility. As mortuary rites renewed the primary spiritual relations of the Wari' universe, so they also revitalized relations on the social plane with the gathering of affines in support of the dead person's family. Wari' cannibalism involved not the recycling of vital energies or body substances, but the renewal of vital institutions of socio-ecological security.

A Wari' elder recalled that shortly after the contact, a missionary lectured him, saying, "Eating is for animals. People are not animals, people are not meat to be eaten." In Western thought, the revulsion that cannibalism provokes is related to its apparent blurring of distinctions between humans and animals, in treating human substance like animal meat. For Wari', however, the magic of existence lies in the commonality of human and animal identities, in the movements between the human and nonhuman worlds embodied in the recognition through cannibalism of human participation in both poles of the dynamic of eating and being eaten.

NOTES

1 The final syllable is stressed in all Wari' words. *Wari'* is pronounced "wa-REE," ending in a glottal stop.

2 Most reports of endocannibalism involve eating only small bits of flesh from specific body parts (the typical Melanesian pattern) or consuming only the ashes of cremated bones, which appears to have been the most widespread Amazonian pattern (see Dole 1974; Meireles 1986; Zerries 1960). In lowland South America, consumption of substantial amounts of fellow tribesmembers' boiled or roasted flesh has been reported among the Guayakí of Paraguay (Clastres 1974) and Panoan peoples along the Peru-Brazil border (Dole 1974).

3 In excluding exocannibalism from this discussion, I do not mean to imply that it had no relation to mortuary cannibalism. Vilaça (1992:289–94) has emphasized that Wari' cannibalism of both enemies and affines expressed a broad "cannibal logic" of reversibility in the positions of predator and prey in Wari' relations to social others. Erikson (1986), Overing (1986), and Viveiros de Castro (1992) have noted that the traditional anthropological distinction between exo- and endocannibalism blurs in the face of the complex forms of cannibalism envisioned in lowland South American myths, cosmologies, and rituals.

4 All translations of Wari' oral texts are my own, as are all translations of written texts (with foreign titles).

5 The assertion that eating corpses involved no transfer of biosocial substances or energies is consistent with the logic of Wari' ethnomedicine, conception theory, and shared substance concepts, in which attributes are transferred among individuals only by blood and its analogs (breast milk, semen, vaginal secretions, and perspiration), not by ingesting roasted flesh (see Conklin 1989:274–304). Roasting is believed to dry up or neutralize the potency of blood and other body fluids; contact with corpses is polluting, but eating well-roasted flesh was not believed to transfer any qualities from the corpse to those who ate it. Clastres reported a similar idea in Guayakí thought about endocannibalism: "On eating human flesh one does not acquire anything more, there is no positive influence" (1974:316).

6 Extensive incest prohibitions promote dispersed affinal alliances (Meireles 1986:273), and families generally intermarry with two or more different groups of affines. At the same time, there is an emphasis on repeating as well as proliferating affinal ties by taking spouses from families already linked by previous marriages.

7 The Wari' traditionally practiced cremation as an alternative way to dispose of corpses whose flesh was considered dangerous to eat because it was contaminated by specific disease conditions. Corpses were cremated, not eaten, when they had pus in their lungs, or symptoms resembling liver disorders (ascites and cirrhosis). The outsiders who suppressed Wari' cannibalism, however, did not present cremation as an option, perhaps because cremation is discouraged in Latin American Catholicism.

8 For more detailed discussions of funeral practices and variations, see Conklin (1989:407–17) and Vilaça (1992:208–21). Funerals for people who died in massacres and epidemics often deviated from normal

patterns. When a village had been attacked, or a person killed close to home, Wari' sometimes feared that the assassin(s) would return. In such cases, they dispensed with much of the usual ceremony and quickly roasted and consumed the corpse(s). The mass death and social chaos of the contact-era epidemics brought similar disruptions of funeral practices, including painful episodes in which corpses were abandoned, and subsequently ravaged by vultures, because the survivors were too sick to cut the large amounts of firewood needed for roasting or cremation.

9   *Nari* is a verb meaning "to be related." The proper nominative designations for consanguines and affines, respectively, are *iri' ka-nari* and *oro-ka-nari paxi*. In this text, I follow Vilaça (1992) in using simplified verbal forms, iri' nari and nari paxi. Similarly, mixita, ton ho' and hwet mao are verbs; the nominative designations are *ka-mixita-wa, ka-ton ho'-wa*, and *ka-hwet mao-wa*.

10   This antihomeopathic idea recurs in Wari' shamanism and ethnomedicine. A shaman shares body substance with his animal spirit companion and falls violently ill if he eats that animal's flesh. Similarly, certain illnesses are attributed to ingesting substances that are similar to one's own body substance, but in a more potent, incompatible state (Conklin 1989:302–12). Corpses' flesh and body fluids, transformed by putrefaction, are considered dangerous only when ingested by their close consanguines. When eaten by affines and non-kin, roasted flesh is not believed to cause illness, although it is regarded as polluting.

11   Most women in the Rio Dois Irmãos region said that they participated in mortuary cannibalism. In the Rio Negro-Ocaia region, many women said that they did not eat human flesh because they disliked its stench. Vilaça (1992:216–17) cited one senior man who also claimed never to have eaten the dead. In addition, some women who usually participated in cannibalism told of decisions not to eat a specific affine's corpse because they felt too close, emotionally, to the dead person. Men were expected to perform impassively the duty of consuming the corpse, regardless of their feelings of intimacy with the deceased or the revulsion provoked by the smell and taste of decayed flesh.

12   Rosaldo (1989) has called attention to the power of emotions in shaping cultural responses to death. Wari' anger over relatives' deaths generally appears to have been directed outwards, into sorcery accusations against Wari' in other communities or retali-

atory attacks on Brazilians or other indigenous populations. Wari' testimonies about mortuary cannibalism give little reason to think that it expressed or vented anger or resentment, although the possibility cannot be ruled out entirely.

13   In a provocative discussion that is beyond the scope of this article, Albert (1985) and Overing (1986) have discussed associations between affinity and images of cannibalism among the Yanomami and Piaroa, respectively, in relation to issues of social harmony, violence, warfare, and the internal dynamics of endogamous, egalitarian societies. Carneiro da Cunha and Viveiros de Castro (1985) have addressed related dynamics of vengeance and reciprocity in Tupinambá exocannibalism.

14   A similar rationale shaped affines' roles in euthanasia: when an elderly person suffering from a terminal illness wished to die, he or she summoned a male affine to perform the killing. Funerals were only one of several contexts in which Wari' traditionally called upon affines to perform such services.

15   A horror of burial, and preference for being cannibalized or cremated, has been reported among Panoans (Erikson 1986:198), Yanomami (Lima Figueiredo 1939:44), Guayakí (Clastres 1974:319), and Tupinambá war captives (Viveiros de Castro 1992:289–90).

16   Efforts to extinguish material traces of the dead are widespread in lowland South America. Especially common are name avoidances and the destruction of dead people's houses and personal property (see, for example, Albert 1985; Gregor 1977:264; Jackson 1983:200; Kracke 1981:262; Métraux 1947). The dual rationales of discouraging ghosts from returning to their homes, and removing reminders that cause sadness to the bereaved, are recurrent themes. Kracke commented that among the Kagwahiv, these two different rationales are given "so interchangeably that it almost seems as if they are different ways of phrasing the same thing" (1988:213–14).

17   According to Vilaça, "Only after the body is roasted and devoured, is the *jam* [spirit] of the deceased bathed under the water, and [it] passes to full living in the world of the dead" (1992:247).

18   Vilaça has emphasized that "for the Wari' culinary preparation (which is initiated with the cutting of the prey) and devouring are interrelated and indissociable processes. The cadaver is roasted in the fire that, in its origin, is cooking fire (see the myth of *Pinom*). In this sense the cadaver is prepared as prey and should be ingested as such" (1992:263).

19 Viveiros de Castro (1992:213) has noted Tupi ideas of a connection between the persistence of a corpse's flesh and the persistence of memories linking the dead and the living.

20 Vilaça's Wari' informants echoed these sentiments. She cited one man's explanation: "'If we bury, we think about where he [the deceased] walked, where he worked; we think about his skin being there in the earth still. With the fire it is good, it finishes all the body, we don't think more'" (Vilaça 1992:265).

21 White-lipped peccaries are prominent in native American myths and rituals, from Mexico south to the Argentinian Chaco (see Donkin 1985:83–94; Sowls 1984:185–7). They often are considered closely related to people. In *The Raw and the Cooked*, Lévi-Strauss (1969:84) identified peccaries as an intermediary between jaguars (the quintessential animal predators) and human beings.

22 Hüroroin parties are structured around oppositions between a host community and visitors from elsewhere who sing and dance for their hosts. Male visitors stage dramatic raids on the hosts' village, destroy property, and perform parodies of sexual intercourse with host women. Hosts punish these transgressions by forcing the visitors to drink and vomit vast quantities of maize beer. With repeated vomiting, some lose consciousness and enter itam, in which they bleed from the mouth and experience involuntary muscular contractions that force the body into a rigid fetal position. When this occurs, the party's sponsor cries, "I've killed my prey!" ("*Pa' pin' inain watamata!*"). Submission to the physically painful "death" of itam affirms both a man's physical stamina and his trust in the allies who care for and revive him (see Conklin 1989:148–54; Vilaça 1992:186–91).

23 Metaphors of reciprocity pervade relations to the peccaries. Just as precontact party hosts sent their guests home bearing gifts, Wari' hunters traditionally gave presents to the spirits of slain white-lipped peccaries, and occasionally do so today. Before butchering, a peccary carcass is surrounded with items such as bows and arrows, baskets, chicha, shotguns, clothing, and cigarettes. The peccary is told to carry the "images" (jami-) of these items home and tell fellow Water Spirits that they, too, will be given gifts when they visit the Wari'.

24 Pollock has described strikingly similar eschatological beliefs among the Kulina of Acre, Brazil. At death, Kulina spirits journey to the underworld and receive a ritual welcome from their ancestors who, as white-lipped peccaries, fall upon the spirit and consume it. Like Wari', Kulina believe that the ancestors return to earth as white-lipped peccaries that are hunted by living people. Unlike Wari', the Kulina system carries this cycle one step further: white-lipped peccary meat becomes the souls of Kulina babies.

25 Kiltie observed that "[w]hite-lippeds are distinctive among all the terrestrial herbivorous mammals in neotropical rain forests in being the only species that forms large herds, which may include over 100 individuals" (1980:542). Hunting white-lipped peccaries is an unpredictable business, for the herds range over huge territories, never lingering long in one place and disappearing for weeks or months at a time. However, when the herd does appear, it offers relatively easy targets and multiple kills are common, making white-lipped peccaries the single most important terrestrial game in the diets of the Wari' and many other native Amazonians. Fishing involves similar patterns of high potential yield with a high quotient of procurement uncertainty; in the flooded forest, dense concentrations of huge numbers of small, easily-caught fish occasionally appear, quite unpredictably, in the fluctuating waters of temporary streams and ponds.

26 Although the spirit was believed to be revived when its corpse was dismembered and roasted, this revival does not appear to have been contingent on the corpse's being eaten. Several individuals described scenarios in which a spirit, revived when its corpse was cut, returned to earth and saw its own, still uneaten body roasting. Without exception, informants asserted that Towira Towira revived all spirits alike, regardless of whether their corpses were cannibalized, cremated, or buried. Vilaça (1992:265) has suggested that, since the change to burial, Wari' have come to see the rotting of the corpse as a kind of natural "cooking" that substitutes for the roasting at traditional funerals.

REFERENCES

Acosta Saignes, Miguel, 1961 Estudios de Etnologia Antigua de Venezuela. (Studies of Early Ethnology of Venezuela.) Caracas, Venezuela: Universidad Central de Venezuela.

Albert, Bruce, 1985 Temps du sang, temps de cendres. Représentation de la maladie, système rituel et espace politique chez les Yanomami du Sud-est (Amazonie

Brésilienne). (Time of Blood, Time of Ashes. Representation of Illness, Ritual System and Political Space among the Southeastern Yanomami [Brazilian Amazon].) Ph.D. dissertation, Université de Paris X.

Arens, William, 1979 The Man-Eating Myth: Anthropology and Anthropophagy. New York: Oxford University Press.

Battaglia, Debbora, 1991 The Body in the Gift: Memory and Forgetting in Sabarl Mortuary Exchange. American Ethnologist 19:3–18.

Berlin, Elois Ann, and E. K. Markell, 1977 An Assessment of the Nutritional and Health Status of an Aguaruna Jívaro Community, Amazonas, Peru. Ecology of Food and Nutrition 6:69–81.

Bloch, Maurice, 1992 Prey into Hunter: The Politics of Religious Experience. New York: Cambridge University Press.

Bloch, Maurice, and Jonathan Parry, eds., 1982 Death and the Regeneration of Life. New York: Cambridge University Press.

Briggs, Charles, 1992 "Since I Am a Woman, I Will Chastise My Relatives": Gender, Reported Speech, and the (Re)production of Social Relations in Warao Ritual Wailing. American Ethnologist 19:337–61.

Carneiro da Cunha, Manuela, and Eduardo B. Viveiros de Castro, 1985 Vingança e temporalidade: Os Tupinambás. (Vengeance and Temporality: The Tupinambá.) Journal de la Société des Américanistes (Paris) 71:191–208.

de Carvalho, Bernardino, 1962 Pakaanovas: Antropófagos da Amazônia. (Pakaa Nova: Cannibals of Amazônia.) O Cruzeiro (São Paulo) February 10:118–24.

Chagnon, Napoleon A., and Raymond B. Hames, 1979 Protein Deficiency as a Cause of Tribal Warfare in Amazonia: New Data. Science 203:910–13.

Clastres, Pierre, 1974 Guayakí Cannibalism. P. Lyon, trans. In Native South Americans: Ethnology of the Least Known Continent. Patricia J. Lyon, ed. Pp. 309–21. Boston: Little, Brown.

Conklin, Beth A., 1989 Images of Health, Illness and Death Among the Wari' (Pakaas Novos) of Rondônia, Brazil. Ph.D. dissertation, University of California at San Francisco and Berkeley.

Crocker, J. Christopher, 1977 The Mirrored Self: Identity and Ritual Inversion among the Eastern Bororo. Ethnology 16(2):129–45.

Crocker, William, and Jean Crocker, 1994 The Canela: Bonding through Kinship, Ritual, and Sex. New York: Harcourt Brace.

Cruzeiro, O, 1962 Pakaanovas. (Pakaa Nova.) O Cruzeiro (São Paulo), March 23:152–60.

Dole, Gertrude E., 1974 Endocannibalism among the Amahuaca Indians. In Native South Americans: Ethnology of the Least Known Continent. Patricia J. Lyon, ed. Pp. 302–8. Boston: Little, Brown.

Donkin, R. A., 1985 The Peccary. Transactions of the American Philosophical Society, 75. Philadelphia: The American Philosophical Society.

Dufour, Darna L., 1983 Nutrition in the Northwest Amazon. In Adaptive Responses of Native Amazonians. Raymond B. Hames and William T. Vickers, eds. Pp. 329–55. San Francisco: Academic Press.

Erikson, Philippe, 1986 Altérité, tatouage, et anthropophagie chez les Pano. (Alterity, Tatooing, and Cannibalism among Panoans.) Journal de la Société des Américanistes Paris 72:185–210.

Folha de São Paulo, 1962 Sertanista não conseguiu impedir que os Índios devorassem a menina morta. (Government Indian Agent Did Not Manage to Prevent the Indians from Devouring the Dead Girl.) Folha de São Paulo, January 13.

Freud, Sigmund, 1981[1913] Totem and Taboo. In The Standard Edition of the Complete Psychological Works of Sigmund Freud, 14. James Strachey, ed. Pp. 100–55. London: The Hogarth Press and The Institute of Psychoanalysis.

Gillison, Gillian, 1983 Cannibalism among Women in the Eastern Highlands of Papua New Guinea. In The Ethnography of Cannibalism. Paula Brown and Donald Tuzin, eds. Pp. 33–50. Washington, DC: Society for Psychological Anthropology.

Graham, Laura, 1986 Three Modes of Shavante Vocal Expression: Wailing, Collective Singing, and Political Oratory. In Native South American Discourse. Joel Sherzer and Greg Urban, eds. Pp. 83–118. New York: Mouton de Gruyter.

—— 1995 Performing Dreams: Discourses of Immortality among the Xavante of Brazil. Austin: University of Texas Press.

Gregor, Thomas, 1977 Mehinaku: The Drama of Daily Life in a Brazilian Village. Chicago: University of Chicago Press.

Harner, Michael, 1977 The Ecological Basis for Aztec Sacrifice. American Ethnologist 4:117–35.

Harris, Marvin, 1977 Cannibalism and Kings: The Origins of Cultures. New York: Random House.

—— 1985 The Sacred Cow and the Abominable Pig. New York: Random House.

Hertz, Robert, 1960[1907] Death and the Right Hand. Glencoe, IL: Free Press.

Jackson, Jean E., 1983 The Fish People: Linguistic Exogamy and Tukanoan Identity in Northwest Amazonia. New York: Cambridge University Press.

Kensinger, Kenneth M., 1991 A Body of Knowledge, or, the Body Knows. Expedition (University of Pennsylvania Museum) 33(3):37–45.

Kiltie, Richard A., 1980 More on Amazon Cultural Ecology. Current Anthropology 21:541–44.

Kracke, Waud, 1978 Force and Persuasion: Leadership in an Amazonian Society. Chicago: University of Chicago Press.

——— 1981 Kagwahiv Mourning: Dreams of a Bereaved Father. Ethos 9:258–75.

——— 1988 Kagwahiv Mourning II: Ghosts, Grief, and Reminiscences. Ethos 16:209–22.

Lévi-Strauss, Claude, 1969 The Raw and the Cooked. New York: Harper & Row.

——— 1977 Structural Anthropology, 2. New York: Basic Books.

Lewis, I. M., 1986 Religion in Context: Cults and Charisma. New York: Cambridge University Press.

Lifton, Robert J., 1979 The Broken Connection: On Death and the Continuity of Life. New York: Simon & Schuster.

Lima Figueiredo, José, 1939 Indios do Brasil. (Indians of Brazil.) Brasiliana (São Paulo), 5th ser., 163.

Lindenbaum, Shirley, 1979 Kuru Sorcery. Palo Alto, CA: Mayfield.

Mason, Alan, 1977 Oranao Social Structure. Ph.D. dissertation, University of California at Davis.

da Matta, Roberto, 1979 The Apinayé Relationship System: Terminology and Ideology. In Dialectical Societies: The Gê and Bororo of Central Brazil. David Maybury-Lewis, ed. Pp. 83–127. Cambridge, MA: Harvard University Press.

Maybury-Lewis, David, 1974 Akwe-Shavante Society. New York: Oxford University Press.

Meigs, Anna, 1984 Food, Sex and Pollution: A New Guinea Religion. New Brunswick, NJ: Rutgers University Press.

Meireles, Denise Maldi, 1986 Os Pakaas-Novos. (The Pakaa Nova.) Master's thesis, Universidade de Brasília, Brazil.

Melatti, Julio Cezar, 1979 The Relationship System of the Krahó. In Dialectical Societies: The Gê and Bororo of Central Brazil. David Maybury-Lewis, ed. Pp. 46–79. Cambridge, MA: Harvard University Press.

Métraux, Alfred, 1947 Mourning Rites and Burial Forms of the South American Indians. América Indígena 7(1):7–44.

Metcalf, Peter, and Richard Huntington, 1991 Celebrations of Death: The Anthropology of Mortuary Ritual. 2nd ed. New York: Cambridge University Press.

Milton, Katharine, 1984 Protein and Carbohydrate Resources of the Makú Indians of Northwestern Amazonia. American Anthropologist 86:7–27.

Murphy, Robert, 1960 Headhunter's Heritage. Berkeley: University of California Press.

Overing, Joanna, 1986 Images of Cannibalism, Death and Domination in a "Non Violent" Society. Journal de la Société des Américanistes (Paris) 72:133–56.

Pollock, Donald, 1992 Culina Shamanism: Gender, Power and Knowledge. In Portals of Power: Shamanism among South American Indians. E. Jean Langdon and Gerhard Baer, eds. Pp. 25–40. Albuquerque: University of New Mexico Press.

Poole, Fitz John Porter, 1983 Cannibals, Tricksters, and Witches: Anthropophagic Images Among Bimin-Kuskusmin. In The Ethnography of Cannibalism. Paula Brown and Donald Tuzin, eds. Pp. 6–32. Washington, DC: Society for Psychological Anthropology.

Ramos, Alcida Rita, 1990 Memórias Sanumá: Espaço e tempo em uma sociedade Yanomami. (Sanumá Memories: Space and Time in a Yanomami Society.) São Paulo: Editora Marco Zero.

Reichel-Dolmatoff, Gerardo, 1971 Amazonian Cosmos. Chicago: University of Chicago Press.

Rosaldo, Renato, 1989 Culture and Truth: The Remaking of Social Analysis. Boston: Beacon Press.

Rosenblatt, Paul C., R. Patricia Walsh, and Douglas A. Jackson, 1976 Grief and Mourning in Cross-Cultural Perspective. New Haven, CT: HRAF Press.

Sagan, Eli, 1974 Cannibalism: Human Aggression and Cultural Form. San Francisco: Harper & Row.

Sanday, Peggy Reeves, 1986 Divine Hunger: Cannibalism as a Cultural System. New York: Cambridge University Press.

Seeger, Anthony, 1987 Why Suyá Sing: A Musical Anthropology of an Amazonian People. New York: Cambridge University Press.

Seeger, Anthony, Roberto da Matta, and E. B. Viveiros de Castro, 1979 A construção da pessoa nas sociedades indígenas brasileiras. (The Construction of the Person in Brazilian Indigenous Societies.) Boletim do Museu Nacional (Rio de Janeiro), Antropologia (n.s.) 32:2–19.

Sowls, Lyle K., 1984 The Peccaries. Tucson: The University of Arizona Press.

Staden, Hans, 1928[1557] Hans Staden: The True History of His Captivity, 1557. Malcolm Letts, ed. London: George Routledge & Sons.

Turner, Terence S., 1980 The Social Skin. In Not by Work Alone. Jeremy Cherfas and Roger Lewin, eds. Pp. 112–140. Beverly Hills, CA: Sage Publications.

Urban, Greg, 1988 Ritual Wailing in Amerindian Brazil. American Anthropologist 90:385–400.

—— 1991 A Discourse-Centered Approach to Culture. Austin: University of Texas Press.

Vilaça, Aparecida, 1989 Comendo como gente: Formas do canibalismo Wari' (Pakaa Nova). (Eating like People: Forms of Wari' Cannibalism.) Master's thesis. Museu Nacional, Universidade Federal do Rio de Janeiro.

—— 1992 Comendo como gente: Formas do canibalismo Wari'. (Eating like People: Forms of Wari' Cannibalism.) Rio de Janeiro: Editora UFRJ (Universidade Federal do Rio de Janeiro).

Viveiros de Castro, Eduardo B., 1992 From the Enemy's Point of View. Chicago: University of Chicago Press.

Von Graeve, Bernard, 1972 Protective Intervention and Interethnic Relations: A Study of Domination on the Brazilian Frontier. Ph.D. dissertation, University of Toronto.

—— 1989 The Pacaa Nova: Clash of Cultures on the Brazilian Frontier. Peterborough, Canada: Broadview Press.

Wilbert, Johannes, and Karin Simoneau, 1990 Folk Literature of the Yanomami Indians. Los Angeles: UCLA Latin American Center Publications.

Zerries, Otto, 1954 Wild-und Buschgeister in Südamerika. (Wild- and Bush-Spirits in South America.) Studien zur Kulturkunde, 11. Wiesbaden, Germany: F. Steiner.

—— 1960 Endocanibalismo en la América del Sur. (Endocannibalism in South America.) Revista do Museu Paulista (São Paulo), n.s., 12:125–75.

Part VI

Remembrance and Regeneration

21

Sacrificial Death and the Necrophagous Ascetic

Jonathan Parry

My aim in this paper is to outline two opposing ways in which the problems of temporality and man's mortality are handled within Hinduism. The first section focuses on the case of the householder. For him, I argue, the 'good' death is a sacrificial act which results not only in a re-creation of the deceased, but also in a regeneration of time and of the cosmos. In the second section I turn to a group of ascetics who are intimately associated with death, corpses and the cremation ground. By contrast with the householder, the somewhat macabre practice of the Aghori ascetic is directed at a suspension – rather than a renewal – of time, and is thus an attempt to escape from the recurrence of death implied by the endless cycle of rebirths.[1] The singularity of his means to this end lies (as Eliade (1969:296) perceived) in a peculiarly material and literal play on the common Hindu theme of the combination of opposites; but both the end itself and its theological justification are – we shall find – expressed in thoroughly conventional language.[2]

Although the life of the householder and the life of the ascetic are oriented towards two different goals, both share in the same complex of interconnected assumptions about the relationship between life and death. As Shulman (1980:90) puts it:

> The Hindu universe is a closed circuit: nothing new can be produced except by destroying or transforming something else. To attain more life – such as a son, or the 'rebirth' of the sacrificial patron himself – the life of the victim must be extinguished. Life and death are two facets of a single never-ending cycle.

Consistent with this, we shall encounter an image of life as a limited good: thus a barren woman may conceive by causing the child of another to wither away and die. Death regenerates life: the householder sacrifices himself on his funeral pyre in order than he may be reborn; while the power derived from his intimacy with death and decay enables the Aghori ascetic to confer fertility on the householder (and this despite his own disparagement of the ordinary mortal condition). What is more, the power to convert death into life is seen as intimately connected with the performance of ascetic

From Jonathan Parry, "Sacrificial Death and the Necrophagous Ascetic," in *Death and the Regeneration of Life*, eds. Maurice Bloch and Jonathan Parry (Cambridge: Cambridge University Press, 1982).

austerities – not just in the obvious case of Aghori, but also in the case of the austerities performed by the corpse of the householder on his cremation pyre, and by the chief mourner during his regime of mourning. The cremation rituals of the householder – with their insistence on the complete elimination of the remains of the deceased – recall, moreover, the ascetic's denigration of the 'gross' physical body. Seen from this point of view the opposition between ascetic and householder would not appear radical. But from another perspective the difference *is* fundamental, for while the renouncer's goal is a permanent state of being unfettered by any material form, the cremation rituals of the householder hold out only the promise of a renewed existence which is itself impermanent, and in which the immortal soul is unbreakably chained to a particular transient form.

At the outset I should acknowledge that – for reasons which will become obvious – there are many gaps in my data relating to the Aghoris, and should explicitly state that I have not personally witnessed many of the secret performances with which they are most closely associated. What needs to be kept firmly in mind then is that at various points the account relates, not so much to what these ascetics actually do, as to what they say they do and what other people believe them to do.

My ethnography is from the city of Benares,[3] one of the most important centres of Hindu pilgrimage in India. Benares is sacred to Siva, the Great Ascetic, the Lord of the Cremation Ground and the Conqueror of Death; and the cornerstone of its religious identity is its association with death and its transcendence. All who die here automatically attain 'liberation' or 'salvation' (*mukti, mokṣa*) – an inducement which attracts many elderly and terminally-sick people to move to the city. Each year thousands of corpses of those who have been unfortunate or undeserving enough to expire elsewhere are brought to Benares for cremation on one of the two principal burning *ghāṭs*; while vast numbers of pious pilgrims come to immerse the ashes of a deceased relative in the Ganges or to make offerings to the ancestors. Death in Benares is big business, which – as I have outlined elsewhere (Parry, 1980) – involves an elaborate division of labour between a number of different kinds of caste specialists variously associated with the disposal of the corpse, the fate of the soul and the purification of the mourners.

Sacrificial Death and the Regeneration of Life

Manikarnika *ghāṭ* is the best patronised of the city's two cremation grounds. It was here that at the beginning of the time Lord Visnu sat for 50000 years performing the austerities by which he created the world, and here that the corpse of the cosmos will burn at the end of time. But these events occur not only at the start and finish of each cosmic cycle. They also belong to an eternal present which is continually reactualised on the *ghāṭ* in the uninterrupted sequence of cremations performed there.

A recurrent theme in Hindu religious thought is the homology which is held to exist between body and cosmos. Both are governed by the same laws, are constituted out of the same five elements and everything that exists in the one must also exist in the other (cf. Goudriaan, 1979:57). Hence all the gods and the whole of space are present within the human body – a notion which is explicitly elaborated in the *Garuda Purana* (part 15), an eschatological text to which the Benares sacred specialists continually refer. The homology is also one of the basic principles underlying the architectural theory of the Hindu temple, which is constructed on the plan of a cosmic man (Beck, 1976); while many forms of worship involve a 'cosmicisation' of the body of the worshipper (Gupta, 1979). A case in point is provided by the rituals described in the *Kalika Purana*. The worshipper begins by symbolically effecting his own death which is identified with the death of the world; and in subsequently re-creating his body he reconstitutes the universe. It is of some significance for what follows that the sacred space within which all this occurs represents 'a stylised cremation ground' (Kinsley, 1977:102).

Body and cosmos are thus equated; and this – combined with our last example – would seem to imply a further equivalence between cremation which destroys the microcosm of the physical body and the general conflagration which destroys the macrocosm at *pralaya*, the time of cosmic dissolution. (Indeed certain of the texts classify an individual death as *nityapralaya* – a regularly-enacted doomsday (Biardeau, 1971:18, 76)). But just as the world's annihilation by fire and flood is a necessary prelude to its re-creation, so the deceased is cremated and his ashes immersed in water in order that he may be restored to life. Since the body is the cosmos the last rites become the symbolic equivalent of the destruction *and rejuvenation* of the universe. Cremation is cosmogony; and an individual death is assimilated to the process of cosmic regeneration. Popular thought certainly presupposes some intrinsic association between cremation and the scene of original creation, for one of the reasons given for the bitter opposition to a Municipal plan to relocate the burning *ghāṭ* away from the centre of the city was that it is not possible to sever its connection with the place of the prolonged austerities (*tapas*) by which Visnu engendered the world.

Now such austerities generate heat, which is in many contexts represented as the source of life and fertility. Thus Agni (the god of fire) is represented as the 'cause of sexual union' (O'Flaherty, 1973:90). Through the heat of his austerities the ascetic acquires a super-abundant sexual potency, and a creative power by which he may rival or even terrorise the gods; through the cremation pyre the seven storm-gods are born (O'Flaherty, 1973:109); and through bathing in the tank of Lolark Kund in Benares, fecundity is conferred on barren women – the tank being sacred to the sun, the source of heat. Consistent with this, Visnu is described as burning with the fire of the *tapas* by which he created the cosmos at Manikarnika *ghāṭ*. By entering the pyre here the deceased – as it were – refuels the fires of creation at the very spot where creation began. Indeed I have heard cremation described as a kind of *tapas,* and certain of the texts clearly represent it as such (Knipe, 1975:132; cf. Kaelber, 1976, who puts it in terms of Agni imparting *tapas* to the corpse).

Another way of developing the same argument would be to note that cremation is a sacrifice,[4] and that the essence of the textual conception of the sacrifice is that it is a cosmogonic act. Thus – to invoke a different account of the origins of the universe – every sacrifice may be said to replicate the primal act of Prajapati who produced creation by the sacrificial dismemberment of his own body. As Heesterman (1959:245–6) puts it: 'The sacrifice

may be described as a periodical quickening ritual by which the universe is recreated . . . the pivotal place is taken up by the sacrificer; like his prototype Prajapati he incorporates the universe and performs the cosmic drama of disintegration and reintegration'. *Any* sacrifice then is, as Eliade (1965:11) affirms, a 'repetition of the act of creation' and maintains or repairs the cosmic order (Zaehner, 1962:245–6; Malamoud, 1975; Biardeau, 1976:22; Herrenschmidt, 1978 and 1979). It therefore represents a renewal of time.

What, then, is the evidence that *cremation* is a sacrifice (and hence an act of cosmic regeneration)? Here we might start by observing that the term for cremation in Sanskrit and in the Sanskritised Hindi of my more literate informants is *antyeṣṭi*, or 'last sacrifice'; and that one of the manuals of ritual practice regularly used as a guide to the mortuary rites (the *Śraddha Parijat*) explicitly equates cremation with a fire sacrifice. Or, to cite a different authority (though not one which my informants ever invoked), the *Śatapatha Brahmana* represents the sacrifical fire altar ritual as symbolic re-enactment of the story of Prajapati, and then goes on to lay down precisely the same rules for handling the corpse of a deceased sacrificer as for treating the sacrificial altar which represents the body of the god (Levin, 1930).

The parallels between cremation and the sacrificial procedure are, as Das points out, almost precise.

> Thus the site of cremation is prepared in exactly the same way as in fire-sacrifice, i.e. the prescriptive use of ritually pure wood, the purification of the site, its consecration with holy water, and the establishment of Agni with the proper use of *mantras* . . . The dead body is prepared in the same manner as the victim of a sacrifice and is attributed with divinity. Just as the victim of a sacrifice is exhorted not to take any revenge for the pains which the sacrifice has inflicted on him (Hubert & Mauss, 1964) so the mourners pray to the *preta* to spare them from his anger at the burns he has suffered in the fire (*Garuda Purana*). (Das, 1977:122–3)

The corpse is given water to drink, is lustrated, anointed with ghee and enclosed in sacred space by being circumambulated with fire – which is precisely what Hubert and Mauss (1964:31) describe as happening to the sacrificial victim. Further, the same set of ten substances (known as *dasang*) which are offered in the pyre are also used for the fire sacrifice (*havan*); while according to the standard manual of mortuary practice – the *Preta Manjari* (p. 4) – the wood used for the pyre should be that which 'pertains to a sacrifice' (*yāgyik*).

All this poses a puzzle. On the face of it there would seem to be a flat contradiction between our received wisdom that the corpse is pre-eminently polluting and dangerous, and the notion that it is a fit sacrificial offering to the gods. The situation is complex and the evidence is hard to interpret and often appears contradictory. Much of my data would certainly support the view that the corpse is contaminating (and indeed the enormous symbolic power of the association between corpses and the Aghori ascetic rests on this fact). But this is far from the whole story, for in certain respects the dead body appears to be treated as an object of great purity, even as a deity. It is said to be Siva, is greeted with salutations appropriate to Siva (cries of 'Har, Har, Mahādev'), and continual play is made on the phonetic similarity between Siva and *śava* ('corpse'). It must be guarded against pollution, may not be touched by the impure, is wrapped in freshly-laundered cloth, is circumambulated with the auspicious right hand towards it and the pyre is ignited by the chief mourner only after he has passed through an elaborate series of purifications (cf. Stevenson, 1920:144–8). He offers the fire with his right hand; and at this time his sacred thread hangs over his left shoulder towards the right-hand side of his body, as is the rule when offerings are made to the gods (whereas it hangs from right to left when the offering is to the ancestors or to an unincorporated ghost). Or again, in the custom of certain regional communities represented in Benares, the corpse of a woman who has died in childbirth or during her monthly course must undergo special purificatory rites before she is fit for the pyre, as if only those in a state of purity are eligible for cremation (cf. Stevenson, 1920:151; Kane, 1953:231; Pandey, 1969:270–1).

I cannot confidently claim to be able to provide a definitive explanation for this apparent contradic-

tion. I believe, however, that the most revealing place to start is with the definition of death as the instant at which the *prān*, or 'vital breath' leaves the body. Now according to the theological dogma expounded by many of my informants, this occurs – not at the cessation of physiological functioning – but at the rite of *kapāl kriyā*, which is performed mid-way through the cremation, and at which the chief mourner releases the 'vital breath' from the charred corpse of the deceased by cracking open his skull with a stave. Before this stage it is commonly said to be completely inappropriate to use the term *preta* meaning 'a disembodied ghost'.

The corollary which is often derived from this is that it is precisely at the moment of breaking the skull that death pollution begins. Accordingly, the *śrāddha* ceremonies which mark the end of the year of mourning are celebrated on the anniversary of the cremation rather than on the anniversary of the actual death. That on this view impurity does not emanate from the corpse itself is neatly illustrated by the case of those who have died a 'bad' death and whose corpses are not burnt but immersed in the Ganges. In such an instance, it is often claimed, no death pollution is incurred until after the *putlā vidhān* ritual at which the deceased's body is re-created in the form of an effigy, into which his soul is invoked, and which is then cremated. Since this rite may be delayed until several months after the disposal of the actual body, and since there is no impurity in the interval, it is clear that death pollution springs from the act of cremation rather than from the corpse or its physiological demise. It is, in the Benares idiom, a consequence of 'the sin of burning the body hairs of the deceased'. Hence as Pullu Maharaj explained, the chief mourner remains in a state of great purity before igniting the pyre, 'because he is performing a *mahāyugya* – a great sacrifice. It is we who pollute him by our touch and not he us.' After cremation, however, he is defiled 'for he has burnt the flesh'.

What this definition of the point of death implies is that before the cremation the corpse is not a corpse but an *animate* oblation to the fire. As another informant spontaneously put it: 'he does not die but is killed. He dies on the pyre.' Cremation, he went on, is violence (*hatyā*) and death pollution (*sutaka*) the consequence of that violence.[5] On such a theory cremation becomes a sacrifice in the real sense of the term: it is a ritual slaughter which makes of the chief mourner a homicide, parricide or even slayer of the gods. It is hardly to be wondered at, then, that his subsequent purifications – like that of any sacrificer – resemble the expiation of a criminal (Hubert & Mauss, 1964:33). It should not be thought, however, that the victim is a reluctant one for – as we shall see – a crucial aspect of the 'good' death is that it is a voluntary offering of the self of the gods. The corpse is thus not only alive but also a willing victim, and hence a being of extraordinary sacredness.[6]

I hasten to emphasise that all this refers only to a somewhat esoteric level of theological discourse, and that at another level it is of course universally acknowledged that a man is dead once the physical manifestations of life are extinguished. Reasoning from this starting point, other informants held that death pollution begins at the moment of physiological arrest, and that the corpse itself is a source of severe impurity. Those best versed in the texts, however, tended to steer a middle course between these two theories by distinguishing the case of the Agnihotri (by whom sacrificial fires are continuously maintained) from that of the ordinary householder. While for the former there is no death pollution before cremation, for the latter it begins when respiration ceases (cf. Abbott, 1932:177, 192, 505; Pandey, 1969:269).

What is common to both theories, then, is the view that death pollution starts when the body ceases to be animated by its 'vital breath'. The disparity arises over the point at which this happens. On the view that it occurs during the cremation, the deceased's body represents a pure oblation to the gods; while on the view that the 'vital breath' departs at physiological arrest it is merely an impure carcass.[7]

Given that the good death is a sacrifice and sacrifice is an act of regeneration, it is only to be expected that the beliefs and practices associated with cremation are pervaded by the symbolism of embryology. According to one well-known text which deals with sacrifice (the Śatapatha Brahmana), there are three kinds of birth: that which is had from one's parents, from sacrifice and from cremation (Lévi, 1898:106–7; Levin, 1930). Indeed the ritual techniques involved in both of the latter might be seen as a branch of obstetrics. Having dispersed his own body in the sacrifice, the sacrificer reverts to an embryonic state and is then reborn (cf. Heesterman, 1959; Kaelber, 1978); while at death – as I have often been told – the body is to be taken to the cremation ground head first because that is the way a baby is born; while the corpse of a man should be laid face down on the pyre and the corpse of a woman face up, for this is the position in which the two sexes enter the world. During the fifth month of pregnancy the vital breath enters the embryo through the suture at the top of the skull and it is from here that it is released during cremation. Throughout pregnancy the baby is sustained by the digestive fire which resides in its mother's belly, and at death it returns to the fire from which it came and is thus reborn (cf. Knipe, 1975:1). At both parturitions an untouchable specialist acts the indispensible role of midwife – cutting the umbilical cord at birth and providing the sacred fire and superintending the pyre at death.

At other points the symbolism of the maternity ward is replaced by that of the bridal chamber. The funeral procession of an old person is described as a second marriage party and is accompanied by erotic dancing; while a husband and wife who die within a few hours of each other are placed on a single pyre in what is explicitly represented as a position of copulation. In some texts the corpse is described as rising as smoke from the pyre, turning into clouds, rain and then vegetables, which when eaten are transformed into semen (O'Flaherty, 1973:41–2; 1976:28). The destruction of the corpse is thus converted into the source of future life.

The connection between death and sexuality is a theme which is constantly reiterated in both textual and popular traditions. In myth, for example, death enters the world as a result of sexual increase (O'Flaherty, 1976:28, 212) and childbirth is given to women as a consequence of the god Indra's brahmanicide; in folk dream-analysis a naked woman or a bride is a presentiment of impending death; and in ethno-medicine the loss of semen results in disease, old age and death, while its retention confers vitality and even immortality (cf. Briggs, 1938:324, Carstairs, 1957:84–5, 195–6; Eliade, 1969:248–9). If death regenerates life, it is equally clear that in turn the regeneration of life causes death.

It is this endless cycle which the ascetic seeks to evade. As a consequence he is not cremated. The bodies of small children, and of victims of certain diseases like leprosy and smallpox, are also immersed in the Ganges rather than burnt. Except in the case of the ascetic, however, an effigy of the deceased should later be burnt; and this also applies to one who has died a violent or accidental death (whose body will normally have been cremated). Unless this substitute corpse is offered to the fire the deceased will indefinitely remain as a marginal ghost (preta). In all cases, then, a real or surrogate cremation is a prerequisite for the proper re-creation of the departed.

While piecemeal explanations of each individual category have often been suggested, the crucial point about the list of exceptional cases given in the previous paragraph is – as Das (1977:123) has pointed out – that it constitutes a single set. It consists of those who are not fit sacrificial objects (e.g. the leper), those who have already been offered to the gods (e.g. the renouncer who has performed his own mortuary rituals at the time of his initiation and who subsequently exists on earth as a marginal ghost), and those whose death cannot be represented as an act of self-sacrifice (e.g., children and victims of sudden or violent death).

This last case ties in with the notion that the 'good' death is one to which the individual voluntarily submits him- or herself: one of the prime exemplars of such a death being the satī-strī, or 'true wife' who mounts her husband's funeral pyre. In the ideal case the dying man – like the sacrificer before the sacrifice (Kaelber, 1978) – forgoes all food for some days before death, and consumes only Ganges water and charan-amrit (the mixture in which the image of a deity has been bathed), in order to weaken his body so that the 'vital breath' may leave it more easily; and in order – as I would see it – to make himself a worthy sacrificial object free of foul faecal matter. (A similar interpretation may be placed on the bathing and occasional tonsuring of the corpse prior to cremation.) Having previously predicted the time of his going and set all his affairs in order, he gathers his sons about him and – by an effort of concentrated will – abandons life. He is not said to die, but to relinquish his body.

In the case of a man of great spiritual force a kind of spontaneous combustion cracks open his skull to release the vital breath; while the vital breath of one who dies a bad death emerges through his anus in the form of excrement, through his mouth as vomit, or through one of his other orifices. Such an evacuation is a sure sign of damnation to come, a notion which is perhaps not unconnected with the idea that it is best to die on an empty stomach. An image of the way in which the soul might ideally emerge was provided by the case of an old householder, whose extraordinary spiritual development had gained him a circle of devoted disciples, and whose subsequent mortuary rituals I attended. His copybook death was said to have been consummated on his funeral pyre when his burning corpse successively manifested itself to a privileged few in the forms of the celebrated religious leaders Sai Baba, Mehar Baba and Rama Krishna Paramhamsa, as the terrifying god Bhairava (Lord Siva's kotvāl or 'police-chief' in Benares) and finally as Siva himself. A rounded protuberance was seen to move up the spine of the corpse, burst through the skull, soar into the air and split into three parts. One fell in Benares, another went north to the abode of Siva in the Himalayas and nobody knows what happened to the third.

The best death occurs in Benares, or failing that in another place of pilgrimage. But in any event death should occur on purified ground and in the open air rather than in a bed and under or on a roof. One would hope to die to the sound of chanting of the names of god, for one's dying thoughts are often said to determine one's subsequent fate, even to the extent of redeeming the most abject of sinners. There are not only places but also times to die well – 'the fortnight of the ancestors' (pitri-paksha) for example, or during the period of uttarāyaṇa (the six months of the year that start with the winter solstice); while five of the twenty-seven lunar mansions (nakṣatras) of the Hindu almanac are from this point of view inauspicious and require special rituals of expiation. But such inconvenience is unlikely to affect the paragon, whose spiritual force gives him a degree of mastery over the time of his own death.

By contrast with 'good' death, the 'bad' death is one for which the deceased cannot be said to have prepared himself. It is said that 'he did not die his own death'. The paradigmatic case is death by violence or as a result of some sudden accident; the underlying notion being that the victim has been forced to relinquish life prematurely with the result that his embittered ghost is liable to return to afflict the survivors unless the appropriate propitiatory rituals are scrupulously observed. Whether these have been successful can only be judged by their results, for the ghost that is yet to be satisfied will return to haunt the dreams of the mourners or to vent his malevolence in other more destructive ways. As a consequence, bad death in the family tends to be cumulative, the victim of one causing another.

The most common expression for what I have called 'bad death' is *akāl mrityu*, literally 'untimely death' (though some of the resonance of this expression might be better captured by glossing it as 'un-controlled death' – by contrast with the controlled release of life which is the ideal). Strictly speaking, it is not the age of the victim but the manner of dying that is diagnostic of an *akāl mrityu*, and the death of an old person may be 'untimely' if it was caused by leprosy, violence or a sudden accident. The expres-sion *alp mrityu* (meaning 'death in youth') is however often used as a synonym for *akāl mrityu* – such a death being almost *ipso facto* bad. The good death occurs after a full and complete life – the lifespan appropri-ate to our degenerate age being one hundred and twenty-five, and this a mere fraction of that of former epochs. The fact that few attain even this modest target is a consequence of the sins of this and former lives; and the greater the burden of sin, the greater the shortfall. Those who die before the age of forty are certainly destined for hell; while the still-born infant is probably some reprobate expiating his crimes by a succession of seven such births. There is also, however, the notion that the sins of the father may be visited on the son, and that the attenuation of this life may be a consequence of the wickedness of those with whom the individual is most closely associated. The quality of life thus determines its duration. But it also determines the quality of death. A group of Funeral Priests who – with some rancour – were regaling me with the story of the seizure of their hereditary rights by one of their rich and powerful colleagues, clinched their evidence of

his iniquity with the gleeful recollection that he had died vomiting excrement. As for his son, their pre-sent employer, 'he will reap; . . . leprosy is coming out on him. He will rot as no one in our caste has ever rotted before.'

Although I cannot deal here with the extremely elaborate sequence of post-cremation rituals, there are two aspects of these rituals on which I would like to comment briefly. At death (*dehānt*, 'the end of the body') the soul becomes a disembodied ghost or *preta*, a marginal state dangerous both to itself and to the survivors. The purpose of the rituals of the first ten days is to reconstruct a physical form for this ethereal spirit – though this new form is of a less 'gross' kind than the one the deceased had formerly inhabited. Each day a *piṇḍa* – a ball of rice or flour – is offered in the name of the deceased, each of which reconstitutes a specific limb of his body. By the tenth day the body is complete, and on the eleventh life is breathed into it and it is fed. On the next day a ritual is performed which enables the deceased to rejoin his ancestors. The wandering ghost (*preta*) becomes an incorporated ancestor (*pitṛ*). A ball of rice represent-ing the departed is cut into three by the chief mourner and is merged with three other rice balls which represent the deceased's father, father's father and father's father's father. The soul then sets out on its journey to 'the abode of the ancestors' (*pitṛ lok*) where it arrives on the anniversary of its death, having endured many torments on the way – tor-ments which the mourners seek to mitigate by the rituals they perform on its behalf. In order to cross over into 'the kingdom of the dead' (*yamlok*) at the end of its journey, the sould must negotiate the terrifying Vaitarnī river which is invariably repre-sented as flowing with blood, excrement and other foul substances.

The first point that I want to make is that in a number of ways the symbolism of this whole phase of the mortuary rituals continues the theme of death as a parturition. The word *piṇḍa* is used not only for the rice or flour balls out of which the deceased's body is reconstructed, but also for an actual embryo (cf. O'Flaherty, 1980); and the body is completed in a ten-day period paralleling the ten (lunar) month period of gestation (cf. Knipe, 1977). What's more, there is a striking correspondence between the image of crossing the Vaitarnī river and the birth passage of the child out of the womb, the latter also being explicitly represented as negotiating a river of blood and pollution. What we seem to have here is a case of ritual over-kill; the deceased is reborn out of the fire and then born all over again in the subsequent rituals.

It is perhaps also worth noting that, in relation to the twelfth-day rituals, both the textual commentaries and the more knowledgeable ritual specialists in Benares make a rather different kind of link between death and regeneration. If the chief mourner's wife is barren, then in order to conceive a son, she should consume the rice ball used in the ritual to represent her husband's father's father (cf. Kane, 1953:346–7, 480). The *piṇḍa* identified with the ancestor thus has the quality of semen and may beget a new *piṇḍa*-embryo (cf. O'Flaherty, 1980). Though the notion is clearly inconsistent with the theory of reincarnation postulated by the doctrine of *karma*, the idea is that the great-grandfather comes back as his own great-grandson; and I would add that even those who deny the efficacy of any such procedure often assert an identity of character between the two.

My second point relates to the regime of mourning and its striking similarity to the code of the ascetic. The chief mourner must not shave, use soap or oil his hair, wear shoes or a shirt; throughout the mourning he must wear a single garment, must sleep on the ground, avoid 'hot' food and abstain from sex – all of which recalls the conduct prescribed for the renouncer. Each year tens of thousands of pilgrim-mourners go to the holy city of Gaya in order to make offerings there which will ensure the final salvation of their deceased parents. Many of them wear the ochre-coloured garments of the ascetic and it was several times explained to me that this is a symbol of their temporary assumption of the renouncer's role. Dumont (1971) and Das (1977:126) have both remarked on this parallel, and Das interprets it in terms of the liminality of both statuses. Her point is unexceptionable but, I believe, insufficient; for what she fails to note – but what some of my informants explicitly said – is that it is by taking on the role of the ascetic and performing austerities (*tapasya*) that the chief mourner acquires the power to re-create a body for the deceased.

I have thus returned to my starting point: the creative power of asceticism, by means of which Visnu engendered the cosmos. Austerities produce heat, the source of life – the corpse being subjected to the heat of the pyre that the departed might be reborn. Cremation is thus an act of creation, even a cosmic renewal. The paradox is that such austerities have the odour of an opportunism repudiated by the 'true' renouncer, in that they are oriented towards a regeneration of life. For the latter the value of such a goal is dubious, since the world is suffering and the corollary of rebirth is the relentless recurrence of death. The real aim of renunciation is rather an escape from this endless cycle, and it is this – I will suggest – that makes sense of the baroque excess with which the Aghori is associated.

The Necrophagous Ascetic and the Transcendence of Time

Before the creation was a void. According to the myth of Visnu's cosmogony recorded in the best-known eulogy of Benares' sanctity, the *Kaśi Khanda* (Chapter 26), all that originally existed was Brahma, which cannot be apprehended by the mind or described by the speech, and which is without form, name, colour or any physical attribute. Creation proceeded by differentiation from this primal essence, duality emerging from non-duality. Much of the endeavour of the world-renouncer may be seen as an attempt to recapture the original state of non-differentiation and to re-establish the unity of opposites which existed before the world began.

The discipline of yoga is – as Eliade (1969; 1976) has shown – directed at precisely this goal. By his physical postures the yogi subjugates his body and renders it immobile; by concentrating on a single object he frees his mind from the flux of events and arrests mental process; and by slowing down and eventually stopping his breath 'he stops the activities of the senses and severs the connection between the mind and external sensory objects' (Gupta, 1979:168). Sexual intercourse may be converted into a discipline in which the semen is immobilised by the practice of *coitus reservatus*, or its normal direction of flow reversed by reabsorbing it into the penis after ejaculation. By thus controlling his body he acquires magical powers (*siddhis*) by which he may defy nature and control the world. But above all, the yogi's immobilisation of mind, body, breath and semen represents an attempt to return to what Eliade describes as a 'primordial motionless Unity'; and to attain *samādhi*, a timeless state of non-duality in which there is neither birth nor death nor any experience of differentiation.

This suspension of time and conquest of death is also, the aim of Aghori asceticism. The theological premise on which their practice is founded would appear to be a classical monism. Every soul is identical with the Absolute Being; all category distinctions are a product of illusion (*māyā*), and behind all polarities there is an ultimate unity. But what *is* peculiar to the Aghoris is a very literal working-out of this monistic doctrine through a discipline which insists on a concrete experience of the identity of opposites, and on a material realisation of the unity between them. It is a matter of a kind of externalised fulfilment of what is more orthodoxly interpreted as a purely internal quest.

Although there are many similarities of practice, and perhaps also a direct historical connection, between the Aghoris and the skull-carrying Kapalikas of certain late Sanskrit texts, they themselves trace the foundation of their order to an ascetic called Kina ('rancour') Ram, whom they claim as an incarnation (*avatār*) of Siva, and who is supposed to have died (or rather 'taken *samādhi*') in the second half of the eighteenth century when he was nearly one hundred and fifty years old. The *āśrama* (or 'monastic refuge') Kina Ram founded in Benares (which is also the site of his tomb) is one of the most important centres of the sect – though only one or two ascetics actually live there. Each of the succeeding *mahants* ('abbots') of this *āśrama* is supposed to be an *avatār* of (Siva's *avatār*) Kina Ram; the present incumbent being reckoned as the twelfth in the line.

There are probably no more than fifteen Aghori ascetics permanently or semi-permanently resident in Benares and its immediate environs,[8] but others from elsewhere congregate at Kina Ram's *āśrama* during the festivals of *Lolārk Chhath* and *Guru-Purnīmā*. The evidence suggests that at the end of the last century their numbers were several times greater – (Barrow, 1893:215, gives an estimate of between one and two hundred) – though it is very unlikely that they were ever a numerically significant element in the ascetic population of the city. Their hold on the popular imagination is, however, out of all proportion to their numbers, and some Aghoris acquire a substantial following of lay devotees. Recruitment to the sect is theoretically open to both sexes and to all castes. In practice, however, all the ascetics I knew, or knew of, were male and of clean caste origin (though some of their devotees were female).

The Aghoris, wrote Sherring (1872:269), are 'a flagrantly indecent and abominable set of beggars who have rendered themselves notorious for the disgusting vileness of their habits'. Indeed the 'left-hand' discipline (*vām panthi sādhanā*) they embrace was hardly likely to commend itself to the English missionary. The Aghori performs austerities at, and probably lives on, the cremation ground – in some cases in a rough shack, into the mud-walls of which are set human skulls (Morinis, 1979:258). He may go naked or clothe himself in a shroud taken from a corpse, wear a necklace of bones around his neck and his hair in matted locks. His eyes are conventionally described as burning-red, like live coals; his whole demeanour is awesome, and in speech he is brusque, churlish and foul-mouthed.

Rumour persistently associates the Aghoris with human sacrifice, and there is said to have been a notorious case in the recent past just across the river from Benares. What is certain, however, is that during the British raj more than one Aghori was executed for the crime (Barrow, 1893:208); and only recently the *Guardian* newspaper (Thursday, 6 March 1980) reported the death in police custody of an old ascetic who was living on a south Indian cremation ground and who was suspected of the sacrifice of five children whose blood he collected in bottles for the performance of rituals by which he sought to attain immortality. The article goes on to cite a recent (unspecified) survey which claimed that there are still probably a hundred human sacrifices offered each year in India in order to avert epidemics, ensure the fertility of crops or women, or confer supernatural powers on the sacrificer.

As part of his discipline the Aghori may perform the rite of *śava-sādhanā*, in which he seats himself on the torso of a corpse to worship. By means of this worship he is able to gain an absolute control over the deceased's spirit, through which he communicates with other ghostly beings. The Aghori sleeps over a model bier (made from the remnants of a real one); smears his body with ash from the pyres, cooks his food on wood pilfered from them and consumes it out of the human skull which is his constant companion and alms-bowl, and which he is supposed to have acquired by some crude surgery on a putrid and bloated corpse fished out of the river. My informant Fakkar (meaning 'indigent'/'carefree') Baba, however, shamefacedly admits to having obtained his from a hospital morgue, though he claims to have taken precautions to ensure that it was a skull of the right type (see below). It belonged, he says, to a young Srivastava (Trader) who died of snake-bite. The provenance of Lal Baba's skull is reputedly more immaculate. Several of my friends at Manikarnika *ghāt* recall the day when he waded out into the river to retrieve the corpse to which it belonged, and one of them claims to have unwittingly lent him the knife with which he performed the operation. Before eating I have seen Lal Baba offer the food it contains to a dog, thus converting it into the 'polluted leavings' (*jūṭhā*) of the most debased of animals, and one which is also – like the ideal Aghori – a scavenger living off the carrion of the cremation ground. The 'true' Aghori is entirely indifferent to what he consumes, drinks not only liquor but urine, and eats not only meat but excrement, vomit and the putrid flesh of corpses.

While I myself have been present when an Aghori drank what was said to be the urine of a dog, and swallowed what was undoubtedly ash from a cremation pyre, I cannot personally testify to their necrophagy. All I can say with complete assurance is that they readily own to the practice; that as far as my lay informants are concerned the matter is not in question, and that several of them claim to have seen an Aghori eating corpse flesh. One highly revered ascetic has hung a large portrait of himself in the leprosy hospital which he founded, in which he is shown sitting cross-legged on a corpse, a bottle of liquor in one hand while in the other is a morsel of flesh which he is raising to his lips. Apart from its very existence, the interesting thing about the

painting is that the corpse which he is devouring appears to be his own (which would conform with the theology of monism I describe below). What is also relevant here is that another of my ascetic informants insisted that the crucial point about the corpse on which the Aghori sits to worship is that it is identical to his own.

Starting with the *Dabistan*, a seventeenth-century Persian source (cited by Barrow, 1893 and Crooke, 1928), the historical records treat necrophagy as an indisputable fact and provide several supposedly eye-witness accounts of the practice – though some of these are far from credible. The narrator of *The revelation of an orderly* (a semifictional work published in Benares in 1848) claims, for example, that: 'I once saw a wretch of this fraternity eating the head of a putrid corpse, and as I passed he howled and pointed to me; and then scooped out the eyes and ate them before me'. Another nineteenth-century British account claims that 'near Benares they are not unusually seen floating down the river on a corpse, and feeding upon its flesh' (Moor quoted in Oman, 1903:166); while according to a third, the drunken Aghori 'will seize hold of corpses that drift to the banks of the river and bite off bits of its flesh . . .' (Barrow, 1893:206). Or again, Tod (1839:84) reports that 'one of the Deora chiefs told me that . . . when conveying the body of his brother to be burnt, one of these monsters crossed the path of the funeral procession, and begged to have the corpse, saying that it "would make excellent '*chatni*', or condiment"'.

While such reports would certainly do little to allay the doubts expressed by Arens (1979) about the nature of our existing evidence for anthropophagy, what is perhaps more serious witness to its occurrence is provided by the series of prosecutions which followed the special legislation passed by the British to ban – as Crooke (1928) phrased it – 'the habit of cannibalism'. One Aghori, for example, who was tried in Ghazipur in 1862

was found carrying the remains of a putrid corpse along a road. He was throwing the brains from the skull on to the ground and the stench of the corpse greatly distracted the people. Here and there he placed the corpse on shop boards and on the ground. Separating pieces of flesh from the bones he ate them and insisted on begging. (Barrow, 1893)

The defendant later admitted that 'he ate corpses whenever hé found them' (Barrow, 1893:209). Convictions were also obtained in subsequent prosecutions brought before the courts in Rohtak in 1882, and in Dehra Dun and Berhampore in 1884. In one of these cases the accused testified that 'he frequently ate human flesh when hungry' (Barrow, 1893:210); while the newspaper report of a further incident asserts that it forms 'the staple of their food' (The Tribune (Lahore), 29th November 1898, cited in Oman, 1903:165).

Despite the impression which such accounts may create, I am convinced that if necrophagy is indeed practised by any of the Aghoris I encountered, it has nothing whatever to do with the requirements of a balanced diet (as Harris 1977, has somewhat implausibly claimed for the Aztecs); but is an irregular – perhaps even a once-off – affair, performed in a ritualised manner at night during certain phases of the moon (associated with Siva). (In view of Arens' caution, it is perhaps as well to retain an open mind on whether necrophagy ever really occurred in any but freak instances. In this context it may be worth pointing out that even the admissions of the ascetics themselves are not beyond suspicion, for – quite apart from the possibility of police duress – the hallmark of an ideal Aghori is that he consumes the flesh of corpses, and any acknowledged failure to do so is a confession of inadequacy. On balance, however, I think that the probability must remain that at least some Aghoris have always taken this aspect of their discipline seriously.) Details of the precise ritual procedure surrounding such an event are supposed to be secret; and there is a considerable discrepancy between the accounts I was given. Some said that the consumption of flesh should ideally be preceded by an act of intercourse on the cremation ground; others that having eaten of the flesh the ascetic should cremate the remains of the corpse and smear his body with the ashes. But almost everybody agrees that after eating the real Aghori will use his powers to restore the deceased to life (cf. Barrow, 1893:221; Balfour, 1897:345–6), and that the flesh he consumes should be that of a person who has died a bad death.

This association recurs in the notion that the skull which the Aghori carries should have belonged to the victim of an 'untimely death', as should the corpse on which he sits to meditate (cf. Morinis, 1979:258–9). The preference is not just a question of the practical consideration that, since such corpses are immersed, their remains are the ones most likely to be available. It is also a matter of the power that resides in such skulls, which is said to render even the most virulent of poisons innocuous. That of a Teli (Oil-presser) and of a Mahajan (Trader) who has died a bad death is especially prized. Oil-pressers, it is explained, are a proverbially stupid caste and their skulls are therefore easy to control; while Traders tend to be sharp and cunning and their skulls are particularly powerful. With the proper mantras (sacred formulae) an Aghori can get his skull to fetch and carry for him, or cause it to fight with another. It is as if life resides in the skull itself, only waiting to be activated by one who knows the proper incantations. It is because the vital breath of a person who has died a bad death has not been released from his cranium on the cremation pyre that his skull remains a repository of potential power.

Like other sects with a close affinity to Tantrism, the Aghoris perform (or at least claim to perform) the secret rite of cakra-pūjā involving the ritual use of the so-called 'five Ms' (pancañmakāra) – māns (meat), machhlī (fish), madya (liquor) mudrā (in this context parched grain or kidney beans) and maithuna (sexual intercourse). A group of male adepts, accompanied by one or more female partners, sit in a circle. The woman is worshipped as a manifestation of the goddess and is offered the food and drink which is subsequently consumed by the males who feed each other. The first four Ms all posses aphrodisiac qualities and thus lead towards the fifth – in which the adept and his partner incarnate Siva and his consort unite in coitus reservatus. As far as my subsequent argument is concerned, the crucial point here is that the female partner should ideally be a prostitute or a woman of one of the lowest castes; and she should also be menstruating at the time and thus doubly polluted. But what is also significant is that the sexual intercourse which is supposed to occur is a calculated repudiation of procreation. (By contrast the duty to sire offspring was frequently represented by my high-caste householder informants as the only legitimate pretext for coitus.) Not only is the semen withheld, but the act takes place at a time when the female partner is infertile. Moreover, she is preferably a prostitute: the one class of women who have a 'professional hostility' to fertility and who provide the perfect 'symbol of *barren* eroticism' (Shulman's, 1980:261–2, apt phraseology; my emphasis). Consistent with the discussion of Aghori aims which follows, the act of ritual copulation thus reveals a certain disdain for the regeneration of life, and identifies the male adept with Siva locked in a union with his opposed aspect which is both without end and without issue. It is a sexual pairing rid of its normal consequences – progeny and death (the latter being commonly used in popular speech as a metaphor for ejaculation, and being caused – as we have seen – by a failure to retain the semen).

This liaison between the Aghori and the prostitute recurs in several other contexts. The prostitutes of the city not only visit the burning *ghāṭs* to worship Siva there in his form of Lord of the Cremation Ground (Smaśan-Nāth) but each year on the festival of *Lolārk Chhath* they used to come to sing and dance at the tomb of Kina Ram (though the practice was abandoned in the late 'fifties after a serious disturbance among the university students). Moreover, it is said that the bed of a prostitute is equivalent to a cremation ground in that it is an equally proper place for an Aghori to perform his *sādhanā* (ritual practice).

By his various observances the Aghori acquires *siddhis*, or supernatural powers, which give him mastery over the phenomenal world and the ability to read thoughts. If he is sufficiently accomplished he can cure the sick, raise the dead and control malevolent ghosts. He can expand or contract his body to any size or weight, fly through the air, appear in two places at once, conjure up the dead and leave his body and enter into another. All this, of course, is exactly what one might predict from the Aghori's dealings with corpses and bodily emissions, for – as Douglas (1966) points out – that which is anomalous and marginal is not only the focus of pollution and danger, but also the source of extraordinary power.

While *siddhis* may, of course, be won by ascetics who follow quite different kinds of regime, it is

widely believed that they are acquired more quickly and more fully by those who pursue the path of the Aghori. This path, however, is more difficult and dangerous than that which is followed by other orders; and one whose discipline is inadequate, who is overtaken by fear during his austerities, or who fails to retain his semen during *cakra-pūjā*, pays the penalty of madness and death (cf. Carstairs, 1957:232). He then becomes an *Aughar-masān*, the most recalcitrant and difficult to exorcise of malevolent ghosts.

The association between madness and the Aghori is not, however, an entirely straightforward one. The genuine Aghori, it is acknowledged, is – almost by definition – likely to seem demented to ordinary mortals, and is apt to talk in a way which they cannot comprehend. But this is merely evidence of his divine nature and of the fact that he has succeeded in homologising himself with Siva, who is himself somewhat touched, and with Lord Bhairava – one of whose manifestations in Benares is as *Unmat* ('mad') Bhairava. Moreover complete lucidity is not the best policy for one who shuns the world and does not wish to be endlessly importuned for spiritual guidance. But while there may be an element of both divine and calculated madness in an authentic ascetic, it is also recognised that some Aghoris are simply insane in the medical sense. Their affliction, however, is generally attributed to a failure of nerve or an insufficiently fastidious attention to ritual detail during the performance of such dangerously powerful rites, rather than to any notion that their attraction to these practices suggests that they were unbalanced already.

By virtue of his magical powers, the Aghori who has – in the local idiom – 'arrived' (*pahunche hue*), is likely to attract a large lay following who bring their pragmatic problems to him for solution. Baba Bhagvan Ram, for instance, has an extensive circle of committed devotees. Most of them are of high caste, and many are members of the professional middle-class. (Amongst the inner circle of disciples are, for example, a retired Collector and a retired Police Inspector, a post-doctoral research fellow and an administrator from the university, a College Lecturer, a student now studying in north America, two lawyers, an engineer, a Customs and Excise officer, a factory manager, a public works contractor, and a well-to-do shopkeeper). Two other Aghoris I knew also had a significant middle-class following. Even in the presence of an ascetic other than their acknowledged *guru*, the humility of such devotees – who would in other contexts brook no trifling with their dignity – is really remarkable. When Pagila ('mad') Baba wilfully defaecated on the string-cot on which he was reclining, a Rajput police officer and a Brahman businessman undertook the cleaning up.

Although motives are hard to be confident about, for what it is worth I record my strong impression that what attracts many of these people to the Aghori's following are the *siddhis* which he is believed to have obtained and which he may be induced to use on their behalf in an insecure and competitive world. To my knowledge several of them joined Bhagvan Ram's entourage at times of grave personal crisis – the Police Inspector when he was under investigation for corruption, the contractor when his business started to fail, the Customs and Excise Officer when the prospect of providing a suitable dowry for his daughters became an immediate problem. Not of course that this is an aspect of the matter to which they themselves would publicly call attention. As at least some of these middle-class devotees were inclined to present it, the initial appeal was rather the egalitarian social ethic which Baba Bhagvan Ram preaches, and about which I shall say more later. As I would somewhat cynically interpret it, however, his considerable success amongst such people is at least in part attributable to the fact that this message is one which they can identify as 'progressive' and 'modern' and which they can casuistically use to legitimise a more shamefaced and surreptitious concern to tap the source of a fabulous supernatural power.

The paradox of the situation, however, is that in order to gain and maintain a reputation as an ascetic worthy of the name, the laity require miracles as evidence of his attainments; yet the brash display of such powers is regarded with equivocation for it testifies to an incomplete spiritual development. While proof that he has taken the first step, it demonstrates that he has gone no further, for the one who has really 'arrived' is the one who scorns to indulge the laity with such trifles, who is indifferent

to reputation, and who pursues his own salvation with a complete disdain for the world. In order to attain his goal of *samādhi*, a double renunciation is necessary: first a renunciation of the world and then of the powers that are thereby acquired (cf. Eliade, 1969:89; 1976:106–7).

The man-in-the-world, however, remains thirsty for miracles and his compromise is the ascetic who is seen to work wonders – as it were, under the counter and in spite of himself – while denying his capacity to do so. It is not uncommon, in my experience, for one ascetic to be disparaged by the followers of another on the grounds that he is a mere performer of supernatural tricks. But at the same time the follower feels obliged to justify the claims he makes for his own *guru* by reference to a personal experience of the marvels he can accomplish. Did he not witness, or even himself benefit from, this or that miraculous cure? Was he not actually with his *guru* in Benares when the latter was unmistakably sighted in Allahabad? The fact that the ascetic himself disclaims such reports merely confirms his spiritual authenticity.

The curse of an Aghori is particularly terrible and virtually irrevocable. The food of the accursed may turn to excrement as he raises it to his lips, or his heir may die. When a filthy Aghori dressed in the rotting skin of a fresh-water porpoise was, some generations ago, refused admission to the Maharaja of Benares' palace during the performance of a magnificent *yagya*, the sacrificial offerings became immediately infested with maggots and the sacrifice had to be abandoned. As a result of this incident, the Maharaja's line has continually failed to produce heirs, and has been forced to perpetuate itself by adoption; while the curse also stipulated that any Aghori who henceforth accepted food from the palace would be afflicted by a fistula in the anus (*bhagandar*). When the late *mahant* of Kina Ram's *āśrama* was at last induced to revoke the curse and eat from the royal kitchen, the Maharani immediately conceived a son – but the *mahant* himself succumbed to the foretold disorder.

For the development of my theme the story is particularly instructive in two ways. The first is that it draws our attention to the fact that the curse of an Aghori, and – as we shall see – his blessing too, is as often as not concerned with reproduction and fertility. But what is also significant is that the exclusion of the ascetic from the Maharaja's *yagya* appears to be merely a transposition of the well-known mythological incident in which Siva is excluded from the sacrifice of his father-in-law, Daksa, on the pretext that he is a naked, skull-carrying Kapalika (O'Flaherty, 1976:278) – the sectarian precursor of the Aghori. But Siva is essential to the sacrifice if the evil it unleashes is to be mastered (Biardeau, 1976:96). Denied of his share, he spoils the whole event and precipitates a disaster of cosmic proportions. Though the scale of our story is admittedly more modest, it is not difficult to see that the Aghori is merely playing the role which was written for Siva – as well he might, for we shall find that he aspires to be Siva.

The blessing of an Aghori is as beneficent as his curse is awesome. By it he may confer inordinate riches, restore the mad, cure the incurable or bestow fertility on the barren. In order to conceive a child, both Hindu and Muslim couples go in large numbers to Kina Ram's *āśrama*, where they visit his tomb, bathe in the tank of Krimi Kund ('the tank of worms') and take ash from the sacred fire which is fuelled by wood brought from the cremation pyres and which is a form of the goddess Hinglaj Devi. The tank is the one beside which Kina Ram performed his austerities – thus again making a direct link between *tapas* and the powers of creation. The same procedure should ideally be repeated on five consecutive Sundays or five consecutive Tuesdays – days of the week which are special not only to Kina Ram but also to the god Bhairava. An identical procedure will cure children of the wasting disease of *sukhaṇḍi rog* which is caused by a barren woman touching or casting her shadow on the child immediately after she has bathed at the end of her period. She will then conceive, but the child will start to 'dry up' (*sukhnā*) and wither away.

An Aghori's blessing is characteristically given by violently manhandling and abusing its recipient. Bhim Baba, for example, used to live on the verandah of the City Post Office, stark naked, morosely silent, and generally surrounded by a crowd of onlookers and devotees. Every so often, as if infuriated, he would lumber to his feet (for he was massively fat)

seize a small earthenware pot and hurl it with a roar into the crowd. The fortunate target of his missile could leave assured that his problem was about to be solved or his aspirations met (cf. Morinis, 1979: 244; Barrow, 1893:226). It is said that on festival occasions Kina Ram would throw his urine on the crowds by way of blessing. Indeed the bodily emissions of an Aghori are charged with a special potency and have miraculous medicinal qualities. The sister of one of Bhagvan Ram's university-educated devotees, for example, was said to have been cured of a grave illness after her brother had obtained for her a phial of his *guru*'s urine. A lay follower may be initiated by the *guru* by placing a drop of his semen on the disciple's tongue; while at the initiation of an ascetic the preceptor fills a skull with his urine which is then used to moisten the novitiate's head before it is tonsured (Barrow, 1893:241).

Now my informants continually stress that as a result of his *sādhanā* an Aghori does not die. He realises the state of non-duality I referred to earlier; he 'takes *samādhi*', and enters into a perpetual cataleptic condition of suspended animation of deep meditation. His body is arranged (if necessary by breaking the spine) in a meditational posture (known as *padmāsan*), sitting cross-legged with his upturned palms resting on his knees. He is then placed in a box which – in Benares – is buried in the grounds of Kina Ram's *āśrama* (and which is everywhere oriented towards the north). Unlike the householder or ascetics of most other orders his skull is not smashed in order to release the 'vital breath'. A small shrine containing the phallic emblem of Siva is erected over the site of the grave, the emblem transmitting to the worshipper the power emanating from the ascetic's subterranean meditation.

By entering *samādhi* (the term refers to his tomb as well as to his condition within it) – which he is represented as doing by conscious desire at a time of his choosing – the ascetic unequivocally escapes the normal consequences of death: the severance of the connection between body and soul, the corruption of the body and the transmigration of the soul. Provided that he has 'taken' *samādhi* while still alive (*jīvit-samādhi*), rather than being 'given' it after death, his body is immune to putrescence and decay although it remains entombed for thousands of years. It is still the occasional habitation of his soul, which wanders the three *lokas* (of heaven, earth and the netherworld) assuming any bodily form it chooses and changing from one to another at will. The real ideological stress is here, rather than on the incorruption of the particular body he inhabited before he took *samādhi*. Endless stories nevertheless testify to a conviction that the body of the model ascetic is perfectly and perpetually preserved in its tomb; and it is widely believed that this body is at times animated by his peripatetic soul which may be brought back to its former shell in an instant by the fervent prayers of the devotee.

A *samādhi* (in the sense of tomb) which is reanimated by the presence of the soul is described as a *jāgrit-samādhi* ('awakened *samādhi*). Baba Bhagvan Ram's disciples credit him with thus 'awakening' the occupants of every one of the fifty *samādhis* within the precincts of Kina Ram's *āśrama* since he took over its effective management; and this makes it possible to induce them to take a more direct hand in the affairs of men. As for himself, Bhagvan Ram denies the appeal of heaven, where – as he wryly informed me – 'all the celestial nymphs (*apsaras*) are now old ladies'. His intention is rather to spend eternity 'watching and waiting' here on earth where he is within easy reach of ordinary mortals. It is out of compassion for the sufferings of humanity that such an ascetic denies himself the final bliss of complete dissolution into Brahma, for once he is finally liberated 'who will give the sermons?'.

What sense, then, can we make of the ethnography I have provided? One preliminary observation here is that Aghori ideology, if not always their practice, insists that members of the order do not solicit alms. This relates to the familiar South Asian contradiction that, while the ascetic is enjoined to remain completely independent of the material and social order, he must necessarily depend on the gifts of the householder in order to support himself, and can therefore never entirely escape from the lay world. Aghori practice may be seen as one radical solution to this dilemma. His loincloth is a shroud, his fuel the charred wood of the pyres, his food human refuse. By scavenging from the dead (who have no further use for what he takes), the Aghori escapes the clutches of the living, and in theory at least realises the ascetic ideal of complete autonomy.

We may also note that the Aghori's vigil on the cremation ground may be represented as an unblinking meditation on the classic Hindu themes of the transience of existence and the inevitability of mortal suffering. 'Surrounded by death in the place of death, those aspects of reality that end in the fires of the cremation ground become distasteful . . . attachment to the world and the ego is cut and union with Siva, the conqueror of death, is sought' (Kinsley, 1977:100). Like ascetics of other orders, the Aghori aspires to die to the phenomenal world, to undergo the 'Death that conquers death' (Kinsley, 1977), and to exist on earth as an exemplar of the living dead. But what makes him different from others is that he pushes this symbolism to its logical limits.

The theological line which the Aghoris themselves most forcefully stress, however, is the notion that everything in creation partakes of *parmātmā*, the Supreme Being, and that therefore all category distinctions belong merely to the world of superficial appearances, and there is no essential difference between the divine and the human, or between the pure and the polluted. As Lal Baba represented his own spiritual quest to me, it is to become like that ideal Aghori, the sun, whose rays illuminate everything indiscriminately and yet remain undefiled by the excrement they touch.

The doctrine that the essence of all things is the same may clearly be taken to imply a radical devaluation of the caste hierarchy, since from this point of view there is no fundamental difference between the Untouchable and the Brahman. What is less obvious, however, is whether this teaching is one which relates only – as Dumont's model (1960, 1970) would suggest – to the ascetic (caste is irrelevant for *him* but not for the world at large), or whether the Aghori's devaluation of the social order is to be interpreted as a message for *all* men. My Aghori informants themselves were not altogether unequivocal on the matter – sometimes denying to caste any relevance whatsoever, while at others presenting equality as a matter of the ultimate *religious* truth of the enlightened rather than as the appropriate goal of social policy. This lack of clarity is perhaps only to be expected, since for them the central concern is with dissolving the barrier between god and man (or more precisely between Siva and the individual ascetic himself), rather than with tearing down that which divides men from each other.

It is, however, clear that the *social* implications of Aghori doctrine are far from absent from the teachings of Baba Bhagvan Ram, their most illustrious representative in Benares, who has derived from its religious truth a this-worldly ethic of equality and community service – though I concede the possibility that this may be a modern reworking of the renouncer's message. The *āsrama* Bhagvan Ram founded just across the river from Benares includes a hospice for lepers, a primary school, dispensary, post office and printing press. Amongst his circle of followers inter-caste marriage is positively encouraged. But what might also be said is that within the egalitarian order which he would have his disciples realise, a position of unquestioned privilege is nonetheless preserved for the *guru*. He drives about in a jeep, and while he sleeps over a grave, he does so in a well-appointed room under an electric fan. Even his teaching is not without its streak of ambivalence. While caste may be dismissed as a conspiracy of the powerful, the vow by which his male devotees should offer their daughters in marriage leaves considerable doubt about the equality of the sexes within marriage, and the doctrine of *karma* is not in question. Lepers are paying the price of past wickedness. (I regret that I neglected to ask whether the same might not also be held to apply to the Untouchables.) What is at issue, he told me, is rather the right of others to use this fact as justification for their exclusion from society.[9]

If, however obliquely, Aghori doctrine poses questions about the ultimate legitimacy of the social order, there is a rather different way in which their practice reinforces this message of doubt. In orthodox caste society, polluting contacts between castes must be eliminated in order to preserve the boundaries of the group, for which – as Douglas (1966) argues – the boundaries of the body often serve as a metaphor. The Aghori's inversion of the same symbols of body margins implies exactly the opposite message. With the destruction of boundaries entailed by the consumption of flesh, excrement

and so on, goes an affirmation of the irrelevance of caste boundaries. Coming at the issue in a more general way suggested by Turner (1969), we might also note the relationship which exists between liminal states, the suspension of the hierarchical structure of everyday life, and a stress on a vision of an unhierarchised and undifferentiated humanity. By contrast with that of the initiand in tribal society, the Aghori's liminality is permanent – and it is also of a somewhat extreme character. It is hardly surprising, then, that he should represent something of the equality which is generally associated with those liminal to the routinely ordered structure.

Perhaps the most striking aspect of the data, however, is the remarkable similarity between the character assumed by the Aghori and the person of Siva. Indeed the description of Siva given by his disapproving father-in-law perfectly fits the stereotype of the Aghori:

> He roams about in dreadful cemeteries, attended by hosts of goblins and spirits, like a mad man, naked, with dishevelled hair, laughing, weeping, bathed in ashes of funeral piles, wearing a garland of skulls and ornaments of human bones, insane, beloved of the insane, the lord of beings whose nature is essentially darkness. (Briggs, 1938:153)

The epithet *aughar*, by which the Aghori is widely known and which implies an uncouth carefreeness, is one of the names of the god. Like Siva, who ingested the poison that emerged from the Churning of the Oceans and thereby allowed creation to proceed, the Aghori is a swallower of poison who liberates the blocked-up fertility of women. Like his prototype he is addicted to narcotics, is master of evil spirits, is touched with madness and his most salient characteristic is his moodiness. He is *ambhangi* – one who follows his whims with truculent intransigence. He adorns his body with the ornaments of Siva, plays Siva's part as spoiler of the sacrifice when denied admission to it, is greeted in a way appropriate to the god with cries of *Bom, Bom* or *Har Har Mahādev*, and indeed claims and is acknowledged to be Siva. So, for example, the *mahants* of the Kina Ram *āsrama* are explicitly said to be his *avatars*. In the rite of *cakra-pūjā*, the Aghori becomes the Lord of Forgetfulness wrapped in a deathless embrace with his consort; while his necrophagy on the cremation ground may be seen as an act of communion in which he ingests Siva (represented by the corpse), and thus re-creates his consubstantiality with him. The skull he carries associates him with Siva's manifestation as the terrifying god Bhairava who – to atone for the sin of chopping off Brahma's fifth head – was condemned to wander the earth 'as an Aghori' with a skull stuck fast to his hand. Dogs, which like the Aghori scavenge off the cremation ground, are his familiars – as they are of Bhairava in whose temples they wander freely. The special days for visiting these temples are the same as those for visiting Kina Ram's *āśrama*; the god too blesses his worshippers in the form of a (token) beating delivered by his priests, and in ritual intercourse the Aghori's female partner is often identified as his consort, Bhairavi. In short, as Lorenzen (1972:80) has noted, the ascetic homologises himself with the god and acquires some of his divine powers and attributes. Above all, like Siva – the Great Ascetic and Destroyer of the Universe whose emblem is the erect phallus and whose sexual transports shake the cosmos – he transcends duality by uniting opposites within his own person, and thereby acquires Siva's role as *Mahāmritunja*, the 'Conqueror of Death', who amongst the gods is the only one who survives the dissolution of the cosmos and who is truly indestructible (*avināśī*).

This, it seems to me, is the crux of the matter. The theme of inversion and the coincidence of opposites runs throughout the material I have presented. The ascetic becomes the consort of the prostitute, the menstruating prostitute becomes the goddess, beating a blessing, the cremation ground a place of worship, a skull the food-bowl and excrement and putrid flesh food, and pollution becomes indistinguishable from purity. Duality is abolished, polarities are recombined, and the Aghori thus recaptures the primordial state of non-differentiation. He passes out of the world of creation and destruction and into an existence which is beyond time. He attains that state of unity with Brahma which characterised the atemporal and undifferentiated void which existed before the world began. So while I have argued in the first section of the paper that the mortuary rites of the householder represent a re-creation of the deceased,

a renewal of time and a regeneration of the cosmos, I am arguing here that by embracing death and pollution, by systematically combining opposites, the Aghori aims to suspend time, to get off the roundabout and to enter an eternal state of *samādhi* in which death has no menace.

NOTES

1   Although I try here to make some sense of the path of Aghori asceticism by contrasting it with that of the householder, it is of course clear that much of their practice might also be usefully seen in opposition to the discipline of other ascetic orders. Such an analysis is, however, beyond the scope of the present paper.

2   Cf. Bharati's observation (1976:17) that the unique contribution of Tantrism lies not so much in any philosophical novelty as in its ritual methods.

3   Fieldwork in Benares was carried out between September 1976 and November 1977 (supported by the Social Science Research Council) and in August 1978 (supported by the London School of Economics and Political Science). I am deeply obligated to Virendra Singh for his language instruction, and to him and Om Prakash Sharma for their research assistance.

4   On the conception of death as a sacrifice see Biardeau (1971:76 and 1976:38); Das (1976 and 1977: 120–6); Levin (1930); Malamoud (1975); Pandey (1969:241, 253) and Knipe (1975:132–4).

5   I should note, however, that while the breaking of the skull is generally seen as a release of life from the body, most of my informants shied away from the explicit conclusion that it therefore amounts to an act of violence against the deceased.

6   In this sense, then, the deceased is himself the sacrificer; which would seem to contradict the implication that, by taking upon himself 'the sin of burning the body hairs', the chief mourner assumes this role. In fact, however, there is no incompatibility between the two, for in the Indian theory of sacrifice – as in many others – the sacrificer's offering is his own body homologised with that of the victim. Or, to put it more simply, the chief mourner is symbolically equated with the deceased.

7   The notion that the sacrificer is the real victim of the sacrifice (see note 6) perhaps suggests another way of looking at the ambiguity surrounding the ritual state of the corpse (i.e. whether it is pure or polluted). According to the classical theory, the sacrificer has acquired –

through the initiatory rite of *dīkṣā* – a sacrificial body sufficiently august to be offered to the gods in sacrifice, while his profane body remains behind in the safe-keeping of the presiding priests (Malamoud, 1976: 161, 193). The problem with cremation, however, is that it is impossible to disguise the fact that it is not only this sacred entity which is dispatched by the fire, but also the sacrificer's profane and mortal being. My tentative suggestion, then, is that it might be possible to see the ambiguity over the condition of deceased as a reflection of the difficulty of retaining, in this instance, a clear conceptual distinction between the two bodies of the sacrificer. As representative of his sacrificial body, the victim is pure; but as his patently profane and incipiently putrescent corpse it is also impure.

8 I personally encountered twelve, but with only eight of them did I have any but the most fleeting contact. Although some Aghoris spend a significant amount of time on pilgrimage (in particular to Pryag, Pasupatinath in Nepal and Kamakhya in Assam), most appear to have a home base, and none that I came across was rigorously peripatetic.

9 I encountered a very similar ambivalence in the case of another Aghori whose public pronouncements continually stress the brotherhood of all men and the meaningless character of the social hierarchy. It was clear that he regarded himself as a member of a small spiritual elite karmically qualified for the attainment of *samādhi*.

What is also striking is that both of these ascetics not only repudiate caste but also the divisions between Hindus and others; and both are prepared to appropriate Christian symbols to make this point. Bhagvan Ram's leprosy hospice is surmounted by a Christian Cross; while Sadhak Basudeb showed me a pictorial autobiography he had made for the instruction of his devotees which contains a drawing in which he is receiving the stigmata from Christ who appeared to him during his wanderings in the Himalayas. This element of religious syncretism is also apparent at the shrine of Aughar Nath ka Takhiya, which contains several Aghori *samādhis* and which is said to belong equally to Hindus and Muslims. The influence of a devotional *bhakti* ideology is also particularly clear in much of the Aghoris' discourse.

REFERENCES

Abbot, J. 1932 *The keys of power: a study of Indian ritual and belief*. London: Methuen and Co.

Arens, W. 1979. *The man-eating myth: anthropology and anthropophagy*. New York: Oxford University Press.

Balfour, H. 1897. 'The life-history of an Aghori Fakir', *Journal of the Anthropological Institute* (London), 26, 340–57.

Barrow, H.W. 1893. 'On Aghoris and Aghoripanthis', *Journal of the Anthropological Society of Bombay*, 3, 197–251.

Beck, B.E.F. 1976. 'The symbolic merger of body, space and cosmos in Hindu Tamil Nadu', *Contributions to Indian Sociology*, (n.s.), 10, 213–43.

Bharati, Agehananda 1976. *The trantric tradition*. Delhi: B.I. Publications.

Biardeau, M. 1971. 'Etudes de mythologie hindoue (III): 1. Cosmogonies Puraniques', *Bulletin de l'école française d'extrême-orient*, 58, 17–89.

—— 1976. 'Le sacrifice dans l'hindouisme', in *Le sacrifice dans l'Inde ancienne*. M. Biardeau and C. Malamoud, pp. 7–154. Paris: Presses Universitaires de France (Bibliothèque de l'école des hautes études, sciences religieuses, vol. 79).

Briggs, G.W. 1938. *Gorakhnath and the Kanphata Yogis*. Calcutta: YMCA Publishing House.

Carstairs, G.M. 1957. *The twice-born: a study of a community of high caste Hindus*. London: Hogarth Press.

Coomaraswamy, A.K. 1941. 'Atmayajna: self-sacrifice', *Harvard Journal of Asiatic Studies*, 6, 358–98

Crooke, W. 1928. 'Aghori', in *Encyclopedia of Religion and Ethics*. ed. J. Hastings. 1: 210–13. New York.

Das, Veena 1976. 'The uses of liminality: society and cosmos in Hinduism', *Contributions to Indian sociology*, (n.s.), 10 (2), 245–63.

—— 1977. *Structure and cognition: aspects of Hindu caste and ritual*. Delhi: Oxford University Press.

Douglas, M. 1966. *Purity and danger: an analysis of concepts of pollution and taboo*. London: Routledge and Kegan Paul.

Dumont, L. 1960. 'World renunciation in Indian religions', *Contributions to Indian Sociology*, 4, 33–62.

—— 1970. *Homo Hierarchicus: the caste system and its implications*. London: Weidenfeld and Nicolson.

—— 1971. 'On putative hierarchy and some allergies to it', *Contributions to Indian Sociology*, (n.s.), 5, 58–78.

Eliade, M. 1965. *The myth of the external return*. Princeton: University Press (Bollingen series 46).

—— 1969. *Yoga: immortality and freedom*. Princeton: University Press (Bollingen series 61).

—— 1976. *Patanjali and Yoga*. New York: Schocken Books.

Garuda Purana (n.d.) (With Hindi commentary by Sudama Misr Shastri.) Varanasi: Bombay Pustak Bhandar.

Goudriaan, T. 1979. 'Introduction: history and philosophy', in *Hindu tantrism*. S. Gupta, D.J. Hoens and T. Goudriaan, pp.3–67. Leiden: E.J. Brill (Handbuch der Orientalistik).

Gupta, S. 1979. 'Modes of worship and meditation,' in *Hindu tantrism*, S. Gupta, D.J. Hoens and T. Goudriaan. pp.121–85. Leiden: E.J. Brill (Handbuch der Orientalistik).

Harris, M. 1977. *Cannibals and kings*. New York: Random House.

Heesterman, J. 1959. 'Reflections on the significance of the Daksina', *Indo-Iranian Journal*, 3, 241–58.

Herrenschmidt, O. 1978. 'A qui profite le crime? Cherchez le sacrifiant', *L'Homme*, 18 (1–2), 7–18.

— 1979. 'Sacrifice symbolique ou sacrifice efficace', in *La fonction symbolique*. eds. M. Izard and P. Smith. Paris: Editions Gallimard.

Hubert, H. and Mauss, M. 1964. *Sacrifice: its nature and function*. London: Cohen & West.

Kaelber, W.O. 1976. '"Tapas", birth and spiritual rebirth in the Veda', *History of Religions*, 15, 343–86.

— 1978. 'The "dramatic" element in Brahmanic initiation: symbols of death, danger and difficult passage', *History of Religions*, 18, 54–76.

Kane, P.V. 1941 and 1953. *History of Dharmasastra*. vols 2 and 4. Poona: Bhandarkar Oriental Research Institute.

(Sri) *Kaśi Khanda* (n.d.) (Compiled and rendered into Hindi by Baikunthnath Upardhyay.) Varanasi: Shri Bhragu Prakashan.

Kinsley, D.R. 1977. '"The death that conquers death": dying to the world in Medieval Hinduism', in *Religious encounters with death: insights from the history and anthropology of religions*. eds. E. Reynolds and E.H. Waugh. pp.97–108. University Park and London: Pennsylvania State University Press.

Knipe, D.M. 1975. *In the image of fire: Vedic experiences of heat*. Delhi and Varanasi: Motilal Banarsidass.

— 1977. 'Sapiṇḍīkaraṇa: the Hindu rite of entry into heaven', in *Religious encounters with death: insights from the history and anthropology of religions*. eds E. Reynolds and E.H. Waugh. pp.111–24. University Park and London: Pennsylvania State University Press.

Leach, E.R. 1976. *Culture and communication: the logic by which symbols are connected*. Cambridge: Cambridge University Press.

Lévi, S. 1898. *La doctrine du sacrifice dans les Brahmanas*. Paris: Bibliothèque de l'école des hautes etudes, sciences religieuses, 11.

Levin, M. 1930. 'Mummification and cremation in India', *Man*, 30, 29–34, 44–8, 64–6.

Long, B. 1977. 'Death as a necessity and a gift in Hindu mythology' in *Religious encounters with death: insights from the history and anthropology of religions*. eds. F.E. Reynolds and E.H. Waugh, pp.73–96. University Park and London: Pennsylvania State University Press.

Lorenzen, D.N. 1972. *The Kapalikas and Kalamukhas: two lost Saivite sects*. Berkeley and Los Angeles: University of California Press.

Malamoud, C. 1975. 'Cuire le monde', *Puruśartha: Recherches de Sciences sociales sur l'Asie du sud*, 1, 91–135.

— 1976. 'Terminer le sacrifice: remarques sur les honoraires rituels dans le brahmanisme', in *Le sacrifice dans l'Inde ancienne*. M. Biardeau and C. Malamoud, pp.155–204. Paris: Presses Universitaires de France (Bibliothèque de l'école des hautes études, sciences religieuses, vol. 79).

Martin, M. 1838. *The history, topography, and statistics of Eastern India*. London: W.H. Allen & Co.

Morinis, A. 1979. Hindu pilgrimage with particular reference to West Bengal, India. Unpubl. D.Phil, thesis, University of Oxford.

Myerhoff, B.G. 1978. 'Return to Wirikuta: ritual reversal and symbolic continuity on the Peyote hunt of the Huichol Indians' in *The reversible world: symbolic inversion in art and society*. ed. B.A. Babcock, pp.225–39. Ithaca and London: Cornell University Press.

Newby, E. 1966. *Slowly down the Ganges*. London: Hodder & Stoughton.

O'Flaherty, W.D. 1973. *Asceticism and eroticism in the mythology of Siva*. London: Oxford University Press.

— 1976. *The origins of evil in Hindu mythology*. Berkeley, Los Angeles and London: University of California Press.

— 1980. 'Karma and rebirth in the Vedas and Puranas', in *Karma and rebirth in classical Indian traditions*. ed. W.D. O'Flaherty. pp.3–37. Berkeley, Los Angeles and London: University of California Press.

Oman, J.C. 1903. *The Mystics, ascetics, and saints of India: a study of sadhuism, with an account of the Yogis, Sanyasis, Bairagis, and other strange Hindu sectarians*. London: T. Fisher Unwin.

Pandey, Raj Bali 1969. *Hindu samskaras: socio-religious study of the Hindu sacraments*. Delhi and Varanasi: Motilal Banarsidass.

Parry, J.P. 1980. 'Ghosts, greed and sin: the occupational identity of the Benares funeral priests', *Man*, (n.s.), 15 (1), 88–111.

— 1981. 'Death and cosmogony in Kashi', *Contributions to Indian Sociology*, 15: 337–65.

Preta Manjari. (Samvat 2032. Compiled by Sudama Misr Shastri and revised by Mannilal Abhimanyu.) Varanasi: Bombay Pustak Bhandar.

(The) Revelations of an orderly. (by Paunchkouri Khan (pseudonym) 1848.) Benares: Recorder Press (Selections reprinted in *Calcutta Review* 1849, 11, 348–96).

Rigby, P. 1968. 'Some Gogo rituals of "purification": an essay on social and moral categories', in *Dialectic in Practical Religion*, ed. E.R. Leach, pp.153–78. Cambridge: Cambridge University Press (Cambridge papers in social anthropology, no 5).

Sahlins, M. 1978. 'Culture as protein and profit', *The New York Review of Books*, November 23, pp.45–53.

Sherring, M.A. 1872. *Hindu tribes and castes as represented in Benares*. London: Trubner & Co.

Shulman, D.D. 1980. *Tamil temple myths: sacrifice and divine marriage in the South Indian Saiva tradition*. Princeton: University Press.

Sinha, S. and Saraswati, B. 1978. *Ascetics of Kashi: an anthropological exploration*. Varanasi: N.K. Bose Memorial Foundation.

Sraddha Parijat (n.d.) (Compiled by Rudradatt Pathak). Gaya: Shri Vishnu Prakashan.

Stanley, J.M. 1977. 'Special time, special power: the fluidity of power in a popular Hindu festival', *Journal of Asian Studies*, 37 (1), 27–43.

Stevenson, S. 1920. *The rites of the twice-born*. London: Oxford University Press.

Tod, Lt. Col. J. 1839. *Travels in Western India*, London: W.H. Allen.

Turner, V. 1969. *The ritual process: structure and anti-structure*. Chicago: Aldine Publishing Co.

—— 1977. 'Sacrifice as quintessential process, prophylaxis or abandonment', *History of Religions*, 16 (3), 189–215.

Vidyarthi, L.P., Saraswati, B.N. and Makhan, J.H.A. 1979. *The sacred complex of Kashi*. Delhi: Concept Publishing Company.

Zaehner, R.C. 1962. *Hinduism*. London: Clarendon Press.

22

The Nineteenth-Century Tlingit Potlatch: A New Perspective

Sergei Kan

Introduction

A number of Northwest Coast rituals labeled "potlatches" have been the subject of anthropological analysis.[1] Functionalist, ecological, psychological, structuralist, and other theories have been applied to this phenomenon since the time of Boas (Benedict 1934; Barnett 1938; Codere 1950; Suttles 1960; Piddocke 1965; Drucker and Heizer 1967; Rosman and Rubel 1971; Adams 1973; and so on). Only recently has it been subjected to symbolic analysis, which has generated interesting new interpretations but has led to the neglect of the sociology of the ritual (Snyder 1975; Goldman 1975; Walens 1981; Seguin 1984, 1985). The Tlingit potlatch has, by and large, escaped the attention of anthropologists concerned with interpretive theory.

The major ethnographers of Tlingit culture have emphasized the significant role played by the dead in the potlatch and the native view of the ritual as a memorial (Veniaminov 1886; Swanton 1908; Emmons 1920–45; McClellan 1954; Olson 1967; de Laguna 1972). By incorporating this native model of the potlatch and by drawing on previous accounts as well as data collected during fieldwork in 1979–80 and 1984 (including active participation in several potlatches), I have tried to produce a more holistic analysis of this ritual as it existed in the period between 1830 and 1890, which predated massive Christianization and other significant sociocultural changes.

I begin with . . . a discussion of the 19th-century Tlingit funeral, the first stage in the cycle of mortuary rituals that culminated in the memorial potlatch. By focusing on the native characterization of the ritual as the "finishing of the dead body," I show that it resembles other rites of secondary treatment of the dead analyzed by Hertz (1960). Models of the mortuary ritual developed by Van Gennep (1960), Hertz (1960), Huntington and Metcalf (1979), and others are applied to the potlatch; the transformation of the deceased, the mourners, and their affines is also discussed. Finally, the symbolism of the various forms of ritual discourse and exchange is examined to broaden our understanding of the relationships among the four categories of potlatch participants: the hosts, the guests, and the deceased matrikin of each. I conclude the paper with suggestions about the

From Sergei Kan, "The 19th-Century Tlingit Potlatch: A New Perspective," *American Ethnologist*, 13, 2 (1996): 191–212.

possible use of some of the methods and findings of this study in analyzing potlatches in other Northwest Coast societies.

[. . .]

Nineteenth-Century Tlingit Funeral

The Tlingit were divided into two matrilineal exogamous moieties, the Ravens and the Eagles (Wolves), further subdivided into matrilineal clans. Each clan possessed crests, origin myths, songs, and dances, which presented its sacred history and symbolized its members' collective identity. Clans also owned names (titles), subsistence areas, and other forms of tangible and intangible property. Many were not localized but were represented in villages by their segments (subclans), each occupying one or several houses. Each house was identified with a matrilineage, which also owned a stock of lands and ceremonial property. The society was ranked, with house heads and their immediate matrikin forming the aristocracy. Junior matrikin of the aristocrats constituted the commoners. Slaves, consisting of some impoverished Tlingit and their neighbors captured in warfare, were perceived as being outside the Tlingit society and were not granted full personhood (Kan 1982:101–2). Lineages and clans were ranked, but ranking was inexact and subject to dispute and reevaluation, ultimately tested in the potlatch.

The funeral began with the washing and dressing of the corpse in ceremonial garments depicting the crests of the lineage and clan of the deceased.[2] The body was placed in the back of the house in a reclining position, knees drawn up and bound, hands placed on them. The deceased wore gloves or mittens, boots, and (a male?) was provided with a spear. Frequently he also wore a headdress representing his clan or house. Other regalia of the matrilineal group of the departed were placed near the body, along with personal possessions. The number of the deceased's matrikin affected by the death depended on his status and rank. A standard unit involved was the subclan. All of its members suspended their mundane activities and visited the house of the deceased several times throughout the wake. Most strongly affected were the lineage kin of the departed, who had to fast, cut their hair, paint their faces black, and observe other taboos. These mourners expressed their sorrow and honored the deceased by wailing, singing "crying songs" (*gaax daasheeyí*), and speaking to and about him. During the wake, the ghost was believed to remain in the house, and when it departed to the cemetery, there was a danger that it would take a beloved relative along.

In the meantime, the paternal/affinal relatives of the deceased (members of the opposite moiety) were busy preparing the funeral pyre, dressing, feeding, and comforting the mourners, and carrying out other practical tasks. The length and elaborateness of the wake were determined by the rank and status of the deceased and of his lineage and clan. A commoner's wake lasted for 4 days, while that of an aristocrat (*aanyádi*) could continue for 8 days. Every evening, affinal/paternal relatives of the deceased came into the house to comfort the mourners with speeches. They received tobacco, food, and some gifts, tokens of the much larger donations to be made to them in the potlatch (Shotridge 1917:106–8; Olson 1967:59–60). Food and tobacco were also burned as an offering to the matrilineal ancestors of the mourners.

The body was taken out through the back of the house or the smokehole and cremated. Some personal belongings of the deceased were cremated as well, while others were subsequently distributed among his lineage kin. The male "opposites" of the departed cremated the body, while the female ones collected the ashes and the bones, and placed them in a temporary container, a box inside a grave house. Following cremation, the matrikin of the deceased removed the signs of mourning, cleansed themselves, and conducted the first in a series of small feasts, in which they thanked their "opposites" and feasted them. Once again, food and tobacco were sent to the matrilineal ancestors of the hosts. The end of these feasts coincided with the arrival of the spirit of the deceased in the "village of the dead" (*s'igeekáawu aaní*), but its final separation from the living did not occur until the memorial potlatch. The term *s'igeekáawu aani* (literally "village of the bones' people") was applied to the cemetery located behind the village of the living, as well as the distant, noncorporeal dwelling place of the spirits. The cemetery consisted of grave houses containing several boxes, each filled with the remains of a single person. Every clan's cemetery was located behind its houses, so that the "village of the dead" mirrored that of the living. Boxes with the remains of aristocrats were also often deposited in the back of mortuary poles.[3]

My analysis of the Tlingit funeral (Kan 1982: 190–266), influenced by Van Gennep (1960), Hertz (1960), Turner (1967), and Huntington and Metcalf (1979), focuses on the transformation of the corporeal and the noncorporeal attributes of the deceased, the mourners, and the members of the opposite moiety involved in the funeral. In the course of the mortuary ritual, several elements constituting a complete human person in the Tlingit culture were separated from each other. The decaying corpse was a source of great danger for the living matrikin of the deceased. In the native theory of personhood (Kan 1982:45–80), a clear distinction was made between the temporary physical attributes, which I label the "outside," and the more permanent corporeal and noncorporeal ones, that I refer to as the "inside."[4] The former included the skin and flesh, seen as the surface upon which the social identity and emotional state of the person were reflected. Representations of the social identity also appeared on ceremonial garments, seen as an additional layer of the "outside." Despite the preoccupation with the perfect state of the "outside," the "inside," consisting of the bones and several noncorporeal entities, was perceived as a more significant element controlling the "outside." In contrast to the "soft" and "wet" flesh, the bones were considered "solid," "dry," and "heavy," and occupied an intermediate position between the flesh and the spiritual entities.[5]

Cremation may be interpreted as a quick way of separating the polluted flesh (no longer controlled by the "inside") from the pure bones and releasing the noncorporeal entities of the "inside."[6] The bones were "dressed" in blankets and placed inside a "house" in the "village of the dead." The spiritual entities included a ghost that dwelled with the bones, a spirit located in a noncorporeal replica of the house of the deceased in the distant "village of the dead," and another spirit that returned to this world

to be reincarnated in a matrilineal descendant of the deceased.[7] Cremation ensured that the spirit remained warm in the afterlife, while the fireplace inside the house of the living served as their medium of communication with departed matrikin, who depended on the food and gifts placed in it by the living.

Despite the pollution emanating from the corpse, the Tlingit displayed it in the most conspicuous part of the house, associated with the house chief (hít s'aatí) and the sacred objects representing the lineage crests (at óowu). In the native view, the clothing put on the deceased equipped the spirit for a difficult journey through the interior forest to the "village of the dead," while the songs performed by the mourners "cleared the underbrush from its path" (McClellan 1975:373; Kan 1982:207). At the same time, the display of the corpse was described as "showing respect to the deceased" (Wallis 1918:80; Swanton 1908:429). The focus of the wake was on the social identity of the deceased (cf. Hertz 1960:77). The death of each member of a matrilineal group (particularly an aristocrat) caused a social crisis. Hence, the wake involved a collective assessment of the social career of the deceased and reiterated his ties with each member of his lineage or clan. The first stage in the transformation of the deceased into an ancestor (cf. Hertz 1960:79–80),[8] the wake was a period of the greatest solidarity among the matrikin of the deceased, united in their common grief, and in what they called "love and respect" for the deceased. Their mourning attire underscored that unity, while deemphasizing the important distinctions and inequalities among the aristocrats and commoners, old and young, men and women. The transformation of the mourners during the funeral paralleled that of the deceased, consisting of the three stages of the rites of passage (Van Gennep 1960; see also Hertz 1960; Huntington and Metcalf 1979; Kan 1982:222–3).[9]

The mourners' behavior contrasted sharply with that of their paternal/affinal kin. While the former were passive, if not socially dead, the latter were engaged in handling the polluted corpse, and helping the mourners practically and morally. This enabled the mourners to concentrate on the pure "inside" (social persona, spiritual attributes) of the deceased, since their "opposites" dealt with the polluted "out-side." By the end of the funeral, the mourners returned to normal, active life and became donors, while their "opposites" turned into the more passive recipients, a role they continued to play throughout the remaining rituals of the mortuary cycle, including the potlatch.

Thus the funeral reaffirmed the two fundamental principles of the Tlingit sociocultural order: matrilineal unity and solidarity, and the reciprocity between moieties. It began as a dramatic disruption of normal social life and ended with its restoration as well as reaffirmation of basic cultural values, including the "love and respect" between the living and the dead, and between affines. Finally, it allowed the mourners to display their sacred crests and perform the ancestral songs and dances that enhanced the status of their matrilineal groups.[10]

Memorial Potlatch as the Secondary Treatment of the Dead

The funeral and subsequent memorial feasts did not complete the mortuary cycle. The remains of the deceased were not considered "finished" until a new container had been provided for them. This could be a new box, a new or repaired grave house, or a mortuary pole. The remains were "finished" by the same paternal/affinal relatives of the deceased who had earlier participated in his funeral. At the memorial potlatch they were remunerated for their services, while the matrikin of the deceased ritually ended their mourning. The ceremonial regalia, names, and other attributes of the deceased were bestowed upon his matrilineal descendants. Only those on the very bottom of the social hierarchy were not memorialized in a potlatch. The rest of the people were either honored in a special potlatch or included in the rites honoring their matrikin of higher rank.

The liminal nature of the period between the funeral and the potlatch was clearly expressed by the notion that the deceased had not yet found a permanent place in the "village of the dead," while his matrikin had not yet been released from mourning taboos, and were still considered indebted to their "opposites," who had helped them during the funeral. To refuse to give a potlatch was to risk illness and death, and to show a total lack of "love and respect" for one's matrilineal ancestors and "opposites."

By approaching the Tlingit potlatch as a secondary treatment of the dead, I incorporate the native view into the analysis and thus broaden its scope. I also suggest that the data indicate a similarity between this ritual and various forms of the secondary treatment of the dead found throughout the world (Hertz 1960; Bloch 1971; Huntington and Metcalf 1979; Bloch and Parry 1982).[11]

Outline of the memorial potlatch

The hosts' preparation for the potlatch included an accumulation of wealth and an observance of various rules similar to those imposed on persons preparing for a dangerous task requiring magical power and good fortune (laxeitl). Brothers-in-law of the hosts (naa káani) were sent to invite the guests from distant communities, while the local guests were invited some time before the ceremony by the naa káani who stopped in front of their houses and called out their ceremonial names (titles) — hence the Tlingit term for the potlatch, ku.eex', from the verb ya-.eex', "to call out," "to invite."[12]

The arrival of the guests was marked by mock battles and an exchange of dances and songs between the guests standing in their canoes and the hosts on the beach. Once the guests had landed, they were taken to the houses of the hosts' clan, where they stayed through the entire period of feasting and ceremonies, which lasted for at least a month. Preliminary rites included dancing, singing, and masked performances by the two sides, as well as the feasting of the guests by their hosts. The potlatch proper usually lasted 4 days. It began with the hosts "mourning their dead [matrikin] for the last time." Sad ("heavy") songs belonging to the mourners' clan were performed, tears were shed, and speeches of condolence were delivered by the guests, to which the hosts responded with speeches of gratitude. With this part of the ritual completed, the mood and behavior of the participants became less somber. The hosts now performed songs describing their ancestral crests (called "national songs" by the present informants) and displayed them in the form of ceremonial garments and other regalia. The guests were feasted several times, while some food was put in the fire for dead members of the hosts' clan, who were believed to take part in the potlatch. The guests told jokes to entertain the hosts and help them forget their sorrow. "Love songs" (kusixán daasheeyí) were also exchanged between the two sides.

The climax of the potlatch was the distribution among the guests of the gifts contributed by individual hosts. Before making his or her donation, each host was given an opportunity to deliver a speech or sing a song illustrating his or her relationship to the deceased and to thank the guests for their help. Just before the distribution of gifts, the hosts named members of their group, many of them youngsters. A small portion of the gifts was burned for the benefit of the donors' matrilineal ancestors. The name of each deceased member of the hosts' lineage or clan was called out, followed by the name of a particular guest who was to receive the gift. The dead received the noncorporeal essence ("inside") of the gift, and the living its corporeal form ("outside"). Having collected their presents and packed the leftover food, the guests thanked the hosts for their generosity, and performed a few dances and songs as a form of gratitude. Often they would stage a small return potlatch, distributing among their hosts a portion of the gifts they had just received.

The Potlatch Participants

The deceased

The potlatch completed the distribution of the various attributes of the deceased among the several domains of the universe. The bones and the ghost finally found a permanent home in the cemetery, while the spirit became forever established in the distant "village of the dead." Another noncorporeal entity, the yaahaí, returned to the living to be reincarnated in a matrilineal descendant of the deceased. His ceremonial title(s) or name(s) as well as festive attire depicting his lineage or clan crests were bestowed on his successor. The rebirth of the deceased and the death's failure to interrupt the continuity of the matrilineal group were dramatically expressed by addressing the new owner of the title or

the regalia as if he were the deceased himself (Kan 1979–84).

In the potlatch, the mourners'/hosts' attention began to shift from the recently deceased person to other dead members of their matrilineal group, whose names were also invoked and who were also "warmed," "clothed," and "fed" through the fire. The key value of the unity and solidarity of the matrikin was thus confirmed, since the rite, which had begun as a memorial to a single person, became the main occasion for remembering, honoring, and helping the matrilineal ancestors of the mourners/hosts. Every member of the group was given an opportunity to mourn his or her own departed matrikin.

One of the most dramatic and effective forms for expressing the continuity between the generations of lineage or clan relatives were the "sad songs" (tuwunukw daasheeyí), also called "heavy songs" (yaadaali daasheeyí). Some were identical to those performed during the funeral, but others (the most sacred and valuable) were reserved for the potlatch. For example, one popular "sad song" of a Sitka clan is believed to have been composed by a woman of that group, after the canoe containing her baby had been carried away by the tide. The woman mourns her beloved child's death and compares it to the tragic deaths of several of her clan ancestors, killed while riding in a canoe in the early 1800s, during the war with the Russians (Olson 1967:44–5; Kan 1979–84). The image of the canoe carrying dead bodies links the two events. When the descendants of the song's author perform it during their potlatch, they lament the deaths of all of their matrikin, both the recently deceased and those of long ago, including the unfortunate infant and the brave warriors. Since kinship terms rather than personal names were used in most songs, and since many deaths resulted from the same causes, a mourner could usually find an appropriate song to express his or her sorrow about the loss of a particular clan relative (cf. de Laguna 1972:632).

The participation of the matrilineal ancestors of the hosts in the potlatch was emphasized throughout the ritual by invocation of their names and reference to their lives. The custom of inviting them to the potlatch was believed to have originated in ancient times, when Raven, the culture hero, was shaping the world into its present form. According to Veniaminov (1886:623–4), Raven once invited the dead to a feast and tried to feed them. However, they were able to consume only the food placed into the fire. After his guests had departed, Raven discovered that the food in their dishes remained intact. "This is why today the Tlingit have memorial feasts for their dead relatives in order to feed them, but with one difference: they throw just a little bit into the fire and [their living guests] eat the rest," concludes Veniaminov (1886:623–4).

The notion that everything given to the guests in the potlatch belonged to the dead member of the hosts' lineage/clan explains why the food and gifts have been referred to as "dying" or "being killed."[13] Once the property had been collected and prepared for distribution, it could no longer be used by the donors, since that would bring great misfortune upon them. As one informant explained, "You can't touch that food, gifts, and money. They already belong to the dead" (Kan 1979–84). The presence of the dead accounts also for the taboo on continuing the potlatch proper into daylight hours.[14] The association between the dead and the nighttime is not surprising, since animal and superhuman spirits were active at night, magic power was more accessible to humans after dark and, in comparison to this world, day and night in the "village of the dead" were reversed.

The potlatch played a number of important roles in the sociopolitical domain of Tlingit life, including the validation of claims to certain rank and status. However, the Tlingit themselves saw it first and foremost as a *memorial ritual* (de Laguna 1972:612; Kan 1979–84). Having no corporeal "outside," the dead were invisible, but through various forms of symbolic media they were, as one informant put it, "brought back to life." In the performance of the "heavy songs," the living not only described the lives of their matrilineal ancestors but ensured that the "voices of the dead could be heard." This seems to be more than a metaphor, since a number of informants said that they could see their beloved mothers and maternal uncles among the dancers and could distinguish their voices among those of the singers (Kan 1979–84).

The continuity between the living and the dead matrikin was made manifest in most of the ritual performances, but especially when the ancestral regalia and the "heavy" ceremonial names/titles were used. The garments passed from one generation of clan members to the next could be interpreted as the "outside" layer of the dead appropriated by their living descendants. The names were also perceived as tangibles placed on the living as clothing. Thus, according to Olson (1933–54, notebook 5:52), "Those to be reincarnated go to a place no one knows where and when they come back they carry (as a bundle) under their arm that same name which is therefore given to them." Names were said to be given "to the face" of the recipient (Johnson 1979:6). This notion was reinforced by the practice of rubbing some of the gifts to be distributed in the potlatch on the forehead of the recipient of a name. The Tlingit were concerned with preventing their names/titles from "dying out" and accomplished that by perpetually recycling them among their descendants. Each potlatch name/title, as opposed to a birth or a pet name, had a certain prestige and social value and indicated the rank of its holder (Olson 1967:48). According to Olson (1933–54, notebook 9:65), "A man who repays his debt may pay only the original amount but usually would pay back more for the honor of his name. But if the debt is passed on for a generation or more, a larger amount is always paid. *Idea is not of interest but of honor of the name*" [emphasis added].[15]

The relationship between the living and the dead dramatized in the memorial potlatch was that of reciprocity. The living provided the dead with food, warmth, gifts, and, most importantly, love and remembrance. In return, the dead passed on their valuable names and other sacred possessions and prerogatives, used by the living to maintain and raise their rank, status, and prestige.[16] Although this could not be called "ancestor worship" (contra Emmons 1910), the Tlingit did believe that the dead could not only help but harm the living with illness and death, if the latter did not remember, honor, and help them. As long as the dead were remembered by their living matrikin and could participate in their potlatches, they remained immortal and sat close to the fire in their noncorporeal houses

(Swanton 1908:462). The forgotten ancestors, on the other hand, moved further and further away from the fire, suffered from hunger and cold, while their "houses" in the cemetery crumbled. Ultimately, the continuity of the matrilineal clan, as a cultural category, depended upon a human ability to *remember*.

The mourners as hosts

Just as it is necessary to include the deceased in the analysis of the potlatch, it is essential to incorporate the native view of the ritual as the last public expression of the mourners' grief. Thus, in the 1980s potlatches I witnessed, the hosts were encouraged by guests "not to hold back their tears" and "let all their sorrow out." This was accomplished through the mourners' performance of the four special "crying songs," one of their most treasured possessions. This singing was followed by the four prolonged *oo* sounds made by the mourners, said to "expel sadness from their *toowú* [mind/soul, "inside"]." The male mourners also struck the floor with their staffs four times, "putting all of their grief" into that act (Kan 1979–84; Olson 1967:61).

The Tlingit thought that emotions originated in the *toowú* and were expressed on the "outside" through tears, laughter, words, and facial expressions. Grief was perceived as a particularly powerful emotion, somewhat independent of human will and consciousness. According to Swanton (1908:437), "It is not through man's own will, but the way that Raven made people, that brings forth a new song, when people are called together after one has died." The "crying songs" were the most appropriate expression of grief, perceived as something tangible, which could be manipulated and expelled during the potlatch. Thus, in Olson's account, the mourners followed the singing of the four "sad songs" with the shedding of their coats (in lieu of blankets) and holding them before the fire to "dry their sorrow" (1967:62). The ritual was also seen as a way of strengthening the mourners' *toowú*. Their mood was expected to change and no more tears were supposed to be shed in public after that. In a recent potlatch, the hosts expressed this change by using two carved representations of their main crest, a certain type of salmon. At the beginning of the ritual, the two fish were hung on the wall with their heads pointing downward to represent sorrow; after the ceremony of "pushing away sorrow," their heads were turned upward, to make them "look happy" (Kan 1979–84).

In the expression of their sorrow, the hosts were unified. Throughout the potlatch, this solidarity was maintained and repeated in word and action. Thus, all of the hosts remained standing during the potlatch, occupying the front of the house, its least conspicuous area, so as to show their deference to the guests (Kan 1978). Every member of the hosts' group, regardless of rank, could express his or her feelings (de Laguna 1972:632–3).

The hosts were also united in their subsequent performances aimed at displaying their ancestral regalia and prerogatives. While justified as a show of "love and respect" for their ancestors, they were also intended to confirm the hosts' claims to their sacred possessions and to raise their status. As Olson (1967:59) notes, *the potlatch was not a duty but a privilege*. In fact, it was the only major opportunity for the display of the sacred crests (*at óowu*), the performance of songs, dances, and myths embodying the sacred history, identity, and destiny of the matrilineal group (its *shagóon*). A generous distribution of property accompanying this display increased the value of the crests. Thus, a distribution of $6000, while displaying a headdress representing one of the hosts' major crests, was described as "killing $6,000 to bring out the headdress" (Swanton 1908:442; see also Oberg 1973:125). In addition to displaying their old possessions, the hosts could validate their claims to new ones, including houses and lands. This was said to make the property and its owners "heavier," that is, increase their value and status by bringing them into direct contact with the wealth to be distributed to the guests. Thus, in a recent potlatch, money placed inside a headdress representing the hosts' major crest was later rubbed on the faces of those who were to be given names (Kan 1979–84).

These and numerous other examples indicate that actions aimed at raising the hosts' rank and status were justified as ways of honoring their matrilineal ancestors. The names of the dead were also invoked to restore peace, whenever conflicts occurred among the participants. I suggest that the "love and respect" of the living toward the dead served as an ideology, enabling the living to present actions aimed at raising their status as noble and morally correct. While statements of grief and love for one's ancestors, made by some of the hosts (especially the chief mourners), expressed sincere emotions, other used them as a rhetorical device in a struggle for power and prestige. At times the desire for prestige outweighed the mortuary/memorial purpose of the potlatch.

Nevertheless, it is incorrect to consider competition over rank, status, and prestige to be the only significant purpose of this ritual, as some scholars have done (Oberg 1973:124–5; Tollefson 1976:203–34). On the other hand, it would also be a mistake to restrict the analysis to the native ideology, which emphasized such commemorative aspects of the potlatch as "dignity, sympathy, high respect for all, with the exalted chief and the poor and lowly united in sorrow and honor for the ancestors" (de Laguna 1972:612). In my opinion, the complexity of the potlatch and its centrality in Tlingit culture and society resulted from a dialectical relationship between competition and cooperation, between the struggle for power and prestige on the one hand, and the "love and respect" for the ancestors on the other.

Thus, while united in their grief and pride in their clan's shagóon, the hosts competed with one another, and different categories of persons played unequal roles. For example, if the deceased was a house or a clan chief, several of his successors might compete for his title and position by trying to contribute the largest amount of wealth to his memorial potlatch and to play the leading role in it. Although most of the negotiations and debates between them would occur in private, the amount of wealth each would contribute and the order in which these individual presentations would be made served as a form of public competition. The head of the hosts made the last and the largest donation. Lower-ranking hosts could also use the wealth they contributes to compete with clan relatives of a similar rank. Although each host was supposed to contribute in accordance with his or her present rank and status, there always remained some room for competition and mobility. Such behavior was explained and justified as an effort to emulate the "illustrious prece-

dents set by one's maternal uncles and grandfathers. However, the abstract standards of noblesse oblige or the legendary examples of dead ancestors were readily replaced by the challenging marks set by the present acts of fellow chiefs and clanmates" (de Laguna 1972:613). Bitter disputes between hosts also centered on the right to use crests and bestow valuable names on their immediate matrikin. Thus, if several houses acted as hosts, one of them would sometimes try to "grab" a high-ranking name before others had a chance to do so or would refuse to recognize the right of another house to display a particular crest (Oberg 1973:125; Kan 1979–84).

Among the hosts, the superiority of aristocrats over commoners, old over young, and men over women was stated by their respective location inside the house as well as the different tasks assigned to them. At the same time, the complementarity of different social categories was also expressed, for example, in the relationship between male and female styles of dancing. On the whole, the potlatch was dominated by the aristocrats, who acted as guardians of the ceremonial regalia, as song and dance leaders, as key orators, and as contributors of the largest amounts of wealth. The esoteric language used in the potlatch and the numerous metaphorical references to the participants' shagóon were used and understood mostly by the aristocrats who were specially trained for this ceremonial role. On the other hand, the cooperation of the entire matrilineal group of the hosts was necessary for the success of its potlatch, while the glory of the aristocrats reflected on their lower-ranking kin. Even a small contribution made by a poor host or a child was welcomed, and those with nothing to give were helped by their matrikin.

The opposite side as guests

Much of the potlatch was focused on the relationships between hosts and guests, the latter activated by the same combination of competition and cooperation already discussed. To compensate one's "opposites" for the services provided during the funeral was just as important as the other functions of the potlatch examined above. This explains why today the Tlingit refer to this ritual in English as the "pay off (party)." In the potlatch guests continued to play their crucial role as mediators between the hosts and their deceased matrikin, since the spiritual essence of things given to the guests became the property of the dead. The guests also acted as representatives or impersonators of their own matrilineal ancestors, whose songs and dances they performed, and whom they frequently mentioned in their speeches. Finally, the presence of the guests was the prerequisite for the validation of the hosts' claims to their sacred crests.

In Tlingit society, relationships between matrilineal groups belonging to the different moieties were delicate and required a great deal of care to maintain balanced reciprocity. Feuds and wars between the Ravens and the Eagles broke out over minor insults and injuries. Unlike conflicts between members of a single moiety, these could not be settled informally, but demanded an elaborate peace-making ceremony before normal relations could be restored. One major prerequisite for peace was that the rank of all the slain members of one moiety should equal that of the other (de Laguna 1972:592–604).

Intermoiety relations in the potlatch must be viewed as a restoration of balance and a transformation of potential hostility into peace. This interpretation is supported by the use of war symbolism and rhetoric in the initial and sometimes later stages of the potlatch. Before the guests from another community could land in front of their hosts' houses, a mock battle occurred between the hosts on the beach and the guests standing in their canoes (Olson 1967:61–2; Billman 1964:59). The ceremony began with the chief host appearing on the beach with a bow and arrows and wearing his war costume, and ended with his welcoming the guests by walking into the water towards them and having his junior male relatives carry them ashore in their canoes.

In comparison to the late 19th-century Kwakiutl, the Tlingit potlatch was characterized by relative peacefulness and a general lack of openly adversarial behavior. The killing of slaves and drowning of copper sheets and other valuables, labeled the "destruction of property" by anthropologists, was done not so much to challenge rivals, but rather to offer gifts to the hosts' matrilineal ancestors. At the same time, the aggressive rhetoric of some Tlingit potlatch speeches was not unlike that of the Kwakiutl potlatch

described by Codere (1950). However, her interpretation of this phenomenon as a substitute for warfare does not seem to apply to the Tlingit, who waged war against and potlatched with each other throughout most of the 19th century. After the Americans put an end to warfare, the scale of the potlatch did increase, but that was due to the enrichment of the Tlingit from the fur trade and wage labor. A comparison of Tlingit and Kwakiutl potlatch rhetoric leads me to accept Drucker and Heizer's intepretation of the Kwakiutl references to war as a "verbalization of conflict," rather than a survival from an earlier era dominated by fighting (1967:125–9).[17]

The next issue to be discussed concerns the identity of potlatch guests. While existing evidence supports Rosman and Rubel's argument that the guests were divided into two competing groups (1971:51–3), they were not necessarily the only groups linked to the hosts through marriage. Swanton's (1908:435) data, the evidence used by Rosman and Rubel, does not show that the hosts' clan (the Chilkat Gaanax.-ádi) had affinal ties only with two of the subclans invited to the potlatch (the Chilkat and the Sitka Kaagwaantaan). All of the existing data indicate that a Tlingit matrilineal group intermarried with more than two other groups (Olson 1967:7; Tollefson 1976:209–10; Kan 1979–84; and so forth).[18] If this is the case, how then can we explain the dual division of the guests? First, the structure of the Tlingit house encouraged this; guests occupied the two sides, where they sat facing each other (Kan 1978). Second, out-of-town guests were always treated with somewhat greater deference than local ones. Since any major potlatch required the presence of the former, the division of the guests seems natural. If only local guests attended, they were divided along clan and lineage lines. The point is that it was the opposition itself and not the identity of the groups that mattered (cf. McClellan 1954:86). Competition between the two parties was expressed in dancing and eating contests, as well as in other performances, adding excitement to the ritual and underscoring the unity of the hosts.

The hosts carefully watched their guests to prevent competition from turning into serious conflict. The most effective way of restoring peace was for the chief host to appeal to the memory of his predecessor whose ceremonial attire he was wearing and whose crest(s) he was displaying. These objects were called "masterless things" (*l s'aatí át*), which resembles the term for widow, *l s'aatí shaa* (a woman without a master) (de Laguna 1972:614). This suggests that the violence between the guests threatened to turn the hosts into "widows," that is, to deprive them of potential spouses.

In addition to this dual division, the guests were also differentiated according to rank, age, gender, and the degree of relatedness to the chief hosts and the deceased. The guests' seating arrangement was the hosts' own statement of the current hierarchy within and between the kin groups of their "opposites." The ranking of guests was reconfirmed by the order of the distribution and the size of the gifts they received. In most cases, guests accepted the hosts' evaluation of their rank and status, but occasionally a guest showed displeasure and even attempted to leave. This called for a quick reaction from the hosts, who offered the offended person a different seat or increased the size of the gift. Thus, the potlatch became the main context in which members of the two moieties negotiated their positions in the social hierarchy, doing it not through open confrontation or argument, but by couching their actions in the rhetoric of "love and respect" for each other and for the ancestors.

Although the rank of a guest and the degree of closeness of his or her paternal/affinal relationship with the host were the main determinants of the nature and the size of the gift, the hosts' rhetoric emphasized that the feelings of "love and respect" between the donor(s) and the recipient were the determining factors. The main guests were paid especially generously for the services they had provided during the funeral and subsequent memorial rites, including the "finishing of the corpse." Of course, high-ranking persons and the close paternal/affinal kin of the lineage of the deceased were usually selected for those honorable tasks. Once again, the dead served as a vehicle for potlatch participants to justify their actions, lifting them above the level of mundane politics and personal likes and dislikes.

The special position of the hosts' close paternal/affinal relatives was emphasized not only by their places in the house and the size of gifts received, but also by assigning to them the prestigious task of serving as the hosts' *naa káani*. The latter were usually the brothers-in-law of the deceased and of the chief hosts, who performed the most delicate tasks of inviting the guests, escorting them to their seats, and counting and distributing the wealth amassed by the hosts. The most remarkable manifestation of this special relationship between close paternal/affinal relatives was the assistance provided to the hosts by their "fathers" and siblings-in-law. Swanton (1909:438) reported that a woman whose husband was preparing a major potlatch in the early 1900s obtained $2000 from her clan relatives in another community, thereby increasing her husband's contribution by 50 percent (cf. de Laguna 1972:640–1). The wife of the chief host could also refuse the money and gifts given to her with the words, "I give myself up for my husband" or "I give it [return the money and gifts] for the face of my husband" (McClellan 1954:84). According to McClellan (1954:84), only high-ranking women attempted this maneuver, which increased their own and their husbands' prestige. In current potlatches, financial help given to the hosts by their paternal/affinal kin is quite substantial and the practice itself seems more prevalent than in the 19th century. An individual host may receive money from up to two dozen guests who wish to honor and show their "love and respect" to him. The amount received constitutes up to 30 percent, if not more, of the total monetary donation made by such a host. Of course, the guests making such contributions usually expect a generous return when the money is distributed.[19]

Forms of Exchange

The reciprocity between hosts and guests involved, in addition to tangibles, a flow of words, bodily movements, food, and gifts. The hosts dominated this exchange, since they had to restore the balance in their relationship with their "opposites," threatened by the hosts' indebtedness to them. Food and gifts flowed mainly from hosts to guests. On the other hand, guests played a greater role in the ceremonial oratory, since their role was to comfort the hosts and help them forget their sorrow, to which the hosts responded with words of gratitude.

The oratory of condolence and gratitude

The potlatch oratory of condolence and gratitude was a complex genre, made into a true art form by the Tlingit. Since a detailed analysis of its structure, symbolism, style, and function has appeared elsewhere (Kan 1983), a brief summary is presented here.

The effectiveness of oratory was based on the notion that the spoken word had the power to heal and hurt, depending on how it was used. Guests' speeches were thus supposed to "smooth out," "strengthen," and "heal" the mourners' "inside" (*toowú*).

The structure of each speech was invariable, beginning with a "genealogical catalogue" (Dauenhauer 1975:186), which reaffirmed the speaker's ties with the different categories of the hosts and reminded them of the culturally appropriate emotions that characterized specific paternal/affinal relationships (for example, "love and pity" of fathers toward their children). The next step was a presentation of an episode, usually from the myths of the speaker's clan, which involved a human being or an animal in mortal danger and his miraculous deliverance, thanks to a human being or a superhuman helper. The hosts' sorrow was linked to the protagonist's suffering, the guests' love and compassion to the actions of the mythical helper. The opposition between the *grief* and the *absence of grief* was metaphorized and repeated by a series of oppositions involving physical conditions frequently experienced by the Tlingit, such as hunger/eating, darkness/light, wet/dry, war/peace, and so on. The speaker could dramatize the healing effect of his words by using a crest of his clan to "save" the story's protagonist. For example, if the frog was his crest, he could say that the frog had swallowed up the mourners' sorrow. He could also strengthen the message by invoking his own matrilineal ancestors, saying that they were the ones helping the hosts. The references to the speaker's own matrilineal ancestors also reminded the hosts that their guests had previously suffered similar losses and hence could better understand their feelings. A condolence speech

ended with a repetition of the opening genealogical catalogue.

The hosts interrupted the condolence speeches with their own exclamations of agreement and approval, and later thanked the guests and reiterated the message of their speeches in their own statements. The structure of the latter was the same as that of the guests. The words of the guests were said to "have healed" the mourners, "covered them with warm blankets," and "brought them good fortune" (*laxeitl*). The metaphors of the condolence oratory linked the past and the present, denying death the power to disrupt the process of social reproduction (Kan 1983:53–6).

At the same time, potlatch oratory allowed the participants to invoke their ancestral history, crests, and other sacred possessions. Thus, as with other forms of symbolic action involved in this ritual, it delivered messages of "love and respect" between relatives, as well as competition and the desire to increase their rank and prestige. This multivocality characterizes the other types of ritual exchange discussed below.

The "love songs"

The solemnity of the condolence oratory and especially the "crying songs" contrasted sharply with the mood of the "love songs" (*kusixan daasheeyí*), also called "songs about the children of the clan" (*naa yátx'i daa sheey'i*). These were sung by the hosts, after the completion of the sad portion of the potlatch, when the hosts began to entertain the guests and to express their gratitude. A Tlingit "love song" addresses the children of the singers' clan, that is, those members of the opposite moiety whose fathers are their clan relatives. Thus, if the hosts were members of the Kaagwaantaan clan, they would sing about the "children of the Kaagwaantaan." (They could also mention the children of other clans of their moiety.)

To address a Tlingit as a "child" of his or her father's clan was meant to flatter and please him or her. The category of a clan's "children" included the singers' actual or potential spouses. Thus the "love" referred to in these songs included the feelings of fathers toward children as well as the love between men and women. As Dauenhauer points out,

The term "love" is used here also to mean respect. Love songs may be to a person of the opposite sex, but they may be in a deeper sense directed to one's own family [paternal kin], regardless of sex. Although the song may function on different emotional levels, the pattern will be structurally the same. (Dauenhauer 1975:153)

Many "love songs" were composed by persons expressing their feelings toward spouses and sweethearts, but the latter were never mentioned by name: the plural form of the word "child" was instead used. Thus, a particular "child" of the composer's clan was inseparable from his or her own clan, and love and social identity were linked together. As Dauenhauer (1975:153) puts it, personal emotion was expressed to a specific individual by a specific individual, but the relationship was controlled by the marriage rules.

The clan identity of the addressees remained unknown until the latter responded by joyfully dancing in a special style. This acknowledged their paternal ancestry and returned the "love and respect" to the singers. The guests also responded with a few "love songs" of their own, prompting the hosts to react in a similar manner.

"Love songs" underscored the cultural emphasis on "love" between "opposites," seen as being responsible for sexual and social reproduction. They stressed the lighter side of intermoiety relations, contrasting sharply with the war rhetoric exchanged earlier between hosts and guests.[20] "Love songs" were more than a simple relief from the solemnity of much of the potlatch, although the importance of participants' enjoyment should not be underestimated. The use of images that alluded to heterosexual love in a ritual marking the end of mourning is not surprising. This was, after all, a celebration of life's victory over death, a common theme of mortuary rites throughout the world (cf. Huntington and Metcalf 1979; Bloch and Parry 1982).

Feasting and the distribution of gifts

The feelings and attitudes of the hosts to the guests were also expressed through the distribution of food and gifts, the climax of the potlatch. The spectacular nature of the distribution of huge amounts of fish, meat, fish oil, berries, animal skins, blankets, and so forth, has been the subject of a number of analyses (for example, Benedict 1934; Suttles 1960). However, "this powerful quantitative impression" of the wealth has "obscured for many scholars the traditional ... regard for both the quantity and the symbolic significance of each item" (Goldman 1975:134).[21]

The Tlingit themselves referred to the feeding of guests and showering them with furs (or blankets) as giving them physical strength (*latseen*) and warming them by covering them up (Olson 1967:19). These images were appropriate, since the hosts were, in fact, reciprocating the guests' earlier efforts to "warm" their "inside" and to "give it strength." Thus, the spiritual comfort was exchanged for the physical comfort and strength. Feeding the guests was an effective way of demonstrating one's feelings toward them, since gifts of food were a standard form of exchange between affines. Gifts bestowed on a person by his or her paternal/affinal kin outside the potlatch were also referred to as "blankets" (McClellan 1975:638). The special nature of these gifts as expressions of the hosts' "love and respect" for the guests was emphasized by physical contact. As mentioned above, gifts were rubbed on the donors' foreheads or wrapped around them, thus absorbing part of the donors' selves. This quality of the potlatch gift was well understood by Mauss (1967:10; cf. Walens 1981:80).

Feeding the guests and giving them gifts was also an expression of the hosts' generosity. No object given could be refused, since its spiritual essence belonged to the dead. To refuse meant to "close the door to the land of the dead" (Olson 1967:66), that is, to disrupt the reciprocity between the living and their ancestors. Thus, food and gifts linked the four categories of the potlatch participants: the hosts, the guests, and the deceased matrikin of each. To this day, the favorite food of the hosts' deceased clansmen is served in the potlatch. Some of it, specially marked as belonging to the dead, is put in dishes called *gan kas'íx'i* (or *x'aan kas'íx'i*) (fire dish) and given to close paternal/affinal relatives of the deceased hosts. The donor announces their names as well as those of the guests who received the dishes. In the past some of this food was burned, but today all of it is consumed by the recipients (Kan 1979–84; Worl 1984).

The symbolism of the animal skins and furs, as well as the blankets that replaced them as primary potlatch gifts by the end of last century, also pointed to a special relationship between the living and the dead. The act of giving them was called to "dress the guests" (Emmons 1920–45, Shukoff's Account:9) or to "put on something," and it elicited statements of gratitude from the guests, who thanked the hosts for "warming" them (Olson 1967:65).[22] It is possible that originally furs and blankets were actually placed on the guests, as is still done by the Koyukon Athabascans (distant relatives of the Tlingit), in their memorial rites. Among them, the guests who represent the dead are dressed by the mourners/hosts on the last day of the potlatch and their departure is described as the dead leaving their relatives forever (Carlo 1978:67).

The potlatch gifts and food had other meanings appropriated by the hosts in their efforts to raise their rank, status, and prestige. In Tlingit society, presenting a person with a gift was not necessarily an act of "love and respect." It could also be a request for a larger return gift as well as a way of placing the recipient in an inferior position vis-à-vis the donor (cf. Oberg 1973:99).[23] Challenged by their hosts' generosity, the guests tried to match or exceed it in their own potlatch, in which the former acted as guests.

Another message carried by potlatch gifts was the donors' success in subsistence activities, which reflected their skills and magical power. Thus, according to one of Emmons' informants, a chief host might sometimes boast of his hunting achievements and the wealth that they had brought him (1920–45, Shukoff's Account:8–9).

The hosts tried to create the impression of an endless supply of food, including forcing on the guests more than they could consume. The latter were expected to overeat and vomit, and then were given additional gifts for their "suffering." If nobody vomited, it spoke badly about the hosts and their food (1920–45, Shukoff's Account: 8–9).[24] Finally, the practice of providing the guests with extra food to take home served as a reminder of the hosts' generosity and power long after the end of the ceremony.

Similar to potlatches in neighboring coastal societies, the Tlingit potlatch involved several types of gifts, some of them reserved for the aristocracy (cf. Goldman 1975:136–7). Along the entire Northwest Coast, slaves and copper sheets ("coppers," Tlingit *tinna*) were the most valuable, their symbolism similar but not identical to that of other ritual prestations. Both slaves and coppers were brought from the "outside," the former through warfare with the neighbors to the south, the latter through trade with the interior Athabascans and later with Europeans (Keithahn 1963b). Their acquisition and distribution were controlled by the aristocracy. Neither slaves nor coppers were used for utilitarian purposes, since the former were purchased just before the potlatch and did not do any work (Oberg 1973:116) and the latter were reserved exclusively for ceremonial exchanges. Slaves, like other gifts, were placed in physical contact with the hosts' crests: they were killed with a special club depicting their master's crest, or held a rope tied to a headdress owned by their master (Olson 1967:63). The freeing of slaves, which increased in the postcontact period due to European pressure, was equivalent to killing them, since both acts made them socially dead (freed slaves had to leave their owner's community; cf. Goldman 1975:54). The slaves sacrificed in the potlatch became the servants of the hosts' matrilineal ancestors, while those given away became the guests' property. The spirits of the latter most likely became the property of the dead as well.

Coppers were the most expensive gifts, their value measured in several slaves. Like aristocrats, they were described as being "heavy," "hard," and "shiny." They were the most high-priced gifts exchanged between the families of a bride and groom. Several myths described coppers as "everlasting living things" and their origin was associated with the sun (Swanton 1909:252–62). They often had their owner's crest depicted on their surface, and each copper had a central "T" cross segment called the "backbone" (Keithahn 1963b:59; Olson 1933–54, notebook 10:34). Coppers were usually drowned rather than thrown in the fire and, like human bones, were "heavy," indestructible, and contained their owner's spiritual essence (Billman 1964:59). Coppers and slaves were the only gifts requiring a return presentation of equal or greater value (Olson 1967:66–7). Ultimately these two categories of potlatch gifts represented the aristocrats' control over life and death, since the latter could either kill them or give them away, that is, "spare their lives."[25]

The discussion of the symbolism of the various forms of the potlatch exchange shows that songs, dances, and speeches, as well as food and gifts, served as a code for communication between hosts and guests. The various messages sent repeated the themes of competition and cooperation that, as I have demonstrated, characterized the entire potlatch. These various forms of symbolic media allowed the participants (particularly hosts) to mask assertions of superiority and make them appear to be statements about "love and respect." At the same time, they served as aesthetically powerful forms for expressing gratitude and other emotions that strengthened the cooperation and harmony among the participants.

Conclusion

In this analysis of the symbolism as well as the sociology of the Tlingit potlatch, I have demonstrated its internal symbolic logic and linked it to various symbolic premises in other aspects of the Tlingit sociocultural order.

The study clearly shows the key role played by the dead in the Tlingit potlatch, both as participants and as a source of sacred values, an ideology used by the living to explain and justify their behavior.[26] The potlatch periodically imposed order on the flow of social life, and provided temporary agreement among members of society about their relationships and their relative positions in a social hierarchy. The ritual was characterized by a dialectical relationship between competition and cooperation, which both united and differentiated its participants.

Beliefs about the dead and the desire to honor and emulate them both encouraged and limited competition, and reconciled such contradictory ideological principles as matrilineal solidarity and social hierarchy, and cooperation between affines and inter-moiety competition. It also prevented conflicts generated by the social praxis from undermining the fundamental cultural values and structural principles. The ability of the potlatch to serve as the key link between the "thought-of" and the "lived-in" sociocultural order explains its centrality in 19th-century Tlingit life, as well as its survival into the present, despite years of criticism from missionaries and government officials and significant changes in the native culture and society.

The potlatch could not have played this central role in Tlingit life if it did not have a strong emotional effect on its participants. Although the data available on the 19th-century potlatch is insufficient for a detailed analysis of this aspect of the ritual, some existing accounts and information derived from current potlatches indicate that such powerful emotions as grief, joy, love, and so forth were a significant part of the participants' experience. Just as competition and cooperation existed in a dialectical relationship, so did positive and negative emotions. By wearing the regalia of their ancestors, performing their songs and dances, and giving and consuming objects created through hard work, the actors experienced fundamental cultural values as personally held orientations.

I suggest that the analysis presented here could be applied to other Northwest Coast potlatches and ceremonies, and that the role of the dead in them has, so far, been neglected or underestimated. A considerable amount of data on the Kwakiutl, Tsimshian, Haida, Bella Coola, and other potlatches could be used to generate more holistic interpretations.[27] Much work remains to be done and we are fortunate that, despite the loss of some of their "religious" aspects, present-day Northwest Coast potlatches are "alive and well," still linking the living and the dead through various forms of ceremonial exchange and strong emotional bonds (cf. Holm 1977; Kenyon 1977; Blackman 1977; Stearns 1977; Miller 1984; Seguin 1985).

NOTES

1 The category "potlatch" is a creation of Europeans (including anthropologists). As Goldman points out in a discussion of Kwakiutl ceremonialism (1975: 131), "There never were, at least in precontact days, such events as 'potlatches.' Rather, there were specific

ritual occasions commemorating marriage, death, the construction of a house, investiture of an heir," and so forth. However, since many Northwest Coast ceremonies did share basic features, and because the Indians themselves have incorporated the term "potlatch" into their vocabulary, I will use it in this paper.

2 For a detailed reconstruction of the 19th-century Tlingit funeral see Kan (1982:156–266). The best accounts of this ritual are by Emmons (1920–45, ch. 6:14–25), Olson (1967:58–66), and de Laguna (1972:531–47), although all of them focus on the funerals of aristocratic males. However, for the purpose of my study, these are the most important rites, since they were the most elaborate and served as the model for those of the rest of the population. This explains the use of the male pronoun in my paper.

3 The origin and evolution of Tlingit mortuary architecture is a complex issue that has not been fully resolved yet. See Keithahn (1963a), de Laguna (1972:539–45), and Kan (1982:184–7, 1985).

4 A structural analysis of the Tlingit model of the world (Kan 1978; 1982:163–71) revealed the centrality of the "inside"/"outside" opposition. The "inside" was usually positively marked and associated with the Tlingit people, the village, the warmth of the fire, dryness, abundance of food, and so forth. The "outside" was associated with the non-Tlingit, the dangerous domains of the forest and the sea, cold, wetness, famine, and so on. The Tlingit had to venture into the "outside" to obtain wealth and superhuman power, but preferred to return to the safety of the "inside."

5 "Heaviness" was also associated with aristocratic status, moral righteousness, and sacredness (Kan 1982:48–51, 98–115).

6 There is some evidence that the person's "inside" (spiritual attributes and bones) was provided by maternal ancestors, while the "outside" (for example, facial features) by the maternal as well as the paternal ones.

7 The data on Tlingit beliefs about noncorporeal attributes of the human being is sketchy and contradictory. In addition to the three major spiritual entities already mentioned, there were others, such as the breath, the toowú (mind, feelings, thoughts), and a spirit that reincarnated in a matrilineal descendant of the deceased (Kan 1982:59–71); see also de Laguna (1972:758–71) and Emmons (1920–45: ch. 6).

8 According to Emmons (1916:17), the most important painting on the face of the deceased was the crest of his moiety. This suggests that in death the Tlingit rose above lineage and clan identity, and returned to primary affiliation with the moiety. This paralleled the journey of the spirit of the deceased back in space (toward the interior) and in time (retracing the route followed by the ancestors said to have migrated from the interior down to the coast).

9 The mourners' behavior was also believed to affect their future. If they followed all the rules, they were to become wealthy and live longer. This was the "positive aspect of liminality" discussed by Turner (1967).

10 Cf. Hertz 1960; Huntington and Metcalf 1979:93–118; and Weiner 1976:85–6 on the emphasis on "life values" in death-related rituals.

11 The Tlingit treatment of the remains of the dead bears a special resemblance to those of such northern Athabascan groups as the Carrier (Jenness 1943:534) and the Kutchin (Hardisty 1866:319), who were probably their distant relatives.

12 This sketch of the Tlingit potlatch is based on Swanton (1908:434–43), Olson (1967:58–69), McClellan (1954), de Laguna (1972:606–51), and Kan (1979–84, 1982:268–79).

13 Goldman (1975:245) presented linguistic evidence from Kwakiutl suggesting a similar concept: the verb *yaxwede* (to give away property) is related to *yaq* (to lie down, dead body), and *yaqwe* (to be beaten, to lie dead).

14 If it could not be completed before sunrise, the participants had to sing a special song that asked the Raven to allow them to go on.

15 Several recent symbolic analyses of Tsimshian and Kwakiutl cultures suggested that the people were given to eternal names, rather than the other way around, because "the name is an institution or the soul of a corporation that exists forever" (Miller 1984:29; cf. Goldman 1975:37; Walens 1981:65; Halpin 1984; Seguin 1984:114–15).

16 Goldman came to a similar conclusion in his analysis of the relationship between the living and the dead in Kwakiutl culture (1975:197).

17 McClellan was the first to note the "strong stress on symbolized warfare" in the Tlingit potlatch (1954:96).

18 In the case of the Chilkat Gaanax.ádi, their spouses were selected from the Chilkat Daꞣl' aweidí and other clans and subclans, both local and nonlocal.

19 I do not know yet whether this practice became more popular in this century, with the strengthening of ties within the nuclear family, or whether my predecessors simply failed to report it fully. In any case, this reversal of the flow of the potlatch wealth is an interesting new dimension of the Tlingit potlatch that has not received sufficient attention.

20 This explains why "love songs" were used during the ceremonies that reestablished peace between groups belonging to the opposite moieties.

21 The work of Goldman (1975), Walens (1981), and Seguin (1984, 1985) has finally addressed the issue of the symbolism of the potlatch gifts.

22 Cf. the guests' use of pieces of blankets and cloth received at potlatches to make clothing.

23 Cf. Walens' interpretation of the Kwakiutl food giver as superordinate and the food receiver as subordinate (1981:80ff.).

24 Walens' analysis of the symbolism of vomiting in Kwakiutl culture might be applicable to the Tlingit potlatch (1981:16–17). According to him, vomit, like fire, does not destroy, but transubstantiates, and is thus a paradigm of transformation and rebirth. If the Tlingit guests, like the Kwakiutl, vomited into the fire, the food thus returned could immediately reach the dead.

25 The data on coppers from other Northwest Coast cultures is more extensive than the Tlingit material. Goldman (1975 passim) suggests that Kwakiutl coppers were associated with blood, salmon, sun, and fire. Coppers had the shape of a human torso and were carried like children. They died and were reborn like human beings. The most honorable way to kill a copper was to dismember it (Walens 1981:148–9). Goldman calls it an "overloaded and hence elusive symbol," which synthesized all forms and realms of life (1975:225). The most remarkable was an association between coppers and bones of the dead chief of the host group, mentioned in several accounts of the Kwakiutl (Drucker and Heizer 1967:137), Tsimshian (Garfield 1939:238), and Bella Coola (McIlwraith 1948:252) potlatches.

26 Cf. Weiner's (1976:56) discussion of the role of the dead in the Trobriand system of ceremonial exchange.

27 Many aspects of the potlatch that continue to puzzle anthropologists might be understood if their symbolism was examined within the context of the broader sociocultural order. Thus, the famous destruction of wealth in the late 19th-century Kwakiutl potlatch might have had its roots in an effort to supply the ancestors with food and gifts (cf. Piddocke 1965:257; Wike 1952).

REFERENCES

Adams, John W., 1973 The Gitksan Potlatch: Population Flux, Resource Ownership and Reciprocity. Toronto: Holt, Rinehart & Winston.

Adams, John W., and Alice B. Kasakoff, 1973 *Review of* Feasting with Mine Enemy: Rank and Exchange Among Northwest Coast Societies, by Abraham Rosman and Paula Rubel. American Anthropologist 75:415–17.

Barnett, Homer G., 1938 The Nature of the Potlatch. American Anthropologist 40:349–58.

Benedict, Ruth F., 1934 Patterns of Culture. Boston: Houghton Mifflin.

Billman, Esther, 1964 A Potlatch Feast at Sitka, Alaska. Anthropological Papers of the University of Alaska 14(2):55–64.

Blackman, Margaret, 1977 Ethnohistorical Changes in the Haida Potlatch Complex. Arctic Anthropology 14:39–53.

1982 During My Time. Florence Edenshaw Davisona, a Haida Woman. Seattle: University of Washington Press.

Bloch, Maurice, 1971 Placing the Dead. London and New York: Seminar Press.

Bloch, Maurice, and Jonathan Parry, eds., 1982 Death and the Regeneration of Life. Cambridge, England: Cambridge University Press.

Carlo, Poldine, 1978 Nulato: An Indian Life on the Yukon. Fairbanks, AK: N.p.

Codere, Helen, 1950 Fighting with Property. American Ethnological Society Monograph No. 18. Washington, DC: American Ethnological Society.

Dauenhauer, Richard L., 1975 Text and Context in Tlingit Oral Tradition. Ph.D. dissertation. Department of Comparative Literature, University of Wisconsin–Madison.

de Laguna, Frederica, 1952 Some Dynamic Forces in Tlingit Society. Southwestern Journal of Anthropology 8:1–12.

1972 Under Mount Saint Elias: The History and Culture of the Yakutat Tlingit. Smithsonian Contributions to Anthropology, vol. 7, 3 parts. Washington, DC: US Government Printing Office.

Drucker, Philip, and Robert F. Heizer, 1967 To Make My Name Good: A Reexamination of the Southern Kwakiutl Potlatch. Berkeley: University of California Press.

Emmons, George, 1910 The Potlatch of the North Pacific Coast. The American Museum Journal 10(7):229–34.

1916 The Whale House of the Chilkat. Anthropological Papers of the American Museum of Natural History 19(1):1–33.

1920–45 Unpublished Manuscript on Tlingit Ethnography. New York: American Museum of Natural History, Archives.

Garfield, Viola, 1939 Tsimshian Clan and Society. University of Washington Publications in Anthropology 7(3):167–340.

Goldman, Irving, 1975 The Mouth of Heaven: An Introduction to Kwakiutl Religious Thought. New York: Wiley.
1983 *Review of* Feasting with Cannibals: An Essay on Kwakiutl Cosmology, by Stanley D. Walens. American Ethnologist 10:615–16.

Halpin, Marjorie, 1984 Feast Names at Hartley Bay. *In* The Tsimshian. Images of the Past: Views for the Present. Margaret Seguin, ed. pp. 57–64. Vancouver: University of British Columbia Press.

Hardisty, W., 1866 The Loucheaux Indians. *In* Smithsonian Institution Annual Report for the Year 1866. pp. 303–27. Washington, DC: US Government Printing Office.

Hertz, Robert, 1960 Death and the Right Hand. R. And C. Needham, transl.; E. E. Evans-Pritchard, introduction. New York: Free Press.

Holm, Bill, 1977 Traditional and Contemporary Kwakiutl Winter Dance. Arctic Anthropology 14(1):5–24.

Huntington, Richard, and Peter Metcalf, 1979 Celebrations of Death. Cambridge, England: Cambridge University Press.

Jenness, Diamond, 1943 The Carrier Indians. Bureau of American Ethnology Bulletin 133, Anthropological Paper no. 25. Washington, DC: US Government Printing Office.

Johnson, Andrew P., 1979 Kaax'achgook. College, AK: Tlingit Readers, Inc. and Alaska Native Language Center.

Kamenskiĭ, Anatoliĭ, 1906 Indiane Aliaski (Tlingit Indians of Alaska). Odessa, Russia: Fesenko Publishing House.

Kan, Sergei, 1978 The Winter House in the Tlingit Universe. MA thesis. Anthropology Department, University of Chicago.
1979–84 Ethnographic Notes from 14 Months Among the Tlingit Indians of Southeastern Alaska. (Unpublished ms. in author's possession.)
1982 "Wrap Your Father's Brothers in Kind Words": An Analysis of the Nineteenth-Century Tlingit Mortuary and Memorial Rituals. Ph.D. Dissertation. Anthropology Department, University of Chicago.
1983 Words That Heal the Soul: Analysis of the Tlingit Potlatch Oratory. Arctic Anthropology 20(2):47–59.
1985 Memory Eternal: Orthodox Christianity and the Tlingit Mortuary Complex, 1840–1940. (Unpublished ms. in author's possession.)

Keithahn, Edward L., 1963a Burial Customs of the Tlingit. The Alaska Sportsman 29(4):18–19, 33–6.
1963b Origin of the "Chief's Copper" or "Tinneh." Anthropological Papers of the University of Alaska 12:59–78.

Kenyon, Susan M., 1977 Traditional Trends in Modern Nootka Ceremonies. Arctic Anthropology 14(1):25–38.

Mauss, Marcel, 1967 The Gift, Forms and Functions of Exchange in Archaic Societies. Ian Cunnison, transl.; E. E. Evans-Pritchard, introduction. New York: Norton.

McClellan, Catharine, 1954 The Interrelation of Social Structure with Northern Tlingit Ceremonialism. Southwestern Journal of Anthropology 10:76–96.
1975 My Old People Say. An Ethnographic Survey of Southern Yukon Territory. 2 parts. National Museum of Canada Publications in Ethnology, No. 6(1–2).

McIlwraith, T. F., 1948 The Bella Coola Indians. 2 vols. Toronto: University of Toronto Press.

Miller, Jay, 1984 Feasting with the Southern Tsimshian. *In* The Tsimshian. Images of the Past: Views for the Present. Margaret Seguin, ed. pp. 27–39. Vancouver: University of British Columbia Press.

Oberg, Kalervo, 1973 The Social Economy of the Tlingit Indians. Seattle: University of Washington Press.

Olson, Ronald L., 1933–54 Unpublished Fieldnotes on the Tlingit of Southeastern Alaska. Archieves, Bancroft Library, University of California–Berkeley.
1967 Social Structure and Social Life of the Tlingit Indians in Alaska. University of California Anthropological Records 26:1–23.

Piddocke, Stuart, 1965 The Potlatch System of the Southern Kwakiutl. Southwestern Journal of Anthropology 21:244–64.

Powers, William K., 1983 *Review of* Feasting with Cannibals: An Essay on Kwakiutl Cosmology, by Stanley D. Walens. American Anthropologist 85:203–4.

Ringel, Gail, 1979 The Kwakiutl Potlatch: History, Economics and Symbols. Ethnohistory 26:347–62.

Rosman, Abraham, and Paula Rubel, 1971 Feasting with Mine Enemy. Rank and Exchange Among Northwest Coast Societies. New York: Columbia University Press.
1972 The Potlatch: A Structural Analysis. American Anthropologist 74:658–71.

Seguin, Margaret, 1984 Lest There Be No Salmon: Symbols in Traditional Tsimshian Potlatch. *In* The Tsimshian. Images of the Past: View for the Present. Margaret Seguin, ed. pp. 110–33. Vancouver: University of British Columbia Press.

1985 Interpretive Contexts for Traditional and Current Coast Tsimshian Feasts. National Museum of Man Mercury Series. Canadian Ethnology Service Paper no. 98.

Shotridge, Louis, 1917 My Northland Revisited. Museum Journal 8:105–15.

Snyder, Sally, 1975 Quest for the Sacred in Northern Puget Sound: An Interpretation. Ethnology 14: 149–61.

Stearns, Mary Lee, 1977 The Reorganization of Ceremonial Relations in Haida Society. Arctic Anthropology 14(1):54–63.

Suttles, Wayne, 1960 Affinal Ties, Subsistence, and Prestige Among the Coast Salish. American Anthropologist 62:296–305.

1984 *Review of* Feasting with Cannibals: An Essay of Kwakiutl Cosmology, by Stanley D. Walens. American Indian Quarterly 8(2):138–9.

Swanton, John R., 1908 Social Conditions, Beliefs, and Linguistic Relationship of the Tlingit Indians. *In* The 26th Annual Report of the Bureau of American Ethnology. pp. 391–486. Washington DC: US Government Printing Office.

1909 Tlingit Myths and Texts. Bureau of American Ethnology Bulletin 39. Washington, DC: US Government Printing Office.

Tollefson, Kenneth D., 1976 The Cultural Foundation of Political Revitalization Among the Tlingit. Ph.D. dissertation. Anthropology Department, University of Washington.

Turner, Victor, 1967 The Forest of Symbols. Ithaca, NY: Cornell University Press.

Van Gennep, Arnold, 1960 The Rites of Passage. M. B. Vizedom and G. L. Caffee, transl.; S. T. Kimball, introduction. Chicago: University of Chicago Press.

Vaughan, James Daniel, 1975 Haida Potlatch and Society: Testing a Structural Analysis. Paper presented at the Northwest Coast Studies Conference, Simon Frazer University, Burnaby, Canada.

1985 Tsimshian Potlatch and Society: Examining a Structural Analysis. *In* The Tsimshian and Their Neighbors of the North Pacific Coast. Jay Miller and Carol M. Eastman, eds. pp. 58–68. Seattle: University of Washington Press.

Veniaminov, Ivan, 1886 Zapiski o koloshakh (Notes on the Tlingit). *In* Tvoreniia [collected works] of Ivan Veniaminov. Vol. 3. Ivan Barsukov, ed. pp. 573–658. Moscow: Synodal Press.

Walens, Stanley, 1981 Feasting with Cannibals. An Essay in Kwakiutl Cosmology. Princeton, NJ: Princeton University Press.

1982 The Weight of My Name is a Mountain of Blankets: Potlatch Ceremonies. *In* Celebration. Studies in Festivity and Ritual. Victor Turner, ed. pp. 178–189. Washington, DC: Smithsonian Institution Press.

Wallis, W., 1918 Ethical Aspects of Tlingit Culture. American Journal of Psychology 29:66–80.

Weiner, Annette B., 1976 Women of Value, Men of Renown: New Perspectives on Trobriand Exchange. Austin: University of Texas Press.

Wike, Joyce, 1952 The Role of the Dead in Northwest Coast Culture. *In* Indian Tribes of Aboriginal America. Selected Papers of the 29th International Congress of Americanists. Vol. 3. Sol Tax, ed. pp. 97–103. Chicago: University of Chicago Press.

Worl, Rosita. 1984 Spiritual Food for the Dead. Tlingit Potlatch Bowls. Alaska Native News (May/June):43.

23

Dead Bodies Animate the Study of Politics

Katherine Verdery

Dead people belong to the live people who claim them most obsessively.

James Ellroy

[. . .]

I see politics as a form of concerted activity among social actors, often involving stakes in particular goals. These goals may be contradictory, sometimes only quasi-intentional; they can include making policy, justifying actions taken, claiming authority and disputing the authority claims of others, and creating or manipulating the cultural categories within which all of those activities are pursued. Politics is not restricted to the actions of political leaders but can be engaged in by anyone, although such actors often seek to present their goals as in some sense *public* ones. That is, some of the work of politics consists of making claims that create an issue as a "public" issue. Political actors pursue their activities in arenas both large and small, public and private; the overlap and interference of the arenas shape what goes on in any one of them. Because human activity nearly always has affective and meaningful dimensions and takes place through complex symbolic processes, I also view politics as a realm of continual struggles over meanings, or signification. Therefore, I stress those aspects in my discussion, and I find dead bodies a particularly good vehicle for doing so.

Politics happens in contexts. Because the context of postsocialist politics is unusually momentous, I preface my discussion with a brief sketch of what I think it is. I start with the assumption that for the last two decades or so, we have been both creating and living through an epochal shift in the global economy. Among its elements is a change in the operation of capitalism, responding to a global recession evident as of the early 1970s. A large literature, beyond my purposes here, has arisen around this transformation. Sometimes called a change to "flexible specialization,"[2] it has produced a massive shift in the tectonic plates of the world economy; one sign of that was the 1989 collapse of Communist Party rule in Eastern Europe, and soon thereafter in the Soviet

From Katherine Verdery, "Dead Bodies Animate the Study of Politics," in *The Political Lives of Dead Bodies: Reburial and Postsocialist Change* (New York: Columbia University Press, 1999).

Union. I have suggested elsewhere how I think that happened, underscoring processes internal to the Soviet system that connected it more fully with international capital flows and, as a result, altered both the form of socialist political economies and their place in global capitalism.[3]

Although I am not alone in seeing the postsocialist transformation in such earthshaking terms, my view is far from universal. Some observers find increasing evidence that as the dust from 1989 settles, persistent continuities with the socialist order are at least as striking as disruptions of it. The centralized economy and socialist property rights, in particular, have proved highly resistant to change. Nevertheless, much of what set socialism most clearly apart from other forms of political economy was wholly compromised after 1989: the Communist Party's relative monopoly over the formal political sphere, the degree of central control over the budget and over economic redistribution, the mechanisms that sustained socialist property as the dominant form, and the illusion of the party-state's omnipotence (brought into question by Poland's Solidarity in 1980 but smashed altogether in 1989). Even if some of these features continue in postsocialist societies, they no longer index the distinctive cluster of institutions that was "actually existing socialism."

Moreover, the context in which those features operate has changed. The various barriers that socialism had fumblingly erected no longer insulate it from the "outside." Global capitalism exerts its pressure particularly against the institutions by which socialism defined itself as noncapitalist, such as party and state forms, property arrangements, and openness to market forces. Although the results of outside pressure will not necessarily be "transitions to capitalism," the context in which we should assess postsocialism's emerging forms is – far more than before – the international one of global capital flows. When I speak of a shift in the world's "tectonic plates," then, I do not mean that a plate called "socialism" has buckled before one called "capitalism"; I mean, rather, that an alteration in the entire system of plate movements compels us to reconsider the dynamics in any one part of it. For the postsocialist part, those dynamics affect the full gamut of politicoeconomic and sociocultural life.

Where do dead bodies figure in this? I believe they offer us some purchase on the cultural dimension, in the anthropological sense, of postsocialist politics. (By this I do not mean the so-called concept of political culture, as underspecified as it is overused.[4]) They help us to see political transformation as something more than a technical process – of introducing democratic procedures and methods of electioneering, of forming political parties and non-governmental organizations, and so on. The "something more" includes meanings, feelings, the sacred, ideas of morality, the nonrational – all ingredients of "legitimacy" or "regime consolidation" (that dry phrase), yet far broader than what analyses employing those terms usually provide. Through dead bodies, I hope to show how we might think about politics, both as strategies and maneuvering and also as activity occurring within cultural systems.

Hinted at in my wording is a view similar to Max Weber's: that the pursuit of meaning is at the heart of human activity, and that social analysis aims to understand meanings rather than to explain causes. In his work, Weber described some overarching processes he believed characteristic of modernity, such as rationalization, secularization, and the "disenchantment" of the world. In hands other than his, however, such concepts have tended to desiccate how politics is treated. I prefer, in examining postsocialist politics, to speak instead of its *enchantment*, so as to enliven politics with a richer sense of what it might consist of.[5]

In speaking of enchantment or enlivening, I have two related things in mind. The first is an analytic one: I hope to show how we might animate the study of *politics in general*, energizing it with something more than the opinion polls, surveys, analyses of "democratization indices," and game-theoretic formulations that dominate so much of the field of comparative politics.[6] Where else, I ask, might we look for "politics," in perhaps unexpected places that arrest the imagination? The second sense is a descriptive one, concerning the specific forms that political action is taking in the postsocialist world. Do we find there the ritual murders, pyramid schemes, and images of zombies and clandestinely circulating body parts described, for example, by Jean and John Comaroff in their work on postapartheid

South Africa?[7] Perhaps not, but we do find UFO movements in Armenia, invocations of the devil as a source of wealth in Transylvania, and radio-based mass hypnotism in Russia.[8] My two senses of enchantment (the analytic and the descriptive) are interconnected: we more easily broaden our conception of "the political" in the face of empirical surprises like those.

The analytic and descriptive senses are also, however, importantly distinct. In trying to animate or enchant the study of politics, I am not saying that secular socialism dried out a politics that must now be reinfused with meaning (or even "reborn," as some would have it[9]). To the contrary: communist parties strove continually, as Jowitt has argued, to establish their sacrality and charisma.[10] Rather, I am protesting that perhaps from too much rational choice theory, our standard conception of "the political" has become narrow and flat. Therefore, I propose turning things around: instead of seeing nationalism, for instance, in the usual way – as a matter of territorial borders, state-making, "constructionism," or resource competition – I see it as part of kinship, spirits, ancestor worship, and the circulation of cultural treasures. Rather than speak of legitimacy, I speak of reordering the meaningful universe. I present the politics of corpses as being less about legitimating new governments (though it can be that, too) than about cosmologies and practices relating the living and the dead. And I see the rewriting of history that is obviously central to dead-body politics as part of a larger process whereby fundamental changes are occurring in conceptions of time itself. These are the kinds of things I mean when I speak of analytically enlivening or enchanting politics.[11]

Investigating the political lives of dead bodies, then, enriches our sense of the political while providing a window onto its specific forms in the transformation of socialism. The rest of this book offers some examples of how such an analysis might proceed. A number of themes contribute to the enlivened sense of politics that I am advocating, and most of this chapter is devoted to discussing them. Before I continue, however, I believe I must raise a difficult question, albeit with only tentative answers: Why dead bodies? What is it about a corpse that

seems to invite its use in politics, especially in moments of major transformation?

Why Dead Bodies?

To ask this question exposes one to a flourishing literature on "the body," much of it inspired by feminist theory and philosophy,[12] as well as potentially to poststructuralist theories about language and "floating signifiers." I will not take up the challenge of this literature here but will limit myself instead to some observations about bodies as symbolic vehicles that I think illuminate their presence in postsocialist politics.[13]

Bones and corpses, coffins and cremation urns, are material objects. Most of the time, they are indisputably *there*, as our senses of sight, touch, and smell can confirm. As such, a body's materiality can be critical to its symbolic efficacy: unlike notions such as "patriotism" or "civil society," for instance, a corpse can be moved around, displayed, and strategically located in specific places. Bodies have the advantage of concreteness that nonetheless transcends time, making past immediately present. Their "thereness" undergirded the founding and continuity of medieval monasteries, providing tangible evidence of a monastery's property right to donated lands.[14] That is, their corporeality makes them important means of *localizing* a claim (something they still do today, as I suggest in chapter 3). They state unequivocally, as Peter Brown notes, "*Hic locus est*."[15] This quality also grounded their value as relics.

The example of relics, however, immediately complicates arguments based on the body's materiality: if one added together all the relics of St. Francis of Assisi, for instance, one would get rather more than the material remains of one dead man. So it is not a relic's actual derivation from a specific body that makes it effective but people's belief in that derivation. In short, the significance of corpses has less to do with their concreteness than with how people think about them. A dead body is meaningful not in itself but through culturally established relations to death and through the way a specific dead person's importance is (variously) construed.[16] Therefore, I turn to the properties of corpses that make them, in Lévi-Strauss's words, "good to think" as symbols.

Bodies – especially those of political leaders – have served in many times and places worldwide as symbols of political order. Literature in both historiography and anthropology is rife with instances of a king's death calling into question the survival of the polity. More generally, political transformation is often symbolized through manipulating bodies (cutting off the head of the king, removing communist leaders from mausoleums). We, too, exhibit this conception, in idioms such as "the body politic."

A body's symbolic effectiveness does not depend on its standing for one particular thing, however, for among the most important properties of bodies, especially dead ones, is their ambiguity, multivocality, or polysemy. Remains are concrete, yet protean; they do not have a single meaning but are open to many different readings. Because corpses suggest the lived lives of complex human beings, they can be evaluated from many angles and assigned perhaps contradictory virtues, vices, and intentions. While alive, these bodies produced complex behaviors subject to much debate that produces further ambiguity. As with all human beings, one's assessment of them depends on one's disposition, the context one places them in (brave or cowardly compared with whom, for instance), the selection one makes from their behaviors in order to outline their "story," and so on. Dead people come with a curriculum vitae or résumé – several possible résumés, depending on which aspect of their life is being considered. They lend themselves to analogy with other people's résumés. That is, they encourage identification with their life story, from several possible vantage points. Their complexity makes it fairly easy to discern different sets of emphasis, extract different stories, and thus rewrite history. Dead bodies have another great advantage as symbols: they don't talk much on their own (though they did once). Words can be put into their mouths – often quite ambiguous words – or their own actual words can be ambiguated by quoting them out of context. It is thus easier to rewrite history with dead people than with other kinds of symbols that are speechless.

Yet because they have a single name and a single body, they present the illusion of having only one significance. Fortifying that illusion is their materiality, which implies their having a single meaning that is solidly "grounded," even though in fact they have no such single meaning. Different people can invoke corpses as symbols, thinking those corpses mean the same thing to all present, whereas in fact they may mean different things to each. All that is shared is everyone's *recognition* of this dead person as somehow important. In other words, what gives a dead body symbolic effectiveness in politics is precisely its ambiguity, its capacity to evoke a variety of understandings.[17] Let me give an example.

On June 16, 1989, a quarter of a million Hungarians assembled in downtown Budapest for the reburial of Imre Nagy, Hungary's communist prime minister at the time of the 1956 revolution.[18] For his attempts to reform socialism he had been hanged in 1958, along with four members of his government, and buried with them in unmarked graves, without coffins, facedown. From the Hungarian point of view, this is a pretty ignominious end.[19] Yet now he and those executed with him were reburied, faceup in coffins, with full honors and with tens of thousands in attendance. Anyone watching Hungarian television on that June 16 would have seen a huge, solemn festivity, carefully orchestrated, with many foreign dignitaries as well as three Communist Party leaders standing near the coffins (the Communist Party of Hungary had not yet itself become a corpse). The occasion definitely looked official (in fact it was organized privately), and it rewrote the history – given only one official meaning for forty years – of Nagy's relation to the Hungarian people.[20]

Although the media presented a unified image of him, there was no consensus on what Nagy's reburied corpse in fact meant. Susan Gal, analyzing the political rhetoric around the event, finds five distinct clusters of imagery, some of it associated with specific political parties or groups:[21] (1) nationalist images emphasizing national unity around a hero of the nation (nationalist parties soon found these very handy); (2) religious images (which could be combined with the nationalist ones) emphasizing rebirth, reconciliation, and forgiveness, and presenting Nagy as a martyr rather than a hero; (3) various images of him as a communist, as the first reform communist, and as a true man of the people, his reburial symbolizing the triumph of a humane socialist option and the death of a cruel Stalinist one; (4) generational images, presenting him as the symbol of the younger generation whose life chances had been lost with his execution (this group would soon become the Party of Young Democrats); and (5) images associated with the ideas of truth, conscience, and rehabilitation, so that his reburial signified clearing one's name and telling the story of one's persecution – an opportunity to rewrite one's personal history. (That some people presented communist Prime Minister Nagy as an *anti*-communist hero shows just how complex his significances could be.)

Perhaps attendance at Nagy's funeral was so large, then, because he brought together diverse segments of the population, all resonating differently to various aspects of his life. And perhaps so many political formations were able to participate because all could legitimate a claim of some kind through him, even though the claims themselves varied greatly.[22] This, it seems to me, is the mark of a good political symbol: it has legitimating effects not because everyone agrees on its meaning but because it compels interest *despite* (because of?) divergent views of what it means.

Aside from their evident materiality and their surfeit of ambiguity, dead bodies have an additional advantage as symbols: they evoke the awe, uncertainty, and fear associated with "cosmic" concerns, such as the meaning of life and death.[23] For human beings, death is the quintessential cosmic issue, one that brings us all face to face with ultimate questions about what it means to be – and to stop being – human, about where we have come from and where we are going. For this reason, corpses lend themselves particularly well to politics in times of major upheaval, such as the postsocialist period. The revised status of religious institutions in postsocialist Eastern Europe reinforces that connection, for religions have long specialized in dealing with ultimate questions. Moreover, religions monopolize the practices associated with death, including both formal notions of burial and the "folk superstitions" that all the major faiths so skillfully integrated into their rituals. Except in the socialist period, East Europeans over two millennia have associated death with reli-

gious practices. A religious reburial nourishes the dead person both with these religious associations and with the rejection of "atheist" communism. Politics around a reburied corpse thus benefits from the aura of sanctity the corpse is presumed to bear, and from the implicit suggestion that a reburial (re)sacralizes the political order represented by those who carry it out.

Their sacred associations contribute to another quality of dead bodies as symbols: their connection with affect, a significant problem for social analysis. Anthropologists have long asked, Wherein lies the efficacy of symbols? How do they engage emotions?[24] The same question troubles other social sciences as well: Why do some things and not others work emotionally in the political realm? It is asked particularly about symbols used to evoke national identifications; Benedict Anderson, for instance, inquires why national meanings command such deep emotional responses and why people are "ready to die for these inventions."[25] The link of dead bodies to the sacred and the cosmic – to the feelings of awe aroused by contact with death – seems clearly part of their symbolic efficacy.

One might imagine that another affective dimension to corpses is their being not just any old symbol: unlike a tomato can or a dead bird, they were once human beings with lives that are to be valued. They are heavy symbols because people cared about them when they were alive, and identify with them. This explanation works best for contemporary deaths, such as the Yugoslav ones I discuss in chapter 3. Many political corpses, however, were known and loved in life by only a small circle of people; or – like Serbia's Prince Lazar or Romania's bishop Inochentie Micu (whose case I examine in the next chapter) – they lived so long ago that any feelings they arouse can have nothing to do with them as loved individuals. Therefore I find it insufficient to explain their emotional efficacy merely by their having been human beings.

Perhaps more to the point is their ineluctable self-referentiality as symbols: because all people have bodies, any manipulation of a corpse directly enables one's identification with it through one's own body, thereby tapping into one's reservoirs of feeling. In addition (or as a result), such manipulations may mobilize preexisting affect by evoking one's own personal losses or one's identification with specific aspects of the dead person's biography. This possibility increases wherever national ideologies emphasize ideas about suffering and victimhood, as do nearly all in Eastern Europe.[26] These kinds of emotional effects are likely enhanced when death's "ultimate questions," fear, awe, and personal identifications are experienced in public settings – for example, mass reburials like those of Imre Nagy or the Yugoslav skeletons from World War II.

Finally, I believe the strong affective dimension of dead-body politics also stems from ideas about kinship and proper burial. Kinship notions are powerful organizers of feeling in all human societies; other social forms (such as national ideologies) that harness kinship idioms profit from their power. Ideas about proper burial often tie kinship to cosmic questions concerning order in the universe, as well. I will further elaborate on this suggestion later in this chapter and in chapter 3.

Dead bodies, I have argued, have properties that make them particularly effective political symbols. They are thus excellent means for accumulating something essential to political transformation: symbolic capital.[27] (Given the shortage of investment capital in postsocialist countries and the difficulties of economic reform, perhaps the symbolic variety takes on special significance!) The fall of communist parties devalued much of what had served as political or symbolic capital, opening a wide field for competition in which success depends on finding and accumulating new capital resources. Dead bodies, in short, can be a site of political profit. In saying this, I am partly talking about the process of establishing political legitimacy, but by emphasizing symbolic capital I mean to keep at the forefront of my discussion the symbolic elements of that process.

NOTES

1   My thanks to Fay Cook and Laura Stoker for two stimulating conversations about "politics."
2   See, e.g., Harvey 1989.
3   See Verdery 1996: ch. 1. I will not take up here the many questions my phrasing points to – such as whether there is such a thing as "capitalism," whether "socialist" systems were a form of state capitalism or something sui generis, etc.
4   Nor do I mean the concept of "framing," with which some political scientists think to bring in culture by showing how politicians package something so it sells (e.g., Snow et al. 1986; Snow and Benford 1992). I borrow my phrasing from Doug McAdam, whom I thank for his assistance with this paragraph.
5   I am indebted to conversations with Fay Cook, Lynn Hunt, and Kirstie McClure that helped me to see this as my goal.
6   For a similar critique, see Karl 1990. My thanks to her, as well, for a helpful conversation on the themes of democratization and legitimacy.
7   Comaroff and Comaroff 1998.
8   See Platz 1997; Verdery 1996: ch. 7; and Ries 1997.
9   E.g., Urban 1997.
10   Jowitt 1987.
11   I alternate among these words and others like "animate" or "enrich," rather than resting with the word "enchant," hoping thereby to make my meaning clearer. One might too easily read "enchant" to imply fairy tales and magic; although in postsocialism we indeed find some of that, I have in mind something a bit more down-to-earth.
12   See, e.g., Butler 1990, 1993; Bynum 1995a, 1995b; Scarry 1985.
13   My thanks to István Rév, Laura Stoker, and Dorothea von Mücke for stimulating my thoughts on this question.
      Jean and John Comaroff (personal communication) offer a different answer to the "Why dead bodies?" question from the one I present here. They suggest that changes in the global economy have made the body (as raw labor power) the only salable commodity that everyone has, and that advances in the process of its commodification (the sale of organs and sexual services, the marketing of smiles, etc.) place it at the forefront of capitalist development.
14   István Rév employs this argument in his discussion of the "Why dead bodies" question (the work is in progress under the title Covering History). I am grateful to him for sharing it with me.
15   Brown 1981:86.
16   This is not to say that such "construals" are unconstrained. Efforts to grapple with the problem of what impedes the complete invention of pasts include those of Michel-Rolph Trouillot in his book Silencing the Past (1995) and (quite differently) of Milan Kundera, in The Book of Laughter and Forgetting (1980).

Both see checks on invention as coming from the *materiality* of certain objects and processes. The hat of Clementis on Gottwald's head in the opening scene of Kundera's novel, the packets of letters, the flash of a gold tooth – all signal events and people who cannot be simply airbrushed out of history. Although we can variously interpret the *meanings* of these material things, we cannot make them up – or unmake them – entirely. I am grateful to Michel-Rolph Trouillot for a stimulating conversation on this theme.

17 Most symbols share these properties. I claim only that corpses are particularly effective in politics because they embody the properties unusually well.

18 My account draws on those of Gal 1989, 1998; Rév 1995; and Bruszt and Stark 1992.

19 Barber (1988:49) observes, however, that people may bury a corpse facedown when they fear it is dangerous; this posture will make the corpse burrow further into the earth rather than emerge from his grave.

20 The initiative for Nagy's reburial did not come from official circles, but from the Hungarian diaspora (who had organized an anniversary in Paris the year before) and from the families of Nagy and others hanged with him or purged later. The families had repeatedly sought official permission but were put off. At length the Hungarian government agreed to a small family burial, then (under pressure) to a non-official public funeral; from that point on, the government had nothing to do with the arrangements. By the time of the funeral, however, the Party leadership was so divided and its position in society so compromised that they asked to be included! The initiating families at first refused, then finally agreed that three officials could attend as private persons; they would be excluded from the private family burial that followed the public gathering. For those who would see Nagy's reburial as a political effort to build legitimacy for the communist regime, I note that it should, rather, be seen as crucial to the Party's downfall (see Rév 1995:24; Bruszt and Stark 1992:40).

21 Gal 1989:8–9.

22 For a book-length study of comparable funeral politics in South Africa, see Garrey Dennie's fascinating dissertation (Dennie 1996).

23 These cosmic associations contribute to the well-known ethnological fact that death rituals are the slowest of all practices to change (Barber 1988:48; Brown 1981:24; Kligman 1988). Their stability, in turn, makes them good instruments for nationalists who – as sometimes happens with new regimes – want to reaffirm a connection with or return to "older" national "traditions." Claims of that kind have been rampant in building anticommunist identities since 1989. (Thanks to Pam Ballinger for suggesting this point.)

24 For a particularly interesting treatment, see Obeyesekere 1990.

25 Anderson 1983:4, 141.

REFERENCES

Anderson, Benedict. 1983. *Imagined Communities: Reflections on the Origin and Spread of Nationalism*. London: Verso.

Barber, Paul. 1988. *Vampires, Burial, and Death: Folklore and Reality*. New Haven: Yale University Press.

Brown, Peter. 1981. *The Cult of the Saints: Its Rise and Function in Late Christianity*. Chicago: University of Chicago Press.

Bruszt, László, and David Stark. 1992. "Remaking the Political Field in Hungary: From the Politics of Confrontation to the Politics of Competition." In *Eastern Europe in Revolution*, Ivo Banac, ed., pp. 13–55. Ithaca, N.Y.: Cornell University Press.

Butler, Judith. 1990. *Gender Trouble: Feminism and the Subversion of Identity*. New York: Routledge.

——. 1993. *Bodies That Matter: On the Discursive Limits of "Sex."* New York: Routledge.

Bynum, Caroline Walker. 1995a. *The Resurrection of the Body in Western Christianity, 200–1336*. New York: Columbia University Press.

——. 1995b. "Why all the Fuss About the Body? A Medievalist's Perspective." *Critical Inquiry* 22:1–33.

Comaroff, Jean, and John Comaroff. 1998. "Occult Economies and the Violence of Abstraction: Notes from the South African Postcolony." *American Ethnologist* 26.

Dennie, Garrey Michael. 1996. "The Cultural Politics of Burial in South Africa, 1884–1990." Ph.D. diss., Johns Hopkins University.

Gal, Susan. 1989. "Ritual and Public Discourse in Socialist Hungary: Nagy Imre's Funeral." Unpublished MS.

——. 1998. "Political Culture and the Making of Tradition: A Comment." *Austrian History Yearbook* 29:249–60.

Harvey, David. 1989. *The Condition of Postmodernity*. Oxford: Blackwell.

Jowitt, Kenneth. 1987. "Moscow 'Centre.'" *Eastern European Politics and Societies* 1:296–345.

Karl, Terry Lynn. 1990. "Dilemmas of Democratization in Latin America." *Comparative Politics* 23, no. 1:1–21.

Kligman, Gail. 1988. *The Wedding of the Dead: Ritual, Poetics, and Popular Culture in Transylvania.* Berkeley: University of California Press.

Kundera, Milan. 1980. *The Book of Laughter and Forgetting.* New York: Alfred A. Knopf.

Obeyesekere, Gananath. 1990. *The Work of Culture: Symbolic Transformation in Psychoanalysis and Anthropology.* Chicago: University of Chicago Press.

Platz, Stephanie. 1997. "The Transformation of Power and the Powers of Transformation: The Karabagh Movement, the Energy Crisis, and the Emergence of UFOs in Armenia at the Dawn of Independence." Unpublished MS.

Rév, István. 1995. "Parallel Autopsies." *Representations* 49:15–39.

Ries, Nancy. 1997. *Russian Talk: Culture and Conversation During Perestroika.* Ithaca, N.Y.: Cornell University Press.

Scarry, Elaine. 1985. *The Body in Pain: The Making and Unmaking of the World.* New York: Oxford University Press.

Snow, David A., and Robert D. Benford. 1992. "Master Frames and Cycles of Protest." In *Frontiers in Social Movement Theory,* Aldon Morris and Carol Mueller, eds., pp. 133–55. New Haven: Yale University Press.

Snow, David A., E. Burke Rochford, Jr., Steven K. Worden, and Robert D. Benford. 1986. "Frame Alignment Processes, Micromobilization, and Movement Participation." *American Sociological Review* 51:464–81.

Trouillot, Michel-Rolph. 1995. *Silencing the Past: Power and the Production of History.* Boston: Beacon.

Urban, Michael, with Vyacheslav Igrunov and Sergei Mitrokhin. 1997. *The Rebirth of Politics in Russia.* Cambridge: Cambridge University Press.

Verdery, Katherine. 1996. *What Was Socialism, and What Comes Next?* Princeton: Princeton University Press.

Index